THE WORLD SHE EDITED

The World She Edited

Katharine S. White
at *The New Yorker*

Amy Reading

MARINER BOOKS

New York   Boston

Grateful acknowledgment is made to the following for permission to quote from both published and unpublished material:

Estate of Roger Angell for the unpublished letters of Ernest and Roger Angell. The Authors League Fund and St. Bride's Church, as joint literary executors of the Estate of Djuna Barnes. Estate of Kay Boyle for permission to quote from a letter to Katharine White Copyright © 1932. Estate of Bessie Breuer for permission to quote from letters to Katharine White Copyright © 1932 and 1970 and a letter to William Maxwell Copyright © 1942. Condé Nast for the unpublished letters of *New Yorker* employees, including Katharine and E. B. White, Harold Ross, William Shawn, Harriet Walden, Roger Angell, Wolcott Gibbs, William Maxwell, and Daise Terry. Extract from letter from Roald Dahl to Howard Moss (April 14, 1949) from the *New Yorker* papers held in the Manuscript and Archives Division of the New York Public Library Copyright © 1949. The Roald Dahl Story Company Limited. Estate of Babette Deutsch for permission to quote from a letter to Katharine White Copyright © 1952. Estate of Stanley Edgar Hyman for permission to quote from a letter to Gus Lobrano Copyright © 1946. The Mary McCarthy Literary Trust for permission to quote from a letter to Katharine S. White Copyright © 1951 and Linda Davis Copyright © 1978. Letter from Vladimir Nabokov to Katharine S. White dated September 24, 1954, Copyright © 1954 by The Vladimir Nabokov Literary Foundation; letter from Vladimir Nabokov to Katharine S. White dated February 3, 1954, Copyright © 1954 by The Vladimir Nabokov Literary Foundation, used by permission of The Wylie Agency LLC. Estate of May Sarton for permission to quote from letters to Katharine White Copyright © 1955 and 1960. Estate of Nancy Stableford for permission to quote from a letter to Dana Atchley Copyright © 1961. White Literary LLC for permission to quote from the unpublished personal letters of Katharine Sergeant White and E. B. White; *Onward and Upward in the Garden*; *The Letters of E. B. White, Revised Edition*; "Lady Before Breakfast" and "Natural History" from *Poems and Sketches of E. B. White* Copyright © 1981, White Literary LLC, reprinted by permission of White Literary LLC.

HarperCollins books may be purchased for educational, business, or sales promotional use. For information, please email the Special Markets Department at SPsales@harpercollins.com.

FIRST EDITION

Designed by Chloe Foster

Library of Congress Cataloging-in-Publication Data has been applied for.

ISBN 978-1-328-59591-1

24 25 26 27 28 LBC 5 4 3 2 1

Contents

PART IV: EDITING A LITERARY POWERHOUSE
(1930–1938)

PART V: INTERREGNUM
(1938–1943)

PART VI: THE YEARS OF GREATEST INFLUENCE
(1943–1954)

Prologue

February 1953

On a February day in 1953, Katharine Sergeant White sat in her corner office at *The New Yorker* on the nineteenth floor at 25 West Forty-Fifth Street. Snow was falling outside and her desk was piled with manuscripts and mail, all overdue because she'd only just returned to the city from a week at her farmhouse in Maine. One letter solicited her attention above all else, a writer's cry of distress.

The short-story writer Frances Gray Patton, typing from her home in Durham, North Carolina, confessed to Katharine that she was creatively paralyzed and suffering "guilt and shame" over not being able to write, her mind like a broken phone. "You know how sometimes when you're only half through calling your number something in the instrument clicks back to that empty, buzzing dial tone? Well, that was what would happen to me when I was halfway through a story." She further confessed that she had been on the verge of asking Katharine for help several times before, but she hadn't wanted to bother her, so instead she forced herself to write a new story—"rather dull and contrived"—which she was sure Katharine wouldn't like and which hadn't yet worked to lift her out of her "doldrums."

Katharine's reply, twice the length of Patton's letter, scrawled in her clear, definite handwriting in pencil on unlined paper, gorgeously and robustly responded to her author. I recognize you, she began, and I know your distress is real. "All I can say to reassure you is that I know—I mean I <u>really</u> know—that this sort of trouble happens to every good writer at intervals." She would know, as an editor going on her eighteenth year at *The New Yorker* and the wife of one of the country's most celebrated writers, E. B. White, who was just then enjoying the runaway success of his children's novel *Charlotte's Web*, only four months old. But Katharine's husband, known as Andy, had a troubled relationship to his own craft and Katharine often used his travails as an example for her authors. She described to Patton Andy's "one horrible year" of not writing in the 1930s, and then mentioned several other briefer and more recent dry spells. In fact, she said, just about every fiction writer she knew suffered from Patton's doldrums. "They start stories and never finish them. Or they finish them and decide they are unsuccessful. Or they like them and send them out—these are distinguished writers whose names you would know well—and then get rejections." These episodes happened with such frequency that Katharine had realized they were not symptoms of brokenness but the very opposite. "Fanny, I'm sure that what you are suffering from is merely the disease of being creative, plus the trouble of having the written word as your medium."

Then Katharine dug into some potential solutions. Might Patton take a short trip to write elsewhere, or might she do a different kind of writing, perhaps switching from third to first person, or from fiction to memoir—or "casuals" and "reminiscences," in *New Yorker* parlance? Perhaps she could write under a pseudonym? Katharine even generated a few concrete story ideas from the funny, newsy personal letters that Patton had written to her recently. She ended the letter squarely on a rejection—the story that Patton thought she wouldn't like had, in fact, been met with a resounding "no" vote among the magazine's editors. "At the same time I think you were right to submit this manuscript. A writer half the time can't judge his own work fairly, especially when in a self-doubting mood, so it is better to send out manuscripts than to mull over them." In a letter bursting with generous and buoying sentiments, Katharine was saying: I can help you read your own work; I'm right there inside it with you. Then she edited her own prose—crossing out words and sentences, adding new ones in the margins—before handing it to her secretary to be typed in duplicate, one copy mailed to Durham and the other filed in the *New Yorker*'s "Patton" folder for 1953.

Good editing is invisible, but masterful editing makes visible the unsaid, because a great editor receives what is not on the page: the unrealized, the unthought, the assumed, the retracted, the tentative, the implied. Once in a while, the art of editing consists of reading not words but their author, of stepping into the private compositional process to help build the architecture of the writer's inner life. This kind of editing can be intensely personal, and this is the kind of editing that Katharine S. White perfected. Katharine's relationship with Patton typified the method she had refined with dozens of other women writers by this moment in the 1950s, the high point of her editing career. Fanny Patton was herself a late-blooming author. She was the daughter of two writers and had studied playwriting at the University of North Carolina, but then she married a Duke University literature professor and focused on raising their son and twin daughters. Only when her daughters were nearing their high school graduation did Patton turn to short stories, publishing her first one in *The Kenyon Review* in 1945 and winning a spot in that year's *O. Henry Memorial Award Prize Stories* collection. Katharine bought a story from her the next year and began a warm correspondence. Patton traveled north to New York, and she was so intimidated and keyed up by the city that when Katharine invited her to "a little family dinner," just the Whites and Harold Ross, founder of *The New Yorker*, Patton's "bones turned to water." But the evening of such august company was "easy and charming," and Patton comported herself well even when S. J. Perelman sat down for some light banter. By that point, Patton had published four stories with Katharine, and three more were in the pipeline. She had also earned a bristling sheaf of Katharine's famous rejection letters, scrupulous and detailed explanations for why a given story would not work for the magazine; Katharine frequently found Patton's stories too "artificial" or "overdrawn" or "unconvincing." Patton introduced Katharine to her friend and fellow Southerner Peter Taylor, who contributed to *The New Yorker* for the next three decades. Katharine, in turn, introduced Patton to her dear friend and short-story virtuoso Jean Stafford.

Now, in the winter of 1953, Patton's gratitude burst out of her to fill two letters. You have given me back my confidence, she wrote, first by the very fact of her long and engaged letter, but also by conveying that Patton had risked nothing by writing a poor story or confessing her trouble.

"It was almost as if you had assured me of my inalienable right to fail if I had to!" And this, Patton had suddenly realized, was a necessary precondition for writing herself out of her paralysis, this "prevailing mood of quiet optimism" that came from not having to "pull myself up taller than I really am <u>all the time</u>," from being able to share her flawed work with a responsive editor to whom she was equal. What Katharine elegantly communicated was that their relationship and Patton's position within *The New Yorker* was secure, so that she need not endlessly audition to be read seriously.

Katharine's sensitive editorial work would pay dividends for Patton for years to come. Patton sent a new story with her second letter, called "The Game," and Katharine accepted it at once—provided that Patton would agree to work with her to shorten and tighten it, to edit it over several intense rounds of marked-up manuscripts and long explanatory letters. "The Game" tells the story of two women, once childhood friends and now reunited after seventeen years apart. Lillian has moved to Baltimore and married a wealthy man, while Maria has stayed in their small Southern town. When Lillian runs into Maria in a Baltimore department store, she remembers why she was drawn to her when they were young: in Maria's company, "you were safe and free. You could assume any whimsical attitude that struck your fancy, or indulge in that hyperbole of the moment that is the leaven of conversation, without the danger of being held to account later." The story is not about Katharine and Fanny, but the whisper of Katharine's influence can be heard. When Lillian brings Maria home to her posh town house, Maria asks for money for her sick child; Lillian goes over to her desk and presses a panel to open a concealed drawer in which lies a bundle of bills. Did Patton know that Katharine had just such a hidden cabinet in her tambour desk at home, holding the same cache for unforeseen circumstances? "The Game" was published in the May 9 issue of *The New Yorker* that year and then was selected for the 1954 volume of *The Best American Short Stories*. Fanny and Katharine would work together right up until Katharine retired from the fiction department, and she would hand her over to her son, Roger Angell, whom she'd hired as a *New Yorker* editor in her own mold. Katharine and Fanny would continue writing personal letters for the next decade.

This was the secret of Katharine's success: what she called "the personal-editorial letter." Eliciting good work from her authors meant connecting with them in an intimate space and being receptive to whatever they brought her. She gave of herself to her authors, and she got back their whole selves in return. She called out the best in an entire generation of women writers: Emily Hahn, Janet Flanner, Kay Boyle, Mary McCarthy, Elizabeth Bishop, Jean Stafford, Nadine Gordimer, Elizabeth Taylor, May Sarton, Louise Bogan, Christine Weston.

These women crafted literary careers between first- and second-wave feminisms, without the benefit of legible categories for their labor. They wrote from deeply personal experience but, under Katharine's pencil, strove to appeal to a wide readership; their work gave feeling and sentiment a very particular role to play in a liberal, middle-class worldview. In their long and plentiful letters to Katharine, they included telling details about the conditions for their literary work amid families, travel, health burdens, financial straits, and world politics. They wrote knowing they could count on Katharine's equally personal responses as a powerful and sympathetic woman. She cleared obstacles, advanced them money, rescued them from despair, introduced them to each other, turned dry spells into headlong rivers, and suggested now-classic stories and essays. She made a life of the mind possible for herself, and in so doing, she made the same thing possible for dozens of female writers—and their thousands of readers. She edited just as many men as she did women; she would later point to her long and lively relationships with Vladimir Nabokov and John Updike as career highlights.

Katharine wrote (and dictated) a near-bottomless trove of letters to authors, but she was not a writer. She published a handful of essays, but she was never willing or able to reveal herself in print. And yet time and again, she gently summoned hard truths from other women, conjuring their best work from the silence of what she never wrote about herself. Her editorial letters show an interplay between revelation and withholding, a pattern of generosity off the page that enabled generativity on it, the evolution of her understanding of when to edit and when to incite.

To read Katharine's letters and memos and manuscript marginalia, then, is to do far more than simply resuscitate and pay homage to her career, buried as it has been under the larger-than-life male personalities at *The New Yorker*. To peer over her shoulder as *she* reads is to discover something new about reading as an act of intimacy and of community.

She spent the last decade of her life curating her and her husband's legacies by sorting through mountains of papers. She was the caretaker of centuries' worth of letters, daguerreotypes, recipe books, and last wills and testaments from both the Shepley and Sergeant sides of her family— and both clans saved everything, even the envelopes in which the letters were delivered, attached by rusty paper clips. From these stacks of papers, Katharine compiled five different university archives. She donated her papers to Bryn Mawr College, E. B. White's papers to Cornell, the Shepley papers from her mother's family to Bowdoin College, her sister Elizabeth Shepley Sergeant's papers to the Beinecke Library at Yale, and the Sergeant family papers from her father's family to Sterling Memorial Library at Yale. She read virtually every sheet of paper before she donated it, and annotated many of them. Ancient letters sit in acid-free boxes in climate-controlled warehouses up and down the Northeast with tiny little pink slips—routing slips from *The New Yorker* with a circled "T" for "timely"—paper-clipped to them, the slips repurposed for Katharine's penciled notes about the letter and her hasty initials, KSW.

In other words, almost every source for this biography comes to us already interpreted by Katharine's reading. *This* was her life's work, these notes a kind of autobiography. Reading over her shoulder means paying attention to the layers of reading happening across time on any given sheet of paper. Her words are a framing device that, somewhat surprisingly, gives us emotional immediacy rather than scholarly distance. We can read her mind at work, read her own fascination with the life of the mind, feel her reading expand within our own. Much of what I will tell you comes from Katharine's own curation of her papers.

But some of what I will tell you comes from what she did not say, what she purposefully did not save, what I've discovered outside her archive, what she never knew. She zealously destroyed primary sources and had no scruples about noting so. Like Katharine, I too will attempt to read the silences packed thickly around the many words bequeathed to us from her busy life, and I will note them for the record even if I cannot fill them.

The art of editing consists of a thousand tiny pencil strokes that add up to something far greater. Frances Gray Patton once told Katharine, "You've done a remarkably clever and delicate piece of editing and I take it as a generous act of friendship as well." Cutting a writer's words can be a gift; silences can be audible. And at the heart of editing, there is reading and immense receptivity. Patton returned to that letter about paralysis later in her career at another moment of aridity and drew yet more strength from Katharine's "great sympathy and understanding." Rereading can be enormously creative.

Part I

The Family
Glamour

(1892–1909)

1.

Katharine Sergeant's birth certificate could have used an editor. She was the only baby born in Winchester, Massachusetts, on September 17, 1892, so it's not as if the clerk was busy, but he or she nonetheless recorded her existence as "Katherine D. Sargeant." Two errors, and then there's that middle initial, an intriguing cipher that appears on no other document in Katharine's enormous archive.

In a family where everyone held until their death the nicknames acquired in the cradle, Katharine Sergeant was only ever Katharine Sergeant (pronounced "SURGE-ent"). She was *never* Kate or Katie or Kittie (except to Groucho Marx, who addressed her as "Katie" in exactly one letter). She was registered for school as Katharine Sergeant, and she signed every letter as Katharine. Most family letters were addressed to her that way, too, although her aunt Crullie (whose real name was Caroline) and her second husband, Andy (whose real name was not Andrew but Elwyn), could get away with calling her Kay, as did a few close male friends; her first husband called her Katrina. When she was a grown woman, her colleagues would call her Mrs. White despite her pleas to be more familiar. All her life, something about Katharine seemed to rebuff the diminutive.

Yet she was a little girl once, the youngest of three children, doted on by her two older sisters, Elsie (whose real name was Elizabeth) and Ros or Rosie (short for Rosamond). To peel back the layers of the formal, impressive woman she became, to begin at the beginning, it helps to start with an image rather than a name. When she was four years old, her aunt Poo (full name: Annie Barrows Shepley) painted her portrait, and there, underneath an enormous plumed hat and above an enormous ruffled white blouse with puffed sleeves and a maroon bow, we find a little girl with enormous gray eyes. The lavish clothes make her look like a little Dutch burgher, and her long blond ringlets and Cupid's-bow lips are the very essence of a nineteenth-century Romantic girl child, but even these features do not overwhelm her forthright gaze. In contrast to Aunt Poo's portrait of Ros, whose face is shadowed and whose expression is troubled, almost bereft, Katharine's portrait shines from within. She seems utterly sure of herself as she gazes back at her aunt.

Photographs reinforce this impression. There's four-year-old Katharine sitting on a rococo bench in a photographer's studio, wearing perhaps the same white dress with its exuberantly ruffled bib, hands folded obediently in her lap. This time we can see her blond bangs and ringlets, and this time she is smiling. And further back—an even tinier Katharine in a voluminous white ruffled dress and black stockings, standing beside the library fireplace. Also, a triptych of baby photos, back, side, and front. Fast-forward to a framed but undated studio portrait of her from perhaps her teenage years, another white blouse, high collared and ruffled, presenting her face as if on the pedestal of a bust, her long hair pulled back and just a few wisps escaping. From infant to teenager, the gaze is the same. Katharine Sergeant White began as a little girl preternaturally secure in her place in the world. It wouldn't be long after Aunt Poo's oil painting before Katharine's life would be terribly riven, but she kept her sense of herself.

No baby portraits exist of Elsie and Ros, and almost no childhood photos of the elder two daughters at all until a beautiful group portrait of the three sisters as grown young women. Katharine, however, was the youngest daughter in an affluent family who was regularly put in front of a camera lens, her hair curled, her blouse starched and fluffed up. Katharine's confidence came from her family, from her never doubting that she was loved.

She always remembered her childhood as happy, and what made it happy were the gardens around her home and the company of her sister Ros, who was four years older than Katharine and closer to her than to Elsie, who was eleven years older and busy growing into a young woman. The Sergeants lived in a large, comfortable home in Brookline, Massachusetts, at 4 Hawthorn Road, and the backyard held the hawthorn trees for which their street was named—three of them, a red, a white, and a pink. A signal memory of her childhood was picking the blossoms of those enormous trees. Katharine would write many years later, "we children had to carry a stepladder into the empty lot next door, use it for the first boost up, and then scramble the rest of the way to a narrow ledge on top of an enormously high lattice fence that backed our shrubbery. Standing there perilously, trying to keep our balance, we had to reach *up* to break the branches." They'd arrange the flowers in the tall Japanese vase their father had purchased in the city for their gold-papered parlor.

Katharine and Rosamond would play Millinery, a game they invented to embellish the boring straw hats they wore as students of Miss Winsor's School. They'd browse among their father's flowers—everything was free for the taking except the rhododendrons and azaleas—and pick blooms to stick into the plain ribbons around their hat crowns; then they'd parade in front of the adults and receive their praise. Their garden offered them not only hawthorn but forsythia, Japanese crab, Japanese quince, mock orange, flowering almond, lilac, bridal wreath, weigela, deutzia, althea, and shrub roses. In addition to the curving bed of shrubs and the flower beds, there was a privet hedge and a wide lawn, where Katharine and Ros would "as good as live" when school was not in session. They played croquet, baseball, ring toss, diabolo, and battledore and shuttle-cock. They played Statues, "a very violent game," Katharine remembered, where one girl would whirl another girl around and around by her wrists and then fling her away, shouting out a state of mind—"Grief, Anger, Grace, Hatred, Love, or Defiance"—into which the poor dizzy girl must freeze as soon as her feet touched the ground. The child who struck the most outlandish pose would get to be the next whirler.

Their family's land was surrounded by undeveloped plots ripe for the exploration. Even more enticing, one block to the east, a beautiful new park had just been made. The Brookline Land Company had sold some of its acreage to the town, which hired one of its most famous residents, Frederick Law Olmsted, to turn the brackish, tidal Muddy River into Leverett Pond and connect it up to his other Boston parks, finally closing the chain of parks known as the Emerald Necklace. The year after

Katharine's family moved in, and five years after Olmsted retired, the city voted to change the names of Leverett Park and Jamaica Park to Olmsted Park. Everywhere around her, Katharine could see both gardens and country vistas, and those sights shaped her mind's eye for her entire life.

Hers was an outdoor childhood. Each summer, the Sergeants would rent a cottage at Chocorua Lake in New Hampshire, and the girls would turn tan from boating and hiking. Katharine and Ros would take their canoe out to the calm waters at the head of the lake in the early morning, just as the white water lilies were beginning to open in the sun. It was another delicate picking operation: "The stern paddle had to know precisely how to approach a lily, stem first, getting near enough so the girl in the bow could plunge her arm straight down into the cool water and break off the rubbery stem, at least a foot under the surface, without leaning too far overboard." They'd row home amid the scent of the *Nymphaea odorata*. They'd visit Aunt Poo at Apple End, the house she'd purchased in Woodstock, Connecticut, when she came into an inheritance. Katharine and Ros would walk down the country lanes and make a game out of who could collect the most food to bring back home from farms and gardens: "nuts, apples, peaches, berries, and unharvested tomatoes and carrots."

So many of Katharine's memories revolved around plants. She was as close an observer of plants as she was of her father and his very particular gardening aesthetic. She remembered, three decades after his death, how disappointed he'd been when the assortment of rhododendrons he'd specially selected by color bloomed, but all in the same "pallid lavender-white flower trusses." She remembered too, with sharp specificity, the roses that he grew under the east window of the library, "their heavenly fragrance and the way they grew a half-story high, and the clusters of white single roses, with gold stamens turning to a rich brown." Her father called them Guelder roses, but later when she tried to find them for nostalgia's sake, she learned he had the name wrong, and she never solved the mystery of his shrub roses, though she suspected they were musk roses. She grew dahlias, not because she liked them—she was embarrassed by their showiness—but because her father had. She remembered that every morning at breakfast, the girls would be asked, "Who will pick the flowers today?" and one of them would be tasked with arranging them for the house. Once a year Charles would pile his daughters into a trolley and take them to a certain hillside on the north side of Boston so they could pick mayflowers. He taught them the plants to identify and avoid (deadly nightshade, poison ivy, poison sumac) and the plants to eat (young checkerberry leaves and sassafras root).

Charles Sergeant was a disciplined patriarch whose routines the young Katharine well knew but whose playful side she could access. She remembered him leaving the house each morning, six days a week, by eight o'clock to reach his office in Boston, and he was never home until seven o'clock. But his interest in gardening meant that even before breakfast he'd be out on the lawn, digging up dandelions with his penknife. One year, the dandelions spread so vigorously that he bought jackknives for Ros and Katharine and paid them ten cents for every hundred dandelions they extracted. But Katharine knew that he really only wanted to arm his daughters for his favorite game, mumblety-peg, where players compete to throw their knives close to their opponents' feet. Charles taught Katharine several expert throws that she could still execute as an adult.

Each May and June, he would bring his daughters to a nearby estate, Holm Lea, to see its enormous, naturalistic plantings of rhododendrons and azaleas in their full glory, a swath of color that was reflected in the estate's pond. Holm Lea belonged to Charles Sprague Sargent—no relation—who was an eminent dendrologist, the first director of Harvard's Arnold Arboretum, and the man who brought Frederick Law Olmsted to Brookline. Katharine's father, a middle-class engineer with a solid but unremarkable career with the Boston Elevated Railway, and his neighbor, a wealthy Boston Brahmin and nationally known scientist, would have their annual conversation in which they would rue the mix-ups in the mail occasioned by their nearly identical names. Perhaps their similar surnames were behind the misperception that dogged Katharine her entire life; even her obituary in *The New York Times* called her a Boston Brahmin, but she was not descended from the same family as Holm Lea's owner, nor that of the painter John Singer Sargent.

A small point, but with large ramifications. Katharine's parents had both experienced their own parents' poverty and business failure; Katharine's experience of plenty did not come with a guarantee. Moreover, these freedoms might not have been available to her as a daughter of the leisure class destined to further her family's status through marriage. The childhood that her father gave her was characterized by its liberality.

So for Katharine, Holm Lea meant not a faint social embarrassment but quiet roads through which she and her friends were allowed to bicycle all year round, provided they did not pick any blooms from Mr. Sargent's shrubs. In the late 1890s, bicycling was still controversial for girls and young women. Conservatives worried that bicycles would harm girls' growing bodies, deforming or overstimulating the pelvis, damaging reproductive organs, and unfitting the future women for childbearing. They also worried that unsupervised free time would translate into expectations for political independence. Both fears stemmed from concern for the continuity of white supremacy—if women were too busy bicycling into their new future to birth babies, then the ruling class would have no descendants to carry on their interests. Katharine was allowed to bike with her sisters and her friends from Hawthorn Road to Walnut Street and then west to Holm Lea, where she would enter at Heath Street, because it was close to "a lovely swamp" where she would pick skunk cabbage and cowslips—Mr. Sargent couldn't object to those bouquets, could he?

Katharine's father influenced her to become a gardener and a naturalist, the kind of person who would always remember the first time she found a fringed orchid in New Hampshire. With her ruddy health and her preference for outdoor activities, she was a tomboy, a cultural category promulgated just after the Civil War to correct the definition of white womanhood as frail and inactive, a definition that many thought was the reason for rampant illness among white women and a declining birth rate. For girls of Katharine's class and race, a hearty diet and physical exercise were new ingredients for growing the strong wives and mothers their generation needed. Her father's parenting destined Katharine to become a New Woman, that much-discussed creature of the day, a specific cohort of women born at the end of the nineteenth century—between the Victorian embodiments of "true womanhood" and the flapper—who achieved unprecedented levels of education, a cohort of women portrayed in the popular press as athletic, independent, and socially mobile. The New Woman most frequently appeared in the popular press astride a bicycle.

2.

Though Katharine's astonishing memory retained into old age the precise way that her father's rose stamens shifted from gold to brown, she could not remember a single detail about her mother, who died when she was six years old, just a year after the family moved to Hawthorn Road and its idyllic gardens.

Katharine never wrote about her mother. She never mentioned hearing the news of her mother's sudden death or attending her funeral service. She never referred to herself as motherless. None of her accounts of herself included this trauma—indeed, she almost certainly wouldn't have called it a trauma. This silence can be explained not only because her mother was so quickly supplanted within the Sergeant household, but also by the family's emotional reticence, by a logic in which too much feeling was dangerous.

Everything that Katharine learned about the Shepley side of her family, she learned from Aunt Poo, most of it from a remarkable book that Poo wrote toward the end of her life when she was the last surviving Shepley—or rather three identical books, one for each of the Sergeant sisters. She typed out the family story in triplicate, over two hundred single-spaced pages, and she pasted in old photographs and had each of the large books luxuriantly bound in antique Japanese brocade. Her book is a long, loving, and deeply mythologizing account of the Shepleys, its author desperate to honor her forebears and assure her nieces they come from good and ancient stock. Even within Aunt Poo's sentimental account, though, the cracks in the mythology show plainly. Not only did Poo's book fail to draw Katharine close to her mother's memory, it also stumbled in portraying the Shepleys as American nobility. Their gentility was always aspirational and sometimes quite imperiled.

Katharine's mother, Elizabeth Blake Shepley, was known as Bessie. Both of Bessie's parents, James Cunningham Shepley and Mary Fessenden Barrows, came from Maine. James attended Thornton Academy and Bowdoin College, then read law at a firm in Saco, Maine, following in his father's career, before heading west to open his own practice. Mary, the daughter of a country doctor in Fryeburg, Maine, married James in 1853 and joined him in St. Cloud, Minnesota. Bessie was the eldest; Poo came next; and then a son, George.

Bessie's father was active in civic life and helped to write the new state's constitution, but he lived in the Shepley family imagination as a doer of dangerous deeds, including a heroic and physically grueling rescue of a group of white settlers who'd been trapped in Fort Abercrombie by the Sioux and Chippewa, as well as a stint in the Civil War. One thing he was not adept at was making money, and the war had broken his health, so after the war the Shepleys lived in a carriage house on a relative's vast country estate in Naples, Maine. Bessie's happiest years unfolded in this remote and beautiful landscape, and that's what she would seek to re-create for her daughters. She had twenty cows for company, and dogs and cats and horses and hens and pigs, in addition to her brother and sister, and orchards, pastures, forests, a trout brook, and a pond. "We read *Little Women*," Poo recalled, "and liked it because it was a family just like ours, we thought"—the Shepleys were the Marches with the patriarch back home. Their family formed, according to Poo, a "charmed circle" that was united by their parents' obvious love for each other, even through the difficult years of James's protracted illness. Poo also referred to the "family glamour," their own bedrock certainty of Mary and Bessie's beauty, James and George's intelligence, and Poo's wit.

As the girls grew older, the charmed circle opened a bit so they could attend school. Bessie first attended the North Bridgton Academy and then a school in Boston, both times staying with family. But her future was cut short by the early death of her father. James Shepley moved to California to start a sheep-raising business with two other men. It never prospered. One day in May of 1874, he was found dead up in the hills, garroted, with his money and gold watch still on his body. The murder was never solved, and its effects rippled outward in Bessie's life.

On the advice of relatives, Mary moved the family to Boston and bought a house on Charles Street, turning it into a boarding home, which began to fail almost immediately. As a widow with three children newly thrust into moneymaking, Mary did not run the business well and struggled to afford food for her family and her boarders. The children would remember going hungry as they descended into extreme poverty. It was an enormous downfall for the family: from the lush country to the city, from cash-poor abundance to privation, from close-knit togetherness to loss and absence.

The Shepleys loathed their boarders, purely out of resentment, though all of them were, in Poo's telling phrase, "a very superior set of people." One of them was "a quiet young man with beautiful dark eyes" who liked to sketch, didn't particularly like the business world of Boston in which he worked, and found the boardinghouse to be homelike and comfortable. At Christmas in 1879, he and Bessie announced their engagement to the family. Bessie was twenty-three years old and Charles was twenty-eight.

Charles Spencer Sergeant rescued the Shepleys. He analyzed Mary's finances with a businessman's eye and induced her to give up the boardinghouse. On June 3, 1880, Charles and Bessie were married in the flat by one of her uncles, the bride in fashionable olive green. Charles moved everyone to a small, newly built double house in Winchester shared with a family of three, with oak trees in back, a veranda in front, and a park across the street. Elsie was born eleven months later and named after her mother. Mary helped Bessie keep house, furnished it with her eighteenth-century family heirlooms, and cooked extravagantly from her storehouse of country recipes. George paid board for a room in the crowded household while Poo studied art in New York.

The Winchester years give a glimpse of what Katharine's childhood might have been like had her mother survived. The Sergeants were social and active with a wide circle of friends among the young families of Winchester. Bessie doted on her daughter, but she worried about her too, and doubted her own abilities as a mother. Elsie was frequently ill, especially with earaches. On the night that Rosamond was born, six-year-old Elsie was sent to a neighbor's, where she succumbed to an earache so intense that when she learned the next morning that she had a sister, she felt a distinct sense of unreality; her family seemed like strangers who had played a trick on her. When Ros was little, she too was plagued with poor health.

As an adult, Elsie's words for Bessie were "quiet unassertive and saddish now and then." She remembered her mother crying as she pored over the household accounts, afraid to spend money—surely haunted by the boardinghouse years—yet unable to counter her husband's appetite for rich breakfasts consisting of steak or fish, plus eggs, muffins, and griddle cakes with maple syrup.

Perhaps she was overshadowed in their tight household by stronger personalities: Charles as the patriarch and Bessie's mother, Mary, whom the children called Garty. Elsie, who would grow up to become a writer who specialized in portraits of writers and other artists, once attempted but never finished a memoir of her own evolution as an artist. Elsie would call Garty a "dominiser," a powerful figure who stood taller than Charles and exerted as much control over him as she could, given that he was the breadwinner and she was perfectly penniless. Every single day since James's ghastly murder, she wore old-fashioned widow's dress, including a black gown with a tight-fitting bodice and a bonnet over her gray crimped hair with a veil that fell down her back to her waist. She was deeply competitive at games: chess, dominoes, cribbage, hearts, Old Maid, bezique, solitaire. Her main way to engage the children was to have them button her shoes or run errands. In Elsie's memoir, these "two murderous antagonists"—her father and his mother-in-law—formed the internal structure of her own mind, a powerful male and a powerful female locked in combat. She also remembered many loving moments with her father, as when he told her "Mr. Greenheart" stories every evening, a character he invented who lived behind a little door in a tree, or when he took her on canoe trips every Sunday morning. She called her father and her aunt Poo, the painter who lived on her own in New York, the "rousers of [her] inner imaginative life." But of her mother, she wrote almost nothing; Bessie left barely a trace on her eldest daughter, the one who knew her longest.

Bessie gave unwavering support to Poo in the pursuit of her icono-clastic artistic career. She encouraged her to go to Paris to study paint-ing, and to devote herself to her art full-time upon her return, rather than teach. Poo did, traveling to the Académie Julian, which, unlike the École des Beaux-Arts, admitted women. She received the same artistic training there as previous students, such as Henri Matisse, John Singer Sargent, and American painters Cecilia Beaux and Elizabeth Gardner. Bessie sent encouraging letters during the tough times, telling Poo, "You have great and unusual ability, and we know you have a strong character and wonderful courage and perseverance." She sent money, and she did her best to bridge the distance between her life ("a person with a com-fortable home and an assured income," as she called herself) and Poo's spinster life in the city.

Garty did not exert her influence on Katharine. Bessie's mother had moved with the Sergeants from Winchester to Walnut Street, the orig-inal road in Brookline, Massachusetts, and she moved with them again as Charles's fortunes grew. In the summer of 1898, the Sergeants bought the large and handsome house that would form the basis of Katharine's memories. Charles paid $23,500 to Anne Appleton for the house that her mother, Mary Appleton, had commissioned from Henry F. Bigelow and William Rutan only four years earlier. The Sergeants' new home at 4 Hawthorn Road was a three-story, 4,300-square-foot, pink-brick Georgian Revival with a half-circle driveway, six bedrooms, and six fireplaces, at the front of a 17,600-square-foot parcel of land.

Garty must have approved of this move. The town of Brookline and the house itself signaled a rise in stature. Brookline, a suburb of Boston, grew not from farmland but from small country estates belonging to wealthy retired merchants or businessmen who commuted into the city center by carriage. In 1860, the Brookline Land Company formed to develop the town while still preserving its exclusivity. The company sold plots with a deed preventing "occupation or erection of any building which could work injury or annoyance to residents." Brookline became an even more desirable neighborhood once the Brookline Branch Rail-road carried residents into Back Bay. Charles joined the men commuting into the city, while his wife and mother-in-law ran the big house.

But Garty enjoyed the splendid new home for only a month before she died in October of 1898, on the forty-third anniversary of her marriage to James Shepley. The funeral took place in the Episcopal church she helped to found, and she was buried not with the Shepleys in Maine but with the Sergeants in a plot in Winchester, Massachusetts. In Poo's mind, it was Ros who loved Garty the most but Katharine who most resembled her in character.

The following spring of 1899, Bessie decided to visit Poo and their brother, George, at 96 Fifth Avenue in New York, where they "kept house on a windowsill," as Ros described their artistic poverty. Bessie was finally coming into her own as a wife and mother. Elsie, the oldest, was taking an extra year after graduating from Miss Winsor's School before applying to Bryn Mawr College. Katharine was growing into a sturdy young girl and all three daughters were thriving. But Bessie had been feeling unwell and thought a change of scene and a reunion with her siblings would help.

On May 8, Bessie and Poo visited the Metropolitan Museum of Art, but Bessie experienced abdominal pain so great it prevented her from walking. Back at Poo's studio, they called their rich neighbor's doctor and he soon arrived but refused to treat Bessie. He suspected she had appendicitis, and if so, her case was beyond his expertise. Appendectomy was a recent surgical technique; only in 1894 did Charles McBurney describe the incision that could split the muscles so the inflamed organ could be removed. While Bessie lay in agony, George spent the night tracking down the one surgeon in Manhattan who could help her—it may have been Dr. McBurney himself—and when he arrived first thing the next morning, he confirmed the diagnosis and rushed her to the New York Hospital on Fifteenth Street for the operation. Bessie wanted to wait until Charles could come down from Brookline, but the delay had already cost her too much, so she went into surgery without him. He arrived just as she emerged and had about ten minutes alone with her before she died.

The girls learned the news when Aunt Poo stepped off the train in Brookline the next afternoon, but Katharine never recalled this moment. Elsie had had an ear operation that morning and was pale and gaunt with a bandage around her head. That evening, the ear began hemor-rhaging and Elsie was again treated by a doctor. Elsie never commented on the link between her earaches and monumental changes to her family, first Rosamond's birth and then her mother's death.

The Sergeants held a service for Bessie at home, and then they all journeyed to the family burial ground in Winchester, where Bessie was laid to rest next to her mother. Aunt Poo remembered that Elsie was un-der Charles's strict injunction not to cry or show any emotion during the service and burial. She privately wondered if this is what caused Elsie's mental health to suffer just a few years later. Did Katharine cry, and was she scolded? Certainly one of the lessons she absorbed as a child was that decorum was crucial even at a moment of deep internal anguish.

Aunt Poo stayed with the Sergeants all through the summer, when they took a house in Marion, Massachusetts. And then, as the school year commenced, Aunt Poo returned to her brother, George, in New York, and Charles brought the two younger girls back to Hawthorn Road. Elsie began her first year at Bryn Mawr College, having passed the demanding entrance exams. She settled into her rooms in Denbigh Hall and enrolled in English literature, medieval history, and biology. That fall she acted the part of Queen Elizabeth in a play called *The Quest of the Lantern*. Curiously, Elsie's departure for Bryn Mawr and their mother's death became linked in Katharine's mind in the tiny fig-ure of a teacup, a real-life incident that she later tried to work up into a short story that she heavily revised but never finished. "So many things happened that year, ^good things and bad things that Kathy could never quite sort them out in her mind or know which had happened first," the story begins. ". . . The best of them all was the teacups. and the worst was Mama." Kathy, who is six, and her next-eldest sister, Penelope, receive bone china teacups done up in fancy paper from a distant aunt. "'What a Christmas present for children!' said Marguerite scornfully. Marguerite was 17 years old ^and was apt to talk that way." In real life, Katharine, who col-lected china animals and miniature shoes from foreign countries, was enchanted with the delicate teacup, white with tiny bunches of roses—and then devastated when she was forced to give it to Elsie to use in her proper Bryn Mawr dorm room.

Ros returned to school at Miss Winsor's. Their father returned to his routine: up at dawn to head directly to his garden to dig weeds and to supervise the work of William Hickey, his handyman, before an early breakfast and then the train into Boston, returning home to eat supper and tell his daughters stories or read to them. Somehow he found the time to visit his many clubs, the exclusive Algonquin, the professional Engineers, and the artistic St. Botolph's, where he might have shared a drink with fellow member Frederick Law Olmsted. The Sergeants' cook, Mary Hillen, and two young Irish maids, Louise Fallon and Catherine Evans, took care of the family.

3.

It was Katharine's life that changed the most. Into her mother and grandmother's absence stepped another aunt, this time from the Sergeant side of the family: Caroline Belle Sergeant, or Aunt Crullie. At six years old, Katharine was too young to follow in her sisters' footsteps at Miss Winsor's, so Crullie resigned her position as headmistress of the Norwood School in Newark, New Jersey, to live with her brother and care for Katharine. No one at that time could anticipate that she would live with Charles for nearly four decades, until his death in 1936.

The graft between aunt and niece took. "My feeling for you was love at first sight—such a dear little girl, who accepted me so sweetly," wrote Crullie, on her ninetieth birthday, to Katharine. The feeling was mutual. Katharine would refer to Crullie her entire life as "really [her] mother." Crullie, as given to sentimentalizing as Aunt Poo, told a story of those early months that metonymically expressed their relationship. It was evening, and she and Charles were sitting peacefully by the fire in the library, when Crullie heard Katharine calling to her from the top of the stairs. She went to the little girl, shivering in her nightgown, and asked her what was wrong. "Aunt Crullie, I told you a lie. I haven't studied my lessons for to-morrow," Katharine replied, according to Crullie, whose heart melted. "From then on I think we understood each other," she wrote to her niece. Crullie was Katharine's teacher, plus her aunt and mother, until she was eleven. From Katharine's earliest memories, love and learning were bound up together in the person of her impressive aunt.

Caroline Belle Sergeant was the youngest of seven siblings in the Sergeant family, born on Charles's tenth birthday. Charles was the oldest son and the third sibling of George and Lydia Ann (Clark) Sergeant of Northampton, Massachusetts. Lydia died just a year and a half after Crullie's birth. George, a grain merchant, died of pneumonia in 1875, when Crullie was twelve. Katharine later noted for the family archive that her father was headed to Harvard when George died penniless because his partner embezzled funds, forcing Charles to go into the business world to support his family. This was not strictly true. Katharine also mythologized her family's history.

Charles was twenty-two when his father died, long past the age of Harvard College matriculation. After graduating from Northampton High School when he was sixteen, he went straight to work in a bank in Easthampton, climbing his way up in four years from sweeping the floors to serving as a teller. In 1872, he turned his banking experience into his first position with a railroad. Like many young men before him, he escaped the conservatism of his close-knit Boston family by going west; he moved to Lake Superior to serve as cashier and paymaster of the Marquette, Houghton & Ontonagon Railroad. Charles asked his father to alert him to openings at railroads back east, but his next position, as clerk for an iron company, kept him in Michigan. It wasn't until the year after his father's death that he was able to return to Massachusetts, when he took a position as chief clerk of the Eastern Railroad, which was where he was working when he met Bessie Shepley four years later.

It made sense, then, that Charles would take the Shepleys' finances in hand and lead them to firmer ground. He was the only one on any branch or twig of Katharine's family tree with business sense—but in all other respects, the two sides of Katharine's family had almost everything in common. As white Anglo-Saxon Protestants whose ancestors had been in New England for generations, they were from the same world and shared the same unspoken assumptions. Neither family was wealthy; neither possessed a house or estate to display their prominence in material terms. But both families saved furniture, daguerreotypes, and thousands of letters from their ancestors; both families believed in their own American nobility. Both the Shepleys and the Sergeants reminded themselves of their family legacies in their letters to one another and kept alive the feeling that though they may have struggled financially, they were nonetheless set apart by the deeds of their forebears. Aunt Poo, for instance, repeated the story of her father's daring rescue of the white pioneers from the barbaric Native Americans. Growing up, she had been accustomed to "thinking and reading people," she wrote to Katharine, to the "First Families" of New England, so that when she moved to Palatine Bridge in the Mohawk Valley of New York as a young woman to take a teaching job, it was "a different sort of place, as foreign to anything [she] had known as Russia would have been."

The Sergeants always invoked the one about Katharine's great-great-great-grandfather, "the famous John Sergeant," in her words, "the first missionary to the Hoosatonic Indians in Stockbridge." She wrote that he was "famous for many things, among others that he was the first missionary to any American Indian tribe to make a grammar in their own language. A member of one of the earliest classes to graduate from Yale, he went directly to his missionary work, and his house is now a museum in Stockbridge called 'The Mission House.'" Reading deeper into this story reveals slightly different contours.

John Sergeant graduated from Yale twenty-eight years after its founding. He did indeed become the first missionary to "the praying town of Stockbridge" in Massachusetts, and learned the language of the Mohicans, into which he translated all his sermons and portions of the Old Testament. But he also found the Mohicans "as fickle and irresolute in their Determinations, as any People in the World." He gave up on the adults and focused his work on a bold solution for Mohican youth—children would be separated from their parents to break their dependence on their Native culture and sent to learn at a Christian boarding school that he founded in the 1740s. He married Abigail Williams, the daughter of a land speculator, and built the Mission House high on a hill, from which he preached while his father-in-law steadily dispossessed the Mohicans of their lands down below, some of which would become Williams College. Stockbridge's most famous resident, Norman Rockwell, would nonetheless mythologize the white and Native alliance by painting Konkapot, the Mohicans' leader, and John Sergeant in the Mission House parlor, Abigail peeking around the corner in wariness.

Charles and Crullie grew up in the Mission House, as had all the Sergeants before them, but all that remained of their family legacy was

John and Abigail's wedding furniture and the stories of John Sergeant's deeds. Their father, George, was not a successful businessman. A decade after he married Lydia Ann Clark, Katharine's grandfather and a partner started a dry goods store, Thayer and Sergeant, but they also tried to expand the store and speculated in real estate, so that their small empire ballooned and then collapsed. Just before her death, Lydia's grandfather sold her a house on Bridge Street in Northampton, a house that her seven children inherited, and in which many of them would die during Katharine's lifetime.

There was emotional truth, then, to Katharine's statement that Charles was forced to make his own way in the world as the only son of a struggling merchant, but her version of the facts glides past the family's firm grasp on patrimony. Katharine's father felt an innate connection to the communities built by his ancestors, an ownership that had nothing to do with landed wealth. He was a member of the Sons of the American Revolution (and his sisters were Daughters), listing five different ancestors whose deeds entitled him to join that club, including Erastus Sergeant, the Reverend John Sergeant's son. But what separated him from the other side of Katharine's family is that he inherited from his father a modern standard of success, as well as a model of what *not* to do. Charles appears to have avoided speculating in real estate and never partnered with other businessmen. He internalized his father's standards of success by providing for his family and by steadily improving his position in the public realm of business, and his proud maintenance of the home at Hawthorn Road proved his investment in visible markers of prosperity. He believed in bootstrapping, but he disdained anything that deviated from the world of public enterprise. He made no disguise of his contempt for Bessie's brother, George, who left his mother and sister to work on the Mexican Central Railway, where he eventually spent seven years. No matter that George's biography dovetailed with Charles's own; he had even gone to work in a bank at age twelve, beating Charles to that distinction by four years. George struck Charles as a failure, someone who hadn't "made good in business," lacking as he did a house, a family, and a slate of club memberships. Charles resented his "coming back without a penny" and found him too much like his father, the failed sheepherder. He obtained a job for "the family scapegrace," as Katharine later called him, on the Boston-Worcester streetcar line of the Boston Elevated. Unlike George, Charles was conservative and prosperous precisely because his own father was not. Thus, both Katharine's father and mother grew up with their parents' business failures as structuring principles of their adulthood. The material comfort of their suburban estate was new to them.

When his sister Crullie came to Hawthorn Road to help ease some of her brother's responsibilities, she brought with her another facet of the Sergeant family legacy, another modern difference from the Shepleys—the high value they placed on female education. Charles and Crullie's oldest sister, Kittie (full name Catharine De Forest Sergeant), for whom Katharine was named, was herself named after her aunt Catharine Sedgwick Sergeant De Forest. This Catharine had served as a missionary in Beirut and Lebanon with the American Board for twelve years and helped to found a girls' school—this was another cornerstone story of the Sergeant family. And this Catharine, for her part, was likely named after Catharine Maria Sedgwick, a novelist and Stockbridge relative, who in 1839 advised girls, "Be sure to be so educated that you can have an independent pursuit, something to occupy your time and interest your affections; then marriage will not be essential to your usefulness, respectability, or happiness." Female education was built into Katharine Sergeant's very name.

Aunt Crullie, the youngest of the seven siblings left motherless when Lydia died the year after her birth, might have grown up with pinched prospects. But her sister Kittie, who lived in George and Lydia's house at 82 Bridge Street in Northampton her entire life, and her brother Charles made sure that Crullie had an advanced education. After graduating from Northampton High School, she attended Smith College, then only five years old, graduating in 1884. As a pioneer at a women's college, Crullie was entirely too educated for her time; the only ambitious future open to her was teaching. She moved to the South and began a girl's school on the plan of Smith College, which was successful enough that after two years she could leave it to run without her when she returned north. She taught at the Clarke School for the Deaf in Northampton, then a private school in Connecticut, before moving to Newark to become co-headmistress of the Norwood School. Her sister-in-law Bessie's death cut short her career, but she stressed to Katharine that coming to live with her brother and to take care of his daughters was not sacrifice but "a rare blessing." Perhaps she joined Charles's household because she felt she owed him for all he and Kittie had given her; perhaps she joined the family because she had grown up motherless and financially insecure, and she wanted to give her nieces a better life.

4.

Charles and Aunt Crullie gave the youngest Sergeant daughter a childhood filled with books. Katharine had a few of her mother's books: the moralistic Franconia stories by the Reverend Jacob Abbott and Juliana Horatia Ewing's *Jackanapes*, "the romantic story that our grandmothers and great-grandmothers used to weep over," as she later wrote in *The New Yorker*, and which made her cry too. Another of Ewing's stories featured a little girl nicknamed Traveler's Joy, who went around planting flowers along the highway to cheer up tired travelers. Country lanes in Woodstock, Connecticut, were thus similarly adorned with perennials dug up from Aunt Poo's flower beds, because "Mrs. Ewing had power," as Katharine would write in *The New Yorker*. She remembered Aunt Poo reading Br'er Rabbit and the Tar Baby stories to her. Katharine would certainly have read Charlotte F. Daley's books of poems and stories, *Sundials*, *The Skating Party*, and *When Three Are Company*, because Aunt Poo illustrated all of them, but she might not have liked them. Katharine's taste ran away from the sentimental.

She read an abundance of fairy tales and preferred Andrew Lang's collections—*The Blue Fairy Book*, *The Red Fairy Book*, *The Violet Fairy Book*—to Arthur Rackham's "gloomy" illustrations with their "darksome forests and tortured tree trunks." Her appreciation for the genre was sophisticated enough to encompass satires of it, such as *The Feather* by Ford Madox Ford. She read Laura E. Richards's *Captain January*. She had beautiful editions of Lewis Carroll's *Alice* books and *Robin Hood* and *Aesop's Fables*. She did not own—and therefore ardently yearned for—*The Adventures of Baron Munchausen* with the Gustave Doré illustrations, a friend's treasured possession. She had no time for what she considered sappy books like *Heidi* or *Hans Brinker*, she far preferred the gritty world of *Black Beauty*.

She loved *Evelina* by Fanny Burney, the epistolary novel about a young girl buffeted by the cruelties and pleasures of aristocratic society. Katharine considered it deliciously scandalous. Best of all were the novels of Louisa May Alcott, and she declared as a fifty-four-year-old, "They are still the best that have been written." Like many intellectual women before and after her, Katharine discovered in *Little Women* a story rooted in realism and female domesticity that opened an imaginative space of possibility, of ambition, for its young female reader.

Charles sent his youngest daughter to the public library in Brookline once a week with the grave responsibility of choosing two books for him to read to himself at night. Crullie choose his novels; Katharine was responsible for autobiographies and travel narratives. He would be stern with her if she slipped up and selected a book he had already read, so from the youngest age, she was paying close attention to adult reading habits, the curation of an interior life.

Katharine was lucky to live in the town that housed the nation's very first children's reading room. The city of Boston opened the first free public library in 1848, but it wasn't until 1890, two years before Katharine was born, that the Brookline Public Library turned its basement over to children's books, and in 1899 it added a children's librarian. Katharine was not, though, confined to the children's room, and she read widely: "Eliza Orne White, and Lily Wesselhoeft, and Howard Pyle to Dumas and Sarah Orne Jewett, and Scott and Thackeray—all at the same age."

Katharine read what she could, and she listened to her father or Aunt Crullie read aloud what she could not yet read, and she listened to what they were reading to Ros: *Ivanhoe* at age seven or eight, then *Oliver Twist* and *David Copperfield*. She was set loose in the library of her aunts and uncles at Bridge Street in Northampton, where she was captivated by her first magazine, *Harper's Young People*, an eight-page weekly that she read in bound volumes dating back to the 1880s.

But a glimpse of Katharine's future lies in the pages of another children's magazine, *St. Nicholas*, which might with no little exaggeration be called *The New Yorker* for the precocious author and artist. It was founded in 1873 and edited by Mary Mapes Dodge, the author of *Hans Brinker*. In 1899, the same year that *Harper's Young People* folded, *St. Nicholas* introduced a wildly popular new department called "the St. Nicholas League," a subscribers' competition in poetry and prose, drawing, photography, and puzzles, for which winners won silver or gold badges and publication in the next issue. An incomplete list of *New Yorker* artists whose careers began with bylines in *St. Nicholas* includes Ring Lardner, Cornelia Otis Skinner, Robert Benchley, Edmund Wilson, Elinor Wylie, Theodore Roethke, Eudora Welty, Faith Baldwin, and Rachel Carson. One month a poem by Edna St. Vincent Millay was featured in the same issue as a photograph by Scott Fitzgerald. William Falkner submitted a drawing just a few years before he added a vowel to his last name. Ernest Hemingway used to sneak copies with him to the outhouse, "for this was the best reading time of all," and years later the smell of lime on a battlefield would bring back to him a memory of the magazine. When *New Yorker* writer Stephen Vincent Benét's epic poem, *John Brown's Body*, achieved bestseller status in 1928, the magazine noted that Benét had begun his career with a gold medal from *St. Nicholas* and wondered "how many other American poets did too," noting, "Our theory is that all of them must have. . . . We doubt if any poet could retain his lyric heart until reaching his majority, were it not for the gold badge of *St. Nicholas*, clutched against his thin and palpitant breast."

The Sergeants were *St. Nicholas* subscribers, naturally, and in the early months of 1902, Rosamond saw her name on its honor roll three times for her photography. Not to be outdone, that August Katharine achieved a silver badge for a short piece of prose, "A Discovery (A True Story)." It is a fact almost too good to be believed that her true story was about a spider and its web, "all soft and silky," foreshadowing her future husband's biggest success. She was nine years old, not yet a schoolgirl, and she beat both of her future husbands into the magazine. Her first husband, Ernest Angell, wouldn't see his name in *St. Nicholas* until the following year, when he began earning gold badges and honor roll mentions for solving the magazine's mercilessly difficult puzzles, and submitting his own. Elwyn B. White (whose first prize was from *Woman's Home Companion* for a poem about a mouse when he was nine) won a silver badge in 1910, when he was eleven, for "A Winter Walk" ("All the trees wore a new fur coat, pure white, and the pines and evergreens were laden with pearl"), then a gold badge in 1913 for "A True Dog Story," and several honor roll mentions.

Ros kept at her photography, and in 1903 she won third prize in the "wild-animal photograph" category for a picture called *Wild Ducks*, but Katharine—ever the worshipper of truth—called that "a sinful hoax" because the ducks were tame ones living on a pond and eating from their hands. E. B. White possessed a far more ecumenical stance toward the magazine's editorial policy. A boy who lived two houses up the block clued him in: if he wanted to get published in *St. Nicholas*, he just had to put in some kindness to animals. As a result, his early writings showed "an amazing note of friendliness toward dumb creatures, an almost virulent sympathy for dogs, cats, horses, bears, toads, and robins. [He] was kind to animals in all sorts of weather almost every month for three or four years." Two children, one in Brookline, Massachusetts, and the other in Mount Vernon, New York, both critically scrutinizing the criteria for submission to a literary magazine.

Katharine was a promiscuous reader as well as a precocious one, and her father and Crullie seemed to have provided only support, never censorship. Katharine was allowed to read books that scared her and books that she didn't understand—and these were "often the ones that meant the most" to her. Years later, when she reviewed children's books for *The New Yorker*, she worried that the abundance of juvenile books scrolling off the presses would "divert children from adult books they otherwise would be reading." She valued intellectual risk, because she herself had profited from wading into books that made her stretch to encompass them.

In many respects the Sergeants conformed to the socioeconomic patterns of other white, middle-class, urban, professional families in the Northeast at the turn of the century. Charles was a strict, class-conscious, and politically conservative patriarch, one who held his entire extended clan to a rigorous standard of propriety, but he deviated from the parenting values of his peers in several important ways, perhaps because his own hold on his newly acquired social class was more tenuous than it appeared. The Romantic vision of childhood that reigned among the Sergeants' class held that children were magical, fragile, innocent creatures who needed protection from the savage world for as long as possible. The pioneering children's reading rooms in public libraries such as Brookline's were as much about keeping curious readers away from adult books as they were about fostering children's native imagination. But not only was Katharine allowed to read widely, for a time she escaped the confines of structured schooling and was not taught the feminine arts of sewing and needlework, though she did play piano. Charles did not attend church except for holidays, and this meant his daughters did not attend Sunday school. For Charles, books were an instrument of social betterment, an ongoing project in his household.

More important, Charles had ensured Crullie's education, and she in turn brought to his household a conception of childhood that jibed perfectly with teenage Elsie's own burgeoning modern independence as a Bryn Mawr student. Though Elsie left for college when Katharine was only eight years old, she continued to nurture her littlest sister—perhaps even more than she did Rosamond, with whom she had less in common. When Katharine was quite young, Elsie gave her a book of British verse, and this made an enormous impression on Katharine. She would say that this volume taught her "there was more to poetry than Sir Walter Scott and the early American poets," but the gift was even bigger than that. The gift was Elsie's attention and her cultivation of Katharine's intellectual life. If Elsie's inner world was shaped by the "murderous antagonism" between Charles and Garty, Katharine's was shaped by the dovetailing sympathies of Crullie and Elsie, for though she was motherless, she was nonetheless raised in a household of ambitious, educated women, plus one forceful man. Her family was typical of its era in that adults took priority over children—"their comforts, their needs, their pleasure," in Katharine's words—but this youngest daughter grew up in a kind of loophole created by the loving attention of her aunt and sister, both single, both educated, both interested in her as a project of their own feminism. Katharine would later say, "[Elsie] was a most important person in my life until I was about twenty-five and I owe her more than

I can say." Her sister and aunt gave her an unself-conscious security and she remembered gradually realizing how the rest of the world saw her: "I was short, with a great knot of hair at the back of my head. I had not particularly worried about my appearance, though, until an old friend of the family said to me, 'I suppose you realize, my dear, that your *hair* is a deformity.'" Elsie and Aunt Crullie cared about propriety but not beauty, style, or fashion; they took specific interest in the growth of Katharine's mind and gave her a wide-open vision of what her future might hold.

And Charles, for the most part, agreed that Katharine's intellect should be fostered. Before long, Elsie would battle him about a wildly consequential decision for Katharine's future. But mostly Katharine remembered her father's nurturing qualities along with his strictness, which came together in the view of him as a gardener sculpting his land into formal beauty. It was her father who mixed "preventative hot whiskey lemonades" and "restorative eggnogs" when his daughters were sick. When Charles celebrated the opening of a new line of the Boston Elevated that he had engineered—it may have been the L, which began service in the summer of 1901—it was Katharine who got to push the throttle of the train forward on its maiden voyage.

The year 1903 brought significant changes to Katharine's world. Not only did she obtain another honor roll mention in *St. Nicholas* for an essay, but she also began school that autumn at age eleven, becoming the third Sergeant girl to attend Miss Winsor's School. Elsie had entered the school for girls at age thirteen; Bessie and Charles had chosen it for her because Miss Winsor's father, Frederick Winsor, had been the Sergeants' family doctor when they lived in Winchester. Sending their eldest daughter to an elite private school was surely a signpost of upward class mobility for Bessie and Charles, a repudiation of their respective parents' business failures. The fit was so apt for Elsie that Rosamond and Katharine followed her there.

Ros was a tenth-grade pupil, and each morning she'd walk Katharine up the hill to High Street, then back down the hill to Brookline Village, where they would catch the streetcar to 95–96 Beacon Street. How could Katharine fail to be ennobled when she joined the other seventh-graders for classes in the elegant, high-ceilinged rooms of the two brownstones connected by doorways on each floor, with marble fireplaces, gilt paneling, crystal chandeliers, and a Louis Quinze ballroom? She plunged right into the demanding curriculum: *The Bible for Children*, English (which meant spelling, composition, and phonetics), literature (which meant ancient texts and Shakespeare plays), Roman history, mathematics, zoology, French, Latin, art, sewing, and gym. Each morning at eleven o'clock, the girls of Miss Winsor's would pour out the front doors and flood the Boston Public Garden for recess, "liable at any time to overlook the 'Keep Off' on ice or grass, to block the walks with games of marbles, or to play tag, inadvertently, on tulip beds," in Miss Winsor's words.

Headmistress Mary Pickard Winsor was straight out of a Frances Hodgson Burnett novel. She had entered Smith College in 1879 (a year before Aunt Crullie) but was called home after only one year to help her mother with her private girls' school, Miss Ware's in Winchester. Education was her destiny: her grandmother had also run a private school, three of her six siblings would go into higher education, and eight other women from her class at Smith would go on to become headmistresses. Miss Winsor did not teach by the time Katharine enrolled. The youngest Sergeant daughter felt her influence most keenly through the school's summer reading prize, a contest to gladden the bookwormish hearts of all three Sergeant girls. On the last day of the school year, the students were given a list of ten or fifteen books selected for their grade, of which they were required to read about five. But this list was supplemented by dozens of recommendations. Each girl returned to school with a list of her own—all the books she'd read over the summer, with a few reports on the ones she'd liked the most. Miss Winsor collected these lists and held her students in suspense for the entire school year; on the very last day, she'd award a prize for the best list, which was not necessarily the longest, though many girls read over a hundred books a summer in pursuit of Miss Winsor's approval. In her second year, Katharine faced stiff competition in the form of her best friend, Katharine "Katie" Gericke, the Austrian daughter of the conductor of the Boston Symphony. To their relief, they both won, and when Miss Winsor awarded the prize, she said how dreadful it would have been had it gone to only one of them. Katharine kept her prize—a leather-bound copy of James Russell Lowell's complete works inscribed by Miss Winsor—for the rest of her life. Professor Lucy Martin Donnelly, the head of the Bryn Mawr English department, told Katharine a few years later that Miss Winsor's girls were *too* well-read and she could introduce nothing new to them.

5.

The spring prior to Katharine's matriculation at Miss Winsor's, Elsie graduated from Bryn Mawr. She'd had a rocky time; her transcript shows that she repeatedly deferred exams, though when she finally did take them, her marks were stellar. She graduated among the top ten in her class with a concentration in history, politics, and economics, and was awarded the prestigious George W. Childs essay prize. She was, though, in very poor health. Her doctor recommended that she go abroad to regain strength, and Elsie asked Aunt Poo to accompany her. Elsie's postcollegiate trip nearly knocked Katharine off the path of her own life, though it would take some time for the effects to be felt.

Elsie and Poo set sail for Italy that autumn: Taormina, Syracuse, Agrigento, Palermo, Naples, Rome, Assisi, Perugia, and Florence. With each change of city Elsie's state of mind worsened. The very thing that was supposed to cure her was instead weakening her to an alarming degree.

"Nervous strain," in Aunt Poo's words, or "extreme nervous strain." In her doctor's words, "moral depression and continual disquiet" shading into "profound nervous prostration." In a single word, neurasthenia, or "nerve weakness," a disease invented in 1869 by Boston neurologist George M. Beard and embellished by another neurologist, S. Weir Mitchell, who became its foremost expert. Neurasthenia gave doctors a conservative, Victorian framework to counter modern Gilded Age values, which they saw as dangerously accelerated, overextended, and unhealthy. The body possessed a finite supply of nervous energy, which was created by digestion and distributed by the nervous system; some of the uses of human energy, like productive work and physical exercise, were beneficial and increased the body's own supply, but other uses were wasteful, such as masturbation and gambling, and if too much indulged would deplete the body and generate an indistinct constellation of symptoms. Elsie's list included fatigue, headaches, backaches, sleeplessness, digestion trouble, "unhappy" menstruation, thinness, a pale complexion, and a perceptible lack of vitality.

Neurasthenia, though, could function as a backward mark of distinction. It often indicated a sensitivity, a refinement, that characterized the upper classes, and most frequently afflicted artists and intellectuals. George M. Beard connected it directly to women's expanding rights and "the mental activity of women." Women could succumb to neurasthenia if their path to meaningful work was blocked. Jane Addams, who spent seven years in the 1880s in a neurasthenic depression, wrote in *Twenty Years at Hull House*, "I have seen young girls suffer and grow sensibly lowered in vitality in the first years after they leave school. In our attempt then to give a girl pleasure and freedom from care we succeed, for the most part, in making her pitifully miserable." Part of the problem, in her diagnosis, was that the educated young woman is confused by "this apparent waste of herself, this elaborate preparation, if no work is provided for her."

The Sergeant family never referred to this time in Elsie's life with anything more than euphemism, but her trouble appeared to peak during her senior year at Bryn Mawr. Though she initially seemed to do better when she first reached the sunny shores of Sicily, she had a relapse in Taormina, when whom should she encounter but Lucy Martin Donnelly, her Bryn Mawr English professor. Donnelly was acting as chaperone to Mildred Minturn, the youngest daughter of a wealthy family who had periodically suffered from neurasthenia since her own Bryn Mawr graduation in 1897. (Aunt Poo: "One of her troubles seems to be having too much money, I should say.") Aunt Poo was wildly distressed at the reunion. Though she liked Donnelly and saw the obvious affection she had for Elsie, she also observed that Donnelly had "brought back to E. some of the old feeling of strain and tension—merely from seeing every day someone so closely associated with that time." Elsie should at all costs avoid "contact with someone who brings back her interest in work and study." The root of Elsie's sickness was, apparently, the intellectual life she had worked so hard to achieve.

In deference to Poo's orders, Donnelly left Elsie alone, and the two pairs of women parted ways in Palermo. Poo kept Elsie's days peaceful, with breakfast in bed, Italian lessons, light exercise, and no mental exertion whatsoever. "I must try to find as foolish and amusing society as we have had through the winter," Poo wrote to her brother-in-law. They managed to spend six months in Italy without going to a single art museum. But Elsie continued to decline throughout the spring, and Poo's letters to Charles grew more panicked.

In May of 1904, Poo abandoned the notion of Venice and instead rushed Elsie to Paris to visit Dr. Gorodichze, the same doctor Mildred Minturn had consulted the previous year. Within an hour of meeting the bearded Russian, Elsie was committed to the Institut Médical de Champs-Elysées. Had she been a man, the prescription would have been the "camp cure," several months on a ranch in the western United States for vigorous exertion with horses, rope, and cattle; the West functioned in the American cultural imagination as a wellspring of energy that brought out the civic best in overworked white urbanites. A straight line can be drawn from Theodore Roosevelt's own cure for neurasthenia— his stint in the Dakotas from 1884 to 1886—to his part in the creation of the National Park system. But Dr. Gorodichze gave Elsie the female equivalent: the "rest cure," pioneered by Dr. Mitchell for the most severe cases among his upper-class white female patients. Elsie was forbidden from seeing anyone for a month and from writing to anyone for two weeks. She was on a strict diet meant to increase her weight, which would then increase the supply of energy circulating through her system, and she was on a rigidly structured schedule of virtually no exertion besides sitting in the garden, to combat the psychological irrationality that came with depleted reserves. Charlotte Perkins Gilman, a patient of Mitchell, famously suffered more from the intellectual starvation of the rest cure than she did from her initial illness, as she portrayed in the horrific short story "The Yellow Wallpaper."

Elsie, too, failed to bounce back. At the end of her first month, she was out of bed for only one to two hours a day, and her doctor warned that autumn would be far too soon for her to return to her family. Over the next year and a half, she moved from hospital to luxury hotel to hospital in Neuilly-sur-Seine, Switzerland, and England. Aunt Poo returned to the United States at the end of 1904. Sometime during this period, Charles left his youngest two daughters with Aunt Crullie and moved to London for six months, where he had been invited to consult on the design and building of the London Underground. He was offered the presidency of the London rapid transit system but declined, possibly because of Elsie's needs.

Katharine may not have known precisely why her sister didn't return from her European tour. It is perhaps telling that Poo and Elsie's letters from abroad are addressed to Charles at his business address, 101 Milk Street in Boston. But for the second time in Katharine's young life, a beloved family member—a woman who nurtured her—went away and did not return. Katharine never wrote about the effects of this disappearance, either, on her emotional life. The incident is striking by the palpable silence that surrounds it.

Elsie returned to the family sometime in 1905, the year Katharine turned thirteen. It had been two years of illness and recovery, and Elsie would take a few years to get back on her feet and begin the writing career that would become her life's work. She would never write about or refer to these years, continuing the Sergeant family tradition of burying pain under silence, but she would become quite interested in the role of the unconscious in the creative process. Katharine too would draw connections between mental health and the writing life, but she would draw them differently from her older sister. They did agree on one lesson, though: even as it must have felt as if she had been punished for her collegiate success as a scholar, Elsie was not deterred from a life of the mind, and nor would her littlest sister be. In the winter of 1906, Elsie felt well enough to undertake some social work among the Italian immigrants in Boston; the next spring, she returned to Europe with Pauline Goldmark, the social reformer, activist, and Bryn Mawr graduate, and soon she would publish her first book, *French Perspectives*, a collection of essays observing French manners.

That previous spring, Ros had graduated from Miss Winsor's. Her

academic record was unremarkable but Miss Winsor praised her character, and she had developed an interest in music and studio art that would
last all her life. Upon graduation, she studied French and music and
tutored two children in Boston, before taking her own (uneventful) trip
to Brittany and Paris. She did not go to college. She had been the steady
sister in Katharine's young life, the one who was there when she left the
classroom to ride the streetcar home; the one who traveled with her to
Connecticut, where they rambled together, eating wild berries and stolen
apples; the one who traveled with her to New Hampshire to splash in
creeks and row on the lake. Their relationship appears to have been easy
and placid, the natural companionship of two girls often alone together,
sharing a love of the woods and a bent for artistic pursuits.

Katharine's relationship with Elsie would grow far pricklier over the
years. Perhaps the origin of their eventual unease can be found in Elsie's
absence and reappearance, and in how changed she must have been upon
her return. But in one respect, Katharine looked to Elsie as a model
for how to grow up. She had her sights firmly fixed on college, and she
wanted to follow in Elsie's footsteps and apply to Bryn Mawr.

Charles said no. In his mind, everything that Elsie had suffered resulted from her overeducation; the fault for her nervous breakdown lay
with the college. Perhaps he had already stifled Ros's desire to continue
her education—the family record is silent about her ambitions. Elsie
recognized the drive in her littlest sister. She was as accustomed to
mothering Katharine as she was to arguing politics with her politically
conservative father and campaigning for the modern ideas she'd learned
at school. She went to battle on Katharine's behalf and argued with her
father to convince him to let Katharine attend college. Finally she prevailed, one of the most consequential acts of nurturing in Katharine's
life, and Katharine would never forget it.

The autumn of 1907 began an intense two-year period during which
Katharine prepared for matriculation. As a college preparatory school,
Miss Winsor's offered two distinct tracks for the students' junior and se-
nior years: Radcliffe and Bryn Mawr. Katharine buckled down to study
English, French, German, Latin prose and poetry, geometry, algebra,
physiology, and American history, in addition to Miss Winsor's required

classes. Physiology—the branch of biology that studies the normal functions of living organisms and their parts—set her on fire, and when she came home bursting to tell her father all about it, he "raised his hand wearily and stopped [her], saying 'Do I have to go through that course a *third* time?'" Acceptance to Bryn Mawr at that time required bright young women to score at least 60 percent on at least fifteen of twenty tests in not only physiology but plane geometry, Latin grammar, prose composition, and much more.

It wasn't all study and rigor. In October of Katharine's junior year, she got to stand in attendance at her aunt Poo's wedding at 4 Hawthorn Road. After her European sojourn with Elsie, Poo had returned to Apple End, her stone house in Woodstock, Connecticut, where she had a studio and garden. She hired a Japanese man, Hyozo Omori, as a housekeeper, only to realize that he was "a gentleman of ancient lineage and culture" and a graduate of Stanford who knew many things, but not how to cook. She kept him on through the summer to help her in the garden, and when he professed his love and asked her to marry him, she eventually accepted. Omori was thirty years old to her fifty, and the relationship scandalized many.

Charles, for one, would have nothing to do with Omori. This presented an obstacle for the couple because Omori's traditional beliefs demanded that he get permission for the marriage, and Poo's brother-in-law was the closest thing to a father she had. Charles had similarly disapproved when his brother-in-law George Shepley had married a young, flirtatious reporter for Hearst's *Boston American* but hadn't any power to stop that union. (All he could do was ban the *Boston American* from his house.) But eventually Charles softened, and he even hosted Poo's wedding and provided the breakfast. All three Sergeant girls, who'd already fallen under Omori's spell when he taught them to make green tea and sip it with sweetened rice cakes, attended in finery. Poo and her new husband set sail for Tokyo, where they used their own money to open a pioneering settlement house, Yurin-en, in a poor suburb of the city. Yurin-en mainly served disadvantaged children, and eventually became the nation's first kindergarten. Aniko, as Annie "Poo" Barrows Shepley Omori became known, was its first and longtime headmistress.

Katharine would see her aunt Poo only once more after the wedding. In 1912, Omori would organize the first Japanese team to participate in the Olympic Games, and he and Poo would travel with the team to the Summer Olympics in Stockholm, then swing by Boston on their way home to Tokyo. Hyozo Omori would contract tuberculosis on their return voyage and would die in San Francisco. Aunt Poo would return to Japan and live there for another thirty years until her own death. It was from Tokyo, with the war that would destroy Yurin-en looming on the horizon, that she would sit down to write the Shepley history that would become known to the Sergeant sisters as Aunt Poo's manuscript.

Wedding excitement aside, Katharine mostly studied and dreamed of college. A year and a half after Aunt Poo's departure, in the spring of 1909, Katharine graduated from Miss Winsor's and sat for her Bryn Mawr exams. She failed the algebra test, thus jettisoning her acceptance to Bryn Mawr. She later attributed it to a fever caused by tonsillitis, a perennial affliction of her childhood. But Katharine would write of the episode, "One of the strongest feelings I have about my education at school is that it taught me how to work and how to be thorough. I have never stopped being grateful for that. It set standards for the rest of my life." She had learned one lesson very well: decorum above all in the face of personal disappointment.

The next year, then, unfolded at Hawthorn Road and Miss Winsor's, just like the previous ones. Katharine took an extra year of Latin and brushed up on her mathematics. The next spring, she retook the entrance exams and sailed over the benchmark. She was launched, and the next four years of her life rose up before her eyes, a future that she had chosen with determination.

Just two weeks before she moved to campus, though, something monumental happened that would set her apart from all the other young women in her cohort. Katharine got engaged.

6.

Katharine and Ernest Angell had known each other since the
summer before Katharine's twelfth birthday. It was the summer
that Elsie was sick in Zurich and their father was helping to engineer the London Underground. Aunt Crullie took Katharine and Ros
to New Hampshire, where they stayed at the Hotel Chocorua instead
of their usual cottage. There, Katharine met a friend her own age named
Hildegarde Angell, and her tall, dark, slender older brother, Ernest, who
at the age of fifteen had absolutely no interest in Katharine.

The Angells had traveled from Cleveland, Ohio, where Ernest lived
with his mother, Lily Angell, and Hildegarde. He too had experienced the early death of a parent. His father, Elgin Adelbert Angell,
attended his twenty-fifth reunion at Harvard in the summer of 1898
and then boarded the French steamer *La Bourgogne*, en route from New
York to Le Havre, where he intended to meet up with his wife and
daughter. Family lore says the women were in Europe for six months
so Lily could recover her strength after nursing Elgin through a trying
bout of typhoid. Ernest, too, was booked on *La Bourgogne*, but at the last
minute was felled by chicken pox and left with his uncle Frederick in
Connecticut. Just before dawn on the Fourth of July in 1898, *La Bourgogne* encountered heavy fog off the coast of Sable Island in Nova Scotia and smashed into the British iron ship *Cromartyshire*. The captain
and most of the ship's 725 passengers were drowned, including every
first-class passenger. Elgin was forty-eight years old, Ernest only nine.

Four years later, Ernest published a story in *St. Nicholas*. "Polly's
Fourth (A True Story)," takes place on board a steamer off the coast of
Newfoundland in the early hours of the Fourth of July. In this version,

the heroine, a young girl traveling with her parents, awakes to eerie stillness—the ship has been enclosed by ice "stretching as far as the eye could reach, tumbled, irregular, of a pale green color!" Polly marvels at the booming and cracking of the ice, which substitutes for the fireworks back home, and she watches, fascinated, as the ice breaks up and black water shows through. The passengers learn "that the steamer had grazed a large iceberg in the night, but had gotten safely away. Had any ice fallen from the huge mass it would have crushed the boat." The next day, the ship is able to wend its way through the iceberg and reaches Liverpool without further incident. "But that Fourth in the ice Polly will never forget." As his son Roger would write in *The New Yorker* many decades later, Ernest had "rewritten the worst moments of his life, and, at whatever price, put them behind him."

Ernest did well at his private university school, but he was happiest outdoors, where he grew up camping, canoeing, and fishing; like Katharine, he was equally at home in physical and intellectual pursuits. He passed through a series of nicknames: he was "Sincere Cupid," and then "the Great Man" among his outdoorsy friends, and later "the King of the Forest" among his family for his relentless spirit at every endeavor, from gardening to skiing to his "thunderous but erratic" tennis game. Katharine would later say of him, "He was a very sociable person who liked to have many people around him." That first summer in Chocorua, he had pursued not Katharine but a girl with his sister's name of Hildegarde (who happened to be a distant cousin of Katharine's). He spent a year in Paris and Munich perfecting his French and German before entering Harvard in the fall of 1907.

It was Ernest, as well as Elsie, who provided Katharine with a template for a successful college education. Ernest was a serious, ambitious student who added Greek and Latin to his list of languages, and taught himself trigonometry, and took physics, and majored in history, and decided to do whatever he must to graduate Phi Beta Kappa. He tried out for both the baseball team and *The Harvard Crimson*, the college newspaper, in his freshman year, and failed at both. He courted a young woman named Evelyn Bolles, who lived right there in Cambridge.

Somewhere along the way, he fell in love with Katharine. As she grew

older, she joined a "mountain-climbing and camping group" of teenagers at Chocorua Lake, which included Stuart Chase, later to become a
well-known economist, and his friend Ernest. Perhaps the spark was
struck the day Katharine won the Chocorua Lake boat pageant in a
scene straight from an Alcott novel. What more beguiling sight was
there on the lake than a young, blond, suntanned Katharine, lying supine
on an old door over the gunwales of her canoe, powdered to within an
inch of her life to render her lily-white, arms crossed over her chest, and
a sweltering cloth that her aunt Crullie had embroidered with golden-
rod pulled up to her chin? She was Alfred, Lord Tennyson's Elaine on
her death barge, her final letter to Lancelot clutched in her fist, and her
father was the black-draped oarsman, a Mexican sombrero covering his
bald head. Slowly, with sweat dripping off both father and daughter, they
advanced around the lake, Katharine striving in her misery to look both
dead and "demurely love-lorn." When they finally reached the judges'
stand, Charles reached down, plucked the letter from Katharine's stiff
fist, and handed it up to the judges: "I loved you, and my love had no
return, / And therefore my true love has been my death."

In the summer of 1910, Ernest skipped his family's trip to Chocorua
in favor of a volunteer mission to St. Anthony, a town on the northern-
most tip of Newfoundland, not far from the spot on the map that must
have continued to haunt him since his father's death. He was under the
spell of the charismatic Dr. Wilfred T. Grenfell, a British doctor who'd
begun a nonprofit organization to improve the lives of fishermen in
Newfoundland and Labrador. Dr. Grenfell, "a man-of-action, a 'muscu-
lar Christian' and a social reformer," raised money for his mission among
the New England elite, and his supporters founded Grenfell Associations, which recruited young people as WOPs, or "workers without pay,"
for summer volunteering. Ernest, toting a large .45–90 rifle that he never
got to shoot, was in charge of maintaining the reindeer herd on which
the fishermen subsisted.

At the end of that summer, on Katharine's eighteenth birthday and
just two weeks before she was to begin college, Ernest proposed, and she
accepted. In their minds, they were engaged, but they had one further
step to complete before it was official: Ernest asked Katharine's father

for his daughter's hand in marriage. The Sergeants had known the Angells for some years; they socialized in the same Chocorua circles and belonged to the same white, professional-managerial class. Ernest had the
making of a prosperous man who could provide for his eventual family.
Moreover, though she was the youngest, Katharine was the first Sergeant
girl to attract a beau. With Elsie and Rosamond's futures still tentative,
and with the negative analogue of Elsie's health crisis in mind, Charles
must have been relieved to secure Katharine's place in the world. He said
yes, though he would not formally announce Katharine's engagement for
another two and a half years. How much did such considerations affect
Katharine's own acceptance of Ernest's proposal? Was she as eager to
please her father and avoid Elsie's fate as she was in love with an attrac-
tive young man?

There may or may not have been a ring, but there were most definitely
enormous hairy boots. Ernest brought her back from Newfoundland
a pair of mukluks, and she proudly packed them with her to college,
thinking the knee-high sealskin boots would provide both warmth and
distinction in the Pennsylvania winter. But the hides had been improp-
erly cured and they would stink up her closet, her room, and indeed that
entire end of the hallway, not to mention all her clothes. Her roommate
would make her throw them out, unworn, and for months afterward her
room still smelled "like an Eskimo igloo."

Ernest was about to start his senior year at Harvard and would then
continue to Harvard Law School before joining the Cleveland firm
where his father had been a partner, so he and Katharine knew their
engagement would be long. That year, Ernest would make the baseball
team. He would be elected to *The Harvard Advocate*, the college's literary
magazine, just as his father had before him; he would edit the *Advocate*
alongside his classmates T. S. Eliot and Conrad Aiken. He would win
a Harvard College scholarship and a teaching assistantship. He would
graduate Phi Beta Kappa, just as he'd hoped. Presumably, he and Katharine corresponded, but no letters from their college years survive. She
had reasons for keeping her fiancé at arm's length, and she was busy
laying the groundwork for her professional life.

Part II

The New Woman Gets It All

(1910–1925)

7.

If you will tell me why the fen
Appears impassable, I then
Will tell you why I think that I
Can get across it, if I try.
—Marianne Moore '09, *Tipyn o'Bob*, June 1909

Katharine Sergeant was most definitely a type. She went to college in the autumn of 1910 and became a Mawrter, one who attends Bryn Mawr. Under the very firm leadership of President Dr. Martha Carey Thomas, a Mawrter was a highly specific sociological designation that revealed much about its bearer. Katharine was, in fact, the consummate Mawrter, and she came of age within an extremely narrow window of time in which, just for the merest sliver of American history, it looked as if women could have it all. She graduated in 1914 expecting to have both a family and a substantial, rewarding career. And she did, taking her place in the ranks of the New Women who were remaking Progressive Era America.

When Katharine moved into her suite of rooms in Pembroke West on October 3, 1910, she was on familiar territory, having visited the campus and that very dormitory when Elsie was a Mawrter. She had a monthly allowance from her father and the promise of letters from home every few days. She quickly made a new home with her roommate, Eleanor Washburn, the daughter of a reverend who had been "prepared" by Miss Henry's private school in Colorado Springs. In fact, she already knew Eleanor well from summers at Chocorua Lake in New Hampshire.

Young women who attended Bryn Mawr in the 1910s were overwhelmingly white, native-born Northeasterners from the middle class. In Katharine's incoming class of 126 girls, she was one of 87 who had graduated from a private school. Her family was able to afford the cost of tuition, which was $200 a year, and room and board, which began at $300 a year. Her fellow students were almost wholly the daughters of professionals: lawyers, teachers, doctors, merchants, bankers, and technical engineers, not to mention three clergymen. Katharine was one of twelve Unitarians in her cohort. There were five Catholic girls in the class of 1914, and there were four Jewish girls, who were roomed separately from the other students. Black applicants were quietly guided to other colleges and universities. Mawrters' families were likely to be close-knit, because such support was crucial to girls in only the second generation to attend college. Their parents were likely to be educated, and unsurprisingly, many girls had mothers—or aunts—who had pioneered the cause of women's education. Perhaps less obvious is that many fathers were as committed to female suffrage and education as they were to temperance and other social reforms. They raised their daughters to be athletic and to vigorously enjoy the natural world. They stressed civic service over moneymaking. They viewed their daughters as contributors to progress, not as eligible debutantes to bolster their families' fortunes.

Katharine checked every one of those boxes. Moreover, she was one of half the girls in her class who entered with the label "clear" on her transcript, indicating that she had no academic conditions on her record or exams to retake. In early October she sat down with President Thomas and decided on her classes: English literature, elocution, composition, general philosophy, general psychology, and biology.

Katharine the freshman hit the ground running, and not only in field hockey, which she played for all four years under the training of Constance "the Apple" Applebee, the person who introduced field hockey to the United States despite deep resistance to the idea of women armed with clubs. Katharine's team won the championship each of those four years. The Apple gave Katharine a nickname—Serge—but it didn't stick. In her first year, Katharine served as class secretary and Philosophy Club secretary.

In November of her sophomore year, Katharine directed *The Taming of the Shrew*, in which she had a small part, and the production led directly to one of her first college bylines in the *Tipyn o'Bob* (Welsh for "a little bit of everybody"), Bryn Mawr's monthly literary magazine.

She published an intriguing little essay called "A Plea for the Satirical," in which Katharine urges sympathy for Kate, for though she has "a tongue with a tang" (a line that actually comes from *The Tempest*), it is Katharine's sincere opinion that Kate's sarcasm stems from self-consciousness, not malice. She knows this, writes Katharine, because she has been called a Kate herself. "Can you not see that what appears to be unfeeling cruelty in her sarcastic epigrams about her best friends is merely a disguise by which to cloak her real feelings, for, above all else, Kate in her shyness fears to become ridiculous. Kate is always reserved,— for that very reason she hides her emotions. Some people even deny to her these emotions, but she really does feel as other human beings do." Nineteen-year-old Katharine understood sarcasm only as a personality trait; she would learn that the charge of "unfeeling cruelty" had far more to do with female ambition and power than with native shyness. Yet she already felt misunderstood: "Here my own bitterness appears, and discretion urges me to stop or my own sarcasm, hiding, I assure you, a sensitive, reserved and shyly retiring nature, will prepossess you against all Kates." Still, though, no one called her by that nickname.

Katharine truly hit her stride in her junior year. Bryn Mawr made use of the Johns Hopkins group plan, in which students selected two or more closely aligned subjects as their majors. Katharine declared her group as English and philosophy—though her philosophy grades were not stellar—and she took classes in Greek, the English Romantics, and descriptive writing. Lucy Martin Donnelly's Greek poetry class gave her the first real trouble of her academic career, and her grade in it sank over the course of the year from 75 percent to 65 percent, knocking her out of the running for an honors citation, "but who cares," she blithely wrote to her father. She was evidently not laboring under Charles's stern expectation that she master every class and had no trouble admitting that she had read Kant three times a week—"which, incidentally," she noted, "I can't understand in the least."

There were plenty of other ways to test her prowess and prove her mettle. She joined the debating society, one of whose topics was "*Resolved*, A weekly college newspaper is desirable at Bryn Mawr." As a member of the English Club, she sat in Denbigh Hall one November evening and listened as Walter Hines Page, the vice president of Doubleday and the editor of *The World's Work*, gave a speech titled "Making a Magazine." She was elected stage manager for *Cyrano de Bergerac*. "It is the most terrific job and I feel very incapable," she effused to her father, filling several pages with the list of her duties, then another list of all the ways the production could go wrong. "And tact! my I shall have to have it." There was basketball too, just for exercise. "They say I play a horrid rough game which is a disgrace, but I don't mean to." But then she injured her toe, which became infected. "You must expect me to look very fat. I warn you now," she wrote to her father three days before a visit. "No exercise for more than a month, draw your conclusions. The play will make me thin again, however."

In *The Lantern*, the school's literary annual, she published a short and lovely essay about a steeplechase. But it was the *Tipyn o'Bob* in which she expanded on the confident, wry voice of her letters home to her father and Crullie, in the form of a jaunty short story from the perspective of a young businessman living in Japan—surely inspired by her new uncle. Katharine told her father that she loved writing stories and was looking forward to submitting them to Professor Regina Crandall.

Most portentously, in her junior year, Katharine served as one of the staff editors of *Tipyn o'Bob* alongside Mary Coolidge, Jean Batchelor, and Sarah R. Smith, sometimes writing the lead editorial column. Years later, Katharine took credit for helping to revive the *Tip* after it had died, though it appeared continuously from 1903, seven years before Katharine arrived on campus, onward; indeed, the poet Marianne Moore was one of its editors (and a prolific contributor of poetry and prose) from 1907 to 1909. Katharine's actual contribution was to increase its frequency from monthly to fortnightly. She was also the one to convince President Thomas that students should have sole authority over the contents, with no faculty advisor, making the *Tip* the first undergraduate publication to appear without censorship. President Thomas nonetheless took a lively interest in their literary works, and one day called Katharine into her office. Brandishing a copy of Winifred Goodall's essay on Christopher Marlowe, she pointed to the line "He died in a brawl in the stews of London." Did Miss Sergeant know what the word "stews" meant? President Thomas inquired. "I gulped and said I did and said it had to be in there because it was a fact. I won out," recalled Katharine (and somewhere out there in the vast nation, a young tramp reporter named Harold Ross smiled without knowing why).

"We have all, at one time or another, felt a wild desire to break things, to throw stones through windows, to crush tumblers in our hands, to hurl books about promiscuously," begins one of Katharine's essays, before going on to counsel against both revolutionary passion and the blasé attitude of the world-weary Mawrter. "Enthusiasm for what there is good in the present and for what there may be better in the future, is greater than any present effort to destroy. And by wholesome enthusiasm alone do we attain the real spirit of the age we live in,—the spirit of solid and able construction." Construction of what? Katharine doesn't say, but suffrage was one of the most oft-invoked social themes of the journal, and no wonder, given the views of President M. Carey Thomas.

By far the greatest influence at college on the young Katharine Sergeant was the impressive and intimidating President Thomas. Though she had stopped teaching by the time Katharine arrived on campus, Thomas exerted almost complete control over the workings of the college, in a time before academic administrators ran the day-to-day operations. By Katharine's freshman year in 1910, she was at the height of her national renown as an educator, an advocate for equal opportunity for female education, and a suffragist. When she wasn't traveling to give speeches testifying to the rigors of Bryn Mawr and the right of women to collegiate and graduate education, she would expound upon her views to her students in her famous chapel talks, daily ten-minute speeches that ranged over everything from her opinion on the latest student theatrical production to the lessons the students should learn from their suffragist forebears. Bryn Mawr women lived in delighted fear of their leader. In Katharine's senior year, the debating society took up the question of feminism. The student on the negative side had dutifully prepared her argument about why the Victorian woman was to be admired for her skills as a wife and a mother, and she was ready to speak when in walked President Thomas. The students fell silent as Thomas set aside her umbrella, removed her rubbers, pulled out a handkerchief, and looked expectantly up at the debaters. The miserable student found she could not break the silence and she never gave her antifeminist speech. Decades later, in the 1970s, Katharine would carp to a younger woman that the feminists of the day, the ones who called themselves Ms., acted as if they had invented women's liberation, but to have gone to Bryn Mawr in the 1910s was to hear it "shouted from the college chapel" every single day.

Thomas's vision for her students was highly specific and arose from her own exceptional life story. Bright and well loved, she was the oldest child of Baltimore Quakers and was allowed an active and lightly supervised childhood, followed by education at the Howland School, a Quaker academy for girls in Union Springs, New York. There she learned Latin and struggled mightily to learn Greek. Her father, James Carey Thomas, helped to found Johns Hopkins University from the bequest of a Baltimore Friend. The president of Johns Hopkins gave Thomas a letter of recommendation for her application to Cornell University, which was coeducational from its founding, and in 1875 she enrolled in the Classical Course and graduated in just two years, one of 20 women in a class of 240. That very year, 1877, Thomas's father and two other relatives met with Joseph Wright Taylor to discuss forming a Quaker women's college—what would in eight years become Bryn Mawr.

Also that year, the Johns Hopkins board of trustees, which included Thomas's father and uncle, debated whether or not to admit women, without coming to a conclusion. That September, Thomas became their first test case when she applied to the graduate program under the renowned classicist Basil L. Gildersleeve. The board equivocated. They allowed Thomas to enroll but prohibited her from attending classes. She studied Greek grammar eight hours a day, but it was hardly a real education. Fully conscious of how much her failure would cost the women lined up behind her, she withdrew from the university in 1878, instead studying comparative literature and philology at the University of Leipzig and the University of Zurich, earning a PhD summa cum laude from the latter in 1882.

She returned home to take up what she had considered her rightful position since she'd first heard of Taylor's idea for a women's college: she expected to be its first president. Instead, in 1884 she was named professor of English and dean of the faculty, to serve under a male president, James E. Rhoads. Bryn Mawr opened its doors to students in 1885, and it wouldn't be until Rhoads's retirement in 1893—and months of extremely contentious board meetings, and Mary Garrett's offer of a $10,000 donation contingent upon Thomas's appointment—that Thomas would finally be inducted as Bryn Mawr's second president. She had no inauguration.

The year Elsie arrived at Bryn Mawr, 1899, was also the year that Thomas famously rebuked Harvard president Charles Eliot for his assertion that women could not possibly benefit from the classical traditions of learning, that women's colleges should have a separate curriculum consisting largely of manners ("bearing, carriage, address, delicate sympathy, and innocent reserve"), and that women could never live up to the standard set by men. Thomas's response created national headlines. She agreed with President Eliot that "gentle breeding" should supplement "scholarship and character." But she was not simply educating "some rather peculiar well-to-do girls," as Eliot had called them. She was molding them to be a recognizable type, and for a model to emulate she looked right over President Eliot's head; she wanted the Bryn Mawr woman "to become as well known and universally admired as the Oxford and Cambridge man." The women at her college were going to study the classics and train their bodies and teach each other by mixing across cultural backgrounds in their residential colleges, and they would emerge as strong women for not having had to justify their pursuits to men for four years—her college would be an "Adamless Eden." If women had one difference from men, it was in her mind an understandable and a correctible one: "As yet college women are not as ready to accept criticism." Of which President Thomas had rather a lot to give.

Thomas could be harsh with her students as she drove them forward in pursuit of a public life. Perhaps her most famous line from a chapel speech is "Our failures only marry" (though many remembered it as "Only our failures marry"). This, then, is the crucible in which Katharine Sergeant's sensibilities were forged, a highly self-conscious environment in which feminism was inextricable from ambition. She was expected, along with every single one of her classmates, to delay or refuse marriage, to pursue a career or a graduate degree, and to make a substantive contribution to the greater good.

But she had already accepted an offer of marriage. For all that she fit the mold of the quintessential Mawrter, in the fact of her engagement, Katharine was a conspicuous oddity, almost antifeminist. When she told her friend Leah Cadbury Furtmuller about Ernest, Leah replied, "Oh, Katharine, how perfectly awful!" This only echoed President Thomas's own response to a Bryn Mawr senior who appeared at a party in a new rosy dress and announced her forthcoming marriage: "Oh, you poor little pink thing!" It took a strange kind of strength, then, for Katharine to move through all four years of college with marriage directly in her future. If her engagement mollified Charles, it flouted President Thomas; Katharine had something to prove to both.

President Thomas was astonishingly successful at cracking open the door of possibility for her graduates. Between 1889 and 1908, only 10 percent of Bryn Mawr graduates did not work—President Thomas's failures. The majority of Mawrters did not marry (55 percent)—a group that included Marianne Moore and Katharine's sister Elsie—and most of those women pursued graduate education (62 percent). The majority of those who did marry pursued a career and economic independence (54 percent), while among the female population at large, only 5.6 percent of married women classified themselves as breadwinners. The Mawrters were making Thomas proud.

Katharine, though, was at the tail end of this emancipatory trend, and the door was about to close behind her. One of the many serendipitous facts of Katharine's iconoclastic life is that, had she been born a few years earlier or a few years later, she would have faced a radically different set of circumstances for white women's education and employment. Only by coming of age in this small window of time could she have enjoyed the career that she did.

The first generation of women college students, the pioneers, were a decidedly serious lot. The women who attended the first coeducational and women's colleges from 1865 to 1890 had much to prove, no room for error, and no career prospects. The vast majority of them, such as Katharine's aunt Crullie, went into teaching at the secondary or collegiate level. The next generation, the women who attended college from 1890 to the 1910s, often distressed their forebears with their frivolity. The stakes felt lower for these women, the opportunities greater. Like Katharine, they could afford not to ace every class. They had the luxury of expecting self-fulfillment, and their values reflected an individualism that their forebears lacked. But they also had the security and the moral mandate to join the social reformers of the Progressive Era, to use their education to better society through paid and volunteer work.

What most separated this second wave of women from their forebears, though, was their attitude toward men. Even just a few years prior to Katharine's arrival in 1910, Bryn Mawr was an extension of the Victorian era of separate spheres. Women were cordoned off and left alone to form intense bonds of love that sometimes were and sometimes were not sexual—lesbianism was not yet stigmatized. Marianne Moore at Bryn Mawr had a series of "smashes" on her classmates, including Peggy James, daughter of William, who broke up with her: "She is a sweet 'piece of fur' but I am too rough I guess." These smashes, which were chronicled in a daily newsletter called *The Bird News*, merely recapitulated M. Carey Thomas's experience at Cornell in the 1870s, when she wrote about her own smashes to her mother and aunt. President Thomas lived in a house on the Bryn Mawr campus (called the Deanery even after she achieved the presidency), first with Mamie Gwinn, a literature professor, and then with Mary Garrett, an heiress who'd helped to found the college. Official Bryn Mawr calendars would list the "at home" hours of President Thomas and Miss Gwinn as if it were the most natural thing in the world, and indeed, such "Boston marriages," in which two upper-class women lived together without the financial support of men, had become acceptable in New England at the end of the nineteenth century.

Women in Katharine's cohort faced a shifting set of pressures and opportunities. Same-sex relationships were now becoming pathologized by the medical establishment, and the coming years would witness a far greater surveillance of female relationships at women's colleges. Yet Katharine's generation expected greater equality with men, and they fought for greater heterosexual freedom. Theirs was an egalitarian feminism, not a separatist one, and it included room for marriage within its ambitious vision of social activism and substantial careers.

How quickly that vision would fall apart. By the middle and late 1910s, the statistics on marriage and careers completely reversed themselves; now 65 percent of Bryn Mawr graduates chose marriage and only 49 percent continued their schooling. The trend slid from there. Among the classes of 1946 through 1950, a full 93.1 percent of Bryn Mawr graduates were or had been married. The average age of marriage, which in Katharine's time was just over twenty-seven, crept down to twenty-three and then twenty-two. Women's education underwent a wholesale redefinition, fitting women not for careers or reform work, but for marriage—the so-called MRS degree. Educated women faced a rising backlash against their full participation in the labor market, and after the passage of the Nineteenth Amendment to the Constitution in 1920, they lacked a central issue around which to rally. The easiest way to discredit a woman in power became to accuse her of being a lesbian, and the pressure to conform to a heteronormative family structure grew immense. Perhaps educated women of the second and third generations had no coordinated response to the backlash precisely because they'd embraced an individualist ethos that stressed sexual liberation over political power. Opportunities for Bryn Mawr alumni slipped backward almost as soon as Katharine Sergeant graduated.

And yet for a time the world was hers for the taking, and in college she practiced balancing schoolwork with a long-distance romance. Ernest appears only infrequently in her letters to her father, and she even confessed to him that she was neglecting her fiancé: "I guess there's no danger of my writing Ernest too much. I'm ashamed—I am so horrid to him." She implored her father not to let Ernest meet her at the Back Bay train station when she visited home in March of her junior year because there would be "oodles of girls" at the train station, and presumably she was reluctant to remind those girls of her tall, handsome fiancé.

Katharine's vibrant social life revolved almost exclusively around Bryn Mawr. She went for long country walks with her classmates, building fires to make coffee and toast so they could stay out longer. Her philosophy professor, Theodore de Leo de Laguna, and his wife, Grace, a former Bryn Mawr graduate student in philosophy, invited her over for dinner; she had tea with her English professors, Dr. Regina Crandall and Miss Elizabeth Daly; wealthy alumnae treated her to outings in Philadelphia. In one banner week, she saw a production of *Kismet* starring Otis Skinner, followed by the opera *Die Walküre*, which made her feel "limp from the greatness of it." She told her father that she was determined to repeat the experience as often as possible in the next year, writing, "Once I get to Cleveland I fear I'll hear little opera"—it was apparently agreed that she would follow Ernest to Cleveland after their marriage. But perhaps she could share her aesthetic appreciation with her beau now? Katharine appended an urgent postscript: "P.S. This is very important. Don't you think it would be all right for me to go to the opera some night with Ernest. Loads of girls do go with men, and we could go 2nd balcony and no one would see us." The answer was apparently no, because no mention was made of Charles's permission or of a subsequent outing. Her letters returned to a breezy, casually anxious catalog of all her assignments and the results of all her quizzes.

At the end of Katharine's junior year, Ernest graduated from law school. Once again, the Sergeants and the Angells met at Chocorua Lake for the summer, and then the couple parted ways, Ernest to Cleveland to begin practicing law at Webster, Angell, & Cook, Katharine to Bryn Mawr for her final year of college.

8.

Every one has at some time the sense of a new appreciation of old things. It is the feeling of a moment, when, all at once, the commonplace everyday round of affairs becomes very precious. You feel it here when you come up from the station at night after having been away, perhaps only a day, but long enough to realize an absence; then, the lighted halls, the voices, the sense of life within become suddenly a rare thing, a new experience to which you are coming.
—Katharine Sergeant, "Daily Themes," *The Lantern*, 1914

Looking back at her college years, Katharine would repeatedly marvel at one fact: she was never assigned an American author in any of her literature classes. The literary career she would build for herself over three and a half decades was in no way foretold by her English major. Elsie too would note that she read only the likes of Flaubert at Bryn Mawr: "No Melville, no Hawthorne, no Poe, no Dickinson, no Whitman. Henry James and Edith Wharton were the only modern fiction writers; expatriates, you see; and we read them for pleasure, not for study." Even the European curriculum progressed no further in time than the Romantic poets.

In this, President Thomas, the radical educator, was entirely conventional. In the 1910s, the study of literature was still mostly divorced from the production of literature. The invention of creative writing as a discipline was still a few years in the future. It would arise from the philosophy of John Dewey and progressive education. In fact, creative writing—not to mention MFA programs and an enormous portion of twentieth-century American literature—would begin at the Lincoln School, an experimental private school in Manhattan, in the early 1920s, the very time and place where Katharine and Ernest's children would go to school. An English teacher at the Lincoln School named William Hughes Mearns would elaborate on Dewey's idea that children learn best when their own interests guide their willpower and exploration, coining the term "creative writing" to mean writing that expresses the author's own experience of selfhood. Mearns used this new idea to break apart the old pedagogy of teaching grammar and rhetoric by rote; his methods were so successful they quickly colonized secondary education, then undergraduate courses, and then the creation of new graduate programs that used the workshop method of criticism. It wouldn't be long before the individual would be her own metric when writing or reading.

But for Katharine, the study of literature involved the disciplining of the mind, rather than its unbridled self-expression, the buckling down to the monumental tomes that had educated her forebears. The Bryn Mawr English department, which Martha Carey Thomas chaired even while she was president, owed its curriculum to German universities with their heavy emphasis on philology, the scientific study of literature as a linguistic phenomenon rather than as human expression. President Thomas's mentor at Johns Hopkins, Basil Gildersleeve, wrote that philologists were like botanists and *littérateurs* were merely florists, concerned only with "aesthetic charm" and not the enduring principles by which language is preserved. President Thomas thus designed a two-year English course required of all Bryn Mawr students that was split evenly between linguistic studies and the history of literature, with a long list of books to read on the side, much as laboratory work accompanied science classes. Only in the upper years might an English major in good standing take advanced composition classes, which were the first fledgling attempts to teach students to sound on the page like the books they read.

So in her senior year, Katharine took English Renaissance Lyrics, English Renaissance Drama, Greek Plato and Composition, Greek Sophocles, and Reading of Shakespeare (plus an economics class and a psychology class, and oral exams in German and French). She took two electives from Dr. Crandall: Daily Themes and Narrative Writing, which taught her "the style and methods of the best modern writers of short stories, both English and French." She received her lowest grade of the year (78 percent) in Narrative Writing, and for the rest of her life she would demur whenever an author-friend urged her to turn one of her memories into a short story for *The New Yorker*.

President Thomas herself mourned the absence of a strong literary culture at Bryn Mawr in a chapel talk during Katharine's senior year. She seemed to be almost scolding the women, taking them to task for not being creative enough. "In looking over the alumnae and working out a type it seems to me that we are not creating here a literary type. It does not seem to me we have a strongly marked school of younger writers. I am hoping all the time it may come. There are very few poets, very few artists or artistic people." Never mind that Elsie had, by then, published her first article in *McClure's*, where she met and befriended Willa Cather; the two of them would help found *The New Republic* that very year. Marianne Moore had not yet begun publishing poems in *The Egoist* and *Poetry*; that would come the following year. President Thomas does not consider that her own English curriculum itself might have something to do with the general lack. Instead, she attributes the distinctive character of the Bryn Mawr type to the fact that all of their families are second-, third-, or fourth-generation Americans and have fully absorbed the go-ahead values of the national culture. "The Americans are an extraordinarily efficient and competent people. That does not go with the dreamy, vague, unsuccessful people who turn out every now and then a great genius or a great scholar." No, the typical Mawrter was "executive," "a competent type."

Yet Katharine was doing an extraordinary amount of writing and reading that year, because she had been elected editor in chief of *Tipyn o'Bob* along with Winifred Goodall. The pair also served as editors in chief of *The Lantern*. Like Marianne Moore before her, Katharine's true education came from editing and writing for the literary magazine in the fervent company of her peers. Moore had suffered the indignity of hearing Professor Lucy Martin Donnelly say she shouldn't attempt to major in English because her writing was so uneven she'd risk not graduating (she chose history, politics, and economics instead), but then found encouragement and admiration from women in the class above her on the *Tipyn o'Bob* editorial staff; their criticism meant more to her than her professor's. Elizabeth Bishop and Mary McCarthy would discover much the same dynamic a decade and a half later at Vassar when they cofounded the avant-garde literary magazine *Con Spirito*, which was influenced in part by Moore's poetry. Moore, Bishop, and McCarthy consciously and strategically used their college literary magazines to launch their writing careers against the constraints or indifference handed down to them by their professors.

Katharine would take a more meandering path to her career, but with hindsight the parallels and lines of influence from her senior year at Bryn Mawr to her position at *The New Yorker* eleven years later are marvelously clear. In addition to increasing the frequency of *Tipyn o'Bob*, Katharine and her coeditor also expanded the unsigned editorials, often printing four or five short pieces on different topics, not unlike what *The New Yorker* would someday call Talk of the Town. Their first editorial nails a perfect wry-earnest tone while claiming not to: "We editors have been trying to catch at that desirable acquisition, vaguely termed an 'editorial standpoint.'" They announce their artistic intentions:

> The demand has been for a popular magazine. "The *Tip* is too high-brow, too literary," we are told and obviously only by those who never write for it. But, quite seriously, we wish you to know that there is no set standard of art, style or rhetoric to which *Tipyn o'Bob* contributors must conform. Subject matter of interest and sentences that parse are all we ask. We editors must reserve for ourselves alone the Greeks' quaint method of expressing irony or humor in a bit of bad grammar. That is our privilege and our recompense.

Over the years of their tenure on the staff, the magazine drifted away from newsy articles, listings of events, and college songs, and toward polished stories, essays, and poems. Katharine and Winifred Goodall so redefined the *Tip* that they opened space for a campus newspaper, something they campaigned for at the end of their reign, and by the next year, the classes below them would launch the Bryn Mawr *College News*.

Katharine and Winifred, both star students in the English department (Winifred would win the department's prestigious essay prize at the end of the year and later earn a master's degree from Columbia University), had no problem hectoring their cohort into greater intellectual seriousness. As their college careers drew to a close, they lamented the downplaying of their own education when away from the ivy-covered walls of Bryn Mawr: "During vacations she must be as silent as possible on her college life unless she wants to be branded as 'hopeless.' . . . Just so the average person at college avoids being 'different' or 'high-brow' by a studious abstention from over-much interest in anything academic." Katharine knew she would soon face pressure to disavow the education she'd worked so hard to attain. Some people avoided "high-brow" art because they disliked it, didn't understand it, or feared being seen as pretentious. For college-educated women, the question of taste was refracted through gender, something Katharine would spend much of her career elaborating.

In their last editorial, Katharine and Winifred congratulated themselves for breathing new life into the *Tip*, both by its new fortnightly form and by inviting more controversy into the editorial pages. They detailed their hopes that the future *Tip* would broaden its coverage to political, scientific, and philosophical topics. And they pointed to a glaring absence in the college's literary landscape. "The college papers need an office," its two retiring editors wrote. Neither the *Tip* nor *The Lantern* had a dedicated space for editorial meetings; the members of the editorial board, "guided by written signs and verbal messages," hunted for the next meeting place like seekers on a quest. "The 'copy' itself is carried about piecemeal from place to place, in sweater-pockets, or crumpled in the hand, like the 'doll-rags' with which we used to play." But they were no longer playing dolls, Katharine and Winifred flatly stated. In 1914, at one of the most privileged, protected spaces for female intellectuals in the country, these women were still seeking a room of their own. Their plight symbolizes the still-tenuous nature of the literary profession for women, and the energy with which women in the Progressive Era created their own institutions. Katharine experienced both the empowerment of leading a team of equals and the necessity of defining for herself the exact shape her ambitions would take in the face of relative indifference. *Tipyn o'Bob* existed as a lively community of opinionated women because Katharine and her friends made it so. She would remain friends with the literary women of Bryn Mawr for the rest of her life.

The point truly cannot be overstated in the context of Katharine's future career. At Bryn Mawr, she found a marriage between friendship and ambition that she would replicate in her career. In her junior year of college, she roomed in Pembroke West with three other women: Helen Carey, who went only by "Carey"; Wynanda "Nan" Boardman; and Helen "Knick" Knickerbacker Porter. By their senior year, Katharine's intense friendships had fused into a group so integral it acquired its own name, the Inner Shrine. Decades later, Katharine would delight in telling Mary McCarthy, author of *The Group*, about her own clique of six suitemates, a clique distinctive enough to warrant an article in the Bryn Mawr yearbook for the class of 1914. Outsiders shouldn't be jealous of the Shriners, the anonymous yearbook author insists. Their membership merely consisted of "six shy, unassuming girls" who banded together when "uninvited by the rest of the world." True, they benefited from some overstuffed laundry trunks full of food enough to feed "six fairly hungry girls"—but not a seventh. True, too, that the Inner Shrine spent many an evening "discussing why all the affairs of the nation are wrong" and giving "a little gentle criticism" of each other's "clothes, faults, or general conduct." For Katharine, no boundary existed between her intimate female friendships and the work of her mind. Bryn Mawr College enabled that marriage, and the Progressive Era, into which she would shortly graduate, necessitated that she carry it forth into the unstructured, not-yet-invented life of the married, educated woman.

But first, Katharine had one last duty to perform as a Mawrter. What did she feel on the morning of Friday, May 8, 1914, when President Thomas stood at the front of the chapel and sternly orated on the momentousness of the next afternoon's May Day festivities? Bryn Mawr's May Day was a daylong pageant that happened once every four years, functioning as both a fundraiser and an opportunity to prove that the college was producing healthy, talented, poised young scholars. President Thomas needed to counter the tenacious assumption that scholarship deformed the female body—the same bias that connected neurasthenia to overeducation. In other words, on May Day nothing less was at stake than Thomas's legacy. And in 1914, Katharine Sergeant was the student leader of the entire occasion.

The scale was immense: All students were required to attend acting, dance, and music lessons upon threat of fines. Thousands of spectators would arrive on special Pullman cars and pay $2 apiece to see a pageant, a maypole dance with five hundred dancers, and seven old English plays, each performed three times throughout the day. This year, former president William Taft would watch his daughter, Helen, play the part of King Richard the Lionheart in *Robin Hood*.

Saturday, May 9, dawned dark and cloudy. There was a heavy shower just before the start of events at half past two o'clock, but then the sun appeared and shone on the campus in its spring glory, the dogwood and Japanese cherry in full bloom. *The Philadelphia Inquirer* estimated that between eight thousand and nine thousand people watched the theatricals. President Thomas, in a chapel talk, declared May Day a finished and remarkable success. Katharine had pulled it off, the grand spectacle that was the single best showcase of Bryn Mawr values.

With May Day, as with her editorial work at *The Lantern* and *Tipyn o'Bob*, Katharine had illuminated individual talent while orchestrating it into a seamless whole. Certainly it is possible to spot in these senior-year endeavors the faint stirrings of Katharine's later success with a magazine, itself a cohesive collection of individual talents. But in the spring of 1914, as she listened to President Thomas's praise of May Day, Katharine may have been musing about how she'd soon have to leave behind all the ritual and pageantry of Bryn Mawr to move to Cleveland, where she knew no one and had nothing waiting for her. She may have been thinking of Elsie's fragility, and how by contrast she had proven she could carry the weight of her studies, her engagement, her literary hobbies, and a public position of leadership without faltering.

Katharine had, in fact, caught the eye of President Thomas. She wrote to her father a few weeks later that she was invited to a luncheon at the Deanery on Commencement Day, "to [her] astonishment as she usually ask[ed] only the Presidents of the big organizations." She beseeched her father to accept if he, too, received an invitation, saying, "I want protection."

Katharine's senior year roared to a close. At the end of May, she had a solid four days of exams, which she soldiered through despite having eaten bad meat in the dining hall. She and Winifred sponsored the election of a new editor in chief at *Tipyn o'Bob* and passed her the baton. She took her last oral exams and then joined in the hoop races down Senior Row. She made a speech at her class dinner. She shot down the rumor that she and Ernest had eloped, a worry that engulfed her father and Aunt Crullie. She had her hair shampooed and she took the train into Philadelphia to buy a garden party hat.

And then at last came commencement. On June 4, 1914, at eleven o'clock, President Thomas handed Katharine her diploma. Despite her regular confessions of academic defeat to her father, and despite the fact that fully one-third of her entering class failed to make it through the rigorous Bryn Mawr curriculum (including her freshman roommate, Eleanor Washburn), Katharine Sergeant performed extremely well, graduating fourth in her class of eighty-five girls. Her father, Aunt Crullie, and both sisters were there to celebrate with her. There is no record of whether or not Ernest was there too.

9.

Stature: 5 feet 2½ inches
Forehead: High
Eyes: Grey
Nose: Roman
Mouth: Small
Chin: Medium
Hair: Brown
Complexion: Medium
Face: Oval

One month after her graduation, Katharine Sergeant applied for a passport. In front of a notary public, she swore that she was a native-born citizen, as was her father, and she appended a handwritten note before her signature: "I am unmarried." Her name was spelled correctly and included no middle initial. She promised to return to the United States within two years. Like her sisters before her, Katharine likely considered a trip to Europe a requisite part of her education; the Continent was still the epicenter of culture. In precisely ten years, Katharine would help change that with the founding of a consequential American magazine. Her trip ended quickly. Austrian archduke Franz Ferdinand was assassinated just twelve days after Katharine was granted her passport, and Charles called Katharine home as more countries joined the war.

She returned to live at Hawthorn Road until her wedding in the spring. Just as she had followed Elsie's footsteps to Europe, she now followed her into the city of Boston and into the new progressive discipline of social work. Beginning at the turn of the century, a tight cohort of politically radical New Women used their excellent education to found a series of organizations that solved several problems at once. Jane Addams's Hull House in Chicago, the quintessential progressive institution, enabled Addams to employ educated women in the meaningful work of ameliorating some of capitalism's offenses against poor women. The settlement house movement educated, studied, and advocated for the working class; it sought to "Americanize" immigrants; and it also fused a network of women who went on to innovate other left-wing responses to industrial capitalism's exploitation of the poor, like Florence Kelley's National Consumers League and Alice Hamilton's founding of the discipline of industrial medicine. Katharine, as she was casting about for useful work in the years after college, would be influenced by both Kelley and Hamilton.

Katharine first volunteered at Massachusetts General Hospital, where she worked under Ida M. Cannon, the newly installed chief of social work, who served alongside only two other chiefs, those of medicine and surgery. Cannon formed a special interest in industrial diseases and tasked various professionals with studying topics like "Dust, Fumes, Monotony, etc." as well as the hazards of specific occupations, like loss of voice among telephone operators. Katharine sat at a desk in the outpatient department and waited for someone to come out of treatment and show her a big card that a doctor or nurse had given him or her, reading, for instance, "eczema on hands and arms." She was then tasked with asking the relevant questions to discern if the patient was a butcher or a rabbi preparing kosher meat. If the large card read "lead poisoning," she'd note the telltale signs of wrist-drop and a blue-gray line along the gums and ask the patient how often he washed his hands in between painting and eating. She was even able to attend lectures at the hospital. Like Elsie, she was putting her education to civic use and opening her eyes to a world beyond Brookline, Chocorua, or Bryn Mawr. Her volunteer work would lead directly to two paying jobs. Medicine suddenly seemed like a possibility for her future career; at this moment, her stated ambitions were to become a writer, a doctor, or an archaeologist, in that order. She kept the Mass General position for six months in the winter of 1914–15, resigning when her wedding day approached.

First there was a pre-wedding dinner party for Katharine's fellow Mawrters, at which the couple was surprised by a booklet of terrible songs written about them that Ros had collected. On May 22, 1915, Katharine and Ernest became the second couple to be married at 4 Hawthorn Road, in a simple ceremony presided over by Ernest's Harvard classmate, the very freshly ordained Reverend Frederick May Eliot, later the president of the American Unitarian Association. The newlyweds took the train to northeastern Ontario and canoed and camped on Lake Temagami, a protected reserve with no cottages on its shores, only on the twelve hundred islands within it; Ernest had fished there since his teens. Katharine never described her wedding or honeymoon—those details became overshadowed by later events. A photograph from about this era survives, and though it is undated, it is not hard to imagine that it was taken on her honeymoon. Katharine sits on a pristine lakeshore beside a canoe loaded with provisions. Her long hair is wound round her head in a milkmaid braid. Her eyebrows are straight, her mouth is a horizontal line, her gaze, over her right shoulder at the photographer, is level. She would later write to her granddaughter Callie that she and Ernest had "two, possibly three, good years together." Then she would amend herself, telling Callie, "The first seven years were happy ones."

Once back in Cleveland, Ernest, who had been living with his mother and sister at 8903 Euclid Avenue, moved with Katharine to 1933 East Seventy-Third Street, sixteen blocks south. Just as soon as they moved into their own home, Katharine discovered something interesting about her new husband: He talked to himself. Constantly, argumentatively, ruminatively. He would be startled to find that he'd voiced his thoughts in the presence of his wife, who, for her own part, was unsettled. "I could only believe that he was unhappy in his new life," she would later write. "What else could I think? What had I done wrong? I was deeply in love and I was anxious." But as time passed and she overheard Ernest debating with himself about which tie to wear or trying out a line of thought to use at work, she realized his muttering had nothing to do with her and relaxed into bemusement.

The Angells began their married life in the middle of an era that sought to reform marriage. One of the many changes that progressives sought was the redefinition of heterosexual marriage as an alliance of equal partners who choose each other based on mutual love and sexual attraction. They argued that the economic basis of traditional marriage, in which a wife is financially dependent on her husband, bent the institution away from emotion and toward subjugation. So the mandate for women to work outside the home, the very nectar that Katharine had drunk at Bryn Mawr, aimed not just to bolster women's financial security but also to redesign their inner lives, to open the possibility for a new kind of intimacy within a marriage of class equals. The Angells proudly believed in this marriage of equals. In so many ways, they exemplified their cohort as vigorous and outdoorsy, socially committed and community minded, willing to effect generational (if not structural) change within their own intimate partnership. But in one way, they were unusual. Just as Katharine stood out from other Mawrters with her early engagement, so did the Angells stand out by starting a family right after their marriage.

But even before the couple began their own family, they helped form another. Their matchmaking must only be inferred, because the family mythology does not preserve the origin story of Rosamond's marriage, but the facts say that she met a Cleveland man who traveled in the same social circles as Ernest's family, presumably while she visited her sister and new brother-in-law just after they settled in Ernest's hometown. Did Katharine and Ernest fix her up with the eligible bachelor, or was theirs a chance meeting at the Mayfield Country Club, where Ernest's mother and the groom were both members?

Ros's fiancé was John Strong Newberry, the son of Arthur St. John Newberry, head of the Sandusky Portland Cement Company (and grandson of the eminent physician, explorer, and geologist for whom he was named, John Strong Newberry). He was five years Ros's senior, a graduate of Yale College and an executive in his father's company, but also a literary scholar with an interest in French translation who must have appreciated Ros's interest in music. In other words, Ros made a similar bid for stability as her younger sister. She chose a modern, elite young man from a conservative family—John's mother was listed in various *Social Registers* and *Who's Who* directories as "against woman suffrage" and a member of the Country, Mayfield, Twentieth Century, Tea and Topics, and Garden clubs. Ros and John were married at 4 Hawthorn Road in May 1916, almost exactly on the Angells' one-year anniversary, with eight Yale men as ushers. For the rest of her life, Katharine would have a hard time remembering which anniversary was hers and which was Ros's. *The Boston Globe* described the ceremony as "a very pretty home wedding." Only immediate family were in attendance; Ernest was best man.

Katharine was two months pregnant at the wedding. The Newberrys settled in Cleveland on East Eighty-Seventh Street, fourteen blocks north of the Angells, and Ros would have been on hand when Nancy Angell was born in December of 1916. (Nancy was born into a kind of inheritance; as the first child in Katharine's Bryn Mawr cohort, she became the Class Baby of the 1914 women, forever referred to as such in alumni publications.)

Despite her sister's presence, Katharine felt lonely in Cleveland as a new mother. She felt exiled from all that was familiar in the Northeast. She'd grown up as a staunch Red Sox fan, and after center fielder Tris Speaker joined the Cleveland Indians, she liked to say, "Tris Speaker and I were traded to Cleveland in the same year." That spring and summer, she would push Nancy's stroller past League Park near the Angells' house, and if there was a game in progress and she could hear the crowd cheering, she would imagine it was Speaker making her proud.

Both sisters cast around for causes in which to place their energies. Ros found hers at the Cleveland Music School Settlement, a new organization that gave piano, violin, and voice lessons at discounted prices to underserved children.

Katharine hired a young girl with six weeks of training as a nanny to take care of Nancy so that she could head into the workforce. Her immediate boss at her old volunteer job at Massachusetts General Hospital, Amy M. Hamburger, now directed the Cleveland Cripple Survey, the first citywide census of physically handicapped children and adults in the nation. Katharine's task was to visit each house on a list of addresses that

Miss Hamburger gave her, ask for the mother or female head of house, and attempt to gain entry. She remembered that it was generally easier in tenements and slums than in the posh homes on fashionable Lower Euclid Avenue that she knew from her own social life. The census had already identified the 4,186 disabled people in their geographic area of 150,000 families, and it was Katharine's job to fill in answers concerning the conditions in which the individual was living, the family income, and whether or not the individual was able to work or attend school. A trained nurse would follow behind her in a day or two. The Cleveland Cripple Survey surprised the social workers who undertook it. They had no idea there were so many individuals who met their definition of disabled, nor that there were so many who had found fulfilling occupations. Though in later years the survey would be criticized for the way it carved out the disabled population from the rest of the public body, made them visible with a pernicious label, and focused only on their right to work at the expense of other rights, at the time it represented a step forward in advocating for the most vulnerable, including the 246 school-age children who were not being educated because no institution could meet their needs.

One morning in the autumn after she settled into newlywed life, Katharine attended a meeting of the Cleveland Woman's Suffrage Party at its headquarters on Euclid Street, passing underneath an enormous sign that read "Men of Ohio! Give the Women a Square Deal." One important man of Ohio had already been radicalized—Ernest had been a member of the Men's Equal Suffrage League since at least 1914, when he worked to rally one thousand men to join in a suffrage parade of ten thousand women, "the strongest jolt to indifference" they could muster. The party had won an important victory that year. Under the leadership of Vassar graduate Minerva Kline Brooks, East Cleveland had voted to give women municipal suffrage, the only place east of Chicago where a woman could cast a vote.

But on this particular morning, the talk was not about political strategy. A young woman named Grace Treat had seen an extraordinary theatrical performance the previous night, and she described it in such excited detail to Katharine and her friend Minerva Brooks that they asked her to arrange for them to see it too. Several nights later, the Angells, Minerva Brooks, and her husband, Charles, visited the home of Raymond O'Neil, the drama and music critic for *The Cleveland Leader*. He had constructed a tiny model stage on which sat a cardboard cyclorama. He turned down the lights and turned up a rheostat—a brand-new invention—to illuminate a mountain peak against a faint dawn sky. As the couples watched, morning colors swept behind the silhouette of the mountain range, brightened to noon, then shaded again into dusk. They were utterly captivated by the new lighting effects and by O'Neil's theories for how they could reinvigorate the rather stale conventions of American theater. "I think we should form a little theatre group to produce plays in this new art form," declared the energetic Minerva Brooks. Improbably, that was the spark for America's first and longest-running regional theater, still staging plays today. It was in the Brooks's drawing room that a group of ten "businessmen and Bohemians" officially formed the Cleveland Play House with O'Neil as its director—but not a single actor among them. Ernest, decidedly from the "businessmen" side of things, was elected treasurer and soon also became a trustee, helping to guarantee a bank loan from the Citizens Savings and Trust Company.

In May of 1916 the Cleveland Play House performed its first work, Maurice Maeterlinck's *The Death of Tintagiles*, a puppet show with O'Neil's cyclorama of a moody castle and atmospheric lighting controlled by the rheostat. The production featured Grace Treat's fabric dolls, thirteen inches high, with completely blank or symbolically minimalist features. Katharine operated a marionette and read the part of a character who uttered a terrified scream, and she would later write that this production roughened her voice for the rest of her life (she made no mention of the possible influence of her lifelong smoking habit).

The relationships Katharine formed at the Play House would last her lifetime. Grace's sister Ida, a professor of Romance languages at Western Reserve University with a doctorate from the University of Paris, wrote *Forty at a Blow*, a play adapted from a Grimm fairy tale and performed as a shadowgraph against a bright white screen. Katharine found O'Neil difficult to work with, but Ida married him. Katharine and Ida became close friends. The two collaborated to edit a book of local poetry, which included a few poems from each of them, Katharine's first postcollegiate publication. Later, Katharine would publish seventeen of Ida's stories in *The New Yorker*. The Play House staged August Strindberg's symbolist play *Motherly Love*, starring a young Cleveland actress just returned from theatrical training in Paris, Clare Eames, in her first professional role. The play, though daring, was a success, and Eames left Cleveland right afterward for New York. The Angells would continue their relationship with her through the 1920s as she earned great acclaim on Broadway and in silent films; they introduced her to the playwright Sidney Howard, whom she married in 1922, and from there the lines of affection and influence would grow quite tangled. Sidney Howard was a close friend of Elsie Sergeant; he corresponded with and visited her often in Europe at about the same time that Eames was starring at the Cleveland Play House, and the drama in which these players would someday find themselves enmeshed would rival anything Strindberg could have written for them.

But for these years in the middle of the 1910s, the Cleveland Play House, like Bryn Mawr College, called out from Katharine her creative energies and delivered her happiest relationships. Her brother-in-law John Newberry joined in (perhaps Ros did too, but her name does not appear in the Play House records), and he served as president in 1919 and 1920.

With hindsight, this theatrical interlude before Katharine discovered her literary career offers an intriguing counterfactual. What might her life have been like had she stayed in the theater? She threw herself into the work, designing costumes and painting scenery, and must have felt an enormous sense of ownership at having been present at the creation of a new cultural institution and at the introduction of European modernism into the heart of America. But she was, after all, a marionette at the command of an autocratic male, at whose behest she lost her voice. She would shortly have to leave both the theater and modernism behind.

Ernest enlisted as an officer in the war in November of 1918.

10.

And then freedom from ties . . . of course one wouldn't, of one's own volition, drop below the surface of life, and duck off to another world, leaving behind everything one most values. Wife and baby . . . job, house, and committees . . . one did it because it was the right thing to do, because one had to take a part with the rest of humanity. But it is nevertheless a precious and wonderful opportunity.

—Ernest Angell, quoted in Elizabeth Shepley Sergeant's
  Shadow-Shapes, 1920

Nancy was six months old when General Pershing's American Expeditionary Forces were established, and by the time she was ten months old, Ernest was ready to join. He had been obediently practicing law since graduation. "My most vivid recollection from those four years," he would tell his Harvard classmates just after the war, "is of an unending and overlapping series of committee meetings and committee reports. Everything was in the process of being administered; one never stopped to ask why." Now his "civic conscience" was pricking him. He was ready to drop the reports and do his part.

Ernest's war career was likely bound up in an almost invisible chain of associations with the start of Katharine's literary career. He was recruited by Willard Straight, a New York banker and an active member of the Preparedness Movement, to join the Bureau of War Risk Insurance, a new endeavor that aimed to correct the federal government's historic indifference to soldiers and their families' welfare by compensating families during a soldier's service, providing disability and death benefits, and offering voluntary insurance at low rates. Perhaps Ernest came to Straight's notice because of his legal career, but there is another reason why a lawyer way out in Cleveland might have attracted his attention. In 1914, Straight and his wealthy wife, Dorothy Whitney Straight, had founded and funded a new progressive weekly magazine, *The New Republic*, which, in addition to urging the United States to join the war since the sinking of the *Lusitania*, had also published a book review by Katharine Sergeant Angell in 1916. Katharine lavished praise on the translation of journalist V. Doroshevitch's account of the refugees who poured into the western Russian provinces from Poland in the summer of 1915, finding his remarkable prose unlike anything in English: Doroshevitch "achieve[d] the effect of not having tried for effect," a documentary style that was decidedly not realism.

Katharine's first magazine byline almost certainly came through her sister. Elsie Shepley Sergeant had been writing for *The New Republic* since its founding. Her own first byline arose from her social work among the Italian immigrant community in Boston. She wrote an angry, tightly argued, and statistically supported exposé of the "home-work" or "sweated" system of labor, in which entire families of Eastern European immigrants earned fifty cents for twelve-hour days spent fashioning the accoutrements of the Gibson Girl, including the rolls of hair they wore under their pompadours. Elsie showed up unannounced at the offices of *McClure's Magazine* on East Twenty-Third Street, clutching her manuscript pages and a letter of introduction for the esteemed Willa Cather from their mutual friend Pauline Goldmark. Cather accepted Elsie's article for publication at the front of the magazine in 1910, thus beginning a lifelong friendship between the two writers. When Cather joined *The New Republic*, she brought Elsie along with her to write reviews and articles about European culture. In 1918, the magazine sent Elsie to France as its war correspondent. Perhaps, along the way, she recommended her brother-in-law to Straight.

Ernest answered Major Straight's invitation and enlisted as a first lieutenant. His draft card: "Tall, medium, or short (specify which)? Tall. Slender, medium, or stout (which)? Slender. Color of eyes? Brown. Color

of hair? Brown. Bald? No." He was sent to France, where he rose to
the rank of captain and helped the insurance program succeed mightily,
though he must have chafed in his role of uniformed sales agent and he
almost certainly sat in yet more committee meetings. Katharine would
later say that he didn't stay long with the Bureau of War Risk Insurance.
His French was so good that he was recruited to counterintelligence,
which is why he remained abroad until September of 1919, nearly a year
after Armistice. She said that he caught two spies.

Meanwhile, Katharine chafed under the very condition that Straight's
bureau was trying to improve: she received half of Ernest's pay, which she
remembered as $1,800, and she quickly found that it was not enough to
support her and Nancy. If her article in *The New Republic* had stirred up
literary ambitions, she briskly cleaned them away in a domestic version of
embracing the war effort, and she wouldn't publish again for another six
years. Instead, she turned a volunteer job into a paid position. Throughout
the war, she continued to be an active member of the suffrage movement,
and when it shifted its energies over to the volunteer war effort, Katharine assumed a leadership role in the Woman's Committee of the Council
of National Defense. She was also a steady leader of a standing committee within the Consumers League of Ohio. She did not share Ernest's
antipathy to committees; no progressive woman could have afforded such
a stance, not if she wanted to make improvements in the lives of those
around her. The Consumers League was begun by Jane Addams and
chaired by Florence Kelley, who became Katharine's new boss. The league
worked for food safety, privacy laws, and a label testifying to a product's
manufacture under fair working conditions. Katharine's job required her
to obtain an Ohio State factory inspection badge. She traveled to facto-
ries that were thrumming with war production and inspected their safety
conditions. Her previous work at Massachusetts General Hospital cued
her for what to look for: workers who were not given a chance to wash
their hands between using lead paint and eating their lunches, workers
who had no protection from the fumes of the banana oil they sprayed on
airplanes. Her reports resulted in changes on the factory floor of an alu-
minum can company and an airplane manufacturer, and she was called to
Columbus to testify on behalf of a new law for worker protection.

At the same time, the shortage in natural gas soon meant that the temperature in the Angells' house dipped down to thirty-two degrees. Katharine made the decision to leave her work and move with Nancy back to Brookline, joining Charles and Crullie at the comfortable Hawthorn Road house.

Charles had just retired as vice president of the Boston Elevated Railway Company. He'd had a long, distinguished, and lucrative career, and he'd weathered turbulence toward the end of it. Back in the summer of 1916, the Massachusetts lieutenant governor chaired a special commission to investigate the railway's finances; facilities had fallen into disrepair, and the railway was unable to raise capital. Charles rode out the ensuing changes, twice passed over for promotion to the presidency but never fired with other executives. In November of 1918, he retired at the age of sixty-six and took up oil painting.

The reunited family moved about the rooms of the Hawthorn Road house that winter of 1918: Charles; Aunt Crullie; Katharine; Nancy, just about to turn two years old; and her Cleveland nanny. If Katharine was relieved to return to Brookline—traded back to her home team—she may have also felt as if her heart were being stretched. Not long after she left, Rosamond discovered that she was pregnant with her first child, and John "Jack" Newberry Jr. would be born the following summer.

And across the ocean, Elsie was lying alone in a hospital in France, a striking repetition of the winter of 1904. In October, Elsie and three other American women had traveled to a battlefield in Marne that was crucial for the defense of Rheims. They were escorted by Mademoiselle de Vallette, head of the American section of the Press Department of the Foreign Office, and a lieutenant, who exhorted them not to pick up anything from the battlefield. As the women walked toward the German lines, they could not resist stooping down to peer at a German prayer book or the inside of a German gas mask. Suddenly, Elsie felt "a stunning report, a blinding flash"—Mlle. de Vallette had picked up an unexploded "potato masher" hand grenade. The Frenchwoman died instantly, the lieutenant lost an arm, and Elsie found that she could not stand, though she felt no pain—not at first. One of the other journalists recalled not understanding that Elsie was injured, "for she made no sort of fuss, but spoke as calmly as ever." In fact, she had sustained compound fractures of both ankles, and it would be months before she could walk.

Once again, she lay in isolation at a hospital in Neuilly, unable to communicate with her family, though the *New Republic* articles and the diary that she wrote and soon published about her experiences do not draw the parallel with her earlier illness. She merely watched her own abstract fascination with the wartime procedures of the hospital and said, "As so often in the past, my mind has come to life and helped largely in saving my nerve."

Elsie had proposed to Ferris Greenslet at Houghton Mifflin that she turn fifteen of her *New Republic* articles plus additional material into an account of the American participation in the war. *Shadow-Shapes: The Journal of a Wounded Woman*, in other words, was not the manuscript she'd contracted to publish. But when her injury—and the Armistice that was announced a month later—cut short her original story, she used the disruption creatively. She found herself in a highly unusual position, because American and European forces included no women soldiers, so she was likely the only female to be wounded on a battlefield by a weapon and treated in a military hospital. *Shadow-Shapes* reflects Elsie's unique circumstances with modernist style and structure; she dispenses with journalism and reaches for a new, nonrealist way of writing to convey the life of the American Hospital of Paris before and after the war's end, intercut with flashbacks to her own witnessing of the war itself. Impressionistic, baldly factual at times, sharply funny at others, devoid of self-pity (bending her stiff knee joint is "a process which sounds and feels very much like an effort to separate the wainscoting from the wall"), her own subjectivity undercut with indirect speech that takes on the perspectives of her many visitors—Elsie created a modernist wounded narrator nine years before Ernest Hemingway's *A Farewell to Arms*.

The book sold modestly when it was published in 1920 and has been all but forgotten. Rereading it now with the Sergeant family as a frame brings certain passages into high relief. Elsie befriends her doctor and convinces him to let her watch an operation for appendicitis. "How bloodless and decent the procedure, how delicate and exquisitely sure the hand of science." The surgery that could not save her mother be-comes one of the experiences that allows Elsie to recover.

She writes extensively in the book of her friend "Rick"—the play-wright Sidney Howard—of his aliveness in the face of a combat pilot's daily danger and his unfitness at war's end for the American business mindset. The book's other main character is Ernest, her brother-in-law, with his "fine, frank, judicious brown eyes," "doing his responsible job in the rear of the A.E.F" in Dijon. In the spring, he was transferred to Paris, and she rejoiced in the company of her brother-in-law as she recovered. But what she wrote about him is strange. In a long, stodgy passage that concludes the book, she re-creates his thoughts on "the gallant comrade-ship of the sexes on which our civilization rests," which is not something "the home-keeping women folk will ever know." This passage wants to be a tribute to women's worth on the battlefront, but it reads as an elab-orate defense, before any accusation had been made, of Ernest's behav-ior toward women while away from his wife. He speaks passionately of something Elsie experienced with Sidney Howard, *amitie* between the sexes, affectionate friendship without sentimental complications." Ernest compares himself to the callow American soldiers who had rev-eled in their temporary sexual freedom, but he maintains that American values "have fundamentally stood the test," and that if anyone had been changed in the encounter, it was French women, who would now mea-sure themselves against independent American women like Katharine, with whom he could not wait to be reunited.

At last, in May of 1919, after nearly seven months in the hospital and much therapy to regain the use of her legs, Elsie boarded a steamer for New York. But Ernest stayed in France for another four months, at work with the U.S. Liquidation Commission to settle foreign claims against the War Department—or perhaps that was merely his cover story. Kath-arine had tried to keep herself productive during this time. She did not work for pay—it was the winter of the influenza pandemic, and when the nanny caught it, Aunt Crullie was tasked with nursing her while Katharine cared for Nancy—but she did volunteer, at a Brookline ele-mentary school playground and at the Children's Hospital Boston, and she audited a few writing classes at Boston University.

Ernest returned to his young family in September. Elsie had noted that often returning soldiers "propose to seek not only new occupations, but new American habitats." Ernest continued in the law profession, but the Angells at once sought a new habitat. On the advice of Emory Buckner, the legendary New York trial lawyer and a fellow Harvard Law graduate, Ernest set his sights on New York; Buckner had himself arrived as a young man with a wife and children and no prospects, and had quickly made a name for himself cleaning up corruption with meticulous facts and dramatic courtroom presentations (he would be the subject of a two-part profile in *The New Yorker* that Katharine would edit). Ernest took the risk of moving away from the comfortable Midwestern city of his father's success. To pave their way, the Angells enlisted Elsie's help. Could she find them an apartment in New York?

11.

The Angells moved, sight unseen, into the furnished apartment Elsie found for them at East Eighty-First Street, and in November of 1919, Ernest resumed practicing law. Now the Angells could count on a bigger salary than Ernest's wartime pay, but Katharine found work as soon as they settled into their new home. The Bryn Mawr Alumnae Endowment Fund employed her in the New York chapter office, and she traveled to organize additional chapters in Toledo, Detroit, and Pittsburgh. She enjoyed the job, but she had to give up the work when she became pregnant a second time.

In August of 1920, the Nineteenth Amendment to the United States Constitution was ratified, and one month later, Ernest and Katharine had a son, Roger, born two days after Katharine's twenty-eighth birthday. They moved to a bigger apartment and acquired a summer home not far away in Snedens Landing, a hamlet across the Hudson River on the steep hillside of the Palisades.

Katharine spoke of these years only once, just a few months before she died, in a heavily redacted and edited account. These were the years when the architecture of her life began to crack.

In the summer of 1921, the Angells experienced such pinched financial straits that they gave up their Manhattan apartment and moved to their Snedens Landing cottage to live year-round. Nancy was four and a half and Roger was still a baby. It isn't obvious why the young family with a lawyer at the head of the household should find themselves unable to afford their home. They had perhaps overextended themselves with the class imperative of two dwellings. Katharine and Roger would both say in later years that Ernest never had a head for business.

Snedens Landing (named after the palindromic family who ran the boat to Dobbs Ferry for two centuries) was an enchanted place, almost otherworldly in its overgrown remoteness, with winding roads around steep terrain. It was close to Manhattan but a world away: after a forty-four-minute train ride from Grand Central Terminal to Dobbs Ferry, the ferry captain could row across the river in fifteen minutes—eleven on a calm day. Electricity arrived in the village only a few years before the Angells. Their house, which dated to 1780, was made from light brown Dutch fieldstone that had come over the Atlantic as ship ballast. It had belonged to Captain Larry Sneden, who ran a store out of it, and it would later be named to the National Register of Historic Places.

The house was at the bottom of a twisting hillside road, right along the Hudson River. There were two gardens—a vegetable garden for Ernest and a flower garden for Katharine. The south side of the house held an arbor on which grew the grapes that Nancy and Roger, when they were a bit older, would stomp into wine for their parents during Prohibition. Under the arbor was a patio where the family ate dinner beside a free-standing stone fireplace. At the bottom of the property there was a porch at the river's edge. The river provided the Angell children with a place to fish for eels and crabs and to watch the river traffic go by. On Sundays the family would picnic with neighbors at a nearby pergola overlooking a brook that plunged over a natural waterfall and filled a small, deep pool adorned with a water-spouting gargoyle. There Ernest would perform his famous trick: he would climb nearly thirty feet above the pool and then dive over the boulders into the precise center of the deep water. Snedens would soon become home to a crowd of wealthy artists—actors like Katharine Cornell, Ginger Rogers, and Laurence Olivier—but the Angells were among the first of that wave, and they found themselves right at home.

That summer, they befriended a brother and sister from England who lived just across the little road in the old Mollie Sneden house: Marian Powys, a renowned lacemaker with a shop on Fifty-Seventh Street that catered to women in the Morgan, Frick, and Rockefeller families, and John Cowper Powys, a writer who would become well-known at the end of the decade for his novel *Wolf Solent*. John was then working as an itinerant lecturer, and he was only just stopping by Snedens Landing when he met the Angells. A few days after he left, he wrote to his sister: "I did remark how much he admired you! and, as you know, I myself took quite a fancy to him at once, it is the most important of all events to you." The important event was Marian's love affair with Ernest. Her brother was in full support of the liaison, and in fact he offered Marian his services, writing, "[I could] indulg[e] in a timely flirtation with Madame . . . ha! eh? towards whom I recollect—yes; . . . I *was* rather attracted—certainly more than to anyone else in your Landing!"

Ernest had had at least one French lover during the war. It is unclear when Katharine learned about this. Elsie had strenuously portrayed Ernest as the exception among American soldiers for whom wartime was a suspension of the rules. Ernest, in Elsie's version, had "so many close friends among women and still care[d] for only one." But Elsie had in fact gone out of her way to whitewash Ernest's sexual escapades in a book ostensibly about her own trauma.

Now Ernest decided that he'd like to continue the French tradition. That summer, he and Marian spent weeknights in Manhattan, perhaps at the apartment over her shop, and on weekends they returned to their respective houses at Snedens Landing, an arrangement that Katharine felt compelled to abide to keep her family together. But Ernest must have spent at least some time with Marian in Snedens, because he taught her to swim in that deep, cold pool below the waterfall.

Ernest was the one great love affair of Marian's life. She was thirty-nine years old, seven years older than Ernest, and she'd spent the first part of her life breaking free of her large and storied family. She was the seventh of eleven children born to a vicar in Dorchester, but from a very young age she wanted something other than her parents' traditional world. She learned about lace at a William Morris–inspired art school and then traveled to Belgium, Italy, France, and Switzerland to learn its craft, design, and history. Then, when her beloved older brother John, ten years her senior, moved to the United States, she campaigned to be allowed to follow him there, ostensibly to take care of him. But John needed no care, and he collaborated with Marian in launching her new life as an independent woman. In 1916 she opened her Devonshire Lace

Shop on Washington Square; her first visitor was Mrs. J. P. Morgan Jr., and her first customer was Isadora Duncan. In the fall of 1920, Marian moved her shop to West Fifty-Seventh Street, a sign that her business was thriving. John, her lifelong admirer, described her as "adamant in her heroic strength" at making a living by her artistic passion. Marian was handsome, with a distinctive profile, a haughty-sounding British accent, and an informal manner that charmed people from all walks of life but that would harden if opposed.

In October, a month after Roger Angell turned one, Marian became pregnant with Ernest's baby. She may have deliberately meant to conceive a child, but she soon learned that she could not count on her lover for support. In her seventh month, the cottage she rented was sold, and she asked Ernest to lend her money to buy a nearby house. He said no; the Angells were still living year-round in what was supposed to be their summer home and were perhaps saving to return to Manhattan. So Marian borrowed the money from a relative and purchased Hagen House, a ramshackle wooden house dating to 1805, in which she would live for the rest of her life.

John invented the story that Marian had married a man in the diplomatic service in October who promptly went off to Italy and died of malaria. Marian's situation, according to John, was "neither absolutely black, nor absolutely white, but *grey*," thus the fabricated husband who widowed her was named Peter Grey. They even produced a portrait of the unlucky man. And when Marian's son was born on July 14, 1922, she named him Peter Grey after his fictional father. That summer, Mrs. Ernest Angell traveled without her husband to the Chateau Frontenac in Quebec.

Peter would grow up in Snedens Landing with only that portrait to stand in for his absent father. Marian and her son would form an intense two-person family in their messy house, with various Snedens women helping out over the years. His parents would hide the true identity of his father well into Peter's teenage years, but he would suspect there was more to the story than a conveniently dispatched diplomat. John nervously forestalled Peter's questions, privately "wishing that his origin was yet *more* mysterious & unusual than it was!" Finally, as a Harvard student, Peter would meet his father, and every year around the time of his birthday, they'd have lunch at the Harvard Club. Sometimes Ernest would give him cash, but the two of them would never be close.

But for now, in the tiny hamlet of Snedens Landing, Katharine's knowledge of Ernest's affair was "making [her] sick," as she later wrote in a letter to her granddaughter just six months before she died, the only surviving testament to her feelings about Ernest's infidelities. She does not seem to have been open to Ernest's attempt to redefine their marriage to include a mistress. She merely put up with his weekday absences from her bed—for a time—and worked hard to maintain an outward appearance of normalcy. She did not work or volunteer. She stayed at home, a long way from the city, caring for her two young children, looking out across the river with a view of the ferry as it moved toward or away from the long, narrow dock.

Finally, she told Ernest that she could not abide his idea of marriage, and in her words to her granddaughter, he "bravely gave up his mistress." The Angells decided to repair rather than end their marriage. Their efforts began with another move, this time back into the city. Incredibly enough, they kept the Snedens Landing house for weekends and summers. It is this fact that casts doubt on the idea that Katharine knew the identity of Ernest's lover, or even the existence of his son. Either Katharine knew about Marian and Peter, in which case she made a monumental concession to Ernest in the name of family harmony, responding unconventionally to his infidelity in order to maintain a conventional family life; or she didn't know about them, and Marian and Ernest successfully pulled off a stunning deception right under her nose in a town that was supposed to be a refuge and a home. It clarifies little that Peter and Roger casually knew each other from the time they were boys and would slowly grow a friendship over their summers in Snedens, a friendship that coalesced around playing tennis. It's possible too that the affair between Ernest and Marian continued past when Katharine asked for Ernest's "brave" renunciation; many years later, when Katharine and Ernest would finally divorce, Marian's friends would wonder if now Ernest would marry her (he wouldn't).

Ernest's mother, Lily, helped the Angells buy a brownstone at 61 East

Ninety-Third Street, a block and a half from the Central Park Reservoir, and Manhattan once again became their primary home. The house was narrow, sixteen feet wide, with one bay window and one smaller window for each of the three stories above a basement apartment, with a steep stoop up to the front door, a coal chute under the steps, and a small garden in the back. It represented a distinct step up in the world for the young family. In time, they'd hire a French couple, Joseph and Edmonde Petrognani, to cook, keep house, and wait on the table. Katharine, however, continued to have no meaningful work outside the home to give shape to her days.

Katharine was not the only one moving house. Lily Angell left Cleveland for Park Avenue, just around the corner from her son and daughter-in-law. Katharine's sister Ros also moved from Cleveland; John Newberry retired from his father's cement company in 1920 and they relocated to Boston, where John taught literature at MIT. Katharine's father, Charles, sold the big house on Hawthorn Street in October 1921. He and Crullie moved west to join their sisters Helen and Mollie at the Bridge Street house in Northampton.

With hindsight, these few years at the beginning of the 1920s seem like a lost time for Katharine, after the promise of college. One thing was certain: she knew how *not* to behave in the face of betrayal. Katharine and Ernest had introduced Clare Eames, their actress friend from the Cleveland Play House, to Elsie's friend Sidney Howard, who cast her in his Broadway play, *Swords*. The play was a failure, but Howard wrote to Elsie, "It became suddenly evident to Clare and me that the real purpose of the play was to marry us." The news plunged Elsie into an emotional crisis, the exact outlines of which are mysterious except that she reacted like a woman scorned. Elsie made Eames's life "complete hell" and did everything she could to break the engagement. Eames came to Ernest for help. Ernest, surely cognizant of Elsie's nervous breakdown after college, told Elsie that if she did not back down, he would have her committed to an institution. A terrified Elsie signed a written retraction of her accusations and kept her distance from Eames and Howard, who married in Cleveland on June 1, 1922 (they would divorce at the end of the decade, and Ernest would represent Howard in their protracted fight). Elsie recognized that part of her mental fragility arose from her battlefield injuries, and she sought out the care of Dr. Thomas Salmon, a psychiatrist who studied "shell shock." Dr. Salmon helped Elsie regain equilibrium, and the two would collaborate to bring mental health care to World War I veterans.

Elsie and Katharine both felt betrayed by the men who had fought in France and returned from the war, but this hardly brought the sisters closer. This moment, like so many others at this time, swirls with dark silence. It isn't clear what role Katharine played in Ernest's brutal handling of Elsie's crisis, or what lessons she drew about mental health, the display of deep feeling, and the dangers of emotional attachment, or about her husband and the lines he wouldn't allow others to cross, despite his own transgressions. Katharine's life in the early 1920s can best be intuited by the negative spaces. Ambition still thrummed inside her, but she did not write poetry or fiction, or join a theater in New York, or seek to transform her experiences into any genre of art. She did not pursue public health or other progressive causes. This extended moment of disappointment was perhaps a continuation of the forbearance she'd learned when her mother died.

In 1922, Ernest took a new job at the law firm Hardin, Hess & Eder, where he would remain for the next fourteen years. The couple took a Caribbean trip that they could not afford, the result of what Katharine called her "bad mathematics." Ernest had been invited to join Senator Medill McCormick's select committee on the United States' 1915 invasion of Haiti and the Dominican Republic, which was formed in response to Haitian allegations that US Marines had behaved brutally toward civilians when squashing a resistance to the occupation. Ernest traveled first to Washington, DC, and then to the island as a representative of the Haiti–Santo Domingo Independence Society, the National Association for the Advancement of Colored People (NAACP), and the Union Patriotique of Haiti, on whose behalf he questioned witnesses at hearings in Port-au-Prince and Santo Domingo. Katharine was invited too, but the committee would not cover her fare. She bought her own ticket, only to discover afterward that she'd overestimated the Angells' checking account by $1,000 and that they couldn't afford the fare. She solved that problem in an admirably straightforward fashion by selling two fiercely argued essays on the invasion of Haiti to *The New Republic*, which appeared respectively in March and July of 1922. In an echo of Elsie, she described a foreign culture with telling detail and a distinct political argument. Katharine reported the Haitian "insistence that the Americans leave, utterly and entirely," saying, "They will accept no compromise." Katharine's essays put *The New Republic* in rare company. Only *The Nation*, which published NAACP secretary James Weldon Johnson's indictment of the invasion, broke through the bland message of cultural uplift peddled by *The New York Times* and other mainstream news outlets. But this political reporting was a one-off, a path not taken, a momentary experiment with Elsie's writing practice.

Katharine went back to work, likely because she needed something to take her out of her unhappy home and because the Angells still lived slightly beyond their means on the Upper East Side with household staff. She worked for a society decorator, Amy Richards Colton, who was a friend of Elsie's and a neighbor in Snedens. Katharine staffed Colton's shop at East Fifty-Seventh Street and ran errands to wholesalers and antique stores, but she found Colton's taste ridiculous—"brown and green and very drab"—and the work boring.

Next came Katharine's first professional editing job, and it was a flat failure. A poet friend of hers, Scudder Middleton, recommended her to Dr. Beatrice Hinkle, a psychoanalyst with a book manuscript in progress. Katharine's mandate was to help turn Hinkle's "very Germanic English" into "good English" (the description is Katharine's; Hinkle was born and raised in San Francisco and earned her MD at what became Stanford's medical school). She quit after only two weeks. The reason, which Katharine would explain sotto voce in letters to several correspondents over the years, was that Dr. Hinkle was "more messed up than her patients—having an affair with another woman, oppressing her son, etc." The editorial mismatch between Katharine and Hinkle—Katharine's refusal to identify with an ambitious career woman whose interest in medicine and public health she shared—raises questions on the eve of Katharine's new career. Hinkle was a pioneer in medicine, the first female city physician in the country (and a single mother), and then the founder of the first psychotherapeutic clinic in the United States. She traveled to Europe to meet Freud and Jung, then became both an important early feminist critic of Freud and the one who introduced Jung to American readers.

Katharine had recoiled from either homosexuality or psychoanalysis—or both. She again wondered if writing was the solution to some of her problems. She had Elsie as a forerunner, but she broke away from Elsie's *New Republic* and began publishing book reviews in *The Nation*, succinct, confident, and learned essays. She reviewed St. John Ervine's *Some Impressions of My Elders*, a journalistic account of Russia, a mystery novel, a novel in the Sinclair Lewis tradition of satirizing Main Street ("The picture which it gives of a provincial, respectable, mean-spirited, overfed, over-comfortable, and under-thinking existence seems perfect to one reader at least whose lot was cast for a time on just such a plane"). She reviewed books for *The Atlantic* and *The Saturday Review of Literature*. She waxed rapturous over a translation of Lady Murasaki's *The Tale of Genji* with a preface by poet Amy Lowell, which likely intrigued her because Aunt Poo had recently published a translation from Japanese of Murasaki's journals, also with a Lowell preface, and because Lowell hailed from Brookline.

And then everything changed in the summer of 1925. Katharine was at home in Snedens Landing when her neighbor Fillmore Hyde suggested she apply for a job at a new magazine, *The New Yorker*, for which he was writing. The magazine was then just six months old and struggling badly. Hyde was the only true New Yorker on a magazine staff run by young men from the hinterlands. *The New Yorker* was "nothing," said Henry Seidel Canby, editor of *The Saturday Review of Literature*, when Katharine ran Hyde's idea by him.

Still, Katharine traveled to the ninth floor of the Central Building at 25 West Forty-Fifth Street. As she exited the elevator, others turned right to get to work on a two-year-old magazine named *Time*. She turned left and marched into *The New Yorker* for a job.

Part III

Editing a Humor Weekly

(1925–1929)

12.

The *New Yorker* offices were chaotic. Katharine walked into a maze of partitions, crowded with writers hunched at desks, and other writers standing over them waiting their turns in a never-ending game of musical typewriters. She presented herself to Gladys Unger, the receptionist and switchboard operator, who passed her to Helen Mears, the boss's secretary. Katharine didn't know it, but all these people—writers, administrative staff, editors, the art director Rea Irvin—were on the verge of losing their jobs, at just the moment she came to ask for one. Launched in February, the magazine was losing money so briskly that by May the publisher had wanted to kill it. He rather miserably gave founding editor Harold Ross a few more months to attempt a comeback in the more profitable fall season, when advertisers might return to their pages. Until such a time, Ross's specific directive was to save money. That August, his magazine had a circulation of fewer than three thousand copies, and he was reduced to running ads for free just to make his magazine look prosperous.

Katharine was brought into Ross's office, where she found a tall man in a dark suit and plain dark tie with a wild head of hair. She introduced herself to Ross, flourished the reference of Fillmore Hyde, and said she wanted to work for *The New Yorker*. Ross was impressed with her education and patrician bearing. Her employed her on the spot as a part-time manuscript reader for $25 a week.

Ross hired Katharine with a jaunty impulsivity that she would soon learn was a defining trait of his management style. If she'd had to apply for the position, she never would have gotten the job. If someone had asked her to design her perfect career, this might be precisely what she would have come up with.

She joined an organization that was spinning its own mythology even as it was floundering, a myth still intact today. The origin story goes like this: there, in a cramped set of midtown offices, elbowing for room in a building with more established publications, such as *Saturday Review* and *Smart Set*, was Harold Ross, a barely civilized former reporter, emitting an unbroken stream of curses and running his hand anxiously through his plush, upright pompadour. "I'd like to take off my shoes and stockings and wade in Ross's hair," sighed the actress Ina Claire.

By day, Ross managed his staff with chaotic intensity from inside his many contradictions. The Colorado transplant, who looked, in Alexander Woollcott's words, "like a dishonest Abe Lincoln," had the nerve to publish a high-class humor magazine to rival *Vanity Fair* for cultural prominence in the glittering city. The very first issue took the shape that has persisted to this day, with Goings On (current listings for theater, moving pictures, art, and music events), Talk of the Town (punchy anecdotes that give an insider view of work and play in Manhattan), and profiles (not full portraits, but vivid descriptions of the interesting men and women of the day).

At *The New Yorker*'s founding, Ross partnered with an unlikely investor, Raoul Fleischmann, reluctant heir to the Fleischmann Yeast enterprise. Ross was given office space in a building constructed by a group that included Raoul's older brother Charles, rent-free, in exchange for advertising Fleischmann's Yeast. The two men fought all the time but stayed together for decades, because Fleischmann kept to his own side of Ross's strict partition between business and editorial. Ross, the high school dropout, read every word of the proofs, insisted on fanatical accuracy even within fiction, and scrawled queries that instantly entered magazine lore. "Who he?" Ross would write if a character appeared in a story without proper introduction.

By night, he sat with Dorothy Parker, Alexander Woollcott, Robert Benchley, Frank Sullivan, and other wits at the Algonquin Round Table, a group that understood self-mythologizing. One evening, he accosted Dorothy Parker and asked her why she hadn't come into the office to write for him as she'd promised. She looked at him balefully and said, "Somebody was using the pencil." Everyone all over town laughed and repeated the comeback.

In the early days, *The New Yorker* drained money and failed to retain readers. Just three months into its life—and three weeks after its few readers encountered the first casual, "A Step Forward," bylined "E.B.W." (E. B. White)—the founders decided to cut their losses and end the magazine, then drunkenly changed their minds after a champagne-infused wedding reception, but they still couldn't attract advertisers to its foundering pages. Most ominously, the page inside the front cover remained empty, so they filled it with a series by Corey Ford called "The Making of a Magazine: A Tour Through the Vast Organization of *The New Yorker*." Ford's satire tells how the paper for the magazine is made from gowns that 7,600 dressmakers have made for 5,000 young women to wear on the subway, where they are crushed into pulp. He recounts the growing of punctuation in hothouses, where periods are watered to become the commas of which Harold Ross was inordinately fond. Look at what we are trying to do here, the series shouted; notice the heroic efforts of all these clever men! *The New Yorker* was, in James Thurber's words, "the outstanding flop of 1925." It was also "the only flop that kept on going."

But there's another way to tell the magazine's origin story: by traveling along the networks forged by the women who were there from the beginning and who have been barely mentioned in histories of the magazine. This story shows quite simply that so many of *The New Yorker*'s early successes were due to the efforts of feminist women who interpreted the magazine's obsession with sophistication in a way guaranteed to appeal to readers like themselves—educated, active participants in the city's cultural life.

Peer closer at the magazine that fetishized peering closer, and there was Janet Flanner wearing a top hat and the occasional monocle. Flanner, whose Letter from Paris was crucial in establishing the tone of the magazine in its earliest issues, was the discovery not of Harold Ross but of his wife, Jane Grant, the first full-time female reporter in the *New York Times* city room. The artist Neysa McMein had introduced the two women years before, and Grant and McMein visited Flanner in 1923 when she moved to Paris's Left Bank. Flanner's subsequent letters to Grant were so lively and evocative that Grant asked her simply to submit them unchanged to *The New Yorker*, and the first one appeared in the September 12, 1925, issue. Flanner told New Yorkers at which restaurants they should dine (Ciro's and the Château Madrid), which waning nightclubs were about to rise again (the Perroquet and the Florida), and which wealthy dowagers they would be likely to spot at these watering holes, as well as which of their features were available for mockery (the Marquise de Chateaubriand, whose bosom is "always ornamented with what looks like the bottom of a tumbler—in reality a colossal diamond," and "Mme Bobe of robbery notoriety, than whom no one is blonder"). From the very first, Flanner had already perfected her arch tone, her juxtaposition of French and American mores, her treatment of larger national events through the sparkling lens of gossip. Flanner never wrote in the first person singular; as with Talk of the Town, her columns issued forth from a collective "we" that implicitly invited the reader into her Parisian world. The only trace of Ross's hand was in the byline: after the first unsigned column, he Frenchified Janet to Genet (later changed to Genêt), and she would write under that pseudonym for decades. Her real name, however, had remained unaltered during her short marriage to William Rehm, because she was a Lucy Stoner, a member of the Lucy Stone League.

Jane Grant started the league in 1921 with Ruth Hale, also a journalist and the wife of journalist Heywood Broun, after both women realized how hard it was legally to use their birth names on mortgages and passports. Ross, tetchy at hearing them raise the subject yet again, shouted, "Aw, why don't you two hire a hall?" So they did, in a manner of speaking, forming one of the first feminist organizations in the aftermath of women's suffrage. The Lucy Stone League's slogan was "My name is the symbol of my own identity and must not be lost."

Another Lucy Stoner was Alice Duer Miller, frequenter of the Algonquin Round Table, Barnard graduate, and friend of Hale and Grant. Miller too was a writer, known for her collections of satirical poems in support of suffrage, *Are Women People?* and its sequel, *Women Are People!* She'd lent her name to *The New Yorker* from its beginning, appearing on its purely symbolic masthead—most of the members of the Round Table contributed cachet but no writing—and allowing a public relations firm to sign her name to telegrams sent to all the city newspapers announcing the magazine's debut. As a member of a vast Colonial family, she had a lot of cousins, and she steered one of them to Ross, telling him *The New Yorker* better hire him or Ross would never again be invited to her parties. That's how Wolcott Gibbs, a humorist, theater critic, and playwright, became a pillar of the magazine as a writer and editor until his death in 1958. Miller knew a good piece of writing when she read it. She came to Grant with an essay that a niece had written called "Why We Go to Cabarets—a Post-Debutante Explains." Ross refused even to read the essay, certain it was rubbish. Ellin Mackay, Miller's niece, was a celebrity, a glamorous young socialite from a wealthy family, famous for no reason. How could she write anything *The New Yorker* would want? Grant's city-desk instincts were hardly literary. "Even if she has written it with her foot you can't turn it down," she told her husband. Grant had, after all, just conducted a subscription campaign in which she hired college women to cold-call people whose names were in the *Social Register*.

The article ran in the November 28, 1925, issue, which instantly sold out. Grant and Miller were right; Mackay's exposé was the perfect intersection of the magazine's dream of a cultured readership and its desire to hold itself apart from the class-bound rituals of New Yorkers to scrutinize and ironize them. Mackay pulled back the curtain on her generation's preference for nightclubs over the parties and balls stage-managed by their "Elders." "Cabaret has its place in the elderly mind beside Bohemia and bolshevik, and other vague words that have a sinister significance and no precise definition," she wrote. The novels of F. Scott Fitzgerald and Gertrude Atherton had led her elders to believe her generation preferred to socialize indiscriminately with people from all walks of life. Nothing could be further from the truth. "We do not like unattractive people," Mackay maintained as a matter of staunch principle. The social demographics had shifted, and the "numberless, colorless men" of her class were even worse in her eyes than the "poisonous" poseurs who dissembled about their social standing. "Yes, we go to cabarets," Mackay ended defiantly, "but we resent the criticism of our good taste in so doing.

We go because, like our Elders, we are fastidious. We go because we pre-fer rubbing elbows in a cabaret to dancing at an exclusive party with all sorts and kinds of people."

This piquant, askew analysis of the glitteriest corner of the social world was solid gold for readers who'd been to a cabaret but never a debutante ball, or readers who had only been to cabarets vicariously, through the literature of the flapper generation. Mackay's insider tone invited read-ers into a criticism of what they'd never experienced, conveying instant sophistication to the holders of that opinion. This would become a *New Yorker* hallmark. Mackay's piece encapsulated everything *The New Yorker* yearned to be, the way it educated its readers about the fashionable life while pretending to assume they already knew it, the way it flaunted taste and discernment, not inherited wealth, as the marker of rank, the way it upended expectations without seeking to upend the social order.

But how many readers noticed that Mackay merely whitewashed an argument that Chandler Owen, the coeditor of the most radical Black magazine, *The Messenger*, had been making since 1922? Owen had ar-gued that the cabaret was "one of the most democratic institutions in America," able to do what the church, school, and family had failed to do: break down the color line and allow Black and white urbanites to enjoy each other's company. And it was precisely the cabaret's informal-ity that allowed it to function as "the dynamic agent of social equality." Mackay's essay expresses a longing for this social freedom but only in class terms, leaving race off the pages of *The New Yorker*. It is a missed opportunity right there at the beginning: the magazine would not aspire to provide or portray that kind of easy mixing between Black and white cultures.

Still, the November 28 issue of *The New Yorker* sold out, thus rescuing the magazine from the brink—but not simply because it happened to contain a one-and-a-half-page article that titillated its readers. It sold out because Jane Grant knew how to press the levers of the city's vast, interconnected publicity machine. She told city editors at the *New York World*, *New York Times*, and *New York Herald Tribune* about an essay by the glamorous young woman who everyone knew had been defying her father's wishes in dating a young Jewish songwriter named Irving Berlin.

All three newspapers believed they had a scoop, and the story about the *New Yorker* story made all three front pages, and news syndicates and international papers picked it up too.

F. Scott Fitzgerald wrote wearily in the *Tribune*: "People simply have to escape from a milieu largely composed of young women who write articles for newspapers about the necessity of escaping from such a milieu." But the milieu was inescapable. A newspaperman named James Thurber first heard of *The New Yorker* when he sat on the terrace of the Café du Dôme and read about the Mackay exposé in the Paris *Herald*.

The milieu further thrilled to Mackay's words when, in a follow-up *New Yorker* essay about the decline of society balls, she wrote, "Modern girls are conscious of the importance of their own identity, and they marry whom they choose, satisfied to satisfy themselves." Mackay eloped with Berlin four weeks later; she called Ross moments after the ceremony to tell him she was Mrs. Berlin now—she would not be joining the Lucy Stoners. Her father disinherited her, but no matter, because her new husband gave her the lifetime rights to his song "Always." Not to be outdone, Ross gave her a lifetime subscription to *The New Yorker*.

Ross complained that he was "surrounded by women and children," and that the magazine was "in a velvet rut." *The New Yorker*'s pages included almost as many women as men. The contributors were young and sometimes monied, sometimes struggling but aspirational. Many of the magazine's female writers did not live in the city, but they knew how to channel urban attitudes. They wrote for the women they wanted to resemble. The gendered appeal to readers like themselves, though, was never obvious simply by peering closer at the table of contents or the bylines, because *The New Yorker* used neither. For the first few years, many pieces were unsigned, or signed only with initials, or signed with gender-neutral pseudonyms, such as their book reviewer named "Touchstone" (and all of them were signed at the end, not the beginning, of each article, story, or poem). The editorial "we" was capacious enough to encompass a range of implied identities.

Though he was married to one, Ross could hardly be called a feminist, and the *New Yorker* archives contain hundreds of letters to female job applicants telling them that the position to which they were applying could only be filled by a man. Ross to a Miss Joseph: "I regret to say that you won't do. I need a man, and one with considerable newspaper or some kind of journalistic experience. A man, not a woman, because this person would have to run a lot of people, work all sorts of hours, tramp around in the slush, go to the printers, etc." ("Miss Joseph" was Nannine Joseph, the head of nonfiction at the Brandt & Brandt literary agency, and in a few short years she would start her own agency and represent Franklin and Eleanor Roosevelt.)

From the very first issue, he was perennially in search of "an infallible omniscience," a "superhuman engineer" (in James Thurber's words) who would manage the office. Ross needed a genius, and he went through great handfuls of them, twenty-two managing editors in the first dozen years, according to Wolcott Gibbs. The procession of geniuses soon became known as Ross's jesuses, and to a jesus they were all men. Ross's prejudice that no woman could handle the responsibility meant that, when Katharine Angell walked into *The New Yorker* offices that summer day in 1925, she was not caged into an administrative role. Her boss's underestimation is what allowed her to rise to a position of creative power. Half a month later, he promoted her to full time, doubled her salary to $50 a week, and tasked her with a wide swath of editing duties, practically everything except reporting.

She read manuscripts, while the reigning jesus, Ralph Ingersoll, co-ordinated schedules. Ross added Katharine's name next to Ingersoll's on the masthead a year later, and they served as co–managing editors. She did everything but type her own correspondence; for that, she had a secretary, Ralph Paladino, or "rdp" on the memos, reader's reports, and letters that she dictated to him all day long. Katharine would later remember with pure affection, "Ross was furious that I was a woman but he soon came to depend on me and accept me."

Theirs was a platonic love affair carried out in the language of bureaucratic procedure. They were evenly matched in their devotion to the magazine, and they expressed that devotion in long, excruciating memos to each other about office policy, memos that managed to be at once deadly serious about the magazine and wry about everything else. Katharine never hesitated to dress Ross down. Unlike all the other editors, who were required to trudge to him with their concerns, Katharine sat and waited for Ross to come to her, which he did a thousand times a day. She offered her opinion about what advertising to accept, whom they should hire as book or fashion critic, and which employees should be eligible for stock options.

Katharine's swift ascent, from manuscript reader to co–managing editor, meant more than an increase in responsibility. What her job title didn't capture is that she was second only to Ross in the shaping of the magazine's voice, and that her job faced both outward, to the myriad contributors and would-be contributors, and inward, to the staff—and Ross himself. She carried around in her mind a conception of what was—and what most decidedly was *not*—*The New Yorker*, and every decision large and small was filtered through this vision.

Katharine was not a pioneer or an exceptional woman. Fully 20 percent of her fellow Bryn Mawr graduates joined the publishing industry in the 1920s, during a time when literary skills honed in college opened doors to public life for women even while other doors remained firmly closed, because cultural taste was an arena in which women were allowed to be experts. Women had been editors since the founding of the American republic: Sarah J. Hale took the helm of *Godey's Lady's Book* in 1837, and over six hundred other women edited American periodicals in the nineteenth century. The suffrage movement required its own magazines, and women like Lucy Stone of the *Woman's Journal*, Elizabeth Cady Stanton and Susan B. Anthony of *The Revolution*, and Clara Bewick Colby of *The Woman's Tribune* rose to the occasion. Margaret Fuller was the first editor of the Transcendentalist journal *The Dial*, beginning in 1840. Mary Booth edited *Harper's Bazaar* for its first twenty-two years, beginning in 1867, and Elizabeth Jordan ran it for the first thirteen years of the twentieth century. In the 1920s, an astonishing number of women edited the little magazines that curated modernist literature; many of the century's masterpieces were first published in the pages of Harriet Monroe's *Poetry*, Margaret Anderson and Jane Heap's *Little Review*, and Marianne Moore's *Dial*.

Of utmost importance to Katharine's story is the fact that in the 1920s, she could rely on a healthy network of female literary agents representing female writers to female editors, women who knew each other from college, women's clubs, and family ties along the Eastern Seaboard. In a business that is all about facilitation, these women relentlessly made connections for each other in ways that often were invisible to their male counterparts, and thus to history. The ease with which Elsie ushered Katharine into the pages of Willa Cather's *New Republic* and Jane Grant brought Janet Flanner to Katharine was utterly typical for women who had grown up as the Sergeant girls had, reading the same books, editing their school literary magazines, expecting the same freedoms. Their success came from talent, varying levels of material comfort and privilege, and the hard work of creating relationships to sustain one another and meet each other's needs.

Katharine's new job in the summer of 1925 was extraordinary not because she was a woman, but for the sheer naturalness with which she assumed command, the perfect use she made of her skills, the confidence with which she simply began doing what needed to be done. She swiftly grasped what *The New Yorker* wanted to be. She saw the whole, even while it was still a ragtag collection of little parts, and helped bring it fully to life.

13.

It is hard for me to picture a happier, more rewarding existence than my own. I find myself, strangely enough, actually living to some degree the life I had visualized for myself fifteen or more years ago.
    —Katharine S. Angell, "Home and Office," 1926

Each morning, Katharine would wake up in her bedroom on the second floor of the Angells' three-story brownstone on East Ninety-Third Street. She would wind her never-cut, heavy brown hair into a nest at the back of her head, fixing it into place with an armory's worth of bone hairpins. She would dress in tastefully understated clothes of excellent quality: tailored tweeds and, as they came into fashion, Ferragamo shoes and Sally Victor hats.

She would wake Roger and Nancy from their beds on the top floor and help them with dressing and breakfast, sharing these duties with the family's cook, maid, and nurse. She would plan out the children's day and see them off. Eight-year-old Nancy Angell would take the number 3 crosstown bus up Fifth Avenue and then west on 110th Street and then up Manhattan Avenue to the Lincoln School on 123rd Street, an experimental coeducational private school formed with Rockefeller money under the aegis of Columbia University's Teachers College. Roger Angell, age five, crossed the street from their house to get to the Nightingale School on East 93rd Street, a private school for girls that the Angells somehow persuaded to take Roger for kindergarten. Ernest traveled the length of Manhattan to his law firm, Hardin, Hess & Eder, across from

Trinity Church in the Financial District. And Katharine traveled forty-five blocks south to the *New Yorker* offices at 25 West 45th Street.

If it was a Monday, Katharine attended a meeting to critique the just-published issue, assign articles for the various departments, and revise, accept, or reject cartoons, pointing at them on an easel with knitting needles. These meetings could take hours as they waded through all the submissions, including two-sentence scenarios that needed art and art that needed captions. She critiqued and suggested covers. Soon, the magazine had developed such a coherent sense of humor—Katharine's phrase was "killingly funny"—that she was tasked with drawing up a list of "the more familiar art ideas" to avoid, including anything to do with manholes, the gentleman-in-bed theme (gentleman to his butler: "You may remove the moon, Blodgett"), and children talking like adults (one little boy to another: "You lay off that woman, see!").

If it was a Wednesday, she attended a meeting to dole out ideas for the next issue's Notes and Comment page (the unsigned lead editorial, often just called Comment), Talk of the Town column, Reporter at Large column (a journalistic take on the city, initially written by Morris Markey), and the features that fell specifically in her domain: casuals (a term she coined for short amusing essays on the city, sometimes merging fiction and memoir), Profiles, and special features. Talk of the Town was written anonymously and ideas for topics came from anywhere—reporters, editors, readers. Katharine, like the rest of the staff, was a prolific contributor of ideas and sometimes stories themselves, sending Ross dozens—hundreds—of memos with ideas for Talk items from her own excursions in the city. She and Ernest ate at the Granada Grill near Carnegie Hall, where they were stopped by the doorman, a Black man named Terry who greeted Ernest by name, identified his hometown as Cleveland, and proceeded to inform him what grades he'd received in each of his classes in college (a B in English 45, apparently). Terry's previous position had been in the dean's office at Harvard, where his ironclad memory had been legendary. "Such a doorman is an asset," Katharine wrote to Ross. He appeared in the magazine two months later.

In just a few years, Ross would learn from Katharine's Talk memos that a young man named Joseph Kennedy had become "about the most significant figure in the motion picture and vaudeville worlds," and that Mrs. John D. Rockefeller Jr. was starting the still-secret Museum of Modern Art. But Katharine's instinct was fallible. A hot tip from a Southern contributor, A. B. Bernd, alerted her to the yo-yo craze, but she dismissed it as a flash in the pan—only to be scolded by her daughter, Nancy. A few weeks later, Talk of the Town ate crow: "This backwater hamlet has been very slow to discover Yo-Yo. Cities like Dallas and Birmingham knew about it long ago." Then the column helpfully described how the toy worked: "If you have uncanny gifts or are in cahoots with leprechauns, you can make it twirl its way back up the string again."

Katharine and Ross had a weekly meeting at which they would discuss "manuscript, payments, picture proofs, staff, plans, policy, ideas, everything." In between meetings and lunches at the Algonquin around the corner on West Forty-Fourth, there was the writing—Mrs. Angell could always commandeer a typewriter—and it is an open question whether she directed more letters to Ross or to all *The New Yorker* authors combined. She wrote to him about everything from the state of the women's bathroom (its single toilet was forever clogged, and if the "unsanitary and intolerable" conditions were not addressed, she would not work there any longer) to the year-end bonuses among employees, and everything in between. Ross and Raoul Fleischmann leaned heavily on her to oversee the tenor of the ads, promotional materials, and shopping guides like Lois Long's fashion column, On and Off the Avenue—though her comments were always retrospective. To her and Ross's mind, the following items were "suspect": "undergarments, 'functional' advertising, drug advertising, cosmetics that made false or unsubstantiated claims, advertising that tried to be funny and wasn't, pompous ads and distasteful ones, and just plain badly designed or poorly laid out ads" (but they were fine with "cigarette ads and hormone cream ads"). More than thirty years later, Fleischmann would name as one of Katharine's signal contributions to the magazine her insistence that the magazine should adhere to a high standard for the "honesty, decency, and believability" of all ads it accepted, a standard that defined their readership and positioned the magazine within a niche market, a newly visible socioeconomic class of discerning consumers with disposable income and leisure time. It was good business for *The New Yorker*, even in those desperate days, to reject some advertisers.

Ross entrusted Katharine with two duties essential for shaping the voice of the magazine: critiquing previous issues and spotting talent for future ones. She performed both with ardor, though they required precisely opposite stances toward the magazine, alternately negative and hopeful. One memo might take down a writer or an entire department on the basis of a single word:

> Mr. Ross:
> In the issue of June 2nd, page 49, last paragraph, in Markey's "Reporter at Large" piece, you will find this sentence:
> "It is not unlikely that when this interest crystalizes a little further into action" etc.
> This is an absurd statement, for if there is one thing you cannot do, it is to <u>crystalize</u> anything into action. What Markey meant to say was <u>galvanize</u> into action, and the makeup room should have caught this point.
> *KSA*

The very next day, she brought to Ross's attention a writer whom she considered "one of the best people now writing critical stuff," a sentence that would lead to Lewis Mumford's three-decade-long association with the magazine.

Katharine wrote more than memos. She wrote continually for *The New Yorker* from her very first months in the office, but she never wrote much, and for decades her published writings were anonymous or pseudonymous. Even now a full reckoning of her literary output is impossible, though some of her archived memos give clues that can be followed into the pages of the magazine. Her first *New Yorker* byline was a short poem under the name Angelina. She then alternated with using her initials, KSA. It was *The New Yorker*'s style to sign all short verse with the poet's initials, since a triple-barreled name could sometimes visually outweigh a slight poem. The magazine was not offering fame and glory to its published authors in those early days, and Katharine did not seek it.

As Angelina, she wrote a casual about the pleasure of fly fishing up north and how the pursuit was ruined by the sheer tedium of dealing with the other fishermen at the lodge who condescended to the "little lady." There were Talk stories, concise book reviews, an obituary, and steady handfuls of other tiny, unsigned contributions, such as this one, titled "Feminists' Confession":

March is the month I chose to be
The Clinging Vine on the Strong Oak Tree
I may sell my soul—but I win redemption
By helping my spouse to his tax exemption.

If a common thread can be drawn out from these minor pieces without their unraveling, it would be their dyspeptic sense of humor. Katharine relished taking the opposing stance or puncturing pieties. A March 1926 casual, "Sweetness and Light," takes place in a modern, tastefully decorated obstetrician's waiting room (nearly six years after the birth of her son, Roger). The interior begins to influence the narrator, who is so cross that she wishes she'd never been born. "Your temper slightly improves until you pull yourself up with a jerk lest that infernally cheerful atmosphere should 'get' you again. No, it takes determination but you *will* be cross, nobody *shall* stop you." But Angelina eventually succumbs to gaiety, much to her own disappointment.

It was not just staff who contributed to *The New Yorker*. For a magazine whose identity rested almost entirely on the word "sophisticated," it is counterintuitive to realize how much of *The New Yorker* was sourced from its wide readership, its archives thick with reader-submitted entries from all over the country. Ross and his staff do not appear consciously to have designed this editorial strategy, and the magazine rarely asked for submissions. Yet somehow the editorial tone, with its wry "we" and its habitual references to insider knowledge, invited readers to join in the grand project of authoring the city. The magazine developed a set of recurring rubrics under which they published poems and short pieces, such as Taxi Driver Philosophy and If I Were King (which Katharine changed to If I Were Queen when she contributed a poem). Readers sent tips for Talk of the Town and clips from hometown newspapers of miswordings and other gaffes that could be used as newsbreaks to fill space at the bottom of columns. What proportion of those readers had sent photographs, puzzles, and essays into *St. Nicholas* when they were children? Harold Ross simply recapitulated Mary Mapes Dodge's idea of harnessing reader energy, only without the gold and silver badges.

Right away, this relationship to readers set *The New Yorker* apart from the competition. The magazine taught its readers how to read the city in a self-reflexive loop that tightened their bond to its weekly installments. Its reporters tramped and scribbled in notebooks just like any others, but they did not attempt exhaustively to cover any particular beats. They gave editorial space to what caught and held their curiosity, teaching their readers an urbane kind of attention and discernment. And the magazine covered newspapers and other magazines with a fascinated obsession, digesting and interpreting everything from pulp magazines to avant-garde monthlies, offering readers its "sophisticated" read on them. What were newsbreaks but an unusually succinct projection of this restless reading consciousness?

And *The New Yorker* covered itself, though it liked to say that it didn't. Katharine constantly rejected poems, casuals, and stories that were too "writer conscious," in the magazine's internal vocabulary; she was forever relaying to authors Ross's strict injunction against writing as a topic of interest to their readers. Yet *The New Yorker* broke this rule all the time, and the effect was to invite readers behind the scenes and into the magazine as a living, changeable entity, and to turn reading into something active. Taken together, this editorial stance made the city feel smaller, more encompassable. One of the magazine's contributors regarded *The New Yorker* as replicating what a young Washington Irving had done for New York in the early nineteenth century with *Salmagundi*; it was "reviving the old feeling of intimacy, by means of gossip, light satire, and anything that happens to fit, not neglecting the occasional element of charm." Within this village, it felt utterly natural for many readers to put down the magazine and pick up a pen.

It was Katharine's job to sift through all those submissions. Ingersoll edited most of the writers who contributed to *The New Yorker*'s regular columns, such as Lois Long's On and Off the Avenue and Tables for Two, Morris Markey's Reporter at Large, and all the sports commentators. Katharine edited verse, fiction, and profiles, and corresponded with readers wishing to submit. *The New Yorker* did have a form rejection letter, a half slip of paper that read, "The New Yorker regrets that it is unable to make use of this offering but desires to thank you for its submission." But Katharine was forever on the hunt for readers who could be turned into reliable contributors, so she wrote thousands of personal, specific rejections, all of them from K. S. Angell. It was not obvious that K. S. Angell was a woman, and the replies often came to Mr. Angell, and subsequently to Mrs. Angell—but never to Katharine.

So part of each day was devoted to the opening of the mail and the creative act of criticism and rejections, because the mathematics of the early *New Yorker* were punishing even for treasured contributors, who were turned down ten times more often than they were accepted. Katharine was thus simultaneously engaged in dozens of conversations, stretching across weeks and months, with dozens of writers, who would fire back with a story as soon as she rejected a bundle of poems. In the 1920s, many of *The New Yorker*'s stories, poems, and casuals came not from professional writers or even from people in journalism or publishing, but from stay-at-home wives and mothers. Only in *The New Yorker* could William Butler Yeats share space with poet Jacqueline Embry from Louisville, Kentucky.

The slush pile was more vital to *The New Yorker* than to comparable magazines because it had no money to pay established authors, and because Ross's Algonquin circle could only infrequently be nudged to contribute. Era-defining authors such as F. Scott Fitzgerald, Ernest Hemingway, Sinclair Lewis, and William Faulkner all published in *Collier's*, *The Saturday Evening Post*, *The Smart Set*, and *Scribner's Magazine*. Edna St. Vincent Millay's agent sent Ross a sonnet that he would have loved to publish, but he couldn't afford the $100 price for such a short piece, and Millay never offered the magazine anything again. Katharine grew *New Yorker* contributors from the loamy soil of the slush pile, steadily watering them with her letters until they produced something that she could pluck for the magazine.

After she accepted a piece, she'd invite the writer to her office to edit in person, the pages spread across a big table, along with Ross's queries, and they'd comb through each phrase and sentence until it was time for lunch on Katharine's expense account, usually at the Algonquin, occasionally the Ritz if the writer was a gourmand, and 21 if John O'Hara was her date, because he'd never let her sign for the check and always wanted to impress her with his ability to get a table at the city's most exclusive speakeasy.

The volume of mail and the specificity of *The New Yorker*'s needs meant that in the 1920s, Katharine did little developmental editing and much rejecting. Her letters would offer at most a few sentences of explanation for why a poem or story did not pass muster ("For one thing it has in it 'halitosis' which we have really succeeded in not mentioning," and for another, "You really can't couple 'heiress' with 'Paris'"). She might occasionally point to a flaw that could be fixed and the piece resubmitted, but she did not mark up manuscripts or edit pieces over many rounds of revisions. Contributors were simply expected to nail *The New Yorker*'s tone on the first try, and the fact that *The New Yorker* got steadily better and more focused throughout the 1920s demonstrates that Katharine's discernment was justified.

An astute reader of the magazine hoping to break into print would notice, by 1927, that *The New Yorker* operated by several principles guiding almost all of its writing. It was, first, foremost, and forevermore, a magazine about New York, a tireless, ceaselessly fascinated record of a roving consciousness observing street corners, ballrooms, nightclubs, and ball fields within the five boroughs. Ross learned early in his journalism career that a strict definition of a periodical's identity was what allowed it to flourish.

Related to the tight attention paid to this single patch of earth was the magazine's focus on a single word: "sophisticated." It showed up in Harold Ross's initial prospectus for the magazine ("It will be what is commonly called sophisticated, in that it will assume a reasonable degree of enlightenment on the part of its readers") and in nearly every other invocation of *The New Yorker*'s identity and unique place in culture after that. The magazine's readership was sophisticated; in contrast to magazines like *The Atlantic* or *The New Republic*, *The New Yorker* addressed a peer culture of young, college-educated professionals, transplants to the city, often unmarried, often without children, and with much disposable income to spend on the perfumes and clothing advertised in its pages. Its topics of consideration were sophisticated: nightclubs and speakeasies, relations between the sexes, breaking away from the small town and learning the intricate ways of the city.

Most of all, its tone was sophisticated. *The New Yorker* traded on a kind of misdirection, offering to its readers the feeling of being inside a small club of smart, witty, and well-off young people, a feeling it engendered by seeming to assume the reader knew certain cultural markers while in fact teaching those markers to them as newcomers to the club. Thus it was crucial that the magazine never be too obscure or experimental or highbrow or erudite—that would immediately dispel the aura created by its dry, knowing irony, its winking address to its readers, its air of collusion—so Katharine wrote dozens of rejection letters for stories or poems that were "too special" or "unavailable" to their readers. This explains an important myth contributing to Ross's aura, the one about him as a philistine who would not publish anything he couldn't understand. He simply used himself as a measure and insisted that there was no value in pretending to understand something, in assuming that because a poem or story was mystifying it must be good. *The New Yorker*'s editors worked extremely hard to eliminate too-high thresholds into the pieces they published so that readers could saunter directly into the pages of the magazine and casually join its sophisticated world.

If *The New Yorker* was strung with the tension of sophisticated writing that was nevertheless easy to understand, the magazine was also balanced on a line between anonymous writing and an editorial "we" that nonetheless expressed an individual consciousness. By omitting a table of contents and placing the writer's name, initials, or pseudonym at the end of each piece, *The New Yorker* subsumed authors' identities into the magazine's own. Yet it demanded that its pieces be particular, idiosyncratic, forever new. Katharine constantly rejected submissions because they dealt with an interesting topic in an expected way. This demand for specificity arose in part from the magazine's refusal to cover larger topics in the politics and public affairs of the city. Not only did Ross's magazine remain politically unaffiliated with any cause, it also remained aloof from more journalistic coverage of events. Thus its editors were forever hungry for pieces that could report the political, the economic, even the national through the particular, through a smaller story of one person roaming the city and encountering the surprising.

Ross's mania for accuracy expressed itself early and often in the magazine's history. Representative internal memo: "Where is New York? The New York Central time tables are in tenths of miles and the employees' time tables are in hundredths of miles, or less than a car length. At exactly what point in Grand Central Station is this figured from—the ends of the platforms or what? There must be some point which is officially New York." But "his demon checking department" (Katharine's words) did not get started until 1927, when an untried writer named Griffin Barry published a profile of Edna St. Vincent Millay that was riddled with errors (and which ran in the same issue as Hemingway's only contribution to the magazine). Millay's mother, Cora, stormed down to the office, "a rather small, angry woman" whom Ross sent to Katharine. She listened to Mrs. Millay and suggested that she write her corrections as a letter, which Katharine then edited and published in the magazine two months later. She also added to her own job description the editing of profiles, and she never published Barry again. Ross established his fact-checking system whereby even fiction would be tethered to verifiable reality. If the checking department missed something, Katharine would catch it. In a heated memo to Ross, she cast aspersions on the department when the checkers missed an error in a review of the movie *State Fair*, which repeatedly referred to a sow, when in fact the hero was "a prize hog (a boar, male animal)—not a sow. His name was Blue Boy and his masculinity was stressed throughout. Sows are ladies."

Katharine frequently rejected pieces that she personally liked. In those early days, the usual reason was length. Most pieces—casuals, profiles, and stories—were under three pages in length. If Katharine didn't feel she could preserve an essay or a story's quality through drastic cutting, she would turn it back to the author with a suggestion for where else to submit it. She would also turn away pieces if the magazine had recently run something on a similar topic or if that topic was reserved for another author. *The New Yorker* strove for utmost topicality, so the magazine would not run a piece that described something that happened a few weeks ago, even if it was a story that mentioned, say, horse racing in the most general way but the racing season had just concluded. This idiosyncrasy, called "pegging" a story to a season, holiday, or event, would drive *New Yorker* writers bananas over the years; sometimes, instead of rejecting a piece for occurring outside the current season, the editors would buy it and hold it for months or even years. There was an ancillary rule prohibiting anything "intramural": any mention of other *New Yorker* writers or the magazine's competition among magazines and newspapers. Ross was squeamish on sex and even more horrified by mentions of anything related to a bathroom (Ross: "The word toilet paper in print inevitably presents a picture to me that is distasteful and, frequently, sickening. It would, for instance, ruin my meal if I read it while eating. It might easily cause vomiting"). Any flavor of debauchery needed to be aesthetically justified for it to be considered (Katharine to a fiction writer: "Oh dear, oh dear, here you are being just too alcoholic for words, and it is such a shame because we think your story is good"). Though he cursed with abandon in the office, Ross wouldn't allow it on the page unless the writer could find no other way to express the point. He hewed to his idea of decent taste, and it was Katharine who occasionally, arduously persuaded him otherwise. She told Dorothy Parker, "I have the reputation with our editor for possessing the dirtiest mind on the magazine because I've fought so many times for phrases or drawings that seem to his puritanical mind slightly off color." Ross even had a prejudice against snakes. Katharine observed, "If anyone mentions snakes to him he always says 'Talking about snakes gives women miscarriages!'"

Somehow, amid all these rules, they managed to get out a magazine.

Katharine would head home right at five o'clock with a thick brown portfolio bulging with galleys and manuscripts. She would set the folder aside for two hours of focused time with the children, to have tea and read aloud or play games. She would devote Saturdays and Sundays to them, and in spring and autumn the family would often head out to Snedens Landing for the weekend, before spending the summer months there full-time. The Angells were social but frugal; they ate out two or three times a week at friends' houses and hosted dinner parties at their own house twice a month, but only rarely went to the theater and almost never to nightclubs. Most nights were for working, and after the children's bedtime, both Katharine and Ernest would pull out their papers to resume where they'd paused earlier that day.

This, anyway, was how Katharine depicted her daily routine in an essay that she wrote a year into her tenure at *The New Yorker* for a special issue of the magazine *Survey* devoted to the topic of working women. Katharine offered herself to her peers as an exemplar, a particularly prideful one. She worked, she declared, for "countless" reasons: because it was her duty to help support her family; because she was not happy unless she was engaged in productive work; because she didn't enjoy housework; and because she could earn more by working and paying for help than she could save by not working; and she added, "If honest, I must admit to a distinct personal ambition." And the most important reason: because she was a better wife and mother when she worked. The essay even notes the setting in which it was written: a tent in the woods, probably in the Adirondacks but maybe in New Hampshire, at the tail end of the summer of 1926. Roger was away, probably with his grandmother, while Katharine and Ernest camped and canoed with Nancy. The only way to write about her perfect work-life balance was to snatch some time away from the "wholly concentrated family life" the essay claims she is having at the very moment of its composition.

If this tension was palpable to the essay's readers, another one was not: the strain of her marriage. Katharine instead highlighted the coziness of this hardworking young couple, each building a future in the absorption of their own mind. "Neither of us finds that working side by side is any less companionable," she claimed, "than reading our separate novels, or even than playing bridge together."

Katharine finished her article and returned from the north woods to settle back at her desk. One of her writers, William Rose Benét, had a story forthcoming in September and a poem in October. Janet Flanner had left Europe for a visit to California, and her piece was scheduled for November. For each story or essay there would be a letter with Katharine's reaction to the piece, followed by a list of queries for the author to clarify in his or her next draft. Then the story would be set in proof, and copies sent to Ross and perhaps another editor. Katharine would collate their responses and write another long letter to her author. Then galleys, more small changes, and publication. E. B. White had pieces coming up in quite a few issues that autumn, including one about bungling the conversation in the receiving line of a wedding.

14.

As a member of an old Boston family and as a graduate of Bryn Mawr, militantly proud (as the Bryn Mawr graduates of those days especially were) of her fitness to take part in matters of importance, she knew perfectly well who she was . . . and she took care to make her weight felt at every turn.
—Brendan Gill, *Here at "The New Yorker"*

N*ew Yorker* mythology had a thing or two to say about Katharine, the working mother. She had a distinct editorial persona, which shaped not only how she was regarded at the magazine and in the larger literary world of New York City, but also how she viewed urban social dynamics and what kinds of writing she sought to acquire to exemplify them. Time and again, after a nod to her indispensability, a chronicler of the magazine would bestow on her a heavy laurel: the word "formidable." John Updike used the word, as did Katharine's son, Roger, and the biographers of E. B. White, James Thurber, and Wolcott Gibbs. Then there were the variations on the theme. She was "intelligent, no-nonsense," "opinionated . . . imposing, even austere," "a strong woman—too strong," "a cold-blooded proposition," someone who "thrived on the role of office pit bull" and who looked "like a dour, switch-wielding schoolmarm."

It is impossible not to hear the gendered connotations. "Formidable," the word most often used to describe Katharine—ostensibly conveying respect but also fear, with a coded warning about boundaries transgressed—is almost never used to describe men. One sentence should suffice to counter this bias: Katharine was paid precisely to have opinions. Male editors who fulfilled their job duties were deemed not "formidable" but "genius," a term used for both Harold Ross and Maxwell Perkins. Andy White had his own opinion about the adjective: "Katharine was as formidable as a yellow warbler."

But it is worth peering closer when a woman who successfully edits a famous humor magazine is called humorless by her male colleagues. In fact, though Katharine's ear for "killingly funny" jokes and sardonic narrators was finely tuned, there was one subject about which she completely lacked a sense of humor, and that was her job. She took her position at the magazine very seriously, which meant that she was never self-deprecating or ironic toward her own status as a female boss. Lurking within the word "formidable" is this original sin: she did nothing to prop up male authority or disguise her own, nothing to make it easier for men to defer to her.

Katharine may have had reasons for holding herself apart from her office colleagues, ranging from the sparser options available for highly educated women in the backlash of the Nineteenth Amendment and the way female authority was perceived in the pre-feminist years to her own conservative embrace of hierarchy. But as she grew on the job, she did not hold herself apart from her authors, as the thousands of letters that fill *The New Yorker*'s editorial files prove. Indeed, editor William Maxwell and writer Jean Stafford both described Katharine as "maternal." She was as blunt as she was tactful, as snobby as she was compassionate, as imperious as she was hardworking. She was never interested in being a female role model and did not comport herself as if she thought history was watching.

To many of her colleagues, she was surprising. They knew exactly how highly Ross esteemed her and how crucial her opinions were. Edmund Wilson would say a few decades later, Katharine and Ross "complemented and admired one another. Each had his [*sic*] respective way of scaring and impressing the other. Their relations were, I thought, quite emotional; they seemed to go from crisis to crisis." The stormy relations between the reigning couple added to Katharine's prestige, and many staffers tiptoed around her, only to discover that their fear of her was entirely misplaced. Hobart "Hobie" Weekes, an assistant fact checker, described her as a "universal housemother" who worried about absolutely everyone's health. "People unacquainted with this employee benefit would emerge from the elevators rattled because Mrs. Angell had been looking them up and down closely during the ride. They would later learn that she had heard they had a cold, or were scheduled to be operated on, and was only being kind and solicitous." Some people could not mentally translate what seemed like sternness or criticism into empathy. Weekes was one of them: "I was never able to shake the feeling at such a time that either my nose was running or my trousers were open." But other employees came to appreciate the way she had as much interest and concern for junior staff as she did for her senior colleagues, sending notes when they were ill and gifts at Christmas—indeed, her own archives are filled with notes from secretaries and clerks, thanking her for her thoughtfulness. Katharine's self-presentation (serious, reserved, authoritative) did not entirely match her character (curious, generous, sympathetic).

Even beyond its inaptness, the description of Katharine's character as "formidable" misses something essential about her work as an editor: her fundamentally optimistic nature, her belief in the perfectibility of the work. Katharine's ceaseless stream of memos to Ross represented a creative act born from a generous imagination. Just as Fleischmann understood that turning down some advertisers was good for business, so Ross understood that Katharine's criticism of the book (industry parlance for "magazine") was a way to feed their shared conception of it. You can't say that something isn't right for *The New Yorker* if you don't have a glittering and very real vision of what *The New Yorker* actually *is*—even if it's *not yet*.

There is nothing in Katharine's vast archive to indicate that she was ever anything more than puzzled and impatient by this perception of her as formidable. But she was certainly aware of how her criticism might land. Buried deep within a five-page memo to "Dear Harold" is a nicely encapsulated theory of her critical practice:

> Naturally, every time I take issue with the content or
> scheduling, I know perfectly well that every issue is a hazard

and a makeshift and that it has to be put together like a jig-
saw puzzle from what is on hand. However, it seems to me my
reports will have more value if I take a sort of Olympian view
and assume you have a bank of perfect stuff to choose from.
Therefore, if you approve, I'll shoot at each issue with perfection
in mind and some of the time what I criticize will make a point
and other times it will have been unavoidable. But I don't want
to feel I have to be sparing one or another person's feelings.

So she proposed that she deliver her criticisms to Ross for his eyes
only, because he was the only other one up there on Olympus, shooting
for perfection.

If she wasn't bothered by the perception of her, she certainly understood gender as a key to the modern city, and her editorial choices
in these years of the magazine's awkward youth show her interest in
a gimlet-eyed view of the relationship between men and women. *The
New Yorker* operated by way of contradiction. As a sophisticated urban
magazine with writing from rural and suburban readers all over the
country, it was also a brittle commentator on modernity fostering connection through its attitude of aloofness. And it was Katharine's assiduous reading of the slush pile that turned up the new writers who spoke
this very particular language, best exemplified by Dorothy Parker but by
no means confined to her work. (Ross handled Dorothy Parker himself.
"She'd murder you," he told Katharine, and she had to agree that she,
Katharine, was "fair game" to Parker, though the writer was always "kind
and friendly" when they met outside the office.) Katharine's discovery of
four unknown female poets in 1926—Patience Eden, Margaretta Man-
ning, Margaret Fishback, and Elspeth—helped increase the amount of
poetry in each issue and turn comic verse into the satiric playground
for women's attitudes on the war between the sexes, work, family, and
the inner life of a modern, educated female. Under Katharine's hands,
The New Yorker's light verse got darker, more attuned to the discord of
urban single life. Long before E. B. White, Robert Benchley, and James
Thurber began writing on the theme of the Little Man, forever befud-
dled by modernity and humorously inadequate to his domineering and

competent women, Katharine curated hundreds of poems by these four writers that did something she did not—they used self-deprecation and irony to comment on gender norms.

Patience Eden was a single woman, educated at Middlebury and Smith, just a few years before Katharine attended Bryn Mawr. She submitted poems from Old Lyme, Connecticut, behind several secrets. Her real name was Martha Banning Thomas, but she didn't confess this to Katharine until a few years into their relationship, when she tried submitting verses under that name in an attempt to outsmart her editor, only to have them come winging back to her (Katharine to Martha Banning Thomas: "I have always had a suspicion"). She was also crippled by polio, which had cut short her career as a kindergarten teacher, and she was supporting herself through writing—something that Katharine never knew. Eden wrote steadily, heedlessly, as if she couldn't help herself, and one year she withstood thirty-six rejections from Katharine to earn just six acceptances.

Or take Elspeth MacDuffie O'Halloran, a poet from Springfield, Massachusetts, who shed both her maiden and married names to publish simply as Elspeth. Her specialty in *The New Yorker* was rue at her own susceptibility to men, and the difference between the poet's sleek exterior and messy interior, as in the poem "Possibly."

> He wore a frock coat
>   And a silk hat.
> He wore a gray tie—
>   It might have been that.

> I could hear his bitter voice
>   From where I sat.
> I could see his bitter smile—
>   It might have been that.

> A nice man to listen to,
>   And to look at,
> He never glanced my way—
>   *It might have been that.*

Her specialty in her letters to Katharine was wild gratitude for every acceptance. "Do you like to know you are saving a life, negligible though that life may be!" Again: "I'd rather be rejected by you than any other editor in the whole world!" The implied readers of these glinting shards by Patience Eden, Elspeth, and Dorothy Parker (Elspeth was similar in tone and theme to Parker) were women just like them, women who could understand how the sophisticated stance that marked them as modern and liberated could also injure them. They used humor and irony to note the discrepancies between their bodies and the feminine ideal, between their lives and the lives they should have been leading, and they consistently invoked the heart as a counterpoint to the blasé flapper—sentiment as the refuge from *The New Yorker*'s own exhausting, sometimes desiccated sophistication. Katharine soothed Elspeth's jittery heart and asked for more work, always more. It was what the poet needed. She wrote in 1928, "The only thing I care about in the world is writing. This isn't meant to be funny."

What an unfashionable statement. *The New Yorker* had planted its flag against earnestness. In a letter to potential contributors, the editors declared, "Our list of prejudices still includes certain types of social bores—all hundred-percenters and go-getters (includes Rotarians, Kiwanians, and conventioneers) all lecturers, society doctors, society painters, all musicians when off the platform, out-of-towners, all advocates of intolerance, the nouveau, etc. In general, *The New Yorker* wants to be against everything that is vulgar and dull." The magazine was forever sidestepping into an ironic distance from whatever it observed, and its contributors likewise often chose to confront serial rejection with sarcasm and frenetic performances of taking themselves lightly. But at the heart of it all was Katharine—the deadly earnest center of gravity, scrupulously polite, sometimes reflecting a correspondent's joke back at her, always game, never flippant.

Above all, she was unfailingly respectful of the act of writing itself. The often biting editorial stance of the magazine did not infect Katharine's understanding of the relationship between editor and writer. She was equable whether accepting or rejecting, which sometimes sent her writers off into wild passions. Phyllis Crawford, who published the Elsie

Dinsmore series under the name Josie Turner, wrote, "It seems to me that everything I send you comes flying back. I suspect you of sarcasm when you say, 'Do keep up the good work.'" But if there was one tactic Katharine lacked, it was sarcasm. She treated everyone as if they were just about to hit that sweet spot between their talent and *The New Yorker*'s needs. She wrote to one of the magazine's mainstays, the poet Baird Leonard, "In other words, this will have to be something quite different, and I just bet you will wake up some morning with a perfectly clear idea of how to do it."

How conscious was her unflappable editorial persona? How much of it stemmed from her understanding of the way a woman needed to conduct herself in a sometimes raucous male environment with no respect for boundaries? Katharine remembered taking her first vacation from *The New Yorker* to go camping with Ernest for two weeks in the Adirondacks. Upon her return early in the morning, she was ordered to Ross's house to read through the backlog of manuscripts that had arrived in her absence—a not unusual occurrence because "Ross would summon [her] there to work alone or with him." She took the ferry home to Snedens Landing to change her clothes and rushed back into the city to get to Ross's apartment on West Forty-Seventh Street on time, where she was shown into the bedroom. There, on her boss's bed, she "began manfully to read" the pile, before she fell sound asleep. "Luckily, both Ross and I thought it was a good joke and I soon caught up on the back manuscript reading." Though Ross "resented" (her word) that Katharine was a woman, he heavily relied upon her authority; at the end of their weekly conferences, Ross would then turn to Mrs. Angell for advice on his personal matters: "should his wife have a charge account (this one was very funny), what to do about [his daughter] Patty and her schools and her music and her reading," as well as sticky office matters like "Gibbs' drinking" and "secretaries who fell in love with him, etc. etc."

If she did not tramp through the slush, as Ross imagined his corps of reporters did, she often visited the homes of her contributors to edit in person, a potentially risky situation. While Ross saved Katharine from Dorothy Parker, he refused to edit Alexander Woollcott's Shouts and Murmurs column though the two were old friends and former housemates; he sicced Woollcott on Katharine. She remembered "Old Foolish" as "a time-consuming bother" and said "he liked to try to embarrass [her] when [she] went to 'Wit's End,' his East River apartment," by appearing in unbuttoned pajamas. Katharine learned to ignore Woollcott's inappropriate dress but to pay heightened attention to his inappropriate prose, into which he forever tried to sneak "hidden dirt," or references to things he thought the proper, middle-class matron would not understand. She did. "Oh dear, Mr. S.S. Van Woollcott, what a trial you have been to us this week, but what can you expect, Sir, when you send in a piece that is really very dirty when you are so far away and this is a Must Go This Week's story."

One day, the poet John Peale Bishop came to see Katharine and Gibbs. He pulled a manuscript out of an envelope, and a few condoms dropped onto Katharine's desk. She simply pulled her blotter over the condoms and they "went on talking about commas," Gibbs reported, adding, "Great poise, I thought." The reporter St. Clair McKelway took Gibbs aside and confided that Mrs. Angell had finally asked him to call her Katharine. Gibbs, who at that point had worked for her for six years, confessed he had never called her by her first name: "I always had a feeling it would [be] like taking your finger out of the dike."

She learned what to ignore, when to play along, and when to draw the line. Ross was a self-described "straight old-fashioned double-standard boy," with one vocabulary for men and another for "women, children and ministers." Katharine counted as a man. During one particularly heated battle, she shouted at him, "All right, all right, but you needn't be so goddamn rude about it." She got through to him that time, and she said, "He was never rude or violent in his speech to me again. He was profane, of course, and I picked up on his profanity, as you see."

But she was always the straight woman, always the upright, middle-class citizen. When Charles Lindbergh came to town for his ticker-tape parade, the writer Corey Ford, who was meeting with Katharine over a manuscript, persuaded her to come to his office overlooking Fifth Avenue to watch. She immediately regretted it, as his entire workplace devolved into a party with bad gin and a secretary on Ford's lap and no one paying the slightest attention to the parade—just Katharine, alone at the window.

She never seemed to mind the antics going on around her, never mustered a feminist critique of such power differentials, and probably considered such treatment a rueful and inescapable part of being the only woman on the editorial staff. She never sought to change this dynamic, merely to endure it. In the early years of the magazine and of her career, she was personable without being personal, withholding something of herself even as she fussed over others. No contributors or staff members could possibly know, for instance, that Katharine's home life was still miserable.

15.

I wonder whether there are not many other couples like us in the middle thirties who, having safely passed that stimulating and adventurous period of keeping-the-wolf-from-the-door, are engaged in the dreary business of living beyond their income, and this from the highest of motives.
—Anonymous, "Living on the Ragged Edge," 1925

Neither the move to the Upper East Side nor Katharine's new focus and steady income had healed the Angells' marriage. Katharine wrote about the stressors of their home life in an essay she published outside *The New Yorker*, but even so, she wrote anonymously, and she kept the worst off the page.

Like "Home and Office," the essay that she wrote in that tent in the woods, this essay, "Living on the Ragged Edge: Family Income vs. Family Expenses," describes her daily life as a working mother, but in a darker and more sardonic register. She published it in *Harper's Monthly Magazine* in December of 1925. She writes to answer the question of why she and "Tom" are perpetually "dead broke." The span of time since they purchased their brownstone has been "two thoroughly unhappy years," and they exist in a state of "dull, nagging, insistent hurt." Katharine can find no misstep to account for their misery, no outlay expendable enough to be trimmed for the greater family good. True, they could save piles of money by moving to the suburbs, but she says, "Tom and I are not made temperamentally for suburban life, for neighborliness." They choose instead "the concentrated, brimming, independent life of a city alternating with the calm and beauty of real country and real soil." Is this too high a standard, she wonders, and then in the next breath answers that it is not. The problem is not that she and Tom buy high-quality shoes for the children or own a home that is expensive to maintain, both of which are certainly true. The problem, she intimates without having the nerve to say it—even anonymously—is that their families and their elite educations have trained them for culture but not capitalism. They are willing to work hard, but only at what enriches them intellectually, and the problem is that the marketplace does not reward what they are good at. Set against the backdrop of the first ten years of their marriage, all those committee meetings and marches and reports to Congress, the even more unspeakable problem might be that the Angells wanted to resist the world and reshape it while still enjoying the spoils of their social status.

The tensions between husband and wife lay behind both of Katharine's essays on being a working wife and mother. After the financially straitened years in New York, the Angells were doing better, but largely because Katharine's salary, rather counterintuitively, exceeded Ernest's. It galled Ernest that she earned more than him; this was a fracture not only in their companionate marriage but in his progressive principles. It isn't clear from this vantage why Ernest never made much money as a corporate lawyer. Perhaps his heart just wasn't in it—later he would become the chairman of the American Civil Liberties Union, a position much more aligned with his values—or maybe he had expenses that drained his accounts. But if he did not value money, he did value the male breadwinner as the cornerstone of the family, and Katharine had usurped this role.

She was also fighting against the prevailing political winds. The years after suffrage had seen the attenuation of one strand of feminism, the largely white middle-class movement for legal rights, when its tentpole cause had been resolved; many such suffragists now considered women as individual citizens with a direct relationship to law and government, rather than an oppressed group requiring collective action. But antifeminism had continued apace through the passage of the Nineteenth Amendment, and the flapper cohort prided itself on lack of seriousness.

Katharine must have felt the importance of testifying from within her experience of the working world, at a time when the pages of mainstream magazines were filled with essays questioning women's fitness for public life. In fact, not long after "Living on the Ragged Edge" appeared in *Harper's*, the same magazine published the reactionary essays "Seven Deadly Sins of Woman in Business" and "Equality of Woman with Man: A Myth." Katharine was proud to give permission for parts of *Survey's* "Home and Office" to be excerpted in a pamphlet about the place of married women in business produced by the YWCA and sent to 125,000 young women around the country.

What the essay didn't say was that Ernest was still having affairs, some of them with married women—some of them with Katharine's own friends. One night, Ernest was assaulted near Riverside Church and robbed of a gold watch that he had inherited, but he did not report the crime because then it would be known that he was with another woman when it happened. Katharine, though, knew the story, and she would someday tell it to Roger, though she would not tell him how she found out.

There is the merest suggestion, among Katharine's ferociously scrubbed archive, that she too had an affair during this time. Years later, James Thurber would refer to "that old romance between Katharine and Ordway Tead," and Katharine wrote obliquely about a relationship with Tead much later in her life. She and Ernest were friends with Tead, a professor of industrial relations at Columbia, and his wife, Clara, president of the Katharine Gibbs secretarial school. The Teads gave big parties that the Angells frequently attended at their home in Forest Hills and their apartment on East Fifty-First Street. Katharine perhaps knew Ordway through *The New Republic*; they both appeared in the same March 1922 issue. Katharine grew to know the Teads' household so well that later, when their housekeeper, Verinda Brown, became a source for a profile that *The New Yorker* was running of the sensationalist Long Island minister Father Divine, she would go on record only if Katharine told her it was okay. Katharine would say of this time, "I have always tended to forget purposely painful events, and all this business about a friendship with the Teads is part of it." From the time of her mother's death onward,

Katharine's strategy for dealing with personal pain was "to forget purposely" whenever she could, to look to the future.

She trudged through the life she and Ernest had built together. Roger had followed his sister to the coeducational Lincoln School after his thrilling kindergarten year at the Nightingale School. Katharine joined Elsie, who lived in the city on East Fifty-Second Street, at the Cosmopolitan Club, a private club for women of distinction in arts and letters. She maintained the outward appearance of propriety and ambition, in her writing and in her self-presentation.

Her personal life was far apart from her professional life but drawing ever closer as she grew on the job and went on the hunt for new writers. Many of Katharine's authors came from tightly wound circles of friends and relations. *The New Yorker* would publish sixty poems by Jean Batchelor, Katharine's old *Tipyn* coeditor, over a fifteen-year span. She repaid Scudder Middleton's dubious favor of recommending her to the psychoanalyst Beatrice Hinkle by hiring him as a manuscript reader, and he would eventually join the storied ranks of fired jesuses. She began publishing Elinor Wylie in December of 1925, as well as Wylie's husband, William Rose Benét; her sister, Nancy Hoyt (some of whose contributions have been obscured because she, like Dorothy Parker, reviewed books anonymously); and her in-laws, Laura Benét, Rosemary Carr Benét, and Stephen Vincent Benét. Katharine accepted three contributions from her own sister-in-law, Hildegarde Angell.

One family member she never edited—not once did she appear in *The New Yorker*—was Elizabeth Shepley Sergeant, a meaningful absence given that one of Katharine's main duties was editing the profiles that quickly became a cornerstone of the magazine, and that Elsie's main literary output during the 1920s consisted of profiles of prominent Americans. Elsie had published steadily in *The New Republic*, and in the early part of the decade she branched out into *The Nation*, *The Bookman*, and *Harper's*. She had purchased land and built a house in New Mexico, hoping the desert climate would ease the aches from her wartime injuries, and she split her time between New York and the Southwest, writing about both. She chronicled the building of her adobe house in a four-part series for *Harper's*, bringing the Southwest into the comfortable living rooms of the professional class in the Northeast, and she soon began campaigning for the rights of Indians upon her radicalization at the hands of John Collier.

Two sisters, one a prolific writer of magazine articles, the other a perennially hungry editor of a magazine—why weren't Elsie and Katharine closer? Why hadn't Elsie, a long-standing member of the Cosmopolitan Club and a member of its literary committee, been the one to nominate Katharine for membership? Instead, Katharine was nominated by Miriam Kimball Stockton, a lawyer's wife and theater supporter whom Katharine never otherwise mentioned as a friend. Why did Elsie's profile of Alice Hamilton, the doctor and founder of occupational health whose work shaped both sisters' volunteering in Boston, appear in *Harper's* rather than *The New Yorker*? Katharine ostensibly would have been a natural editor for Elsie's profiles of poet Amy Lowell or for *The New Yorker's* very own Elinor Wylie. In 1927, A. A. Knopf collected Elsie's profiles into a book, *Fire Under the Andes: A Group of North American Portraits*.

Family legend says that Elsie considered herself too highbrow for a popular magazine like *The New Yorker* and that she disdained her sister's willingness to taint literature with commerce. Aligning their careers across the chasm of their silence reveals this to be inaccurate. Elsie sought a wide readership for her varied work. And in fact, she did try to place her writing in *The New Yorker* through her agent, Elsie McKeogh. She submitted a profile of Alva Belmont, the well-known millionairess of Newport and radical suffragist. Katharine delayed responding as long as she could, and when she finally wrote to McKeogh, she rejected the piece, confessing that she felt "pretty sick about the whole thing." But she minced no words. "It was a surprising piece of work to come from my sister, because I thought it was rather carelessly written." She included with her letter an edited version of the article with many cuts, hoping that McKeogh could place it at *The New Outlook* or the *Herald Tribune*. The Belmont profile never saw the light of publication, but it would not be Elsie's last attempt to break into *The New Yorker*.

In these early years, when the mail brought piles and stacks of letters and manuscripts to her desk every day, Katharine was not curating a body of American literature. Magazines had been central to the middle class since the 1890s, when newsstand prices dropped to a dime an issue and suddenly many different people across the nation would be reading the same articles in *Munsey's* or *McClure's* or *Ladies' Home Journal*. Magazines became the crucial intersection of industrial capitalism's need to advertise its wares and middle-class consumers' need for information, entertainment, and connection shared across regions. But the book industry lagged far behind the magazine industry in consolidating a mass literary culture. Even into the 1920s, bookstores and department stores stocked mainly hardbound books aimed at scholars and the educated elite, as well as inexpensive reprints of classic and international literature, while newsstands sold dime and pulp novels. For now—until the middle of the decade brought innovations in publishing—Katharine merely curated an American moment, one that appealed to her, an educated and wry New Yorker at once enchanted with and disillusioned by the identity of the modern American woman.

The sheer volume of unsolicited manuscripts meant that Katharine needed another editor, and in 1926 she hired John Chapin Mosher as her first manuscript reader. Mosher, who was Katharine's exact age, a graduate of Williams College, and a sometime playwright, had begun writing for the magazine, little sardonic pieces that slotted right in, like the story about the young man who was disinherited but retained the box at the Metropolitan Opera that had been entailed to him, so he moved in and made it his home ("But I shall never be in a position to keep any pets"). Mosher lived openly as a gay man, which was a problem at *The New Yorker* when his review praising *Mädchen in Uniform*, a German film about a young girl's lesbian awakening, was reprinted in huge letters and posted outside the Criterion Theatre (he criticized "how few meanings we Americans have for the word 'love'"), embarrassing Ross, who sent Katharine to ask Mosher to tone it down. He kept writing for *The New Yorker* (becoming the film critic in 1928) and he kept his sexuality off the page, and he soon proved to have a fantastic eye as a reader, discovering James Thurber and John O'Hara in the slush pile. In 1927, Wolcott Gibbs moved from copyreader to manuscript reader, and Katharine headed a new three-person team. She instituted the policy that two readers would need to approve a manuscript from the slush pile for her to read it, but that she would have first look at anything from literary agents and the magazine's regular contributors.

She was also forever on the lookout for contributors who could become staff writers. Could Elspeth, who had recently been fired from her job at Pilgrim Press, a conservative Christian publisher, for smoking in the dressing room, be put to use reviewing books alongside Parker and Nancy Hoyt? No, that idea wouldn't fly, perhaps because of Elspeth's rivalry with Parker.

Well, could E. B. White, a young, talented, and unencumbered contributor, be roped in to write more regularly?

16.

This I say, and this I know:
Love has seen the last of me.
Love's a trodden lane to woe,
Love's a path to misery. [. . .]
Look! A lad's a-waiting there,
Tall he is and bold, and gay.
What the devil do I care
What I know, and what I say?
　　—Dorothy Parker, "Wisdom," *The New Yorker*

Katharine met her future second husband through his writing, and he met his future wife through her editing. While this statement is perfectly true, neither of them would ever have phrased it this way—certainly not the editor who was publishing the anti-romantic poems of Parker, Elspeth, and Patience Eden. It was not love at first sight or even an office infatuation, nor was it precisely a meeting of two literary minds. Katharine was simply doing her job, which involved paving the way for E. B. White to discover his.

The last issue of *The New Yorker* in 1925 had contained a casual called "Child's Play." With hindsight, this 650-word essay, the longest piece under the byline EBW, out of the dozen he had published in the magazine so far, struck him as the beginning. He tells of lunching at Childs' and finding himself suddenly baptized by a glass of buttermilk down his blue serge suit, the waitress muttering, "In the name of John." Far from upset, he notices the "terrific" humor of the situation. "'Perhaps,'

I mused, 'this is one of those "smart backgrounds" *The New Yorker* is always talking about.'" He stands, commanding the attention of the entire restaurant, "a perfect audience," and with great magnificence, he places a dime under his plate, walks to the cashier's cage, pays the bill, and refuses the change. The city as theater, a Little Man managing to rise above himself for one glorious moment—it was classic E. B. White, already. Later, he would give this incident, and the publishing of it, to a fictional character, Mr. Volente, who would "mak[e] for himself the enormously important discovery that the world would pay a man for setting down a simple, legible account of his own misfortunes."

Katharine accepted two more of his casuals and then suggested to Ross that he hire the young man as a staff writer. Ross made the appointment but Katharine kept it, striding into the lobby and asking, "Are you Elwyn Brooks White?" He was, but everyone called him Andy, a name from college that had stuck (a Cornell tradition bestowed the nickname of founder Andrew Dickson White on every student with the last name White). He would write of their meeting, "I sat there peacefully gazing at the classic features of my future wife without, as usual, knowing what I was doing."

She offered him the job. He said no.

Andy White was never really called Elwyn. His childhood nickname was En. Like Katharine, he grew up in a large, comfortable house in the suburbs as the youngest and most petted child, surrounded by books, a pen in hand, the green world just outside to tempt him. His family was larger than hers, and intact; he called their three-story turreted house in Mount Vernon, New York, and its eight inhabitants "a small kingdom unto [them]selves." His mother was forty-one when he was born in 1899; his father was forty-five; the next-youngest sibling, Lillian, was five; and the oldest, Marion, was eighteen. Samuel White, the vice president of a piano manufacturer, and Jessie Hart White, a traditional "Victorian mother," were shy and unsocial. Andy wouldn't realize until later how atypical it was that their fashionable house rarely welcomed visitors, and until he went to college, he "never even knew there *was* such a thing as a dinner party." The family gave Andy everything he needed: His brother Stan taught him to read in kindergarten with the help of

The New York Times and *Webster's Dictionary*. His father gave him the neighborhood's first child-sized bicycle, and as he grew older he was allowed to ride to his sister Marion's house. His father also gave him his very own canoe when he was eleven, to use on the family's August trips to Belgrade, Maine, which were to Andy "the golden time of year" and "sheer enchantment." His mother, along with a maid and a cook, tended the household. His dog Mac, for whom he built a sheepskin-lined stall in the barn, met him each afternoon on the same corner and walked him home from elementary school, PS 2.

Andy inherited his parents' shyness but not their reticence. By the time he was nine, he and Lillian were the only White children still living at home, so he divided his time between busy exploits with neighborhood boys and solitary explorations of the house, the garden, and the stable, which housed the carriage, occasional chickens, plus the coachman and his living quarters. Andy was indifferent as a student but terrific at being a kid, all that ice skating at the Dell, and frog- and snake-hunting at Snake Pond in Willson's Woods. He did not read; he was too busy. But he wrote letters to his many siblings, and poems, and almost daily journal entries. In high school, he was assistant editor of the literary magazine, *The Oracle*. He did well enough to earn a few scholarships, and since he was denied entry to the army because he didn't weigh enough, he decided to follow in the footsteps of his brothers Stan and Albert and enroll at Cornell in 1917, where the tuition was inexpensive because part of the university is a land-grant institution. He felt right at home amid the region's lakes, gorges, and waterfalls. Just like at home, he split his time between writing and the outdoors, and was elected to the board of editors of *The Cornell Daily Sun* in his sophomore year; by his junior year he was editor in chief. He was adopted by a dog, called the Mutt, who followed him between the *Sun* office and his fraternity house. Like Katharine, he fell under the spell of several teachers, including English professor William Strunk Jr., journalism professor Bristow Adams, and historian George Lincoln Burr. And he fell in love. Alice "Burch" Burchfield, a chemistry major and actress, was the lucky object of his poems in the *Sun*, including one that compared her eyes to those of his dog.

Upon graduation, Andy moved home to Mount Vernon and commuted to Manhattan to begin his long-awaited journalism career—
which began with a splutter, as his job with United Press lasted for a
single week. Next was public relations, which he quit after a few months.
He proposed to Alice and she turned him down. He was floundering
and desperately unhappy, so he did what many before him had done—he
went west, motoring across the wide United States with a college friend,
Howard "Cush" Cushman, working his way to Seattle, where he got a job
with *The Seattle Times*. After only six months, he was asked to write his
own (unsigned) column, but he was fired a mere three months into that
elevated position. His writing was too ambitious and elevated, and as he
later conceded, "a youth who persisted in rising above facts must have
been a headache to a city editor." He was putting together the pieces of
what would become his career but having a hard time slotting himself
into larger organizations and torquing his prose to fit editorial require-
ments. So he went to Alaska. He paid for a first-class ticket on board a
ship, and then worked in the saloon of the same ship to afford the return
passage. A train journey brought him to New York, back to reality. He
took a job in advertising, and at night he wrote and submitted squibs
and poems to Franklin P. Adams's column, The Conning Tower, in *The
World*—which was then the premier place for a writer to publish and the
launchpad for many a career. Then, in April 1925, he published a casual
in *The New Yorker*, a poke at his current job, in which he described spring
as an advertising man might: "If the new 1925 crocuses were not the
most remarkable VALUE in the field, they wouldn't be appearing at the
rate of a million a day. Nothing satisfies like a good crocus!" He remembered that during this time, he "burned with a low steady fever, just because [he] was on the same island" with writers like Robert C. Benchley,
Dorothy Parker, Frank Sullivan, and Alexander Woollcott. He shared a
third-floor Greenwich Village walk-up with Cornellian Gustave "Gus"
Lobrano, who would one day become a *New Yorker* editor, and two other
men. When Katharine met him, he was twenty-seven years old, working
part-time for an advertising agency, perched on the island of Manhattan
but not immersed in any of its literary centers, its newspapers or publishers or popular magazines or literary journals.

Andy would later cite many different sparks to his desire to make a life out of writing, from the excitement of borrowing his brother's Oliver typewriter to his poem about a mouse published in the *Woman's Home Companion*—which prompted him to keep a journal, with some entries later appearing in his book for children *The Trumpet of the Swan*—to meeting Professor Strunk at Cornell. As he put it, "I took to writing early, to assuage my uneasiness and collect my thoughts." Writing helped make him feel more integral. He had many fears: fear of the attic; fear of platforms, which made public speaking unthinkable; fear of school and sex and death; fear that the brakes of the trolley that had carried him up and down Ithaca's steep hills would fail. His shyness, what a future *New Yorker* writer would call "the tyranny of his modesty," manifested as a sometimes crippling self-subtraction, a desire to escape out into the anonymous natural world.

So it seems almost inevitable that he would so thoroughly misrecognize his destiny when Katharine offered it to him. His account of that meeting was only that Mrs. Angell "had a lot of back hair and the knack of making a young contributor feel at ease." He meant her long hair twisted in a bun. He didn't just turn Katharine down; he left the country, temporarily turning down his entire life in the city. His roommate, Burke "Bob" Dowling Adams, worked for the Cunard Line and had wrangled a job making a motion picture of a new "college class" of cabins. The morning Adams was to depart, he invited Andy along to write the script. In the span of a day, Andy obtained a passport, visas, and shirts, then jumped aboard with Bob to visit England, Belgium, France, Holland, Germany, and Switzerland. The crossing took nine days, the trip lasted five or six weeks, and all of it was free to the unencumbered young man, his first trip to Europe.

Andy kept publishing with *The New Yorker*, and Katharine kept offering him a job. It took innumerable lunches among Katharine, Ross, and Andy—not to mention a felicitous mail day after his return from Europe when he opened six envelopes from the magazine containing payments totaling $178—before he finally agreed to their offer, and another few lunches before he agreed to occupy an office, though not regularly. He worked part-time as a staff writer at $30 for several months before he felt secure enough to renounce his other part-time job and officially assume the role of staff writer in early 1927.

Andy's first assignment was writing newsbreaks—or, more precisely, sifting through and choosing typos, malapropisms, and unintended ironies from the clippings that readers sent in, a thousand a week, and writing the "snapper" at the end of each one—something he did so well that he would continue to do it until 1982, some thirty thousand of them in all.

> She was then about sixteen, and dressed herself always in black dresses—dozens of them—falling away from her slim, perfect body like strips of clay from a sculptor's thumb.—*F. Scott Fitzgerald in the* Saturday Evening Post.

In that case, dozens of them would be none too many.

> Prior to his return to work this morning he spent the weekend at his fiancée's home and is now back on the job better versed in business methods.—*Waterbury (Conn.) Republican, regarding John Coolidge*

Atta fiancée!

> Turning the corner, the gigantic skeleton of New York's newest and the world's highest building comes into view.—*The Herald Tribune*

It naturally would.

> Mrs. Grace Wright is being wired for electricity, which will be a great improvement and add considerably to her value in the community.—*Medina (O.) Sentinel*

Women are more restless every day.

He was soon writing Notes and Comment, rewriting ideas and tips for Talk of the Town, and writing or rewriting captions to cartoons. He continued to publish casuals and light verse, and soon expanded to theater reviews. Every tap on his typewriter produced seemingly effortless and pitch-perfect prose or verse. Ross had him write full-page ads for the magazine's subscription campaign, and so in addition to being the writer buried within the editorial "we," he was often quite literally the voice of the magazine.

Andy shifted away from Talk pieces and took over Notes and Comment after he brought on board the man who was to become a literary partner and lifelong friend: James Thurber. Thurber had tried to break into *The New Yorker* with limited success. Finally he met Andy through Russell Lord, a mutual friend, and Andy brought him into the offices to meet Ross, who, true to his nature, hired Thurber on the spot to be a jesus. Thurber was a spectacularly inept jesus but soon graduated to staff writer and a tiny office that he shared with Andy, big enough only for the two men, their typewriters, and a stack of copy paper. Andy described the incredible productivity of his officemate as that stack of paper rapidly decreased and he wrote about "discarded sorrows, immediate joys, stale dreams, golden prophesies, and messages of good cheer." Thurber later credited White with teaching him to discipline his outpourings and to reach for precision rather than profusion. Thurber learned the rhythms of Talk paragraphs from Andy and soon became the twin pillar of the front of the book.

Andy needed very little editing. Katharine would take her pencil to his typewritten sheets and maybe she would change "And there comes an hour in the afternoon of these little dogs when they are to be exercised because it is ordained they shall be" to "There comes an hour in the afternoon of these little dogs when it is ordained they shall be exercised." And then she would scrawl "anytime" at the top if it was an evergreen paragraph to hold in the bank, or an "A" to go in the next issue, "B" for the one after that.

Autobiographical though his verses may have been, minutely attuned to the beating of his own heart, they were not revealing. Was the sonnet he published in *The World*, in which he mocks himself for being unable to kiss his beloved under the forthright stare of a statue in Washington

Square, addressed to Katharine? No, probably not, for he was then seeing a young Southerner named Mary Osborn. How about the *New Yorker* poem in which he climbs the fence into Gramercy Park late one night, only to be startled by the statue of Edwin Booth admiring the woman he is with: "She's awfully sweet, I admire your taste, / I notice your arm is around her waist— / You haven't a pass and you haven't a key, / But give her a little kiss for me." No, that would be Rosanne Magdol, a nineteen-year-old secretary at *The New Yorker* who was pretty and vivacious but not terribly serious. Katharine found her a job at another magazine.

A poem appeared in *The New Yorker* in January of 1928, suggesting that in between walks around the city with young women and old statues, Andy spent a bit of actual time in the office, where an unlooked-for feeling was beginning to grow.

Notes from a Desk Calendar

Monday
Now grows my heart unruly
   At mention of your name,
And if I love you truly
   Is anyone to blame?
      (No answer required.)
Tuesday
Suppose the glance you gave me
   While standing by my chair
Struck home, could aught then save me?
   And am I one to care?
      (No answer desired.)
Wednesday
The persons who have seen us
   Together—have they guessed
There stands so much between us
   Which has not been confessed?
      (No answer requested.)

> Thursday
> Does earth, with each new sun-up,
>   Abundantly proclaim
> My heart in yours is done up?
>   And do you feel the same?
>   (No answer suggested.)
>   Friday
> The trays upon my table
>   Are labelled "Out" and "In";
> Was ever man less able
>   To have his day begin?
>   (No answer projected.)
>   Saturday
> Were I more plain and artless
>   In setting forth this love,
> Could you continue heartless
>   In re the lines above?
>   ("No" answer expected.)

Two weeks after this poem was published, Elspeth wrote to Katharine, "You certainly stirred up E.B.W." In the absence of any concrete biographical data (neither Katharine nor Andy would later pinpoint how and when their attraction grew), this tiny comment holds outsized importance. It implies that the addressee of the poem was an open secret among Andy's friends (the poem was signed "Beppo," one of Andy's childhood dogs), and it further implies that it was Katharine who did something to provoke the poem. Of course she could "continue heartless." She was seven years Andy's senior, a married woman with two children, his superior in the office—as a well-heeled and authoritative executive, she was not the obvious match for this feckless, shy youngster with a phobia for commitment. But that only lends support to the idea that she, as the stronger of the two personalities, initiated their relationship.

At some point in the first half of 1928, Andy and Katharine began an affair.

17.

Someone once said that if you took a ms. for The New Yorker to the post office & mailed it there, you found it, with a courteous rejection slip, on your return home.
—Babette Deutsch

The timeline of Andy and Katharine's deepening attraction aligns with a change in the literary sensibility of the magazine. Andy's writing introduced a more generous note into the magazine's caustic humor, and the tone of the book as a whole shifted from snobby jabs at social inferiors and pretentious elites to first-person ironic monologues that just as often mocked the narrator as they did another social group.

Even this late in the decade, *The New Yorker* did not see itself as engaging in a literary project. Just as the magazine refused to print photographs, so did it sometimes publish an issue without any stories in it; even when it did, it refrained from drawing a dark line around fiction to separate it off from the more capacious genre of "casuals." Katharine told one contributor in 1928, "This matter of fiction for The New Yorker is difficult and since we do not regularly run stories they must either be just so perfect that we cannot see our way clear not to use them or so appropriate and so much a part of New York experience that they belong in this very specialized magazine because of the theme."

This extreme choosiness makes it interesting to read the stories Katharine did publish and to track the authors whom she worked hard to make her own. Katharine thought the magazine had room to run short stories more often than they did, so she sent a letter asking contributors for more serious fiction. *The New Yorker* would always prize terseness and humor, but now that it had hit a healthy circulation number (fifty thousand subscribers by the end of 1927), Katharine was able to talk Ross into departing from their reliance on tropes and comic conventions to take a chance on individualistic literary expression.

One unknown writer who answered the call was Sally Benson, the younger sister of Agnes Smith, who had obtained a job on the *New Yorker* staff through Ross's wife, Jane Grant. Katharine accepted Benson's short story "Apartment Hotel" just eleven days after it was submitted. Only two pages long, the story begins with a matter-of-fact description of the Morrisons, a couple who have lived in a hotel for thirty years, content in the small world created by their routines. The story abruptly changes tone when it relays a conversation that Mrs. Morrison, riding the bus, overhears between a younger man and woman who gauzily discuss their previous night's wild time of drinking, dancing, and a hansom cab ride to Atlantic City, before making more plans for dinner that night at a speakeasy. Mrs. Morrison goes home and suggests to her husband that they try a new restaurant. "Someone, I forget just who it was, was telling me of a little place in Eleventh Street. I think she said it was an Italian place." They show up at the unmarked brownstone, but the man at the door turns them away—they are not the right kind of patrons. Back at their hotel, Mrs. Morrison picks a dead leaf off the fern at their usual table. Sally Benson had certainly made a study of her intended readership. From its economy, to the flat narration of Mrs. Morrison's life wrapped around the irruption of Jazz Age dialogue at the center (overheard speech was a *New Yorker* staple), to the juxtaposition of the generations and the implied judgment arising from well-chosen details, "Apartment Hotel" was a character study aimed right at Katharine's acquisitional heart. She wrote to Benson, "We are so glad you sent it to us because we feel sure that you should contribute regularly to the magazine and we consider this one of the best first pieces we have had from someone who has never written for us."

Benson was an ambitious twenty-nine-year-old mother and wife whose previous writing had been confined to movie reviews and interviews in

places like *Screen Play*, *Photoplay*, and *The Morning Telegraph*. She replied
with exuberance. Would *The New Yorker* like another Mrs. Morrison story,
plus two art ideas, plus another story? Katharine had unlocked something
by accepting the story, the first one she'd ever written, Benson told her;
immediately after, she had submitted two long stories and one short one
to *Life*, and all three were accepted. Katharine rejected Benson's art and
story ideas but carefully worded her rejection as encouragement to write
more, and she extracted from "Apartment Hotel" a guideline for Benson's
future work: "We feel that the effect of your other story was in the lack
of elaborateness, and the lack of plot." Benson understood perfectly, and
the next two stories of hers *The New Yorker* published resembled the first
in structure and tone. Both begin with a brisk, omniscient narration of
a quiet scene in progress, then break into dialogue that rapidly inflates,
and just as suddenly crashes down to a resigned reality. Her protagonists
were almost always female, almost always middle-class, and frequently
subjected to the compassionately critical eye of their author. Ross would
reject stories that crossed the moral line (such as one whose female protagonist he read as an "on the town, a tramp"), but she was so good that
he let her write awfully close to that line, with stories that discussed even
adultery—as long as none of the characters committed it. (Katharine enforced Ross's editorial proscription against adultery even as she herself
continued her affair with Andy. Ross's magazine, aspirational and upbeat,
was always an idealized version of the modern urban life.) Wolcott Gibbs
marveled at the Benson exception: "Harold Ross vs. Sally Benson. Don't
bother about this one. In the end it is a matter between Mr. Ross and
his God." Benson would publish over 125 stories in *The New Yorker* well
into the 1950s, so many that she gave some of her stories a pseudonym,
Esther Evarts. Her only rivals for prominence in the magazine were John
O'Hara and Robert Coates. She would collect these stories into bestselling books that would then be made into plays and movies that would
endure, including *Junior Miss* in 1941 and *Meet Me in St. Louis* in 1942.

Katharine cultivated two other writers in the late 1920s who would
become crucial to the magazine's identity. Thyra Samter Winslow, like
Sally Benson, was a Midwestern transplant to New York City, who
wrote semiautobiographical stories that de-sentimentalized their rural

characters. Like Benson and indeed like Katharine herself, Winslow was only loosely tied to her husband, giving her the emotional distance to observe the sexual politics of Manhattan. Unlike Benson, though, she was a known writer when she began submitting her stories to Katharine in 1927. H. L. Mencken had published her in *The Smart Set*, which was *The New Yorker*'s closest competitor; he ran well over a hundred of Winslow's stories under her own name, as well as her male, female, and gender-neutral pseudonyms, and she moved on from those pages only when Mencken renounced the editorship. Sometimes she wrote from within a breezy first-person jadedness ("I am for neater and, under certain circumstances, fewer murders"), and other times she narrated her characters from an ironic remove, one that indicated their moral failings without stating them ("She took time to admire her legs as she pulled on her new evening stockings. A good shade, nude, when you're not fat").

Winslow's voice was distinctive; as a Jew who could "pass" yet who wrote critically of Jews who assimilated, she was skeptical of the very upward mobility she had practiced upon coming to New York, and willing to be unlikable in saying so. Yet even within her distinctiveness, she was recognizable as part of a cohort defined by Dorothy Parker, a class of writers for whom style was critique and the modern city held as much disappointment as it did seduction.

In 1927, Katharine received a batch of letters that a young woman had written to her brother while on a road trip to Santa Fe. Without her permission—and in an inadvertent echo of Janet Flanner's introduction to the magazine—he forwarded them to *The New Yorker*, thinking they might be published as is. Katharine agreed, but Ross vetoed the letters on their subject matter—Santa Fe, he noted, was out west. When the writer in question moved to New York, her brother tried again, and Emily Hahn learned she had been accepted by *The New Yorker* before she knew she'd submitted anything. The magazine printed three of her letters-turned-stories within ten weeks. Two of them are almost pure dialogue. The first, "Lovely Lady," begins in the middle of a conversation between a first-person speaker and her friend, a majestically drunk young woman married to an older man, sapped of purpose in life, and envious of the speaker's need to earn her own living. It is a character portrait painted by the gap between what the friend says and what she unintentionally reveals, a gap filled with a knowing look between author and reader. Hahn mined this same trope in the next two stories, and though *The New Yorker* rejected her subsequent three attempts, she'd already gained Harold Ross as a fan. "You're cattier than anyone I know, except maybe Rebecca West. Keep it up!" She did, through more than two hundred articles for *The New Yorker*. It wouldn't be until 1930, when *The New Yorker* turned down her two separate requests for a job, that Hahn would leave for Africa and then China, launching her long career as an international correspondent.

Hahn's "Lovely Lady" ran in the same issue as F. Scott Fitzgerald's sole contribution to *The New Yorker* in the 1920s, a casual called "A Short Autobiography," submitted by his first agent, in which the speaker chronicles his life through exceptional wines and champagnes he has drunk. *The New Yorker* had previously contented themselves with sniping at his reputation, including John Mosher's profile in 1926, "That Sad Young Man" (opening line: "All was quiet on the Riviera, and then the Fitzgeralds arrived, Scott and Zelda and Scotty"). Katharine tried to get Fitzgerald to write a profile of Ring Lardner, but he declined, telling his literary agent, Harold Ober, "As for Mrs. Angell (whoever she is) I will gladly modify my style and subject matter for her, but she will have to give me her beautiful body first, and I dare say the price is too high." Ober translated that for Mrs. Angell: "He says he wishes he could have done one of Ernest Hemingway." Fitzgerald would not maintain his aloof attitude for long. In the early 1930s, he and Zelda would submit stories and poems to *The New Yorker* and receive their rejections, and Katharine would dutifully ask after him about once a year, and lunch with Harold Ober to discuss ideas she had about work for Scott Fitzgerald to do for *The New Yorker*.

Mostly, though, Katharine largely refrained from chasing after famous authors, though she certainly kept tabs on them in rival publications. Nor was she particularly dazzled when well-known authors submitted to her, as they'd now begun to do as *The New Yorker*'s reputation grew. The editorial vision of the magazine was always at the forefront of her mind. Margaret Foley and Rowe Wright, the two women who headed up the

Magazine Department in the Curtis Brown Literary Agency, sent Katharine three stories by a prominent client. "We always have such high hopes when a D. H. Lawrence manuscript appears," she replied, "but somehow always seem to be disappointed because none we have received thus far are really New Yorker material" (Lawrence never made it into the magazine). She turned down Theodore Dreiser for a piece that was "too much an inside newspaper controversy for us," a one-act play called *Anthropos* by e. e. cummings for being—what else?—"just too obscure and difficult to follow," and a poem by Upton Sinclair because, though the scrubwoman "aroused [their] indignation," the subject was too far afield for *The New Yorker*.

Janet Flanner put Katharine in touch with her friend Djuna Barnes, who came through with a deft casual called "Reproving Africa" about how she had failed upon traveling there to find the exotic continent of her imagination. Buoyed, Katharine suggested that she try some short sketches of humorous female types. Barnes was delighted that Katharine had "as smart an idea as this one for [her] particular kind of genius!" She submitted three: "The Woman Who Goes Abroad to Forget," "The Crasher," and "The Lost." It was, perhaps, a branching fork in *The New Yorker*'s history—would Barnes's elliptical, linguistically exuberant takes on female identity sit on a magazine page next to Dorothy Parker's bitter wit and the anti-romanticism of Benson and Winslow? No, they would not. Katharine invited modernism to submit and then largely rejected it.

She accepted "The Woman Who Goes Abroad to Forget," but only with significant edits because, as she explained to Barnes, her "piece was pretty 'dizzy' for [*The New Yorker*'s] rather straight forward [*sic*] and not esoteric public." "Dizzy": this was a pet word of Katharine's in the late 1920s, and she awarded it ecumenically; John O'Hara, William Rose Benét, reporter Alva Johnson, and S. J. Perelman all learned that their prose was "dizzy" from Katharine's editorial letters. She wasn't singling out modernist writers, but it was certainly they whose writing was most likely to stumble over *The New Yorker*'s insistence on a low threshold of comprehensibility.

So triumphantly had the humor weekly transcended its lighthearted beginnings that now Gertrude Stein thought it an appropriate venue for her work; she submitted two unsolicited poems. *The New Yorker* might have chosen to publish this talked-about modernist writer for her celebrity value. Katharine not only turned down Stein, she rejected a profile of Stein by (a then unknown) Paul Bowles.

Modernism pervaded the pages of *The New Yorker*—an issue with Barnes's work featured an ad for an angular floor lamp with the tagline "Modernism you can live with!"—but the magazine was never a home to experimental writing. The shock of the new interested the editors not at all, at least not as an effect they wanted to create in their readers. Instead, Ross's de facto strategy was to survey modernist art through the magazine's critical review columns, to allow Janet Flanner to drop references to it throughout her Paris Letter, and to parody it mercilessly in casuals by the likes of Corey Ford and James Thurber. Taken together, these modes hold up modernism as an aesthetic movement to know and understand, to mobilize in one's mind as a critical, discerning sophisticate, without particularly endorsing it (though *The New Yorker* did often champion modernist painting). Katharine let writers like Stein who sought a larger readership publish in *The New Yorker*'s rival in the category of "smart magazines," *Vanity Fair*. But *Vanity Fair* would soon fold in the midst of the Depression, placing *The New Yorker* in the ascendancy.

A second, much more deafening silence was the absence of Black writers. No writers of the Harlem Renaissance published in the pages of *The New Yorker*, and with one tiny, failed exception, no editors cultivated Black writers or showed any curiosity about their work. Race was a regular topic of observation—if not frank conversation—in Talk pieces, within cartoons, and on covers. The magazine played into racist conventions, but it just as often satirized them; barbs frequently targeted bigots who supported the Ku Klux Klan, but also white liberals who considered themselves enlightened about race because they were friendly with their Black servants.

But the magazine's attitude toward African American culture is better detected in what submissions never appeared in its office, rather than what did make it into the magazine's pages. A partial list of emerging writers, artists, and thinkers whom *The New Yorker* ignored includes Gwendolyn Bennett, Charles Chesnutt, Countee Cullen, Aaron Douglas, Rudolph

Fisher, Zora Neale Hurston, Georgia Douglas Johnson, Nella Larsen, Claude McKay, and Jean Toomer, not to mention established figures like Alain Locke and W.E.B. Du Bois. For all the competing magazines that Katharine read regularly in order to poach talent—*The New Republic*, *Daughters of the American Revolution Magazine*, *Life*, *Judge*, *College Humor*, *Vanity Fair*, *The Saturday Evening Post*, *The Nation*, *The Atlantic Monthly*, *Bookman*, *Forum*, and *Scribner's*—she ignored *The Crisis* and *Opportunity*, in which these Black writers regularly appeared. "It was a period," Langston Hughes would later write in *The Big Sea*, "when every season there was at least one hit play on Broadway acted by a Negro cast. And when Negro authors were being published with much greater frequency and much more publicity than ever before or since in history." Hughes in *The Nation*, Cullen in *Bookman* and *Harper's*, Du Bois in *The Nation* and *Survey*—but none of them in *The New Yorker*.

Imagine the conversation if Katharine and Jessie Fauset—a would-be Mawrter who'd been steered to Cornell and who now fostered Black authors as the literary editor of the NAACP's official magazine, *The Crisis*—had met at a cabaret and compared their editing careers. The parallels between the two women are striking. Fauset edited *The Crisis* from 1921 to 1926, second in command to a powerful male editor, W.E.B. Du Bois, whose overweening authority she often countermanded to win over writers. She was the first person to publish work by Countee Cullen, Arna Bontemps, and Langston Hughes, but like Katharine she went to especial lengths to publish work by women. She discovered Nella Larsen and gave immense support to Georgia Douglas Johnson, among many others. Unlike Katharine, though, Fauset was a writer with ardent ambition. She had published poems, stories, articles, book reviews, and travel essays in *The Crisis*, and a novel, *There Is Confusion*, with Boni & Liveright, publisher of Pound, Eliot, Anderson, and Faulkner. She may have left *The Crisis* in 1926 because of conflicts with Du Bois, but certainly she also wanted more time for her own writing. She looked for a new job and hoped to find a position as a manuscript reader, telling a colleague that if race was a barrier, she'd work at home rather than in an office. She would do anything but teach—yet that's precisely what she did when she couldn't find publishing work, teaching French at a public high school in New York. She would publish *Plum Bun* in 1929, a novel about a light-skinned Black woman who chooses to live "ambi-racially" (as *The New Yorker* put it in their one-sentence mention), but she would not publish much of anything before then and she would stop publishing in 1933. Her work would struggle to find traction with Black and white editors, critics, and readers, because her focus on middle-class Black characters met no one's expectations for the self-conscious pre-sentation and advancement of Black culture—too conservative for some, too unexotic for others. But Fauset's writing could have slotted right into *The New Yorker*. Katharine could have altered the trajectory of Fauset's life, just as much as Fauset could have enriched *The New Yorker* with her work and her connections to dozens of other writers.

The New Yorker's incuriosity about the fervent art scene at the north of the island, even extending to the absence of book, music, art, and the-ater reviews or notices in the Goings On About Town pages, perfectly coincided with the magazine's address to the well-to-do rather than the avant-garde. Among the magazine's white, educated, affluent readership, beliefs about race lagged behind beliefs about gender.

One exception came in the late 1920s, when Katharine reserved James Weldon Johnson as a profile subject for Walter F. White; the magazine kept meticulous records of reservations, but they were no guarantee of publication. Johnson was then the secretary of the National Associa-tion for the Advancement of Colored People, as well as the editor of several poetry anthologies; the writer of what was then known as the Negro national anthem, "Lift Every Voice and Sing"; and the author of a novel, *The Autobiography of an Ex-Colored Man*. White, as the acting secretary of the NAACP, knew him well, a relationship that promised to enhance his piece rather than compromise it because *The New Yorker* did not consider profiles to be objective journalism. Over the next year, Katharine sent White four separate queries to tell him how eager she was to receive his Johnson profile. Finally, White submitted it, only to receive a rejection letter two days later. He had erred, Katharine said, in writing too scholarly a portrait of Johnson, too insistent a view of him as an important man, when what *The New Yorker* wanted was to make him "come alive as a human being." A profile of James Weldon Johnson appeared in 1933, written by Robert Wohlforth, a white writer; the first paragraph lists all the important white men Johnson knew personally, including every president from McKinley to Coolidge. A year prior to that profile, Herbert Seligmann Jr., the publicity director for the NAACP, pitched to Katharine a profile of Walter F. White himself, "who looks much blonder and more Nordic than most accredited Teutons" and who "joined the Ku Klux Klan by an error on their part which led [sic] to their undoing" through his undercover investigations of lynchings." She wrote back immediately, saying the magazine knew White well and admired him. But she declined.

Just as she had solicited more serious fiction, so did Katharine send out a letter to advertise her openness to more serious poetry, which "would be not only useful but important to the magazine"—a most unpoetic but heartfelt manifesto of *The New Yorker*'s take on poetry at this time. William Carlos Williams responded with a poem, "rather long, rather stringy," and an exclamation of surprise: "Really I didn't know that The New Yorker was interested in poetry as poetry." It was another missed connection: with anguished politeness Katharine rejected Williams, and his next offering produced a form rejection.

Katharine's letter reached another poet whose work would be instrumental in shaping the empty space that Katharine had created by pushing aside some of those droll casuals and forgettable verses. Louise Bogan had published poetry and reviews in *The New Republic* and *Poetry*, as well as two volumes of poetry, and had worked as an editor at *The Measure*. She had published a tiny, unsigned poem in *The New Yorker* in 1926, and so she was on Katharine's list to receive the unexpected invitation for more literary work, prompting Bogan to submit her weightier, allusive lyric poetry—and just in time, too, because weeks later her house in the Berkshires burned and she lost almost all of her notebooks and manuscripts. The fire prompted her and her husband, Raymond Holden, to move back to the city, where Holden took a job as *The New Yorker*'s newest jesus. Katharine eagerly accepted four of Bogan's poems and dispatched them into the pages of the magazine within the next five months, where they sat within the columns like small bright-dark rocks, obdurate though the voice spoke clearly. Bogan drew the intensity of her lyric voice from reticence and withholding. She said of her poetry, "I have written down my experience in the closest detail. But the rough and vulgar facts are not there." For a magazine whose self-definition rested on a bedrock of facts, Bogan's work marked a small, consequential shift.

So many things were going well for Katharine. The magazine was succeeding, and she had the enormous personal satisfaction of bringing her own literary talents and tastes to bear on its flourishing and deepening content. When the opportunity arose for her to purchase additional *New Yorker* stock, she took it, perhaps using family money. The part-time job that Katharine had taken to add money to the family bank account during a difficult time had turned into a lively career. Ernest's mother, Lily Angell, died in 1927, and Ernest and his sister, Hildegarde, split her substantial estate between them, further easing the Angells' financial strain.

So highly regarded were Katharine's contributions to the magazine by this time that Raoul Fleischmann approached her secretly to offer her Ross's job. Fleischmann had grown frustrated with his inability to control Ross; the independence of the editorial department from the business side meant that Ross sometimes embarrassed Fleischmann and made his job more difficult, as when Ross ran parodies of advertisements in the magazine. Fleischmann wanted to fire him, and he traveled up to Katharine's home on East Ninety-Third Street one day while she lay sick in bed with an infected ear to offer her the job, or at the very least obtain her blessing for firing Ross. Katharine rejected him, just as she had so many potential contributors. She told him, not for the last time, that she would quit if he fired Ross, and so would many of the other editors. Ross was *The New Yorker*, and no one could do his job as well as he did. Fleischmann backed down and Katharine got back to the work she had made for herself.

18.

You don't have to know any history to love Corsica, and you don't have to know any history to love Katharine, and both of them found favor in my eyes.

—E. B. White to Scott Elledge, 1970

Despite their robust finances, the Angells' marriage continued to worsen, and now their fighting had broken out in front of Nancy and Roger. For this, Katharine blamed Ernest: he had a volatile temper, which she thought he had inherited from his mother, a "holy terror." Did they argue about Andy? Ernest almost certainly knew about him; Andy had even been to dinner once at East Ninety-Third Street with Roger and Nancy. Katharine, who would never fully open up about the dissolution of her marriage, insisted in the staunchest terms that her affair with Andy did not cause her divorce. Andy was, perhaps, a lightness for her during a dark time, but neither of them considered their relationship serious enough to lead to marriage. Andy did not ask for, and she did not offer, a divorce as a condition of being together; he would later say that she and Ernest had been heading for a divorce when he first became acquainted with her, long before their affair.

On June 15, 1928, a string of taxis pulled up in front of the Angells' house on East Ninety-Third Street. Katharine, Ernest, Nancy (age eleven), Roger (age seven), and their French governess piled in with their luggage and were driven down to Pier 54. There, they met up with Katharine's sister Rosamond, her husband, John, and their son, Jack (al-

most nine), who were joining them on a six-week trip to Europe on the
SS *France*. At the festive send-off, the adults celebrated with friends and
alcohol. Nancy remembered Ernest uncharacteristically drinking too
much and being sick, which made Katharine "absolutely livid." Roger
remembered being on board the ship, proudly wearing French berets
with his sister and older cousin, and disembarking and being chauffeured
around France in a limousine, courtesy of the Newberrys' wealth.

The trip was a vacation in grand style at least three months in the
planning and the first time the Angells had left the country with their
children. It was, in very small part, a work trip. Katharine visited Janet
Flanner in Paris, where they had several lunches together, lobster and
champignons Provençal, and where Flanner introduced Katharine to
Djuna Barnes in person. In Paris Katharine also called on Ralph Barton,
the caricaturist and one of the magazine's founding editors, to press him
for drawings and articles, carrying with her a letter of introduction from
Harold Ross: "This is to introduce Mrs. Angell, who is not unattractive."
(This, Katharine dryly noted, was "the highest personal comment [she]
ever got from him.") She met the *New Yorker*'s Paris fashion correspondent, Beatrice Mathieu, who helped her shop for handmade lingerie and
a designer dress called the Flag, navy silk with a red, white, and blue sash.
They moved on to the Riviera, where they stayed with the writer Charles
Brackett and his wife. Katharine stepped outside for her first view of the
blue Mediterranean, and there below her, floating in resplendent naked-
ness, was Alexander Woollcott.

But the European trip was mainly "a last attempt to save [their] marriage," in Katharine's words. If only that statement could be opened up
and picked apart. How would a lavish, crowded trip abroad help the couple through the difficult emotional work of forgiveness and reconnec-
tion? How would returning to the site of Ernest's first indiscretions help
them rebuild trust? In fact, Ernest broke away from the family to visit
his wartime paramour in France. Ernest felt his marriage had entered a
new and modern phase, that he and Katharine could stay married while
pursuing other relationships; Katharine would later tell her children that
Ernest had urged her to see other people. Andy would remember this as

well, that "Ernest wanted to be in the right place at the right time doing the In thing," and that being unfaithful "was the In thing to be in that era, and he kept urging her to go and do likewise."

And in fact the trip afforded Katharine and Andy a few intensely romantic days in exotic locales. On June 1, 1928, he came over on the SS *Corinthia* with his roommate, Gus Lobrano, who was traveling for business. After banging around London and Paris with Lobrano, Andy struck out on his own. He found Katharine in Paris and they took a train to the outskirts, where they canoed on the Seine and stopped to eat dinner at a little restaurant, the two of them in sports clothes and sneakers among the Parisians in evening dress. They met up in Saint-Tropez and Corsica, and the island days made the clearest impression on him. They drank too much white wine and rode bicycles, and Andy ended up in a cactus. They stayed at the Hôtel des Étrangers and wandered the garden among lizards and vines and sunshine and listened to someone playing the piano in the "dead afternoon."

And the children? Nancy, Roger, and their cousin Jack had been deposited at the home of a French family in Grasse on the French Riviera. They lived there for several weeks, speaking French and playing with the family's donkey. Nancy knew something of what her parents were doing and was abashed; Roger knew nothing, only that his parents were suddenly gone, and that they'd left separately. Years later, he transformed his impressionistic memories from this time into a *New Yorker* story, "Côte d'Azur," in which the little boy is far more unsettled by his mother's absence than his father's, and is temporarily returned to himself, "in such a whirl of happiness and excitement," on the few times that his mother comes to visit.

The two couples and their children, and the bachelor, returned to New York and to their everyday lives. It would appear that nothing had changed. Katharine dove back into work at *The New Yorker*, reviewing the pieces that other editors had bought in her absence and pestering her writers for the pieces they'd promised but failed to deliver. At night she went home to a man she did not love. They tried to keep up appearances by maintaining their social life, for instance inviting friends over for a "stand up party" at their house after ten o'clock one Thursday evening.

Andy published five more poems to Katharine in The Conning Tower, including "Of Things That Are," which began:

> In the warm sun
>   Of a strange land,
> I beheld your life
>   And possessed your hand.
>
> In the real cold
>   Of things that are,
> I have lost hold
>   Of a caught star.

Nothing, it seems, could dislodge them from their interlocking misery. On New Year's Day 1929, Andy wrote in his journal, "Walking twice around the reservoir this afternoon in the fog, resolving a problem: whether to quit my job and leave town telling no one where I was going." He didn't quit, but a few weeks later he tried a smaller version, hopping into his new Model A Ford roadster and heading straight north to Belgrade, Maine, where he stayed for a week to ice-skate and "let a lot of cold fresh Maine air blow through [his] brains." He was in love with Katharine, that much he knew; what he couldn't figure out was what to do with his feelings.

Only a few weeks later, in February of 1929, the decisive moment arrived. Katharine described it only once, forty-seven years later, in the same letter to her granddaughter Callie, written at Christmastime just six months before her death, in which she divulges Ernest's affair with Marian Powys Grey. It is a letter heavily edited by an editor, additions made after the fact. She wrote, "Then we got to quarreling?sp (and this was bad for Nancy and Roger) and when ^one day he ^slapped my face and knocked me down, ^to the floor I walked out for good and all."

This heartbreaking statement would have been subjected to another kind of editing, too, if Katharine had had her way. In the final decade of her life, she read and sorted her boxes of letters before donating them to

Bryn Mawr. She annotated many of them, adding dates, clarifying names, scribbling all those notes on pink routing slips. None of the letters she ultimately donated hint at any strife or unpleasantness in her own life; she frequently noted when she had destroyed part of a letter because of its sensitivity. The reason that her letters to Callie survived her editing and remain securely in the Katharine Sergeant Angell White archive at Bryn Mawr is that Callie donated them after her grandmother's death. Katharine did not want this letter about Ernest to be known outside the family. She ends it by writing, "Burn this letter. Ever so much love, Grandma."

After the incident, Katharine left the house on East Ninety-Third Street and headed to Greenwich Village, to Althea and Jim Thurber's large and often raucous apartment at 65 West Eleventh Street. The Thurbers were having marital troubles of their own, which Jim Thurber had been transmuting into the Mr. and Mrs. Monroe stories that Katharine had been publishing in *The New Yorker*. They had attempted to stave off divorce not with children but with puppies; when Jeannie, their beloved Scottie, gave birth to eleven, they gave one to Katharine, who named her Daisy. Now Katharine came to stay with them for only a few days. Not long after her visit, they would split apart, Althea to a rented Connecticut house and Jim to the Algonquin Hotel.

Andy and Thurber helped Katharine move some furnishings and clothing from the East Ninety-Third Street brownstone to the Snedens Landing house, and as Thurber's marriage crumbled, the three New Yorkers banded together. Just hours before Katharine had sailed for Europe, Thurber confessed to her that his eyesight was failing, and she had held his hand and arranged for him to see an oculist. Now, with the loss of his apartment, Thurber intended to stay at Snedens Landing for a week, bringing Jeannie and her remaining puppies, certain of finding the support he needed. Ernest knew how close Katharine and Thurber were and during these months he leaned on Thurber to help him persuade Katharine to return to their marriage. How Thurber brokered those conversations has remained off the page.

Katharine and Andy discussed marriage, but without seriousness. Katharine couldn't muster faith that a man seven years her junior would make a better match than the one she was leaving, nor could she believe Andy would want to become a stepfather to two older children. Andy, for his part, was having his usual aversion to commitment. Pictures taken on the front porch of the stone house show them, two people at a time with occasional dog, draped languorously down the steps, despite the February cold. Proof that marriage did not seem a viable option for the two of them comes from the fact that the three of them vowed to return to that exact spot in twenty-five years, each folding a newspaper clipping into his or her wallet as a talisman. The men still had theirs when the date arrived. Did Katharine?

As the winter gave way, Katharine struggled to keep up at *The New Yorker*, but she missed many days in the office because of her emotional overwhelm. She had found time, though, to shepherd Andy White's first book into print. He collected sixty-four poems—including all those written to her—in a volume called *The Lady Is Cold*, which referred not to his paramour but to a stone statue standing in front of the Plaza Hotel. Katharine found him an illustrator, her friend Ernest F. Hubbard, and an editor, her friend Eugene Saxton at Harper. The book went out into the world on May 1, 1929. If there was a celebration, none of its participants remembered it. Katharine was overextended and her home life was untenable.

Katharine had the bad luck to want a divorce in the very state with the nation's most restrictive divorce law, dating back to Assemblyman Alexander Hamilton's law of 1787. The only grounds for a divorce in New York was adultery, and only with proof. This meant not that thousands of unhappy but faithful couples were caged in their marriages, but that divorce in New York became a theater of the absurd, with a script and a corps of actors springing up to manufacture the necessary evidence. Typically the husband would agree to be "caught" in a hotel room with a scantily clad woman; the wife would burst in upon them with her lawyer and a private detective, as well as a photographer to harvest the necessary evidence. After just a few seconds of indignity, the play would break up, and the divorce papers would eventually list the charge of infidelity—one last consensual act before the marriage was over, one enduring act of chivalry encoded in the legal record.

Raymond Holden agreed to be discovered with his lover, Louise Bogan, in order to obtain a divorce from his first wife; his daughter remembered a commotion in the living room one night, followed by Holden and Bogan's marriage not long afterward. This was also how Harold Ross and Jane Grant were divorcing, at just the same time that Katharine was deciding on her own divorce. The Ross/Grant marriage had been rocky for at least two years, and Ross would later attribute their strife to Grant's feminism: "I never had one damned meal at home at which the discussion wasn't of women's rights and the ruthlessness of men in trampling women. You go through several years of that and you can't take it anymore." So they learned their parts, enacted the drama, and were divorced in 1929.

This model, though, required both parties to agree on the farce, and Ernest did not want a divorce. When Katharine confided in Ross, he suggested that she follow in the footsteps of their mutual friend Margaret Case. Case was a writer for *The New Yorker* and *Vanity Fair*. As the daughter of Frank Case, the owner of the Algonquin Hotel, she was famously the only person ever to have been born at the hotel, making her a sibling of *The New Yorker*. She was just then in Reno, Nevada, to obtain a divorce from Morgan G. Morgan, her stockbroker husband. Perhaps Katharine should join her at the Circle S Ranch?

Reno, which by 1929 was synonymous with divorce in popular culture, provided Katharine with an alternative script to follow. The state offered nine different grounds for divorce, with lower standards of proof in uncontested cases, and had by then settled upon a three-month residency period (soon to be lowered to six weeks), calculated to bolster its economy with Eastern dollars. Well-off clients from restrictive states wore a groove on the earth: first they boarded the luxurious express train, the 20th Century Limited, at Grand Central, then they changed at Union Station in Chicago to the Overland Limited, and three days later, they disembarked at the Reno Union Pacific station.

Katharine wrote to many of her authors that she had been sick lately and was taking a few months away from the office to recover her health. Fortunately, she had just that year hired a new secretary named Daise Terry, an expert stenographer and typist who came to the magazine from

Budapest, where she'd been serving with Herbert Hoover's postwar relief agency. She proved herself so competent that she would eventually
head the entire secretarial staff and also work closely with the magazine's
artists, staying with *The New Yorker* until her retirement in 1968. But
for now, she was the perfect partner in Katharine's enterprise, because
(in the words of her boss) she was "a hard taskmaster and she did not
approve of romance or marriage." Neither, at the moment, did Katharine.

On May 10, 1929, Katharine brought Daisy the puppy to Andy's
apartment for the duration of her absence. Andy and Ross accompanied
her to Grand Central, and after saying goodbye, she left on the four o'clock
train.

Andy White then offered a small departure from the script. He went
back to his apartment and took a nap, which was briefly interrupted by a
neighbor calling to invite him over for a drink the next day. He fell back
asleep and then into a disturbingly vivid dream of the phone ringing
again; this time it was Katharine, and she was calling off their relationship. He woke again in the middle of the night, and the two phone calls
combined in his confused mind. He thought Katharine was in trouble.
Bold action was needed; Andy made his way to Long Island, chartered a
plane, and flew to Chicago. But, as Katharine's posh train was making its
comfortable way through the winter snow, the plane was unable to make
headway through a storm that blew up. She completed her twenty-hour
journey, and eventually Andy found her at the house of her friends John
and Evelyn McCutcheon in Chicago, where she was staying overnight.
She could hardly reassure him of her commitment to him, since they'd
made none, but she could at least debunk the phantom phone call. They
said goodbye again, after making a pact—which they would very shortly
break—to not write while she was away, and they each boarded a train,
she onward to Reno, he back to New York.

19.

The nightmare quality of the place has never been set down so far as I know and all one gets is short stories about cowboys and silly ladies taking the cure. . . . The greatest lack I felt in anything I have read about Reno is the idea that the place is tragic, which it certainly is. Writers always emphasize the frivolous and bawdy element, whereas there are a lot of people, serious-minded and sad, going through hell.

—Katharine White to Nancy Hale, 1935

Katharine carried to Reno a letter of introduction from her New York lawyer, Morris Ernst, and once there she engaged the firm of Ayers, Gardiner, and Pike to accomplish her divorce. Ernest, too, was represented by a Nevada firm but never set foot in the state. Katharine's attorneys prepared the complaint for her to file a day or two after she'd established residency, and then her only job was to live in Reno, which she did with gusto—and with the observational acumen of a reporter.

She had read plenty of Reno, all the women getting beauty treatments and cavorting under the sun, but what surprised her was the "tragic" nature of those seeking divorces—and the people who were eager to exploit them "in the most doubtful moments of their lives." Katharine would get caught up in both the frivolity and the sadness. She was a full participant in the surreal divorce culture of Reno, even though she lived not in the Riverside Hotel, the downtown center of it all, but at the Circle S Ranch, north of Reno near Pyramid Lake.

The first thing she did, upon moving into her first-floor room, was fall in love. Her name was Snowball, and she was a trim and sure-footed white mare. Katharine impressed the ranch's improbably named owners, Hy and Mae West, with her ability to ride, which she likely learned in Chocorua, and soon she and Snowball were traveling as far as twenty miles a day on the never-ending ranch chore of rounding up horses from the surrounding desert, the old ones destined for the chicken feed factory next to the racetrack. One perennially missing Circle S horse was named the Lord, so they got a lot of mileage out of looking for the Lord and not finding him anywhere. The sere land around the Circle S fascinated Katharine. Her letters to Andy were filled with descriptions of the hills, the lizards, and always the horses. She involved herself in roundups, rodeos, and branding. There were dogs at the ranch too, but for perhaps the only time in her life, another species took precedence in her heart and she could not get enough of the horses.

She had gained weight, she warned Andy, and had a sunburn that peeled and turned to a tan. She had taken to wearing her hair in braids wound around her head, her younger style from her teenage years in the New Hampshire woods. Her lips were chapped and her eyes bloodshot. She had gone west for a divorce, but what she also got was a rejuvenation. Quite without meaning to, she found herself undergoing the male version of the cure for neurasthenia, which called for an escape from the effete civilization of the Northeast out into the rugged authenticity of the West, where recovery would come from vigorous physical exertion and contact with the simpler values of the natural world. The Circle S was the direct antithesis of Elsie's rest cure in France, Switzerland, and England.

She heard that Ross, recovering from his own divorce, had departed Manhattan for the Austen Riggs sanitarium in her ancestral home of Stockbridge, Massachusetts, and that disgusted her. "I should like to send him a little piece of tatting or a kindergarten mat to weave. If that isn't intellectual poverty for you." He was obviously doing it wrong.

Elsie's cure had prevented her from using not only her body but also her mind, and Katharine too initially found relief in voluntarily setting down a heavy intellectual burden. She described her three months in

Nevada as "suspended animation," a time when she could be a "vegeta-ble," a place where "critical judgment degenerates." She wrote, "A ranch wipes out intellectual and emotional complications—everything is sim-ple and spread out like the land." She preferred not to think, saying, "That I don't find comforting." She read novels but she edited not a single word, and that began to worry her a bit: "I wonder if I'll ever be able to earn my living with my head again."

Katharine was aware that her suspended state was a kind of luxury. Many of the divorce-seekers couldn't afford to spend their residency on vacation, and so Reno responded with short-term jobs. "Everyone you encounter is tied up in the divorce industry," Katharine noticed, "the girl who waves your hair and even the bellboys in the hotels and the people who sell you in the shops are also there temporarily to get a divorce."

The Circle S, though, was full of literary women. In addition to Kath-arine's friend Margaret Case, she shared the house with the writer Agnes Boulton, who was divorcing the playwright Eugene O'Neill. Boulton loved the "wide open" town of Reno—bars and casinos and prizefights and no speed limits in the entire state—but she especially loved being hit on by "a violent suitor" at the Circle S. Boulton described him as "25, six feet three, wild and handsome, and the crack 'Bronk rider' of the west." (Katharine, too, admired "a few beautiful ones who were most objectionable"—but she only admitted that many years later.) Boulton snapped out of it eventually, and returned home to her lover and her two children. But the Reno respite provided Boulton with literary material, and she wrote an unpublished essay about marriage inspired by women like her housemate Katharine "really just enjoying life—or themselves." These intellectual and culturally adept women would only relearn to love, Boulton believed, once they'd truly experienced independence.

Katharine too conceived of her stay at a divorce ranch as outside the chronology of her life. She visited a fortune teller, a gambling joint, a Reno bar, the racetrack—many times—and a late-night party at a coun-try general store where she danced with a man who had killed someone. She swam at the Reno hot springs to the sound of amplified Victrola records. She swam at Pyramid Lake, a turquoise gem surrounded by chalky banks and miles of bunchgrass and sagebrush, and soon enough she was skinny-dipping in the moonlight. She was "amused" by the automobile industry, all the predatory car dealerships that offered payment plans to appeal to the people who came to Reno and "decided that this was the moment to learn" to drive—but she was not immune to the appeal. She bought a Ford, a roadster that was a twin to Hotspur, Andy's beloved car, and she named it Bonnie Gray, conscripting some visiting high school boys to teach her how to drive it. Mostly she rode, a physical challenge to heal her emotional raggedness. She relished riding alone, as soon as she'd earned that privilege: "You get away from human beings and everything assumes its proper proportion yet you have a great sense of companionship with the horse who seems for the moment to be the wisest, most sympathetic, most omniscient of creatures." She was kicked by a horse, "a distinction of which [she was] a trifle vain."

The exile was, in many ways, the worst of both worlds, because she was deluged with letters from her family filled with admonishments and advice, but she could do nothing to care for her children or repair her relationships from afar. The children moved to Snedens when school let out, as usual, with Miss Heyl, their governess, and went on outings with Aunt Elsie and Aunt Rosie. Elsie gave Katharine an earful about Nancy's reticence; her unwillingness to talk was, to Elsie, a clear sign that she needed psychoanalysis, which, come to think of it, would also benefit Katharine. Elsie had begun studying analytic psychology with a student of Carl Jung's at the same time that she was writing her first novel, *Short as Any Dream*—based on the Shepley family stories of traditional farming life in Maine and settling the frontiers of Minnesota and California—and she deeply believed in the centrality of the unconscious to both art and life. The next month she would publish the novel, and then she would move to Zurich for two years to study with Jung himself. But she would never convince her sister of the worth of excavating memories and pain from where they lay buried in the mind. Katharine dismissed Elsie's concerns about Nancy as overwrought.

As near as Katharine could tell, both children seemed fine, though of course a child's correct and polite letter on classroom notepaper could hardly divulge his or her inner state. "I hope you are having a good time out west. Are there any cowboys down there?" wrote Roger. Katharine initially held out hope that Nancy could come visit her, but that was soon dashed. Roger headed up to his Maine sleepaway camp, Camp Chewonki, for the northern version of her own relentless physical exertions. And her family kept writing to her: "If only they'd leave me alone—letters and letters that almost drive one frantic."

Well, only some of the mail was unwelcome. Katharine received letters from Thurber, and surprisingly long and caring ones from Ross. And she wrote to Andy every few days, an outpouring of words that were rarely emotional but always vivid, charming, full of life. In these letters, Katharine sounds fifteen years younger than in the editorial letters she had written at the office just weeks earlier: "Andy, when you're around the world looks all silver and mauve and pearlescent. I'm looking very beautiful today, Andy, and I love you." Oh, Katharine could write a parody with the best of them. In fact, she was practically producing her own sophisticated magazine from Nevada, complete with profiles of cowboys, divorcées, and drunk cowgirls; Talk of the Town items derived from day trips in Bonnie Gray to Reno and Carson City; and Notes and Comment pieces on happenings back east. As soon as she was settled in May, she lobbied hard for Andy to come visit her. Bring Ross, she urged, or Thurber ("I'll find lots of girls for Jim"). She wrote, "[I] want you to see me when I'm healthy and normal so that you can forget the abnormal half mad woman." But he didn't come, and so she kept writing.

Once again, what she declined to write signifies as much as what she did. She did not write about marriage, other than to say, most emphatically, that she would refuse to discuss it if he came for a visit. She did not write about her divorce proceedings; Ernest's name was never mentioned. She wrote often of her mood swings, her "outbursts of enthusiasm or depression," and didn't hesitate to mention when she'd had a day so miserable she couldn't get out of bed, but she did not lean on Andy for reassurance. She merely reported her emotional state as she did Snowball's minor injuries. Here too she saw herself as part of the crowd: "Almost every woman seems to arrive [here] sick and goes to the doctor in her first week." Katharine's doctor prescribed iodine to prevent "exophthalmic goiter," and she suspected he told the same thing to all the divorcées. Thus she minimized her own troubles.

Andy did seek reassurance from Katharine. On July 11, he reached his thirtieth birthday, and he was filled with thoughts of his own inadequacy, his failure to achieve anything of note as a mariner, a poet, or a reporter (his categories). He hadn't produced a major book. Should he quit *The New Yorker*? It was a nice enough life, and he could be content with it, if he knew for certain that was the limit of his writing talent, but while a higher ambition still burned in him, didn't he owe it to himself to leave aside the "palpitating paragraphs," the work for hire, and create a life where he could write from within himself?

Katharine, the editor with several dozen authors at her fingertips, all of them trying to craft writing lives for themselves, had a thing or two to say on the matter. She began with the obvious: Andy was "preeminently a writer." "Everything you do has a certain perfection that is rare," she told him. His fears of being a hack thus brushed aside, she went on to say that maybe he *should* quit the magazine; she wouldn't pressure him to stay, but said, "I do know this: there's no real freedom or happiness for the person who vagabonds, throws over the idea of being a responsible member of society and says 'This year I can live on 50¢ a day and work my way to the coast.'" Sure, that can be valuable for a little while—and was this perhaps a bit tactless because that's exactly what Andy had done after college?—"but a lifetime of it would leave you pretty blank after a year or two." She rejected his terms, his false dichotomy between the routine, confining work of the magazine and the free, unencumbered life of the starving artist. Look at Willa Cather, who wrote for magazines and hadn't published a book anyone noticed until she was almost forty. She asked him to think of his position at *The New Yorker* as "a comparatively gracious and free life," the very condition for the kind of writing he'd like to do. "Oh, stop preaching Katharine," she concluded. "I ought to be the last person in the world to hold forth on how to arrange one's life, having made a pretty disgusting mess of my own and other people's."

In fact, Katharine had thought she herself might not return to *The New Yorker*, that it had filled a dark hole during her unhappy marriage but was not worth the demands it made on her time and her health. But by the time she answered Andy's fears, she had grown nostalgic for the magazine, its staff, and the city itself, and she was ready to return to her desk, but with a much stricter limit on her time in the office. So she re-acted with alarm when she heard a rumor that Andy had gone ahead and resigned from *The New Yorker*. She dispatched a telegram with instructions on how to telephone her immediately, and she hurtled into Reno to take the call. The next day she wrote to him from her hotel, reassured that he had not quit as she had feared. "I thought I was perhaps included in The New Yorker resignation."

Andy did skip town and leave the country, but he went only as far as Camp Otter in Ontario, where he'd been a counselor, and in which he was now acquiring a part interest. He wrote Katharine, "Ontario is wonderful (haven't you been up here, I seem to remember that you have)"—and this was perhaps a bit tactless given that her Ontario trip was her honeymoon with Ernest. To Ross, he wrote that his return would be delayed indefinitely: "On account of the fact that The New Yorker has a tendency to make me morose and surly, the farther I stay away the better."

In early August, Hy and Mae West both grew ill, forcing Katharine to move to the Mayberry Dude Ranch, closer to Reno—and forcing her to give up Snowball, who was likely pregnant, and whose foal would be named Kay if male and Katharine if female (another mare's colt had already been named after her: Pyramid Angel). She traded horses for lawyers as her trial date approached.

Katharine's New York attorney, Morris Ernst, added an addendum to the conventional divorce proceedings, and this one would have deep and lasting consequences for Katharine, Ernest, Andy, Roger, and Nancy. Ernst was not yet famous for his defense of Joyce's *Ulysses* on behalf of Random House in its obscenity trial, nor was he yet *The New Yorker*'s lawyer, nor had he yet published one of his many books, *For Better or Worse: A New Approach to Marriage and Divorce*. But he was already working out his idea for how to respond to the crisis of divorce, a crisis that virtually every magazine—except *The New Yorker*—had bemoaned. Katharine's old nemesis Beatrice Hinkle had written about it in a cover story for *Harper's*: divorce rates were on the rise, nearly double what they were at the beginning of the century, and they were markedly higher for women who worked outside of the home. Women, wrote Hinkle, were "fast awakening from their long sleep—a sleep in which they were unconscious of themselves as individuals and conscious only of the object—the man and the child for whom they lived." Suffrage and education led women to expect companionate marriages, and their increasing autonomy outside the home afforded them the means to leave less ideal marriages that in the past might have caged them. Katharine's divorce swept her into this cohort of modern women.

Her father, for one, deplored what he considered the selfishness of contemporary values. Charles wrote to Elsie, "I hate to see these dear children become victims to these modern ideas of individuality." Morris Ernst did not share Charles's conservatism, but he too worried that the law was cold to moral concerns about the impact of divorce on children. It was common for couples to present to their Nevada judge an agreement they'd written for the custody and care of their children. In theory, the judge would be guided by such an agreement but not bound by it; in practice, judges never looked too closely and simply rubber-stamped the addendum. Ernst believed the law owed more to children, and he rewrote the literary genre of the custody agreement to better shape their welfare. In particular, he strongly advocated the use of arbitration clauses, which, though rarely invoked, allowed the language of the agreements to stay flexible, always open to renegotiation. "The purpose of all this," he would later write, "is to avoid the temptation of writing the children's future in fiction, for that is what any attempt to anticipate the possible changes of twenty years means."

A week and a half before their trial date, Katharine and Ernest signed a highly unusual three-page memorandum to guide their family's new arrangement. They agreed to joint custody, something that was extremely rare—and even radical—before the legal reforms of the late 1970s and 1980s. Had Katharine wanted sole custody of Roger and Nancy, she almost certainly would have prevailed in court. Judges during this era overwhelmingly preferred mothers to fathers in custody disputes, even in cases when the mother's adultery had been proven, and this era has been called the nadir for fathers' rights. But Ernest was very clear about his willingness to fight, and Morris Ernst persuaded Katharine not to drag the sordid details of their marriage through the courts because it would harm the children; his highest value, the word he used to her and that would pepper the book he would eventually write on the subject, was "civilized." Instead, the arrangement of joint custody was intended as an olive branch to smooth the contested divorce. Despite their inability to collude on the divorce itself, the Angells managed to agree on something far ahead of their time and deeply consequential.

In another unorthodox choice, and in accordance with Ernst's philosophy, the rest of their custody agreement was only a loose set of principles to guide their evolving decisions over the years, not a mandated structure for the division of the children's time. They started by agreeing that the children's education was paramount and that they should be educated to the fullest extent of their parents' finances. All else evolved from this fundamental, shared principle. Nancy and Roger would be kept together as much as possible. "Their care, custody and control shall be equally divided between the parents," and the exact division of their living arrangements would depend upon their schooling. Both parents would decide together anything concerning their health, education, and "moral questions." The agreement notes that Katharine was not requesting alimony but that Ernest agreed to pay $5,000 yearly to cover six months of the children's expenses, plus all education, medical bills, governesses, and clothing. The memorandum closed with provisions for changes in parental income, remarriage, and the arbitration of disputes.

Ninety years later, as he approached his centenary, Roger Angell would talk about how his mother "abandoned" him and his sister after the divorce. He said that it "never should have happened; she never should have given up her children." As an adult with grown children of her own, Nancy used nearly the same language: her mother "in essence renounced all claim to Roger and me, the two children, and walked out on us and said, 'Okay, your father can have the responsibility, he can have the custody, and anything else.'" To the end of their lives, both children experienced joint and equal custody as their mother's desertion, and both believed that Katharine regretted "giving" them to Ernest, a regret they believed shaped the rest of *her* life. At the center of the emotional logic by which Nancy and Roger understood their family is Katharine's silence. It was not until much later that she would divulge Ernest's affairs and her reasons for the divorce to her children, or that she would work hard to exonerate herself to chroniclers of the magazine from Ernest's rancorous assertion that Andy broke up their marriage. She shielded her children for so long because she herself had been raised to avoid unpleasantness, and because she wanted to preserve their relationships with Ernest. She never explained the nuances of the legal agreement and never tried to clear herself of the charge of abandonment. She chose silence and peace rather than bitterness and a conflict that might make the children distrust their father. And she left no record that she regretted their joint custody agreement.

The idea of abandonment would also crop up in *New Yorker* histories that touched on Katharine Sergeant Angell's scandalous personal life. Her divorce would get fused with her "formidable" demeanor to paint a picture, over and over, of a cold and ambitious woman who pursued success at the expense of her children's well-being. The emotional truth of her children's lived experience of the divorce trumped Katharine's emotional truth and the legal facts; the equal division of custody between two parents persistently damned one of those parents to a lifetime of criticism, but not the other.

On August 17, 1929, Katharine appeared in front of Judge H. W. Edwards at the Second Judicial District Court of the State of Nevada, accompanied by her three lawyers. The complaint entered by Katharine was as notable for what it did *not* say as for what it did, reading in part: "Defendant has treated plaintiff with a long line and continual and systematic course of unkind and cruel treatment," "defendant has been at all times extremely critical of and sharp tongued toward plaintiff, and in a sharp manner and a loud tone of voice has adversely criticized plaintiff," and "defendant has been extremely disputatious and contentious, easily provoked to anger and has become angered at plaintiff, nagged at, complained of and found fault with her, and at times was rude to her in public and in the presence of friends and acquaintances, made remarks which humiliated her and caused her to suffer great mental pain."

Katharine did not mention any of Ernest's affairs. She made no mention of his son, Peter Powys Grey. She did not accuse him of domestic violence. She made no mention of anything prior to "the last two or three years before the separation of the parties." Instead, she sought a divorce on the grounds of extreme cruelty, arguing that Ernest's treatment "caused plaintiff great mental pain, was without plaintiff's fault or provocation on her part, seriously affected her health, destroyed her happiness, frustrated the objects and purposes of the marriage and made further cohabitation unendurable."

Ernest's answer was to "deny each and every allegation" and ask that the action be dismissed. He made no countercharges, and therefore he made no mention of Katharine's infidelity.

Judge Edwards heard "certain evidence," which the divorce decree does not specify, but it was persuasive enough for him to decide, two days later, that "each, every and all the allegations of said complaint are true." He ratified and approved the couple's memorandum on child custody and declared an absolute divorce from the bonds of matrimony. Newspapers in cities around the country, including New York and Boston, announced Katharine's successful suit the next day. None of them mentioned Katharine's position at *The New Yorker*. Papers in Texas and California called her a "society writer." All of them misspelled her first name.

20.

Katharine packed her belongings, sold her Ford, and headed back to New York on the same trains that had brought her to Reno, arriving on August 23. She was tanner and heavier than when she'd left, but perhaps also lighter. Her mood can perhaps be adduced from a Comment she published in *The New Yorker* upon her return: "Travelling is more fun west of Chicago." When the train headed west and crossed an invisible line in Illinois, passengers began to relax their clothing, manners, and behavior. And those same passengers, stepping onto the 20th Century Limited in Chicago to head east, would snap themselves upright, toss aside their ice cream cones, and pull on their gloves for dinner. "The effete East—it's where we belong, but we can't avoid a sigh at the admission." She returned to an empty city, no Angells or Sergeants, no children, and no Andy (he was still in Ontario), and she moved into an empty apartment.

Andy had found and leased the apartment for her while she was in Nevada. It was in the same building as Kate and Russell Lord, the friends who'd introduced him to Jim Thurber, a six-story stucco building one block from Washington Square Park at 16 East Eighth Street. The apartment on the third floor had lots of windows, a kitchenette, a wood-burning fireplace, and a living room spacious enough for a sofa bed for the children's visits, but she needed to have her own double bed cut down to three-fourths size. She was meticulous about taking only her own ancestral furniture from the Upper East Side brownstone, leaving behind everything that she and Ernest owned together. She found space for the Steinway baby grand piano that she had proudly purchased just a few years earlier with her first earnings from *The New Yorker*, and she took the tambour desk that her Sergeant aunts had given her when she got married. It was a cheerful apartment, and she outfitted it to be comfortable for her new three-person family as well as for occasional dinner parties. She would soon learn that her rear windows looked down on the garden of Sherwood Anderson's apartment in the Washington Mews (his wife had obtained a Reno divorce from him in 1924).

She still used the Snedens Landing house, and it was here that she spent a rare day alone with Roger at the tail end of August, before Nancy returned from her summer with the Sergeants. They walked down the woodland path to the waterfall that made a deep pool a few yards away from the Hudson River. It was where Roger had learned to swim, where Ernest would do his daredevil dive, and Katharine knew Roger particularly loved that spot. On the way home, Katharine pulled him over to the steps of an empty house, and there, nestled into the overgrown lawn, she told him about the divorce. He would not remember the weeks she had lived in Snedens Landing or the months she had lived in Nevada, because it was common for him to spend extended time away from his parents, but he would viscerally remember his devastation at hearing she wouldn't be coming back to the home at East Ninety-Third Street. Katharine explained what she and Ernest had agreed after the divorce was granted: Nancy and Roger would live with Ernest during the week and continue to attend the Lincoln School. On weekends, they would travel down to Katharine's apartment in Greenwich Village. Katharine got a fast start on her new life by establishing the children's weekly routine, hiring a part-time housekeeper named Josephine Buffa, and hosting a dinner one night with Harold Ross when Janet Flanner was in town from Paris.

Inevitably she and Andy began to talk seriously of marriage. It was a time of "many a tedious discussion," in Andy's words, and it carried on into the early autumn, through Black Tuesday, and into the colder months. The divorce hadn't changed any of the reasons for or against marriage. Andy had by now moved to 23 West Twelfth Street, just four blocks in a straight line north of Katharine's apartment. Their debate was "like a floating poker game," Andy recalled, "moved from place to place and went on at all hours of the day and night." Very early on an unremarkable Wednesday morning in November, they found themselves at Katharine's apartment, "with pros and cons flying around the room like saucers." Suddenly, Andy resolved to marry her, and just as suddenly, Katharine agreed. "We spent the rest of the day getting married—no mean feat."

First they made phone calls: Katharine had a man coming over for dinner that night, but it was hardly a date; it was a work dinner with the openly gay John Mosher. Katharine canceled the plans and called her housekeeper to tell her she needn't cook for two. Next, they packed Daisy into the car and set off on the world's least-romantic set of errands: to the Guaranty Trust for Katharine's divorce papers, to the city license bureau for a marriage license, and to a truly dispiriting jewelry store on Sixth Avenue where the rings were so ugly they forewent them altogether. They ate lunch at a speakeasy, Louis & Martin's, where they bumped into Emily Hahn, who was in a rotten mood because she had just been stood up. They drove to Bedford Village, where they failed to raise a justice of the peace. So they stopped in at the Bedford Presbyterian Church on the village green, an imposing white Gothic Revival church, where they met Reverend A. F. Fulton. It appeared that their matrimony was nigh, but then Daisy got into a fight with Reverend Fulton's police dog. They put their wedding on hold long enough to shut the dogs up in the reverend's house and then walked back to the church, where at last they were married, amid the flowers left over from a funeral the previous Sunday.

They drove back to Greenwich Village and had supper in the back room at Marta's, an Italian restaurant, and the very next day Katharine was back at work, dispatching rejection letters. "By the way," she wrote to Gilbert Seldes, "you will see my signature is different which is because I was married to E. B. White not very long ago. Mr. Ross seems to insist that I change my name for office purposes, which is a bit confusing." But more typically she simply signed the next round of letters "K. S. White (former K. S. Angell)" and let her correspondents draw their own conclusions. One of them would write, "I don't know whether one congratulates a lady on changing her married name or not, but whatever is the friendly and well wishing thing to say, that's what I am saying."

Katharine hadn't relinquished Ernest's name after her divorce and she seems never to have entertained the idea of reverting to Katharine Sergeant—no Lucy Stoner she.

So much of Katharine's life that year had been out of her control, and the next few days proved no different. She was likely planning to tell her children about her elopement when she saw them that weekend, but before she could do so, Walter Winchell broke the story in his gossip column in the *New York Daily Mirror* and Ernest's sister, Hildegarde, read it and told Nancy, who would for the rest of her life say that she learned of her new stepfather from the newspapers—another strike against Katharine.

Winchell scored cleverness points by posing Andy's marriage as a resounding answer to the question of his and Thurber's just-published book, *Is Sex Necessary? Or, Why You Feel the Way You Do*, which came out just ten days before his elopement.

Thurber and Andy had hatched the book back in the spring, when they and Katharine were relishing their singlehood together. It didn't escape any of them how extraordinary it was that three people, two of whom were getting divorced and two of whom were falling in love, would collaborate so productively at this intense moment in each of their lives. Writing and sex perfectly collided. Katharine's friend Eugene Saxton, now Andy's editor, acquired the book immediately, though he was dubious at first about Thurber's drawings, which Andy had painstakingly retraced with India ink. The mock sexology book had the bad luck to come out just as the stock market tanked, but it still found a robust audience for its gentle derision of modern courtship rituals. (Andy on writing a letter to one's beloved: "Now, you have written the words 'Anne darling' and have put a punctuation mark there. You pause for just a second, and in that second you are lost. 'Darling?' you say to yourself. 'Darling? Is she my darling, or isn't she? And if she *is* my darling, as I have so brazenly set down on this sheet of paper, what caused me to take such a long, critical look at the girl in the red-and-brown scarf this morning when I was breakfasting in the Brevoort? If I can be all aglow about a girl in a red-and-brown scarf in the early morning, is Anne my darling, or am I just kidding myself?'") The book hit the bestseller list, selling out its initial print run of twenty-five hundred, and the publisher reprinted it twenty-five more times for a total of forty thousand copies sold in its first year. *Is Sex Necessary?* launched Thurber's second career as a cartoonist, and he was well aware of how much he owed to Katharine and Andy for this.

Viewed one way, Katharine's decision to marry Andy was scandalous, reckless, perhaps selfish, maybe a little risible. Viewed another way, her decision was conservative and conventional. In the wake of betrayal and disillusionment at the hands of her first husband, she chose stability and a second chance at a warm, stable, emotionally rich home life. She knew that marriage with Andy would provide no barriers to her professional life. She also likely knew that he would depend on her far more than Ernest ever had. She chose to give up her short stint as a single woman in favor of this mutual support. She also gave up some defining interests of her teens and twenties that she'd taken up in part because of her love for Ernest, including camping and canoeing, and activism for liberal social causes. Now she'd turn inward, toward making a new home with her funny, sensitive, shy husband.

Andy gave Katharine time to acclimate her children to the idea of him, so it wasn't until two weekends after they were married that he moved into Katharine and Daisy's sunny Greenwich Village apartment at East Eighth Street. The new couple lived close to Thurber, the Lords, and Thurber's friends Robert Coates—who would soon become one of Katharine's treasured authors—and his wife, Elsa. They bought a Ping-Pong table. They restored Katharine's bed to full size.

Part IV

Editing a Literary Powerhouse

(1930–1938)

21.

Here was this very beautiful, rather stout, long-haired woman (hair in a huge bun in back) with a sort of diffident, wry way of talking.
—Nancy Hale

Don't shoot till you see the Whites of The New Yorker.
—John O'Hara

Getting married did not end Andy's agony over deciding to get married. He wasn't at all sure how to integrate himself into Katharine's life. Just a few weeks after their elopement, he sat down on a Saturday night and wrote to her. "I've had moments of despair during the last week which have added years to my life and put many new thoughts in my head." Not the most amorous way to address his bride. "This marriage is a terrible challenge," he wrote, pointing bitterly to all the people who wished the Whites well "with their tongues in their cheeks." He alluded to troubles between him and Nancy: "That I could assimilate Nancy overnight is obviously out of the question—or that she could me." He did not find it as easy to connect with an adolescent girl as he did with a young boy—not to mention that Ernest wrote the new couple long letters in which he prohibited Andy from being with Nancy unless Katharine was present, and though Nancy was too young to know this, she certainly heard her father's many bitter words about her new stepfather. But Andy wanted to tell Katharine that his thoughts always "ended on a cheerful note of hope, based on the realization that you are the person to whom

I return." His love hit him especially strongly one day when he walked into her office at work and there she was, "real and incontrovertible"— Katharine in her element. "Being with you is like walking on a very clear morning—definitely the sensation of belonging there."

That same month, he found another way to express the idea of Katharine as home.

> Natural History
> The spider, dropping down from twig,
> Unwinds a thread of his devising:
> A thin, premeditated rig
> To use in rising.
>
> And all the journey down through space,
> In cool descent, and loyal-hearted,
> She builds a ladder to the place
> From which she started.
>
> Thus I, gone forth, as spiders do,
> In spider's web a truth discerning,
> Attach one silken strand to you
> For my returning.

Despite Andy's resolve that their families "had probably best be kept in their respective places," the Whites braved the Newberrys' house in Boston for the holidays with Nancy and Roger. They returned to work, but only for a few months, and in March of 1930 they took a twelve-day trip to Bermuda for a delayed honeymoon. They stayed at Waterville, a grand home right on the water's edge built in 1725 by the Trimingham family and still run by Ada Trimingham as an exclusive guesthouse. Naturally it was a working holiday for at least one of them; Katharine romantically brought with her a sheaf of manuscripts by the crime writer Herbert Asbury.

In May, Katharine discovered she was pregnant. It was so soon, and presumably the couple hadn't solved all the "terrible challenges" of their marriage in the intervening five months. That the news was a surprise can perhaps be inferred from a letter Andy wrote to Katharine, a letter that on the surface evinces nothing but charm, unfolding as it does in the voice of Daisy the terrier: "White has been stewing around for two days now, a little bit worried because he is not sure that he has made you realize how glad he is that there is to be what the column writer in the Mirror calls a blessed event." Andy had Daisy explain not only his joy but also the reason for his reticence: his "not wanting to appear ludicrous to a veteran mother." Well, no, in truth it was more than that. Daisy went on to say, "I know White so well that I always know what is the matter with him, and it always comes to the same thing—he gets thinking that nothing that he writes or says ever quite expresses his feeling, and he worries about his articulateness just the same as he does about his bowels, except it is worse, and it makes him either mad, or sick, or with a prickly sensation in the head." So the upcoming blessed event, on some initial level, sent Andy right into his anxieties, which might not have been what Katharine was hoping to hear as she faced the expansion of her family. "Daisy" went on to reassure her that Andy loved her not only as "a future mother" but also as a "present person"—"Quite apart from this fertility, he admires you in all kinds of situations or dilemmas, some of which he says have been quite dirty."

This funny, formal device of ventriloquizing Daisy at once put distance between Andy and his feelings and revealed perhaps more than the writer realized. Katharine may have understood her new husband to be announcing a pattern: she would need to be strong and steady, the home to which he could always return, even when she was herself at the center of tumultuous events, such as adding a third child to a split household. Offering Katharine Andy's emotional support was not a task Daisy was particularly suited to perform. Instead, Andy asked from Katharine a kind of emotional acuity that was tied to his identity as a writer and hers as an editor: he asked her to read through his anxiety, inarticulateness, and silence to discover his true feelings buried underneath, the very interpretive work that she performed every day. Again in the fall, Andy used Daisy's voice to reassure his pregnant wife: "Don't let Mr. White's depression worry you, as it is my experience that usually it is his stomach, or what he wistfully refers to as his 'work.'"

Katharine was the rock not only for Andy, but for her writers and the staff of *The New Yorker*, as an awful incident proved just days after the Whites' return from Bermuda in March. Katharine's fellow editor, Wolcott Gibbs, had married his second wife, Elizabeth, the previous August, and they lived in one of the Tudor City apartment towers on Manhattan's east side, not far from *The New Yorker*. Elizabeth also worked at the magazine as a promotion writer; young and lively, she was well-liked around the office. One Saturday, the Gibbses went to see a play called *Death Takes a Holiday*, whose plot induced in Elizabeth a morbid fascination with the idea of jumping from a window to her death. Gibbs spent the weekend watching over her, staying up all night on Sunday and skipping meals. Both missed work on Monday. He brought his sister over for reinforcement, and they finally persuaded Elizabeth to take a sleeping pill and get some rest. After she fell asleep, Gibbs left the bedroom to get a bite to eat. When he checked up on her at lunchtime, her bed was empty. She had only pretended to sleep, so that she could slip into the bathroom, where she jumped out the seventeenth-story window. Gibbs looked down at her body on the sidewalk of the north court, where a crowd was gathering, and then he pulled his head back into the apartment, picked up the telephone, and called Katharine. "Could you come right over—Elizabeth has just killed herself!"

Katharine, who was eating lunch at her desk, put down the sandwich and hurried over, not knowing how the woman had died or what she would confront. She found a distraught Gibbs, repeating aloud, "I never should have left the room." As the police and detectives arrived, his mood worsened, and he began saying he would kill himself. Obviously he could never return to *The New Yorker* and taint the magazine with such bad publicity, he thought, so it was clear to him that his life was over. Katharine spent the entire day keeping the police at bay and persuading Gibbs to see a doctor; she only left when he was admitted to a hospital and sedated. Gibbs would soon return to work, where he would continue to be "professionally ambidextrous," as Andy called him, writing and editing in equal measure. He would move in with his younger sister, Angelica, who would also write for *The New Yorker*. He would meet Katharine's author Nancy Hale, and the two of them would have an affair, until John O'Hara introduced Gibbs to his third wife. His best years were yet to come.

Of course Katharine was the one whom Gibbs called. No one seemed to wonder if the woman on whom they all depended ever needed a bit of help herself. That summer, Katharine took Nancy and Roger upstate to Bedford. She and Ernest had continued their unconventional custody agreement, which meant that in the summers each had the children for a month. Ernest had given up the Snedens Landing rental, unable to afford it, and instead he would pile Roger and Nancy in the car and take them on adventurous trips: a Montana ranch; a boat ride down the Laguna de Tamiahua near Tampico in Mexico, where his sister, Hildegarde, lived with her husband; a Missouri cattle farm; and Chocorua, naturally. He even took them out to New Mexico to visit Elsie in Tesuque, their relationship having persisted after her break with Sidney Howard and his divorce from Katharine.

By contrast, Katharine stuck much closer to home for her summers with the children, opting for a version of domestic life transposed to a rental property. While Andy went to Camp Otter in Ontario, bringing Thurber with him, Katharine stayed in a cottage on the historic Palmer-Lewis estate in Bedford, New York, where she oversaw a crowded household; Andy's letters from Ontario sign off with love to "[Katharine], Serena [the unborn baby], Daisy, Roger, Nancy, Josephine [their cook], Willy [Josephine's son], Miss Heyl [a governess], [Katharine's] father, and the two cats. Or is it eleven cats?" Katharine always needed to work during her vacations, and that particular summer she told a friend, "I am standing on my ear trying to get Nancy off to school"—Nancy was transferring from Lincoln School to Concord Academy, a boarding school in Massachusetts. And it was Katharine who took care of Andy when he was hospitalized for two weeks with paratyphoid that autumn. But Ernest, for one, had little sympathy for Katharine's overcrowded lifestyle and thought that her Bedford summers were detrimental to Roger and Nancy. They were, he noted to his sister, "left 4 days a week to their own devices with only the cook and the nurse to look after them," to him a clear demotion of the children's interests in the face of Katharine's career despite "all the talk K puts up about making everything right for them." Ernest had initially given Katharine money for her to take the children to Bedford, a favor she requested of him despite asking for no alimony, but now that she had remarried, she took over the expense herself—which she felt insulated her from his criticism. But it left him "disgusted by all the cant and usual complacency."

Soon it was Katharine's turn for a stay in a hospital. On December 21, 1930, she went into labor and Andy took her to Harbor Hospital at Sixtieth and Madison. But the birth became complicated, and her doctors determined that she would need a Caesarean section, and soon after that, Joel McCoun White was born, hale and healthy. But Katharine was in danger and needed a blood transfusion—Andy later remembered that the doctors and nurses thought she might die. In his telling, a taxi driver was hailed and he agreed to donate the blood that Katharine needed. She lay there, weak in her bed, only rousing when a well-intentioned nurse whispered, "Do you want to say a little prayer, dearie?" "Certainly not," she answered.

The next few days brought the biggest snowfall of the year and a white Christmas to New Yorkers, but it was a tense one for the Whites. Katharine and Joel remained in room 823 of the hospital through the holidays while Katharine recuperated. Ernest brought Roger and Nancy to meet their new half brother on Christmas Day (after which the children traveled up to Boston to be with their aunt Rosamond for a week). On the momentous occasion of the New Year, Andy once again ventriloquized a letter from Daisy to Joel, a rambling and slightly intoxicated six-pager, concluding it just as the bells rang for 1931. "White tells me you are already drinking milk diluted with tears," he begins, "so I take it life is real enough for you, tears being a distillation of all melancholy vapors rising from the human heart."

On January 7, Katharine and Joe—as he was already being called—came home to the Greenwich Village apartment. But just a few days later, Katharine was back in a different hospital, this time with a kidney infection that pinned her in bed. Joe stayed home in Andy's care, and for a few weeks Andy was, as he put it, "in complete charge of his life and character." He'd recently acquired a 16 mm movie camera, and he took long and boring films of the baby being bathed by his nurse, drinking a bottle fed by his nurse, lavishly spitting up all over his nurse's white starched uniform. Katharine, meanwhile, recovered slowly in the hospital with a low fever, "feeling defeated, whipped, and mad," in Andy's words.

So the year, and the all-too-swift newborn days of Joe's life, did not start well for Katharine. She eased back into her job that February—nudging Janet Flanner for her profile of Coco Chanel, critiquing Lois Long's fashion column for Ross's eyes only—and returned to full-time work in the beginning of March, but even then, the year did not improve. She took the three children to Bedford Village for Nancy and Roger's weeklong Easter break at the end of March, but she was unable to bring them to *New Yorker* author Bessie Breuer's Easter party as planned, because she was again bedridden, this time with an infected antrum that laid her low for two weeks. When summer arrived, she and the children spent most of June in Bedford. Then she returned to New York for a week to helm the magazine while Ross was away, before she and Andy spent July and August on their usual working vacation.

Katharine was struggling, but the main source of stress was largely hidden from those around her. Relations with Ernest were as fraught as ever, and whatever goodwill had powered them through the crafting of their flexible child custody agreement was now rapidly dissipating in the enactment of that agreement. Everything was up for renegotiation, and though not much changed in the children's lives, behind the scenes each parent pulled on the other to get more time, more concessions. Katharine tried to get Nancy and Roger for all of Christmas Day, but Ernest defended his right to have them in the morning; Ernest tried to pare Roger's summers with the Whites down to two weekends a month, but Katharine refused. Ernest's distrust of Andy persisted and grew. Not only did he not want Nancy to be alone with him, he now wanted to wrest Roger away. "I intend to have a talk with White," he wrote to his sister, "about the part he seems to be starting to play, by taking Roger around to the theater and the like. That's just more than I intend to stand from the little blighter."

Animosity roiled between Katharine and Ernest on one particular subject that year: Roger's education. Katharine wanted him to begin boarding school; Ernest thought that would be a grave mistake, that Roger was too young and needed *more* parental involvement in the wake of the divorce, not less. In March, just after Katharine returned to work, she agreed to meet Ernest to discuss the issue in the lobby of the Commodore Hotel. The meeting proceeded miserably: Katharine nearly broke down; Ernest nearly lost his temper; she called him the next day to apologize. Ernest told his sister Hildegarde, "You can't cooperate with a person whom you cannot basically trust because they don't keep to engagements, forget them, distort them; because she won't answer letters on any subject that is at all unpleasant to her; because it is just too saddening for me to have to see her at all." Katharine would not have recognized herself in such a description, she who assiduously answered every letter that crossed her desk, but if it was true, it demonstrated what effect high emotion could have on her otherwise straightforward work ethic. Ernest was ready to have "an open fight, arbitration," if necessary. He spoke darkly of "a definite break."

The next month, their mutual friend from Chocorua, Stuart Chase, had lunch with Katharine and then dinner with Ernest, and was able to broker a peace between them. Roger would not change schools; he would stay at Lincoln School. Ernest had the idea to hire a college student as a companion for him and he sent an ad to the student affairs office at Columbia University. Soon, Arthur "Tex" Goldschmidt, a junior at Columbia, was spending five evenings a week with Roger, and they got along so well that Ernest invited him to give up his college accommodations and live in Nancy's old room in the town house on East Ninety-Third Street, where he was included in parties and holidays. Ernest was an engaged and concerned parent, the one to sign his kids' report cards each quarter and save them in boxes until the day he died. He worried about his children's emotional needs and how fit he was as a single man to fulfill them. He gave a dance for Nancy when he was concerned that her social circle was too constrained, and he bragged about her good grades. Roger, to him, was more naturally curious and brilliant but almost entirely lacking in discipline, and he used their summer outings to tame and funnel Roger's creative energy. His letters to his sister overflowed with worry about and pride in his children, and most letters also contained a line about how "any active cooperation with Katrina [was] apparently impossible"—worry and pride in Nancy and Roger was not something they could share across the taut line of their continual arguments.

Katharine had no one to help her navigate these post-divorce tensions. Her poor health was plain to anyone, but even Elsie, who continued to correspond with Ernest, chalked it up to "the whole New Yorker atmosphere" and thought she should go away for a year. Katharine couldn't lean too heavily on Andy, because his own mental and physical health was so precarious.

Andy especially needed rest that summer of 1931, Katharine wrote to Ross, saying, "He's been half sick this month with some obscure thing that has given him a queer blood pressure." They decided to try Maine—their first time there as a couple—and landed in Blue Hill on the recommendation of a friend, renting a stone cottage owned by the wealthy Miss Nila Slaven. Blue Hill was a town invaded each summer by the "rusticators," people exactly like the Whites who came for long summers to balance the frenetic lives they led in the city. The Whites' cottage, though, was just a bit removed from the main summer scene because it lay outside the town by an old stone pier built to export the area's native granite to the Panama Canal. The location served them well. "Did we like Blue Hill? I should say we did and we weren't a bit snappy, as we were in East Blue Hill—not a cocktail or a Chriscraft [sic] in sight," Katharine wrote to her author Donald Moffat. "Most of the time we lived on a very rickety sloop among the seals and rocks." Louise Bogan and Raymond Holden visited the Whites, the first of several Maine visits between the two families.

The Whites returned to New York, but not to their Greenwich Village apartment; they rented a place in Bedford for three weeks while construction workers poked a hole in their apartment ceiling and built a staircase to the apartment above to accommodate their growing family, doubling their rooms from three to six. No sooner had they moved back in than Katharine was called away yet again, this time to Vermont, where Roger had been stricken by pneumonia. He and Ernest were visiting the family of Ellsworth Bunker, later the ambassador to Vietnam, at his lively farm in Dummerston, when Roger became sick enough that he couldn't be moved. Ernest returned to New York for work and Katharine rushed north to take his place. Her absence meant that she missed out on Joe's newest trick, and she learned of it in a letter from Andy: "He feeds crackers to Daisy—chuckling softly to himself."

A trick, however, not to be elaborated upon. The day after Joe's first birthday, Mrs. Lardner, the cook, was walking Daisy along University Place when a taxi popped over the rain-slicked curb and hit them both. Daisy was killed and Mrs. Lardner was sent to the hospital. Daisy, by then well-known to *New Yorker* readers, received a loving obituary on page 16 of the magazine: "Her life was full of incident but not of accomplishment . . . she suffered from a chronic perplexity. . . . She was arrested once, by Patrolman Porco. She enjoyed practically everything in life." Mrs. Lardner, who did not return to the Whites' employ, went un-remarked upon, at least publicly. Daisy, in a final letter to Katharine from beyond the grave on the Whites' fifth wedding anniversary several years later, called Mrs. Lardner "the old fool," and then proceeded to more important matters. Daisy informed Katharine that she was controlling from heaven their new dog Morris, a spaniel, saying, "His extreme excitation derives from a faint essence of me." No hearty congratulations from Andy on the big day of their anniversary, just a weary shaking of Daisy's head: "I don't see how you stand Joe and Morris in the mornings—no tranquility, nothing but mussed-up comforters and dragged-out shoes, and White sleeping alone in that study with his bowels."

22.

If there was anything to salvage from this interrupted year, it was the knowledge that Katharine was there to stay at *The New Yorker*. Certainly if Ross had wanted to fire a female employee for the prejudicial reason of being too hampered by family or too female, Katharine had just given him a dozen pretexts. And if Katharine herself still daydreamed about quitting or reducing her hours to part-time, both ideas that she had entertained in Reno, the events of this year had just given her a powerful incentive. But she stayed. She worked from home, from hospitals, and from vacation cottages. When she could do little else, not even care for her baby, she could write to authors and edit their manuscripts.

In fact, 1931 was the year that Katharine ushered into the magazine two women who would have enormous impacts on *New Yorker* fiction: Nancy Hale and Kay Boyle. Hale was a young staff writer who had worked at *Vogue* since 1929 and was just that year beginning to publish short stories in *Scribner's Magazine* and *Vanity Fair*. She sent Katharine a story called "Club Car," and they met for lunch at the Algonquin to discuss it. The *Vogue* staffer was surprised to meet "the sort of person that [she] was familiar with but not in New York; not, for instance, fashionably dressed to any extent that you would notice it." In fact, the reason Katharine was so recognizable to Hale was that their biographies so perfectly mirrored each other. Hale, a decade younger, had grown up too in the suburbs of Boston (the descendant of a famous family that included the Revolutionary War spy Nathan Hale, writer and minister Edward Everett Hale, and writer Lucretia Hale) and attended Miss Winsor's School. Hale and Katharine bonded immediately over their similar childhoods, from their Irish maids to the groceries their parents ordered from S. S. Pierce and the tea dances they attended at Copley Plaza. This made Katharine well positioned to acquire Hale's stories of young women at the boundaries of what was acceptable for their gender, and "Club Car," a story of a woman braving the all-male car on the train to Boston and suffering the implication that she was "a bold adventuress," "bent on seduction," ran in December of 1931. But it wouldn't be until later in the decade, when Hale's own life grew both more entangled and more embedded in her fiction, that she and Katharine would draw tighter together.

Kay Boyle was in 1931 a relatively unknown American expatriate writer in France, author of two story collections and a novel. William Carlos Williams reviewed one of her collections in *transition*, an experimental literary journal published in Paris. Praising her ability to make language new, Williams wrote, "In the United States let us first say Emily Dickinson and then Kay Boyle." But he predicted that Americans would have no use for her work, as she was a modernist, an experimentalist, and a woman. Boyle was going to try. Her friend Bessie Breuer, whom she'd encouraged to start writing in the 1920s, had been publishing in *The New Yorker*, in part because Breuer was a friend of Katharine's sister Elsie. Conveyed along this female network, Boyle submitted "Kroy Wen" in May and Katharine instantly bought it for $200 and published it in July with almost no edits.

"Kroy Wen" represented the perfect intersection of Katharine's tastes, *The New Yorker*'s limitations, and Boyle's modernism. It begins with glances: an Italian couple on a ship peers up at a man on the top deck. "Thoughts and menaces passed through their heads like a passing breeze, or like a feather blowing, and they never thought of any one thing for a very long time." The man peers down at them, and we realize it is his thoughts about the Italians' passing thoughts that we've been hearing. The man is a film director, on his way to Italy to escape "art and humanity" and to soothe his nervous habit of reading words backward, like the name of the steamer: *Kroy Wen*. But the sight of the Italian woman, knitting something in red, perhaps a hood for the baby she is expecting any minute, rouses something in him. "'There's color!' he said. 'I needed a few yards of a pregnant woman. God, what atmosphere!'" He rushes down to steerage, because despite his commitment to the rest cure, "art and humanity pursued him, got him by the eyes and the ears and made him act." He persuades the couple to let him film them, but he needles them to look more anguished. "'She's got to register something,' he said. 'I'm taking a woman in childbirth, you see. She can't just sit there kind of mooning and dozing along.'" But the woman cannot give him the gestures he requires, because she is in labor, something the director does not see or register. "'Maybe it hurts her,' said the Italian. He didn't know what to do." And the story ends.

But it reflected a pattern of literary preferences so marked as to eventually become a formula. The interaction between two characters, both under emotional duress, is bright and intense, as high-contrast as the sun on the steamer deck, eventful but entirely without the traditional plot elements of rising action and resolution—a single moment or mood precisely described. The story is often conveyed at a remove. Sometimes, events are seen through a child's perspective, a child who registers the actions, gestures, and glances without understanding them; other times, that remove is achieved by the narrator's irony. The reader is not meant to identify with the protagonist, to feel at each moment what he or she is feeling. The protagonist's emotions are held up for scrutiny, for criticism. Katharine began curating stories that were congruent with modernism's focus on slices of life while still satisfying Ross's criterion of utter clarity. She was forever hunting for concentrated, distilled life, told in distinctive language.

"Kroy Wen" was the first story Boyle placed in a mainstream American magazine, and it unhooked something inside her. She began writing at a furious pace, sometimes two stories in two days, and she submitted many—but not all—to *The New Yorker*, with mixed results. Katharine unfailingly admired Boyle's writing but found herself turning away stories she liked. She rejected "I Can't Get Drunk" because the "wet" story happened to be "the most persistent theme in [their] manuscripts at the moment," and she refused "To the Pure" for its treatment of male homosexuality, a theme they'd "rather not touch." All of these rejected stories found homes in places like *Vanity Fair* and *Harper's*; all of them found their way into Boyle's story collections. Katharine dearly wanted Boyle's work in *The New Yorker*, and so in order not to lose her to the competition, she would stretch her own editorial limits to meet the writer's needs.

One instance—and there would be more—came in 1933, when Katharine campaigned for Boyle's story "White as Snow," which was about twice as long as the average *New Yorker* story and not only traded in ambiguities but positively relished them. A child tells the story of the summer that her nurse Carrie accompanies the family to the shore for the first time; Carrie, who "would be twenty in a few years," is "coloured sweet and even like sarsaparilla, and she ha[s] never before been near the sea." Carrie becomes fascinated with another teenager, Adamic, a white tennis player of few words. One day Carrie tells the children that Adamic will accompany them to the movies, but once they reach the lobby, he reddens and tells them that there aren't enough seats together, then he quickly flees the scene, with the man in the ticket window shaking his head at him as he retreats. Carrie attempts to laugh it off, but when she takes the children back to their hotel room, she lies down in the dark and won't get up, saying to them, "I'll never tell you what it was. You're too young to know." It is a story precisely about not knowing. Does Carrie, who powders her face and remarks frequently on her sunburn, pass as white, in a story where characters are forever "passing" one another in corridors and along boardwalks, a word that crops up too often to be accidental? Does Adamic believe her to be white, or know that she is Black but accept that she is presenting herself as white? Do either of them believe they are taking a risk by being seen together, or do they believe they are safe until the man in the ticket window indicates otherwise?

Katharine and Ross agreed that two questions needed clarification: Adamic's age, and the point at which he knew Carrie to be Black. Boyle added three paragraphs of dialogue to let a bit of information trickle to the reader through the filter of the child narrator: Adamic was well aware of Carrie's complicated strategy of self-presentation and colluded with it until the ticket-taker made that impossible. (Neither editor particularly wondered about Carrie; it was the white character's perceptions that mattered most.) The story ran its full length in the summer of 1933, and both Katharine and Ross told Boyle how proud they were of it. When Boyle later included "White as Snow" in her collection *The White*

Horses of Vienna, she retracted some small words of clarification that the magazine had added but kept the three additional paragraphs.

"White as Snow" demonstrates that in the early 1930s a risk-taking, stylistically challenging author like Boyle valued publication in *The New Yorker*, that the magazine was not considered too slight or too philistine for an ambitious writer in Gertrude Stein's Paris. This was also the moment when more and more writers signed with literary agents, who then educated their clients about the periodicals market and helped them write toward what they perceived as its needs. Katharine rejected reams of agented stories, and the many missed arrows show how desirable *The New Yorker* had become as a showcase for writers. Even Vita Sackville-West tried to supplant Rebecca West as writer of the London Letter, but Katharine said no and cultivated Mollie Panter-Downes instead. William Saroyan, Conrad Aiken's young friend Malcolm Lowry, Nathanael West just after he published *Miss Lonelyhearts*—all tried and failed to break into *The New Yorker*. The prolific John Fante sent dozens of stories to Katharine but she sent them right back, contributing in her own small, unwitting way to Fante's alter ego, Arturo Bandini, the folk bard of unsuccessful writers in *Ask the Dust* and the other books in the Bandini Quartet. *The New Yorker* never paid well, so the writers weren't in it for the money—they wanted the readership.

But a large readership presented its own new challenges. Early in the decade, editors heard the first grumblings about their particular brand of popular yet discerning taste. For instance, Alexander Woollcott reviewed Wyndham Lewis's biography of Louis XI, *King Spider*, in his Shouts and Murmurs column. Lewis was a valued contributor, but Katharine had no trouble signing off on Woollcott's contemptuous dismissal of the book because everyone knew that Woollcott spoke only for himself; independence was a necessary condition for the magazine's columnists. But Lewis himself objected in unexpected terms to Woollcott's dismissal of Lewis's Catholicism. "When one lightly scratches the sophisticate, the cosmopolite, and the suave," he wrote, "one finds the suburban." Then he repeated the slur, saying it was "terribly suburban to be unaware" of the influence of the Catholic Church on contemporary life, something that "much smarter moderns than [Lewis]" well knew. Katharine spent the next two months mollifying Lewis's feelings and begging him for manuscripts until finally they agreed "that all [was] forgiven and forgotten." But why was "suburban" the epithet that Lewis reached for in his confrontation with bigotry? Why was "suburban" the very antithesis of "modern"?

In October of 1929, the month before Katharine and Andy got married and—perhaps more saliently—the month of the stock market crash, *The New Yorker* expanded into two editions. To the regular city edition, with ads that were specific to New York, they added a national edition, which included most of each week's content but with advertisements for products with countrywide distribution. *The New Yorker* had become suburban. As a business strategy, the dual editions flourished in wildly improbable circumstances. While the country plummeted into the Depression, *The New Yorker* ascended, which, combined with its commitment to avoiding politics, perhaps contributed to its oft-noted indifference to the suffering of the era. Circulation reached over one hundred thousand copies for the first time in 1930, and throughout the decade, circulation, advertising revenue, and after-tax profit rose steadily (with a slight dip in 1932), including 50 percent increases in 1934 over the 1929 figures. Editorially, the dual versions meant that the magazine had somewhat diversified its readership and increased the necessity to publish stories and poems with broad appeal. Again and again through the early 1930s, Katharine found herself asking contributors—especially poets—to simplify their language to allow more readers in.

In 1932, she accepted the first poem from Pulitzer Prize winner Conrad Aiken, who had been sprinkling his "Prelude" verses among periodicals like *The Dial* and *Poetry* as well as *The Saturday Review of Literature* and *The New Republic*. He would publish six poems in *The New Yorker* that year, all of which would later be collected in *Time in the Rock*. It was perhaps the height of Aiken's career, though also a terribly turbulent year in his own life during which he tried to commit suicide. He would continue his association with *The New Yorker* for the rest of the decade, and soon he would take over the London Letter from Rebecca West (after Orson Welles unsuccessfully petitioned for the job), writing under the pseudonym Samuel Jeake Jr. His *New Yorker* "Prelude"s are plainspoken but without easy rewards. In one, the speaker apostrophizes to his "woman" about the very fact that they "do not hear each other," and in another he exhorts a reader to "put a mark down in a book" but adds, "The sum of all your notes is nothing. / Make a rich note of this. And start again." In response to Katharine's inevitable request for clarity, Aiken "lavishly" punctuated his "Prelude"s, but he took the opportunity to preserve for the future his right to stay obscure. "One can never, perhaps, in this kind of symbolic-metaphysical poetry, present a meaning which is rationally analyzable and nothing else," he wrote; "the effect aimed at is a kind of <u>prism</u> of meanings, in which the rational is only a part. Such a poem, if successful, is better, and less understandable, than its obvious meaning: which is to say that it can't be translated, without loss, into plain prose statement."

Aiken merely echoed Kay Boyle, who told Katharine that she "was not attempting to give any feeling of exactitude or truth" in her stories. Exactitude was prized elsewhere in the magazine, of course. None other than Albert Einstein wrote in to comment on a profile of him that Alva Johnston had written and Katharine had edited: "I was extremely surprised not only by the complete accuracy of your information, but particularly by the unusual psychological insight which you show in the articles." But was *The New Yorker*'s famous commitment to fact beginning to limit its literary offerings? Did *New Yorker* readers live, even in their imaginations, only in the material world where meaning was tactile and easily consumed? Katharine entirely agreed with Aiken; his letter, she told him, "ought to serve as a model to literal editors as an interpretation of what the poet is trying to do after all."

But to another poet, William Rose Benét, she wrote, "It is a poem that we like in many ways, but it seems too difficult to follow for our purposes. We do want serious poetry, but we also try to avoid obscurity if we can since we haven't too high an opinion of our readers' intelligence." She often conveyed this not-too-high opinion to her writers, and for an editorial persona of unflappable respect and encouragement, this represented a small crack in the façade, a moment of collusion with writers over the heads of readers, a shared instance of sophistication to soften the blow of a rejection. Whether or not Katharine truly believed the magazine's readership was limited in its appreciation of literature, she most certainly wanted her writers to understand rejection the way she did, as a shaping tool for the overall tone of the magazine, not as an indictment of a given piece or its author.

The tail end of 1932 brought what Katharine would describe as a "red letter event" at the office: the submission of a casual, "Father and the French Court," by Clarence Day, a slight, funny piece about his father's distress when his mother signs up for an expensive book subscription. Day had published a long story about his family in two installments in *Harper's* earlier that year, but it was Ross who saw the potential for turning the story into a series, and it was Katharine who cracked the code that turned Day into a *New Yorker* mainstay. He wrote to her when she accepted his second story, just two weeks after the first, "Somehow your idea about tying these pieces together by having 'Father' in each of the titles, has opened this vein up a lot." He would write story after story, portraying not only his beloved but fallible father, a prosperous stockbroker trying to hold on to Victorian propriety against a rapidly modernizing world, but also the 1890s Manhattan of his boyhood. Katharine and Day, as well as Andy and Day's wife, Peggy, would soon grow very close, and Day's "Father" series would spawn others that would equally come to define *The New Yorker* in the thirties as a reliable source of humor, reminiscence, character studies, and oddity.

So the magazine was thriving, but the same could not entirely be said for Andy. To any observer he looked busy enough. In February of 1932, he got himself assigned to cover the Olympics at Lake Placid. Katharine borrowed ski pants, leather gloves, and wool sweaters from Bessie Breuer, and off they went together. Andy would write in the resulting Reporter at Large piece, "It does something to a man's character to discover that he can still stand up on skis, just as it does something to a woman's character to wear pants and heavy boots and put her hands in her pockets." Katharine did more than stand around in her boots. Andy brought his movie camera. There, amid many, many clips of sled dogs, is a heavily bundled figure in a white knit hat who skis down a small slope and slides directly onto her bottom. She struggles to stand, and then to pole herself up, and when that doesn't work, she just hitches her poles under her arms and sits in the snow, waving them in a way that looks quite merry from behind. Andy filmed Katharine skiing with moderate proficiency, and then a clip of her sitting on a porch in white knit hat and fur coat, gazing out at something snowy and then turning to Andy and smiling in surprise at the camera.

Andy's Reporter at Large piece is largely about ski jumping, which he also extensively filmed before describing it in words. For him, the essence of the sport was best experienced beneath the takeoff point when a jumper launches himself: "As he passes in the air, [hear] the noise his pants make in the wind. That flutter has the sound of death in it—a kind of pr-r-t, pr-r-rt, growing sharper as he drops." The entire piece becomes an expression of Andy's worry for the jumpers' sanity. Roger would later describe Andy as "anxiety plus energy." This Reporter at Large piece reads more as an expression of its writer's psychology than a depiction of the athletes, the wins and losses, the records, the medals, the international relations of the Olympic events.

In fact, 1932 was the year of Andy's slimmest output. It proceeded much as the previous year had, with Notes and Comment every week, but far fewer Talk items or signed pieces. He kept busy with dogs and children. Katharine had continued to attend baseball games since her days in Boston, and now the Whites added hockey to the sports they regularly followed. As soon as Roger was old enough to stay up late, they inducted him into their sports fandom, bringing him two or three times a season to National Hockey League games and six-day bicycle races at the old Madison Square Garden. Roger distinctly felt these outings as a privilege, so different from what his friends were allowed to experience, which he attributed to his mother's newfound youthfulness and Andy's spirit of fun. It was Andy who set up the Ping-Pong table outside in the summer, Andy who organized a painting contest between Nancy, Roger, and Willy Buffa, the son of their cook (Willy won), Andy who took endless pictures and home movies of baby Joe. But he wasn't writing anything in particular.

This was, by contrast, the year that Katharine stepped up her literary output. In February, the same month as the Olympics, she joined her sister Elsie in a newly formed organization, the Prix Femina Américain, the American equivalent of the French organization in which female intellectuals awarded an annual prize for the best book; both male and female authors were eligible, though the prize was formed partly to compensate for the Goncourt, which was not open to women. The organizing committee, on which Katharine sat along with women such as Edna St. Vincent Millay and Dorothy Canfield Fisher, met monthly in the posh rooms of the Colony Club (Katharine said that the writers among them would have preferred her own arts-oriented Cosmopolitan Club). The committee eventually narrowed its selections down to three finalists, then awarded the prize to Willa Cather for *Shadows on the Rock*, what *The New York Times* described as "the most popular novel in America in 1931."

In many respects, Cather was the obvious choice among the finalists— the others were John Dos Passos for *1919* and Phil Strong for *State Fair*—and Elsie was pleased that her good friend was honored, calling her "one of our finest American talents" in an essay about the prize that she published in *The Bookman*. Katharine had edited and published an admiring profile of Cather when Princeton awarded the author an honorary doctorate. She had assigned the profile not to Elsie but to Louise Bogan, who praised Cather as a new kind of American writer who wrote not to "amuse or soothe an American business culture" but to describe a place and character with integrity, "put down almost without accent, keyed to the quietest level, denuded of everything but essentials." Thus Katharine played a small part in helping to canonize the works of this writer. The prize committee afforded Katharine something that *The New Yorker* did not: a chance to rise above the din and fray of publishing—all those endless envelopes containing manuscripts—and read with an eye toward posterity. She never aggrandized her job as a magazine editor; she knew it merely as the unceasing work of producing a weekly issue, not a way to nominate the best of the best.

That same year delivered a new task that brought her down from the literary empyrean and back into the fray. Because she was, as Ross put it, "a mother with children of an age that read books and opinions on the subject," she began an annual children's book review, timed for the holiday season. Suddenly, the two-story apartment in the Village was crammed with books from publishers clamoring for her attention. "Throw open the door of our kitchen cabinet," complained Andy, "out will fall *The Story of Tea*. Pick up a sofa cushion and there, mashed to a pulp, will be a definitive work on drums, tomtoms, and rattles."

Katharine received over two hundred books each season to review, but for that first review in December of 1932 she took on an even mightier task, surveying the seven thousand children's books published in the previous decade for trends. "With expensive paper, type, engraving, color printing, and a generally sophisticated and aesthetic presentation, the publishers have given their all for our pampered young." But the content rarely lived up to the presentation—an apt conclusion for a *New Yorker* editor to draw, given the magazine's refusal to print color photographs or art as a way to distinguish it from other merely clever publications like *Vanity Fair*. She discriminated between "important" books that you might give to please a child's parents, and the straightforward books that actual children would truly love, using as her yardstick the tastes of Joel and Roger. She noted, in a dry reference to Dorothy Parker's infamous review of *The House at Pooh Corner* ("Tonstant Weader Fwowed Up"), that A. A. Milne's verses are "less obnoxious to most children than to their elders." Some books could even please both constituencies, like the cat stories of Wanda Gág: "All my strictures on stylized illustrations succumb to her imagination and wit." Information books fared better under her scrutiny, but not by much. She concluded on a note of nostalgia, noting a few authors from her childhood who were still producing—Eliza Orne White and Laura E. Richards—and finishing pointedly, "And while I am remembering, is there a neglected child who hasn't yet read 'The Peterkin Papers'?" These salty essays, though they were couched as holiday gift guides, contained far too many negative evaluations to be entirely useful to the shopper. Katharine was writing criticism imperfectly disguised as recommendation, and perhaps seeking to nudge publishers, authors, and illustrators in the process.

Katharine seemed, momentarily, the more active of the literary pair. A rumor reached Bessie Breuer that Katharine was writing a book, and she begged for more details, eliciting from Katharine a denial so fierce as to almost sound offended: "I don't know what on earth you mean by my writing a book. Of course, I am not writing a book. Maybe the rumor was about a book that Harper's thinks they are making Mr. White write, but they may be fooled on that too." Breuer wasn't deterred. "I imagine in your job you could write a good funny and rather bitter book on the writing temperament . . . why don't you, anyhow?" The truth was that neither White was writing a book, and Katharine could hardly afford to tackle the subject Breuer suggested; it would be largely about not writing a book.

In the summer of 1933, the Whites again stayed in the Slaven cottage in Blue Hill, Maine, and they chartered a little sailboat named *Alastor*. There is a home movie from about this time that might take place on the *Alastor* and that shows what sailing with Katharine was like. By this time, she had started to grow weary of the movie camera, and she frowned or turned away whenever she noticed it pointed at her. So Andy was forever filming her surreptitiously, which was easy on the boat because there is an oblivious Katharine in glasses and white shorts and shirt, stretched along a bed in the cabin, thoroughly engrossed in the newspaper. The camera comes up behind her, and then sneaks around the other side to face her, panning up to books and magazines wedged in the shelf above her head.

One day, in Allen Cove, about ten miles to the south of Blue Hill, they noticed a traditional saltwater farm, one that stretched right down to the ocean, its farmhouse and barn high up on the hill above them. The next day, they saw the farmhouse from the other side as they drove past, and it had a real estate agent's sign out front.

What made the Whites buy the house in Maine, the farm that changed Andy's life and brought into focus a writing career that was as yet unimaginable in that summer in the midst of the Depression? Andy had no experience at farming. This was no summer cottage for rusticators but a complicated working farm, large but far from grand, and old in the sense of needing repairs rather than possessing pedigree. Andy described their

New Yorker income as placidly piling up in the bank, so they could easily afford the $11,000 purchase price ("when we decided to buy a house in Maine, there the money was"), despite the economic downturn and the expenses of household staff and medical bills and summer travel. They returned to their New York lives at the end of the summer, but Andy's mind was filled with plans for the property, including a long new dock, to get it ready for their sojourn in Maine the following summer.

23.

Oh dear, don't you know yet that we can't use pieces about writers and writing, and editors and all? We really have a strict ruling against this topic because if we didn't have we would have nothing else in the magazine.

K. S. White to Elspeth O'Halloran

There was no slow season at *The New Yorker*. Before Katharine left for Maine, she tabulated the volume of submissions to the magazine in the second half of May: 350 poems, 508 casuals and factual pieces, *each week*. And that was as slow as it got; the memo also listed the averages for each category during the winter months: 600 submissions a week in verse, and between 1,000 and 1,200 pieces a week in casuals and factuals. Still, though, a major portion of her job consisted of noticing which regular contributors had not submitted in a while and prodding them for masterpieces. This job was made more difficult by the 10 percent pay cut that the magazine leveled in 1933, after its profits were nearly halved from 1931 to 1932. Subscriptions had steadily increased every single year of *The New Yorker*'s existence, but the Depression was taking its toll on advertising revenue.

Then came an event of great literary importance: repeal. On December 5, 1933, the Twenty-First Amendment unzipped the Eighteenth Amendment, and Americans were legally free to drink again after thirteen thirsty years; more important, distillers, vintners, and brewers were legally free to advertise their wares (though a 1917 post office appropriations bill made it illegal for liquor advertising to appear in a newspaper or periodical that was sold in a dry state, so during the uneven interval when each state ratified the amendment, *The New Yorker* and other magazines published wet and dry editions, the latter with blank white spaces where the liquor ads should have been). Almost instantly the magazine's gross profits jumped by 17 percent, enabling editors to restore writers' pay rates and to grow the number of pages in the book. The editors—still Katharine, Gibbs, and Mosher on the fiction side, and a stormy succession of jesuses on the nonfiction side that included Stanley Walker, Bernard Bergman, and the future novelist James Cain—set about filling the new pages with new columns. The first was a column they'd run sporadically but had long wanted to feature regularly, Onward and Upward with the Arts, which they described as "reflective pieces of the essay type, written to one theme or another, which will be entertaining, possibly amusing, and perhaps making one or more Valuable Points." In case that didn't narrow it down enough, the letter continued, "Practically everything may be considered an art for the present purposes." Katharine was marginally more helpful in a letter to her friend Sherwood Anderson; the column, while sometimes offering serious criticism, would most often be used to satiric purpose, "to prove more often than not, that there has been <u>no</u> progress in the art in question."

Katharine, though, kept pushing the boundaries of *The New Yorker*, and, after much in-house discussion, she was finally empowered to commission Louise Bogan to write a biannual poetry review column. Though Bogan's husband, Raymond Holden, had been fired from *The New Yorker* like so many previous jesuses, the Whites still socialized with the couple—in part because Holden made the best bathtub gin in town—and Bogan often confided in Katharine. The editor knew that the five stories Bogan had published in the magazine in 1931 were the direct result of a nervous breakdown, and that the three autobiographical essays Bogan was just now publishing had been produced in the midst of another slow disintegration. Holden was unfaithful and sometimes violent, and Bogan was splintering under the pressure. When Katharine finally got Ross on board for the poetry review, she reached Bogan at the hospital in White Plains where she had checked herself in for a six-month stay. Katharine steadily wrote to Bogan and sent her books; she waited patiently for the writing that Bogan tried to do when she was not "walking or reading or bathing or weaving." They both understood that, as Bogan put it, "the real tragedy occurs when the drive that should go into creation becomes unhinged and spills over into personal relationships." Katharine's role, as she designed it on the fly, was to keep expecting that Bogan could write even amid her turmoil, to hold open the space for her words. It worked. Bogan's first regular column was published in April of 1934, and she left the hospital a few months later, strong enough to leave Holden. She would continue writing the poetry review twice a year for the next thirty-eight years (even when Conrad Aiken, who portrayed Bogan maliciously in his novel *Conversation*, tried to take it over). Bogan encouraged her poet friends to submit to *The New Yorker*, telling them not to "snoot" it in favor of more prestigious literary journals; after all, "they might give you a spread, with decorations," as she told Rolfe Humphries.

The New Yorker in 1934 was doing almost too well when other magazines were struggling (*Vanity Fair* would soon be folded into *Vogue*), and it began to suffer problems of abundance and success. What to do, for instance, with all the clever young writers from the college humor magazines coming to the magazine for jobs? "I wish we could start a kindergarten department, a room where we could put these kids to work to be given all kinds of odd jobs," Katharine wrote to Ross. "We have done nothing with the very young, and when the magazine was started and going well, most of us were in kindergarten too. Let's discuss at staff meeting what we should do about it."

But the bigger problem, the identity crisis that consumed much of Katharine and Ross's energies in the mid-1930s, was how to keep authors loyal to *The New Yorker*. She had been so assiduous in cultivating talent that now its artists and writers were valuable enough to swipe away with one big paycheck. The solution that Katharine devised would shape *The New Yorker* for decades to come.

It began when the artist Otto Soglow came into Katharine's office "looking as white as a sheet and saying something awful had happened to him": William Randolph Hearst had offered him a contract to run his *Little King* comics in the Sunday newspapers. Soglow was "very unhappy" about the lavish offer, which worked out to $19,500 a year, and Katharine was too. Soglow had been drawing for the magazine since a few months after it started, and *The New Yorker* had debuted *The Little King* in 1930. The title character was practically synonymous with the magazine, his puffed-up chest instantly recognizable as he cavorted like a child, doing everything but ruling his kingdom. Soglow, as Katharine reported to Ross, "hated to take the King out of the New Yorker, felt sentimental about it, wasn't sure he was doing the right thing for his own prestige, wanted to know how we felt"—but then there was all that money.

Katharine presented Ross with a bulleted plan to solve the problem. Soon *The New Yorker* had drawn up a contract, their first such document, which Soglow signed. *The New Yorker* agreed to buy at least forty of Soglow's drawings, plus pay a bonus of $2,000 for the fortieth. *The Little King* could only appear in other publications with the magazine's consent. Most important, the contract stated that Soglow would submit all his work "first to The New Yorker which shall have exclusive right to their first publication, but you are to have the right to sell elsewhere any of these drawings, with the exception of the Little King drawings, which The New Yorker may reject." The magazine gave Soglow $1,000 upon signing the agreement. As soon as his agreement expired in 1934, Soglow fulfilled everyone's expectations by defecting to Hearst.

It was hard to see him go. "I have been thinking about the list of artists and writers with whom I think we should make some sort of agreement in order to profit by the Soglow experience," Katharine wrote to Harold Ross and Raoul Fleischmann. Her lists are a synecdoche for the magazine in the 1930s. The artists were Peter Arno, James Thurber, Helen Hokinson, William Steig, William Galbraith Crawford, and Gluyas Williams—the most identifiably *New Yorker* artists. The writers they should "aim to hold to [*The New Yorker*] in some manner" were Alva Johnston, Frank Sullivan, James Thurber, Ogden Nash, Dorothy Parker, and Clarence Day, and of course White, Woollcott, Gibbs, and Benchley, but "White would never sign any contract." Others who should have at least verbal agreements to give the magazine first shot at their material included Frances Warfield, Sally Benson, Morley Callaghan, Kay Boyle, Richard Lockridge, Clifford Orr, and Theodore Pratt.

But Katharine could see that verbal agreements were not enough. Not long after they'd settled the Soglow affair, the experience repeated itself: Ogden Nash, *The New Yorker*'s prince of light verse, came to her office and confessed the doleful news that *The Saturday Evening Post* had just offered him a lucrative contract. Nash wanted to continue his relationship with *The New Yorker*, because "his first loyalty" was to the magazine, and he believed "his books [sold] only because his stuff [was] published first in the New Yorker"—but he needed the money. Katharine bumped his line rate up from $1.25 to $2.00 on the condition that he amend the *Post* contract to make sure he could show *The New Yorker* his verse first. Nash agreed, then promptly violated his agreement, thus inaugurating the Nash Hash of 1933–35.

Several Nash poems appeared in the *New York American*, a Hearst newspaper. Katharine instantly wrote to Nash's agent, Helen Everitt at Curtis Brown. She reminded Everitt that she was the one who had discovered Nash; when she accepted his poem "Invocation" in 1929, it was his first sale in three years. Only after finding him in *The New Yorker* did Simon & Schuster and Covici Friede approach him for poetry collections. They negotiated a bonus payment of fifty cents per line at the end of the year if they accepted twenty poems and if he'd give *The New Yorker* the right of first refusal on anything not already under contract.

But the matter was very far from over. That summer in Maine, Katharine paged through the competition, as had become her annual habit, and the September 1934 issue of *Life* brought her up short. She annotated her copy and sent it off with a furious memo to Ross and Fleischmann detailing all the ways it was an ersatz *New Yorker*, from the imitation Notes and Comment and a poorly executed profile of Hugh Johnson to the inevitable Soglow cartoon, and three other *New Yorker* contributors touted right there on the cover: S. J. Perelman, Paul Gallico—and Ogden Nash, with a poem that they hadn't considered first.

If, as Ross put it, "[their] leading artists ha[d] now strayed and the common bunch become [their] leading artists," then what kind of magazine was *The New Yorker*? And now Raymond Moley at *Today* magazine (soon to become *Newsweek*) was gunning for Dorothy Parker, and another Hearst paper wanted Clarence Day. Ross wrote to Fleischmann "to sound a warning that [they were] facing the most serious competition of The New Yorker's existence." It was never simply a matter of line rate; what was the right way to talk about, much less codify, valuable things like reputation? Katharine would later write to another agent, "We have heard repeatedly from our own contributors that one piece in The New Yorker brings them much more publicity, much more intelligent response, and many more demands from other magazines for contributions, than half a dozen in, say, the Saturday Evening Post, and similar magazines." What Nash wanted was a guarantee that *The New Yorker* would not reject his poems—something Ross and Katharine adamantly refused to give. But they learned that Nash published so many poems in other magazines because those editors commissioned verse on topical themes. "This seems to have been our failure," Katharine observed to Ross; "we could have gotten more poems if we had given him specific ideas."

This cut directly to the nature of the enterprise. What was the right way to act toward artists in a commercial setting? Though Ross's background was journalism, he steadfastly refused to assign articles to *New Yorker* reporters. Katharine was forever explaining to her writers that the magazine would happily reserve a subject while they worked on pieces to ensure that no one else duplicated their efforts—especially with profiles—but this reservation was not an order or a guarantee of acceptance. All work was done on speculation and the magazine always retained the right of refusal. What they were truly refusing was a contracted model of production, a factory line in which content was produced within a template. And yet, vexingly, writers needed to eat. What *The New Yorker* vastly preferred, and what they would refine over the next decades without ever naming it as such, was a variation on the idea of patronage, in which they supported their artists and held high expectations for both quantity and quality, while trying not to shade in the broad outline for creative output, a system closer to modernist literary journals than deep-pocketed organizations like the Hearst empire. *The New Yorker* wanted to be generous but not dictatorial; their writers wanted them to be generous and reliable. The trick was balancing artistic freedom with predictable compensation.

For the third time in three years—after Nash's appearance first in *The Saturday Evening Post*, next in the *New York American*, and then in *Life*—

Katharine and Nash hashed out a new agreement that gave Nash a line rate of $2.50 for humorous verse and $2 for serious verse, a guarantee to buy at least thirteen humorous poems if he submitted at least thirty-nine of them, and a retroactive bonus of twenty-five cents a line once the magazine had accepted those thirteen poems. This time it worked, and Nash earned his bonus in just a few months. The Nash Hash concluded satisfactorily for him, and with a new model of doing business for *The New Yorker*. This contract was called the "first reading agreement," and it became a defining principle of *The New Yorker*'s editor-writer relationship.

The first reading agreement was only one example of the magazine's evolution as driven by its writers, not its editors or readers. Another was in the kind of editing that writers could expect. In the early 1930s, Katharine largely confined herself to yes-or-no judgments on stories and poems, with no maybes contingent upon revisions based on her edits. If the answer was no, she always—always—gave a reason. Nash himself marveled at one of her first critical letters to him: "I've never had such an excited and interested rejection," and as a book editor himself, he said, "I've never even written one, in fact." If she had ideas for revisions, she spelled them out, but was always careful to specify that she was not offering an acceptance conditional upon those changes, and that her recommendation could not be construed as an order for the final piece. It became increasingly common for Katharine to have lengthy sotto voce discussions with literary agents about the futility of coaching their authors to write toward a perceived *New Yorker* style. Eugene Joffe was a repeat offender of this particular crime and he earned many rejections—"It's just another frustration story; so little happens, it's all so consciously stark and simple, that it might almost serve as a parody of this type of fiction."

The one thing Katharine did not regularly do was work closely with an author to shape a piece over several rounds of revisions—at least, not until her authors called it out from her. At first, it came in the form of lightly veiled threats to take the work elsewhere. Sally Benson, still one of the *New Yorker*'s stalwarts who published no fewer than ten stories in 1934 in the midst of the Nash Hash, knew just when to drop Charles Angoff's name; he was the editor of *The American Mercury*, and when Benson suggested she might take her story "Wild Animal" over to him because Wolcott Gibbs didn't like the ending, Katharine backpedaled hard and worked with her to fix it. Sure enough, "Wild Animals" ran in the magazine seven months later (wrapped around a Nash poem). Arthur Kober, who'd been publishing stories in the magazine since 1926, employed a similar tactic. When Katharine rejected a story he particularly liked, he announced his intention to publish elsewhere rather than revise it. No, Katharine replied, asking him to send it back "for [their] reconsideration" and adding, "We may have been wrong." Five months later, the very mediocre story, "Rubia," appeared in the magazine.

If *New Yorker* editors cultivated authors over many years and sheaves of rejections, so too did authors develop their editors. In the case of both Benson and Kober, Katharine's compromises paid off magnificently, because each author soon began writing a wildly successful series: Benson wrote the Junior Miss stories, which hit the trifecta of a book, radio series, and Broadway show, and Kober wrote the chronicles of Bella Gross, husband hunter, and her beleaguered parents, Ma and Pa Gross, speakers of a controversial Bronx dialect, which became the books *Thunder over the Bronx* (dedicated to Katharine S. White and *The New Yorker*), *My Dear Bella*, and *Bella, Bella Kissed a Fella*.

Indeed, a series was such a great way to intersect the magazine's rapacious need for material with the authors' stubborn need for money that, in the 1930s, Katharine oversaw a bounty of them; a series could *almost* act as an editorial guarantee of acceptance, and the structure could *almost* serve as a template to speed up the pace of artistic production. The short-story series guaranteed loyalty.

Clarence Day's Father Day series delighted everyone, and Katharine's only problem was how to avoid saturating the magazine with tales of Father. When Day collected the stories into a book, *Life with Father*, Knopf published it, the Book-of-the-Month Club picked it up, and it soon became a runaway bestseller. Day died of pneumonia before he could see the full extent of the book's popularity—it was turned into a Broadway show that still holds the record for the longest run of a nonmusical play.

Day's nostalgic stories, with their effortless capture of a bygone age and their good-natured portrayal of his eccentric parents, inspired James Thurber to turn his typewriter onto his own eccentric parents, leading to *My Life and Hard Times*, a six-part series and then the book that ce-mented his reputation as a humorist. Ruth McKenney, an ambitious but undisciplined writer whose stories Katharine had been rejecting for sev-eral years, began writing about her sister, the beautiful zany foil to her-self as the dowdy straight woman. Though McKenney's sloppy writing needed extensive editing, her voice was crystal clear. McKenney collected her stories into a book, *My Sister Eileen* (dedicated to Katharine S. White), and soon it became a bestseller, a Book-of-the-Month Club pick, a play, a musical (*Wonderful Town*, with music by Leonard Bern-stein), a radio play, two movies, and a television series. John O'Hara's Pal Joey series, Leo Rosten's H*Y*M*A*N K*A*P*L*A*N series, Emily Hahn's Pan Heh-ven series from China: *The New Yorker* was booming.

The magazine's competitors took sharp note of this success during the Depression. A very public problem plagued the editors in 1934, when *Fortune* published a long and detailed feature on the magazine, which it styled as a group profile, an exposé of its finances, and an acerbic review of its tone. The author: Ralph McAllister Ingersoll, Katharine's former co-managing editor, who'd left the magazine after a nervous breakdown occasioned by monumental overwork at Ross's side. With jaunty colle-giality, he asked Katharine in the fall of 1933 for help gathering facts for the article. Then he had a thought: "But I tell you what might be fun—maybe we might collaborate—or maybe you and Andy and I, with a touch of Thurber here and there." After repeating the word "fun" twice more, he breezily threw out the term "labor of love." Katharine wrote that she, Andy, and Thurber were wholly uninterested in free labor: "all are in the business of working for money." But she offered to supply facts, and she dressed up when Mac took her to a posh outdoor restaurant for lunch.

And then the article appeared at the end of the summer, seventeen pages long, with over a dozen *New Yorker* cartoons reprinted without permission and sixteen photographs of its editors and contributors, in-cluding an odd portrait of Katharine shot from below that Ingersoll had purloined by planting a photographer behind a nearby hedge during his terrace luncheon with Katharine. She was "appalled at the malice, both to Ross and [herself]." The unsigned article introduced the outsized character of Harold Ross to the world beyond midtown Manhattan for the first time, and it included hallmarks of his mythos: the "face made of rubber," the "furious intensity" of his "steady unimaginative profanity," the hair that Ina Claire longed to walk through. Ingersoll went into gleeful detail about the magazine's advertising revenue, circulation figures, and profits. Of course department stores flocked to advertise in its pages, when a full-page ad cost $550 to reach 62,000 "active and literate" Manhattan residents, against a $1,500 national ad in *Vogue* to reach just 28,000 New York subscribers.

Ingersoll squarely gave credit to *The New Yorker* for "its editorial kudos." Katharine appeared on page 2: she was from "an old Boston family," and her contribution to the magazine was "taste," a clear result of her superior lineage and education. And then came the backhanded compliment: "Katharine Angell, hard, suave, ambitious, sure of herself, had both kinds, and Ross was bright enough to see it." Ingersoll noted Katharine's salary of $11,000 a year and stock, and credited her for implementing the "rigid formula" of the magazine's famous profiles (which were "secretly prepared"), as well as raising "the standard of verse and prose." He wrote, "She handles people smoothly, with a carefully studied courtesy and tact. Onto her own capable shoulders she takes many a personal office problem shirked by her superiors. Feminine, she may have recourse to tears. But she is preëminently a civilized person and when Andy White married her, a *New Yorker* dynasty was set up." Ingersoll returned to this theme later in the piece: "Editor White is more important than Editor Ross. She is a lady who has her own way. As a one-woman majority on a board of three, she recommends editorial prices [and] editorial payrolls," and, he said, she held such power because she was "shrewd, and able politically."

The entire article damned the magazine at the same time it predicted its continued success. It was pitted with inaccuracies that enraged Ross; the only question was how to retaliate. Katharine had the instantaneous answer: a parody of *Fortune*. Editor St. Clair McKelway said that *Fortune* was only read by businessmen and "ambitious dentists," and that a *New Yorker* parody of *Time* would hurt owner Henry R. Luce far more deeply. Wolcott Gibbs was assigned the task. Luce was made to believe that *The New Yorker* was running a straight profile of him, for which certain facts were needed. How big was his apartment on East Fifty-Second Street?

Luce claimed it was the smallest in the building with four or five rooms. In fact it had fifteen rooms and five bathrooms. But facts, though delicious when obtained, were not needed for a parody. Gibbs invented the weekly salary of an average employee as $45.67890. Ross thought it a little obvious that Gibbs had simply typed sequential numbers, so Gibbs changed it to $45.67802. Dwight Macdonald, then an average *Fortune* employee, later cited the figure as real. Gibbs made sure to print a more believable number for the salary of "Socialite Ingersoll," at $30,000 with $40,000 stock income. The best line in a 4,500-word parody full of best lines was the one that made fun of *Time*'s convoluted style and would forever be associated with Gibbs: "Backward ran sentences until reeled the mind."

Katharine's newly hired junior editor, William Maxwell, remembered what happened next: "Time-Life was in an uproar about it; there was a continuous procession of people in and out of Mrs. White's office. I sat taking in snatches of the excitement." The issue with the parody sold out (for only the first time since Ellin Mackay's debutante article), selling three thousand more copies than the previous issue, and the subsequent issues sold yet more. Ross would declare, "[It was] one of the best pieces ever run by a magazine, unquestionably, and my part in it was satisfying and wholesome."

Only one person wasn't having much fun in the melee, and that was Andy White. Ingersoll described what the White dynasty had wrought: "If you complain that *The New Yorker* has become gentler and gentler, more nebulous, less real, it is the Whites' doing: Andy's gossamer writing—in his increasingly important 'Notes and Comment,' in his flavoring of the whole magazine with captions and fillers—Katharine's buying and editing, her steady civilizing influence on Ross himself." Ingersoll also outed Andy as the anonymous author of Notes and Comment (and revealed one of his pseudonyms, Squire Cuthbert). Ingersoll's words hurt for what they heavily implied. White wrote "delicate fiction"; he was "frightened of life, often melancholy, always hypochondriac." Of Notes and Comment, Ingersoll observed that Andy's "tiny but effective rapiers of thought, exquisitely written," concerned but few subjects: "first his Scottish terriers, then his guppies, more recently a serious interest in economics." There it was—Ingersoll laid the blame for *The New Yorker*'s indifference to the Depression right at Andy's feet, and he delivered the criticism in a soft padding of condescending praise. If this stung, it was only because it dovetailed with Andy's own thoughts and feelings. He even wrote about it in Notes and Comment, a doleful meta-commentary awkwardly couched in the first-person plural on "the paucity of our literary output": "Other than these few rather precise little paragraphs, into which we pour the slow blood of our discontent, we never get around to writing anything at all."

Contrary to Katharine's pessimistic prediction, Harper did succeed in getting a book out of Andy. Two months after the *Fortune* article appeared, Eugene Saxton published *Every Day Is Saturday*, a collection of Andy's writing from Notes and Comment since 1928 (Andy thought highly enough of his own lines on literary paucity to include them in the book). Yet this was hardly the book to put to rest Andy's fears of being a mediocre writer, hardly the book to counter the still-galling sentiment he had expressed to Katharine when he turned thirty—that he would never produce a great book if he continued to churn out a column every single week for a humor magazine. But the reviews were glowing, especially one from his old professor at Cornell, William Strunk Jr.

Katharine's strategy for dealing with Andy's deeply conflicted relationship to his own writing, a strategy she would hone with her authors over the next few years, was to establish as stable and predictable a routine as she could so that he could find pockets of time and peace in which to write. She did not try to persuade him to feel differently. She merely created a home base and took care of the people who inhabited it with executive flair so that he could push aside distractions and expectations and unearth his true subjects. In the next three years, Andy would push this strategy to its limit, and Katharine's own strength would be tested. Just as *The New Yorker* gained power, Katharine and Andy would begin to trade each other for neediness, one of them down with illness and the other one necessarily forced to step up.

24.

It is pretty hard from a distance to figure out just what actuates you and Andy. When I am with you two I can always tell the fact from the supposition because you both have such bad poker faces. As bad as Bob Coates. Bob's eyes give him away but with you and Andy it is your pauses. You also throw lateral passes at each other that a blind end could break up.

—James Thurber to Katharine White

Christmas Day in 1933 unfolded like the two before it; the Whites had established a durable, if not exactly pleasant, routine. First, Katharine, Andy, and Joe celebrated by themselves. Roger and Nancy would spend the morning with their father on Ninety-Third Street, with a tree decorated in Ernest's childhood Victorian ornaments and real candles (plus a kitchen pail in waiting), and they'd open one set of presents and eat one Christmas dinner of goose and plum pudding, then they'd take a taxi downtown to Andy and Katharine. The Whites, by stark contrast with Ernest, decorated with brand-new ornaments and lights instead of candles. Roger said, "Everything is new and young, even the Christmas-tree balls: I can't get over that." Nancy and Roger would play with Joe and Daisy, unwrap a second set of presents, eat a second Christmas dinner, and take a taxi back uptown, knowing they wouldn't be able to tell their glum father much about their afternoon. Nancy would later say Christmas was "just the most terrible day in the world."

In the new year, Katharine took Nancy, now a senior in high school, to visit Bryn Mawr. Katharine had a pleasant time talking with the students and visiting Lucy Donnelly, her old English professor. After Nancy returned to the Concord Academy, she grew alarmingly ill with sinus and lung trouble, but she didn't want Katharine to visit until she'd gotten better and they could enjoy time in Boston together, so Ros supervised Nancy's doctor visits, while Katharine was left to write to her daughter and to the school headmistress to scold her for how she was handling Nancy's illness. Katharine, who was not physically affectionate with her children, often expressed her love in worry, and often felt especially called to parent when either was physically ill. While Roger welcomed this kind of care, as when Katharine left baby Joe to care for Roger in Vermont, Nancy was more independent and more accustomed to meeting her mother as a companion and an equal.

Andy's mental and physical health—which he was beginning to suspect were linked—so troubled him that he decided to try a travel cure. A solo escape from the city, he felt, might allow him to think and write without pressure. He thus began a series of trips that would establish a pattern for the next several years, where he'd take off by himself to explore places that were meaningful to him from his past.

He traveled by train, during which he "wrote hundreds of lines of [his] magnum opus and forgot them too." He arrived in Camden, South Carolina, and checked into the Court Inn, where he had stayed with his parents as a ten-year-old boy. He was delighted to recognize the headwaiter, who was still pulling back chairs in the dining room as he had twenty-five years previously. Many things delighted Andy—the fox terrier in the garden of the inn, who he suspected distrusted him because he was a Yankee; some boys shooting at birds with an air gun—and he wrote about them all in daily letters to Katharine, when he wasn't walking "ten to twenty miles regularly" or attending a polo match. But aside from a single poem, he doesn't seem to have been writing anything for publication, and he didn't stay long. He made no further mention of a magnum opus.

Meanwhile, Katharine held things together at home. She and Joe played all their usual games while Andy was gone, including singing entire songbooks together and playing "driving to North Brooklin," which entailed the imaginative spotting of cows and boats in the urban landscape.

Katharine reported to Andy: "Each morning now he superintends my bath and we do exercises together. The best one we've invented is rolling." Then the formidable editor would stand up, brush herself off, and head to the office, where in one day she and Gibbs looked at 839 picture ideas, and Gibbs read aloud 500 art ideas.

On Andy's way back north, he stopped in Washington to visit his sister Clara, and Katharine came down to join him. They both returned to New York, but just a few weeks later he was back in the sunny South to continue his recuperation, this time in Palm Beach, Florida, with another sister, Lillian, and her family. He also visited Katharine's father, who was there for the winter. Andy fared much better in Florida than on his previous trip to South Carolina, swimming in the ocean every day, people-watching, cycling on the flat paths, and relishing his nieces. But when he experienced a small adverse health event, it sent him spinning into despair. One evening, he touched his forehead, and "it felt as soft as a piece of putty." He rushed to the mirror to see that it was swollen "like the breast of a pigeon." It had to be a brain tumor, but his sister had taken her family to the movies, so he did the only thing he could: he wrote a brief note to Katharine, unlocked the door so no one would have to break it down to find him, and lay down to die. The next evening, he told Katharine the story and said the doctor had diagnosed a sunburn, but he had his doubts. "I still love you & my dying thoughts last night were of you. Kiss Joe," he concluded. Katharine's response gave Andy sympathy but also briskly seconded the sunburn diagnosis and breezed right past his fear of death. "I'm glad you said goodbye to me anyway, but I'm sorry you had a night of farewells," she wrote, before moving on to *New Yorker* office gossip. Clearly she had learned one way to deal with his anxiety.

Back to New York, and then just a few weeks later, in late May, he was off again, this time to the farmhouse in North Brooklin, with a stop in Boston to see Katharine's sister Ros and her family. It was turning into quite a hectic year, but not because of his writing. The Whites traveled to Gaylordsville, Connecticut, to visit writer Robert Coates and his wife, Elsa. Robert began giddily pouring drinks, "and that's what caused the trouble," as he later wrote to Katharine. He does not specify what the trouble was, but he says that he and Elsa both thought "what

Andy should probably do is to cut out drinking entirely for a time, say three months, or six, or something." He had done it himself, Coates said; maybe he'd talk to Andy "as a reformed drunkard." Katharine said only, "These last few weeks have been pretty hard to get through here and I still feel guilty and owe Els a real decent letter of thanks."

Nonetheless, at the end of June, the Whites set off for Maine, the car packed full with "a cat, a puppy, Nancy, and all the usual trappings like typewriter, Victrola, bags, and liquor." Nancy and Roger would come for a month after having spent a month with Ernest. Andy's parents came for a visit—what would be their first and last time at the North Brooklin farmhouse.

Without question, Andy was better in Maine. He was far from isolated, surrounded as he was by family, their visiting friends, local friends, a cook, and farm handyman Howard Pervear. He didn't need solitude, just familiarity, and perhaps a healthy distance from other writers. Nancy recalled a memorable evening from around this time that typified Andy's approach to sociality. Nancy's boyfriend's family, the Parsons, gave a big summer dance for teenagers and their parents. Katharine and Andy went, after much reluctant grumbling from Andy. Nancy watched as Andy made repeated forays to the bar. In the midst of the festivities, Katharine found Nancy and urgently asked her for directions to the bathroom—Andy was in dire straits. When he came back out again, the Whites got ready to leave, but Nancy could see from Andy's movements that he wasn't in a state to drive, and she offered to drive them both home. "Oh no, Nancy, it'll be all right. Andy's always a perfect driver," her mother responded. But the next morning, Nancy could see big branches of evergreen caught in the fender of the car. Even then, Katharine might not have told Nancy the true story, except her handbag had gotten lost in the evening and she needed Nancy to ask the Parsons to look for it. Katharine revealed that Andy had begun the terrifying drive home by plowing into the Parsons' dahlia bed, then clipping every evergreen along their three-quarter-mile driveway, and that it might have been worse if Katharine hadn't pulled up the handbrake. "I think this is one of my mother's very few revelations," Nancy remembered, "almost the only revelation ever that she gave me." Katharine's purse wouldn't be found for another two years, when she lifted up the seat of the car and found it lying there.

All his life, friends would describe Andy as a moderate drinker, in keeping with the mores of his peers. It would seem that he drank more when he needed fortification for an anxiety-producing social scene— and there were fewer of those in Maine than in New York.

During the relaxing bustle of a Maine summer, both Whites worked from afar, and the glorious thing about their new and quite old house was that it was perfectly if accidentally designed for a literary couple. Entering from the front door (which no one ever did), visitors would find themselves in a small hallway facing the stairs to the second story, but there was no living room in sight, no parlor either formal or casual. Instead, the house sat balanced between two small rooms on either side of the front door—an office for Katharine on the right and an office for Andy on the left. Katharine's tambour desk, with its Blackwing pencils and *Modern English Usage* and a secret compartment in which she kept cash, lived under the two windows facing the road, the driveway, and the front garden; to use her typewriter, she swiveled to a small table on her right, looking across the hall to Andy. His desk faced Katharine.

In the fall of 1934, just after the *Fortune* article appeared, Joel White and both Angells began new schools. Joel started preschool at the City and Country School, Roger moved from being a day student at Lincoln School to boarding at Pomfret School in Connecticut (no letters survive to explain why Ernest and Katharine agreed upon in 1934 what so bitterly divided them in 1931), and Nancy matriculated at Bryn Mawr. Katharine took two days off to settle her daughter in at Wyndham, an old fieldstone farmhouse turned into a residence hall. Nancy met with the dean to plan her first year of courses: English, math, German, and physics, and according to her memory, when she emerged and told her mother of the plan, Katharine exclaimed, "I never heard of anything so awful in my life." Nancy was highly conscious of the fact that she was the maverick in a family of litterateurs. "She is taking a pre-medical course," Katharine told her college friend Jean Batchelor, "and I am scared to death about it as it sounds so difficult to me, all the things I couldn't possibly do like Physics and Math." To Katharine, the moment at which medicine seemed possible for her own career was too far back in the distance to remember. Katharine asked Batchelor, who lived nearby, to look in on Nancy when she had a chance. By pure coincidence, Nancy, who was enough like Katharine to find Bryn Mawr amenable, lived in the same room in Pembroke West that had once housed her mother.

Katharine enjoyed a relatively drama-free stretch of time that autumn and into the winter—with the exception of the cook getting poisoned by coal gas at Christmastime—but that only meant that she worked flat out, careening forward with the magazine into the future. In January, she took a week off and stayed at home, telling a friend, "I am awfully tired and am using this as a precaution." The next stretch of months and days were a confusing mix of successes and setbacks, when Katharine and Andy would take turns being needy and strong for each other.

Not long after she returned, Katharine opened an envelope to find two very short stories from a twenty-two-year-old named John Cheever. He was living in photographer Walker Evans's basement apartment, dead broke and striking out with his overly long stories, until writer and *New Republic* editor Malcolm Cowley gave him a kind of dare: write a thousand-word story each day for four days and then send them out. Katharine ran into Cheever in March at a *New Republic* party and told him that she was accepting one of them, "Buffalo," about a man who asks out a young German waitress only to learn that she is the restaurant owner's wife. Katharine paid $45 for the slight story, and it was Cheever's turning point. First, he started "going around like a kid with a broken bank buying scotch and sodas and dating up everyone [he] could lay [his] hands on." Then he landed an agent, Maxim Lieber. Cheever and Lieber proceeded to flood Katharine's office with stories—nine more of them in 1935. Even though she accepted only one more that year, Cheever had learned what he needed to know. "Buffalo" was proof of concept that he could "make a living out of this machine," as he put it. *The New Yorker*'s cultivation of him meant his story would be "written, paid for, printed and applauded in the space of a week." In other words, speed was of the essence. He was puppyishly amenable to revising his stories at Katharine's and Gibbs's direction, but he made them worse in the process. "I wish he'd try a little editing of his own work before he submits stuff," Katharine told Lieber. "I only wish this because I think he has considerable promise." Cheever would eventually publish 121 stories in the magazine.

But he was not yet important enough to warrant an invitation to the gala that the magazine threw at the end of March 1935. To celebrate *The New Yorker*'s tenth anniversary, Ross rented the Jade Room at the Waldorf-Astoria, and the editors drew up list upon list of invitees and sent out tickets admitting two persons at the private entrance ("Dress or not, as you like"). Katharine begged her friend Robert Coates to attend. "It is going to be hardest on people like myself so a few of our friends should at least be there as we won't be able to recognize most of the contributors and they will feel that we ought to recognize them." She and Andy were on the receiving line as hosts for the evening as Ross attended a private *New Yorker* dinner, so she soon met the contributors she didn't yet recognize: over five hundred people attended, including Katharine's good friends and contributors Louise Bogan, Bessie Breuer, and, faithfully, Robert Coates. Ogden Nash was there, and Otto Soglow. Janet Flanner sent Katharine a private congratulations on the magazine's birthday: "You deserve much, very much, of the credit; you've had to hold his hand a lot and wash behind his ears occasionally; it must seem now to have been very much worth it." Only one fight broke out between an editor and a writer (St. Clair McKelway and Morris Markey), so the party was deemed a success, the first large-scale performance of *The New Yorker*'s brand of sophistication.

Many years later, in the midst of his own editing career at *The New Yorker*, Roger Angell would reflect on what made Katharine White a superlative editor. First, "she would never suggest models for writers to emulate. She did not like to urge a writer to be like another writer." The editorial memos in *The New Yorker* archive lavishly bear out this observation. Katharine wanted only to amplify each of her writers. It was a matter of great professional pride that she and the other editors never make the tiniest change without the author's approval. Roger then noted that her language in rejection letters was precise: she was rejecting a given poem or story, *not* the writer herself, who was heartily encouraged to submit again. In fact, at Ross's insistence, the fiction department maintained two enormous gray binders organized by contributor with elaborate schedules for follow-up letters and luncheons, their more valued and responsive writers warranting closer attention than those they knew to be desultory. Roger continued. "She understood that part of an editor's job was praising and building the confidence of a writer, because she was married to a writer, and God knows writers are always plagued with problems, with self-doubt."

It was this last quality that Katharine would continue to develop in the mid-1930s as writers called out more and more from her. The poet Phyllis McGinley sought Katharine's advice about whether or not she should quit her job teaching literature to middle school students in New Rochelle and move to New York City to be surrounded by other writers. Katharine said the same thing she'd said to Andy on his thirtieth birthday: "I have seen so very many people who have written against the greatest odds give up jobs that they thought were holding them down only to find that when they were free they could write much less and write less well." Freedom, to Katharine, did not mean the lack of constraint; it meant, perhaps, a kind of internal freedom that only came from stability and security. Andy used McGinley's predicament as the pretext for his next grumpy Comment: "We encountered a writer this week who wanted our advice," he began (leading McGinley to think that Katharine had written the column). Stay away from "the vortex of letters," he counseled, because "writers tend to magnify the significance and difficulty of writing and to destroy its essential simplicity and directness." Also, they ruined tablecloths with their lead pencils.

Just days later McGinley was back for more advice. ("That's the penalty for being nice to writers," she wrote, "they follow you about like fed kittens.") The publisher Farrar & Rinehart had asked for a collection of poems, then turned down the manuscript, leaving McGinley with sixty-five poems that would soon expire into irrelevance. Could Katharine help? "I'll simply fold up if I have to teach next year again," she wrote. Katharine gave her the names of editors at Simon & Schuster, Harper, and Doubleday, and told McGinley to use her name when submitting the manuscript. Doubleday published McGinley's first book, *On the Contrary*, later that year, and she was indeed able to quit the loathsome job.

But her troubles were not over yet. McGinley moved to East Fifty-Second Street but soon grew ill enough to alarm Katharine, who came to visit her in person and saw that she wasn't eating properly. Katharine then swung into action. She bought a poem, and she invited McGinley to a *New Yorker* party (which McGinley enjoyed, testifying that Katharine was "the prettiest lady there" and saying, "Mr. Ross is swell, even though his hair was a great disappointment"). Katharine advanced her $500 so she could spend a month in Florida and sent recommendations for places to stay. Instead, McGinley checked into the St. Francis Health Resort in Denville, New Jersey, to gain weight under the care of calm German nuns. She wrote about her encounters with psychoanalysis, but Katharine did not accept any of those poems, preferring to hold out for a different topic. Later in the year, McGinley began submitting poems about Oliver Ames, a pseudonym for her new beau, and Katharine published three.

Katharine advanced money to Louise Bogan to help her divorce Raymond Holden when Bogan wrote to her in despair, "There's not only a wolf at the door, but also several jackals, a bear, a mountain lion and several buzzards."

Katharine's support was not confined to money and encouragement. One writer bemoaned the end of her engagement; she and her fiancé were both devout Catholics, but she was divorced and could not marry in the church a second time. Katharine researched the possibility of obtaining an annulment for her—the editor as a full-service consultant for all a writer's troubles and woes.

She provided immensely steady support to Nancy Hale during a turbulent time that appeared successful only on the outside. Hale had placed several more short stories in the magazine after "Club Car" in 1931, and when Katharine read "Midsummer," she went to bat for it with Ross despite its uneditably racy subject matter: a young girl, home alone in her parents' mansion for the summer, spending the sultry afternoons in a secret tryst with her taciturn riding instructor. Ross approved the story, and *The New Yorker* published the frank tale of a young girl's desire in 1934, what Katharine later called "one of the great American short stories of [her] generation."

Hale had published two novels in quick succession with Maxwell Perkins at Scribner and seemed to be on the ascent. But her marriage to Taylor Scott Hardin, with whom she had a son, cracked apart. In the span of two years, Katharine helped Hale through her Reno divorce, her subsequent breakdown and recuperation, and her remarriage to Charles Wertenbaker. As with Bogan, Katharine's strategy was to implacably ask for more material, sometimes suggesting ideas but always expecting that the writer was just about to place her fingers on the typewriter. It would have been easy to give up on someone like Hale, or to back away in respectful silence until Hale emerged from her troubles and returned to the page. But Katharine was developing a theory and practice for helping writers through mental distress, a set of principles that derived from her own histories with Elsie and Andy. She believed that mental illness should not be treated as shameful, that it was an almost natural and certainly understandable part of the creative life, and that it was temporary, and so it wouldn't define the sufferer. She did not believe in psychoanalysis and thought that talk therapy might interfere with a writer's artistic process. Her approach to mental illness was staunchly pragmatic: attempt to alleviate the symptoms and keep trying until the work flows effortlessly.

Katharine made it a point to tell Hale that the path into the magazine was open for her and that she was not written off or forgotten—she consistently put in front of her authors a vision for the resumption of a normal working life. "It is so nice to think that you want my stories," wrote Hale, "even when I am not giving them to you, that sounds rather nasty, but I mean it is kind of nice to know that they will be wanted when there are any there." The writer had lost her knack for expression, it would seem. She asked, rather plaintively, if her illness could have broken her ability to write. Certainly not, Katharine replied. She especially wanted a long feature from Hale on the Reno scene: "Ever since being there myself I have hoped that a real writer would come along and do the subject up definitively." She sent Hale pages and pages of notes from her own experience, an unprecedented outpouring from her personal life, almost a short story in itself. The Reno feature never came about, but Katharine kept trying, even through the birth of Hale's second child. What would you like me to submit, Hale asked, and Katharine responded with three pages of ideas, including a potential series about Hale as a young girl (which she *would* write, but not until the 1950s), a profile, and Footloose Correspondence pieces from the South, where Hale had relocated with Wertenbaker. Hale would continue responding to Katharine's provocations through all the upheavals of her life, including another divorce, remarriage, and breakdown. One year she set the record for the greatest number of stories sold to *The New Yorker* of any author: twelve.

Katharine increased the tenor and variety of support for her authors as she was struggling through her own hidden turmoil. The spring was a bit rocky. Andy's sister Clara brought her manic-depressive husband up from Washington, DC, and asked the Whites to help have him committed to the White Plains hospital where Louise Bogan had gone. But the summer of 1935 started off well, beginning with Andy's purchase of *Astrid*, a thirty-foot cruising sailboat. Joel, who was only five, remembered that day for the rest of his life: he stood on a dock in City Island, New York, and looked down at the double-ended cutter, with its light green deck, dark green trim, and khaki sails, and he fell in love with *Astrid* just as much as his father did. In June, Andy sailed it up to Brooklin with H. K. "Bunny" Rigg, *The New Yorker*'s yachting columnist, who'd brokered the purchase. The short trip turned Andy back into a boy, as enthusiastic as his son. Andy wrote letters home to Katharine: the *Astrid* was "a constant delight." "I'm learning plenty on this cruise—for one thing the importance of always knowing exactly where you are."

Katharine and Joe joined him in July, leaving Gus Lobrano in charge at their apartment, and soon Andy was bragging to Gus about their cool weather and the pleasures of deep-sea fishing in *Astrid*: three hundred pounds of fish in a morning. For Andy's birthday, Katharine gave him a dinghy, "light, well-rounded, rope-edged and elegant." And from afar, while reading manuscripts for *The New Yorker* and scanning the competition, Katharine oversaw the execution of a new project: a new house in New York.

The Whites had decided to give up their beloved Greenwich Village apartment and move to a four-story town house in midtown. Their new neighborhood was Turtle Bay Gardens, which consisted of two rows of ten town homes apiece on Forty-Eighth and Forty-Ninth Streets not far from the Third Avenue El. The backyards formed a shared private garden, low walled and with a fountain copied from the Villa Medici underneath a willow tree. It was a desirable neighborhood on the east side of midtown, a long walk or a short crosstown bus to the *New Yorker* offices and a few blocks away from the Chrysler Building and the Waldorf-Astoria. From Maine, Katharine oversaw the making of custom curtains and supervised the painters who were lightening the walls both inside and on the outside of the house. The plan was to move in September, just after their return from Brooklin.

But the plan went awry, starting in the middle of August when Andy's father, Samuel Tilly White, died in Mount Vernon, New York. Andy's mother decided to move down to Washington, DC, to live with Clara, leaving the family home to be packed up and sold at just the moment when Katharine and Andy needed to pack up their own home.

And then, just as they were preparing to leave Maine and return to New York, Katharine began to have troubling health symptoms: pain, bleeding, and a hard mass in her abdomen. She was confined to her bed with a hired nurse, and Joe stayed with her in the care of a nanny. Andy reluctantly returned to the city, and they wrote to each other every day, but the news was highly ambiguous. Was she pregnant (was that the rationale for the bigger house?) and was she in danger of losing the pregnancy? The doctor thought they just might have headed off a miscarriage in time, but he wasn't sure. Katharine thought that was nonsense. She wasn't having a baby *or* a miscarriage. Her diagnosis was "a good old-fashioned period with trimmings," and by "trimmings" she must have meant the spasms of pain that required hypodermic shots of codeine, not to mention a racing heart and pulse, and weakness and spotting so severe as to keep her in bed. But it was a miscarriage. "So darling," she wrote, "we shall just have to give up our precious hopes for the time being, [because] I am no more pregnant than you are." Her doctor assured her they could try again soon, and she was glad they wouldn't have to wait long to start. She instructed Andy to let the office know she'd be back on October 1. "Much love to you and forgive a disappointing wife."

Her birthday came with little fanfare from Andy and her children, though Ros and her family surprised Katharine with a visit from their nearby vacation home. She was still bedridden, and the symptoms did not abate. She was restless and sent a steady stream of reminders to Andy: switch on the gas, electricity, and phone at the new house, and register Joe for kindergarten, and make sure to get blackout curtains for Joe's room, and get the silver from the bank vault. "I think of you constantly," she wrote, "and feel very guilty to have left those awful female chores for you." But then she added a postscript: "Most of the time my mind is a blank and I don't worry about the moving at all."

It soon became clear that she wouldn't be at work even by the first of October. Her mood dipped and soared, and on good days, Katharine put stock in her doctor's hopeful prognosis for "the future and more babies." In fact, she adored her nurse and doctor. Katharine told Andy, "I must say, I wish he could always take care of us all. We must live in this sensible world some day." As the month progressed, she was able to stand, then walk downstairs, and finally move outside to sit in her garden—chrysanthemum asters, scarlet gladioli, and a lily with blooms half a foot across—and order bulbs for the little patch of garden at Forty-Eighth Street.

She reported on Joe's activities. He played ceaselessly with a toy sloop and together they refurbished it—new paint on the keel, new sails, brass polish on the tiller—little knowing that Joe would someday become nationally renowned for his boatbuilding. The future was being crafted on those pleasant late-summer afternoons, even though it felt like their future had just been curtailed. All Katharine wanted was to return home "to start fresh on a little Serena."

Andy did his level best to hold everything together. During the time the Whites were moving and Andy's mother was selling his childhood home, *The New Yorker* was also moving—a short southward hop, from 25 West Forty-Fifth Street to the nineteenth and twentieth floors of 25 West Forty-Third Street.

Andy boxed up their home. "Just packed specialty box containing Ernest Angell's old catcher's mitt, your ski boots, and a card of admission to 19 Washington Square Club," he wrote to Katharine, boasting of his executive ability. But in truth it was the cook, Marguerite, who did all the work of packing and cleaning, and an army of workmen who prepared the town house for their arrival. Andy reported to Katharine that he'd approved of the decorator's choices, "wearing [his] finest interior expression." Andy did make a few decisions, such as auctioning off their old bookcases now that they had built-ins for their enormous collection and restoring a portrait of his grandmother that his mother had given him as she emptied out the Mount Vernon house. He didn't offer Katharine much in the way of emotional sustenance, at least not by letter. "Got your note and was sorry not to get better news. Be patient. I'm sure you will pull out of this with flying colors!"

In early October, Katharine and Joe returned to New York, and she spent two more weeks resting in her new home. They shared their new neighborhood with another Katharine: Katharine Hepburn, whom they would often see working in her back garden. It was their other neighbors, though, who made them feel right at home, because so very many of them hailed from the world of publishing. Maxwell Perkins, F. Scott Fitzgerald's editor at Scribner, lived next to Hepburn; in his study at the back of the house, with its shelves of books and red leather furniture, he met with his authors over their manuscripts, including two authors whom Katharine shared with Perkins and who also lived in Turtle Bay Gardens: Nancy Hale and Thomas Wolfe. (One night, Wolfe inadvertently awakened Hale at three a.m. by pacing the garden and chanting, "I wrote ten thousand words today—I wrote ten thousand words today.") This suited Katharine just fine. "Do walk down the garden some day and knock on my dining room door," she wrote to Hale. "We are almost always having a cocktail there at 6:30 or so, and I wish you would bring your husband over."

But Andy valued a different set of residents, "a small but distinguished company of white-throated sparrows and hermit thrushes—transient visitors whose presence [t]here seem[ed] miraculous." So the Whites settled uptown, which was counterintuitively both cheaper and a little closer to nature.

25.

In the middle of October, Katharine settled into her new office, which was much the same as her old one, maybe a little roomier, but with a view of the New York skyline that Phyllis McGinley, for one, found very elegant. Life rushed back in. Twice that fall Katharine appeared in The Conning Tower in the *Herald Tribune*, once when Franklin P. Adams came to the Whites' and "met there many friends." Katharine had thrown a cocktail party for G. B. Stern, a British writer whom she had successfully lured into *The New Yorker* the previous year. Ross held court in the entryway; FPA commandeered the living room; Nancy Hale came from across the garden; Thurber introduced his new wife, Helen, to the *New Yorker* crowd; and Andy escaped the throng by bringing a guest up to the top floor to show her Minnie, their new dachshund puppy.

Another evening, Adams and Katharine went to the theater to see Langston Hughes's Broadway play *Mulatto: A Tragedy of the Deep South*, and then came back to the Whites' house, where Andy poured Adams a "beaker or two of beer" and they stayed up late discussing "exhibitionist liberalism." Adams gave his own opinion of the play—despite its "passionate earnestness," parts of it were "repetitious" and the main actress's lines were "pretentious and off key," though well delivered by Rose McClendon—and then he reproduced the Whites' opinion that the play would be "gently dealt with" because reviewers would not want to seem illiberal toward a Black author.

Katharine, for her part, had no problem rejecting Langston Hughes and had been doing it often in the past year. As early as 1933, Hughes had been trying to publish in *The New Yorker*, and in 1934, they accepted "Why, You Reckon," a story in dialect about two "hongry" men in Harlem who rob a white man of "a wallet and a gold watch and a cigarette-lighter and he got a swell key ring and some other little things that colored never use" (at the end, the white man finds the encounter thrilling, saying, "The first time in my life I had a good time in Harlem. Everything else's been fake. You know, something you pay for. This was real"). Publication in *The New Yorker* paid instant dividends to Hughes; though he'd already placed stories in *The American Mercury*, *Scribner's*, and *Esquire*, it was only when he appeared in *The New Yorker* that other mainstream white publications asked his agent for stories, and he bested the $135 that he earned for "Why, You Reckon" with a $400 paycheck from *Woman's Home Companion* for a mildly racy interview he conducted with an ex-wife of a Persian emir. In fact, his new visibility as a Black fiction writer in the major magazines is what led to the production of *Mulatto* that Katharine had just seen (which producer-director Martin Jones had rewritten without Hughes's input). But Hughes was struggling financially. Katharine accepted one more story, "Oyster's Son," but she, Gibbs, and Mosher rejected a dozen more stories, articles, and poems, only a few of which found publication elsewhere. So Hughes searched for a cheap city and chose Reno, Nevada, and while living under the pseudonym James Hughes, he began to write stories under the pseudonym David Boatman. He explicitly framed these to his agent, Maxim Lieber, as a way to pander to the white marketplace, setting aside his radical poetry for conventionally plotted fiction: "Since I must make a living by my pen—typewriter, to be exact—and since the market for Race and Russian stuff is distinctly limited, I see no reason why I should not turn to LOVE, and Love in the best American Caucasian 100% slick paper fashion." He offhandedly wondered, "Maybe we could even sell them once in a while to the movies?" He asked Lieber to keep his identity a secret.

The Boatman stories were a wildly erroneous calculation of *The New Yorker*'s needs and wants. Lieber persuaded Hughes that they were good enough to publish under his own name—"I laughed myself sick" at the stories, Lieber told him—and so he revealed Boatman's true identity to Katharine and offered her the choice of author names. She sorrowfully rejected the first at the tail end of 1934, questioning whether it really had more popular appeal than his other work, though she was encouraging enough to ask Lieber for an informal right of first refusal on Hughes's stories. Gibbs rejected the next two Boatman tales, telling Lieber that no one was "convinced that this kind of comedy [was] Mr. Hughes' forte" and that they "wish[ed] frankly that he'd abandon it because he [was] so gifted the other way." Hughes did abandon Boatman, but he submitted another story the next month, then two more in the next two weeks. Katharine turned them all down, and though Hughes would continue to submit his work to *The New Yorker* for the next twenty years, he would meet with rejection after rejection, only publishing three poems there in his lifetime—no more fiction. Katharine rejected a 1935 story called "Never Room with a Couple" because it wasn't "as colorful a story as his usually are," but seven days later she rejected a Hughes story for being too colorful. "Bastard of Gold" (what likely became "African Morning," published in *Pacific Weekly* and reprinted in Hughes's 1952 story collection, *Laughing to Keep from Crying*) was set in West Africa, and Katharine told Lieber, in *New Yorker* argot, "The remoteness of the setting lets the story out for us." He would have far better luck with *The New Republic*, *The Saturday Review*, and *Harper's*. Katharine never corresponded with Hughes directly and never gave him the slightest hint of how to navigate *The New Yorker*'s moving targets for stories featuring Black characters. Later in the 1930s, William Maxwell, perhaps thinking of the 1934 collection *The Ways of White Folks*, would ask Hughes's agent, "Can't you persuade him to go back and write the kind of short stories about white people, seen through the eyes of negroes [*sic*], that he does so well?"

The New Yorker abhorred the "popular" stories that Hughes and others tried to sell them. Katharine wanted nothing to do with the contrived endings that characterized so many of the stories in national monthly magazines, and she and her editors used a shorthand phrase to dismiss such stories when their contributors slipped up and committed them: "too O. Henry." The insult cropped up repeatedly in the editors' letters to writers—as when Gibbs told Sally Benson, "Those are O. Henry overcoats you've got in there and we don't like them." O. Henry was, of course, the pen name of William Sydney Porter, who rebounded from a stint in prison for embezzling by becoming a writer. From 1904 until his death in 1910, he published over two hundred fifty stories in newspapers, magazines, and book collections. Benson—ever short of money—replied to Gibbs, "I wish they were O. Henry overcoats and I had about a million of them."

Benson did, in fact, sell "The Overcoat," and its fate points to *The New Yorker*'s askew relationship to the literary trends of the early 1930s. *The American Mercury* published the story, and then Edward O'Brien chose it for *The Best Short Stories 1935*—and then chose it again for *50 Best American Short Stories (1915–1939)*. Yet to *New Yorker* editors, "too O'Brien" was another epithet that frequently dotted editorial memos. Katharine elaborated on what the pejorative meant in a letter to Bob Coates's agent: one of Coates's stories was "more literary and artificial, the conventional short story, than the ones he usually [wrote], and as such it [was] less good for" *The New Yorker*. She added, "It may be the very short story that O'Brien chooses to crown, but even so we think we must say 'no.'"

The 1930s were a boom time for the short story, and Edward O'Brien had much to do with that explosion. The rise of English departments and the continued strength of middle-class magazines meant readers were voraciously consuming short stories, and also writing them. The story was seen as a low-threshold entry into publishing, and publication in *Scribner's* or *The Saturday Review of Literature* showered glamour and cultural cachet on the writer. To capitalize on this hunger, industry insiders flooded the marketplace with handbooks and manuals for how to write a short story. Predictably, this fervent art-making from unschooled amateurs disconcerted cultural critics, and the 1930s were also a boom time for essays *about* short stories. What did reading so many short stories *do* to you?

Edward O'Brien had founded the annual *Best American Short Stories* series back in 1915 with the goal of refining and elevating what he considered a particularly American genre. In the mid-nineteenth century, while British periodicals developed the novel through the serialized publication of Charles Dickens, William Thackeray, and Anthony Trollope, American magazines began publishing short stories by Washington Irving, Nathaniel Hawthorne, and Edgar Allan Poe. In fact, it was Poe, writing about Hawthorne's *Twice Told Tales*, who exerted an almost supernaturally strong force on the genre for well into the next century. A short story was defined not by its length, wrote Poe, but by its "unity of effect or impression." It is this intense experience that should dictate the writer's hand. "In the whole composition there should be no word written, of which the tendency, direct or indirect, is not to the one pre-established design." The short story was thus defined from its beginning as an integral whole. This definition put pressure on the plot and the ending of the short story, and the apotheosis of the form—with a detour through satire, courtesy of Mark Twain—was O. Henry and his surprise endings. The 1920s were rife with stories structured around a riddle, an error, a reversal, a twist.

O'Brien, like Katharine, hated this trend. Long before *The New Yorker* began to face the unkillable accusation that its editors published stories according to a formula and twisted writers' work to fit their narrow mold, O'Brien leveled the same charge against all of American short fiction, and his criticism revealed the high stakes of this persistent worry. As a popular genre within the first mass media that grew in popularity during a time of economic acceleration, the short story contained within itself the possibility of becoming mechanistic. O'Brien found disturbing parallels between the industrial machine, the army, and the American short story. National magazines were designed in opposition to art. "The editor's function is to run the machine," he wrote, "the author's function is to build his brain into it." The writer's ease in producing it and the reader's ease in consuming it led O'Brien to worry that the formulaic short story would act like a set of gears and levers on readers' minds, hypnotizing them, overriding their own thoughts, threatening their individual autonomy, and reducing the American reading public to the "least common denominator of sluggish indifference"—a persistent worry about mass culture's effects on gullible consumers. He noted how many short-story writers also wrote advertising copy. This too was a common lament, that America's literature could only appear as "a thin trickle in a deep canyon of advertising." O'Brien edited his yearly collections to resist these trends and encourage artists to develop their own personalities against the machine.

The New Yorker had no such mandate for its editorial choices. Katharine wasn't looking to publish the very best writers on the American literary scene. She wanted only those writers who fit within the narrow canyon of *The New Yorker*'s milieu—local color, an intense moment distinctively told, a small, well-rounded exercise of a writer's personality and wit—and she therefore disparaged stories that she felt were aiming for O'Brien's pantheon, which was at once too elevated and too prosaic for her editorial project. And indeed, O'Brien entirely ignored *The New Yorker* for the first few years of its existence. Soon, *New Yorker* authors started appearing in the *Best American Short Stories* with regularity—Sally Benson, Conrad Aiken, Stephen Vincent Benét, Kay Boyle, Katharine Brush, John Cheever, Nancy Hale, James Thurber—but not for their *New Yorker* stories. O'Brien entirely snubbed John O'Hara. In 1930, *The New Yorker* finally made the cut with a story each from Emily Hahn and Dorothy Parker.

In her pursuit of a different kind of short story, Katharine's criteria coincided with O'Brien's in one distinctive instance. In 1928, Katharine read a story by Canadian author Morley Callaghan in *Scribner's* and wrote to ask if he had any stories for *The New Yorker*. Callaghan checked with his book editor, Maxwell Perkins, who confirmed that the magazine's readership was right for him. Callaghan, like Kay Boyle, saw himself as a modernist, with stories in little European magazines like *The Exile*, *This Quarter*, and *transition*, and so appearing in *The New Yorker* functioned as a kind of Depression-era loophole, a caper of "somehow selling [his] non-commercial stories in the great commercial market and staying alive." In short order, Katharine acquired and published "The Escapade," telling Callaghan she was honored to have it even though it represented a "new sort of material for" *The New Yorker* because the magazine didn't usually publish "straight fictional material," or stories that couldn't be read as loosely autobiographical casuals. Callaghan went on to publish twenty-one stories in the magazine during the 1930s, and O'Brien picked his stories for the annual collection in 1930, 1931, 1932, and 1937 (despite Callaghan's Canadian nationality). Where Katharine and O'Brien converged was on four remarkably similar stories, all centered squarely on the theme of female transgression. Callaghan, like O. Henry and foreshadowing John Cheever, wrote about young, working-class people—for instance, a woman who made eighteen dollars a week in a story that earned

Callaghan several hundred dollars. The four stories dramatize knowability, as in Kay Boyle's first few *New Yorker* stories: will the woman in the story capitulate to the man; can her degree of susceptibility to sexual persuasion be known by her outward appearance?

By the time of Callaghan's fourth O'Brien story, Katharine had begun rejecting his work more often than she accepted it. If Callaghan was seen, at first, as new and sophisticated, and if Callaghan consistently obliged Katharine's requests to change the locations of his stories to New York and its environs, he soon came to seem too provincial for the magazine (Katharine tried hard to convince him to move from Toronto to New York, and she even qualified her recommendation of him for a Guggenheim fellowship by pointing to his stubborn embrace of the hinterland). His work had become predictable and now frequently succumbed to Katharine's bane: "too many coincidences and fortuitous circumstances," as she wrote to his agent.

Callaghan served *The New Yorker* as a vanishing mediator, one of the authors who helped the magazine define its fiction department, only to be rendered moot by the very pages he'd so obligingly filled—and he has been largely forgotten since his last published story in 1938. By the end of the 1930s, *New Yorker* stories filled big swaths of O'Brien's *Best American Short Stories* yearbooks. This was the decade in which *The New Yorker* was fast becoming a literary epicenter, as it evolved from journalism and sketches to its own definition of literary fiction, and Katharine was busier than ever.

In 1936, just after Katharine published Thomas Wolfe's "Only the Dead Know Brooklyn," a subsequent O'Brien pick, she again went to Florida for a short vacation, and she used the same phrase as the previous years in her letters to friends: "I'm just all in and am doing this as a precaution."

Therefore, when Andy was offered an editorship, he turned it down swiftly and decisively. He had a backstage view of the work such a job entailed, and he wanted no part of it. Plus he was still flailing at his own craft. Part of the problem, as ever, seemed to be his conceptualization of himself as a writer—did his poems and casuals and newsbreaks and weekly column add up to anything? He asked Ross if he could begin signing his name in the magazine. Ross said no, and in words least calculated to defuse Andy's anxieties, he added: "I think . . . your page is stronger anonymous, as an expression of an institution, rather than an individual. I feel this very strongly. I feel that the strength of the *New Yorker* is largely that strength." Andy worked from within a contradiction: the writing that he produced most consistently and that found the greatest readership was not the writing by which he could make his name. Ross, whom Katharine called Andy's "personal 'Judge,'" continued to suppress his name and bury his voice in the editorial "we." Andy cast around for another way to define himself. "In a moment of low spirits this winter," Katharine wrote to Clifton Fadiman, the magazine's book reviewer, "Mr. White started to organize his life as if he had only a year more to live, at least that was what he said on a dark day. In doing this he has begun collecting and writing a preface for a book of his poems." That project too went nowhere.

But his struggles were private, and to the literary world he was a writer of unfailing grace and dependability. Christopher Morley offered him the editorship of *The Saturday Review of Literature* in April of 1936. "Please check my name off with a clear, convincing stroke," Andy wrote in response. "I can't edit the side of a barn." He gave several reasons, none of which were that he knew the job well from watching Ross and Katharine and he didn't want it. "I'm a literary defective," he explained, a slow reader who knew nothing of the canon. Furthermore, he said, "My health is always whimsical, and I turn out shockingly little work in the course of a week." He thanked Morley and admitted that he was, in fact, looking for a change. "What I do hope for myself is that before long I can rearrange my affairs so that I can devote my limited energy & curious talents to the sort of writing nearest to my heart & pen." But he did not specify to Morley what that was.

At the same time Andy was turning down an editorship, Harold Ross pared away a large swath of Katharine's job description. He decided to split the fact and fiction departments between two different editors. Yet another jesus, Ik Shuman, had failed to live up to Ross's impossible vision, but instead of firing him, Ross installed him as a liaison between the editorial and business departments, a decision that would prove to be durable. Then he offered the managing editorship to St. Clair Mc-Kelway, a junior editor under Katharine and a talented writer of profiles. McKelway accepted the job on the condition that Ross give him autonomous control over the magazine's journalism, leaving fiction, art, and poetry for Mrs. White (no fool, he also stipulated that he'd hold that job for no longer than three years).

The editorial files give no indication of whether Katharine welcomed this refocusing of her job or resented the diminution of her editorial scope. Though she has since come to be known as *The New Yorker*'s fiction editor, up until this moment in 1936, she helped shape almost every aspect of the magazine, including art, and had a deeply vested interest in nonfiction.

To take only one instance from the months before the fact-fiction split, she had always corresponded regularly with Clifton Fadiman about the direction of his book review column, though Hobart Weekes was the one to edit his copy, and so Fadiman brought his newest idea to her. A friend of his, a "*Nation* contributor, English Instructor up at Columbia, and keen fellow," was extremely eager to write a regular column of radio criticism for the magazine and had drafted a few sample entries. Would she take a look? "We none of us can believe there *is* a person named Lionel Trilling," Katharine responded (she thought Fadiman had written the columns himself under a terrible pseudonym, until she looked up Trilling in the phone book), but the columns were very good—excellent even. They hadn't had radio criticism since a bedridden Ring Lardner had done it for a few issues, and then a bedridden Clarence Day had tried and failed. But Ross was convinced that *New Yorker* readers never listened to the radio "except most dilettantishly." Katharine had an idea: why not survey the readership about their listening habits? If Ross was right, they would have just generated a great line for an ad—*The New Yorker* as a magazine for readers who don't listen to the radio. On the other hand, if their readership would enjoy a radio column, they "might at least improve the quality of the broadcasts"—a telling comment. Katharine was optimistic that their criticism would have heft and weight, would matter to the practitioners of the art form. In the end, Ross did not take up her survey idea, and Trilling did not take up her idea of turning his columns into a few stand-alone entries for Onward and Upward with the Arts. (Trilling kept trying to break into the magazine. He came into the office the next year and unsuccessfully pitched Katharine on the idea of replacing John Mosher as movie critic; he wouldn't publish there until 1949, but not for lack of effort.) The missed opportunity demonstrates the relish with which Katharine conducted daily thought experiments about what the magazine might become and how it might interact with the world it covered.

She was certainly going to miss editing profiles with *The New Yorker*'s finest, and just before the fact-fiction split she had the pleasure of publishing Janet Flanner's groundbreaking profile of Adolf Hitler. Flanner, fresh off a profile of Queen Mary, had the idea in 1935, though he'd "probably be hell on wheels compared even with the Queen, as a job."

Katharine loved the idea—"Just too fascinating for us to resist"—and after the two of them tried and failed to find biographical sources published in the United States, Katharine suggested that Flanner's profile might even grow to become the first American biography of the man. Over the next year Katharine worked to advance Flanner money, get her to Nuremberg and Munich without alerting anyone to her status as a journalist, connect her to reliable inside sources (one of them an old friend of Ernest Angell), and find British and French books and articles (sometimes from pornographic book dealers). The resulting profile stretched to three parts in March of 1936, because Flanner's exhaustive reporting produced a mountain of details, from the recipe for Hitler's favorite gruel to the hierarchy of his influential female friends, his severe neurasthenia, and the number of books in his library—six thousand, most unread. Flanner's profile marked a decided shift in the magazine's stance toward politics. In 1930, Ross had turned down a journalistic scoop, an interview with Benito Mussolini, saying, "We never go in for straightforward treatment of such things as serious articles about famous men." That's exactly what Flanner produced, with Ross's enthusiastic support and Katharine's help—and she signed the articles with her name, not Genêt or a false set of initials, even knowing she'd face criticism in Germany and from those in the United States who felt she hadn't been sufficiently harsh on the dictator in her quest to show the man underneath the state's mythologizing apparatus. She'd tried for a balance that would indicate the political through glittering shards of personal details, as relayed by an interested observer, and therefore the profile could be read as satirical or laudatory, depending on the reader (apparently Germans considered it pro-Hitler). The profile created a stir among American readers. It made Flanner's reputation as a journalist and inaugurated *The New Yorker*'s new willingness to meet the urgent issues of the day with closely reported nonfiction. And Flanner wrote many years later, "[The Hitler profile was] the only job that I ever did on the magazine that I'm really proud of." She swiftly agreed to produce a *New Yorker* profile of the newly crowned King Edward VIII, but he abdicated before she could write it; next was a profile of Elsie de Wolfe, but McKelway took over the fact department before Katharine could edit it.

Katharine's workload further decreased when her friend (and Andy's editor) Eugene Saxton at Harper sent a young author her way to ask for a job. Saxton had just accepted William Maxwell's second novel, *They Came Like Swallows*, and Katharine had published two of his short stories, but Maxwell was floundering in Depression-era New York. Katharine asked him what salary he needed. Maxwell had prepared an answer, on the advice of a friend: thirty-five dollars a week. "Mrs. White smiled and said, 'I expect you could live on less,'" he remembered later. "I could have lived nicely on fifteen." A few days later, a telegram from Katharine offered him a job as the liaison between artists and the Wednesday art committee—at his asked-for salary—though she kept Peter Arno and Helen Hokinson for herself. Before long, Gibbs and Katharine were passing him manuscripts to try his hand at editing, and soon he was a full-fledged member of the team. And when Ross once again threatened to cut serious poetry from the magazine, and when Katharine once again defended the cause of literature with a five-page memo that pointed out, as only one example, Edna St. Vincent Millay's current status on the bestseller list, Ross arbitrarily picked Maxwell to be the standard by which poetry was judged. If the newest hire couldn't understand a poem, they wouldn't publish it. Maxwell was hardly an Everyman when it came to literature; he proved to be a sensitive reader and editor who soon be-friended Louise Bogan, among many others. Katharine had already put Bogan on a weekly salary, instead of paying for her poetry reviews by the word, and she was now making $15 a week, a significant raise. Ross would shortly hire Charles "Cap" Pearce as the magazine's first dedicated poetry editor. Poetry was now safe at *The New Yorker*.

26.

The average contributor to this magazine is semi-literate; that is, he is ornate to no purpose, full of senseless and elegant variations, and can be relied on to use three sentences where a word would do. It is impossible to lay down any exact and complete formula for bringing order out of this underbrush, but there are a few general rules.

—Wolcott Gibbs, "Theory and Practice of Editing *New Yorker* Articles," c. 1937

Katharine's attempts to reorganize her job took place against the backdrop of Andy's continuing troubles. The problem was not New York, and not even really *The New Yorker*, because even during summers and weekends, Andy continued to not write at the farmhouse in North Brooklin. "I have the greatest difficulty making myself do any work here," he confessed to Gus Lobrano. "Even writing a letter seems an imposition. I get out my weekly stint in a sort of lonely rage—shutting myself in a room and lashing out at people who make the slightest noise about the house."

As Morley offered him the job he didn't want, Andy came down with bronchitis, and before he'd fully healed, he was summoned down to Washington, DC, where his mother underwent emergency gallbladder surgery, during which the doctor found cancer too widespread to treat. Andy and his sisters Clara and Lillian decided not to tell her about the cancer. "All that can be done," he wrote to Katharine, "is to give Mother what small amount of happiness and ease life can still hold. It is not much, I fear. The news came very hard this morning, because our hopes had been high." Two weeks later he was back in Washington to say goodbye to her in the hospital, where she lay in tremendous pain. He spent what would turn out to be her last day by her bedside, watching in agony as she tried to convince her children that she wasn't suffering and had made peace with death; she died that night with her daughter Clara by her side. On May 19, 1936, the family held a small funeral and she was buried next to her husband in the Ferncliff Cemetery in Hartsdale, New York.

He'd lost both parents within a year, and his beloved childhood home was gone. Sometime that year, he made a pilgrimage of sorts to Belgrade Lakes, Maine, the place of so many happy memories with his parents and siblings. "Things haven't changed much," he wrote to his brother Stanley in a letter that reads like a perfectly formed *New Yorker* casual. "The lake hangs clear and still at dawn, and the sound of a cowbell comes softly from a faraway woodlot. In the shallows along shore the pebbles and driftwood show clear and smooth on bottom, and black water bugs dart, spreading a wake and a shadow." Twice more he repeated the line about change, before concluding, "Yes, sir, I returned to Belgrade, and things don't change much. I thought somebody ought to know."

But the balm wouldn't last. That fall, he began having dizzy spells, a new filigree to his usual list of physical ailments, which included digestive troubles and hay fever. He consulted specialists, who could find nothing wrong with him, so he made light of the problem in two amusing essays for *The New Yorker*. He described the sensation precisely: "I will be walking along the street, say, and will take three normal steps in a forward direction; then, as I am about to set my foot down for the fourth step, the pavement moves an inch or two to the right and drops off three-quarters of an inch, and I am not quick enough for it." But his condition soon became metaphorical: "The ear must be the very vestibule of the mind," he wrote, and the ringing in his ear "a globule of Thought, caught in a sea puss." His loss of equilibrium could only ever be related to his craft. "A writer, detecting signs of decay in his own stuff, secretes internal poisons which would make even a diseased tonsil sit up and take notice." Oddly, both essays mention tonsils; Katharine had had her tonsils out just before Andy's dizzy spells began.

Her attention could not be wholly trained on Andy. At the end of her usual two months in Maine that year—during which she, Andy, and Nancy took a cruise down the coast on the *Astrid*, sleeping on the boat and eating flounder for breakfast—she left all three of her children with Andy in the farmhouse while she went to Northampton to see her father and aunts. While Andy and Joe cheered Nancy in her last boat race of the summer and while Andy took Joe to visit the Newberrys at their summer home, Katharine took stock of her elders' health under the guise of being feted by them. Her aunts hosted a tea party for Katharine, complete with finger bowls, sponge cake, and Aunt Nellie's specialty, "cheese dreams." Her verdict: "Everyone is old, and everyone is as lively as a cricket." Her father's worst problem was that "he misse[d] the wondering admiration of [her] generation for his sprightly 84 years." His sisters took him for granted.

But his liveliness wouldn't last long. Just after Christmas, having traveled down to Florida for the winter, Charles became gravely ill and landed in the hospital in Hibernia. Katharine monitored his health from afar, preparing herself to rush down to him at any moment. Ros went down from Boston, and Katharine put two of Charles's sisters on a train to join them. When Bryn Mawr's spring break rolled around, she brought Nancy with her to visit Charles in Hibernia, while Andy and Joe traveled to Miami Beach to see his sister Lillian and her family. Katharine wrote to Andy, "[Papa looks] amazingly well outwardly and seems to look the same when you first see him. Then you discover that his life is very much curtailed." The doctors advised them that Charles should never be without the company of a family member and that he do absolutely nothing. Katharine's letters were full of love for her father— "The same old scamp in spirit"—and a bit of annoyance for Nancy, who started off the vacation in a huff about having to be with her mother and elderly relatives but eventually figured out how to enjoy herself ("She's a funny gal"). Nancy took the train back to college, and Katharine joined her husband and son for the rest of their vacation, then traveled back home to New York in early April.

But even before the trip, Andy had made a fateful decision. It was time to stop writing for *The New Yorker*. As he explained to his brother Stanley, he was not quitting, exactly, but taking a year's sabbatical.

1. *Sketch of Katharine Sergeant, four years old*, portrait by Annie Barrows Shepley, her aunt, c. 1896

2. *Portrait of Artist's Niece, Rosamond Sergeant* by Annie Barrows Shepley, 1900

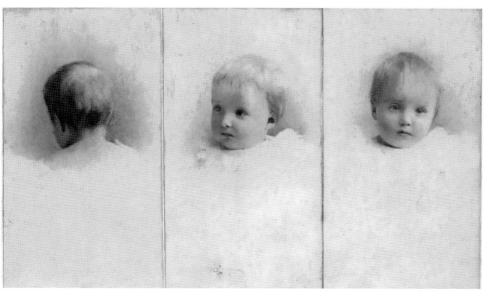

3. Katharine's earliest photos

4. Studio portrait of
Katharine, undated

5. Katharine Sergeant,
undated

6. Katharine in front of the fireplace at 4 Hawthorn Road

7. Elizabeth Shepley Sergeant,
Katharine's mother, 1879
(twenty-two years old)

8. Charles Spencer Sergeant, Katharine's
father, 1904 (fifty-two years old)

9. Caroline "Crullie" Belle Sergeant,
Katharine's aunt, undated

10. 4 Hawthorn Road, Brookline, Massachusetts,
Katharine's childhood home

11. Katharine Sergeant, eleven years old, taken at Chocorua, New Hampshire

12. Three Sergeant sisters: Katharine, Rosamond, Elsie, undated

13. Sergeant sisters, from left: Elsie, Rosamond, Katharine

14, 15. Ernest Angell at Chocorua Lake or Lake Temagami

16, 17. Katharine and Ernest in the 1910s

18. Katharine in Ernest's college sweater

19. Katharine, undated, but possibly on her honeymoon at Lake Temagami

20. Katharine
Sergeant Angell

21. Ernest Angell serving in France during World War I

22. Elizabeth Shepley Sergeant in the garden of the American Hospital of Paris, 1918

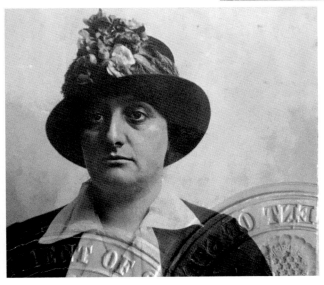

23. Elsie's passport photo, 1918

24. Marian Powys Grey, undated

25. *Marian (May) Powys (1882–1972) with a Lace Shawl*, oil on canvas, 1903, by her sister, Gertrude Mary Powys

26. *Peter Powys Grey (1922–1992)*, oil on canvas on board, 1926, by his aunt Gertrude Mary Powys

27. Peter Powys Grey at Phillips Exeter, 1940

28, 29. Nancy and Roger Angell

31. Elwyn Brooks White at Cornell, 1921, age twenty-one

30. Harold Ross and Jane Grant

32. Katharine Angell, James Thurber, and Jeannie at Snedens Landing, February 1929

33. Andy White and James Thurber, Snedens Landing, February 1929

34. Katharine on Snowball, Circle S Ranch, Nevada, 1929

35. Katharine with infant Joel in the pram and Daisy on a leash, New York City, 1931

36. The White farmhouse in North Brooklin, Maine, early 1930s

37. Katharine aboard the *Astrid*, mid 1930s

38. Only known photograph of Katharine with her three children, undated

39. A publicity photo for *A Subtreasury of American Humor* of Katharine and Andy in *The New Yorker* offices, 1941

40. Jon, Sarah, and Kitty Stableford

41. Evelyn and Roger Angell with baby Caroline, c. 1948

42. Joel White, c. 1945

43. Katharine in her *New Yorker* office, c. 1950

44. Film still of Katharine from Andy's home movies, undated

46. Katharine in her garden in North Brooklin, undated

45. Katharine, Andy, and Minnie, early 1950s

47. Katharine at her desk in North Brooklin, undated

48. Katharine reading to her grandchildren Martha and Steve

49. Katharine's and Andy's graves in the Brooklin Cemetery

50. The tree that Andy planted upon Katharine's death in the Brooklin Cemetery

> I want to see what it feels like, again, to let a week pass by
> without having an editorial bowel movement. It is terrible to
> have to write down one's thoughts before they even get their
> pin-feathers, and I have been doing that for quite a while.
> So toward the end of summer I shall give up my job and
> devote myself to the miasma of leisure and to the backwash
> of spirit. I don't know what I'll live off of, but they say it is
> called the fat of the land. I can always kill a nice fat canary.

In fact, sometime over the next two months, his thoughts for the sabbatical expanded, and by the end of May, he asked Katharine for the extraordinary dispensation of a year away from her and Joe—a year of freedom from his family and all attendant responsibilities. She said yes. Did she feel as if she even had a choice? They had molded their marriage around Andy's needs as an artist for a decade.

Perhaps the idea grew in May when the two of them took a short trip to the farmhouse, bringing with them their enormous new Labrador retriever puppy, Moses (whom Josephine, the cook, called Mr. Mosher). Their turkeys had just hatched ten chicks who needed their care, and their dozens of seedlings needed transplanting to their ambitious vegetable garden. Both of them, during the time they'd spent in Maine alone and together, were seduced by this life. And perhaps Andy had been led to the idea by Thurber, who had given up his desk job as chief Talk writer at the end of 1935—after a breakdown that led to a stint in a sanatorium, a divorce, and a remarriage the month after his divorce—and was now traveling and writing freelance for *The New Yorker*. Andy may have missed Thurber's presence in the office and wanted to emulate his freedom, though the sour truth was that the Whites and Thurber had already begun to drift apart and rarely socialized together. In their view, Thurber's success had begun to alter his character; he was short-tempered, boastful, and quite competitive with Andy, especially when drinking. Not that he needed it, but in Thurber, Andy had a model for how not to build a literary career.

By the end of May, his mind was made up, but Katharine's was uneasy. After their return to New York, he sat down in their town home to write a letter to her in the next room, to explain himself as best he could while leaving certain topics off the table, and though he does not come across particularly well in the long essay he produced, both Whites would agree many years later that it belonged in the volume of collected letters that he published in 1976. He begins by acknowledging her "delicate spiritual tremor" about the whole plan, which he hopes to assuage by telling her "in a general way what to expect of [him] and what not to expect." The reason for the sabbatical was the one that dated back at least as far as his thirtieth-birthday crisis, the time of Katharine's own sabbatical in Reno: the idea that he'd never advance toward the horizon of his talents if he remained shackled to *The New Yorker*'s weekly rhythm. He was going to write, he told his wife, but he was resolutely *not* going to tell her what he planned to write, and he asked her to keep the fact of his writing a secret, to tell others that he was doing "nothing much of anything." He needed privacy—"this aerial suspension of the lyrical spirit"—for his idea to unfold. Without phrasing it this way, Andy asked Katharine for her faith, to let him go on the strength of a "secret project" for which he had long been taking notes "on a theme which engrosse[d] [him]." In case she hadn't quite gotten the point, he added, "I do not, however, want to discuss the literary nature of the project: for altho you are my b.f. and s.c. [best friend and severest critic], I will just have to do my own writing, as always."

His letter does not forthrightly confront the enormity of what he is asking of Katharine. In fact, he figures himself as heroic, turning away from "certain easy rituals, such as earning a living and running the world's errands," in order to do the hard work of artistic creation. Katharine might have retorted that she was left to perform the hard ritual of earning a living and raising their son while he did the easy work of following "a routine of [his] own spirit," as he put it. He truly did not seem to understand that she might take offense when he assured her that by quitting the family, he did not mean to be absent for twelve months. "I simply mean that I shall invoke Man's ancient privilege of going and coming in a whimsical, rather than a reasonable, manner." He planned to travel around the country, always returning to Katharine and Joe, but he said, "I shall not adjust my steps to a soufflé." There is no hint of an understanding that his thoroughgoing rejection of the domestic might feel, to her, like her previous husband's "ancient privilege" of coming and going between home and his mistress's apartment—no hint at all that Andy saw Katharine as anything other than the generic, long-suffering wife of a writer. He says in a postscript, "I realize, too, that the whole plan sounds selfish and not much fun for you; but that's the way art goes."

Katharine likely did not write a response to her husband in the next room; if she did, it does not survive. Indeed, none of the letters to Andy that sit in the archives at Cornell or Bryn Mawr express a disagreement or complaint—from any period of their lives together. If she wrote such letters, she culled them before they could be preserved in research libraries. So perhaps she attempted to persuade Andy that freedom from the magazine and the family would not help his craft, just as she argued when she successfully persuaded him to remain at *The New Yorker* eight years previously. Perhaps she told him in person that she was hurt, or resentful, or outraged at his privilege and the way he took her for granted. But perhaps not. She might have thought about Louise Bogan, Nancy Hale, and her sister Elsie, and she might have feared that Andy was heading for a collapse. She might have defined her role as a spouse, derived from her work as an editor, as giving him precisely what he said he needed, without conditions or judgment, and smoothing as many obstacles as she could for him.

So on July 28, 1937, Andy mailed his last Notes and Comment essay from Maine to *The New Yorker* and began what he called his "year of grace," what he would later describe as "one of the most sensible twelve-month periods" in his life, and what Katharine would later describe in several letters to Roger as Andy's year of not writing—"It scared me to death." That August, while Katharine stayed in North Brooklin with the turkeys, three dogs (Freddy, Moses, and Roger's old bulldog Tunney), three children, and the household help, Andy took off for a cruise in *Astrid* with his Cornell friend Charlie Muller. Katharine reported to Ross that they promptly got lost in the fog, but for the first time in recent memory, Andy felt wonderful: "The dizziness had nearly disappeared before he left, thanks to the local doctor who gave him some medicine as an experiment. Turned out the medicine was for his nerve endings. I always knew it was nerves."

When September arrived, Katharine and Joe returned to New York while Andy stayed in Maine. She resolved to work less. She hired a younger woman to assist Josephine at home. At her friend Peg Day's house, she buttonholed Rosemary Carr Benét, wife of Stephen Vincent Benét and author of *New Yorker* stories and poems, to ask if she'd like to take over the annual children's book review because she "had definitely decided not to do them again." Benét said yes. (But that would only buy Katharine a year's reprieve. The very next December, she would be back to writing the holiday review, and she would add a second review in the spring—to which her initials were appended, unlike Andy's in his column.)

Her attempts to rearrange her affairs were not working very well. She also took on an extracurricular activity, joining the newly formed Elinor Wylie Poetry Fellowship Committee, which awarded $5,000 prizes to American poets. It was a large committee, eventually numbering eighty-eight literary dignitaries (including many *New Yorker* writers, such as Louise Bogan, Nancy Hale, and Margaret Case Harriman). Katharine was interested in functioning as a cultural gatekeeper, but she was not interested in being recognized as such. When the publishers of a book called *Women of Achievement* asked if they could feature her literary accomplishments, she turned them down flat. "I can't see any reason for such a book, other than to satisfy the vanity of the ladies described in it, and can't imagine that such a book would be of any value to students, or as a reference book," she wrote. "Because I hold these beliefs I am probably not one of 'America's representative women.'"

Katharine used her weekends in September to visit family, first taking Joe over to Snedens Landing to picnic with Elsie (Katharine delighted in telling Andy that Joe asked, "'Is Aunt Elsie my aunt or my ancestor?' I've never heard a better characterization of her!") and then traveling by train up to Northampton to visit her father and his sisters for her birthday. Nancy stayed at the Turtle Bay house before her senior year started at Bryn Mawr and Katharine took her to see *The Good Earth*, the film version of Pearl Buck's novel, calling it one of the best movies she'd ever seen.

The Whites wrote long and cheerful letters to one another, chatty and newsy but not personal. Katharine told Andy that her New York gynecologist was impressed with her summer glow and decided that she did not, after all, need the surgery that she had so feared after her miscarriage. "Was glad to get the good news about your health," Andy replied. "Don't work too hard. It would embarrass me to have you working too hard." Katharine's letters always contained a gesture of support: "I don't think I ever missed you so much but I like to think of you there." She told him, "[Stay] if you are doing work of any sort you don't want to interrupt whether it's chopping at a typewriter or a tree."

They discussed money matters, which felt manageable to them because they had always kept separate accounts and split their expenses, an arrangement that Andy continued during his grace year with money he'd already saved and with the proceeds of money his brother Arty had invested for him. He sold their Pierce-Arrow, and Katharine wrote to Andy about using her portion of the money to send her aunt Helen down to Florida for the winter with her father and Aunt Crullie, a plan that Andy approved, admitting that he'd become somewhat cavalier about money in only a few weeks of freedom: "I wouldn't know what to do with a dollar even if I could remember which pants it was in."

Katharine regretted that Andy couldn't be there for Joe's first day of second grade. She recounted a funny story: A young friend named Virginia showed up unannounced at their house to ask Katharine for advice on how to start a career in fashion. She stayed too long after dinner, ignoring hints that Katharine needed to attend to Joe, who soon had a meltdown. After shooing Virginia out the door, Katharine could focus on what he needed: he had composed a poem, and he needed her to take dictation. "Greatly to my surprise he told me the one I enclose, pretty nearly straight off, as it is." Katharine the editor just couldn't help but add, "He corrected one line (not for the better perhaps) as you can see." The poem does not survive, only the mental image of Andy and Katharine passing it between them and marveling at their son. Katharine wrote, with no apparent reference to her poet husband, "I think his fit was all due to the fear that the poem in his head wouldn't get on paper!"

Andy left North Brooklin for Belgrade Lakes and Mount Vernon—clues to his secret writing project, the poem in his head that wouldn't get on paper—and then in mid-October he met up with Katharine and Joe at the Coates's house in Gaylordsville, bringing with him two dressed turkeys. All three Whites returned to New York, a happy family reunion, but the next few months would prove tumultuous for Katharine.

At the end of October, they had a terrible scare when a little girl who lived in Turtle Bay came down with infantile paralysis—polio—the very day that Joe had been playing with her. He was in quarantine for a week until finally they knew he hadn't been infected. Katharine, ever apprehensive of her father's health since his scare earlier in the year, took another trip to Northampton to check in on him.

At work, Katharine's plan to keep reasonable hours and to not overtire herself completely disintegrated when Wolcott Gibbs resigned as an editor (he would continue to write Comment pieces, profiles, and reviews). One week, the editors were so overworked they were forced to hold their staff meeting from eight p.m. to eleven p.m., and most of them didn't even bother going home afterward. Katharine wrote to Janet Flanner that she was training "three or four new men all at once into possible or impossible Gibbses" and confessed, "I have almost gone crazy with overwork."

She charged Gibbs with writing a style sheet for future editors, something to explain "how to edit copy to fit Harold Ross's odd quirks and prejudices on subject matter and style." The resulting document, "Theory and Practice of Editing New Yorker Articles," was meant solely as an interoffice memo but has since become a pillar of the *New Yorker* mythology. The editor, in Gibbs's formulation, existed to save authors from themselves; good writing in *The New Yorker* was made by editors, not authors. "Editing on manuscript should be done with a black pencil, decisively." Would Katharine be able to find and train this decisive editor?

At the holidays, Andy was ready to return to Maine, but Katharine wasn't feeling well. Two days before Christmas, they fought all day, so that by the end they were "in a limp beaten state," by Andy's account. He took Joe up to Maine, but they stayed in nearby Blue Hill, because the North Brooklin house was not winterized. Katharine stayed home with the grippe. Andy wrote wildly happy letters back home about the wintry fun he was having with Joe, as if the snow and the time alone with his son had given him back a sliver of childhood. They sledded and skied and snuck onto their own property to skate on their frog pond. Andy wrote to Katharine, "I wondered again why we crucify ourselves on the spiky ruins of New York."

Meanwhile, Katharine was having a very different holiday. She wrote about it only to Jim Thurber, who had moved to the south of France and, despite the attenuation of their bond from the 1920s, kept up a lively correspondence with both Whites:

> I have been struggling to keep well and spent one week in
> bed. My sinus trouble which kept me in bed seems to have
> cleared up. What I think really was the matter with me was
> a combination of too much work for Christmas and for the
> children's holiday, and too much work at the office, and too
> many worries and anxieties. I never felt so near to having a
> nervous breakdown, but now that is all gone and I feel fine.

But she wasn't fine. Thurber wrote lavish descriptions of his rented cottage at Cap d'Antibes, the food, the scent of mimosa trees, tea at a nearby socialite's estate with Winston Churchill, and he did his level best to persuade the Whites to visit as soon as they could get away. Andy was game; Katharine called the plan "an impossible hope."

In mid-February, the very thing that she feared would happen did: her father became seriously ill in Florida. She rushed down to see him in Daytona, spending four days by his side. Charles Spencer Sergeant died on February 26, 1938, just after she returned to New York. The day of his death, Katharine was at home, sick in bed. He was buried at the house in Hibernia where he had spent so many winters, and Elsie was the only one of his three daughters who was there for the service—but at least Katharine had the comfort of knowing he had died with two of his sisters next to him, courtesy of her Pierce-Arrow money. Aunt Crullie described the "homely and sweet" scene in a letter to Katharine: a grave dug by the house's servants underneath a huge magnolia tree, masses of flowers that Crullie was sure Katharine would have approved—red and pink roses, sweet peas, pansies, violets, purple petunias, and candy tufts—and a committal service read by a young rector who remembered Charles from previous winters. "It was all so friendly and loving that to me there was a complete absence of the usual grim formalities and so it will always be a happy memory."

The same month, amid all this tumult, amid Katharine's overwork, worry, and grief, she and Andy made a monumental decision: they were going to double down on Andy's year of grace, which had not been successful in its first eight months. They were going to move full-time to the North Brooklin farmhouse. Katharine was going to take an immense step away from *The New Yorker*.

27.

As early as January, Andy had called the year 1938 "an unholy mess." He had begun with optimism and resolve. He wrote to Katharine from Maine on New Year's Eve that she was right that he needed to plan his days more, and that he felt "ready and eager for the new year." Katharine was entirely encouraging in her own New Year's letter but hinted that she hadn't always been: "Don't despair of not getting done some of the things you want to. It's what I care most about, that things should be right for you, even though I seem to show it in curious and disagreeable ways. I know I can do better from now on." But over the next few months, something changed. Andy wrote to Thurber—receiver of all the Whites' confidences—"I haven't produced two cents worth of work, have broken my wife's health, my own spirit, and two or three fine old lampshades by getting my feet tangled in the cord."

Katharine, on the other hand, was leaving her beloved job to serve Andy's artistic needs. Once again, if she committed her thoughts and feelings to paper, she edited them out of her archive. For the rest of her life, she would vehemently protest if anyone suggested that she resented following Andy to Maine. "I was not reluctant to go to Maine," she wrote more than three decades later. "I naturally felt sad at leaving, but I was not reluctant to go." But Andy would later express contrition: "I felt I had to get away to our farmhouse in Maine. I liked sailing and Kay loved the country. I tore Katharine loose from *The New Yorker*. It was extraordinarily stupid. She had a desk job. I didn't realize until too late what an awful wrench it would be."

The "unholy mess" of Andy's year of grace arguably proved Ross's stricture against writers' writing about themselves as special people, as members of an elite, urban literary world. His secret project, which was supposed to be an autobiography of sorts, didn't flow when Andy was self-conscious, when he tried to peer into the making of himself as a writer, to write a *Künstlerroman*. His greatest success, still to come, would be when he perfected the *New Yorker* gesture of moving his typewriter out of the frame and writing about himself, but as a farmer and an everyman, not as a writer. So perhaps Katharine knew that this move to Maine, while it might have seemed an escalation of the previous year's bad decision, was a corrective and a necessary condition for his continuing to write. Katharine's move to Maine was an act of faith—despite Andy's unwritten books and his agony of composition—a faith in his style, a faith that whatever he put his pen to would eventually turn out well. She was willing to give up almost anything for that; Andy's career was part of the logic of their marriage.

Thurber, for one, did not approve of this plan, just as he had not been supportive of Andy's decision to walk away from *The New Yorker*. "This is not a time for writers to escape to their sailboats and their farms," he had written the previous fall, arguing that the mid-1930s needed a leftist writer who wrote from his own individual conscience and was skeptical of collectivism. "You are not the writer who should think that he is not a writer." Now an exasperated Thurber pointed out that Andy had just published a long essay in *The Saturday Evening Post* declaring his love for New York and his desire never to leave. Calling himself "a stubborn inhabitant," Andy had claimed that New York's brand of life "in concentrated form" fulfilled in him "a real emotional need" (an echo of Katharine's argument in "Living on the Ragged Edge") and that he didn't seek comfort—he needed the "heroic flavor to the adventure" of living in New York, "nourishing and sustaining a man" through life's routines. Thurber believed this to be true of Andy. He told Katharine that he wasn't persuaded by her reasons, either, that Maine would be better for Andy's mental stability: "The health argument sounds okay, but somehow not okay enough. No decisions made by old New Yorker editors are ever as simple as that." "It would be funny if you became a novelist," Thurber added. "Will you become a novelist?"

But Katharine was resolute. She had begun letting some of her closest authors know of her plan as early as February, just before her father's final illness. She wrote to Janet Flanner that, contrary to rumor, she was not quitting the magazine entirely. "They have said I can still be an editor and work on a part-time long-distance arrangement. I hope it will work out to be feasible. I have done quite a lot of that in the summer already, editing and reading for opinion, etc. in Maine. . . . Of course I won't be around to have a say in scheduling and to comfort and scold contributors, but from a distance one gets a sense of detachment that is sometimes of value and also one can do about twice as much work in less time when in a quiet place." She rushed to add, "What I want you to be sure of, my darling, is that I will always be your friend and that you can consult me about editorial problems just as well when I am not in New York as you ever could before."

The New Yorker had allowed her to become a part-time editor, but not without a fight. Raoul Fleischmann and Harold Ross had been wading through a dense thicket of problems, including Ross's deteriorating emotional health as a result of his unhappy second marriage and Fleischmann's disastrous investment of *The New Yorker*'s operational reserve fund in a failed periodical called *Stage*. When Katharine and Andy announced their plan to move to Maine, Fleischmann saw a way to solve two problems at once, a way to oust Ross while retaining the golden couple: he offered the two of them the editorship of *The New Yorker*.

For each of them, it was the second offer of promotion to the top of the masthead but the first time they considered working together even more intimately than they already did. Fleischmann recalled: "After 'thinking it over' for forty-eight hours, they very charmingly and gracefully turned me down, saying that they were loyal to Ross and the *New Yorker* and could not entertain any such idea and were going to Maine to live anyway."

Throughout March, Katharine worked from New York to settle her father's estate, a burden added to her work life without Gibbs and her home life without Andy. By the end of the month, she was feeling poorly enough to need a vacation. Florida had lost its appeal, so Andy and

Katharine returned to their honeymoon spot of Waterville in Bermuda for a two-week break—but even that did not end the tumult. So violent was the weather during their boat crossing that Katharine was nearly injured when an armchair crashed into the desk at which she had just been working, and their arrival was delayed for a day until the boat could make it into the channel. Finally they disembarked to an island that felt unchanged from their visit eight years previously, and they soon relaxed into the rhythms of swimming, sunning, and dining in the luxury lodge.

The next two months made a mockery of Andy's intention to forgo a schedule and live a life directed only by his whims. He transformed over-night into a dynamo, one who sprinted between New York and Maine in a mad hurry to get the farmhouse ready for their moving day of June 1. He oversaw a noisy crew of workers who replaced the hot water boiler and rebuilt chimneys and burned a pasture—expensive undertakings, es-pecially for a man who wasn't working, but Katharine was able to pay for it by selling some of the securities that she'd inherited from her fa-ther. He was so excited to be in North Brooklin that, on a whim, he stole some lumber from the chimney project to convert the turkey coop into a brooder house for chickens, and he proudly drew before and after pictures for Katharine's benefit. "On a day like this," he wrote as if still trying to convince her of the rightness of the move, "it is inconceivable that we should live anywhere but here." Back in New York, the two of them ruthlessly downsized their belongings. Andy estimated they had twenty-one beds, and he began offering them to anyone he happened to be writing to. They kept family heirlooms, like the cherry furniture that was passed down to Katharine from the Sergeant side, and they kept Katharine's baby grand piano. As if their lives weren't chaotic enough, they got a new puppy, Ezekiel.

By sheer necessity, Andy plunged right back into his identity as a writer for hire. "Any money at all that I can get my hands on these days seems like a fine thing, and nobody gets any back talk from me," he wrote to Ik Shuman, renewing his position of chief writer of *New Yorker* news-breaks. He contributed occasional casuals and started writing paragraphs for Notes and Comment again. But these were stopgap measures to raise some cash, and behind the scenes he began scheming, trading his dreams of literary immortality for a pragmatic assessment of what he had on hand, "in the bank," to use *New Yorker* parlance. He assembled two books of previously published material for Harper, which Eugene Saxton instantly accepted: *The Fox of Peapack*, a collection of poems dedicated to Katharine that would come out later that year, and *Quo Vadimus?; or, The Case for the Bicycle*, a collection of essays and stories that would come out in 1939.

He'd already dusted off some old children's stories, earlier in his year of grace, and with Katharine's encouragement he had set about shaping them into a book. Long ago, before he had a son of his own, he'd begun telling tales to his nieces and nephews of a mouse he had once dreamed about very vividly. His name was Stuart and he was "nicely dressed, courageous, and questing." Andy desultorily wrote a few of the stories down, not intending much, but Katharine showed them to Clarence Day. Day liked them; "Don't let Andy neglect Stuart Little—it sounds like one of those *real* books that last." He did neglect him, until his year off, when Katharine's own questing imagination ran ahead to the problem of how Stuart Little might emerge into the world: "I've been thinking about illustrators for Stuart Little! Guess you wish I'd stop thinking." With his stories being insistently called out from him and his newfound willingness to pull manuscripts from drawers to place on editors' desks, Andy submitted a draft of the first half of *Stuart Little* to editors at Oxford University Press and Viking. Both turned him down. The manuscript went back into a drawer in Maine.

Andy had one last idea, and by June, when the Whites planned to move, it came to fruition. If he needed to write for money, he'd prefer to do it less frequently, to use the first-person singular rather than the first-person plural, and to be able to attach his name to the work—to write from his own conscience and from a grounded place on earth. *Harper's Magazine* contracted with him to write a monthly column called One Man's Meat for the generous salary of $300 per column and with an equally generous allowance of 2,500 words. He would still edit newsbreaks for *The New Yorker* and contribute paragraphs and casuals when the urge struck him. But he would continue to operate independently from *The New Yorker*'s relentless pace.

So would Katharine. Ross and Fleischmann let her go, but with great reluctance and a generous financial deal. A few years previously, in the depths of the Depression, the cash-poor magazine had begun to pay Katharine partly in stock using an escrow arrangement, so that her one hundred annual shares would accrue for ten years, and she could only claim her one thousand shares if she was still employed at the end of that period. Her yearly salary in 1937 was $15,000. Now, as she prepared to step down to part-time work, only occasionally coming to New York for editorial duties, Fleischmann agreed to continue the stock arrangement, unaltered, on top of whatever salary Ross paid her. This was, Katharine understood, a backward-looking gesture that acknowledged that she'd been underpaid from 1925 to 1930, and a forward-looking strategy to earn her loyalty in the hope that she would return to full-time work if the Whites' Maine experiment did not pan out.

To find her replacement, Katharine didn't need to go far. Andy's Cornell friend and former housemate Gus Lobrano had moved from publicity with the Cunard steamship line to an editorship at *Town and Country*. Katharine sent him some pieces to edit as a trial run, one of her possible Gibbses, and she and Ross both approved of the way he handled three short stories and a column by their "premier cliché artist," Alexander Woollcott. With Lobrano in charge and Maxwell growing into the job, the fiction department was in excellent shape. Thirteen years after inventing her job and growing the magazine and performing almost every role on the editorial side of the masthead, Katharine opened her own exit and stepped through.

Part V

Interregnum

(1938–1943)

28.

I just can't forgive Mrs. White for deserting the office. She is the best woman editor in the world, had the best editor's job in the world, and what does she do, leave it all and retire to a farm in Maine. It's just too awful!

—Janet Flanner to Daise Terry, 1939

As her eighteen-year residence in the city was ending, Katharine faced two other endings.

First she traveled to Bryn Mawr to watch Nancy graduate cum laude, after a college career that had included the science and philosophy clubs and the hockey and basketball teams. Nancy had considered pre-medicine, but she'd chosen biology as her major, and she was staying at Bryn Mawr College for another year to earn a master's in zoology.

Then Katharine traveled to Connecticut to watch Roger graduate from Pomfret School. His high school career had been more eventful and less academic than his sister's. Precisely like his mother, he struggled with algebra, failing an exam but managing to squeak through the course without needing a tutor. Unlike his mother, he made the unconscious choice not to focus on his classes. He called it "a form of rebellion against [his] parents who had both been such serious students." Like his mother, he acted in theater, including a part in a French club play. Very much like his mother—in fact, achieving in high school what she did in college—he coedited the weekly newspaper, *The Pontrefact*, for which his mother's connections gave him an advantage he avidly seized.

One of Katharine's authors, a young humorist named S. J. Perelman, introduced Roger to Benny Goodman, the top swing band leader in the country, one night after a set at the Hotel Pennsylvania, and Roger asked to interview him. Sure, Goodman said; come see me at one p.m. the next day. Roger showed up on time and knocked and knocked, until finally Goodman answered the door in his underwear, prompting Roger's lede: "Great bandleaders get to sleep late." He followed that with an interview of Mayor La Guardia, which he obtained by sitting outside his office for hours. Now, as he graduated from high school, he did exactly what was expected of him. He enrolled at Harvard College, like his father and grandfather before him.

Both Nancy and Roger would, of course, spend part of their summer at the farmhouse, where they each had a room. The family went swimming in the morning off the float at the end of the long dock that jutted into the cove, an event always followed by a morsel of semisweet S. S. Pierce chocolate. This was the summer that Joel learned to swim without a life jacket. Andy filmed the family with his movie camera, Katharine on the dock with Nancy, Roger, and Joel. Stills from those few seconds of film remain the only pictures in existence of Katharine and all three children. Another few seconds of film: Nancy, in a plaid one-piece bathing suit, hauling herself up onto the float and struggling to make it, hanging off the edge, when suddenly Katharine swoops into the frame in an identical plaid suit, cigarette in hand, and snatches Nancy's white bathing cap off her head. Nancy finally gets onto the float and stands, only to brace herself as Roger comes flying at her and tries to push her off.

Katharine was proud of the life she could give to her children in Maine—sailing on the *Astrid* for days at a time, fishing for mackerel in the afternoon, and learning to drive on gravel roads—but as the two eldest moved up the educational ladder, her pride was shadowed by money worries. She had taken a pay cut and needed to reach out to Ernest to recalibrate the division of Nancy's and Roger's expenses. In the scant letters that survive between them, financial wrangling had replaced their bickering over weekends, summer vacations, and the disposition of the children's time. For the past three years, at Ernest's request, she had evenly split with him the children's school tuition and expenses (they paid a total of $1,920 a year for Nancy at Bryn Mawr and $960 a year for Roger at Pomfret, plus monthly allowances for both), but she could no longer pay anything and would return to the terms of their divorce agreement. Ernest was affronted by the way she "just announced" her move to Maine and its financial repercussions, prompting another long letter from Katharine in which she tried to justify herself. Her pay cut came at the same time that her obligation to her Sergeant aunts was about to increase from $900 to $1,600 or $1,700 a year (she had stopped supporting Elsie last summer, something she apparently did covertly through their father). Katharine pleaded with Ernest to find her decisions reasonable, "considering how little real expense [she'd] been and how much material help [she'd] been able to give [him] over the years." She added, perhaps untactfully, an attempt to contextualize their unique arrangement: "Most fathers, even with working wives, have to carry all the expenses of their children." She signed her letters "Katrina," his nickname for her. His responses do not survive.

Money troubles aside, Katharine seemed to relish her new life and she was busy in a way that felt right to her. She complained but in a boastful way. She wryly described herself to Ruth McKenney, a younger, single woman earning money by writing about the very life—urban, hustling, social—that Katharine had just left behind:

> My life here is fantastic. You should see me trying to be a good
> farm wife, picking, canning, mopping and dusting, and at the
> same time keeping my 7 1/2 year old from drowning, and my
> 17 year old from killing himself and his girl friends in wild
> night rides, and making my big daughter-scientist be domestic
> when she'd rather be losing all her few dollars on late night
> poker parties. (Not one of the three pays the least attention
> to me.) And on top of this trying to be a long distance editor.
> Then there are the dogs, the pig, the chickens, the turkey (only
> one!), the cows who are our boarders, all meeting disaster daily,
> and the vegetables and flowers that I'm supposed to tend. And
> there's Andy trying to meet deadlines when he'd rather be
> catching mackerel or building a laying house for the pullets.

That bit about the animals was added purely for effect. Katharine had nothing to do with them; Andy and his jack-of-all-trades, Howard Pervear, tended the animals and did all the haying. She ended her pocket essay to McKenney with a patented E. B. White flourish, a portrait of their maid: "The only member of the family with any leisure is the country girl who comes in by the day. She rests all afternoon, reads 'Ulysses,' and washes her hair every five days, and she has to leave on the dot of 8 or her husband gets mad."

Their homestead was a bustling place within a quiet town. North Brooklin, Maine, had narrow gravel roads, few cars, and even fewer tractors. All the work in the fields, including Andy's, was done by horsepower, all that mowing and raking and stowing, with first Roger, and then Joel when he grew big enough, sitting atop the hay wagon. Even beyond the fields, the land was generally bare of woods, and so were the islands out in the cove, because they had been logged for firewood. The town had been served by steamship up until 1934, and descendants of the same dozen families who'd settled the town in the previous century made their living by fishing, lobstering, or canning fish and clams. They had all known each other for decades, and even the men called each other "dee-ah," which charmed Roger, a boy growing up with one foot in the biggest city and one foot in a rural hamlet. It charmed Andy too, and he wrote about it for *Harper's*.

Luckily the Whites had native guides to show them how to live in Maine—their next-door neighbors, Sadie and Charlie Henderson. Katharine saw Sadie almost every day; she had a crucial quality in a friend—she was well-read—and from her Katharine learned things like how to pay the town taxes: you walk to the Bridges' backyard and open the refrigerator in the woodshed and deposit them there, safe against fire. This small-town way of life was getting even smaller. The rusticators who came every summer had dwindled during the Depression and even year-round residents were starting to move away in search of jobs, so the town of Brooklin, with the state's tiniest post office, was shrinking. The Whites lived in North Brooklin, which had its own post office, only very slightly larger. Their postmistress was Edna Pervear, wife of Andy's hired man.

It behooved the Whites to befriend the postmistress because they kept her very busy. Katharine would receive a fat packet from *The New Yorker* in the morning mail run in the farmhouse's large roadside mailbox, and she'd open it, read the memos and manuscripts, comment on them, and have the return packet ready for the afternoon delivery and pickup. It would reach West Forty-Third Street the very next day.

The Whites, too, would frequently travel by train down to the city—sometimes together, often alone—for doctors' appointments, meetings at the magazine, and socializing with friends and family. Katharine would see authors at the Algonquin and Elsie at the Cos Club (Elsie had given up her house in New Mexico; she frequently rented a house in Snedens Landing to write in the warmer months, and she now rented an apartment on East Seventy-Third Street in New York as her primary residence).

When the summer ended and the academic year began, the Whites found themselves with a new daily routine. With Nancy and Roger away, Andy would drive Joe to school each morning while Katharine sat down at her desk with the morning's mail and started reading with a pencil in hand. Joe now attended third grade at the public elementary school, quite a change from his urban private school. "I don't think he'll learn anything much but I don't care," Katharine wrote to Ross. She was happy to distance herself and her youngest son from the high-pressure parenting culture of New York City.

Andy and Howard Pervear tackled the daily chores with the grounds and the animals, plus seasonal tasks like getting a furnace installed before the winter and reshingling the barn roof. There wasn't much time left for writing; Andy had turned in exactly one casual all summer. Behind the scenes, Katharine conspired with Ross to solve the problem of Andy. "I thought his first Comment Dept. was o.k. and his second poor. Don't quote me," Katharine wrote. "I suggest (and don't want him to know this) that an occasional non-timely Comment suggestion that needs rewriting, might start him off on the piece a week habit. I know he wants to write them." But *The New Yorker* was going to need to be patient because they were third in line behind the farm and *Harper's*.

Katharine, for one, looked forward to "the great calm" of her new routine—a quiet household and regular work. But all too soon, she found the daily mail to be a little too calm, a little too boring. Almost the instant that her risky experiment of part-time editing began, she lost footing at *The New Yorker*.

The mailbag contained only non-timely fact pieces that the editors wanted her to clean up. No humor, no poetry, and none of the fiction that was her forte. It felt a little like make-work, and it was mind-numbing. She fired off a letter to managing editor Ik Shuman and stated that she was not willing to serve as "just a doctorer of lousy factual pieces" and that by rights she should be reading casuals and fiction and helping to decide whether or not to buy them (reading "for opinion," in the magazine's argot). "That's what I'm best at and if the magazine will miss me at all, it will be there."

And then she fired off a much longer letter to Ross. She didn't hold back—not that she ever did—when she told him that this was emphatically not what she had in mind when they had designed her long-distance job. Her value to the magazine lay in her ability to read manuscripts and to see their highest potential. Sure, she could tidy up a fact piece or a profile.

> But the best thing I learned to do over the years, it seems
> to me, was to see from a bum casual how to make a good
> one, or to see what trend a writer was taking, and give him
> a steer, or to say how to make a good casual better, or to
> keep up the spirits of and follow up our best writers.

She listed the magazine's most precious authors and sketched out a plan to elicit casuals from them in the coming months: Frank Sullivan, Leo Rosten, Arthur Kober, S. J. Perelman, Dorothy Parker, Robert Benchley, Ogden Nash. And James Thurber—she had three book ideas for him.

It was a slow-motion, long-distance battle of wills, and Katharine was losing. *New Yorker* staffers met to discuss the issue, and Ross and Shuman privately conferred. They held steady in their resolve to use Katharine as a tiebreaker when deciding to buy borderline pieces and a tough-love editor when shaping recalcitrant pieces. But she would no longer help shape the fiction, poetry, and casuals in the magazine; that would be left to Lobrano and Maxwell. In consolation or compensation, Katharine presided over two domains that were hers alone, and she dove in with—arguably—too much energy. The first project was Ross's assignment: reading each "X issue" of the magazine (the just-published issue) and writing a full report of her opinion—"faults, repetitions, typos, merits, and failings"—including the ads.

Katharine opened up the fire hose of her opinionated mind, and if ever she earned the adjective "formidable," it was now. She wrote to Ross, but on the understanding that he would pass along her queries and suggestions to editors, to writers—even to the people profiled in the magazine, as if they too were waiting at the end of this editorial version of "whisper down the lane" for her inner thoughts. She was unsparing. She "never read a more rambling, dull, repetitive, and windy piece" than the As to Men fashion column, which she found both poorly written and offensive in its slavering approach to luxury goods, sure to "driv[e] the reader to the barricades." She was unsparing even when criticizing a story by William Maxwell ("so slight and delicate as to be nearly indistinguishable" from its surrounding text) or pronouncing an E. B. White piece "an obviously minor effort" which should have been relegated to the bottom of the page.

She paid special attention to the balance of the casuals and sounded the alert whenever she felt the magazine had dulled its humorous edge. "We're turning into a little mag. of serious fiction. Coates, O'Hara, Benson, Weidman, Fuchs, are all superb for us but we really shouldn't have to use them so often. And the merit of their stories gets lost in a reader's boredom at seeing their stuff so often." Similarly, she took great offense at Clifton Fadiman's wholesale omission of novels from his holiday book list; they were, after all, "the great Christmas present," and to include them would help "remove the formidable highbrow or specialized taste quality" of his column.

She overwhelmed the *New Yorker* editors with her criticism, and William Maxwell, for one, felt threatened enough to try to respond to her, point by point, with explanations and defenses.

Her response to other editors' response to her is an important key to the structure of her intellectual life. "Just tell the boys I don't want them to explain why such and such a point was missed," Katharine ordered Ross. Her readings were never meant to be action items, she said. These reports were pure analytical exercises, the record of *The New Yorker*'s most interested, knowledgeable, invested reader's thoughts as she read. They were magazine criticism, a genre that didn't exist then and still doesn't, a real-time reader's response to the latest incarnation of that ineffable thing, the magazine's ethos, written by someone with both the previous issues of the magazine and an ever-changing vision of its ideal incarnation alive in her mind. Her reports were meant to be useful, and ignored if they weren't.

The problem, as Katharine knew too well, was that no retroactive report could be as useful in the curation of the magazine as the proactive, creative acquisition of new material. She knew her editing experience was not well used by "destructive post-mortems like this." Once again, she tried to persuade Ross to recalibrate her role at the magazine. She again asked to read new contributions. "It's the pieces that never get to you, though, that I worry about. Perhaps we're losing new writers." She needed to read for the future, not rehash the imperfect past. But nothing changed, other than that Ross gave her permission to slow the frequency of her reports down from weekly to monthly. Everyone in Brooklin and New York City breathed a sigh of relief.

Katharine's other remaining domain was the biannual children's book review, and the deadline for the big holiday column was approaching. So when she wasn't critiquing *The New Yorker* that autumn, Katharine was reading picture books and chapter books. Hundreds of them arrived in the mail sack, stacks of them piling up all over the house as the winter arrived.

That Thanksgiving, Elsie came from New York to visit for a week, arriving in time for a snowfall on Thanksgiving and a feast assembled by the Whites' white-haired cook, Milly Gray. There was a true blizzard the day after the holiday, complete with horizontal snow in the gale-force winds, power and water outages, and Andy in constant motion to thaw frozen pipes and warm frozen animals.

Katharine worked through it all. Another columnist might have been content to choose a couple dozen of the books that publishers' sales teams were pushing the hardest, but not Katharine. Her self-imposed and ambitious mandate was to convey as broad a sense of children's book publishing as possible. Almost no other magazine did so, and Katharine felt called to fill this void. Her goal was a highly edited list of books for parents to tear out of the magazine just before the summer vacation or just before Christmas, to shop for the cream of juvenile books for their kids.

Only by reading reviews, special publications like the bimonthly *Horn Book Magazine*, and publishers' catalogs all year-round could she generate a list of books to consider. And then, for months before each column, she skimmed as many as four hundred books, eliminating half, reading the other half cover to cover, and choosing half of those to blurb for her readers. She could afford no shortcut if she wanted to be able to give her readers pronouncements like those that started her 1938 column: "The age of specialization seems to have caught up with the children's book list; there is hardly a hobby, an art, a craft, or a science that isn't covered." She mapped the current offerings, and only her exhaustive reading enabled her to note what was missing in the marketplace: "There is no new book which one feels sure will be read and reread for years to come, such as Marie Hamsun's 'A Norwegian Farm' of a few seasons back," or "There are no new characters like Mary Poppins to take their place in nursery tradition."

Ross capriciously suggested that maybe *The New Yorker* should run children's book blurbs year-round, three or four recommendations every two or three weeks. Absolutely not, replied Katharine, because then she'd have to read juvenile books "every day of the year, a thought that [was] beyond words repellant." No way would she submit to that "mentally stultifying process." Well, then, could she turn her "too-definitive, too-strenuous" process into something a bit more casual? This request frustrated Katharine to no end. She had grown tired of repeating herself. "How can one choose the cream if you don't have the whole milk to work from?" She needed to read exhaustively to pronounce authoritatively on the field, and she said, "If I am not thorough both the magazine and I look silly."

Through the serendipitous workings of the creative life, Katharine's children's book review created a medium-sized problem with a solution that had a large impact on the White household. The problem—severe enough that Andy twice took it as his subject for his *Harper's* column— was the proliferation of children's books into all corners of their already- teeming farmhouse, what he called the "annual emergency" that found him "gazing hatefully" at all their covers.

Katharine handily solved the problem by donating the books. She began giving them to the district schools, making the rounds monthly, a chore she loved because "the exciting thing is that the children just lap them up." And yet she still had more books to disperse, so she donated many of them to their local library, Friend Memorial Public Library in Brooklin, a one-room building funded by the two brothers who made Friend's Brick Oven Baked Beans and staffed by Annie Dollard, who'd been minding the stacks of donated books since 1901. The tiny, ad hoc collection lacked much of anything for children before Katharine's do- nations began, but soon it was earning notice in *The Bangor Daily News* for possessing "the finest in children's literature." Here was a worthy cause for the mind, Katharine realized. She began donating time and money to the library, and soon she would do much more.

One way to take the creative temperature of the White household was to listen: if it was quiet, Andy was struggling to write and Katharine was muting her own productivity. Katharine told Ross that whenever she handwrote her letters to him, it was because her "batting away" on her office typewriter made Andy feel "uncreative, when he was struggling to put words to paper." That winter, all of Katharine's reports to Ross on the X issue were written in pencil.

But Andy was finding new energy for his children's manuscript, per- haps by invidious comparison to much of what he picked up around the house. He even went so far as to divulge the direction of his thoughts in *Harper's* that Thanksgiving: "Close physical contact with the field of ju- venile literature leads me to the conclusion that it must be a lot of fun to write for children—reasonably easy work, perhaps even important work." He sat back down to complete the story of Stuart Little's quest. He wrote against the headwinds of his own trepidation and spurred by considerable outside pressure. Andy's sentence about juvenile literature caught Theodor Geisel's eye (whose book *The 500 Hats of Bartholomew Cubbins* was about the only children's book Andy actually had praised in his *Harper's* piece). Geisel showed the essay to Anne Carroll Moore, the woman who had founded the New York Public Library's Children's Room in 1911 and its children's programs at all sixty-five branches. Moore immediately launched an intense letter-writing campaign to spur Andy on his writing, a campaign that could not have been more ill advised.

Katharine knew Moore and disliked her. She called her "the Grand Panjandrum of Children's Literature," and though she attended Moore's annual candlelit dinner of authors, librarians, and reviewers in the autumn when children's books were released, she was disgusted by the sentimentality of the event. Moore wielded considerable influence in the world of children's books but, in Katharine's opinion, little taste; Moore preferred the precious and the conventional. Katharine had particular disdain for one of Moore's rules for children's literature, which Moore called one of her four "respects": "If a story was imaginative, it was to be purely so and not have reality mixed up with fantasy." Moore had a rubber stamp that read "Not recommended for purchase by expert," and she'd hold it in one hand while paging through a publisher's catalog. If she unrecommended a book, librarians all over the country would follow suit and decline to order it. But Moore very much wanted a children's book from E. B. White, and in the early months of 1939, she wrote him five times to tell him so—and wrote to Katharine too.

On March 1, Andy sent the unfinished manuscript to his editor, Eugene Saxton, at Harper. "You will be shocked and grieved to discover that the principal character in the story has somewhat the attributes and appearance of a mouse," he confessed. He followed his manuscript down to New York for business meetings, and Katharine excitedly wrote to him about a subject of enduring interest to her: the illustrations. "I think Ernest Shepherd's [sic] style would be good for Stuart Little, but he wouldn't know New York," she wrote. (E. H. Shepard was the British illustrator of the Pooh stories.) "It has to have exact N.Y.C. setting in pictures. . . . What would be best is an American Shepherd." Andy returned home to Maine with Saxton's mandate to finish the book in time for publication that fall, but he did everything he could to tamp down expectations. "My wife is nagging me about Stuart, too," he wrote to Saxton, "in fact today I told her she would have to stop—that she was driving me too hard. I think it made quite an impression on her." Moore also overreached by talking about his *Harper's* essay in her column in *Horn Book*, which led Andy to give her a stern warning too: "I am afraid that between you and my publisher and my wife—all of you at me to finish my book—it will never get done; I pull back like a mule at the slightest goading." Katharine finally wrote to Moore herself: "I've decided that the less we say the sooner it will be done."

But the damage was done. *Stuart Little* went back into the drawer. In fact, Katharine would be the next White with a book flying off bookstore shelves.

29.

There constantly exists, for a certain sort of person of high emotional content, at work creatively, the danger of coming to a point where something cracks within himself or within the paragraph under construction—cracks and turns into a snicker. Here, then, is the very nub of the conflict: the careful form of art, and the careless shape of life itself. What a man does with this uninvited snicker (which may closely resemble a sob, at that) decides his destiny.

    —E. B. White, preface, *A Subtreasury of American Humor*

If 1938 to 1943, the five years the Whites were to live full-time in Maine, turned out to be an interregnum in Katharine's life, it also gives us a glimpse of what *The New Yorker* might have been like without Katharine.

The male editors she'd hired and trained continued to publish women authors—101 of them during Katharine's time in Maine, to be exact. But just under half of those were writers the magazine had previously published, and the vast majority of the women writers not previously published by the magazine had only one or two stories in it. The immense energy Katharine devoted to finding and cultivating women writers— reading rival publications, writing to authors to ask them to submit to *The New Yorker*, taking them to lunch, writing them long and intimate letters even when rejecting a piece—all but dissipated. The new female writers who broke into the magazine during these years found their way in through one of the big New York literary agencies, like Curtis Brown, Maxim Lieber, or Brandt & Brandt, offices that flooded the magazine with stories. These writers continued to submit stories after their initial acceptances but received only terse rejections addressed to their agents, signed by Lobrano or Maxwell, and generally little more personal than the magazine's form letter (which itself went out to seven hundred to one thousand people per week). The only advantage that having an agent gave these writers was a quick turnaround. For many of them, the magazine never even started folders in their own names—a telling omission. Even writers like Agnes Burke Hale and Eleanor Gilchrist, who each had published ten stories, communicated only through their agents—which is to say, they had no real relationship with the magazine's editors, none of the back-and-forth that formed the substance of Katharine's contribution and career. When she would eventually return to her desk in midtown, Katharine would need to reckon with the lost opportunities of these years.

Only with hindsight would the Whites see that their self-exile from the city would have an invisible shape, bounded as these years were by World War II. Katharine paid close attention to the news from Europe, which she mostly received by radio. On the Sunday in September 1939 when England declared war on Germany, Katharine would make Joe put on a suit and Andy would dig up a hat from a closet and the family would go to church to listen to the young minister and sing hymns; that night they would listen to King George on the radio while they ate dinner. Katharine would often stay up late into the night listening to broadcasts, careful to tune in only when Joe was not in earshot, and she would lose sleep from excitement each time the RAF did well. The following year, in the summer of 1940, Katharine would listen to the Republican National Convention and she would be cheered when Wendell Willkie, who advocated that the United States join the war, beat isolationist William Taft for the presidential nomination. That same month, when "Paris became German," Andy would deliver to Ross a particularly heartfelt Comment that would begin to move *The New Yorker* away from its neutral stance to advocate for American intervention as a moral duty. Katharine longed to be useful not just to *The New Yorker* but to the historical moment writ large, and she discussed the news in practically every letter.

In her restlessness, Katharine embarked on not one but two book projects.

The first began almost exactly when Andy tucked away his children's book. The previous year, the publisher Coward McCann had suggested the idea of editing a humor collection, and now, in the spring of 1939, with the war in Europe looming, it seemed like an apt use of the Whites' combined talents. They signed a contract for *A Subtreasury of American Humor*, which would have both their names on the cover. They began writing letters to *New Yorker* humorists to ask for their recommendations of prose and verse: "lost jewels which lie tarnished in old newspaper files and scrapbooks," as Andy put it. But mainly Andy and Katharine would collect whatever they found funny, "a subtreasury designed for the safe-keeping of [their] own valuables." This project, which would take about two years, was an enjoyable distraction for both of them.

Andy grudgingly produced his signed column for *Harper's* only because he needed the money. One Man's Meat was a certifiable success—the first issue in which it appeared brought 11,200 new subscribers and a 20 percent increase in *Harper's* newsstand sales. At the same time, the two collections he'd just released as part of the previous spring's flurry of writing, *The Fox of Peapack* and *Quo Vadimus?; or, The Case for the Bicycle*, had barely sold. There was a mismatch between what he loved to do and what made money, between what he thought when he sat down to write and what people wanted from him.

Katharine was experiencing a similar brand of cognitive dissonance as she sat on the sidelines, reading *The New Yorker* after it was published like any other civilian. She wanted to be reading for inspiration, for vision, for a new author who would electrify her. But instead she was tasked with an exercise in backward curation: editing a book to be called *Short Stories from "The New Yorker."* She worked closely with other fiction editors, but she told one contributor, "If it is good the credit is not mine alone but I put so much work on it that I feel a very maternal interest in its success or failure." Both editors and contributors sent her suggestions for stories, but it was Katharine who edited down those lists, and she often had to shout to make herself heard. "This would be a book of stories, FICTION in the SHORT STORY form, gentlemen, and if any humor got into it, it would be incidental to narrative."

A humor book was already in the works—the Whites' *Subtreasury*—

so this volume of *New Yorker* fiction needed a different reason for existence. But more important, Katharine trimmed out the merely humorous to unearth enough literary stories for a collection that would compete in the marketplace with compendiums like O'Brien's *Best American Short Stories* and *The O. Henry Memorial Award Prize Stories*. Out would go satirical essays, humorous criticism, reminiscences, and even fictionalized autobiographical stories like the beloved Father stories of Clarence Day. No Frank Sullivan, no Robert Benchley, no S. J. Perelman. Katharine's guiding aesthetic would make it difficult even to sweep in anything by E. B. White. But it would have been just as unthinkable to leave him out, so Katharine asked him to add his name to a most uncharacteristic piece he had published earlier that March called "The Door," a phenomenological account of a mental breakdown that he had signed only with his initials, and thus he squeaked into the book. Katharine was adamant that this would not be an omnibus of the best of *The New Yorker*. This would be, in her words, "a distinguished collection of short stories which, though [they] didn't get out to do it, [they] seem to have amassed during the years. It would be mostly savage, serious, moving, or just well written fiction with some that are funny in part." Three stories appeared on every single list of recommendations she received from fellow editors and the few contributors she solicited for suggestions. She put these at the front of the collection: John O'Hara's "Over the River and Through the Wood," Nancy Hale's "Midsummer," and Robert Coates's "The Net." But what should follow them?

She had a secret weapon: Roger, whom she bragged was "the world's living authority on *The New Yorker*," a title he'd held since he was fifteen and surprised Andy and Katharine one evening at dinner by demonstrating his perfect recall of every cartoon the magazine had ever published. They'd immediately put his claim through a battery of tests, and he could match drawings to captions with worrisome accuracy. Had their household's preoccupation with *The New Yorker* deformed their bright child? He was currently putting his peculiar literary education to good use at Harvard, where he majored in English and wrote for and edited the *Crimson*. He breezily told Katharine that he could write a six-thousand-word short story for a creative writing class in a single evening. He'd spent one summer reading manuscripts for Simon & Schuster and another summer as an office boy for *Country Life*. So Katharine and Andy consulted him on the *Subtreasury*, asking him to suggest stories and running their ideas past him. Katharine took almost all of Roger's recommendations.

That autumn, and continuing over the winter and into the spring of 1940, Katharine read and made lists and counted words and remade lists. Managing editor Ik Shuman visited publishers around town and generated so much interest in the fiction collection that he felt the magazine could have its choice of publishers. Simon & Schuster, feeling the collection would bring prestige and the attention of young fiction writers, gunned hardest. S&S promised *The New Yorker* complete control over the contents and mentioned that they were particularly pleased that Katharine was at the helm. Shuman signed a contract that divided the 10 percent royalty entirely among the contributors, with nothing accruing to the magazine itself.

Katharine set to work drafting and redrafting the foreword. "At the time the magazine was getting started, in 1925," explained one immodest version that was soon cut, "the editors had no notion it would become one of the chief outlets for American short fiction." Simply by accepting everything good that came their way, the scrappy little humor magazine "soon found itself printing some of the grimmest and gravest fiction of the grim 1930s." The draft then got pointedly down to business. "Not even the fairy godfather of the 'short story,' Mr. O'Brien, has yet satisfactorily defined this sort of literature." The editors made very clear that, though they'd come late to the game, though they'd never even set out to play the game, they'd been redefining the rules all along. "In gazing on this, our strangest child," the draft concluded, they had at least "shown that the short story is not necessarily the plotted darling of the big-circulation group, and that a short story does not have to run the proper thousands of words and break over into the back among the advertisements." This draft foreword was pared down to a single paragraph, but its point was emphatically made by the stories within.

The work grew to fill all Katharine's available time. Every detail fell to her, including writing the cover copy, which she groused about. In May, she had to beg off from the task of making a dummy edition for the Simon & Schuster salesmen because she was too ill from overwork. To ensure that no superlative stories from the distant *New Yorker* past had gone unconsidered, she traveled to New York to comb through the magazine clip books that secretaries had been assembling for each writer. Her completist approach paid off when she unearthed four stories that everyone had forgotten. At last, in early September, she delivered the manuscript to Simon & Schuster—sixty-eight stories from fifty-four authors, thirty-nine men and fifteen women—and it was published just before the holidays. "The odds are that your best friend hopes to receive a Christmas copy," read one ad.

The reviews performed exactly the interpretive work the magazine needed: "The New Yorker has been blessed with intelligent editors of fiction who have had no faith in formulas or in their own ability to read the minds of their readers, and have merely printed the best stories that they could get," stated *The New York Times*. The stories "form a profound and brilliant mosaic of American life and thought, each piece a rare offering of individual expression," according to the *New York Herald Tribune*, which went on to say, "There used to be a theory that American short stories were written to a pattern; this book is dynamite in exploding it." The writer noticed the restraint of the volume's editors, similar to that of the editors of that year's *O. Henry Memorial Prize Stories*—the war in England and Europe had deflated grandiose theories about the short story's need to capture "the core of life," and the *New Yorker* editors were rightly content to choose stories that "turn away from large generalizations" and instead "cultivate their own poor gardens as best they can," which produced a collection of "intelligent entertainment."

By the end of December, *Short Stories from "The New Yorker"* had gone into its third printing and was briskly selling at $3 a copy; Simon & Schuster's ads trumpeted it as a bestseller. The Book-of-the-Month Club began giving the volume as a premium to new members. The endeavor could rightly be crowned a literary and financial success. The unspoken question within the dozens of memos that flew between Maine and New York, though, was whether this unmistakable announcement of *The New Yorker*'s literary seriousness would change the submissions it received and the stories it decided to publish.

30.

I wish there were a defense factory in which I could make tanks or planes for Russia half a day instead of New Yorker mss.
—Katharine to Andy, 1942

With her role at *The New Yorker* diminished, Katharine had no capacity for stillness and she actively looked for projects to occupy her time, especially those that contributed to something larger than her own household. In 1940 she launched her energetic improvement of the library in Brooklin. The original Brooklin Library Association from 1900 lapsed that year, but it was sorely antiquated anyway. The library had charged a dollar a year for male subscribers, fifty cents for female subscribers, and five cents a week for non-subscribers, and even then, Miss Dollard controlled who was allowed to browse for the one afternoon a week the library was open. Katharine complained that Miss Dollard barred the children of a mother whose morals she did not like, and also that she hadn't cataloged a single book since 1912. So Katharine organized her friends and neighbors into a new association, the Friend Memorial Public Library; helped to draft bylaws; and formed a fifteen-member board of trustees on which she sat, as well as the Ways and Means Committee. The library was now free to all patrons, and the 4-H club and the Girls' Mission Club pitched in to clean the building.

Katharine became the Friend Memorial Public Library's biggest patron. Ledger books list only a few sources of income for the first few years of the 1940s: the town of Brooklin, a small appropriation from the state of Maine to buy books, Miss Dollard's fines on patrons, and Mrs. White.

She created and chaired the Book Committee and began dispatching letters to editor friends to ask for book donations, including Andy's editor Gene Saxton at Harper, Bennett Cerf at Random House, and Tom Coward at Coward McCann. She wrote to all the local authors—Helen Hull, Mabel Robinson, Eleanor Wheeler—to ask them to petition their publishers for books. She hired two professional librarians to catalog the collection that she so zestfully grew. She took a page from Miss Winsor's book and sponsored a yearly prize for children with the best reading lists.

At the same time, Katharine's two eldest children reached significant milestones. Nancy completed her master's in zoology at Bryn Mawr and spent the summer of 1939 at the Marine Biological Laboratory at Woods Hole, Massachusetts. Then in the autumn of 1939 she won a scholarship to Yale University and entered the zoology department in the Graduate School of Arts and Sciences to work with renowned biologist Professor John Spangler Nicholas on "the functional regulation of the teleost embryo after the removal of the ear," the only woman in her department (though women were not admitted to Yale as undergraduates until 1969, they'd been allowed to join the Yale graduate school since 1892). Not for Katharine were her father's worries about the deleterious effects of higher education on the female body and psyche, nor did she worry about Nancy's marriage prospects. She joked in a letter that Nancy was safe because she "seem[ed] to have safety in numbers." But if Nancy had many suitors, they soon narrowed down to one. She met Louis Stableford at Yale and soon they were engaged to be married. Louis Stableford was a first-generation college graduate who had grown up in Meriden, Connecticut. He had preceded Nancy to Yale, studying embryology, and the couple graduated together in 1941. Nancy finished her dissertation in only two years, one of only two women to earn a PhD from Yale that year. Katharine attended the ceremony in New Haven.

That summer, while Louis applied for academic jobs, Nancy planned her wedding. Katharine suggested that Nancy elope, but the couple wanted a traditional wedding, and so Katharine allowed herself to be "cornered" into making lists of people to receive the wedding announcement and invitation, and bemusedly joined Nancy in marking her initials on dish towels. She had some advice to impart to her daughter and eldest child on the eve of her marriage: keep separate checking accounts in order to keep her independence, and (in answer to Nancy's question) sex once or twice a week was her and Andy's standard practice. Ernest (who had married Elizabeth Brosius Higgins Chapin in February 1939) wouldn't commit to attending the wedding, and Nancy was tremendously upset that his bitterness toward Katharine and Andy might prevent him from being there on her happy occasion. Katharine swallowed her pride and reached out to him, ending months of silence, to ask if they could speak on the phone. Let's not rehash the past, she urged; let's simply share this moment. She wanted to compare notes about Louis, whom Ernest had apparently gotten to know better than she ("My great hope of course is that he is a good scientist—of that I know nothing"), and just generally to ease the "stiffness" between them. The olive branch was not exactly seized with gratitude. Ernest wrote back querulously, reopening old arguments. Katharine tried again: "Aren't the facts about as follows? I have said or written things you did not feel to be accurate, you have written or said things I didn't think were accurate. We have told each other this to the point of desperation." She begged him to leave the past behind and think only of the future. "We both know we are far happier when we don't write so let's not begin a correspondence now." Nancy finally planned the day to her own liking and demanded that her father say whether or not he'd be there.

Nancy and Louis were married at the Blue Hill Congregational Church on September 6, 1941, and that night the Whites held the reception at their farm. Ernest and his new wife, Betty, did in fact attend all the events, and it put a strain on everyone. Katharine responded with anxiety; Andy responded by getting drunk the night before and feeling too sick to film the festivities, as he'd promised Nancy. The Stablefords moved to Easton, Pennsylvania, where Louis had gotten a job teaching biology at Lafayette College. Nancy did not work. This moment would remain a mystery to the Stablefords' eventual children. Nancy had worked so diligently toward the highest academic degree in a field that was not particularly welcoming to women and that was such a departure from her parents' and stepparents' fields of expertise—only to stop and settle into a life she could have had without seven years at two of the most rigorous schools in the nation. Two things may have kept her from pursuing a teaching job: she wanted children, and she sensed that their home life was about to be interrupted by the war.

At the same time that Nancy got married, Roger announced his engagement. He'd been dating Evelyn Baker since the summer before his freshman year in college, when he spotted her boldly step in and break up a dogfight. Evelyn's family rented a summer cottage at the nearby Haven Colony in Brooklin, but luckily for Roger, they lived in Weston, Massachusetts, so he was able to visit Evelyn frequently from Harvard. Too frequently: Katharine went behind Roger's back to phone Evelyn's mother and state her wish that the two young people see less of each other; the conversation got back to Roger and he wrote angrily to his mother to say he was old enough to do as he liked. Eventually, Katharine came around to considering Evelyn "a darling," though she noticed that Evelyn was not an intellectual. Did Katharine know that Evelyn's father had prohibited her and her sisters from attending college, like her own father had tried to do to her? She likely buried her doubts about such an early engagement inside the realist understanding that the coming war altered such a calculus.

As the Whites read and listened to and worried about the war news from abroad, as their country tilted away from isolation and toward intervention, they found a welcome distraction in collaborating on their humor book. For over two years, the Whites had been reading through stacks of books and old magazines. They scrabbled up dozens of forgotten newspaper stories and ordered books by the dozens, and they passed their selections and lists back and forth, adding and deleting. It was a monumental task—their book would eventually clock in at over eight hundred pages—but Roger observed that working on it brought a lightness to Andy and Katharine. They laughed together, and they shared in the creation of something that was theirs alone. For the span of this project, Katharine did not have to compromise with Ross, Lobrano, and Maxwell, and Andy did not have to trawl for words at the source of his own creativity for a column on demand. Their only criterion was their own delight. Roger remembered the two of them sitting at their respective desks, doors to their offices open, Katharine facing her window overlooking the front lawn and Andy facing her, the pair ensconced in "two silences," until one of them would break out with something funny that the other needed to hear.

In the summer of 1941, as they finalized their selection of over two hundred poems, stories, fables, parodies, folklore, verse, reminiscences, and other short essays, Andy drafted a preface and Katharine edited it. *A Subtreasury of American Humor* was published in November at a price of $3, just in time for holiday sales.

Coward McCann's marketing traded heavily on the Whites' prestige. The jacket flap notes that the couple had been "perilously involved with humorists for a number of years," and that Katharine had "been the arch-demon of scores of young and middle-aged humorists," while E. B. White was "a humorist in his own right, and ha[d] built up a nice practice in both prose and verse." As expected, many reviewers had quibbles with some of the Whites' selections, but overall they were unanimous in finding the book worthwhile. The *New York Herald Tribune* wrote, "It is rich, variegated, charming, provocative, hilarious, sympathetic, brave, dynamic and, if this is not going too far, probably significant." *The Atlanta Constitution* called it "serious and inspired." The Whites had succeeded in elevating humor to the level of literature. The book soon began showing up on bestseller lists and then achieved a plum: selection as the March and April dividend for subscribers to the Book-of-the-Month Club, guaranteeing the sale of the publisher's new print run of 240,000 copies. The publishers were so pleased by the book's success that they issued a companion volume the following year, *A Treasury of British Humor*, edited by the Whites' friend Morris Bishop.

The *Subtreasury* surely sold well in part because of its timing—it was released just a month before the United States entered the war, and several of the ads and reviews mentioned that now more than ever, Americans needed laughter. The publisher would soon ask the Whites to trim the book for a "pocket book" edition for the overseas troops.

The war was the background and subtext of all the letters that Katharine wrote during these years; even short scrawls to Andy while he was in New York for work or doctors' appointments would contain a sentence or two reacting to the previous night's news on the new radio that he had given her for Christmas. She was, in her own words, "a parlor strategist" with a great deal of skepticism about what she heard on the radio. Would the United States' arms get to Russia in time for a spring offensive? Could the Pacific War be saved? She grumped, "Maybe this country would get down to business if the Japs came to California. And the Germans to Maine." She volunteered to be an air warden but she submitted her registration late and she was not called to duty; she drew scorn from certain townspeople because she was not enrolled in the home nursing course.

She felt "a little too remote," she wrote to Gene Saxton, saying, "I'd rather be nearer a bombing objective." She was handed an opportunity to turn her editing skills to patriotic use when Ralph Ingersoll, former jesus and the writer of the *Fortune* exposé, asked if she would edit a series of columns for *PM*, the left-wing daily newspaper that he had founded two years previously. The idea, brought to Ingersoll "by a committee [he'd] rather not name in a letter," was to profile the "50 worst bastards in Congress," one each week and the more vitriolic the better, to stimulate voter turnout that November. Katharine said no.

She believed she could be most useful to the war effort by working harder at *The New Yorker*. She and Andy petitioned the ration boards in both Maine and New York for extra gas to allow them to drive once a week to Ellsworth for mail pickup and delivery, and their work was considered important enough to be granted that request. As she took on more routine editing, she also used her distant vantage point to strategize on cost-saving measures in the editorial and business offices. She wrote an eight-page memo of recommendations, including the ruthless proposal that they fire the poetry editor and allow the other editors to pick up his slack. Outside of *The New Yorker*, Katharine volunteered at the West Brooklin spotting post as part of the Ground Observer Corps, scanning the skies with binoculars and reporting by phone whenever a plane appeared. Her ancillary wartime contribution was to worry for absolutely everyone and find ingenious outlets for that worry. When she heard of a potential shortage of English muffins, she bought a gross.

When the Japanese attacked the naval base at Pearl Harbor in December of that year, Roger volunteered first for the navy and then the marines but was turned down both times because of his nearsightedness, so he was resigned to finishing out his senior year at Harvard. Andy filed a One Man's Meat column three days after Pearl Harbor, announcing a theme that would grow in importance during the war and its immediate aftermath: "The very patriotism on which we now rely is the thing that must eventually be in part relinquished if the world is ever to find a lasting peace and an end to these butcheries." He registered for the draft in February of 1942, just a few months shy of his forty-third birthday, when the Selective Service Act increased the age through which men were required to register for military service to forty-five. But mainly he farmed while trying to solve problems created by gas and rubber shortages. He announced to the world his production goals for 1942 and 1943: "100 pounds of wool, 14 lambs, 4,000 dozen eggs, 10 spring pigs, 150 pounds of broilers and roasters, 9,000 pounds of milk, and all the vegetables, berries, and fruit needed for home consumption and canning." Andy hadn't yet written anything that he considered a genuine contribution to the nation's thoughts about peace, freedom, and sacrifice.

Upon the United States' entry into war, Andy offered his services to the Office of Facts and Figures in Washington. They swiftly roped him in to help prepare a pamphlet that Roosevelt had requested on "the four freedoms." In January 1942, Andy went to Washington, where the "old dizziness and vapors" attacked him (he'd tried to cover a presidential press conference a few months earlier and had to leave before he fainted), but he held on and managed to work for two days with the other writers—Reinhold Niebuhr, Max Lerner, and Malcolm Cowley. He took himself off to New York to write in solitude and dread. He was charged with drafting the section on freedom of speech and rewriting the manifesto on all four freedoms, knowing it would have to "suit the President and the Supreme Court Justices and Mr. Churchill," and all the young men sent off to fight. He finished the work, though he did have to return home suddenly after taking ill at his hotel.

The effort cost him, and Katharine. Andy's three-week absence from the farm had coincided with a slow-burning health crisis that consumed her with worry. For weeks, Joe was in and out of school with a fever and sinus trouble. Katharine wrote to Andy about the doctors' sometimes conflicting advice and their growing conviction that Joe should have surgery. She said she was at her wit's end with "these baboons," including her old friend Dr. Bliss, the one who'd gotten her through her miscarriage. She wished that they had been smart enough to rent a furnished apartment in the city for the winter, so Joe and Andy could both get top-notch medical care and the family could be together while Andy wrote. In the end, they decided against surgery for Joe and he recovered, but the tug of the city would only grow stronger as the war ramped up. Katharine took on more and more work from *The New Yorker* as staff members were sent overseas.

While Andy was away, Katharine got to work on his next book. He'd been discussing with Gene Saxton the idea of collecting his *Harper's* columns, but it was Katharine who sat down with sheaves of clippings and shuffled them around to find some sort of natural shape. Family lore says that Katharine never edited Andy after those first few years at *The New Yorker*, but she certainly played an outsized role in the making of this book, doing everything from determining its structure to advising on cover art, titles, and subtitles to negotiating his royalty payment. After trying out different shapes, she suggested to Saxton that they publish the columns in diary form, interspersed with just a few *New Yorker* casuals, arguing that many of Andy's best passages wouldn't stand up if severed from their chronological context as the record of one writer-farmer during the run-up to the war. Over several letters to Saxton, she campaigned for that format: "One reason I don't think the book will seem stale, as Andy seems to, is that if you read it with dates, you'll find he made all sorts of predictions which have come true." Saxton agreed, and *One Man's Meat* was published in June of 1942, with three *New Yorker* essays and forty-two *Harper's* columns arranged by month.

This book, as Andy's stepson would say many years later, was the making of E. B. White as a writer. Its publication gathered his signed and originally unsigned magazine pieces and made legible to critics what many attentive readers already knew: that E. B. White's writing had formed a singular project, the processing of national and global news through the life of an ordinary man, far from the centers of power. *One Man's Meat* appeared to wide and unanimous praise; in contrast to the silence his previous two books had elicited, Andy was now reviewed in *Time*, *The Saturday Review of Literature*, *The New York Times Book Review*, and many city papers. *One Man's Meat* charmed all its readers, and reviewers made many comparisons to Montaigne, Emerson, and Thoreau. Many reviews quoted the same passage from Andy's introduction: "The first personal singular is the only grammatical implement I am able to use without cutting myself. It is a book of, for, and by an individual. In this respect it is anathema to our enemies, who find in individualism the signs of decay. It is the I in a man which Hitler has set out to destroy." A book that might have been read as solipsistic or self-indulgent was instead universally greeted as a major contribution to American thought. Clifton Fadiman wrote in a tremendously long column in *The New York Times* that E. B. White is "one of the most useful political thinkers in this country," in part because "he is an abstract thinker who does not write abstractly. His base is always a generalization, which is what makes him more than a journalist; but the development is always concrete."

These paeans in newspapers across the country spurred healthy book sales, about 15,000 copies by the end of the year. But the following spring, the Book-of-the-Month Club would choose *One Man's Meat* as a dividend for subscribers, guaranteeing sales of 240,000 copies and marking E. B. White's arrival as a national literary star with both popular success and critical acclaim. Two years later, Harper would reissue the book with ten columns Andy would write after its first publication (also Katharine's idea); the diary form predicted its own continuation. *One Man's Meat* was both banned by the army for containing "political implications" *and* issued as an "Armed Services Edition" (150,000 copies) and French and German overseas editions (50,000 copies each).

But even as the book's success was proof of concept for the Maine life for which he and Katharine had relinquished so much, Andy was laying the groundwork for the cessation of that life. On the Underwood typewriter that Katharine gave him for his birthday that summer, he typed a letter to Ross in which he finally accepted the invitation to write about the war for Notes and Comment, guaranteeing a paragraph a week at the same time he continued to write the monthly column for *Harper's*. The war was changing everything, even—eventually—the ground beneath Andy and Katharine's feet, as well as their children's.

Nancy and Louis moved to Boise, Idaho, where Lieutenant Stableford was assigned to the Fourth Altitude Training Unit at Gowen Field. Roger graduated from college and in the summer he was drafted to the air force, where he was assigned to the Aircraft Armaments School at Lowry Field in Denver, Colorado. A mechanical aptitude test had identified an affinity for weapons that his boyhood experience with a .22 rifle and twelve-gauge shotgun hadn't revealed, and he was soon teaching machine guns and power turrets to incoming soldiers. As a noncommissioned soldier, he was allowed to live off the post, and he and Evelyn found an apartment and began scrabbling together a wartime wedding.

That October, Katharine spent two days on crowded trains traveling to Denver to be the sole representative of Roger's family at his marriage to Evelyn. She wrote a long letter to Andy on the day of the wedding that forms a striking contrast to her other recent short letters about illness and war and worry; the Denver letter sounds exactly like the ones she'd written to him from Reno just before their own wedding. She took a drive into the foothills of the Rockies and Red Rocks Park and wrote, "It is all breathtaking and stage-setting country. The air is so stimulating I could not sleep at first." She raved about everyone involved in the effort to get Roger and Evelyn married, especially Eleanor Washburn, her first-year roommate from Bryn Mawr, now Eleanor Emery, who opened her "big shabby comfortable house" to Katharine and also hosted the small ceremony. Evelyn's father was the only Baker in attendance, and though Katharine called him "the bane of [her] existence," he did provide a case of champagne and a small monthly stipend for the newlyweds. After a series of absurd errors that threatened to sink the wedding in the short time Roger had leave from the base—the army lost the blood samples he needed to obtain a license, the dean of the Episcopal Church refused to marry them because Roger was not christened and then recanted at the very last minute ("We none of us think that Roger will be able to kneel during the ceremony as required without falling or snickering," wrote Katharine)—the couple was married by candlelight at ten thirty at night, followed immediately by a small reception. Katharine had a grand time and was glad she'd made the trip, despite its inconveniences. "We must all come to Colorado for a trip," she wrote to Andy. "America again has won me completely."

After a winter devoted to pushing the farm through all manner of small crises brought on by shortages and weather, punctuated only by stints at the West Brooklin spotting post to scan the skies for planes, the Whites entered a springtime of illness. Katharine slipped and fell on her back on the ice that February, just as she and Andy were about to leave for a business trip to New York, and that accident quickly compounded into the need for a surgery when the doctors discovered that she had ruptured a benign tumor on her ovary. She underwent a hysterectomy at Mount Sinai, an ordeal that stretched into a miserable two-week hospital stay, as she lay flat on her back while her wound healed and she suffered intestinal pain exacerbated by the medication, including phenobarbital for her nerves. Her room in the private pavilion overflowed with flowers, but she had no visitors at first, not even Elsie, and she begged Andy, who had returned home, for news about the farm. At first she cried every day, which her friend Margaret Ernst assured her was normal after a hysterectomy, but soon her mood stabilized and her letters turned to cheering up Andy. She laughed at Andy's sister Lillian's reaction to the news of Katharine's hospitalization—"the lucky bum."

At the end of two weeks, she sent Andy a list of the items she wanted him to bring from home when he checked her out of the hospital and into a hotel, including her black-and-gold high-heeled mules (or her red fuzzy slippers if he couldn't find those). Katharine faced the future with both worry and squared shoulders: "This operation is going to be much more to recover from than a Caesarian, I can see that." She resigned herself to a temporarily diminished level of energy and girded herself for the onset of surgical menopause.

Two weeks after she returned home, she became a grandmother. Nancy and Louis, who had been recently transferred to Topeka, Kansas, were the new parents of a little girl, whom they named Katharine and nicknamed Kitty. But Katharine was not well enough to travel to meet her namesake just yet.

While the Whites were still in New York following Katharine's discharge, Andy wrote to his editor at *Harper's* from their hotel room to quit his One Man's Meat column, forgoing the job that had brought him so much. His last column, after fifty-five months of writing, was published in May of 1943.

Harper's was not thrilled at Andy's decision and tried to retain him by offering a pay increase of two-thirds, a nod both to his indispensability and to the roaring success of magazines during wartime. He turned down the offer. But others kept coming; Andy's strategy of taking a firm yet modest stance for American intervention and the military advancement of democracy, couched in terms of his own idiosyncratic life rather than grandiose nationalist principles, had proven widely appealing across a middlebrow readership, and the gatekeepers and thought leaders at some of the country's biggest media outlets were taking note. He twice declined a job as one of the Book-of-the-Month Club judges. And he handily turned down the plumpest offer of them all, to replace Alexander Woollcott as a columnist in *Reader's Digest*, the sworn nemesis of Harold Ross and *The New Yorker*.

All this news reached Harold Ross's ears, partially from Katharine's own typewriter. "My admiration for your boldness is unbounded," he wrote to Andy about the *Reader's Digest* repudiation. "You are a man who should not be digested." Ross was extremely alive to the fact that he was writing to a man who was now unemployed, a man to whom his magazine was in debt since he'd resumed writing Comment every now and then. Ross had been complaining for years about the crisis occasioned by the "exodus" of writers and editors as they were drafted: "McKelway, Cooke, Hellman, Whitaker, Weekes, Shaw, Cheever, Newhouse, and God knows who else. I don't know what will become of us." In Ross's mind, Andy's partial return to the Comment page had saved the magazine, and he thought Andy's decision was itself prompted by a higher power: "Damned if I know *what* the page could have been if White hadn't come through this summer. From my standpoint, that was God's doing. We get to the end of the rope here, and then God does something." Now he told Katharine, "Whatever White wants to do, he can do, including taking the magazine over, so far as I am concerned. He's the one man that I'll make any kind of a deal with that he can name."

As for Katharine, Ross admitted that Lobrano was doing a good job of executing the magazine's precise follow-up system of writing to regular authors semiannually to ask for new work, but he said, "Our system for nominating new writers has collapsed almost completely. A total of only two nominees in several months (these from you), which is preposterous." He was so eager to hook and reel in the Whites that he offered them his own Connecticut house.

It took time to iron out the details, but eventually Andy agreed to write four hundred words a week for at least forty weeks a year, and Katharine agreed to work at two-thirds time for $200 a week plus $15 for expenses, half of that time to be spent on acquiring and editing fiction, and another half on a story anthology. Simon & Schuster had been clamoring for another anthology of *New Yorker* writing ever since *Short Stories from "The New Yorker"* had been fueled by the Book-of-the-Month Club in 1941 to skyrocketing sales. The editors repeatedly put off S&S and eventually secured a bit of time by vaguely promising that they'd assemble a collection for the magazine's twentieth anniversary in 1945, and now this became half of Katharine's job description. The Whites declined Ross's offer of his own house, but they accepted the "rather radical" idea (Ross's phrase) to have the magazine subsidize their winter rental of a Manhattan apartment—but only if Ross would also consider giving *all* contributors a bonus to reflect the magazine's wartime prosperity. He did, preferring that the money go to writers and artists rather than shareholders.

Andy's career shift was not enough, at least initially, to stave off the "nervous crack-up" that befell him that spring. While in New York, he sought the care of a doctor who prescribed him strychnine, an extremely toxic compound that had been used since the late nineteenth century to treat the symptoms of neurasthenia. As a nerve stimulant, it blocks the chemical that tells the body's muscles to switch off, leading to spasms even at microscopically low doses, and potentially death. Later, Andy would refer to this episode in several letters to his brother Stanley—

"There seems to be a kite caught in the branches somewhere"—but without going into much detail. He began seeing an eminent psychologist, Dr. Carl Binger, but he told Stanley that doctors were useless. If you ever crack up, he counseled a friend, "take frequent shower baths, drink dry sherry in small amounts, spend most of your time with hand tools at a bench, and play old records till there is no wax left in the grooves."

By the summer, Andy was feeling well enough to perform a family task that he was perhaps dreading—certainly Katharine was. He took Joel to Phillips Exeter in New Hampshire for an admissions interview. Nancy and Roger had, of course, gone to boarding schools at the end of their grammar school years, but for Katharine, this time felt different. "Joe looked so sweet a baby as he set off that it wrung my heart," she wrote to Andy the night after they left. "Somehow the city clothes made him look even younger." She worried that they were perhaps pushing Joe too hard and too soon, and she tried, even at this late date, to ratchet down the pressure. "Remember," she wrote, "Joe doesn't have to go to Exeter this fall, even if they want him. I have the feeling they won't think he's ready for it anyway." She soothed her worry by making nine quarts of berries into jam and doing all the farm chores herself.

Joe was accepted into Exeter and matriculated that fall as a twelve-year-old ninth-grader. Why that school? The Whites' letters give no indication of other schools they may have considered or how this selection was made. Phillips Exeter was, at the time, a boys-only school, one of the oldest schools in the nation, and extremely elite. Joe's time there overlapped with that of John Knowles, who would later model the Devon School in *A Separate Peace* on Exeter. But he did not overlap with Nancy and Roger's half brother, Peter Grey, who had attended Exeter just three years previously, where he acquired the nicknames "Pete" and "Ghastly," excelled at drama just as Roger did, and graduated in 1940 (his private school education was perhaps covertly funded by his father).

For all three Whites, the years of living year-round at the North Brooklin farmhouse were now at an end, the closing of an era. They would continue to spend the months of June, July, August, and September there, with occasional weekends during other parts of the year now that the farmhouse had been winterized, but their lives would now be oriented to New York City. With hindsight, Andy would call this Maine interlude the one time in his life when he was "fully awake, instead of half asleep" and when he was "suddenly seeing, feeling, and listening as a child sees, feels, and listens. It was one of those rare interludes that can never be repeated, a time of enchantment." But in the same breath he confessed that he was "appalled" at his nerve in wrenching Katharine from her job. "My wife was deeply shaken by the exodus, but she never flinched. She was sustained by her weird belief that writers were not ordinary mortals and had to be coddled, like a Queen Bee."

Indeed, the causes and effects of these five years do not neatly align. At the outset, the Whites moved to Maine at Andy's prompting and settled into a life that he designed; he quit the weekly column that had been causing him so much stress and moved to a more leisurely and more remunerative monthly column that allowed him to discover his authorial voice, leading to a book that was a critical and commercial success, not to mention the making of his reputation as a philosophical humorist who could say difficult and critical things without ruffling many feathers. He was leaving *Harper's* at the top of his game and taking a step backward.

Katharine had relinquished the meat of her job and was left to invent a role for herself on the sidelines of the magazine that she so loved, a job she supplemented by coediting three books but only appearing on the cover of one of them. She oversaw the end of her children's childhoods, as two of them got married, one headed into war, one had a baby, and another left home for boarding school—all of that, as she rather abruptly entered a new phase of her own life with an emergency surgery. It was a time of loss and worry for Katharine. And yet it was Andy, not she, who suffered a nervous breakdown.

Katharine and Andy moved back to New York not because they were unhappy in Maine or even because they were reconfiguring their lives around Andy's needs once again, but because they were called to New York to fill the gap left by staffers who'd gone overseas. This was the most and the least they could do for the war. And yet, though her needs were not the instigation of the move, it would be Katharine who would benefit most by their return to *The New Yorker*.

Part VI

The Years of
Greatest Influence

(1943–1954)

31.

The giants have come down from the hills!
—Russell Maloney

The *New Yorker* responded to the war by starting not one but two new magazines. Writer Russell Maloney and secretary Betty Thurlow edited an internal newsletter for the *New Yorker* family called *The Conflict*, a scraped-together affair for everyone serving in the war. It was filled with "dope" from the office on "all the little 4f's and 4h's at 25 West 43rd st," one-paragraph updates from enlisted staff serving overseas, and a "personal" column for sending messages among individuals. It was meant to be weekly, but in only the second issue, Maloney and Thurlow found themselves apologizing for its lateness. "The magazine is quite literally putting up a struggle for its existence these days," they wrote, echoing Ross as they described frantic attempts to get government exemptions to paper rationing and the draft. The situation led to chaos, with new employees hired on every week, none of them sticking around very long, like the sixty-five-year-old "head office boy," a former drummer for the New York Philharmonic who was soon called to serve in the NBC orchestra. In fact, *The New Yorker* was thriving at exactly the time it was fighting for its life. If paper, men, and submissions were diminishing in number—Ross grew desperate for casuals, Comment, and verse—subscriptions and readership were ascending. From 1941 to 1945, subscriptions increased 32 percent, not even including the issues given away for free. Jane Grant, Ross's ex-wife and one of the magazine's founders, had the idea to start a pony edition, a free monthly digest circulated to servicemen and -women, which she edited. It was so popular it soon became weekly and was sent to 150,000 troops. The pony edition instantly reconnected soldiers to the life of the city and to their recent past; it was avidly passed around, a highly anticipated boon to the routine of military service. And it was excellent business: many of those readers would come home from the war and subscribe to the magazine, spiking its postwar success.

"Katharine's news service," as Ross termed her long and detailed correspondence with various women in the office, added more piquant detail to this picture. Daise Terry, who had come aboard as Katharine's secretary in the 1930s, was now head of the secretaries and the manager of the art meetings. She regularly had been stealing a few hours on Sunday to write to Katharine in Maine, the only time when the traffic and noise in the building quieted down enough that she could type uninterruptedly. Terry conjured images of a dozen or more employees "meandering thru the halls with batches of proofs till 9, 10, and 12 o'clock at night" and said, "On Sundays a crew of 6 or 8 is here till all hours; with an office boy racing to and from [William] Shawn's by taxi." She gave Katharine all the news, lighthearted and serious, such as doleful updates on Thurber's unstable antics and poor health (she took the liberty of sending him flowers in the Whites' name when he was ailing). Sally Benson misbehaved horribly, repeatedly coming into the office drunk and raving. St. Clair McKelway was institutionalized in Stockbridge. "Gosh, Mr. Fleischmann would be smart if he built a sanitarium onto this bldg. to house all the crack-ups he's supporting," wrote Terry. William Shawn, the managing editor for the fact department since 1939, suffered through the death of his daughter one day after her birth. Terry praised Lobrano for his steadfastness and jabbed at Maxwell for his restless anxiety and his interest in women. As much as she could, she updated Katharine on the whereabouts of overseas writers, artists, editors, and staffers.

In this whirlwind, the Whites resumed their desks, on the first of December 1943. They discovered that Terry had not been exaggerating. "*The New Yorker* is a worse madhouse than ever now," observed Andy. Earlier in the fall they had settled Joel into school at Exeter with all the attendant rituals, including meeting with his advisor and the dean, inspecting his room, going to church with him, and having coffee with the headmaster. One moment particularly struck Katharine. The three were headed into dinner at the Exeter Inn and she noticed Joel fidgeting. "I wouldn't do that," she said in a quiet aside to him. "It will make you conspicuous." He muttered in return, "If you didn't want us to be conspicuous, you'd cut off your hair." She had known her long hair was unusual but she'd had no idea that it embarrassed her son. She departed Exeter resolved to cut it off, but Andy, Nancy, and Roger all prevailed on her to ignore Joel's comments and keep her hair exactly as she liked it.

Next the Whites traveled to Cambridge for Andy to undergo a turbinectomy, a nasal surgery to alleviate his allergies. Andy was game for the surgery—"Half a lifetime with a middle turbinate is enough to satisfy all but the most avid person"—but it did not relieve his symptoms. It did, though, produce a casual about the culture of a hospital in wartime, staffed by overenthusiastic, undertrained volunteers; in his drugged state, he thought one of the orderlies might actually be Governor Saltonstall. The casual earned him more than the cost of the operation, "a clear-cut victory over the medical fraternity." When Andy was well, he and Katharine made a long-awaited trip out west, first to Denver to visit Roger and Evelyn, and next to Boise to visit Nancy and Louis, and to meet baby Katharine (Kitty) Stableford for the first time. In November the Whites shopped for a furnished rental apartment and moved into a brownstone at 115 East Thirty-Fifth Street, just around the corner from the J. P. Morgan mansion and library, where they planned to stay until the following March.

With Andy's surgery and their travels accomplished, they got to work in December with a renewed sense of purpose. Andy would write about the war, but he would spend even more of his passion on a singular topic: world government, by which he meant not the kind of multinational organization like the soon-to-be-formed United Nations, but an actual authority that was higher than national governments, one that would "lack an enemy" and would therefore be able to prevent war. Andy knew world government was almost unthinkably impractical, but he insisted that it was still worthwhile to elaborate a theory of it, at least in part to counter nationalism, and his move back to the city afforded him a useful metaphor: the big city as "laboratory," New York as a kind of world government writ small with people of all nations loyal to the idea of the city. He would write about world government for the next four years, devoting space in almost a third of his weekly columns to the idea.

Katharine's mission was to shake the branches for fiction writers who could contribute to *The New Yorker* for the first time, and to reconnect with older contributors. She seems to have been guided by the experience of editing *Short Stories from "The New Yorker"* and its excellent reception, which proved that the magazine had a larger role to play in shaping literary taste and that its editors could fulfill this role by being more intentional about what they were already doing. Lobrano and Maxwell had been publishing longer stories, and Katharine's friend Bessie Breuer noticed a distinct change in tone. "Carson McCullers and Kay Boyle were telling me of their pieces for you. I realize that your style has changed, and you want no more feuilletons . . . but serious stories." Yes, Katharine agreed, that was exactly what they wanted, "distinguished" stories, exactly what they were having trouble finding; they needed "fiction that is art and not fictionalized reporting, which seems to be the trend of today." Breuer directed her agent to send them her "real short stories," and even though one of them was on the topic of abortion, Katharine carefully considered it, and when she rejected it in a dense, four-page letter, she noted that it was not the controversial subject but its lack of clarity and emotional resonance that doomed it. *The New Yorker* was at least theoretically willing to go there.

Katharine divested herself of the Christmas children's book column, once again, this time to a staff writer named Sheila Hibben, who'd been writing Talk of the Town paragraphs and short book reviews (but once again the reprieve would be temporary). She began pounding out letters to literary agents, asking after certain authors. Grimly, she picked up copies of *Best American Short Stories* and the *O. Henry* collections to read for potential contributors—a seemingly minor act but with a fairly large paradigm shift behind it. Instead of holding themselves aloof from the yearly story collections and publishing just the short pieces that would work well within the rhythm of any given issue, the editors now entered the conversation about what makes a good story and how the genre could be advanced.

Katharine noted, for instance, that Wallace Stegner had a story in both the 1943 *Best American Short Stories* and *The O. Henry Prize Stories*; she liked those stories very much and thought *The New Yorker* should have published them, but when Maxwell dug into the files, he discovered with some chagrin that Stegner's agent, Bernice Baumgarten, hadn't even bothered to submit the stories to Maxwell and Lobrano because they had turned down so many Stegner stories in the past and had left no doors open for revisions or negotiations. Might Baumgarten put *The New Yorker* back on the list to receive future Stegner pieces? Maxwell asked contritely. Katharine did a similar kind of relationship repair with another agent, Ann Watkins, who felt as if *all* her clients' work was summarily dismissed in two-sentence rejection notes; Watkins had taken to sending new stories in with sarcasm: "I don't expect you to buy this, because it isn't your habit to buy things I send you of late."

Personnel changes on the masthead contributed to the magazine's disciplined commitment to literary fiction and poetry. Charles "Cap" Pearce left to work at the publishing house he'd cofounded in 1939 (leaving behind at least one disgruntled contributor, William Carlos Williams, who had written to Pearce that he'd give *The New Yorker* no more poems to be mangled by editors: "There's something unpleasant to me about submitting anything I value there"). In his place, Peter De Vries, who would soon become a valued *New Yorker* satirist, joined forces with William Maxwell to acquire and edit poetry.

Stanley Edgar Hyman, who had been working with Wolcott Gibbs on Comment since 1941, was now partially freed from that job by Andy's return and was tasked with reading novels in manuscript from publishers and carving out passages that might be excerpted in the magazine as stand-alone stories. Clifton Fadiman stepped down as the book reviewer to take a job that Andy had rejected, a judgeship at Book-of-the-Month Club. He was replaced by Edmund Wilson, the unanimous choice of Ross and the other editors, who changed the tenor of *The New Yorker*'s book criticism. Fadiman was a popularizer; Wilson wrote from an opinionated critical position that, though easy to read, demanded much of his readers (and his editors; Ross lamented to Katharine that Wilson "[fought] like a tiger" over changes to his copy). *The New Yorker* would now, through Wilson, praise British satirists and inveigh against American bestsellers and many genre writers, including H. P. Lovecraft, Raymond Chandler, and Agatha Christie. Wilson delighted in taking aim, most infamously, at Franz Kafka and the cult surrounding his work.

Just as crucially, Hyman and Wilson each helped facilitate his wife's publication in *The New Yorker*: Hyman was married to Shirley Jackson and Wilson to Mary McCarthy. Both women would have lengthy and distinguished careers with the magazine, careers that helped cement the literary reputations they hold to this day. But Jackson and McCarthy had quite different experiences at *The New Yorker*, and the biggest source of this difference was Katharine White.

Jackson's best-known work and one of *The New Yorker*'s most talked-about stories are one and the same: "The Lottery," a story that Jackson wrote in mere hours one morning in 1948, a story that generated more mail than any the magazine had previously published, a polished masterwork of tone and suspense, the cornerstone of a story collection (also called *The Lottery*) that Jackson published the next year, which sold boisterously and vaulted her into the eye of the reading public. So it seems strange to say that Jackson never really stood on firm footing with *The New Yorker*, but then again Jackson's career was built on strangeness.

The magazine's editorial files tell a story of omission. Jackson and Hyman both graduated from Syracuse University in 1940. In 1942, she signed with an agent, Frances Pindyck at Leland Hayward, who submitted Jackson's stories to Hyman's employer, many of them revised at Hyman's suggestions because he knew the magazine so well. That first year, Jackson weathered seven rejections from Maxwell, Mosher, and Lobrano, all of them kind, prompt, and vanishingly terse. Over the next two years, she had four stories accepted but *eighteen* stories rejected (Jackson never suffered from sloth). One of her *New Yorker* stories was selected for the *Best American Short Stories* anthology. So it would seem that Jackson was off to a decent start. But Lobrano communicated exclusively with Jackson's agent, never Jackson herself. He occasionally tempered a rejection with a brief suggestion for revision and an invitation to resubmit, and three times this allowed Jackson to rescue an acceptance from a defeat. But there was no reciprocity in their relationship, not even really a relationship at all, just the polite and swift exchange of stories through an intermediary. Does this matter, given the fulsome shape of Jackson's career?

It matters, because even within Jackson's success it is possible to discern a career that she didn't enjoy but might have. In 1944, Lobrano published four stories and rejected eleven. In 1945, he published two, rejected six, and offered Jackson a first reading agreement. But then he and Maxwell rejected everything Jackson sent to the magazine, even after she changed literary agents, twenty stories over the next three years—some of them more than once—and they decided not to renew Jackson's contract after that first year. Hyman plaintively asked Lobrano why his wife was now meeting with a solid wall of rejection. "Is her stuff flatly unsuitable? What has gone wrong with it? Is it reparable, either in individual stories or in changing her type of writing?" Lobrano's reply, if he wrote one, is not preserved in the magazine's archive.

Jackson didn't publish anything in *The New Yorker* after 1945 until they accepted "The Lottery" three years later (and even then, Lobrano needed Ross to override Maxwell's disapproval of the story). After that, she published only one more story there during her lifetime, though her agent would keep sending stories and collecting matter-of-fact dismissals through the 1950s, over three dozen rejections. Editor Robert Henderson turned down the subsequently famous story "Charles" because it was "too obvious," and Lobrano sent back "The Summer People" because it was too much like "The Lottery." Almost everything that Jackson published was first turned down by *The New Yorker*'s implacable male editors.

Though "The Lottery" forever linked Jackson and *The New Yorker*, this was almost a fluke. The true story is that the magazine did not play a large role in her career as a fabulist. The question becomes: what might Jackson have written had she found a sympathetic editor at *The New Yorker*? Would her career have played out differently had Katharine edited her? It is distinctly possible that the tension that structured Jackson's personal and writing life—she oscillated between horror, myth, and psychological drama, on the one hand, and comic portraits of family life with her children, on the other—might have expressed itself in a different, less bifurcated way under the guidance of a female editor. Perhaps Katharine might have recognized the value of Jackson's domestic writing before Herbert Mayes at *Good Housekeeping* did and shaped it as a comic series in the tradition of Sally Benson and Thyra Samter Winslow. Perhaps she might have seen a way to integrate Jackson's dark literary tastes with her view of childhood as an epoch of magic and possibility. Perhaps she might have edited Jackson through the work of a new and startling reminiscence about a disturbing childhood, much as she did for Jackson's exact contemporary, Mary McCarthy.

McCarthy, like Jackson, first earned a handful of rejections from *The New Yorker*. She was married to Edmund Wilson and already had a sturdy literary career as a founding editor of *Partisan Review* and the author of a novel, *The Company She Keeps*. Finally, in 1943, William Maxwell accepted her story "The Company Is Not Responsible." But he dropped the ball on the edits of that story and didn't respond when McCarthy sent him a first draft of what would become "The Blackguard," a reminiscence. Maxwell went on leave, and McCarthy's work might never have caught on at *The New Yorker* if Katharine White had not swooped in to rescue the relationship.

Everything changed when McCarthy submitted "The Weeds" in 1944. Katharine was electrified. "The Weeds" is quite a long story, not obviously *New Yorker* material, about a woman deciding whether to leave her callous husband, a decision measured against the growth of her garden, with the act of weeding at once a symbol for all creative acts and a way to control passing time. But it *was* quite obviously Katharine White material, she who left her own callous husband and had spent a good deal of time in the garden. As the story circulated around the office, so did the whispers. "The Weeds" must refer to McCarthy and Wilson. Did he know about the story? How could he tolerate it? The answer is that, though he was a violent drunk at home, Wilson was a steadfast supporter of McCarthy's work. The other answer is that he didn't exactly handle the situation with grace. That summer, after McCarthy got pregnant and then miscarried a few weeks later, the couple got into a savage fight and she moved out of their Wellfleet home.

Katharine rushed "The Company Is Not Responsible" into print so that she could publish "The Weeds." At six thousand words, it was one of the longest stories *The New Yorker* had yet run, a moneymaker for McCarthy at sixteen cents a word, not to mention a vigorously discussed story generating a stack of mail from readers. It appeared in September of 1944, and then McCarthy did exactly what she'd written for her protagonist. She left Wilson, and it was as if "she had written herself out of the marriage," in the words of one of her biographers.

Euphoric on the success of that story, Katharine went to extraordinary lengths—extraordinary even for her—to publish more of McCarthy's work. It would be another two years before McCarthy's name appeared again in the magazine, but in the meantime Katharine deluged her and her agent, Bernice Baumgarten, with letters asking for new pieces and inviting them to lunch. McCarthy submitted "The Friend of the Family" and Katharine found it "extraordinarily brilliant," but was forced to reject it purely on length. For any other author, the matter would have ended there, but Katharine wrote a long and agonized letter asking McCarthy to let *The New Yorker* consider it again if she couldn't publish it elsewhere, an offer that Ross called "highly irregular" (the story later appeared in *Town and Country*). Even though she'd bought nothing from McCarthy in 1945, Katharine bumped her pay rate up to eighteen cents and offered her a first reading agreement in 1946.

Finally, McCarthy resubmitted the "The Blackguard," which Katharine hadn't known that Maxwell had already rejected. Without Katharine's encouragement, would McCarthy ever have revisited this piece, or indeed her childhood, in what would eventually become a serialized reminiscence and a book, *Memories of a Catholic Girlhood*? Within Katharine's career, there often isn't a direct arrow between something she said and something one of her authors wrote—the line of influence is not usually that bright and stark. Perhaps McCarthy was always going to write about her ghastly childhood as an orphan in the care of cruel relatives. But with Shirley Jackson's experience for contrast—all those fits and starts and a first reading agreement offered and then not renewed—Katharine's influence on McCarthy becomes less abstract. Katharine offered her continuity and the benefit of the doubt on each draft, a deeply sympathetic reading that might not always become an acceptance but would always be resonant and informed.

Katharine worked overtime to reshape drafts to become stories that *The New Yorker* could publish, and this particular time, her return to New York during the war after her five-year absence from acquiring manuscripts and scouting new talent, shows her evolving a new work rhythm to transcend the impersonality and missed connections that she could see in the editorial files. This moment—1943 turning into 1944—shows Katharine finally enacting the promise she'd glimpsed when editing *Short Stories from "The New Yorker"* in the late 1930s. The magazine could lead the literary marketplace by helping to bring about new fiction, rather than just accepting or rejecting what came in from agents. Her relationship with Mary McCarthy as they worked together on reminiscences proved the soundness of this approach.

She began editing McCarthy's pieces *before* showing them to her fellow editors, a new investment of her time and energy, in order to give the stories the best possible chance of winning a majority of the requisite in-house votes for publication. She couldn't guarantee that the quite extensive back-and-forth between editor and author would be worthwhile, but she did the next best thing—she often sent McCarthy a good-faith advance against the purchase price, money that McCarthy usually needed quite badly. And Katharine continued a practice that she'd begun in the 1920s and would do until her retirement: she brought McCarthy into her office to edit in person at her desk on the nineteenth floor in the heart of *The New Yorker*'s offices on West Forty-Fifth Street.

McCarthy remembered their "almost unvarying ritual": First, Katharine would treat her to lunch at the Algonquin—one martini apiece—at which they gossiped about friends and compared notes about books and recent *New Yorker* stories. Then they'd cross the street and head up to Katharine's office, where they'd go over a piece sentence by sentence, their work punctuated by Katharine looking up words at the Webster's dictionary on a lectern by her desk, and they'd finish the editing in a single session. McCarthy remembered two things that made Katharine's editing superlative. She "saw herself as a defensive bulwark against" Ross's sometimes ridiculous queries, and often she would "draw a line through an editorial question or suggestion and make a little sound of annoy-ance." Katharine was "distinctly on the author's side." Also, she was for McCarthy "the ideal editor" because they thoroughly enjoyed talking over the tiniest of word choices, such as when to use "grey" versus "gray" (the former was, to both of them, a lighter shade). When Katharine re-tired, McCarthy never had another editor who worked with her in that way; William Maxwell became her *New Yorker* editor, but McCarthy said of Maxwell, "The kind of detail Katharine and I hovered over didn't figure in our letters back and forth."

This is what Katharine produced as a magazine editor, these sessions of intense receptivity, of immersive concentration on a writer's piece, of reciprocal reading and sympathetic negotiation over the smallest ele-ments of composition. Her lengthy editorial letters approximated these sessions and were an extended moment in which the writer could be seen and her work read. Taken together with the evolving structure behind Katharine's acquisitions—the first reading agreement, her generous and often unsolicited advances against earnings, her interest in turning one-off stories and reminiscences into serials—what distinguished Katha-rine's editing is the way it offered to her writers the expansion of the solitary moment of reading and writing: a private, intimate partnership, entirely off the page, in which the writer could share her expression from the smallest compositional unit to the largest narrative arc.

In McCarthy's mind, Katharine possessed an almost magical abil-ity to read the as-yet-unvoiced heart of a piece, as when she edited "A Tin Butterfly," the third reminiscence of McCarthy's childhood, which describes the almost incredible beatings she suffered at the hands of her aunt and uncle. *Almost* incredible—Katharine made notes on Mc-Carthy's draft where she wanted the writer explicitly to address the outlandish nature of her relatives' cruelty. McCarthy submitted a new draft just five days after she received Katharine's edits, which had ar-rived with a check for $250. She began by thanking Katharine for the much-needed advance and granting that the edits had improved her story. Then she described "a very strange thing": as McCarthy had begun to revise the passage about the beating, she could suddenly relive the scene in vivid detail, instead of only moving words around on the page.

She wrote, "This seems to indicate that artistic truth and factual truth are inseparable—something I've always believed but that many critics don't. What you sensed as wrong there artistically was wrong, or at any rate cursory, which is really the same thing." Katharine's close reading prompted McCarthy to recall the real "truth" of her past. Katharine was, in McCarthy's interpretation, so empathetically inside the words on the page that she could detect the failure of those words to do their job of touching reality, could sense what McCarthy wasn't saying.

In 1957, when she collected her *New Yorker* reminiscences into a book, *Memories of a Catholic Girlhood*, McCarthy made a narrative choice that was at once inspired by Katharine's editorial process and transcendent of Ross's prohibition against writer consciousness. "A Tin Butterfly" and the other five *New Yorker* essays (plus one that ran in *Harper's Bazaar* and one that was unpublished) appeared largely unchanged, but after each chapter, McCarthy appended a few additional pages in which she reread her own essay and commented on the proximity of her original words to the factual truth as she subsequently realized it. These intertextual passages sound like nothing so much as Katharine's editorial letters, giving broad readings of the essays and gently probing their weaknesses. Within the pages of her avant-garde memoir, McCarthy became her own Katharine White. No wonder Katharine wrote McCarthy an enthusiastic letter upon the publication: "I can't begin to tell you how intensely interesting and how exactly right I find the foreword and the connective links between the chapters. I think their tone is exactly right and their honesty is exciting."

McCarthy and Katharine grew close and visited each other in New York and Maine. Despite his bitter divorce from McCarthy, Wilson too remained on good terms with Katharine and would have occasion, at this same time, to greatly affect her career. Might Katharine advance a sum of money to a friend of his who had published a few poems in the magazine the previous year but was now on very hard times, Wilson asked, an advance "like the one [she] gave Mary"? A brazen request, that the magazine dispense money purely on a writer's promise, purely on the testimonial of a good friend. But Katharine instantly came through with a check, along with an apology: "I'm sorry the sum is not larger than

$500, but I'm sure you'll understand The New Yorker's not feeling they can give more than that to a writer who has never submitted anything but verse and who is still an unknown quantity, so to speak." The writer, a young man named Vladimir Nabokov, would come through with the first of many short stories the next year.

The *New Yorker* was at a pivotal point, as Katharine appears to have realized when she stepped back into the fiction department. Gus Lobrano was still head, as he'd been since she'd left in 1938, but her working underneath him was uneasy for them both. Katharine acted as if she were in charge. She asked the business department for a list of all the fiction writers who held first reading agreements. All nine writers making the highest rates (generally 20¢ for the first two thousand words and 10¢ for the rest, though S. J. Perelman and James Thurber made more) stretched back to the 1920s and 1930s. Only two were women, Nancy Hale and Dorothy Parker, but Parker had barely contributed anything in the 1940s. Katharine knew the magazine vitally needed to build a stable of new authors, and she knew she was playing a long game.

She pursued British novelist Rumer Godden, for instance, beginning in 1942 when she read Godden's debut novel, *Breakfast with the Niko-lides*, right through 1949 when Godden would finally publish in *The New Yorker*. In 1945, Katharine served as one of three judges of the Houghton Mifflin Poetry Competition, and they were unanimous in awarding the prize to Elizabeth Bishop, who had been sponsored by Marianne Moore and Edmund Wilson, and whose book *North and South* was, as Katharine wrote to Ross and Lobrano, "to [her] mind and without question, the best of any of the manuscripts [she] read" out of the pool of eight hundred contestants. Katharine fervently wanted Bishop to write for *The New Yorker*, but there was a problem: Bishop had been submitting poems since 1939, and Charles Pearce had accepted exactly one of them and then rejected the next thirteen. Once again, Katharine engaged in relationship repair, writing two long letters to Bishop and offering to consider poems that had been rejected. Her outreach immediately earned two poems in *The New Yorker*, but both Katharine and Bishop had further ambitions, and several years into the long game, Bishop would begin writing prose for the magazine as well.

Katharine and her fellow editors ignored or rejected some equally distinguished writers. Ralph Ellison tried to break into the magazine, via his friends Stanley Edgar Hyman and Joseph Mitchell, as well as his agent, Henry Volkening. He submitted "In a Strange Country," based on his own experiences, in which a Black merchant marine in Wales is assaulted by a group of white Americans but then welcomed by a group of Welshmen in a pub who sing with him the Welsh, British, and American national anthems and the "Internationale," buoying his optimism for a brotherhood that could transcend racial and class divisions, a theme dear to Andy's heart. Katharine swiftly rejected it, telling Volkening it was "so extravagantly emotional as to sound almost hysterical." She did want to see more of Ellison's work. "We receive so many synthetic stories on race prejudice that I'm particularly sorry we must reject one written with such obviously genuine emotion." Ellison submitted at least five other stories over the next twenty years, but all were rejected, and Ellison's work would only ever appear in the magazine posthumously. William Maxwell used the same justification for rejecting a story by Ann Petry—for its "rather too melodramatic treatment of the negro problem." Langston Hughes was still futilely submitting stories and poems and receiving terse rejections, year after year. Richard Wright, W.E.B. Du Bois, and Alex Haley all submitted writing and all were rejected in 1944 and 1945. Haley, for one, put up a fight after receiving his form rejection letter. Writing from his desk at the US Coast Guard publication that he had started called *The Outpost*, he said, "Of course, I know full well that you are an off-trail market, NEW YORKER—that a manuscript slanted for you and subsequently rejected by you is of no use anywhere else and that you, consequently, are a tough market to crack. I have heard, and firmly believe, that you take in only four (or is it six?) new writers annually." He vowed that even if it took him ten years, he would be published in *The New Yorker*. But Alex Haley never had a byline in the magazine, and neither did Wright or Du Bois. Clearly, if the editors had wanted to include Black writers in its pages, they had plenty of promising people to cultivate, but none of these writers even appeared in the "Potential List" that the editors maintained, in which they tracked the submissions of those they hoped eventually to publish. Wright had twice appeared in *Best American Short Stories* and Petry was just about to be featured there. Wright, Ellison, and Hughes appeared in the inaugural issue of *Cross-Section: A Collection of New American Writing* in 1944, along with Norman Mailer and Arthur Miller. Other publications were besting *The New Yorker*.

After their first winter back in New York, the Whites returned to the farm for the summer of 1944, and they were unexpectedly joined by Evelyn, Roger's wife. Roger had been transferred from Denver to Hickam Field in Honolulu, where he became the managing editor of *Brief*, a fifteen-cent GI weekly for the Seventh Air Force that covered the central Pacific. Roger's life had just more neatly snapped to alignment around his skills. He reported a story about a B-24 bomber that was hit on a mission to Iwo Jima but limped the eight hundred miles home with only one of its four engines intact, and then he expanded this into a longer story that *The New Yorker* published—but this was not his first byline in his mother's magazine. Just a month after he transferred to Hawaii, *The New Yorker* had published his first short story, and the following fall it published another (his mother abstained from voting on his submissions). Meanwhile, in Maine, Evelyn helped Katharine with correspondence and Andy with chores, and her company was very much appreciated by both, even despite the ways she added to the mayhem of the household. Her untamed St. Bernard, Chloe, would race around the farm and "rescue" swimmers from the cove, and that summer she bought a horse, a six-year-old part-Arabian, black with some white on her, broken in for riding and driving but used mainly for plowing the Whites' fields, despite Andy's allergy to horse dander. The mare had a habit of putting her ears back, which Evelyn said was just a trick and not a sign of meanness. Katharine told one of her authors, "I suspect those ears," but she still dared to take the horse out driving in a little cart every once in a while. One day, when Evelyn was driving her, the mare bolted and upset the carriage, so they got rid of her.

Like Roger, Louis Stableford was also posted stateside. Louis and Nancy had moved around the country according to Louis's air force assignments, going from Boise to Topeka to Albuquerque. They were stationed in Rapid City, South Dakota, and were expecting their second child the following March, a son named Jonathan.

Katharine and Andy returned to New York in November of 1944, but they had a difficult time renting a house during wartime. To their surprise, they found themselves back in their old neighborhood of the West Village, at 37 West Eleventh Street, a small duplex that Katharine thought was worse than the previous year's apartment at almost twice the price. They had friends over for cocktails on December 30 and then more soberly watched the next day as 1944 turned into 1945. Paris had been liberated, but the Battle of the Bulge in Ardennes, what would be Germany's last major offensive, was still underway.

Quite apart from their worries about the war and their family and friends in the services, the Whites had a much more proximate cause for fear. Andy felt so mentally "queer" that he thought he might die. That January, he described his mental health to his brother as "mice in the subconscious." "With death at hand," he later wrote in *The New York Times*, "I cast about to discover what I could do to ease the lot of my poor widow, and again my thoughts strayed to Stuart Little." Just eight weeks after moving to West Eleventh Street—after moving back to the place where he'd conceived of Stuart Little a decade earlier—Andy finished up the manuscript. One of the most vaunted careers in children's literature, in other words, began in severe mental distress against a palpable fear of death.

His own account of this time is stark and unexplained. It is one he repeated often, but no one appears to have listened sympathetically enough to his always-modest words. He told Morris Bishop, for instance, that the last few chapters of *Stuart Little* were "a nightmare," telling him, "I wrote them doggedly and while under the impression that I was at death's door and should catch up on loose ends." His biographer would skate right over the conditions under which Andy finished *Stuart Little*, and no one else would wonder what he experienced. He was forty-five years old and not suffering from anything worse than hay fever. He'd always had a fear of death, pure and constant, but something grew acute in this moment and shaped his actions. What was it? *Stuart Little* clearly intensified the mysterious connection between creativity and anxiety in Andy's life's work. We can only know two things: that this fear spurred his productivity, and that Katharine was right there in the center of his thoughts.

Andy submitted the manuscript to Harper. His longtime editor, Eugene Saxton, had died during the war, so the manuscript landed on the desk of Ursula Nordstrom, the director of Harper's Department of Books for Boys and Girls. She later remembered, "Only another children's book editor can know the emotions one has on hearing that a famous writer of adult books is going to send a book for children to the house, for talent in the former does not always carry over to the latter." Nordstrom was nervous. Would she have a crisis of diplomacy on her hands? But she loved the book and immediately forecast that it would appeal to children *and* adults, and thereby increase the tenor and stature of children's literature. She sent a contract to Katharine in March, and they began talking in earnest about illustrators; Andy had suggested Garth Williams, a little-known artist who'd published a few drawings in *The New Yorker*, and Nordstrom sent Katharine a few of Williams's test illustrations as an audition. The book would be published in the fall, she told Katharine, with an initial print run of fifty thousand. Andy, worried, offered to store the extra copies in his barn. Nordstrom thanked him and bumped the print run up to sixty thousand.

The spring of 1945 was a momentous one. At the end of April, Andy convinced Ross to send him to San Francisco to cover the charter conference of the United Nations, the largest international gathering in the globe's history, with delegates from fifty nations. He sent back two Reporter at Large columns into which he poured all his optimism: "If ever there was a time and a place for the wedding of nations, it is San Francisco in the spring." He marveled at the diversity of people gathered together in the city. A week into the conference, when Harold Stassen presented the American delegation's nine objectives, Andy felt that he was present at the brink of a new order: "It seemed more like a turning point than any day I had ever known," he wrote, with Mussolini, Hitler,

Goebbels, and Roosevelt all very recently dead, and everyone's minds focused on human rights and "a neat and precise blueprint labelled the Future." On May 7, Katharine sent him a note from New York: "Looks as if the surrender might come thro tonight when Elsie will be sleeping at our place. Some one whose hand to clasp anyway. I wish it were yours." The war had ended, and although Roger Angell and Louis Stableford wouldn't be home for many more months, it was at last possible for the Whites to peer hopefully into the near future, beginning with a new book by E. B. White.

The publication of *Stuart Little* complicated Katharine's work life in almost comical ways. For starters, it made writing the children's book column infinitely more difficult. (Just as Rosemary Carr Benét had before her, Sheila Hibben lasted only one Christmas at the monumental task and Katharine was back to writing both the spring and holiday columns.) That December she worried: How could she review her own husband's book? How could she *not*? She made the newest book by a beloved *New Yorker* contributor the very subject of her opening paragraphs, and she linked it to three other children's books by the magazine's writers—James Thurber's *The White Deer*, Phyllis McGinley's *The Plain Princess*, and Christine Weston's *Bhimsa*—in which she discerned a very timely theme. "The first season of children's books since the end of the war has the best list of fairy tales in years," she observed. And not just traditional ones, but "pleasant modern stories about a world in which the fanciful happening is the natural one." Right away, Katharine gave readers (or at least their parents) a helpful guide for how to approach Andy's unconventional book, and she placed it within a small but fervent literary trend. But only Andy's book would ignite a controversy. She demurred at commenting on "the small, mouselike being who is the second son of Mrs. Frederick C. Little of this city," since she could hardly be impartial about someone who was "a familiar of [her] own household." (But then she *did* comment, in parentheses: "It is a funny story.") To make all that comprehensible to her readers, she signed her review as K. S. White, the first such time that she gave her identity in the children's column, once again besting her husband, who still wrote in the anonymity of Comment.

Note Katharine's word: "mouse*like*." Andy had spent a few words in the first sentences of the book to elaborate. Stuart Little was "not much bigger than a mouse" and he "looked very much like a mouse in every way. He was only about two inches high; and he had a mouse's sharp nose, a mouse's tail, a mouse's whiskers, and the pleasant, shy manner of a mouse." Stuart Little was a boy who *looked* like a mouse, and the book simply asked its readers to believe this odd occurrence. Consider this delightful sentence: "Before he was many days old he was not only looking like a mouse but acting like one, too—wearing a gray hat and carrying a small cane." The Littles "never quite recovered from the shock and surprise of having a mouse in the family," but even by describing them this way, the book situates its readers among those who have accepted both the unreality and the indeterminacy of a boy who is very much like a mouse.

Anne Carroll Moore would accept nothing of the sort. The New York Public Library's children's librarian, who had so ardently pleaded with Andy to finish *Stuart Little* six years earlier, had now retired, but she still held enormous influence in the field, not least over her replacement, Frances Clarke Sayers. Andy's editor, Ursula Nordstrom, deferentially sent galleys to Moore, who read it and then went on the attack. She summoned Nordstrom to her apartment and told her that under no circumstances should Harper publish *Stuart Little*. When Nordstrom brazenly went ahead with the book, Moore commanded Sayers not to order it for the New York Public Library, which then stifled orders at schools and public libraries all over the country.

Moore wrote Katharine a fourteen-page letter, and though the Whites eventually destroyed the letter in disgust, Andy could not help but remember its stark contents: he should withdraw the book because it was "non-affirmative, inconclusive, unfit for children, and would harm its author if published." Initially, Katharine hesitated to show the letter to Andy, thinking it would upset him, but when he walked into the house an hour or so after she'd received it, he took one look at her face and said, "Well, what's the matter with *you*?" She read it aloud and was relieved that he could shrug it off. She then wrote to Moore a reply of "poisoned courtesy" (Andy's words), informing the librarian that she had completely missed the point of Stuart. Yes, the book deviates from the conventional fantasy tale. "But I can't help feeling that the unpredictable quality of both Stuart, the character, and *Stuart*, the book, is one of the book's merits." The internal mechanism of the book's appeal was the very difficulty of deciding whether the book was for children or adults. "So what I hope," she wrote, "is that children of all ages *may* happen to like *Stuart* for its humor while their elders read it for its satirical and philosophical overtones."

Katharine didn't even remotely convince Moore, who wrote her two more letters of increasing severity. But the book had legions of champions, including Louise Seaman Bechtel, the children's editor at Macmillan and a book reviewer at *Horn Book*, whom Katharine had recently befriended and who acted as her informal advisor for *The New Yorker*'s children's book column. As it happened, Bechtel had been invited to give an endowed lecture on children's books publishing at the New York Public Library that January, an event at which Moore would be seated in the front row. Bechtel told Katharine she intended to use the occasion as a megaphone for *Stuart Little*, and though her plan backfired in one sense—she said from the podium that the book should win all the medals and awards, but Moore subsequently blocked it from the Newbery Medal—she did induce the New York Public Library's director to override Sayers's ban and place *Stuart Little* on the circulating shelves.

Andy was mostly just bemused by the furor, which even made it into the *New York Post*. He later remembered being "shook up" by Moore's letter "but not deflected," and the letter became another building block in his authorial mythology, one that he repeated when *Stuart Little* was turned into a television special in 1966: he wrote that he rebelled against Moore's letter and had followed his "instincts in writing about Stuart, and following one's instincts seemed to be the way a writer should operate"; indeed, "a writer's nose is his own best guide." This was not an entirely accurate statement of Andy's principles; setting aside the fact that he also testified to writing the story in mental distress, what this account leaves out is his awareness of the literary marketplace and his desire to succeed in it.

Andy could afford his bemusement, his emphasis on instincts and noses, because readers loved *Stuart Little*. The book appeared in October of 1945, and by the twenty-fourth of that month, Harper had sold forty-two thousand copies. The following spring, it hit the hundred-thousand-copy benchmark, and it kept on selling, including foreign rights in European and Asian countries. Stuart Little became Tom Trikkelbout in Denmark, Stuart Malutki in Poland, Petit Stuart in France, Bung Kecil in Indonesia, Stuart Mus in Norway, Stūyārta Liṭl in Bangladesh, and, quite simply, Knatten (the Boy) in Sweden. Andy would have the last word after Moore's death: "Children can sail easily over the fence that separates reality from make-believe. They go over it like little springboks. A fence that can throw a librarian is as nothing to a child."

Katharine had her last word the very next year, in a long introductory passage to her 1946 holiday children's book column. She took square aim at those "experts in children's reading" who believed that the child was "sacrosanct." She referred to "a candlelit meeting at which children's books were discussed in a spirit of reverent dedication," an allusion to Moore's annual autumn dinners that few *New Yorker* readers would catch but would stick out like a flame to those who needed to see it. "Let us not overstimulate his mind," Katharine wrote in caricature, "or scare him, or leave him in doubt, these authors and their books seem to be saying; let us *affirm*. Somehow, this modern sentimentality seems to me far more insidious than the simple-minded sentimentality of the Victorians." She staunchly defended the children's books that frighten, that perplex, that outstrip the understanding of juvenile readers—that cause them to stand on mental tiptoes to measure up. She signed her column, once again, as K. S. White.

33.

With the fall publication of *Stuart Little*, the Whites fell into a yearly routine. After their stay in the West Village, they secured a winter rental in Turtle Bay Gardens with their beloved cook, Josephine Buffa, decamping only to drive up to Maine for the Christmas holiday, where they were joined by Joe, Evelyn, Nancy, and her children. Roger wouldn't make it home until the middle of January.

The Whites spent Joe's March break in Sarasota, Florida, staying next door to Ros and her family at the Whispering Sands resort and visiting with author Bessie Breuer. That spring, Katharine and Andy signed a six-year lease for yet another town house in Turtle Bay Gardens at 239 East Forty-Eighth Street, thus ending their frantic summer hunts for winter abodes. Katharine launched into the project of redecorating it over the summer, sending countless letters from Brooklin, detailed and always slightly beleaguered, to Mabel Detmold, the manager of the Turtle Bay complex. She arranged for most of the rooms to be painted, a custom wall of closets and drawers to be built, a special antique china bowl to be turned into a sink in the bathroom, and a telephone line with three extensions installed. She moved her baby grand piano in through the front window, where it would preside resplendently over the living room in front of the four windows overlooking the back garden, along with a pair of lemon-yellow couches. Katharine took to calling it the Henry Poor room because the three artworks she hung in it were a tile, a still life over the fireplace, and a portrait of Joe, all by Bessie Breuer's husband, Henry Varnum Poor. Louise Bogan called it "a dream-duplex" and "the loveliest apartment in N.Y."

But first there was the happy, maddening chaos of summer. Katharine particularly enjoyed the Maine summer scene that year, with all the men home from the war and Allen Cove dotted with boats once again, and the young people enjoying themselves to the hilt, something that gave her pleasure even though her own mobility was somewhat limited by the arthritis in her back that had been plaguing her for months. "I'm disgusted that my entire life these days seems concerned with health and each year I promise myself that six months from now I won't speak of my health," she wrote to Breuer. But she was able to enjoy what she called "innocent diversions" like the Blue Hill Fair, where she snuck off to pee in the bushes just as the trap shooters aimed at their pigeons, and she emerged with a small scrape, to the laughter of her family. Fifteen-year-old Joe was as busy as ever and kept Katharine in a near-constant state of worry, between lobstering during the day with their next-door neighbor, Charlie Henderson, and borrowing the Plymouth convertible at night for dates. Andy helped Joe buy *Shadow*, a classic Herreshoff twelve-and-a-half-foot sloop that he could sail by himself on ever-lengthening trips. He hatched the idea of a three-day circuit around Deer Isle in East Penobscot Bay, but Katharine said no. Andy and Joe worked on her until she relented, then Joe packed a tarp, gas stove, sleeping bag, and food and set off. He weathered a thunderstorm on his first night out and made it home in triumph. He would always remember that trip, and how his mother was "excessively happy" to see him on his return. But really, who could blame her? On the Fourth of July, Joe and a friend were driving around and got the grand idea of firing off a roman candle. It flew into the living room of the first selectman of Brooklin. Katharine grounded him "just about forever," as Roger remembered it.

Summer meant visits with family. Roger and Evelyn came for two weeks, a happy time that was marred when Evelyn suffered a miscarriage. When Roger returned to the city, he wrote his mother a letter saying how very much they had enjoyed their stay; the overall impression of their time in North Brooklin was blissful and the miscarriage felt to them like a thing apart. He tried very hard to wipe away the shadow of sadness from Katharine's mind, the duty of a sensitive son toward an anxious mother. "I really enjoyed being back and it was all I thought it would be and remembered when I was away," he wrote. "I particularly liked the [boat] racing and all that, but just being back with you at the house was the biggest thing of all." (Also, "The only thing that bothered me at all was that you seemed to worry about Joe too much.") Anyway, there was no time to remain sad. Nancy, Louis, Kitty, and Jonathan arrived for their visit. Then the farmhouse's water pump failed (twice), the old refrigerator released its gases and expired in a mess of ruined food, and the dogs chased a skunk into the cellar.

In autumn, Joe returned to Exeter, and Katharine and Andy moved into the Turtle Bay house. Now Andy was just steps away from the site that would become the United Nations headquarters. He regularly took the train up to Lake Success, the temporary home of the UN, to report on events for *The New Yorker*.

In this fall of 1946, another White family rhythm held: in dread and reluctance, Andy published a book that Katharine helped to edit, and it succeeded despite his lack of faith. An editor at Houghton Mifflin had approached him earlier in the spring about anthologizing his editorials about world government. In fact, Katharine had already collected them in a short pamphlet that *The New Yorker* published—without Andy's name—called *World Government and Peace: Selected Notes and Comments*. So Andy, with trepidation, signed a publishing contract for *The Wild Flag*, which meant stepping out from behind the anonymity of Notes and Comment and owning his opinion.

That autumn, as *Stuart Little* continued to sell vigorously, *The Wild Flag* was published in a much smaller print run of fifteen thousand and to more muted acclaim. What Andy intended as a simple, nonideological appeal to end nationalism and agree on a planetary body for the maintenance of peace was received by some readers as naïve, impractical, or insufficiently radical, especially the reviewers in *The Nation* and *Partisan Review*. They read Andy's writing as completely commensurate with *The New Yorker*, his words forever constrained by what they saw as the magazine's relentless conversion of politics into a stance or attitude, part of its middlebrow project of precisely fitting the professional-managerial class to the values of consumer capitalism. A belief in world government, in this critique, required no action other than a vaguely pleasant feeling of loyalty to fellow men.

The book eventually sold over twenty thousand copies and earned many positive reviews, including one from Ralph Ingersoll, who had previously lambasted Andy for avoiding politics. But the experience confirmed Andy's skepticism about taking a stand on a monumental issue. He had begun receiving the kinds of awards that came to a writer of a certain stature—the Limited Editions Club's Gold Medal, the Newspaper Guild's Page One Award, membership in the National Institute of Arts and Letters—but these honors meant little to him and he even declined the latter. In the months after *The Wild Flag* was published, he tried to capitalize on the new visibility for his opinions, finally persuading Ross to allow him a signed column, called Turtle Bay Diary. But he only wrote two installments. Signing his name did not alter his relationship to his own craft, and his anxiety flared up.

Katharine, meanwhile, was so busy working connections on so many fronts that she was forced to abandon the second anthology of *New Yorker* stories that Simon & Schuster wanted in favor of getting out a weekly magazine. Katharine's relationship with the poet Marianne Moore illustrates her farsighted strategy toward future authors in this time of rebuilding. She wrote a short letter telling Moore that she and Louise Bogan had been discussing her recent book of poems, *Nevertheless*, and thought that some of them would have worked beautifully for *The New Yorker*. Katharine invited her to submit, reminding Moore that this was the second time she'd made such a request—the first was when she was an editor of *The Lantern* at Bryn Mawr. Moore was charmed and wrote that she would try to please Katharine a second time. When no poem arrived, Katharine dropped her another line. Moore responded, "It is for one, not a note, but a Christmas or Easter bell, or something of an alpine sound, to know that you really care about having work from me." It would be another eight years before Moore published a poem in *The New Yorker*, but Katharine kept moving pieces behind the scenes. She and a few other Bryn Mawr women wrote to writer friends to obtain money and recognition for Moore, and it paid off handsomely. The

Guggenheim Foundation found itself with extra money in their coffers, and when they approached poets Allan Tate and Louise Bogan to ask who might benefit from it, they were both primed by the Bryn Mawr women to recommend Moore, who suddenly learned that she was to receive $2,500 a month for a year.

Christine Weston may have come to Katharine through her literary agency, Russell & Volkening; they almost instantly became friends, visiting each other in Blue Hill, Maine, within weeks of Weston submitting her first story. Or perhaps Nela Walcott, a painter in Princeton, New Jersey, introduced them; soon Weston and Katharine were almost constantly exchanging news of this troubled friend, also a summer resident of Maine. Weston was a British citizen who had spent her childhood in India, and the stories she began publishing in *The New Yorker* all concerned colonial life. Katharine liked best the stories motivated by nostalgia for a child's-eye view of the country, though she also purchased brittle stories about the fragility of white women at the end of the colonial era. She turned down many other stories, though, including one that she rejected on the familiar *New Yorker* grounds that it was a slight mood piece and only appealed to women, but she fervently wanted Weston in the pages of the magazine and almost immediately offered her a first reading agreement, then bumped up her rates the subsequent year. They wrote frequently and socialized when they could; even their husbands got along well and went duck hunting together in Maine.

But Katharine's admiration of Weston's writing was not unqualified. She believed Weston couldn't write convincingly about America, only India, and vastly preferred that she keep to that lane. In 1946, Weston published *The Dark Wood*, a novel set partly on the coast of Maine. Never mind that the novel hit the literary trifecta—a magazine serialization, a movie in the works with Maureen O'Hara and Tyrone Power, and selection by the Literary Guild book club—Katharine hated it. She was happy for the financial security the novel brought Weston but found the writing itself entirely unconvincing despite the fact that—or in Katharine's analysis, because—it was based on real events. Weston modeled her protagonist, Stella Harmon, on their troubled friend Nela Walcott; both suffered the early deaths of their husbands in Italy during the war, then mentally unraveled, then met and fell in love with men who resembled their first husbands. It was something Weston and Katharine mentioned in their letters, the way John Walcott was a kind of ghost in Nela's subsequent marriage, the way Nela drank too much and was too careless with her own life. It *could* have made an excellent novel for precisely the readership both Weston and Katharine cultivated, but in the latter's mind, it did not. She told Gus Lobrano that she believed Weston had written it honestly, not cravenly in a bid for popularity—but the very closeness of the story made Weston's characters seem unreal to her. Katharine told Weston's agent that she was rather glad for the handful of negative reviews, if they'd spur Weston to spend more time on a given piece and set aside material until she'd achieved emotional distance from it.

This was another principle of Katharine's editing—this ability to keep an emotional distance from her authors to evaluate their work. Did Katharine consciously prevent herself from becoming too attached to any one writer, or was this distance natural to her? Did it feel effective, or lonely in a kind of editorial solitude, in which she faintly humored her authors? There is what feels like a subtle but persistent emotional imbalance in Katharine's archives, in which her authors divulged more to her than she to them, and perhaps many of them thought they were closer to her than they actually were.

The friendship between Katharine and Weston easily survived the editor's lack of regard for *The Dark Wood* (Katharine let her faintly enthusiastic words about the movie and silence about the novel carry the message, which Weston read loud and clear). This was not least because, simultaneous to all of this, Katharine was also working diligently to help Weston return to India for more material. She tried to get Weston accredited as a news correspondent for *The New Yorker*, but the magazine was only allowed one, and that was reserved for a male reporter. Meanwhile, Weston asked for Katharine's help in quite another matter: what should she do about the positive rabbit's test she'd just taken? She laid herself bare for Katharine's advice. Her husband wanted the baby, but she was far more ambivalent. For one thing, it meant canceling her plans for India, and she wrote, "That really gripes me." She wanted to visit Katharine to talk the matter over in person. Meanwhile, she was going to keep the pregnancy secret from her agents and publishers, in case she didn't bring the baby to term. She didn't, and Katharine helped her obtain a British visa, and eventually Weston made it to India, regularly dispatching stories and fact pieces for Katharine's evaluation, and steadily published in *The New Yorker* through the 1940s.

Katharine was working incredibly hard, and the conditions for her job worsened as she and Andy moved through their typical annual routine in 1947: to Sarasota for the February vacation, where Joe recovered from chicken pox and Andy felt so anxious that when they returned to New York he once again visited the psychiatrist he had seen for his breakdown in 1943. Dr. Binger advised him to stop writing, and though Andy always found that practice helpful, he managed to produce two essays that year in which his own poor mental health was the backdrop: "The Second Tree from the Corner" and "Death of a Pig." That spring, Joe graduated from Exeter, and though he had been admitted to Cornell, his father's alma mater, he decided to take a year off to work on a construction crew in New York, building an extension of the *New York Times* building. Katharine was glad about his gap year, because Joe was only sixteen and she didn't want him to go off to college with a bunch of older men, veterans from the war, many of whom were already married—but still she worried about him and his twin obsessions, boats and girls. She worried about everyone. Nancy's third child was due in October, and Evelyn was pregnant again with the auspicious due date of January 1, 1948.

Changes were afoot in the *New Yorker* offices as well. That spring, William Maxwell gave up his job in order to concentrate full-time on writing a novel, and Katharine wrote him a letter wishing him well, but also confessing her own feeling of desolation: "I really feel quite lonely (when a certain type of fiction comes in) at the thought of your not being there to give me support." Gus Lobrano was on leave after what everyone thought was a heart attack brought on by extreme overwork. He stayed out for eight weeks, then only returned to part-time work. Wolcott Gibbs was in the hospital with viral pneumonia and had to have a piece of his lung removed.

Amid all this interruption and worry and illness, Katharine managed to bring an impressive list of new authors into the magazine that year, including Niccolò Tucci, Isabel Bolton (the pen name of Mary Britton Miller), Ray Bradbury, and Rachel MacKenzie, an English professor who would later become the first female editor Katharine hired.

Now that she was playing the long game for the editorial strength of the magazine, Katharine no longer read agents' submissions, all those forgettable stories. But she did read the published story collections, and when *Story* magazine chose its college prizewinner for 1947, she excitedly wrote to its author, "You probably won't remember me but I knew you so well when you were a small boy that it would seem unnatural not to address you as Peter." This was Peter Powys Grey, Ernest Angell's other son. His student days at Harvard had been interrupted by the war and a stint in the army's infantry division, where he saw action in Hawaii and Japan. Back at Harvard, he studied under the literary critic F. O. Matthiessen. "We'll be glad to read anything you'd like to let us see," Katharine now wrote, "new material as well as this contest story if that were available." Peter's story, "Shadows of the Evening," sounds nothing like a college senior's first publication. Senator Greenleaf sits in the back of his chauffeured car, old, infirm, and beginning to lose his hold on reality; nothing happens except the car pulls up to his house and he is helped inside. In disjointed, even disorienting, language, the story sketches the arc of his life as the senator desperately clings to his rapidly diminishing dignity. Peter was not free to submit the story to Mrs. White because *Story* had first dibs, and it was in fact published the following spring. No other correspondence between the two remains in the *New Yorker* files, though Katharine told Ross and Lobrano that she was entering Peter's name on the Potential List. She closed her letter to him by saying how impressed she was at his winning the *Story* prize. "I'm sure your mother must be very proud of that. Please give her my love." This letter, more than anything else, suggests that Katharine did not know the secret history of Marian and Peter Powys Grey, though Peter did by now. At the time she wrote it, Peter was embarked on his first job after college, cofounding the Salzburg Seminar in American Studies, one of the first American studies programs in Europe. He would never publish any other stories.

Katharine told Weston that she'd never worked so hard in her life, days and nights completely crowded with manuscripts and correspondence, with weekends spent in bed to recover. She hustled Andy out of New York on June 1, telling everyone that getting him to Maine was her highest priority no matter what else the magazine demanded of her, because he wasn't well and hadn't been writing. But being in Maine—running a hotel for her family, as she called it—was never relaxing, and Roger, for one, was worried enough to recommend drastic measures. She was in pain and suffering from decreased mobility from her old back injury, the fall on the ice several years previously; what she'd been calling arthritis was turning into something more serious. Roger sternly lectured her that she should follow her doctor's advice to stay in bed for four months. Or she should consider surgery. Or—and he hesitated, asking her not to be sore at him for saying it—she could consider giving up her job.

She did consider the idea of bed rest but then impatiently tossed it aside. Her only concession to poor health and overwork was once again to hand over the Christmas children's book review, this time to Rosemary Carr Benét. The real truth was that she loved being needed by *The New Yorker*. "It's been nightmarish but kind of fun to be back in the old bang-bang twenty-four a day routine," she wrote to Weston. And how could she leave, how could she possibly not be there to open the mail, when it might contain a manuscript by Jean Stafford or Vladimir Nabokov—two authors whom she was in the midst of cultivating? These were, as it turned out, authors with whom she would have two of the very most gratifying relationships of her career.

34.

Katharine's relationship with both Stafford and Nabokov began by rescuing each from the benign neglect of other *New Yorker* editors (just as had her relationships with Mary McCarthy and Elizabeth Bishop). Nabokov submitted his first poem to the magazine, which was itself only his second attempt at verse in English, in 1941. Charles Pearce accepted it, and then two more in 1942 and one in 1944. His editing was confined to rejecting Nabokov's innocent use of the word "horny" to describe a butterfly's anatomy; Nabokov changed it to "sculptured sex." Pearce saw him only as a promising poet fumbling his way into English, but Katharine read his story "Mademoiselle" in *The Atlantic* and clipped it. She wrote to Edmund Wilson to strategize about inspiring Nabokov to write for *The New Yorker*. She spent an evening with him when he came to New York, at Wilson and McCarthy's apartment, and in the midst of the repartee between Wilson and Nabokov, which Katharine found "electric," she managed to pull him aside to explain the magazine's baroque payment system, finally convincing him he could earn more if he switched from *The Atlantic* to *The New Yorker*. She learned how desperately he needed money, and signed him to a first reading agreement and advanced him $500 before he submitted a single word to her. Then she rejected his next poem and the first two stories he sent. She accepted a single poem and then raised his rate. She found a pretext for adjusting his fee for that poem, sending along yet another check. Nabokov loved seeing her notes and checks arrive in the mail one after another like "laggards in a cross country race, or additional puppies." His own output similarly limped along. He told her about a story unwritten, "the pattern showing through the wingcases of the pupa," but an editor could do little with such words but hope.

Perhaps he could finally write something, now that the Wellesley school year and his teaching duties were over, she prodded him in May. And he did, sending her an unlovely and chaotic reminiscence with the completely obscure title of "OUAT." Katharine got to work. She spoke about the essay on the phone to his wife, Véra, perhaps to pave the way for her delicately worded letter. "OUAT" was certainly "full of exciting and beautiful writing," she wrote, but there was no way the magazine could publish it in its current form, as the piece was too impressionistic, too un-unified, too full of personal passages the reader couldn't understand. Under no circumstances could the magazine publish something that quoted from Nabokov's own writing in Russian. Moreover, the essay couldn't be fixed by editing; he would have to cut, rearrange, rewrite. Could they discuss it in person, since she would be coming to Boston to stay at the Ritz for Joe's graduation from Exeter? But unfortunately her back trouble meant she had stamina only for the ceremony and she could not sit down with Nabokov to pore over the manuscript. So he wrote a second draft the next month, and Katharine circulated it to her fellow editors—but the entire editorial staff voted "no" to what they considered a slight portrait.

It would have been easy for Katharine to reject the essay and then rest that summer, as everyone advised her she needed to do. What would have happened to *Conclusive Evidence* (which eventually became *Speak, Memory*) if she had? Katharine spent many hours in July on Nabokov's manuscript, stealing time in the evenings after she'd completed her work on accepted manuscripts, rearranging his sentences for better transitions, rewording his awkward English. It was a risk—maybe she wouldn't be able to convince her colleagues (she later characterized Ross and Lobrano as "anti-Nabokov"); maybe Nabokov would loathe her changes. But at the beginning of August, she wrote to him, regarding her edited version of what was now called "Portrait of My Uncle," "To my intense delight, I got an enthusiastic yes [from Ross]." Nabokov, however, did not accept these edits. He wrote to Edmund Wilson that the edits upset him so much he "almost decided to stop trying to earn [his] living that way." But in time, he wrote to Katharine, "I think you have re-pinned and re-set the story very delicately and sympathetically," and he asked if she could send the check right away. Two months later he sent a second reminiscence, "My English Education." Around this time, in the fall of 1947, when Morris Bishop told Katharine that Cornell was looking for a professor of Russian literature, she told him about Nabokov, leading to a ten-year period of financial stability in which he would write his best-known works.

Nabokov would eventually publish eleven of the fifteen essays of *Conclusive Evidence* with Katharine at *The New Yorker*, and she would help him place the book with Harper, and when it appeared in 1951, she would write, "I feel almost as wrapped up in its success as if I had written it myself. It is by such meager vicarious emotions that editors have to console themselves for the creative work they do not do." Indeed, just before the book would go to press, Nabokov would write but not publish a sixteenth chapter in which he described this very editorial process in the third person, all the minor edits and enforced style compliance to which the magazine subjected him at first, before eventually allowing him his quirks. "Great sympathy, a delicate and loving care marked all editorial queries," he added. "Katharine White, who corresponded with the author in regard to all these matters, took endless trouble to check every hyphen and comma and smooth the creases in an author's ruffled temper and do everything possible to keep Nabokov's prose intact. An excellent proof of the harmonious accord between author and editor is the fact that Nabokov greedily preserved the majority of the corrections in regard to his skittish syntax and also the beautiful 'close' system of the *New Yorker* punctuation." (The magazine infamously favored the generous use of commas to separate clauses for syntax and meaning. Or as Andy put it, "Commas in *The New Yorker* fall with the precision of knives in a circus act, outlining the victim.")

But at the very same time that the two were writing back and forth about the Uncle Ruka reminiscence, Nabokov submitted a short story, and this editorial process revealed rather a different dimension to their dynamic. "Symbols and Signs" concerns a couple and their suicidal adult son, "incurably deranged in his mind" and institutionalized for his "referential mania," in which he believes "everything happening around him is a veiled reference to his personality and existence." The couple's phone rings twice in the night, a wrong number, and the story ends when it rings a third time, leaving the reader to interpret that wordless sign—and risk overinterpretation, the path to madness. The story fascinated but also wrong-footed Katharine, causing her to question her own interpretation.

"I've decided to ask you what your intention is in it," she wrote, because knowing it would guide her edits; if it were parody or satire, "what might be considered over-writing in a straight realistic story ought to be retained and even heightened." She reported being "nagged by the suspicion that there might be more than met the eye in [his] piece." Nabokov played it straight and said he failed to see her point, that it was "a good sample of [his] usual style." Katharine agreed to abide by these intentions and apologized for her misunderstanding. But when she sent back the story, Nabokov was offended by her edits, by how it had been "so carefully mutilated," and threatened to pull the piece.

Predictably, his letter prompted a five-page letter from Katharine with detailed explanations and qualifications. She began by saying he was free to reject their edits, then she explained the rewordings were to be considered "dummy wordings," and she ended by saying, "Distance has been our greatest enemy on this story—indeed in all our dealings." Her battle-tested strategy, so close to how she eased Mary McCarthy through a similarly rocky process, succeeded. Nabokov accepted her edits just as she set to work on the Uncle Ruka draft. "Symbols and Signs" was published in the May 15, 1948, issue ("Signs and Symbols," the story published in the 1958 collection *Nabokov's Dozen*, has many differences from the *New Yorker* version, not least the reversed title, so presumably he reinstated his original draft).

But years later, when he was trying—in vain—to get Katharine to accept "The Vane Sisters" with its second story "woven into or placed behind" the superficial primary story, Nabokov wrote her a letter that has become famous among literary critics. You have already published just such a nested story in "Symbols and Signs," he informed her, fully vindicating White's "nagging suspicion" about his authorial intentions and setting off a decades-long search for the key to unlocking the story's second level. Critics have found such keys in the misdialed number at the end ("I will tell you what you are doing: you are turning the letter *O* instead of the zero," the mother tells the caller) or the characters' movements plotted as chess puzzles; an entire book of essays has been written about the two-thousand-word story. Nabokov had not been honest with Katharine when she asked about his intentions, had not acknowledged her need to understand the story in order to publish it. Though the Nabokovs and the Whites became friends—they would visit each other when the Whites came to Ithaca to see Joe or the Nabokovs came to New York for literary business—Nabokov preserved a distance from his editor that perhaps contained a hint of condescension behind his unflagging courtliness, a willingness to use what he regarded as her mainstream taste for his own instrumental purposes. Katharine would soon be able to discern when Véra signed Vladimir's butterfly signature to his letters.

At the same time she was shepherding "A Portrait of My Uncle" and "Symbols and Signs" into publication, Katharine rescued yet another author from one of her *New Yorker* colleagues. Jean Stafford and Katharine swiftly became intimate friends across geographical distance, their letters creating a sympathetic—and, for one of them, life-changing—closeness. Stafford, a young writer whose second novel, *The Mountain Lion*, was just then making waves, had submitted a few stories to *The New Yorker* during the war through her agent, Marian Ives, a former editor at *Mademoiselle*, but William Maxwell rejected all of them. Now, in the summer of 1947, Ives sent in "Children Are Bored on Sunday," and Donald Berwick quickly sent it back with a "no" with no explanation. But something piqued Katharine's interest, and she asked Ives to send the story back to her. Within two weeks, she had accepted that story, plus another, and offered Stafford a first reading agreement, an offer that came with two checks: $100 for signing the agreement and $1,000 for "Children Are Bored on Sunday." Stafford met with Katharine for lunch, signed the agreement, and fired Ives.

"Children Are Bored" would be the first of twenty-one stories Stafford would publish in *The New Yorker*. Most of those would appear in her 1969 book *The Collected Stories of Jean Stafford*, which would be dedicated to Katharine S. White, nominated for the National Book Award, and win the Pulitzer Prize in 1970 (beating out two of Katharine's other authors, Peter Taylor and John Cheever). Stafford would write one more novel and several children's books, but in this second act of her career she would become best known as a short-story writer, a master of the form.

"Children Are Bored" arose directly from Stafford's previous year, when she'd checked herself into the Payne Whitney Psychiatric Clinic of New York Hospital for what was then called the "psycho-alcoholic cure" (a treatment initially prescribed for her by Andy's psychiatrist, Dr. Carl Binger). The hospital locked the doors behind her and then she was submitted to detoxification from drugs and alcohol, her exercise limited to the courtyard. She was given psychiatric help and careful re-instruction in how to bathe, eat, and sleep. Stafford had been brought to this nadir by her tormented and violent marriage to poet Robert Lowell; both later wrote stories and poems that would suggest their marriage's end was brought about when he tried to strangle her in bed, and in the aftermath of that incident, Stafford feared for her sanity. She moved into the clinic for what was supposed to be three months but stretched to nearly a year and drained the couple's bank account. When she left, Lowell and Stafford were still married but separated, and she needed to build a new life from practically nothing. So she wrote. "Children Are Bored" begins at the Metropolitan Museum, where Emma has gone to while away a Sunday, but when she catches sight of Alfred Eisenburg (based on Delmore Schwartz, a writer and editor at *Partisan Review*), her mind circles back to the last time she saw him, just before "she had closed the door of her tomb," another way of referring to "her collapse." The story makes no mention of a husband; rather, it indicts the intellectual scene of New York. Stafford criticizes the brittle cocktail parties with inferior drinks and arguments about politics and art that disregard the sensual world of Emma's upbringing, her untutored country childhood. She feels like a "rube" despite her college education, never fully able to belong to the "urbane" company of Eisenburg's crowd. But Eisenburg too has suffered a breakdown—she can see it in his face—and the story ends with their mutual recognition of their expulsion from the exalted realm, as they leave the museum in search of a bar.

Katharine's impression of the story remains off the page. The story is mercurial: in one light, it reads as a hazy *New Yorker* mood piece with the magazine's customary ironizing of sophistication itself, but in another, it reads as a tight narrative of a suspended identity, a woman caught between words and images, between her uneducated past and the soulless milieu of intellectuals, between health and ruin: "In so many words, she wasn't fit to be seen." Stafford, and perhaps also Katharine at *The New Yorker*, had a vested interest in portraying the intellectual art scene cracking under its own pretensions. Katharine was awed by Stafford's talent. She was also worried for her health. She only realized, after they met that December, just how nightmarish Stafford must have felt when they lunched together, and now that her anxiety for Stafford was up and running, she would write frequently and find new ways to help her newest author.

Just after "Children Are Bored" appeared in the pages of the magazine, events came to a head for both Stafford and Katharine. Stafford boarded a plane for St. Thomas in the Virgin Islands finally to obtain her divorce from Lowell. She caught typhoid and had a miserable time of it, then came home to New York, where she spent the summer recovering and not writing. Katharine could empathize: "I find myself unable to say how sorry I am about what you must have been through this summer. I know how frightfully my divorce upset me and I did not at that time have much if any feeling left for my husband. If you do, it must be hell itself."

Katharine, for her part, was forced to confront the severity of her back pain. She had resisted surgery as long as she could, even though she couldn't ride in a car or walk a full city block without pain, but X-rays now showed that the joint where her spine met her pelvis had corroded and the bones were roughened from grinding against one another. Her pain would only worsen and her mobility lessen. In the beginning of April, she wrote to her authors that she was about to take a medical leave. Maxwell returned to the office for two months, while she checked into Harkness Pavilion yet again, this time to undergo a spinal fusion on April 15, 1948. Her doctor assured her that he performed this surgery twice a week, then he sedated her, took out a piece of her thigh bone, fashioned it into the right shape, and attached it to her spine with two silver screws. Katharine stayed in Harkness for six weeks (one of her writers, humorist Frank Sullivan, wrote to her there, but said he expected his letter to be returned with a note: "Patient Disappeared After Slaying Nurse"). She underwent physical therapy and gradually built up the amount of time she could sit without fatigue, and she received manicures and phone calls and visitors. Roger came with news of his baby; Caroline "Callie" Sergeant Angell had been born in January, and as a gift to her son and daughter-in-law Katharine engaged the same practical nurse who had cared for Roger as a newborn. Andy and Joe departed for Maine and Katharine scrawled them notes when she was well rested, and occasionally talked to them on the phone. She spent time listening to the radio. A fellow patient across the hall was Walker Cooper, the New York Giants catcher, who had undergone surgery to remove bone chips in his knee after sliding into another player at the plate. Cooper listened to his team's games, and so Katharine did too, and by the time she left the hospital, she had shifted her lifelong allegiance from the Boston Red Sox to the Giants.

At the end of May, she was discharged to her home with a metal brace she wore for the next eight months. She stayed in New York with her cook, Josephine, and a housemaid to help her while Andy and Joe stayed in Maine (Andy had the summer adventure of accepting not one but three honorary degrees in person from the University of Maine, Dartmouth, and Yale). By mid-July she was well enough to join them in North Brooklin (and then Andy departed for New York on assignment from *Holiday* magazine to write an essay, "Here Is New York," a tribute to the bustle, loneliness, and variety of Manhattan). She didn't return to the *New Yorker* offices until October of 1948, and she later said that it took a full year to feel herself again. Though she eventually made a full recovery and could sit and walk without pain for the first time in four years, for a few months alone in Turtle Bay Gardens that summer and then alone in North Brooklin while Andy traveled down to New York, she felt as if she'd never be well again and regretted the surgery.

But she worked throughout her entire ordeal. She wrote to Stafford in St. Thomas to commiserate on the "perfect hell" of her time there, and for the first time she addressed the letter to Jean instead of Miss Stafford ("I always think of you as Jean and perhaps the drugs I am under have made me weak-headed enough to break down the barrier"). She accepted another Nabokov reminiscence, "Colette," just before checking into Harkness, and then she accepted "Russian Education" just after she returned home from the hospital. Practically the first thing she did upon returning home was dash off yet another letter to Mary McCarthy to beg for stories. In May she was answering Andy's fan mail, telling his correspondents that *he* was too ill to write. In August, she produced editorial letters using a Dictaphone that Ross sent to save her the labor of typing. She dutifully spoke into the machine and wrapped and mailed the cylinders to the office for transcription, but she felt self-conscious and apologized into the speaking tube to all her correspondents for her queer letters.

In October, once back at her desk in the *New Yorker* offices, she rejected a Saul Bellow story with far too much profanity to run in their magazine ("[We] are earnestly waiting for the day when he writes something we can publish," she told his agent). She regretfully turned away a story by Elizabeth Hardwick that, to her mind, unwittingly duplicated the plot of *Sense and Sensibility*. She resumed her life exactly where she had left off. In November, the Whites traveled to Cornell University in Ithaca to visit their freshman son, who wore a white Class of 1952 sweater and smoked cigarettes with flair. They sat next to the Nabokovs at Joe's soccer game, and Katharine found Vladimir "positively heavy and plump" after his own recent health troubles but delighted to be known as "the patron saint of the soccer teams," so steady was his presence in the stands.

She even managed to write her annual children's book review for the holiday issue, her longest yet at twenty-three pages, signed with her name and with an ambitious and surprising four-page essay at the beginning, in which she makes her perennial case regarding treating children's reading life with dignity rather than pandering, a theme she advanced by way of a breezy review of a new scholarly book about children's literature throughout American history. She didn't know it yet, but this children's book review, in which she ends her essay by circling around to the beginning, would in fact be her last. In it Katharine writes of the St. Nicholas

League, which had springboarded her into the world of magazines. She deemed the newly published *St. Nicholas Anthology* the family book of the year, guaranteed to please by its excellent selections and the nostalgia they invoked, and she quoted one of its editors, who gave voice to Katharine's own theme: the best children's literature arises from "the constant cooperation of youth and maturity."

Proof positive that Katharine was feeling back to normal by the end of the year: on December 20, she wrote and telephoned around, asking "a few friends, old and young," as she described it to Jean Stafford, to come over to the Whites' house on Forty-Eighth Street for a New Year's Eve party. That night, she and Andy entertained one hundred people—such was Katharine's definition of "a few friends."

35.

Here is a check for your share in the latest royalty on the New Yorker short story book. Sending it to you gives me the chance to say how much we would welcome another short story or casual from you. Is there any hope? Sincerely yours, K. S. White
   —to Mr. White, April 10, 1946

When *The New Yorker* published Jean Stafford's second story, "A Summer Day," in September 1948, it instantly drew a letter from the NAACP objecting to her use of the N-word in the first paragraph to describe a train conductor, classifying an entire people in a "derogatory and insulting" manner. "We would like to receive assurances from you that in the future care will be taken to see to it that such references will not be repeated," the NAACP wrote, noting the "irony" that this insult occurred in the same issue as the second part of E. J. Kahn's profile of NAACP secretary Walter White—the very same White who had tried and failed to publish a profile of James Weldon Johnson, the same White whose profile by the NAACP publicity director Katharine had rejected in 1932. Within this nest of correspondence, much of the magazine's attitude toward racial issues in the postwar era can be discerned.

The NAACP did not receive the assurances they sought. The *New Yorker* editors sent an unsigned reply begging to disagree that the word was gratuitous, because it was uttered in free indirect discourse from the perspective of an illiterate Southern Cherokee boy, and "any other phraseology in the tenor of Miss Stafford's tale would have been false."

Katharine forwarded both letters to Stafford and included her own take on the matter: "Don't let it get you down." She explained, "We have a rule of course against using the word except for a literary purpose as you used it." Even so, she went on, every time the word appeared in the magazine, the editors received such a letter from the NAACP, just as they often received letters from Jewish organizations. The writers of such letters attacked stories that were *against* racial discrimination, she noted. "They don't seem to want the subject mentioned."

Neither woman was deterred by the NAACP letter. In fact, Stafford doubled down in the next story she submitted to Katharine, which might perhaps be read as a direct response to the NAACP. She set "Pax Vobiscum," a title that translates to "peace be with you," on an unnamed Caribbean island in March at a guesthouse filled with young American women staying the requisite six weeks for their divorces. The owner of the guesthouse is Captain Sundstrom, a Dutchman who makes a sport of horrifying the fragile women with deliberately transgressive language— including the N-word and all its variants—and telling shocking, apocryphal stories about the Black people on the island. The center of Stafford's story is an act of unspeakable brutality so beyond the pale that it is obviously untrue, a tall tale told to rile up the torpid, privileged women draped around the pool. "Pax Vobiscum" puts two very different elements into play against one another: on one hand the women's evaluation of their sex appeal and gendered capital, which they'll need to employ in building new lives for themselves, and on the other the undefined presence of racialized others on the island and in these women's lives back home, relegated to the margins of the white mainstream and essentially existing for the women only within the language describing them. Katharine loved the story and bought it immediately. This was definitely not the pastel story for which *The New Yorker* was constantly being criticized, but Katharine's letters to Stafford did not portray their publication of it as a risk, though it extended far beyond "A Summer Day."

If "Pax Vobiscum" drew another letter from the NAACP, the *New Yorker* secretaries did not retain it for the files. The story did provoke a number of readers to write to the editor in exactly the outrage that Captain Sundstrom hoped to stir in his guests, and Katharine forwarded those letters to Stafford for writer and editor to shake their heads over. (One reader was certain that the story snuck past E. B. White on its way into the magazine: "Nothing—nothing will ever make me believe he O.K.'d it.") Katharine was certain that she and Stafford were fighting the good fight. In the words of the letter sent to offended readers, signed only as "The NEW YORKER": "We consider it an excellently written protest against racial ideas prevalent in certain milieus, as well as a biting portrayal of the about-to-be divorced of the Virgin Islands." The editors believed themselves and their subscribers to be subtle enough observers of race relations to be unbound by the NAACP's simplistic rules, and they thought the readers who didn't understand when an author was holding characters up for satire or derision, or when an author was critiquing the very assumptions that she shared with her readers, were in the minority. Katharine also believed that stories that aggressively advanced an "anti-racial prejudice" sounded too much like propaganda and were bad art; she thought these "noble stories" lowered the overall quality of the *O. Henry* and *Best American Short Stories* anthologies.

Instead, Katharine preferred to run stories that indicted the subtle hypocrisies of the liberal readers who were *The New Yorker*'s mainstay, as well as stories that more overtly critiqued the hypocrisies of other groups, including Southern whites, with their easy-to-deplore racism. One story by Frances Gray Patton managed to do both: "The Falling Leaves" portrays a Northern woman named Harriet who marries and moves to South Carolina, where she deplores her new white friends' delight in her Black maid's illiteracy and dialect ("She was an old-fashioned Southern darky, they said, without any fancy modern ideas"), while holding fast to her own condescension ("Harriet was sorry for all colored people") and rank prejudice ("'Don't stand there like a kangaroo,' snapped Harriet"). Neither the NAACP's criticism of *The New Yorker*'s politics nor Katharine's self-satisfied liberalism prompted her to solicit work from Black authors, though she wouldn't have had to look far. Ann Petry, to take one instance, had just won the Houghton Mifflin Literary Fellowship, which had brought Elizabeth Bishop to her attention, and published *The Street*, which was hugely successful; Gwendolyn Brooks, to take another, had published her first book of poetry, *A Street in Bronzeville*, with Andy's publisher, Harper & Brothers, and had been awarded a Guggenheim fellowship.

The postwar years saw a huge expansion in the magazine's readership—subscribers more than doubled in the decade of the 1940s—and a sharpening of its self-definition around the remarkably stable socioeconomic contours of that readership. *The New Yorker* understood its readers to be, in the words of a marketing pamphlet, "at least all of the following: Intelligent, well-educated, discriminating, well-informed, unprejudiced, public-spirited, metropolitan-minded, broad-visioned and quietly liberal." The magazine often pitched itself toward an elite readership but was read—and scrutinized and assimilated—by the newly dominant professional-managerial class.

The Whites saw themselves as good citizens of this sector of the nation, as somewhat reluctant thought leaders who were secure enough in their own self-definition to point out the fault lines within the postwar consensus they were helping to create. Katharine believed herself to be unprejudiced, though her world was almost entirely white. Her vast correspondence does contain one instance of racially insensitive language. She wrote to Ross from Maine, telling him that Andy has "never been able to write in the summer, this year less than ever because he's worked like a n—— on manual labor." Her casual use of this term is shocking and appalling. Her family members do not recall her ever using the term in speech or letters. Why, then, did she use it now? Katharine remarked many times on Ross's use of curses and profanity, and always bragged a bit about how his language rubbed off on her. Perhaps she used the term here, to Ross, precisely to be casually offensive—to prove that she was one of the boys. She could do so because she felt utterly protected within her and Ross's shared white privilege. Elsewhere, she prided herself on her ability to publish many stories about race, and in fact she wished that she could publish more. Many times over the years, she and Andy rued the fact that *The New Yorker* must hold its comedic fire when it came to Black people and others of color. Andy responded to a reader who wrote to him about a casual the magazine had recently published, a first-person account of a Black woman in Amsterdam, "Negroes enjoy a certain immunity to the shafts of satirists and cartoonists. Every week we publish drawings depicting the frailties and idiosyncrasies of the human race, as our artists see them. But we do not feel entirely free to include colored people in comic situations, for the reason that the public is as yet incapable of looking at a Negro as an individual, and persists in looking at him as a symbol." The Whites were tone-deaf to the entitlement required to make such a complaint.

Was Katharine thinking about *The New Yorker*'s power to define and describe the cultural moment to an entire socioeconomic class as she finally set to work editing the next anthology of the magazine's short stories? At the tail end of 1948, publisher Richard Simon reached back out to Katharine, asking if she and her colleagues were ready to tackle the oft-postponed follow-up to *Short Stories from "The New Yorker."* It was now Simon & Schuster's twenty-fifth anniversary, the pretext for reviving the idea.

Katharine and her colleagues agreed, and she set to work making lists, coming up with a rough working draft of *55 Short Stories from "The New Yorker"* in just a few weeks. The editorial files suggest she merely thought of this volume as the best of the last decade, an almost clerical exercise of identifying their major authors and then selecting each author's best story. Simon & Schuster sent over its own list, generated by five S&S editors, and Katharine attacked it with her Blackwing pencil, writing "no" next to anything that wasn't a short story and circling the titles that also appeared on her list. She made exceptions for two reminiscences that "had a real fictional quality": Mary McCarthy's "Yonder Peasant, Who Is He?" and Vladimir Nabokov's "Colette." Katharine decided not to write a foreword, beyond a single paragraph that echoed the disclaimer in the first anthology, that this book was intended as a "representative" collection of the magazine's fiction but that many "notable" pieces were not included because they duplicated themes or were not short stories. She explained to Simon & Schuster that this terseness arose from a need for diplomacy: they couldn't call it the "best" of *The New Yorker*, nor could they even hint that it was the taste and judgment of a single editor, for fear of offending the valued authors in the magazine's stable. She needed a kind of plausible deniability, the cover story that the selection of pieces depended in part on the publisher's needs. As ever, Katharine's mind was trained on the conditions for future production of the stories she so badly needed.

For their part, Simon & Schuster was excited enough about her draft list to begin selling the idea to Harry Scherman at the Book-of-the-Month Club. The publisher also made plans to reissue the first *New Yorker* anthology in a matching format, since it was still selling ten years later.

Perhaps predictably, the extra work on the anthology worsened Katharine's health. Andy had given up responsibility for Notes and Comment at the beginning of the year, though he still contributed when the urge struck him. Now Katharine attempted to decrease her own workload: she got Ross to agree to a new schedule where she'd work four weeks and then take a fifth week off. She visited her doctor, who diagnosed her with overwork and prescribed a warm climate, but she ignored his prescription and traveled to Maine for Joe's break. In May, she finally did make it down to Florida, a convenient place to recuperate because Aunt Crullie, Ros, and John were there, but it was also becoming her least favorite place in the world—"The land where not only man is vile; back again where my bowels constrict and my spirits sag," as she put it to Andy. She also finally confronted the fact that she could not afford to spend all summer reading children's books in preparation for her holiday book review. She turned the book review over to Katherine Kinkead, this time with finality—she would not pick it up again—and with only a little regret for losing her soapbox on a body of literature about which she cared so much.

The very instant she gave up the children's book review, Katharine received a letter from Katherine Gauss Jackson, an editor at *Harper's*, saying she'd heard a rumor that Katharine was now free and asking if she'd like to write the same column for them. Jackson stipulated that a two-thousand-word column be submitted to her in three weeks, for which she'd pay $200. The offer was an almost risible undervaluation of what Katharine had been doing for sixteen solid years and she turned it down with glee. Instead of writing, Katharine spent the summer of 1949 fully relishing the pleasures of the season. Andy described it as "the summer of the grandchildren," with Nancy staying at a cottage only a mile away with Kitty, Jon, and baby Sarah, born the previous October, and Roger and Evelyn visiting with baby Callie. Katharine described it as "a disappointment," because she and Andy could not get away to Nova Scotia as they had planned, and because her enjoyment of the grandchildren was cut with tension when Ernest and his second wife, Elizabeth, came to visit Nancy and Roger. Katharine felt duty-bound to invite the Angells for cocktails (Ernest eventually declined). But mainly she enjoyed the exertions of her increasingly strong body, swimming and rowing in the cove, and of course gardening.

The Whites returned to New York in their new DeSoto Carry-All sedan in October 1949, and just a week later, *55 Short Stories from "The New Yorker"* came out. By the end of the year the anthology had sold fifteen thousand copies, plus another three thousand copies to the magazine itself. It wasn't widely reviewed, but most mentions were positive, finding the collection noteworthy for containing diverse styles but consistent quality.

The exception was a five-page essay in *Partisan Review* by Delmore Schwartz (the real-life inspiration for the male character in Stafford's "Children Are Bored on Sunday," which was included in the anthology) called "Smile and Grin, Relax and Collapse." Schwartz posited that *The New Yorker* existed solely to tutor its readers on the thoughts and buying habits that capitalism required among its dupes in the broad liberal consensus of the middle class. He deplored the magazine's tendency to define the short story as "some form of memoir, reminiscence, or anecdote, especially about childhood or about one's dear, foolish, pathetic, and comical elders." The magazine should be indicted for luring otherwise sterling writers like McCarthy and Nabokov into the lazy and indefensible space of memoir, in which they freely mixed fact with fiction and thereby abandoned the genre's bedrock authenticity. As for the genuine short stories among the lot, they evinced a house style that required the prose to be "chatty, relaxed, not very serious, and certainly never (God forbid!) intellectual." The result was that the magazine was becoming "increasingly nondescript and anonymous." Schwartz hastened to say that he wasn't accusing the editors of a "deliberate conspiracy" to wedge American fiction into a tight formula; he was sure the stories resulted from "a profound and intuitive collaboration between the taste of numerous readers and hard-pressed editors who do the best they can, according to their lights." But he thought those editors could work harder to cultivate the originality of their own gifted authors.

The unvoiced word in Schwartz's review essay was "middlebrow." *The New Yorker* in the postwar era was starting to become confusingly entangled with this loaded term, which had been in use since the 1920s in response to the rise of both modernism and mass culture but was now cropping up in mainstream articles to describe American culture. If highbrow art was rarefied, avant-garde, or intellectual, and lowbrow art was cheap, sensationalist, and disposable, middlebrow art was more than simply everything in between. It sought to use mass culture to convey the values of high culture; it invited its consumers to step up to a higher status. But key to middlebrow's success was its insistence on pleasure; it must never feel like school or homework, but should always be enjoyable and even relaxing, because the acquisition of culture and the climbing of the ladder were themselves pleasurable and desirable. The postwar critics used the term "middlebrow" as an epithet because it implied that art was commensurate with capitalism, tasked with teaching the middle class how to think and strive entirely within market values. *The New Yorker*, with its time-tested editorial ethos of assuming its readers knew the manners and mores of the urban elite (its yachting column, its coverage of polo) while covertly imparting such knowledge through humor, would appear to exemplify this definition in all its facets. To some critics, further proof of the magazine's status was its entanglement with that most quintessential middlebrow institution, the Book-of-the-Month Club. Several books that arose from *New Yorker* series became BOMC hits, such as Ruth McKenney's *My Sister Eileen* and James Thurber's *The Thurber Carnival*, not to mention all three books that Katharine edited during her interregnum from the magazine: *Short Stories from "The New Yorker," A Subtreasury of American Humor*, and *One Man's Meat*. Now, in December of 1949, the Book-of-the-Month Club rejected *55 Short Stories from "The New Yorker,"* but they did select Andy's new book. Harper had republished the essay that he'd written for *Holiday* the summer after Katharine's surgery as a slim book, *Here Is New York*, and that December it was mailed to thousands of BOMC subscribers. The *New Yorker* editors, and the Whites in particular, were far more amenable to partnership

---

with the BOMC than they ever were to the *Best American Short Stories* franchise or the *O. Henry Prize* collections.

The question of what counted as middlebrow fascinated readers at the end of the 1940s. The British writer Stephen Spender took stock of the American literary scene in *Horizon*. He endorsed the familiar criticism of *The New Yorker*, that most writers "are edited (or edit themselves) almost out of existence so that everything in it appears to be by an anonymous body called *The New Yorker*." But when he listed the writers he found most vital in their protest against "vulgarity, commercialization, advertising, exploiting," half of them were Katharine's writers, including Thurber, Stafford, McCarthy, Edmund Wilson, and Marianne Moore.

So which was it—was *The New Yorker* cravenly middlebrow or the organ for the writers most actively resisting the middlebrow? And why did it matter? Russell Lynes, an editor at *Harper's*, published a widely read essay, "Highbrow, Lowbrow, Middlebrow," that split the middlebrow into "upper" and "lower." Right there on the nightstand of the upper-middlebrow consumer, the one who "takes his culture seriously," sat *The New Yorker*, along with *Harper's* and "an occasional copy" of *Partisan Review* ("Membership in any sort of book club he considers beneath him"). Lynes devoted a paragraph to the editor, "caught between the muses and the masses," as the exemplar of the upper-middlebrow worker in the knowledge trades, someone who purveyed highbrow ideas (and read highbrow publications for authors to poach) to the lower-middlebrow consumers. Lynes's cultural mapping proved so popular that *Life* reprinted it with an illustrated chart and it became an influential touchstone in this ongoing conversation, a way to make legible what Lynes identified as a new social structure replacing the old class system. Now prestige would come not from inherited wealth but from "high thinking." In other words, the socioeconomic transformation begun in the 1920s that *The New Yorker* had been founded to observe, shape, and capitalize on was now reaching its apotheosis—and that explained its robust postwar circulation numbers. The magazine's circulation grew from 172,000 at the end of 1941 to 227,000 by the middle of 1945, a 32 percent increase, which didn't even include the free pony edition for servicemen. After the war, *New Yorker* readership would expand by 10 percent every year through 1952.

For Katharine, Schwartz's argument broke down when it moved from the supposed *function* of the magazine within the cultural landscape to its *form*, the actual content of the stories she so assiduously acquired and edited. She was irritated by the continual accusation that the magazine published slight, formulaic fiction that coddled the liberal upper middlebrow, and she relentlessly employed the "but what about" defense, digging through the magazine's rosters to brandish writers with entirely distinct styles. For instance, in 1947, she wrote to an author, "I can't find any other publication that has offered within a three months' period as wide a variation in types of fiction, or in styles of writing, as we have since the first of May, for example, with stories by John Cheever, Kay Boyle, Christine Weston ("Her Bed Is India"), E. B. White, John O'Hara, Niccolò Tucci, Nancy Hale, and Isabel Bolton." She claimed that the only writers the magazine refused to publish were "the pretentious, the totally incomprehensible, and the obscene."

Many of Katharine's stories, poems, and reminiscences evaded a middlebrow aesthetic, and when taken together, as they were in *55 Short Stories from "The New Yorker,"* the pattern was even clearer. The stories might treat the aspirations or discontents of the professional-managerial class, but at a slant. Where middlebrow literature was emotional or sentimental, soliciting the reader's empathy, Katharine's authors often employed narrators who were aloof, dispassionate, intellectualized, or judgmental, as in Sally Benson's contribution to the collection, "Lady with a Lamp," which portrays a vile night nurse without a shred of care or duty toward her patient, a slovenly alcoholic woman. The stories that Katharine published often featured narrators or protagonists who were not mouthpieces for their authors and often did not ask readers to agree with their characters or find them noble, as in Christine Weston's "Her Bed Is India." Where middlebrow literature was earnest, Katharine's authors were often critical, even self-critical, standing at a remove from their own actions or their own pasts to scrutinize them, in story after story about perceiving, a straight line from Kay Boyle's "Kroy Wen" in 1931 to Mary McCarthy's "The Blackguard" in 1946.

Katharine's *New Yorker* offered an alternative to the values that the BOMC advanced, what has since been called "middlebrow personalism," the view that the individual could find refuge from the impersonal, uncontrollable modern world through reading, through connecting with books on the basis of empathy and feeling, a connection so deep as to induce in the reader an experience of absorption and immersion, the highest goal of both the reader and the writer. Instead, she published stories that induced discomfort—such as Astrid Peters's "Party at the Williamsons'," Nancy Hale's "Between the Dark and the Daylight," and Marjorie Kinnan Rawlings's "Black Secret," all of which treated the reluctant or traumatic sexual awakening of children. And she published humor and satire that sought to jolt rather than enchant the reader. Just as Katharine's reminiscences played with genre—never quite fact, never quite fiction—so did the stories she edited transcend the middlebrow. Both were crucial to *The New Yorker*'s success at midcentury, and both fascinated readers because of the way they escaped the familiar categories that tried to contain them.

If Katharine did not listen to intellectual critics in small-circulation journals, she did listen to her authors, and she agreed with them that the editorial staff was overzealous in its queries, fact-checking, and punctuation. Months before beginning work on *55 Short Stories from "The New Yorker,"* she had launched her own internal war against overediting, crusading on behalf of writers like Nabokov. He was grateful when she corrected his invented English words like "museal" but pushed back hard when she sought to shorten sentences and clarify meanings. "I do not think I would like my longish sentences clipped too close," he told her, "or those drawbridges lowered which I have taken such pains to lift." Above all, he wanted his own style, "a certain special—how shall I put it—sinuosity," to survive the editorial process. "Why not have the reader re-read a sentence now and then? It won't hurt him." Katharine discussed Nabokov's work with Edmund Wilson, the perfect intermediary as someone who knew intimately the magazine's internal politics and wanted the best for his friend's work. Wilson, perhaps at Katharine's direction, wrote a three-page letter that he wanted her to use as ammunition against Ross in her campaign. Nabokov's stories were perfect and not a letter should be altered, he wrote. Furthermore, they stood out as rich and precious against all the "pointless and inane little anecdotes that are turned out by the *New Yorker*'s processing mill and that the reader forgets two minutes after he has read them." He went on and on, speaking from his own experience as a rejected author: "The editors are so afraid of anything that is unusual, that is not expected, that they put a premium on insipidity and banality."

Katharine hardly agreed with that, but she discussed the issue with Ross. He professed to have no idea what she was talking about. *Were* people saying that the magazine was overedited? He was baffled but staunchly defended their editorial practice of tightening the prose of "the vast number of semi-literates who write three-fourths of our stuff." Nabokov didn't count in this tally, but too many of their authors didn't actually strike Ross as real writers: "Their stuff has to be rendered into English and can't rise above the plane of straightaway English because that's as high as editing will raise it. But it ought to be edited to that plane." The difference between Wilson and Ross came down to vantage. Ross saw only what came across the editors' desks, and he forever stared glumly into the blank pages of future issues, fifty-two a year, over two hundred fifty short stories a year. He wished that each week he could publish a story as good as one by Nancy Hale or John O'Hara in their prime, but the schedule often called for compromise. Wilson and their other authors looked at the issue from outside, from the finished product sitting on magazine stands next to other finished products, and the entire field of American literary short stories as canonized by story collections, prizes, and syllabi.

Katharine had the overediting conversation at the same time with two other authors, and she told both that she was sympathetic to the charge and was pulling hard on the other editors' reins. She told Christine Weston, "It's entirely your privilege to want a piece to appear as you want it to and I'll fight for that privilege of authors as long as I'm an editor" (just sentences after asking Weston for a host of changes, including to a story's ending). In a long reply of sympathy and explanation to Isabel

Bolton's complaint, Katharine emphasized that the point was for each author to develop her own style. "What bothers us most," she confided, "is when the boys begin imitating each other for that does make for standardization." She begged Bolton not to hold in her head a conceptualization of *The New Yorker*'s style and try to write within that, but to write only to please herself. And, she added, keep reading the magazine, because it was not a static thing, and "in the next year or two [it] may develop some new talent."

It was the prospect of new talent that arguably kept Katharine going, through another big New Year's Eve party to welcome 1950; through the crushing disappointment of having to miss *The New Yorker*'s twenty-fifth anniversary party at the Ritz-Carlton Hotel because she was bedridden with bronchitis; through a European trip that she and Andy excitedly booked—steamer tickets, hotels, a small car for the French portion, a flurry of letters to Janet Flanner and Mollie Panter-Downes for recommendations and introductions—and then canceled because she'd missed too much work due to her illness; through another busy summer at the farm, marred by the sudden and unrelated deaths of two of their employees and her bout of viral pneumonia, but enhanced by the two-week trip to Nova Scotia that she and Andy finally managed to take; through seeing Joe off to MIT, where he had transferred in order to major in naval architecture, even though he'd have to start over again as a freshman with a heavy load of science and math and would miss out on Nabokov's Russian literature class—through all this, Katharine kept her eyes out for new talent. In 1951, *The New Yorker* published sixty-three new fiction and poetry writers, more than one a week.

It was around this time that Andy concentrated on a second children's book, one he'd imagined the previous year, about a spider he'd observed in the barn. And it was right around this time that Katharine finally brought into the magazine three women whom she'd been pursuing for years.

She published her old friend from the Cleveland Play House, Ida Treat, who had just returned to the Unites States to teach English at Vassar after earning not one but two doctorates in France and working as a journalist in Europe, China, and the South Pacific. Katharine had wanted

Treat's work to reappear in the magazine since her first *New Yorker* story in 1941, and now Treat inaugurated a streak that would continue through 1963.

Katharine's many years spent courting Elizabeth Taylor (not that one) and Rumer Godden from across the pond finally paid off (England was still rationing food, and *The New Yorker* sent British writers large boxes of food—ham, roast beef, butter, sweets if they had children—every two months, as well as American reviews of their books). She bought four short stories from Taylor in quick succession and wrote her effusive letters of praise, telling her that she'd devoted an entire summer to reading Taylor's novels and also shared them with Andy and Nancy, who compared them to E. M. Forster's books. They worked well together on the edits even across the distance, in part because Taylor was represented by Bernice Baumgarten, Mary McCarthy's agent, who well knew *The New Yorker*'s idiosyncrasies. Katharine told Baumgarten, "She's the kind of author I think should be allowed as much leeway as possible." But even so, the two hit a bump on Taylor's second story. When Taylor received an overedited proof, she wrote the most genteel and anguished letter of protest, saying that she no longer recognized her work—reading it was "like knocking [her] shins on something in the dark."

And again: when Rumer Godden finally submitted a story, "Time Is a Stream," and Katharine excitedly accepted it, they ran aground on the same polite despair over the magazine's habitual edits. "I agree with Mr. Ross about the attributing of remarks and make this my habit," Godden ventured, "but, in this story, it seems to interrupt the flow as you have sensed and, as it is a story about the flow of time, I think it better to let it flow." More edits, more letters, and three months later, Godden wrote that she'd been ever so gently "wondering if there is a risk of destroying the author's personality." Yes, absolutely, Katharine replied, there was a "grave risk" of just that thing, and she was grateful for Godden's timely letters, writing, "We editors have been making a fighting stand about what we think is over-querying of proofs," and she would brandish Godden's letter as evidence. (She loyally added a defense of Mr. Ross, "the arch queryer," giving the usual line that his edits were only suggestions, "just to be conscientious.") She made a packet of Godden's and Taylor's letters, to which she added a third, by yet another British writer, but this one entirely lacking in politesse. *The New Yorker* worked Roald Dahl into "a howling fury," and only after he calmed down could he write with relative restraint that the magazine "butcher[ed] one's story and mince[d] it up into unrecognizable sausage." Katharine turned over the sheaf of letters to Ross, and she added that even the easygoing American writers who were a breeze to edit, including Jean Stafford and Peter Taylor, discarded the magazine's revisions the instant they republished their stories in book collections. Ross finally conceded the point. He passed the letters along to style editor Hobart "Hobie" Weekes with a strongly worded command for his department to stand down. It was, like the 1930s campaign for fair, dependable payment that resulted in the first reading agreement, a crusade waged by writers against management with a sympathetic editor as go-between.

Not long after this policy shift, Ross began to step away from *New Yorker* duties. In the spring of 1951, he was diagnosed with pleurisy, and the treatment was to spend all but two hours a day on his back. That summer, his doctor discovered cancer in his windpipe, too far advanced for surgery. Ross managed to undergo eight weeks of radiation without disclosing his diagnosis to anyone—not his daughter, not the Whites, not anyone on the magazine staff except Hawley Truax, treasurer, chairman of the magazine's board, and Ross's best friend. He returned to work in September after a five-month absence, but by December the cancer appeared to have spread to his lungs. On December 6, Harold Ross died during the diagnostic surgery that revealed the extent of his cancer.

Katharine and Andy heard the news that night by telephone, and they headed into the office early the next morning to be there for staff and contributors. Andy sat down to write Ross's obituary and he wrote the scene of writing into it, noting that Ross had left them in a "jam" because the next issue was just about to close. "All morning, people have wandered in and out of our cell," he wrote, "some tearfully, some guardedly, some boisterously, most of them long-time friends in various stages of repair." The elevator doors opened and everyone on the nineteenth floor heard an anguished wail: "Andy! *An*-dy!" It was Thurber, feeling his blind way toward Andy's office without his usual helper. Andy's obituary of Ross, written in real time, gives a marvelously alive sense of the scene at the *New Yorker* offices that day, as well as of Ross's distinctive personality and influence on the people who worked for him. It is suffused with feeling and doesn't even attempt to give an account of Ross's life. "Sometimes a love letter writes itself, and we love Ross so, and bear him such respect, that these quick notes, which purport to record the sorrow that runs through here and dissolves so many people, cannot possibly seem overstated or silly."

Katharine greeted the contributors who came in that morning, and the first was Ruth McKenney, who hadn't published anything in the magazine for years, had in fact departed the magazine when she joined the Communist Party and began writing for their publications, but was now back to deliver a note testifying to her regret at leaving Ross, whose belief in a free press she now reaffirmed, before she vanished in a flash. Katharine received a letter from Janet Flanner in Paris that began, "darling Kay, Oh yes, I was thinking of us all, you & [Daise] Terry the first females, with Jane [Grant] after all, & the only ones to outlast him, from that first period. I could not think of anything else but Ross & us."

But none of the women who helped found *The New Yorker* spoke at Ross's service the next Monday, not anyone at all who had known him for years and worked alongside him on the magazine that was the central organizing principle of his life. The service was invitation-only because the funeral parlor at Eighty-First and Madison only held 350 people, but even so there was an overflow crowd to listen in disbelief as a Yale chaplain who had never met him delivered a sentimental eulogy that Ross would have despised. Everyone was baffled by the inaptness; apparently Ross's third wife had too hastily arranged the service without consulting his closest friends. Andy later wrote to reporter Elmer Davis and Frank Sullivan that the real tribute was the preternatural silence of Manhattan's most articulate crowd: "such a bunch of normally noisy and disorderly people sitting so quietly, so respectfully, and so completely forlorn."

For the next six weeks, the staff conducted the work of the magazine under a cloud of uncertainty and suspense. Ross hadn't officially named a successor, and Andy later remembered that there were two candidates for the job: William Shawn and Gus Lobrano. Finally, late in January 1952, Raoul Fleischmann wrote a one-sentence memo and posted it on the editorial floor: "William Shawn has accepted the position of editor of *The New Yorker*, effective today." Lobrano, whom Andy remembered as so upset over being passed over that he "never forgave Shawn or anyone else," continued in his position as head of the fiction department. The editorial staff created a new working protocol: where before it took one man to be "the arch queryer" of every single piece slated to appear in the magazine, now Ross's role would be divided into three, and Shawn would have the final read on fact pieces, Lobrano on fiction, and Katharine on poetry. *The New Yorker* entered a new era, and the Whites began planning a party to usher it in.

36.

The *New Yorker* will blow up like a firecracker if I leave. I am so sure of that that I wouldn't gamble five cents against it, or an hour's time.
—Harold Ross, 1945

In February of 1952, the Whites gave a party for William Shawn to celebrate the inauguration of his reign. They invited 140 guests to the town house on Forty-Eighth Street, and though Katharine was afraid that the crowd would fall right through the floor, the evening went beautifully. Shawn, an accomplished jazz musician, played Katharine's baby grand piano, and then cartoonist Peter Arno took a turn, and lots of people danced. Cartoonist Gluyas Williams had to be helped back to the Harvard Club. St. Clair McKelway got disoriented and walked in on the cook in her bedroom. Christine Weston made several sallies toward the Whites to say good night but was kept at bay by the crowd enveloping the couple each time. The party ended at four forty-five in the morning, right around when Andy felt "the door would presently open and in would walk Scott and Zelda."

The first thing Katharine had done when Shawn was promoted, even before planning the party, was to sit him down to talk about poetry. Though it had been years since she was in charge of it, she still weighed in on it and considered herself the standard-bearer for serious verse that mirrored the magazine's commitment to the best short fiction. What should be the magazine's policy going forward? To her deep gratification, Shawn told her that he personally liked a far greater range of

poetry than Ross ever did, and that they should use their considerable
financial resources to attract more poets. Katharine instantly wrote to
Louise Bogan to ask for her recommendations, saying that now she'd no
longer feel embarrassed to solicit work from distinguished writers like
Marianne Moore. Bogan wrote back with a recommendation for a very
young poet, Adrienne Cecile Rich, a Radcliffe undergraduate whose first
book, *A Change of World*, had just been chosen by W. H. Auden for the
prestigious Yale Younger Poets Prize.

Katharine asked Howard Moss, the junior editor who handled most
of the poetry submissions, to reach out to Rich, "thinking that she might
prefer to get a letter from a young poet than from an aged female editor."
But Rich did not respond. Bogan went to work, writing to Rich at Oxford, where she was spending a year on a Guggenheim fellowship, and by
the end of the year she'd convinced Rich to send her four poems, which
Bogan then forwarded to Katharine. In the ensuing correspondence,
Rich and Katharine discovered a mutual friend in Katharine Gericke,
the girl at Miss Winsor's who vied with Katharine for the summer book
prize, now a resident of Cambridge who frequently had Rich over for tea.

Borne into the magazine by a network of women, Rich became one of
Katharine's authors, not Moss's, and a natural affinity arose between the
two of them across a generation. Their early correspondence is striking
for how deferential the older woman was to the younger. "I feel rather
embarrassed even to make such a revision to a poet of your talent and
ability," Katharine wrote, "and I do hope you will not think it imperti-
nent of us to ask you to think over this possible further change." Rich, for
her part, had no trouble standing her ground against editorial queries,
but she was also game to reword and revise, as she did with two poems
about love in 1953.

"The Marriage Portion" portrays a couple who barricade themselves
from the distractions of daily life and against the clamor of modern
society that would cleave them from each other. The poem's ending
struck the editors as ambiguous: if the couple succeeds in preserving
their aloneness, will they be content and replete, or will they find they've
missed out on life, grown old together in barren sadness? Rich explained
that she meant the former, and she rewrote the final stanza to Kath-

arine's immediate satisfaction. And again: "A Walk by the Charles," a gorgeous autumnal image of a couple holding hands by the river, watching as the oarsmen slice through the reflection of a bridge, an evocation of transience and death—and also the end of sex? Katharine asked. She proposed an alternate version of the last stanza, a version Rich rejected in favor of her own rewrite, to clarify: though their love will end, the couple has not yet recognized it, and still they bridge the autumn air with their clasped hands. In between writing "A Marriage Portion" and "A Walk by the Charles," Adrienne Rich married Alfred Conrad, and Katharine congratulated her, then got right back to the business of editing the exquisite nuances of broken love. She accepted more poems and offered a first reading agreement. At the end of the year, the two finally met in person when Rich came to New York, met Andy at the *New Yorker* offices, and lunched at the Algonquin, where Katharine grilled her for other poets she could solicit for the magazine.

The next year, Katharine gently handed Rich back to Moss, saying that she would have to step away from the added duty of editing poetry manuscripts because of overwork. But when Rich met with rejection after rejection for her second book of poems, *The Diamond Cutters and Other Poems*, it was Katharine to whom she wrote, asking for advice about the next step. Katharine wrote a long and detailed letter recommending three editors at three presses and explaining their relationships to the slim market in poetry. Rich took her advice and used her name to approach Cass Canfield at Harper—she had long been a fan of E. B. White—and within two months she had a contract with Harper and a female editor, Elizabeth Lawrence, to Katharine's pure delight. When the book came out, it contained nineteen poems from *The New Yorker*, including "A Walk by the Charles," with the ending that Rich had revised for Katharine. Both "The Marriage Portion" and "A Walk by the Charles" would continue to appear in Rich's successive volumes of collected poems over the rest of her career.

At the same time that she began courting Rich, Katharine also wrote an encouraging letter to Shirley Jackson's agent—the first time she joined the conversation about Jackson—saying that her recent story in *Harper's*, "The Night We All Had Grippe," was "extremely neat, pointed, and funny," and Katharine wished she'd had a chance to consider it for *The New Yorker*. This was an instance of Katharine doggedly trying to bring an author back into the magazine even though the other editors had steadily rejected every story they'd seen—in Jackson's case, since "The Lottery" appeared in 1948.

In the summer of 1952, she took over Nadine Gordimer from William Maxwell. She had submitted her first story, "A Watcher of the Dead," from South Africa via her agent, and it hit the *New Yorker* sweet spot as a short story about a young child, narrated in the first person so it feels like a reminiscence, and treating an interesting cultural practice, in this case the Jewish ritual of appointing a *wacher* or *shomeir* to guard over a recently deceased person and to recite psalms from sunset to sunrise. Now it fell to Katharine to take over from Maxwell (the files do not reveal why) the hard work of developing Gordimer into a regular contributor, and they began a lengthy and personal correspondence on airmail paper.

The rhythm of Katharine's life held true: she was bringing new writers into the magazine even while struggling with health problems that threatened to derail her career. On July 4, just at the beginning of her vacation, she began to feel ill—feverish, unable to eat, and slowly turning yellow, or, as she called it, "saffron." It took two weeks, but eventually she was diagnosed with infectious hepatitis and was rushed by ambulance to the hospital in Bangor, where she stayed for two weeks. Andy made the forty-five-mile drive to visit her each day, bringing her the paper and stamps she needed to continue her work, until he caught a cold and couldn't risk transmitting it to her. She wrote to Maxwell and Lobrano from the hospital, begging them for proofs and manuscripts and news of the office, and assuring them that she couldn't pass the disease to them through the mail. Finally, she came home in August, but to prevent a relapse or permanent damage to her liver, she was confined to her bed for another month, prohibited from exertion for two months beyond that, and denied alcohol through the end of the year, which she found just too dreary. That August, a local man named Henry Allen came to work for the Whites, and while Katharine lay in bed or sat in the office at the front of the house, he helped take care of the garden and the "ten sheep, eighteen hens, a goose, a gander, a bull calf, a rat, a chipmunk, and many spiders" that lived on the farm.

She paused her editing work in August when all three of her children and their families came to Maine, three generations, including five grandchildren. She and Andy would have everyone over for summer dinners, starting with cocktail hour on the terrace, consisting of macadamia nuts, cigarettes, and several rounds of martinis, which the children liked because it lasted forever and they'd have free range over the farm. Then dinner would follow, all of them seated around the big table in the dining room, everyone dressed up, the boys and men in ties. Katharine would ask the children what they'd been up to; Nancy's son Jonathan would remember his humiliation when she would ask him if he'd had a bowel movement that day. They'd eat several different dishes made from vegetables from the garden. To the children, the dinners felt formal and long and they would look for the right moment to slip away.

Roger taught the children sailing, and Nancy taught them tennis at the courts at the Haven Colony in the town next to North Brooklin where she and Louis had purchased a summer home. But the shared time in North Brooklin was not without tension; family dynamics shaped even their most casual recreations, especially between the Angell siblings. Roger was intensely competitive, and though he had taken up sailing because it was the one sport at which his father did not excel, that did not cause him to relax his intensity when it came to his nephew Jon, who knew that being good at sports was the way to his uncle's heart. But Roger thought Nancy was the one who needed "to relax a trifle." He found her "uncompromising," with a "sometimes humorless attitude about what she [thought was] right and wrong," and one of the things she criticized was Roger's parenting. She was raising her own children to be "anti-snobs," in her son's words, and was proud of their modest life in Easton, Pennsylvania, very different from Roger and Evelyn's metropolitan life, where the girls had a young nanny and Callie had just appeared in an uncaptioned photo in *Harper's Bazaar*. Nancy ran a tight ship, doing all her family's finances and planning their trips herself, and serving breakfasts according to an unvarying schedule: cereal, boiled eggs, cereal, poached eggs, cereal, a free-for-all on Saturday, and eggs again on Sunday. She volunteered with the League of Women Voters, her Episcopal church, and a local clinic for youths with mental health issues, and it never bothered her that she was vastly overqualified for her life, though when someone called the house and asked for Dr. Stableford, Louis would always respond, "Which one?" Roger knew that Nancy judged him and Evelyn, and he tried to understand where she was coming from. He diagnosed her with resentment born of her staunch social conscience, a resentment that he saw her particularly apply to Ernest Angell's children with the wealthy Elizabeth, twins Christopher and Abigail, who lived a privileged life with a governess while Nancy drove herself into an "anxious and nervous state" with her parenting and homemaking.

In fact, Katharine could see that Nancy was strung so tautly that she was in danger of a complete nervous breakdown, so she sat down and wrote Ernest a seven-page letter full of alarm and ideas for salvation. Louis had just been passed over for advancement at Lafayette, because though he was a beloved and effective associate professor, he had poured all his energies into teaching rather than research. So there was no end in sight for what Katharine diagnosed as Nancy's "continual never-ending anxiety about finances and her never-ending labors of hard physical work" as she raised a family of five on $4,100 a year. Even on her vacation, when she grew brown and healthy, she still snapped at the children, snapped at Louis, and broke into tears at small upsets. Katharine asked Ernest for his ideas of how to help the proud family, noting that she'd just given Nancy $300 and had purchased new school clothes for all the kids. Nancy rejected Katharine's offer to pay for a housecleaner, nor would she accept a monthly contribution to her expenses. She had her own solution in mind: she wanted a part-time job. But Louis was staunchly opposed to the idea, and Katharine couldn't support it either, given Nancy's current state of exhaustion. She asked Ernest to join her in connecting Louis to their friends and colleagues at boarding schools and colleges, including Ernest's friend and neighbor Ordway Tead, in the hopes of obtaining him a higher-paying job. She also asked Ernest to contribute financial assistance (which he likely gave). In the meantime, she tiptoed around her volatile daughter, afraid to stress or offend her. And she worried about herself. As she told Ernest, this latest health crisis had reinforced her conviction that she should work less, but that would mean earning less, and this she could not afford with both her daughter and her sister Elsie requiring her financial assistance. "I have felt I just had to go on as long as I could," she wrote, entirely subsuming her thoughts about her career under the burden of moneymaking and caregiving.

She stayed in North Brooklin through the middle of October, later than usual, but she wrote to her authors throughout the entire ordeal. She was worried that her colleagues would think she was pulling "something of a hoax." When the actress Gertrude Lawrence died of hepatitis that September, Katharine used the occasion to tell Shawn that her own doctors had told her how lucky she was to have survived and to be recovering so quickly. "I thought I owed you and Gus a report on my progress," she said, and proceeded to divulge countless details of tests submitted to, results awaited, lingering symptoms, doctors' prognoses. This letter, not markedly different from many that Katharine had been writing in recent years, nonetheless stands out for that phrase: "something of a hoax." How Katharine would have hated to be disbelieved. How fervently she relied, in this low moment of her "black summer," on the marshaling of facts to shape her boss's perception of her. And yet the effect of her prose escaped her intention. For years now, she had been starting many of her letters with a paragraph updating her correspondent on her health to a sometimes startling and often tedious level of detail. People in Katharine's circle were beginning to roll their eyes at the mention of her illnesses, or training themselves to skip ahead to the real meat of the letter.

The topic of Katharine's illnesses could never be detangled from the equally fraught topic of Andy's health. The way people discussed them—lumped together as hypochondriacs fixated on their bodies to the point of making each other and themselves unwell—differed drastically from the way Katharine saw them. She worried constantly about being a drag on Andy, about being unable to fulfill her household duties well enough to enable his writing life. She regarded Andy's health worries as largely nerves and hers as all too real—she had not invented a ruptured tumor, a spine so corroded she could barely walk, an infection that nearly killed her—with the ancillary effect that her maladies heightened his anxieties.

So she talked and wrote about her health, over and over. It had begun as a conscious rhetorical strategy in her correspondence, a way to connect with authors—male and female—with sympathy and realism, by placing the figure of a body in the disembodied sphere of letters to stand in for human connection, and indeed many of her correspondents—male and female—responded in exactly the same register with their own health narratives. Now, though, her letters had begun to mutate into something else, a deeply invested project of self-description or testimony that was going awry, and she was only barely starting to understand how others might perceive her despite her heartfelt words: a hoaxer, a malingerer. What so many people missed when they groaned at Katharine's affliction soliloquys was that behind every single invocation of her body was an invocation of her work ethic—a worried, defensive explanation for silence or a delay, an overly conscientious account of why she couldn't meet someone's expectation though she dearly wanted to—and through every one of her afflictions she continued to work.

Katharine returned to Brooklin again for ten days in November to take the vacation that had been swallowed by illness. She had a genuinely relaxing time because, unlike in the summer, it was just Andy and herself with no children or grandchildren or other assorted summer guests. She demanded nothing of herself. She took naps every single afternoon. She wandered around the quiet farm—always wearing red because of deer hunters—and drank in the mid-autumn colors, "warm browns and grays mixed with the spruce greens," as she wrote to Jean Stafford. She collected spruce boughs and feathery grasses as she meandered and later arranged them into bouquets. She scared up two partridges, was charged by the steer in his pasture, and stood among the Suffolk sheep in theirs as they nudged her with their friendly black faces.

You'd never guess, from this peaceful letter written from a bedded-down farmhouse, that one of the inhabitants had just released a magnificent new book that was storming the bestseller list. On October 15, 1952, Harper's had published *Charlotte's Web*.

Andy had worked on his book without much fanfare for about two years. It is possible that working on this manuscript was the happiest that Andy had ever been as a writer, the time when he was most engaged and least at odds with what he was producing, and that his focus was enabled by the privacy he erected around this particular project. He spent a year researching spiders before he ever committed a word to paper, and he let the facts that he discovered give rise to the story, initially about a pig and a spider, with a girl named Fern added later. He cast about for a way to end the book and remembered a description of himself in a passionate letter that Katharine had written a few years previously. A Brooklin resident named Margaret Murray had published a letter to the editor in *The New York Times* that described rural Maine as so poor the residents of her town fared little better than someone living in a Soviet collective; Andy had published a rebuttal in the *Times*, and then Mrs. Murray and her husband continued to argue with him in private letters. Finally Katharine waded in; she had angrily defended Andy, and she ended by saying the Murrays' criticisms "are not words that should be applied to anyone who is an honest man and an honest writer. Andy is both." The sentiment and the structure rang true to Andy, and he revised them for the final lines of the book: "It is not often that someone comes along who is a true friend and a good writer. Charlotte was both." He set the manuscript aside for an entire year while he continued to let scenes play in his mind.

In March 1952, he finally showed it to Ursula Nordstrom, and within two weeks she'd excitedly contacted Garth Williams for the illustrations. "Any Harper book he ever does is given to him with the understanding that he can stop work on it the minute the E. B. White manuscript arrives," she told Andy. The Whites had Nordstrom to dinner, and they talked about how pictorially to represent a sentient spider, and Katharine gave her notes on the marketing department's advertising copy. Nordstrom really only had one suggestion to make about Andy's manuscript, that he retitle the chapter called "Charlotte's Death" so as not to spoil the ending. Well, Katharine wondered, how had Louisa May Alcott handled Beth's death? Persuaded by Nordstrom and Alcott, Andy changed the title to "Last Day."

It was published in October, and by the end of 1952, *Charlotte's Web* had become the bestselling book on Harper's list. It was beautifully reviewed by Pamela Travers, the author of *Mary Poppins*, in the *New York Herald Tribune Book Review* and by Eudora Welty in *The New York*

Times Book Review. The book received only one bad review: Anne Carroll Moore, writing in *Horn Book*, said, "I step into real trouble and I may as well confess that I find E. B. White's *Charlotte's Web*, illustrated by Garth Williams (Harper $2.50), hard to take from so masterly a hand." Even though she herself grew up on a farm in Maine and found the setting gorgeously described, she once again could not enter into the magic of the book—she found both Fern and Charlotte underdeveloped and unrealistic. But as Ursula Nordstrom merrily observed, Moore's "reservations about *Stuart Little* preceded a wonderful success for that book," so this review was celebrated in the halls of Harper. *Charlotte's Web* would, of course, go on to become possibly the highest-selling children's book of twentieth-century America, and with international translations it would surpass forty-five million books in print, in addition to regularly sitting atop lists of the most beloved children's books of all time. In a tacit rebuke to Anne Carroll Moore, it would become the sixth most borrowed book at the New York Public Library. To this day, it has not lost its power to move readers, including its own author; when Andy would record the audiobook in 1970, it would take seventeen tries before he could get through the ending without breaking down.

But the Whites did not initially enjoy the financial spoils of *Charlotte's Web*, because Andy's contract with Harper specified that he'd receive at most $7,500 in royalties per year to protect his income from the Internal Revenue Service. So their lives stayed level and the peace that Katharine found in the farm that November was real.

When Katharine returned to the office from her Maine vacation, she sat down and wrote a long letter to Elizabeth Bishop. The two had worked together to publish Bishop's poetry over the past seven years, and Bishop had visited the Whites in North Brooklin the previous summer when she drove south after a visit to Nova Scotia; when she returned to New York she told a fascinated Marianne Moore about the farm. Then Katharine had nominated Bishop for an award given by Bryn Mawr College in the name of Katharine and Elsie's English professor Lucy Martin Donnelly. The $2,500 fellowship funded Bishop's life-changing trip to Brazil. And now the two women began to correspond over Bishop's prose. (They'd had a first, brief exchange after Lobrano accepted a short story in 1943 that Bishop wrote under the pseudonym Sarah Foster, not appearing to know whom he was addressing; Katharine later rescued the story from *New Yorker* purgatory, apologized to Bishop, and published it in 1948.) Bishop submitted two stories inspired by her childhood in Nova Scotia but fueled, in a way she herself did not entirely understand, by her new life in Samambaia, Brazil, with her partner Lota de Macedo Soares: "Geography must be more mysterious than we think." Her productivity might also have been fueled by the cortisone shots she was giving herself for asthma, a remedy she ardently wished Katharine would consider as she recovered from hepatitis: "Try it for something sometime." Though both stories Bishop sent at the end of 1952 concerned a young girl in Nova Scotia, they differed significantly in narrative strategy, and thus they met different fates under their editor's pencil.

Katharine quickly accepted the first story, "Gwendolyn," which almost exactly mirrored Nadine Gordimer's "Watcher of the Dead," another story written as a first-person reminiscence set in a foreign land and revolving around a child's fascination with death. Katharine, channeling Ross even now, asked Bishop to trim a passage about soiled underwear—which she did—and to more quickly locate the story in Nova Scotia, a suggestion the writer resisted. "I hope you won't mind my saying so," Bishop wrote, "but I think the convention of situating everything clearly and immediately can get to be boring, make the reader lazy, or else think, oh heavens, here we go again on another of those childhood reminiscences, instead of troubling to absorb the real atmosphere first." Katharine entirely agreed, and said that a conventional childhood piece was the very last thing they wanted.

But the second story, "In the Village," pulled further away from *New Yorker* convention, and the letter that Katharine wrote about it upon returning to the office in November was only the first of many. "In the Village" begins inside an unlocatable perspective, an "I" who remembers an unheard sound: "A scream, the echo of a scream, hangs over that Nova Scotia village. No one hears it; it hangs there forever [. . .]" The story soon switches to a distanced third-person narration of characters with no names, only "the child" and "the mother." Then, another scream and "the child vanishes," only to return as the first-person narrator,

remembering the summer her mother—"It was she who gave the scream"—
came home from a sanitarium before being recommitted. Bishop employs
the detailed, lively descriptions of a vanished world that *The New Yorker*
so loved, but these are nestled within a flickering narrative structure,
with sudden tense changes and that disembodied narrative voice ema-
nating from the same space as the haunting scream. Katharine stepped
carefully through Bishop's story, writing to say that she would preserve
the suggestive tone of the "lovely prose poem" as long as Bishop would
clarify the relationships of the unnamed characters and give the reader
more direction about who is speaking. "In fact we are willing to make all
the concessions we possibly can about the piece and its form, provided
you can give the reader that sense of relaxation that comes from really
understanding it. One does not have to understand *everything* of course,
but one ought not to be so constantly puzzled that one keeps thinking
about the puzzle rather than about your words and your beautiful poetic
and emotional effects."

Again, Bishop pushed back. On a certain level, the story was precisely
about not understanding. "I wanted to give the effect of nervous voices,
exchanging often ambiguous remarks, floating in the air over the child's
head," she explained. After all, the *New Yorker* editors had understood
the plot exactly as she intended. But she admitted that she didn't want
it to be "too mysterious," so she made a few changes and sent a second
draft, which Katharine answered with another long and agonized letter.
"I am really in a state of unhappy indecision over this manuscript because I want us to have it so much, and I somehow feel it's my fault that
I can't persuade you of the obscurities, in a letter." The twenty-six-page
manuscript was too long to reread and would leave the reader "vaguely
dissatisfied"—neither Bishop's nor *The New Yorker*'s aesthetic goal. Katharine risked Bishop's ire by copying the story onto yellow paper and editing the piece to fit her own standard: "The absolute minimum of editing
I thought needed to make this story clear enough to *me*."

Throughout most of the year, Bishop and Katharine would exchange
letters about "In the Village," one of the editor's thorniest stories to date
and a risky venture on which to spend so much of her time, given that
the magazine had not yet purchased it. In between the poet's letters from

Brazil, Katharine fell ill (a ten-day bout of the flu during which she stayed in bed, on the phone solving the problem of the broken furnace at the Brooklin library). Immediately afterward she visited Florida (another ten days spent with Aunt Crullie). But even beyond the routine highs and lows, this March was, as Katharine wrote to another author, a time of "emotional family crises and sorrows and joys." Joe, a twenty-three-year-old junior at MIT, announced his engagement.

Joe had met Allene Messer in Boston when they began running into each other at a deli on Charles Street where they both got their morning coffee. Allene, from Claremont, New Hampshire, was twenty-eight years old, five years Joe's senior, and had studied journalism in college before leaving to work. She had briefly been married nearly a decade earlier and had been supporting herself ever since her divorce. Just like his father, Joe had fallen in love with an older woman, a previously married working woman who had traveled to Europe, more worldly than him in so many ways. Now they were living together in a third-floor walk-up on Charles Street, two or three rooms with a nice view. Joe's parents, in Allene's memory, were untroubled by their living together before marriage, and later Katharine said it could be "a wise arrangement" if it forestalled too-hasty marriages. Andy met Allene, and then one day he brought Katharine to Boston to meet her. Katharine walked into the small living room and peered all around it. She looked at the floor. She moved her foot around on the nap of the rug, and then she raised her head and pronounced, "Clean."

Joe and Allene were married on a Thursday night by a minister they knew at a church around the corner from their apartment. The Whites were not in attendance, saying they both had bad colds. Andy sent Allene a letter that week with his mixed blessing—worry cut with a hefty dose of love for Joe and confidence in their decision. If Katharine could support Joe and Allene's cohabitation, how did she feel about their marriage? Her initial thoughts have not survived, but her disquiet can be inferred, since she worried about her youngest child most of all. Just like his mother, Joe was marrying young, long before he'd established his livelihood. She was open-minded when it came to the unconventional romantics of her authors—but she might have struggled to apply this open-mindedness to her youngest son. It is unclear if Joe and Allene told Katharine and Andy that they were expecting a baby. The new Whites wanted to honeymoon in North Brooklin while Joe's parents were there, so Andy and Katharine traveled up to the farmhouse at the end of March for a short stay to get acquainted with their new daughter-in-law. When Joe and Allene returned to Boston, Allene kept her job and Joe kept his focus on his schoolwork.

Katharine and Andy stayed in New York through July, sitting on the first-base line one day to watch the Giants beat the Dodgers 20–6. That month they began editing Andy's next book. Cass Canfield thought he must have published enough new material in *The New Yorker* since *Quo Vadimus* in 1938 to form a new collection, and Andy thought the success of *Charlotte's Web* meant he might have enough readers to justify such a book. Katharine began arranging pieces and trying out structures for what would eventually become *The Second Tree from the Corner*.

July was also when Katharine finally bought "In the Village" from Bishop. "This purchase of this particular story has made me happier than anything that's happened to me as an editor for months," she wrote, "and I'm ever so grateful to you for your patience in doing the two, long, hard revisions on this manuscript."

And July brought a new story from Nabokov, this one about an old man. The writer warned Katharine, "He is not a very nice person but he is fun." And while you are reading it, he added, please remember that *I* am an American writer, not a Russian one. Thus began the Pnin series, and Katharine had more reasons than most to confuse the protagonist with his author: so many tiny incidents in that first chapter arose directly from her editing relationship to Nabokov. Timofey Pnin, as the story opens, is on the wrong train through upstate New York, poring over a complicated train schedule sent to him by a Miss Judith Clyde. He is about to leave the lecture notes on the train for a talk he is shortly to deliver. Katharine once sent Nabokov a train itinerary for a complicated journey from Ithaca through Elmira to Washington, DC, so he could research a reminiscence about his father (a journey he never took). She also helped him when he wrote to her from Harvard in "acute distress, with hysterical overtones." He was there to deliver the Morris Gray lecture series on poetry and he'd left his poems home in Ithaca; could she give him the numbers of the *New Yorker* issues so he could look them up at Widener Library? Instead she sent him all the clippings the very next day. Pnin, upon realizing his mistake, cried, "What to do? It is a catastroph!," perhaps reminding Katharine of the time she corrected a poem in which Nabokov assumed "syncope" was only two syllables. But though the socially awkward and pitiable Pnin may have caused the reader to cringe (anathema to a middlebrow mode of reading), there could be no misreading the enormous gap between hapless protagonist and erudite author.

"Pnin" needed very little editing—gone were the days when Katharine ran her pencil through such Nabokovian words as "palabral," "photism," "asemia," "hiemal," "intersemestral"—and the story was soon ready for publication but scheduled for late the following year. Katharine begged Nabokov to write more stories about Professor Pnin for a series that could run all next spring and summer, and he told her that he'd already planned a little book about Pnin, ten chapters in all, and that he would send more stories along soon. "It is not the enormous, mysterious, heartbreaking novel that, after five years of monstrous misgivings and diabolical labors, I have more or less completed," he wrote enigmatically. *Conclusive Evidence* and *Pnin* had been pleasant distractions from this other work, its "intolerable spell." "This great and coily thing has had no precedent in literature," he claimed, and though it was absolutely unsuitable for *The New Yorker*, he would honor his first reading agreement and show it to Katharine soon, "under the rose of silence and the myrtle of secrecy." Katharine paid no attention to his certainty that the magazine couldn't publish any part of it. Send it soon, she urged.

That summer was more pleasant than the one before, though just as overstuffed with visiting family in August and September. Joe had a successful season of lobstering before his senior year at MIT, saving up money for when his and Allene's baby would be born in December. "We all of us like Allene," Katharine wrote to Shawn, "and she has been a good sport this summer, in fitting in as a fisherman's wife and fitting into a new family and new set of neighbors and friends. One nice thing is that she and Joe and Roger and Evelyn enjoy each other a lot."

Katharine and Andy stayed in Maine until November 1 to make up for the late start to their summer, giving themselves two months of quiet after the grandchildren left. She had sent Elizabeth Bishop a preliminary varitype proof of "In the Village" in September—"Your annoyance with my small naggings on this story must by now be almost intolerable to you but because this is so outstanding a piece of writing, I must persist, even if you do hate me for it. We don't want a single tiny thing to mar its perfection"—and then in November, upon returning to the office, she looked at the author's proof with its "millions of conventional punctuation and style-rule and clarity queries" and she simply canceled them with a swipe of her Blackwing pencil. We are running your story as you last saw it, she wrote to Bishop, and it will "seem like a breath of fresh air in the magazine" because of the unconventionality they'd managed to preserve through an entire year of edits—"But it does not mean, I'm afraid, that we would do the same thing on all your manuscripts." *The New Yorker* could be flexible, but don't get used to it.

That December, two projects that had built steam all year finally came to fruition. Elizabeth Bishop's "In the Village" ran in the December 19 issue of the magazine, and Katharine sent her a letter filled with the admiring comments she'd heard from the New York literati, as well as her own feeling that "to help get that story into the magazine was the thing that gave [her] the most satisfaction in the year 1953." And Joel Steven White, Katharine's sixth grandchild, known as Steven, was born to Joe and Allene in early December. Andy alone took the trip to Boston to meet him; Katharine was down with the flu.

37.

Write me soon again. You are one of those rare people whose voice comes out so clearly in letters. Mine is generally quite blurred and hoarse, with lots of static.

—Vladimir Nabokov to Katharine S. White, November 24, 1954

Not every literary collaboration ended with such satisfaction. In fact, the years of 1953 and 1954 were a jumbled and confused time when the disorderliness of Katharine's personal life began to affect her work more seriously, and when she missed significant opportunities to make enormous differences in her authors' lives and in the fate and stature of the magazine.

Katharine failed one of her authors who became caught in the McCarthy-era persecution of Communists and sympathizers. *The New Yorker* had for years excoriated the House Un-American Activities Committee through comics, short stories (Mary McCarthy's "The Groves of Academe," for instance), Talk anecdotes, profiles, and especially Notes and Comment. The issue was practically tailor-made for E. B. White, who stood at the intersection of patriotism and free expression, and he repeatedly ridiculed the hypocrisy, paranoia, overreach, and pedantry of HUAC. But when it came time to publicly support an author accused of disloyalty, the magazine did more harm than good, and Katharine did almost nothing.

Kay Boyle and her husband, Joseph Franckenstein, were called before the army's Loyalty Security Board in Germany in the fall of 1952.

Franckenstein, an Austrian who worked in public relations for the State Department, was accused of being a Communist solely because of his wife's political activities—this despite the fact that he'd become an American citizen, enlisted after Pearl Harbor, and been appointed as an espionage agent to the Office of Strategic Services, for whom he infiltrated the Nazi regime in Austria at the greatest possible risk. (Boyle herself had been monitored by the FBI since the 1930s. When she would obtain her file much later, she would be astonished to read in it that she'd had an affair with Ezra Pound when she was ten years old.) Over the next few months and into 1953, Boyle was forced to produce testimonials that her leftist activism and writings were loyal to the United States, and she asked Shawn, Lobrano, and Katharine to write letters on her behalf. Though Boyle collected many letters from editors at other magazines and book publishers, the letters from *The New Yorker* would be the most important for her case because she was then accredited as *The New Yorker*'s Germany correspondent. It was devastating to her, both emotionally and politically, when the magazine failed vigorously to defend her. Because Boyle hadn't published fiction in the magazine since 1949, the editors decided Shawn should be the one to write the letter, but when he did nothing, Boyle began writing to Katharine and Janet Flanner in distress. Flanner instantly wrote a heartfelt and politically useful letter, and Katharine began prodding her colleagues, often from her sickbed.

What followed was a confusing chain of letters and missed connections in which the intentions of the magazine's editors are unclear, but the result was that *The New Yorker* in effect abandoned a longtime writer when it easily could have helped her. All the editors, Katharine included, were far more interested in splitting hairs and finding reasons not to help Boyle than they were in the simple act of claiming her as one of their own. Lobrano wrote an extremely tepid letter that accused Boyle of "political naivete," Katharine wrote nothing in deference to Shawn, and Shawn wrote a letter full of errors—it stated that Boyle was the Germany correspondent "in 1946" instead of "since 1946" and disavowed even knowing her well. The letters were so damaging that Boyle's attorney didn't want to present them, but as expected they were precisely the letters that the prosecutor seized upon in his questioning at the hearing, which began in October 1952 and concluded the following January. Janet Flanner traveled from France to testify in person and was regarded as a representative of the magazine, yet the letters raised doubts that prolonged the hearing.

Franckenstein was eventually cleared of the charges but was fired from his job as a security risk. Boyle was, in essence, fired from *The New Yorker*. Shawn failed to fill out the form necessary to renew Boyle's press accreditation, withdrawing the magazine's sponsorship, though Katharine told Flanner this was because Boyle was not a full-time employee (she hadn't, in fact, published a Reporter in Germany piece since 1950) and had technically been ineligible for the accreditation for several years. To Boyle, it felt like abandonment and betrayal, and she was bitter about *The New Yorker* for the rest of her life. She never submitted her writing to the magazine again, and it does not appear that she and Katharine continued to correspond (though Boyle apparently still hoped they would; she told her agent that Katharine was the main reason why she wanted a connection to *The New Yorker*). For her part, Flanner was deeply ashamed of *The New Yorker*'s silence, a symptom of what she called "syphilitic fascism," a contagious fear of speaking up for the American values of civil liberties and a free press. It took several letters over the course of 1953 for Katharine and Flanner to repair their relationship. Katharine, for a time, defended Shawn's inaction, and Flanner "grieved" that she had lost "[her] oldest friend remaining there in what seem[ed her] only family circle in all these expatriate years." But that fall Katharine admitted that she had written her previous letters to Flanner for Shawn to see; Katharine said she and her fellow editors had lined up behind Shawn, and any letter anyone received about the Boyle affair was "read and edited and fine-tooth-combed by all"; indeed, she admitted that the last letter she'd written "was not really [her] letter at all," and that she'd handwritten a long personal letter but it was returned to her for insufficient postage. She begged for Flanner's forgiveness and they soon made up.

And another very different missed connection, this one even more personal: in October of 1953, Elsie published her biography of Willa Cather, in which she expanded the portrait she had given in *Fire Under the Andes* with material drawn from Cather's own letters to her until her death in 1947. The book was the third biography or reminiscence of Cather to come out that year, all of them constrained by Cather's will, which prohibited direct quotes from her letters. That meant that Elsie's own vivid stories of her friendship with Cather were that much more valuable, and Leon Edel favorably reviewed the book in *The New York Times*. When Katharine read Elsie's *Willa Cather: A Memoir*, was she struck by how much Elsie's description of Cather could apply quite precisely to Katharine and specifically to her relationship with Harold Ross? Elsie wrote of when she first met Cather in 1910, "It made me happy that [Cather]—who to my New England eyes was on the forceful side—could second [Cather's boss, the editor S. S. McClure] without his feeling diminished by her powers. She was not a wily female, a diplomat, she was one to stand to her colors like a trooper, and fight her battles in the open." In a later foreword to a reissue of the book, Elsie again described Cather in words she might also have used for Katharine:

> But she was, as a personality, crisp, blunt, attentive, practical, intellectual—not tactful or deeply aware of the other persons, as born intuitives frequently are to a disconcerting degree. She was sagaciously living as an editor, seemingly with her whole self, solidifying the walls and foundations of her business life.

Katharine recorded her own thought about the Cather biography in several letters to friends and colleagues, but only after Elsie's death. She said that even Elsie's best books were "marred for [Katharine] by her tendency to omit [her subjects'] frailties or discuss their less good books." There was one aspect of Cather's life that she was annoyed Elsie had omitted. She placed her critique in another person's mouth: "Edmund Wilson said to me about the Cather study, 'The trouble is no one dares say Willa Cather was a lesbian.' My sister was not one, incidentally."

Elsie, for her part, was busy looking ahead to her next writing project. She had profiled Robert Frost in *Fire Under the Andes*, had written about his relationship with Cather in her memoir, and knew him as a friend. Might she profile him for *The New Yorker*? Her agent queried the magazine, but the answer was no (in the same year that the magazine turned down pieces by two of the agent's other clients, William Faulkner and F. Scott Fitzgerald's daughter, Frances). It's not clear if Katharine even knew of Elsie's proposal and its quick fate; the rejection was a one-sentence letter by Edith Oliver, a junior reader in the fact department, saying that they'd already run a profile of Frost back in 1931. The sisters could not find a common language for their shared, lifelong devotion to literature. Elsie was intensely curious about the process of artistic creation, as dedicated to writing about it as she was to living a solitary yet social life consisting wholly of manuscripts and letters and summers at the MacDowell Colony. Instead of a *New Yorker* article, Elsie began a full-length biography of Robert Frost.

From the beginning of December of 1953, the Whites slid into "a long-drawn-out succession of melancholy and dreary events," as Andy wrote to his brother. Katharine wrote to Christine Weston halfway through it that 1954 was "about the most confused and difficult year of [her] life." It was a time of death, illness, worry, and disruption.

After Katharine got the flu for Christmas that year, it was Andy's turn, and he was sick when Katharine received the news in January of 1954 that her sister Rosamond was ill and required surgery. Katharine learned that Ros had died on February 3. She was only sixty-six, her death a sudden and ghastly shock, especially because it came just nine months after Ros's husband, John, died after surgery for cancer of the lower bowels (he also suffered from Parkinson's). Rosamond had lived a quiet artistic life, exhibiting her paintings first in Boston and then in Sarasota. Shortly after the Newberrys moved to Florida in the early 1940s, she joined the Sarasota Art Association, and soon she was its president; in 1949 she and her son Jack, also a painter, were founding members of the Florida Artists Group. Katharine had visited her regularly and had at least one of her paintings hanging in the farmhouse. By all accounts the sisters had an easy relationship, but no letters between the two of them survive to shade in the emotional tenor. Rosamond was buried in Cleveland next to John. Katharine's friend Louise Seaman Bechtel thought to send flowers and then reconsidered; instead, she donated a big box of books to the library in North Brooklin in Ros's honor.

The Sergeant family was plunged into an immediate crisis, because ninety-two-year-old Aunt Crullie was now alone in Sarasota and about to be homeless. Katharine barely had time to grieve. She left Andy at home in New York and rushed to Florida with Nancy to sort Ros and Aunt Crullie's affairs. She returned to New York, knowing that she'd be back in just a few weeks. Two days later, Katharine came down with the mumps, while Andy had shingles, and the dachshund, Minnie, had tapeworms. Katharine's doctor gave her a shot of penicillin that prompted an allergic reaction, so it was with a swollen face that she traveled to Maine to start readying the farmhouse for Aunt Crullie. As usual, she carried her work with her everywhere, telling May Sarton, "Most New Yorker work is on the whole soothing and takes my mind off my troubles." Both Andy and Katharine traveled back to Sarasota in mid-March to move Crullie and a nurse into a temporary apartment, with the plan of bringing her up to Maine when the weather was warmer.

When Andy wrote to his brother about this awful sequence of events, he left out one thing: in January, he'd published the book he and Katharine had begun the previous summer, *The Second Tree from the Corner*. By the end of the month it had sold forty thousand copies. Just as *Charlotte's Web* had not materially affected life in the town house or the farmhouse, nor did this book. Andy had made a risky decision a few months previously when he turned down the Book-of-the-Month Club's offer to publish *The Second Tree*, which would have guaranteed him an income of $20,000, but on the condition that he wait until the summer for publication. Andy thought the delay would hurt some of the timely pieces in the book, so he took his chances and let Harper issue it at the beginning of 1954—and then he mostly ignored its passage through the world as he navigated his own disasters. A broken toe. A barn owl that savaged the newborn lambs.

Another book was trying to make its way into the world. The day after Nabokov completed his monstrous, heartbreaking novel in early December 1953, Véra Nabokov wrote to Katharine that they would be in town that weekend and would hand-deliver the manuscript, one copy to her and one to Pascal Covici at Viking; she hinted at but did not divulge the "very special reasons" for all the secrecy. But Katharine was away in

Boston, finally meeting her new grandson Steven, and she didn't learn of the attempted delivery until afterward. Throughout the first months of 1954, as Katharine dealt with Ros's illness and death, she exchanged letters with Véra, pleading with her simply to send the manuscript with a letter from Nabokov explaining its delicacy. She blithely promised pseudonymity in the pages of the magazine, something they'd done for many writers. Véra would say only that the story would jeopardize Nabokov's position at Cornell if it was known that he wrote it, especially because of the deplorable American tendency to associate any first-person narrator with its author, and that it *must* be hand-delivered and *only* if Katharine and Andy could swear secrecy.

Katharine finally understood the scope of the issue when Véra forwarded Pascal Covici's response to the manuscript: pornographic and unpublishable. Katharine backpedaled hard. No, do not show it to me, she wrote. Knowing how high the stakes were, she could not guarantee anonymity in the long run, for surely someone would leak the manuscript, given its value as literary intrigue. Nor could she tell Nabokov how to proceed on what was clearly a brilliant but treacherous book. "My advice would be worthless," she wrote, because she did not know the law. She thought book publishers had more leeway than magazines. But she still held out hope that some part of the book might be excerpted, so she suggested that Nabokov send to her at home only the pages that formed a stand-alone story. "I am afraid the book is so much of an organic whole that no part of it could square the circle of the family lamp light," he responded, and he promised another Pnin story. They continued at cross-purposes; the story he sent later that month met an immediate rejection; the story of Pnin's marriage was "more unpleasant than amusing." Meanwhile, Nabokov's manuscript circulated through the back doors at Simon & Schuster; New Directions; Farrar, Straus; and Doubleday. One Friday afternoon in April, Katharine received a telegram from Nabokov saying that the manuscript would shortly be arriving at her Turtle Bay home by Western Union. She was to read it immediately; speak of it to no one, least of all the editor of *The New Yorker*; and place it in the airmail envelope he was providing and mail it to Olympia Press in France first thing on Monday morning. As it happened, Katharine had houseguests that weekend and a large family dinner planned for Saturday night, and so she mailed the manuscript to Maurice Girondias at Olympia Press, unread, unexcerpted by *The New Yorker*. Many years later, she would write of Nabokov, "Too bad he was so fearsome for I think a few chapters of Humbert's travels through the motels of Florida with his nymphette could have been used. This section is funny." What effect would publication in *The New Yorker* have had on the reception of *Lolita*, first published in Paris in two typo-ridden volumes by Olympia Press, banned in the United Kingdom, and only printed in the United States in 1958? What effect would publication of Humbert Humbert have had on *The New Yorker*? This was a broadening of the magazine's literary standards that Katharine could not afford to consider, a fight for which she had no relish, and ignoring the book had no real consequences for her relationship with Nabokov, who soon signed a contract for *Pnin* with Covici at Viking and sent more chapters her way. *The New Yorker* would eventually publish four Pnin stories from the seven-chapter novel.

Right alongside the dense conversation with the Nabokovs, Katharine was consumed with worry about Aunt Crullie and how much her and Andy's life would have to change to accommodate this fragile, remarkable person in their midst. "She tips the scales at an even 80 lbs., and likes sherry," in Andy's description. "She's quite deaf but I can make her hear after we've both had a couple of rounds." Katharine described her as "[her] favorite of all people aside from Andy but she is very delicate, very deaf, and very old." They booked train tickets for Crullie and her nurse to come to Maine in mid-June, but then Crullie fell ill, necessitating a thousand phone calls between Katharine and doctors, train stations, and hotels. They postponed the trip by a month. When the nurse fell ill, Katharine began to despair more seriously for the months to come. She detested the nurse, but Crullie loved her, so she was resolved to make it work—but what to do about a helper who was "more dead than alive and must be spared stairs and exertion"? Andy built Crullie a special chair to bring her upstairs, and Katharine morbidly envisioned herself carrying the nurse in it. She and Andy joked that they would eat as many meals as they could in the boathouse, but ultimately she was prepared to make sacrifices in order to give Crullie a few happy months at the farmhouse. "So from now on, I expect to be much confined," she wrote to Jean Stafford. She'd travel nowhere for a vacation that year, though she would have been content merely spending a week in New York with Andy watching the Giants ("my dream boys!"). Crullie safely arrived in North Brooklin on July 14 and they soldiered on through a "dreadful" summer.

It was graduation season. Andy collected honorary degrees from Harvard University and Colby College, and the Whites celebrated Joel's graduation from MIT. Allene was pregnant with their second child, due in December, and she stayed in Boston with Steven when Joel was drafted into the postwar army and called to Fort Dix in New Jersey.

In July came Andy's fifty-fifth birthday, but he was the one who gave a memorable gift to Katharine a week later. In her patronage of Friend Memorial Public Library, she had long been bothered by the abandoned house next door. It was owned by the library, but nothing had been done with it, so it was both ugly and a fire hazard. Andy wrote her a card saying that many times in the past he'd considered giving her jewels, only to reject the idea: "You are my precious stone, all the more so because you don't glitter." Now he had the perfect gift—the demolition fee to remove the abandoned house. "Hit it hard and true!" Katharine once more edited the landscape.

But Katharine's summer was plagued by illness. She developed an itchy skin allergy that had her "feeding on anti-histamines and plastered with salves." Nonetheless she worked to ease Aunt Crullie's transition to Maine and to settle the horrible nurse into the household, which, Katharine complained, required her "to spend a great deal of time planning transportation, entertainment, days off, for the nurse who knows noone [sic] and has no resources in this region." Deaf and fragile Crullie was far easier by contrast and she seemed delighted by the household. Katharine's monthlong vacation-at-home was partly given over to recovery from her skin ailment and partly interrupted by work, because she simply couldn't allow the latest McCarthy story, "A Charmed Life," to be edited by anyone but her. But there was another anxiety sabotaging her respite, and that was a live and evolving concern for the fiction department's future. Gus Lobrano was ill, and no one quite knew what the trouble was. He'd come home from the hospital but was not himself, and the list of symptoms that Shawn observed in Lobrano at the office—depression, inertness, seeming beyond caring—struck Katharine as "a set-up for suicide." She laid it on thick to Shawn, telling him it was the magazine's duty to tell Lobrano's wife how he was at work, to encourage her to seek psychiatric help, and to reassure her that her husband could have paid time off so that the financial aspect was no deterrent.

Meanwhile, William Shawn asked Katharine if she would be willing to head the department should Lobrano become incapacitated. She wrote long, fretful letters to Shawn that August in which she considered the matter from every possible dimension. In theory, she was at the ready to do whatever Shawn needed to keep the magazine going. She was especially concerned about the rejection of manuscripts, because she thought that Henderson and Maxwell were too quick to turn away stories, that she and Lobrano were "more optimistic about revises than the others there," and she invited Shawn to send her any manuscripts that needed her optimism even during her vacation, because to her, writing an opinion was "no effort": "I enjoy it." Just that spring, she'd begun cultivating two authors who would need her particular brand of care. She'd read a story by Elizabeth Hardwick in *Kenyon Review* and reached out to ask for submissions, repeating a letter she'd written Hardwick in 1947—as always, Mrs. White was playing the long game. And Nadine Gordimer recommended an African-raised British writer, Doris Lessing, who promptly sent three stories, one of which Katharine bought, followed shortly by another.

In theory, she was ready to assume Lobrano's job, but in practice, she couldn't quite figure out how the logistics would work, between Aunt Crullie's needs, the contemptible nurse, and Andy's wholesale unwillingness to be left alone in the farmhouse with those two. "Andy, you see, is really my first and most important concern," she told Shawn. "He had a lot of head trouble and ill health last month and before, but now he definitely seems better and more cheerful." She simply could not jeopardize his equilibrium; she emphasized this in two separate letters. But nor could she stand by while the magazine floundered. She concocted a contingency plan of checking Crullie into a hospital if she were suddenly called down to the city. She fired the unpleasant nurse and began researching nursing homes, but after visiting six of them, she decided she could not subject her aunt to that lifestyle, and she eventually hired a friend of Ida Treat, her Cleveland friend turned *New Yorker* author, to care for Crullie at the Maine farmhouse after she and Andy returned to the city in the autumn. The weeks went by under an awful suspense about Lobrano, which would not resolve for many more months. Katharine could not know but might have suspected that this situation would structure the entire next chapter of her life.

The summer held an important event in the life of the magazine, but it was only revealed as noteworthy in hindsight. Katharine wrote a note to Lobrano about a package she'd just received. Edward Streeter, a humorist known for *Father of the Bride* and an alumnus of the Harvard humor magazine, the *Lampoon*, had sent her a sheaf of recent *Lampoon* issues to draw her attention to a then-senior who was, in his estimation, one of its greatest contributors. Katharine closely read the verse and prose and gave Lobrano her opinion. None of it made her laugh, but the work showed "mild promise," and they sure needed writers who could reliably produce light verse. "As we know, the chances are 50 to 1 against his developing right, yet I believe we should try kids like this." She recommended that "John Updyke" be entered onto the Potential List for both poetry and prose. "He at least has versatility and isn't afraid to tackle anything."

Updike himself had certainly embraced *The New Yorker* as his weekly correspondence school in creative writing. His family received a subscription to the magazine for Christmas when he was twelve, and he fervently studied each issue, then began submitting his work two years later and collecting an impressive stack of rejection letters. He later wrote, "I loved that magazine so much I concentrated all my wishing into an effort to make myself small and inky and intense enough to be received into its pages." In fact, he would exaggerate the effect *The New Yorker* had on his family when he claimed that his mother, also a writer, who would publish in *The New Yorker* under her maiden name of Linda Grace Hoyer, decided to move the family from a suburb of Reading, Pennsylvania, to an eighty-acre farm about fifteen miles further out in the country when she read E. B. White's columns in *Harper's* during the war. But to Katharine, it was the son, not his mother, who'd made the closest study of E. B. White; Updike, she observed, was just like Andy, from his anxiety to his allergies and his warm heart.

After graduating from Harvard, Updike lobbed dozens of letters and manuscripts to the *New Yorker* offices from his desk in Oxford, where he was spending a year at the Ruskin School of Drawing and Fine Art. As he never employed an agent, his correspondence was directly with Katharine, and occasionally Maxwell. In quick succession that summer, Katharine accepted four poems and a short story, "Friends from Philadelphia," opening the floodgates to Updike's productivity, just as had her acceptances for Kay Boyle and John Cheever. In total that year, Katharine bought nine poems and one story from him (and rejected thirty poems and another story), earning him just over $1,000 in six months, at a time when his father's annual salary as a teacher at his son's public high school was $1,200. It was immediately clear to Katharine that, though his rejections far outnumbered acceptances, Updike would be a prolific writer and an amenable reviser, so that September she offered and he accepted a first reading agreement, and they continued to get to know one another, across the ocean and across their gap in years. Updike wrote to Katharine, sounding a lot like Andy, "The patient and abundant attention you have paid to my offerings this summer is one of the nicest things that has happened to me in my brief and lucky life." And Katharine responded in kind: "Your letter of September 2nd was a great pleasure to get and I confess it made me feel very good. An editor so often wonders whether all the letters he or she sends are just an annoyance."

For the rest of 1954, amid constant interruptions because of Katharine's poor health and other disasters, the two exchanged increasingly bemused letters about Updike's poems. She suffered cystitis in September, which was nothing compared to the weather in North Brooklin that month—two hurricanes roared right over the farmhouse within twelve days of each other. Andy made light of Hurricane Edna in a *New Yorker* essay, depicting Katharine as glued to her radio but otherwise unperturbed, sipping a cocktail and straightening the books on her shelves.

(He also revealed that Katharine hated the American League, which shocked Updike.) Katharine, on the other hand, depicted herself to Jean Stafford as wild with worry in the storm's aftermath over how to care for Crullie with no heat, no power, no water pump, no telephone, and a tree across their driveway. In October, Katharine's cystitis returned so badly that she was flown to New York Hospital on East Sixty-Eighth Street, where she stayed for ten days, working all the while. She was in pain, but her main complaint, as she wrote to Stafford in a letter that accompanied an edited proof, was "hospitalitis—the food, the ennui, the problem of tipping the aids and maids, etc.": "It seems to me I'd be well if only they'd let me go home to my own bed and some decent food." She came home in November and worked a few hours each day in the office as she built back her strength, and she spent part of her energy on letters to Updike.

Two days before Thanksgiving, for instance, she wrote to him about a poem she'd accepted but that contained, to her eyes, erratic and inconsistent punctuation. Could they just change all the colons, semicolons, and dashes to commas? Updike immediately dashed off a three-page letter objecting to her plan, which would produce "a nervous hurry of commas." He thought the rhythm now "hustled" the reader through the poem "as if it were a shabby hall in a house he is thinking of renting." Couldn't *The New Yorker* allow him the same license they granted to prose writers for variety and rhythm? Katharine responded with what she announced at the opening was to be a "treatise on punctuation," a masterpiece of grammatical theory in which she managed to laugh at herself as she drove home her many, many serious arguments. The two were so clearly having fun with each other. Katharine contested him point by punctuation point. Yes, a colon "<u>looks</u> very nice," but "the colon in general usage nowadays has the special function of delivering the goods," while a comma in prose weighs very differently than a comma in poetry. "It was my husband, a light verse writer, who first pointed out to me that stops at the end of lines of verse should be very light because the very fact that a line of verse <u>ends</u> makes a natural stop, both for the eye and for the ear." All this added up to the magazine's general theory of poetic punctuation: "A punctuation mark comes, from habit, to have almost the value of a word. Therefore if used too untraditionally it impinges just the way a misused word does." Updike conceded the commas, at least partially in dazzlement at E. B. White. All this for a ten-line poem, published just before Christmas, which celebrates various celebrities with the last name of Williams. "I want to add that I am delighted to find anyone who cares as much as this about punctuation and who is as careful as you are about your verse," she wrote. (Many years later, Updike would reread these letters and write to Katharine about his amusement and gratitude at her editing, "like a mother retriever cuffing her puppy into shape.")

Katharine ended the year on a grace note, having recovered sufficient vigor to be able to help Joe and Allene in an intense hour of need. Their baby, a girl named Martha, was born just before the holiday, but Joe was still at Fort Dix, so Andy and Katharine traveled up to Boston to bring Allene home to her apartment on Christmas Day, and they spent a week tending the baby and cooking and caring for one-year-old Steven. "It was all quite strenuous but fun," she wrote to one author, and "being a grandmother is almost as strenuous as being a mother," she wrote to another. The generations were on her mind even as she wrote to her newest author, with whom she was becoming increasingly affectionate. "Dear John Updike: Pretty soon, because of my advanced years, I may just break down and start my letters 'Dear John.' After all, you must be a year or more younger than my youngest son." And so she did—but he would never address her as anything other than Mrs. White.

Part VII

The Editor
Becomes a Writer

(1955–1960)

38.

Katharine and Andy began, once again, to plan a trip to Europe, and once again it seemed as if the universe were determined to keep them home. Their February trip to Florida had already been scotched because Andy needed a hernia surgery—"a repair job," in Katharine's words. Optimistically, they booked passage for a six-week journey starting at the end of May, and applied for their passports. When it came time at the passport office to swear her loyalty to country, Katharine said, "I do, except—" and Andy nearly fainted (ever the *New Yorker* editor, she meant that she couldn't entirely swear that she'd gotten her mother's birth date correct).

They set aside two weeks in April to travel to Maine to arrange for Aunt Crullie's care while they would be away. But even that April trip was soon in jeopardy; Roger's five-year-old daughter, Alice, was in the hospital. At first they thought it might be polio, but then she was diagnosed with spinal meningitis. She recovered enough to be sent home to regain her strength, and the Whites arrived in North Brooklin just in time to celebrate Aunt Crullie's ninety-third birthday. And then, two days later, Aunt Crullie had a stroke that put her into a coma. For almost two weeks she lay in the hospital, unresponsive but hanging on, and Katharine did not know what to do.

Caroline Belle Sergeant died on May 13, 1955. Katharine wrote a loving obituary, noting that her aunt's life "followed a familiar pattern of New England devotion and sacrifice—a spinster who took on the role of mother by force of circumstances and who brought to children and friends alike the rectitude of a Victorian upbringing and the warmth of a generous and spirited character." Katharine also couldn't help observing that though Aunt Crullie "never wrote for publication, her letters and communications were small masterpieces of English prose—the sort of exact and elegant expression that is rare in our times and that is the work of a disciplined mind and a feeling for whatever is beautiful and true." The interment of Crullie's ashes and the execution of her will would have to wait. Katharine and Andy set sail for London on May 26.

They boarded the second RMS *Mauretania* of the Cunard–White Star Line, bound for her home port of Southampton, and in a happy coincidence they were joined on board by Frances Gray Patton and her husband, Lewis. For months, Katharine had been writing to her British authors and tentatively making plans for visits, but she'd left their itinerary loose. All they knew at the start was that they'd stay for two weeks in London, and then they'd rent a car to travel outside the city, perhaps all the way to Scotland, and maybe they'd even fly to Germany, where the army had just posted Joe, causing him temporarily to leave Allene and the two babies behind in Boston (that summer they would move to join him).

For their two weeks in London they booked a room at the luxurious Connaught Hotel in Mayfair, and that decision almost immediately revealed itself to be a mistake. Katharine called the Connaught "much too swish and too expensive." Someone had told them it had good food, but they hadn't been expecting such a grand place with such intimidating service. "Never has so much comfort made one man so uncomfortable," Andy wrote to Allene, and he claimed to have lost twelve pounds despite the world-class food. They hadn't been in London for long before they were already worried about getting back home on the *Queen Elizabeth*, because the British papers were full of news about a railway and dockworker strike. Andy had been planning to drive them around the English countryside once they left London, but the roads were so crowded with delivery trucks because of the strike and his nerves were so shot from being pushed around by uppity waiters that he decided he couldn't risk driving on the left side of the road. When *Punch* invited Andy to a staff luncheon, the first such invitation extended to an American since Mark Twain, he turned them down. Both Whites submitted to press interviews; Katharine was interviewed by *The Sunday Times* and Andy by the *Daily Express*.

Andy received another call from a journalist wanting an interview, and this request he attempted to deny, but when the man persisted and asked if he could have a photograph to run with a short caption, Andy asked what sort of photograph he'd like. "A shot of Mrs. White leapfrogging naked over you" came the reply—it was James Thurber, also in London, dissolving into laughter at the kind of telephone prank for which he'd become notorious, and which the Whites did not appreciate. (He used to call Katharine at the office and pretend to be a Black laundress who had lost or scorched the Whites' clothes.) Despite this, they met the Thurbers for dinner, but Jim got drunk and began verbally to attack Katharine. He had done that before. He held Katharine responsible for stealing Andy away from him, he blamed her for his rocky record of acceptances and rejections at *The New Yorker*, and, most of all, he resented her as a woman in power, treating her as if she were the domineering, humorless woman in many of his stories.

A few days later, *Punch* called again, this time inviting both Whites to a tea in their honor, together with *New Yorker* reporter A. J. Liebling. This time they accepted, and Andy thought this might have been the first time a woman had ever entered the offices of *Punch*. (Andy asked for whiskey and soon the tea turned into a cocktail party.) Neither of the Whites knew Liebling, an American journalist whose reporting from Normandy on D-Day and other signal moments of World War II had made his name, since he'd mostly been living abroad, but after the cocktail party, he took them under his wing and showed them the sights. They visited *New Yorker* London correspondent Mollie Panter-Downes at her elegant house, Roppeleghs, near Haslemere in Surrey.

Their vacation immeasurably improved when they left London for Devon, where they stayed for another two weeks in a guesthouse called the Easton Court Hotel, the place where Evelyn Waugh wrote *Brideshead Revisited*, and more recently where their friend S. N. Behrman had stayed to write, a fifteenth-century Tudor house with a genuine thatched roof, gardens out back, and a filling station out front.

The proprietor, Mrs. Cobb, was delighted to have another writer as a guest and graciously agreed to provide the Whites breakfast in their comfortable room with a fireplace, though that was not hotel protocol.

At night, they dined with the other guests, and by day they explored the countryside. Katharine particularly enjoyed walking along the river Teign through deep forests to a small pub about a mile away in Chagford. She marveled at the absence of insects; it all felt so pleasant, and Andy had a reprieve from his hay fever. They visited the Ring O'Bells pub for gin and tonics so frequently that they made a friend, a man whose wife was in London for business—she happened to be a children's book author. He would bring his drink over to the Whites' table and complain about married women who insisted on having careers, until finally Katharine spoke up, telling him that she herself handled a career, a husband, and three children without neglecting anyone. The man apologized, and later made it up to her by sending her a rare book from his collection, a copy of Harriet Beecher Stowe's *A Key to "Uncle Tom's Cabin."* He also asked if she could help his wife's writing career. (She couldn't.)

Their landlady's companion took them in his rattletrap car to Exeter, where they toured the cathedral. They hired a driver to take them to Elizabeth Taylor's house in High Wycombe, Buckinghamshire, where they met the rest of her family, and they so enjoyed Taylor's teenage son Renny that he would come to stay with them in North Brooklin later that summer. They visited the Updikes in Oxford on their way to the Cotswolds, an occasion that intensely embarrassed Andy. The car they had rented was a limousine and the driver wore livery, so they made quite a spectacle when they pulled up outside the Updikes' basement apartment. Updike's reverence for Mrs. White was so great that he assumed she was tall and regal, but if he felt any disappointment at her shorter stature, Katharine soon buoyed him by passing along the message from William Maxwell that a staff job was waiting for Updike in New York when his year abroad was over.

The looming transportation strike forced the Whites to switch their passage home to the *American*, leaving two weeks earlier than they'd planned—but at least they left on a high note, and Katharine would forever remember this trip, which would turn out to be their last, aside from the annual Florida sojourns, as a happy one. When they returned to New York on a lifeless summer weekend, immediately decamping for Maine, she was still only halfway through a three-month leave of absence from the magazine.

It was the longest break she'd had from the magazine since her divorce in Reno in 1929, the longest stretch in which she was healthy but not working full tilt since 1925. She began to think about stepping back from some of her duties at *The New Yorker*. She was approaching her sixty-third birthday, but she wasn't thinking about retiring—not yet. Rather, she thought she should edge away from the fiction department, writing to Shawn, "I am at the end of my rope and feel I cannot go on any longer as is," for her own sake but also because her work there "seem[ed] now to be hurting others as well as [her]self." The issue was Gus Lobrano.

She and Andy reluctantly came down to New York in the middle of August. Their town house had been burgled and they needed to inventory their losses for the insurance claim, and that gave Katharine the opportunity for a private meeting with Shawn. Lobrano had been head of the fiction department since Katharine's departure for Maine in 1938, and for a decade and a half they'd worked well together. But since his return to the office after the previous summer's health trouble, he'd acted entirely unreasonably toward Katharine. In her view, he was exerting a "tyranny" over the entire magazine, Shawn included, in a strange power play that seemed intended to sideline her and get between her and her authors. She regarded this as a ghastly side effect of his untreated mental health trouble. All summer and fall, she and Shawn exchanged letters and phone calls about the situation. Katharine noted that Lobrano withheld manuscripts from her, wouldn't take her phone calls, insisted on knowing when Shawn lunched with Katharine on her New York visits, and threatened to resign over "so many queer things," such as the time when Shawn phoned Katharine to ask how she was faring after another bout of Thurber nastiness. The only solution, in her mind, was to stop editing manuscripts; she wrote, "I fear his feeling against me is now affecting the contributors whose work I handle." This renunciation was absolutely not Katharine's desire. She needed time, she stressed to Shawn. She wrote, "I think it is good for me to be away just now, to regain my equanimity and get over my sadness and sorrow over what I am giving up voluntarily—notably the work I like most of all, which is with the contributors, and the all important (to me, anyway) factor of having a vote on what we buy." She wasn't asking Shawn to choose between her and Lobrano, but to carve out autonomous job descriptions for the two of them, and she'd be willing to take the short straw if it would benefit the magazine.

Even amid this interrupted year of loss and absence, Katharine had been building relationships and soliciting new work. She lunched with Jean Stafford, who told Katharine she'd been feeling blocked and could not write or even think of story ideas. And so Katharine gave her a story, a true event from her childhood that she'd held on to for decades, thinking she herself might write it (she also sent Stafford Blackwing pencils and yellow typing paper). The story took place in Chocorua, New Hampshire, the summer before her senior year at Bryn Mawr, when she was engaged to Ernest. The couple had gone mountain climbing with their friends, and when they returned, they found Aunt Crullie pacing in anxiety. The family's young Irish maids, two friends in their early twenties who had come up from Boston with the Sergeants, had gone swimming but were now long overdue. The story as Katharine relayed it to Stafford arose from her own response to the news. She and Ernest dashed to the boathouse and found the women's abandoned clothes, and then Katharine ran around to neighboring cottages to ask for clues to their whereabouts. She was entirely focused on impressing her fiancé with her heroic deeds and thought little of the women, and it was shame at this superficiality that she meant to evoke in her telling to Stafford. The story continued to its grim denouement: Katharine and Ernest found the bodies of the women floating in fifteen feet of water, and Katharine watched while Ernest swam into the lake to pull them ashore, "the most dreadful happening of [her] life," as she described it. Stafford changed the location to Colorado and timed the tragedy to happen the very day after the narrator, a student at Bryn Mawr, has just gotten engaged to a Harvard man. She does indeed feel, as she races around the lake, "a passion of self-loathing for wanting the girls to be alive chiefly because their being so would set [her] up in Rod's eyes," but Stafford attempted to end the story on a nobler note, despite the two deaths, as the narrator learns to see her fiancé for himself, in his suffering, rather than for how he thinks of her. Stafford submitted "The Mountain Day," which was accepted, just as Katharine was writing long, frantic memos to Shawn, and just as she was ardently courting Stafford's ex-husband Robert Lowell's second wife, Elizabeth Hardwick.

Katharine finally brought Hardwick into the magazine that year. She rejected two more stories by Hardwick until, just days before her departure to England, she sent a long and enthusiastic but provisional acceptance of a third story, "The Oak and the Ax," along with a detailed discussion of the ending and its need for revision. Hardwick sent a new draft within the week, saying, "No matter what the decision, I was very much impressed and pleased by the kind and amount of interest and the thought you've given to all this." But the relationship Katharine was building was in danger of crumbling, as the edits for "The Oak and the Ax" were snarled in the uncertain chain of command at *The New Yorker* that December. Lobrano was back in the hospital. Katharine stopped herself from editing Hardwick's story, thinking that it would be reassigned after the turn of the year when she was no longer in the department. She wrote a letter to Mrs. Lowell apologizing for the magazine's disarray. Stafford's story about Katharine's terrible day would also go to another editor.

In the meantime, Katharine would find another way to be useful to the magazine. She had once before reinvented her job as a work-from-home editor in Maine, and now she would design a job—not editing—that engaged her mind and her knowledge of the magazine. In fact, she designed five. She sent Shawn a memo with five possible roles she could play that wouldn't threaten Lobrano: general planning for future content including fact and columns such as sports and On and Off the Avenue ("This I would love . . . My mind being the way it is, it has darted ahead on ideas about many things . . . I can hardly wait to tell you about them"); writing to agents about rejected fact manuscripts and reading manuscripts of forthcoming nonfiction books for publishable excerpts; starting a translation department to publish work by foreign writers; scouting for new talent by reading anthologies and other magazines (she'd be willing to do this even though she always found it a "deadening and deadly job");

and acquiring verse, given Lobrano's antipathy for poetry and Moss's need for a sympathetic editor as colleague.

But the situation continued to worsen, and finally Katharine wrote Shawn a letter of resignation from *The New Yorker*. A clean break. She could no longer envision a place where she could work "anywhere at all on the magazine and be free of these neurotic Lobrano influences." The crisis was affecting not only her present health but also her retrospective understanding of her career. She wrote to Shawn that while she considered herself "an editor of the magazine as a whole," she was now realizing Lobrano had seen her as "only an assistant editor" who didn't know her place—and, she worried, maybe Shawn had seen her that way too, and she'd literally been laboring under a misconception for years. She spent pages explaining that she thought Lobrano was a "brilliant" editor and she'd always been happy to accept his authority. She'd had a true partnership with Wolcott Gibbs years ago, and she thought she'd replicated that with Lobrano. But now he was undermining her with "spying, suspicions, and military supervision." She positively loathed the idea of resigning—whenever she thought of it, her "sense of justice [was] often outraged and self-pity, that villain, [crept] in"—but she had to do it. "As Andy wisely points out," she said, "I have to accept reality, and life is not usually just, and it is rare when a lifetime of work ends up in a happy way."

Katharine's letter prompted one from Lobrano, a polite and formal letter in which he suggested that she reconsider her decision. He acknowledged that their relationship had been "at times extremely trying to [them] both," but he pointed out that they disagreed only about "procedural or administrative matters," never about literary judgments, and when it came to discussing manuscripts, their conversations were always "stimulating and rewarding and reassuring." Katharine was in no way persuaded. Her worry and anxiety billowed around her. It felt as if everything she had built was draining away from her. In the midst of these long and furious letters, she and Andy took the train to Northampton to inter Aunt Crullie's ashes in the cemetery with the rest of the Sergeants. Katharine felt nothing but loss. "I have done my utmost," she wrote to Shawn, "my absolute utmost to subordinate myself and my happiness and indeed my honor to satisfy and soothe this twisted man, and I have voluntarily abandoned the work I love best and that has been my life." She was petrified that she wouldn't even make it to her January 1 resignation date without a public breakdown in the office. Her mind whirled endlessly through plans to salvage her dignity. She suggested an entirely new project to Shawn: that she announce that she was leaving her position in order to edit Ross's letters into a book about him and the making of *The New Yorker*, because this seemed to her "about the only job there was around there [she] still could do which people like Stafford, Nabokov, McGinley, Shapiro, McCarthy, Wilson, et al. would accept as a natural and good reason for [her] bowing out of Fiction and Verse entirely."

She campaigned hard for this project, adding Andy into the offer and pushing against Shawn's instinct that it was five or ten years too soon for such a book. Who better to edit it, to solicit letters from friends and colleagues, and to write the connective tissue, she said, and besides, it might take them five or ten years to complete it. "We should start *now*," she wrote, "before we have our coronaries, and our total nervous crack-ups, and our arterio-sclerosis of the brain." If he would approve of this idea, Katharine wrote, her "life would be as good as saved." Shawn appears to have said no, but he also said no to her resignation, and the two continued to scheme about what Katharine might do at *The New Yorker*.

As the year drew to a close, they still had not resolved the question, and she was equally frantic about herself and her authors. So many of them would be upset at the news, cut adrift from the person who had worked so hard to cultivate their trust. Telling them of her leaving was one of her "greatest dreads." She stressed to Shawn that they must put a positive spin on her renunciation of the fiction department. It would not be fair to Andy to blame it on his health, as Shawn had done in his explanation to Maxwell. That December, at the end of every editorial letter she wrote, she appended a vague paragraph with the news padded in reassuring words. "After January first I shall no longer be reading poetry and fiction for opinion, or editing either verse or prose," she told Elizabeth Bishop. "I am leaving this department of the magazine and shall instead be working only on general policy and on other matters that concern the magazine as a whole." She gestured toward issues with which Bishop and all her authors would be familiar: "It is, even so, a necessary step for me to take and it is going to be much better for Andy's writing, and for my own health and happiness, that I be freer, able to move about when he wants to and with me less weighed down with the detail of the Fiction Department work than I am now." She repeated these or similar words, and told everyone, over and over, how sorrowful and difficult the decision was.

And the letters poured back to her. May Sarton wrote that Katharine's news sent "a shiver of desolation down [her] spine," saying, "I hate the idea of not being edited by you." Frank Sullivan said, "I don't think I can write coherently about the lamentable news in your note. . . . How am I, and all the writers you have been such a good friend to over all these years going to get along without you?" The agent Bernice Baumgarten saluted Katharine for exactly the skill she herself prized most highly: "No editor I've worked with has been so quick to recognize new talent and so sympathetic toward its development."

Who would replace her on the fiction staff? Katharine had extensive, surprising thoughts on the matter. She proposed a name to Shawn: Brendan Gill. "Please do not jump out of your skin!" she added. "I know that there are hundreds of things against this but please do not dismiss the idea at once." Katharine had accepted Gill's first short story back in 1936, and he'd been almost immediately hired as a staff writer for Talk, profiles, and theater reviews while continuing to publish fiction. Katharine acknowledged that Shawn preferred not to hire writers as editors—Lobrano did not write—but she argued that Gill had "so much stamina, so much vitality," that putting him to work as an editor would not staunch the flow of his writing. She lauded his taste, his sense of humor, his feeling for poetry, his generosity with people, and his "buoyant and optimistic" qualities, which would make him fantastic at spotting new talent. Gill turned down the position, but he likely never knew about Katharine's nomination, never read this generous and excited memo to Shawn in which she envisioned the mature arc of his career as "a first rate writer as well as a major New Yorker editor, the kind of man who has a demanding job and is also a novelist and critic."

Katharine began requesting recommendations from her writers, and May Sarton mentioned a name that rang a bell. Rachel MacKenzie had published a story in *The New Yorker* in 1948 and had continued to submit to it through the Russell & Volkening literary agency, while teaching literature at Wellesley, Radcliffe, and the Bread Loaf Writers' Conference. Sarton had met her at Bread Loaf and thought her "supremely good as a critic, the kind of critic who inspires a writer to revise." It would take almost half a year—and Katharine would have to overcome her own doubts about hiring an unmarried woman, who she assumed would be unexperienced with sex and therefore less good at editing manuscripts on the topic—but she would succeed in hiring Mackenzie as the second female editor at *The New Yorker*, a junior editor who would need extensive training. They'd had women working as scouts and first readers, jobs that Mackenzie also performed, but for the first—and last—time in her career, Katharine brought another woman up behind her. In the summer of 1956, in Katharine White fashion, Mackenzie would instantly begin working her connections, writing to Adrienne Rich, whom she knew from Bread Loaf; reaching out to Muriel Spark and Philip Roth to solicit work in what would become long and rich collaborations; and reconnecting with Wallace Stegner, who lauded her arrival at the magazine, part of what he felt was a sorely needed shake-up in the fiction department.

But as 1955 drew to an end, Mackenzie hadn't accepted the job yet and nothing was certain. The Whites did not travel to Maine for Christmas that year. Instead, they went only across the river to Roger and Evelyn's house. A few years earlier, the Angells had bought a house in Snedens Landing, the site of Roger's happy summertime memories of fishing in the river and swimming in the rocky pool. There, Roger replicated his father's routine of commuting into the city, and there, he reconnected with his childhood friend Peter Powys Grey, and they resumed their fierce tennis games. Peter had married, gotten a job in the public relations department at American Express, and bought the house next to his mother, Marian, where he was raising his two young children, Christopher and Katey. Marian had become a Snedens Landing fixture whom every last person described as eccentric, a woman who never left her tumbledown house with its shabby furniture but who had befriended everyone from heiresses to an entire motorcycle gang. She hosted weekly tea parties for her grandchildren and the other kids in the neighborhood, where she would sit them in front of the fire on her "stinky old couch"—her grand-daughter's words—and read them the classics in her British accent. All the Snedens parents were charmed. Roger's daughters, Callie and Alice, were frequently in attendance.

Elsie too lived in Snedens, where she rented one of the stone houses and frequently called on Roger for help around her house. If she was at the Christmas celebration that year, her presence went unrecorded.

The holiday was a bustle of "food and drink and action and cats and dogs and granddaughters," in Andy's words, and perhaps Katharine too was glad to be at Roger's house instead of hosting the family in Maine. Did she feel strange being back in Snedens Landing, where she had learned of Ernest's mistress, where she had lived after separating from Ernest, where she had broken the news of the divorce to Roger? She certainly felt consumed with thoughts about her near future.

Even on December 29, Katharine's fate was up in the air. She wrote that day to Elizabeth Hardwick, "I myself was to have left the Fiction Department on January 1st, and perhaps I still shall." But she would not leave *The New Yorker* for quite some time. The day Katharine wrote Hardwick, Lobrano underwent a gallbladder operation that began his swift slide into an early death.

39.

When the Whites departed New York in February 1956 for their annual vacation in Sarasota, Florida, they knew that Gus Lobrano was dying, but he did not know. The doctor had discovered that he had an inoperable cancer, but as he lay in his bed at his home in Chappaqua, submerged under the drugs that controlled his pain, his wife, Jean, decided not to tell him. Katharine and Andy were under strict injunction not to spread the news and they kept the secret for nearly the entire month of February. The day before they departed, Andy visited Lobrano, and their conversation felt so much like old times that Andy felt comforted. He and Katharine left knowing they'd never see Lobrano again and that Katharine would stay at the magazine. For now, though, Katharine attempted to put aside thoughts about her role at the magazine as she and Andy began the long drive to Sarasota. They had rented a house sight unseen, and it turned out to be "heavenly," with a patio overlooking a little bayou where mullets jumped and blue herons waded and mockingbirds darted. They swam every day from a tiny island to which they could walk across a bridge. Roger, Evelyn, and the girls came to visit for a few days. But then Jean Lobrano telegrammed on March 1 to say that Gus had died earlier that day, and they found themselves with dozens of letters to write. One evening, Katharine stayed up late into the night with Andy, helping him through the "frightfully difficult" ordeal of writing Lobrano's *New Yorker* obituary, a task so demanding she didn't think Andy would be able to finish it. But he did, praising Lobrano's "flawless" taste in literature but making as big a point of his absorption in his family, trout fishing, and golf, "for it is love of life that enables an editor to work effectively with those who set out, on paper, to interpret life."

Their vacation was further perturbed when Shawn made Katharine the expected offer—to assume Lobrano's job for a few years, during which she would hire and train new editors—and she took several weeks to think it over. Roger wrote that while he hoped she *wouldn't* take on the new role, he knew she probably would. Janet Flanner had written to Katharine years earlier, "Every time there's a shakedown or up in the office, you get the tremours seismographycally [*sic*]; you probably sit so balanced in the center of the whole organization that your mere placing makes it inevitable but it must also be spirit-breaking." She was exactly right. Katharine acutely felt the burden of the magazine's needs and her duty to support William Shawn. She agreed to head the fiction department upon her return from Florida, but only under several conditions: that Robert Henderson be completely amenable to working under her again, that she work from Maine during the summers, that the months of March and August be sacrosanct vacations, and that she retract herself from most of the manuscript editing, because though it was her favorite part of the job, it was also the most physically exhausting. A compromise in the name of institutional continuity was struck. Mollie Panter-Downes wrote to Katharine that Lobrano's death was shocking and sad but said, "If you *had* retired this March, I should have felt that the New Yorker wasn't itself."

The instant she got back to her office, Katharine began—or, really, resumed—looking for a senior editor to be her replacement. She told Fanny Patton, "If you know of any talented young men—we need men, not women—who would make New Yorker fiction editors, do please send me their names or tell them to get in touch with me. We are looking both for those who are experienced and could step into an editing job and for those who could learn to do so after a year or two." Katharine continued to believe that men and women read manuscripts differently and male editors should balance their female manuscript readers. She advised Shawn that they should hire far more editors than they needed, knowing that some wouldn't make the cut and others would take time to mature.

The news of the openings traveled quickly. Malcolm Cowley's son wanted the job, and though Katharine knew Bobby—"I suppose he has outgrown this name long since"—she couldn't encourage his application since he was just out of college and hadn't published anything. Katharine thought Edmund Wilson's daughter Rosamond might be cultivated as a manuscript reader because they had almost bought a piece from her once. The literary agent Henry Volkening put forth the name of two *New Yorker* writers who hadn't published in the magazine in a few years, Dan Wickenden and Gilbert Seldes. Now that Shawn seemed open to considering writers for the editorial position, Katharine advocated for Peter Taylor, a longtime short-story contributor and good friend to Jean Stafford. He considered the position but took a teaching job at Kenyon College instead. None of these candidates worked out. In the meantime, Katharine staved off Elizabeth Bishop's interest in Louise Bogan's poetry-reviewing job (Bogan had no intention of giving it up), told Christine Weston "No chance" when she asked about a part-time office job, and rehired Harriet Walden, who had replaced her husband as Harold Ross's secretary during the war before leaving to have two children. Katharine gave Walden the hard sell; she said that although no job after working for Ross could possibly be as exciting, Katharine's new position in hiring and training editors and reorganizing the department was "enormous." "What I do mostly need," she wrote, "is someone like you: a person whom it is a pleasure to work with, one who is sensitive and intelligent and who can organize me and my work and my life." Walden said yes, and she would stay far beyond Katharine's eventual retirement; she managed the Whites' affairs at *The New Yorker* well into the 1980s. Katharine kept interviewing scores of young men. "The experienced men editors still don't materialize very fast," she told Jean Stafford.

Amid the near misses and unsuitable candidates, one unignorable name kept materializing: Roger Angell. He'd long had his sights on *The New Yorker*, but when he returned from the war, Katharine told him the magazine had no openings for him. He continued writing stories and Comment, and he made a career for himself at *Holiday*, working his way up to senior editor and staff writer and commuting to its offices in Philadelphia two days a week, but he was often unhappy with, as he wrote to Katharine, "the amateurishness and general stupidity" of the magazine, despite the travel perks. As recently as 1950, he'd asked Shawn for an editing job at *The New Yorker*, only to be turned down but encouraged to continue writing, with perhaps a signed column in one of their departments—sports, movies, television—in his future. Then a rumor circulated; Lobrano had apparently said that Roger would never be hired at *The New Yorker* as long as he worked there. Now Roger Angell began to seem like the magazine's most serious candidate for fiction editor, and Katharine considered the matter from every possible angle.

Wouldn't it be best if he joined as an editor in the fact department? she wondered. But the fiction department was in such dire need and Roger was beyond qualified to meet it. Katharine cited his intensive study of the magazine since the age of ten, his indispensability in helping her select pieces for *Short Stories from "The New Yorker,"* and his skill as a "clean writer," in Ross's terms. In fact, virtually the only argument against his candidacy was the optics of working under his mother and alongside his stepfather; Katharine felt guilty "that [their] being there ha[d] deprived Roger of his chance in his most natural habitat." She brainstormed ways that they could discreetly try him out and train him, without ruffling feathers at either *The New Yorker* or *Holiday*, and she gamed out what it might look like if he *didn't* pass the test. She implored Shawn to emphasize to Maxwell and Henderson that he himself was putting Roger forth. "The last thing on earth I want," Katharine wrote, "is to give the impression that the first thing I did when taking the Fiction dept administration again was to put in my son."

Roger's job application began to seem like the solution to their troubles, but it would take months for the idea to gain favor at *The New Yorker*. Over three separate luncheons (shades of Andy White's protracted hiring), Shawn and Roger discussed the terms, and when Shawn offered Roger a $2,000 increase over his salary at *Holiday*, Roger finally accepted. He wrote to his mother, "Sell your stock! Eustace Tilley and I start partnership as of October 1." He would continue submitting his own writing and would edit both fact and fiction, though at first the fiction assignments would come directly from Shawn, "to protect [him] somewhat from any low accusations" among fellow editors. He would soon take over many of his mother's authors—Rumer Godden, Nadine Gordimer, and eventually John Updike. Twenty years later he would even take over his mother's prized corner office, where he would open the door of the closet to find a vanity mirror and a box of her Coty face powder ("Thanks for holding the spot for me all those years," Roger would write to her). But he would begin as the junior editor tasked with following up B- and C-list writers, and he would sometimes find himself sending awkward memos: "There seems to be no one else here to send you this check, so I am sending it to you to my slight embarrassment. But come to think of it, what the hell—why should I be embarrassed? We at the New Yorker like the piece very much," he wrote to Mr. E. B. White. "How about another story real soon?"

While Katharine was strategizing in broad strokes for the magazine's future organization, one that would include Roger, she was also writing to Lobrano's authors, long and heartfelt letters that sought to keep them tied to the magazine despite the freshly broken link. She wrote to V. S. Pritchett, for example, to explain why his first reading agreement had been erroneously allowed to lapse when Lobrano entered the hospital the previous November, and she implored him to continue sending work to the magazine. "I realize that his death will have left you with the feeling that you now have no fiction editor at the New Yorker," she wrote, saying she had long admired his stories and she would give them the closest attention. Indeed, Pritchett would continue publishing stories in *The New Yorker* well into the eighties, and Roger Angell would become his editor and close friend.

Katharine was also vigorously pursuing new authors. Now that she'd finally gotten Elizabeth Hardwick into the magazine, she set her sights on Hardwick's husband, Robert Lowell (something she didn't mention to his ex-wife, Jean Stafford). Lowell had just published a reminiscence in *Partisan Review* of his childhood in Boston, and Katharine was sufficiently embedded in Boston society to know some of his characters, such as her dear friends the Crosbys on Revere Street, who had what she considered the best house in Boston, just steps from Lowell's childhood house. Might he publish future chapters in *The New Yorker*? Katharine would try all year to get more writing from both Lowell and Hardwick, unsuccessfully; when she heard that they were expecting a baby, she sent a fine white English blanket for the layette, congratulating them but in a halfhearted way. "All over the world, children are competing with short stories," she groused, hoping both would soon send her pieces. When the final proofs of Hardwick's latest story were ready, Katharine sent it to her in the hospital where she was recovering from giving birth to her daughter Harriet.

Katharine did enjoy one personal-editorial triumph that summer. Jean Stafford was living in London and had fallen ill; she was living in a depressing set of rooms and not seeing much of the town. Katharine could entirely empathize, and she offered to Stafford the solution that she herself had discovered the previous summer: Stafford should meet A. J. Liebling, who went by the name "Joe." "He is a strange man," she wrote; "often it is next to impossible to get into conversation with him some people think. But he smiles like a Buddha and when he does talk, it is very good indeed. He is a gourmet, who knows the best and least obvious places to eat, and he takes a gusty delight in the English music-hall humors and entertainments." Katharine also wrote to Liebling to introduce him to Stafford. It worked better than she could have anticipated. The pair met in the lobby of Liebling's hotel and had a few drinks. "I was so impressed; he was wonderfully amiable," Stafford would later say. Katharine would never know this part: "Mostly we made jokes about the Whites, about her obsession with illness." Stafford and Liebling would marry two years later and stay together until his death in 1963.

As she played her many roles at the magazine, Katharine alternated between her homes—she and Andy spent May in New York, June in Maine, July in New York, August in Maine—and between work and family drama. In July, a happy drama: Joe, Allene, Steven, and Martha returned from Germany, docking in Brooklyn early one summer morning on what happened to be Andy's fifty-seventh birthday. Katharine and Andy stood at the dock, looking up at the big transport ship, and they could see their grandchildren on deck but waited for over an hour for them to disembark. Meanwhile, Andy became so overwhelmed by the scene, all those soldiers trooping down the gangplank into the embraces of their families, that Katharine needed to lead him over to a bench to regain his composure. Joe was taken to Fort Hamilton for his discharge, and Allene and the children came back to Turtle Bay, where they lived for a few cheerfully chaotic days before all four headed north to visit Allene's family in New Hampshire. They wanted to settle in Brooklin, and Katharine had scoured the area for a suitable house for them to rent. She finally found one just a mile and a half down the road from their farmstead, a house owned by her friend James Russell Wiggins, editor of the *Ellsworth American*, so the entire setup passed muster with Katharine, and the Whites moved right in. Joe bought a boat and returned to lobstering, but that fall he went to work for a local boatbuilder, Arno Day, who would soon offer Joe a partnership stake in his business, cementing Joe's lifetime work at the Brooklin Boat Yard.

Nancy, too, was coming into her own. After years as a homemaker, she now put her doctorate to use as an educator, taking a job that year as a teacher and head of the science department at Moravian Seminary for Girls in Germantown, Pennsylvania. Her two daughters, Sarah and Kitty, attended Moravian while Jonathan, the youngest at eleven years old, attended the local public school. Nancy had been determined to create a stable family life in contrast to the two households in which she split her childhood, and she had done that while also embedding herself in her community and finding ways to act upon her strong social conscience. She had served on the Easton School Board and become active in the Episcopal church and its missions. Now, for the first time, it was Louis who made lunch for Jonathan when he came home from school. Nancy would be home in time for dinner, but then she'd work late into the night. If the first decade of her married life was a conscious effort not to replicate her mother's career-centered life, now she was embracing a teaching career as part of her ethic of service and of a burgeoning feminism that she would pass along to her children.

That summer Katharine executed Aunt Crullie's will, distributing three dozen pieces of small jewelry to Crullie's grandnieces and -nephews. Crullie saved her best jewels for her two surviving nieces, and to Elsie she bequeathed the remainder of her brother George's estate. Katharine sold her stocks as directed and split the money with Elsie.

The flurry of letters the two sisters exchanged about Crullie's estate raised in Elsie an urgent feeling of distress about her own will, now that she was seventy-five, and she wrote to Katharine that it was time for a family conference, one that she had apparently been asking to have for quite some time. Katharine stayed up late for two consecutive nights to write a long response. She wrote that she didn't really want to discuss Elsie's will because she considered it to be "a most personal and private affair," but then she proceeded to write pages and pages of advice. She counseled Elsie to "write what the heart dictate[d]," pointing out that it would surely be amended in future years so Elsie needn't think of it as final. It should be a living document, and in fact, why not write it "in a light-hearted fashion—even a whimsical one if [she] wish[ed]"—"No one is going to care for you more, or less, because of the way you make your will." Ever the editor, Katharine tried to turn Elsie's will into a liter-ary endeavor, but her attempt sounds much more stilted than almost any of the other editorial letters Katharine wrote to her author friends. "My feelings for you, I might say, are entirely sisterly and loving in spite of all our rubs, and you have figured far more over the whole course of my life as a person to whom I owe a great debt than you perhaps realize." Such carefully circumscribed words! "Compatibility is nothing one can create. But affection can exist without compatibility and I do believe we have affection for one another." Money was clearly one fraying strand that tied them together. Katharine had given Elsie money over the years—neither sister's surviving papers record dates or amounts, but Katharine said that the money she gave to their father went directly to Elsie—and she suspected that it hurt Elsie to receive it. She had given Elsie $10,000 some years previously, but her sister worried about paying it back, so Katharine had said, "Okay, leave it to me if it would make you feel better to do so." Now she told Elsie that long-ago comment was only meant to soothe Elsie's anxiety; she never expected that sum as a bequest. She begged Elsie to spend her money over the course of her life, saying it should go toward her own health and happiness. And she made clear, in her heartfelt but dry and formal way, that Elsie need never worry about her future, that Katharine would take care of her just as she had Aunt Crullie. She could never physically care for Elsie—she was too old and infirm and busy earning money to do that—but Katharine wrote, "I

will always, so long as I live, see that you live in a way by which you will
have the best possible care and the most possible happiness should you
become senile or physically totally incapacitated. And I would consider
it my solemn duty as well as my heart's impulse to do this." The letter
exhausted her and she worried about the effects it would have on her
own health. Her physician talked her through these issues, she reported
to Jean Stafford, because he believed "states of mind about sisters, etc. are
just as important as infectious hepatitis or a kidney stone."

Katharine would not have a genuine vacation until the following
March, when she and Andy made their usual monthlong trip to Florida,
and she told Shawn that though she felt guilty about leaving, the respite
came in "the nick of time" for her health. When she got to Sarasota,
she enjoyed a "scandalously lazy month." She and Andy rented a boat
and explored the canals and bayous and sandy keys. Roger could not
visit because he was busy holding down the fiction fort at his new job
(Tom Gorman, the department secretary, reported that Roger was energetically campaigning for a portable bar in his office but that Gorman
was stalling him until Katharine's return). Nancy and Sarah were able
to come down from Pennsylvania, and Katharine enjoyed being able to
focus on just the two of them. She did have one work task to perform,
however, one that was influenced by Sarah's presence. Nabokov had sent
her a copy of the Olympia Press edition of *Lolita*, and now that *Pnin* was
on the verge of publication, he gently chided her for not reading his true
masterwork. She read it in Florida and wrote to him immediately. She
was unable to put it down ("Which is a real tribute," she wrote, "for no
one can put a novel down easier than I can"), and she thought Nabokov
described America with "great virtuosity." But with "five potential nym-
phets" among her grandchildren, including nine-year-old Sarah, "[her]
jauntiest granddaughter," she could only respond with revulsion to his
story. Like so many of *Lolita*'s readers at the time of publication and
since, she interpreted the story through the lens of sympathy and iden-
tification, saying that though Nabokov did manage to elicit a small bit
of her sympathy for Humbert Humbert in the second half, she mainly
repulsed any such feeling, and the experience made her "thoroughly miserable." Of course, she added, she did not believe it should be banned

as it had been in France and England (she would continue to send him letters in support of the book through its 1958 American publication and reviews), and she thought that mainly Nabokov had achieved his objectives: "You raised my hair, gave me the horrors, stimulated my mind, aroused my antagonism and, grudgingly, my admiration." She knew she was risking Nabokov's displeasure by writing this, but she just couldn't not. She signed off with "Please try to forgive my perversity on your perversity."

Just after the Whites returned to New York, Andy found himself launched on another book project. So many of his books were elicited from him or fell into his lap; this one arrived in his mailbox. A college friend sent him a rare edition of *The Elements of Style*, a slim, little-known handbook to language usage that Andy remembered from taking a Cornell English class from its author, William Strunk Jr. He wrote an essay of appreciation for *The New Yorker*, and the very next day, an editor at Macmillan wrote to ask if the essay could be an introduction to a reissue of the book. Andy twirled the idea around and proposed that he revise Strunk's book for a new age, a quick job that he could finish in about a month. Macmillan said yes, but in fact Andy took over a year. Though he spent much of his career denying that Katharine had a hand in his books ("She is a truly gifted writer-helper, and I have had to do my own work in secret for twenty-eight years in order to maintain any feeling of personal accomplishment"), for this book, he did indeed pass the manuscript under Katharine's pencil, and her reading was an asset that he trumpeted to his own editor, telling him that the project would have "the inestimable advantage of coming under her editorial eye" and noting, "She is a better grammarian, organizer, teacher, editor, and mother than I am, and has saved an untold number of lives." *The Elements of Style* would sell millions of copies, become a Book-of-the-Month Club selection, be assigned in college courses everywhere, and be set to music, illustrated, and narrated—an unusual fate for a volume about grammar. It was a triumph of revision and editing.

As Andy wrote and revised and trimmed and rearranged, Katharine's editing practice was coming under fire by a *New Yorker* author and friend. James Thurber sent her a five-page diatribe from Bermuda in May of

1957. He had retreated to the island to recover his health after a slow-motion battle with the fiction department, one in which Katharine was only glancingly involved, but it was to her that he addressed his lengthy complaints. Since Lobrano's death, Thurber had been assigned to William Maxwell, because of his well-known antipathy to Katharine, which the Whites' visit to him in England had not abated. He began submitting to Maxwell a series of fables about contemporary American life, a darker and more dyspeptic version of the fables he had published in the 1930s. Maxwell rejected many of them, and in Thurber's analysis, he turned away the stories that treated national and international politics and issues like Communism and McCarthyism, preferring instead the ones about "husbands and wives and children." Then Thurber submitted *The Wonderful O*, a book-length fable ostensibly for children that also worked as an adult parable about free speech—about a land where a despotic ruler bans the letter "O." Arguably, Maxwell and Shawn simply should have rejected the piece on the basis of its length, but instead they entered into what Thurber called a "destructive collaboration" to trim it to something the magazine could run, and Thurber had many more words for the travesty they produced, which he immediately pulled from consideration. He wrote to Katharine saying that, during the past year and a half when she had headed the department, *The New Yorker* had begun using the word "uncharacteristic" to describe pieces of his that were then rejected, especially anything "not in the comic vain [*sic*]" in which he accused the editors of confining him. Moreover, the magazine's editorial letters were now peppered with phrases like "unanimity of opinion," as if there were a Unanimity Board and every writer must conform or retreat. Thurber was so angry he invented an insult that he knew would wound Katharine: "You have all become, in a curious inversion of Ross's famous byword 'writer-conscious,' extremely editor-conscious." They—read: Katharine—had "made of the New Yorker editorial judgment a rigid thing and [had] developed a certain sense of false infallibility, so that Ross's wonderful ability to see the author's side and to ask for outside opinions ha[d] been lost."

Katharine, uncharacteristically, confined herself to a two-page reply. She invoked her entire thirty-two-year career before saying, "I can't remember a period when there was less unanimity of opinion than in the past year-and-a-half. I consider this healthy—think it gives us more variety." She defended Shawn and said he was the final arbiter of the magazine's contents, just as Ross had been, but said that he would necessarily make a different magazine over time. And she defended the editors' right to make mistakes: "We don't think our judgment was infallible, but I can assure you it was sincere." The fables just simply didn't strike them as fresh. She agreed with Thurber on one point that brought an immediate change—from now on, Roger would edit him. On the surface, Thurber was mollified. But the crack in his relationship with *The New Yorker* began to widen. He had been working in desultory fashion on a set of reminiscences about Ross since even before the editor's death, and this month, in the moment of his greatest discontent and nostalgia for the magazine of the past, he accepted *The Atlantic Monthly*'s offer to polish them up and serialize them (*The Atlantic* had tried to get Andy to write about Ross and offered him $1,000 for an essay, which he promptly declined). Thurber's essays would appear beginning in November of 1957, and he would show Katharine and Andy typescripts of the first two chapters. Andy and Katharine would be utterly charmed, but those feelings would not last when the series continued into the new year and into book form.

Was there any truth to Thurber's accusation that the fiction department was trying to keep its longtime authors in restrictive lanes? Yes, at least a little. Katharine wrote to Shirley Jackson to say that now that *Raising Demons*, her book of family essays, was published, might she return to writing "some short stories in the vein of those in 'The Lottery'"? Jackson had never flagged in submitting her work to *The New Yorker* but hadn't published anything there since 1953 and wouldn't again in her lifetime. And again: Phyllis McGinley had taken an interest in historical figures and had submitted a quite lengthy series of poems about religious leaders and Catholic saints. Katharine rejected them all, then had lunch with McGinley and followed up with a letter to clarify what they hoped to receive from her: "I think of you as the one feminine poet we have who can be witty and wise on all the matters that concern home, children, education, marriage, life in general, and who, I hope, will continue to give us wise and witty comment on the contemporary world in general—not just on domestic matters." This did not go over well. McGinley accused Katharine of anti-Catholic bias and suspected that was the reason why the Whites never invited her to their house, despite the two women's long and heartfelt friendship. From Katharine's perspective, this was wildly untrue—she appended a long note about McGinley to her personal papers that listed all her Catholic friends and explained why Andy's health kept them from entertaining as much as McGinley assumed they did—but she admitted, "I ended up a complete failure as her editor." McGinley published only a handful of poems after this dust-up and then vanished from *The New Yorker*.

Clearly the baton was passing, and Katharine knew it, as when she encouraged Mackenzie to pursue Ann Petry, who in 1958 was likely the first Black female fiction writer to publish in *The New Yorker*, with her story "Has Anybody Seen Miss Dora Dean?" Katharine at least recognized that the magazine needed new voices, even if she herself did not have the right ear for them, and she thought Mackenzie should see Petry often and take her to lunch. The department stood on a sturdy foundation—Shawn at the top, with Maxwell, Henderson, Moss, Mackenzie, and Angell underneath him, plus three manuscript readers, and four secretaries—and did not seem to require an official head. The independent editors functioned well together, and in Katharine's view Thurber's critique of editor consciousness revealed a strength, not a flaw.

That August, Katharine and Andy traveled to Maine, where they were reunited with their new dachshund puppy, named Augie. It was nominally Katharine's vacation, but she spent it in a whirl of motion, as she wrote to Frances Gray Patton: "In this one month I've had to cram in being a farmer's wife (vegetables to freeze, jams, preserves to make etc. against the winter), a mother and grandmother (two young families and five grandchildren here in Brooklin), a gardener, the wife of a man who likes to sail and takes me along to tend the jib sheet, and a woman on vacation who likes to swim and sun." And on top of all that, she wrote, "[I field] daily driblets of work from the office, plus planning remodeling our kitchen, plus, this week, the nasty fact that I limbed up our beloved old car and we have had to try to find another we can bear to buy as a substitute." She nonetheless found time, that month, to write to her favorite, Mary McCarthy, to plead for more stories, citing a dire shortage of good work in the magazine's bank.

The Whites would return to New York again, but only to pack up their belongings. They had made the decision to give up the Turtle Bay town house for good, and from now on, once again, Katharine would work for *The New Yorker* from Maine.

Katharine was still suspended in the perennial state of not retiring, but she was giving up her temporary job as head of fiction and was stepping down into the part-time role that she had designed two years ago—this time officially. She would no longer correspond with authors or edit proofs; she would only read and vote on manuscripts and give her opinions directly to Shawn, much as she did in 1938 when she and Andy first moved to Maine. As she turned sixty-five that September, she spent months dividing furniture among her children's households, selling the rest, and boxing up hundreds of books. Her truncated new role at the magazine began on October 1, 1957, and the couple's lease ended on October 31. Shawn thought to celebrate her by throwing a party, but the guest list was confined to the fiction department lest it look like she was retiring from the magazine. Shawn played the piano; Katharine's newest hire, Bill Murray (son of Janet Flanner's partner, Natalia Danesi Murray), sang in an Irish baritone; and Tom Gorman accompanied them by drumming on the table.

The first thing Andy did when taking up full-time residence in Maine was to acquire new animals—two heifers, some steer, and a flock of sheep to add to the chickens and geese. He had given up writing for Notes and Comment back in 1955, when Katharine first tried to pull away from her duties, and now he only contributed newsbreaks and an occasional first-person essay under the heading Letter from the East (or South, if in Florida—the heading was designed to be flexible), his first signed column in *The New Yorker* at long last.

Katharine resumed the unglamorous work of a consulting editor. She read manuscripts for opinion, voted on everything the other editors sent her, and helped edit tricky manuscripts. For a time, the other editors used her name in their letters to her authors, saying they were only ventriloquizing her critiques, because clearly her judgment still carried authority; many of Katharine's authors continued to write to her about their work even though she firmly steered them toward their new editors and responded only with personal news. She did encourage the other editors to use her as a kind of "bad cop" if needed, and to remind her authors that she was reading their work if it would reassure them. In fact, at least one author felt that it was now time to part ways: Adrienne Rich declined to renew her first reading agreement, saying that her dealings with the magazine had become "impersonal," and this did not suit the new direction that her poetry was now taking. But in most other instances, the editors were easily able to smooth the transition, as when Roger had the unlucky task of rejecting two stories in a row by Nadine Gordimer but convinced her to send a third with a careful and detailed "personal-editorial" letter from one writer to another that demonstrated his admiration for her and his receptivity to her work. Katharine had a double purpose when looking over proofs with other editors' suggested changes: to see if she could add anything useful, and to monitor the progress of the new editors. She wasn't above re-editing her own son's working proof and sending it to Shawn if she thought it had been done incorrectly ("I am disturbed by the editing and can't help feeling that Roger is either scared of Donleavy or else that he has struck a big snag with him"), but she was just as liable to write Roger directly ("I have written Roger a detailed opinion of how I think he can save this story," she told Shawn about a piece Roger was about to reject, "and of how he can perhaps develop a series, with the author's help."

The other part of her job consisted in writing pages and pages of interoffice memos about everything from the rise of expenses in the fiction department to the paucity of manuscripts in her mailbag. As she had with Ross, she sent to Shawn her opinions about recently published issues, and she used her distance from the magazine to rove imaginatively around that bird's-eye view, which led her to make an "iconoclastic suggestion": *The New Yorker* should start to print a table of contents. She knew Shawn might well consider the idea "absurd," but she forged ahead with two different samples, and she argued at length for why the magazine needed it, because of its greatly expanded length, and because it "present[ed] a wealth of the best talent in writing" but "half of it [was] never spotted and read by people who would make a special point of not missing a certain piece of fiction if they could see the name Nabokov or Cheever or O'Connor or Welty or almost any other writer you can name in a Table of Contents." She agreed that part of *The New Yorker*'s distinctive tone came from the absence of an author's name after an article's title within the pages (all pieces were signed at the end), but she thought it was time to present those names at the front. Shawn disagreed, and he wouldn't institute a table of contents until 1969.

She was constantly worried about the dearth of fiction purchased for future issues, and she flogged the editors onward in their quest to discover new writers and to keep old writers loyal via the magazine's patented follow-up system. The part-time and long-distance arrangement had all the same pitfalls it had in 1938, but she would not let her voice go unheard and she would not let the magazine grow complacent in its perennial search for new talent. Despite—or perhaps, in part, because of—Mrs. White's worrying, *The New Yorker*'s fortunes expanded through the 1950s, through all the internal turmoil. Circulation soared and so did advertising revenue, leading *The Wall Street Journal* to report wonderingly on the phenomenon in an article called "Urbanity, Inc: How the New Yorker Wins Business Success Despite Air of Disdain," noting that the magazine was a "remarkably prosperous business enterprise" that was besting its competition with a 10 percent profit margin. *The New Yorker*, it seemed, was going to be just fine without Katharine.

40.

An editor is a person who knows more about writing than writers do but who has escaped the terrible desire to write.
—E. B. White, March 30, 1954

The very first thing Katharine did with her half retirement, as soon as the bustle of the holidays was over, was reinvent herself as a writer. She was poring over her stacks of seed and plant catalogs with the diligence of a scholar when she had an idea: why not treat them as literature? After all, she had arrayed before her such incredible variety, not just in the plants but in the way the nurseries addressed their customers. She had spent three decades attending closely to the nuances of narrative voice, and she could read more in these catalogs than the average gardener. The astonishing thing is that—after a lifetime of demurring whenever anyone suggested that she write anything more than her children's book reviews, inside a marriage built around deference to her husband's creative needs—upon finally reclaiming a bit of time in her daily schedule to design a life outside of the magazine, Katharine discovered an interior landscape of artistic freedom and immediately hit on an idea that was the perfect confluence of her interests and expertise. She would review that season's gardening catalogs against her own distinct aesthetic, and with a sardonic humor. Her innovation was simultaneously to take the catalogs seriously enough to convey useful information to her readers and at the same time to have fun with the stylistic eccentricities and personalities of this large, unexamined subculture.

She wrote to Shawn with the proposal on January 8, and by the end of the month she'd written "A Romp in the Catalogues," just as easy as that. Shawn immediately bought it, sent her a check that seemed quite large to her, and published it in the March 1, 1958, issue of *The New Yorker*. Katharine thought it might be the start of a series, naturally, and she was soon scrawling notes to Shawn with ideas for future essays. Shawn ran the unclassifiable essay, signed KSW, in the Books department. Katharine was once again a columnist for *The New Yorker*. She later wrote, "The two interests often seem to go together—a talent for the soil, a taste for writing and editorializing."

Studying Katharine's close reading of the catalogs reveals much about her narrative persona. She had clear opinions about trends in garden design, and those opinions precisely mapped onto her philosophy of editing. Take zinnias: "clean-cut, of interesting, positive form, with formal petals that are so neatly and cunningly put together, and with colors so subtle yet clear, that they have always been the delight of the still-life artist." Why, then, would the hybridists work so hard to develop zinnias that look like *other* flowers, like "great, shaggy chrysanthemums" or cactuses or asters or dahlias? "The Burpee people, who have always been slightly mad on the subject of marigolds," were now selling fluffy marigolds that themselves looked like chrysanthemums. Katharine the gardener liked plants that were good at being themselves, that showed their own integral principles with clarity and that were not trying to imitate other plants—exactly as she liked her authors.

Then she turned her eye toward the catalog writers, whom she saw as producing a kind of "regional literature." Mary McCarthy and Jean Stafford might have felt a bit slighted to read that Katharine considered these writers her "favorite authors" who "produce[d her] favorite reading matter." Chief among them was "the sage of White Flower Farm" in Connecticut, Amos Pettingill. Katharine was fairly certain the name was a pseudonym but she loved his distinctive "slightly testy" or "peppery" style, "his explicit cultural directions, his odd bits of gardening lore, and his sensible descriptions of what he ha[d] to sell," noting, "I have found that what he says will happen to a plant usually does happen to it." What Katharine did not know is that Amos Pettingill was William Harris, former writer for *Fortune* and husband to none other than Jane Grant, Harold Ross's ex-wife and one of the driving forces behind *The New Yorker*. Harris and Grant had founded White Flower Farm from their own expansive private garden in Litchfield in 1950, and had infused the $1 catalog and bimonthly plant bulletins with their insider knowledge of magazine culture. When Katharine responded to Amos Pettingill as a fitting subject for literary critical analysis, she was in truth responding to her own sensibility already transposed into the world of gardening. For years she would carry on a lively correspondence with "A. Pettingill," until finally in 1965 she would write to him in high embarrassment, having just learned his identity. "Don't blush; I was amused, not angered," he would respond. He wasn't going to break character until she did: "Sometimes I thought you did know and were playing it cool, at others I thought you didn't. So did Jane." He would continue urging her to come stay at White Flower Farm, as he had for years, even offering to send a car for her next time she was in New York, but Katharine would never make the trip.

Katharine's correspondence with Amos Pettingill was only a sliver of the immense body of letters she had been producing with nurserymen for years and which now expanded to include dozens and dozens of letters from readers. Her essay was an instant hit, among non-gardeners as well as those with a natural interest in the subject, and many people admired her entirely unsentimental approach to flowers, so different from everything else that came before her, such a new take on an ancient subject. The correspondence was a slightly mixed blessing for Katharine. She relished the exchange of information, and over the years she would learn about specialty nurseries or vintage garden books or friendly botanists from her network of correspondents. But she also immediately felt a sense of duty toward her readership. Her essays were a service, as were her children's book reviews, and though in the gardening writing she had far more freedom to explore her narrative voice, style must never get in the way of accurate and helpful information. And she was acutely aware of her own status as an amateur. She feared making mistakes and she feared misrepresenting herself. "I hate to sound a fraud," she wrote to Louise Bechtel, worried that Bechtel thought Katharine's garden must be grand and extensive. It really wasn't much, Katharine explained. "I keep saying I've grown this and that, because it is true, but it inevitably sounds like far more than it is. All we have is an old farmhouse set down on a lawn enclosed by picket fences, with borders of perennials along the fences and beds tucked in around the house and on our tiny terrace." (She wrote that she longed for a garden through which she could stroll.) This fear of imposture dogged Katharine. The letters in the mailbag told her how many people were influenced by her words, and that would add fuel over the years to her own innate scholarly bent. She'd awakened a hunger in a broad body of readers and now she must satisfy it. She was quite frequently too technical for the fact checkers at *The New Yorker* (she had to fight to keep them from incorrectly substituting the word "root" for "rhizome," for instance), but she felt she was nowhere near the level of the experts with whom she corresponded.

A month after her essay appeared, Katharine received a letter from a devout fan in South Carolina. Elizabeth Lawrence was herself a gardener and writer, the author of several books and a regular garden column in a Charlotte newspaper, and the two immediately felt a rapport; they began a correspondence that would last until death. Lawrence, too, abhorred the sentimental, and wrote to Katharine of her displeasure when another gardening woman whom she'd never met signed her letter "with love." They both detested the conflation of gardening with gender, the way it signaled a certain kind of female sensibility, approachable and dilettantish. Katharine vented to Lawrence all the too-sharp criticisms and specialist questions that she couldn't include in her column. Lawrence became Katharine's most reliable garden correspondent, but there were several others with whom she conducted years-long conversations that branched out from and fed into her column, including Charles Alldredge, who was Senator Estes Kefauver's speechwriter, and *New Yorker* short-story writer Ambrose Flack.

To those closest to her, Katharine's newfound role as a garden writer was miraculous and surprising. Andy confessed that he "had never thought of her as an authority on horticultural matters" and he "did not regard her as a scientist." To Roger, her competence and professional knowledge seemed almost instantaneous. He'd watched her garden since the Whites bought the Maine farmhouse, but when he opened that March issue of *The New Yorker*, he discovered that she was "suddenly at a very high level of garden writing," and to him her ascension was "like going to the major leagues in your second season."

Katharine found it easy, that spring, to decline Shawn's request that she take up the children's book review for the 1958 holiday issue. It was just too boring now that she had this self-generated writing project, she told him, and the task should go to a younger writer with more enthusiasm (she also knew that some of her opinions—for instance, that Dr. Seuss's work had "degenerated awfully" and that school primers should be boring so that children will reach for more exciting books on their own—would be unwelcome to the younger generation of parents). But she did not find it easy to write. She was plagued by a new physical complaint, a recurring bladder problem that required trips to a urologist in New York and the looming threat of another surgery at Harkness Pavilion. She found it impossible to garden, because her doctor told her she must stay off her feet. The very year when she had dared plan ambitiously to see her garden through all four seasons and "had dreams of glory and of success," she was reduced to pointing at beds and giving instructions to Henry Allen in the leftover time he could devote to flowers when his farm chores were completed.

But she would garden indoors with houseplants and dozens of forced bulbs, and she would write, and in this sphere her ambitions continued to grow. On January 1, 1959, she started a garden journal: handwritten, lengthy, detailed, peppered with news of the household, an exhaustive record of the enormous labor she expended on caring for plants, experimenting with new varieties and recording the results to report back to nurseries and her other correspondents, and doing battle with lice and mites and other diseases. And that January she wrote a second garden catalog essay, "Floricordially Yours." When it appeared that March, it bore a new column heading of Katharine's invention—Onward and Upward with the Garden—and it was signed with her full name. Katharine begins with a simple yet astonishing statement of aesthetic principle:

As I write, snow is falling outside my Maine window, and indoors all around me half a hundred garden catalogues are in bloom. I am an addict of this form of literature and a student of the strange personalities of the authors who lead me on. Gentle and friendly, eccentric or wildly vivid, occasionally contentious and even angry, every one of them can persuade me, because he knows what he is saying and says it with enthusiasm. Reading this literature is unlike any other reading experience. Too much goes on at once. I read for news, for driblets of knowledge, for aesthetic pleasure, and at the same time I am planning the future, and so I read in dream.

This is nothing less than a reader's phenomenology, the navigation and mapping of that interior world that opens up when a mind meets a page, and it results not from her expertise as an editor with a critical approach to literary fiction and poetry, but from her intense amateur engagement with a literature that is meant to be *used*, put into practice, brought out from that interiority. The catalogs induce in Katharine a half-pleasant, half-maddening "state of suspended animation," as she dreams of the growing season, a restless state that, in a later column, she would call "the penalty one pays for the life of culture." That gives a clue to the impetus behind Katharine's writing: the urge to participate, to *do* something with her reading when placing her seed orders was not enough.

Her mind ran ahead, and so did her pencil. In 1959, she published her second essay of the year, explaining to her readers that she could not sit contentedly on the terrace that August but must dash into the house to care for the houseplants and pore over a different set of catalogs to order the bulbs that she would plant in October and November. It seemed as if she might publish her garden column biannually—certainly she had enough to say. The only trouble was a complete lack of time to work. That summer, while Allene was in the hospital to give birth to her third child, John Shepley White, Katharine cared for Steven and Martha with the help of Roger's sixteen-year-old daughter, Callie. Then Andy came down with a nine-week-long stomachache that landed him in Harkness for over a week. "The tests proved it was the same old thing—nerves," she

THE EDITOR BECOMES A WRITER

told a friend, "and we came back and I rushed at the piece before Roger and his family got here at the end of the month for a visit." But she could not finish in time, and she wrote during a five-day stretch when the crowded family was housebound by a storm. Katharine was unhappy about her essay, and when Roger told her that he couldn't read it all the way to the end, her dissatisfaction was confirmed.

Nonetheless, "Before the Frost" ran in the September 26 *New Yorker*, and for the first time, both Whites had an essay—both signed—in the same issue; Andy published "Khrushchev and I," a casual prompted by an insipid newspaper report of Khrushchev's visit to the United States, in which Andy marvels at the many surprising similarities between the two men: Khrushchev is a devoted family man, and Andy can barely believe it because "the phrase that pops into people's heads when they think of [Andy] is 'devoted family man'"; Khrushchev is committed to improving American and Soviet relations, and Andy can't contain his astonishment: "Khrush and I both." It was, he exclaimed, what he was doing right that very minute as he wrote the piece. There's no measuring what Andy's essay produced in the way of marginally improved international relations, but "Before the Frost" produced four hundred letters to Oregon Bulb Farmers after Katharine deemed its owner, Jan de Graaff, "a name to conjure with."

Katharine continued to negotiate her relationship with *The New Yorker*. She wanted to pull away, yet she wanted to stay useful and pitch in with substantive work. Mostly that entailed codifying the editorial practices she had followed for years. She wrote a long memo on the magazine's follow-up system and its internal classification of writers (A list meant "in fairly constant touch," B list meant every six months, C list every twelve, D list was inactive, and P list meant a writer whose work hadn't yet been purchased but who showed potential). She read over the shoulder of the manuscript reader who was assigned to scout writers from other magazines and annual story collections, adding her notes on the stories as well as on the reader's judgments. She stepped back into the role of poetry editor for a few months when Howard Moss took a leave of absence, giving her the pleasure of writing to Louise Bogan again. But mostly she remained in the background, surveying the magazine from afar.

It was from that distance that she sustained the latest assault from Jim Thurber. His book, *The Years with Ross*, was published in the summer of 1959, and it struck Katharine as a disaster and a betrayal. She got out her pencil. First she annotated her copy of the book, then she erased her own words and rewrote them, editing her thoughts as she read: "Never." "Untrue." "Rubbish!" "Impossible," followed by a lengthy correction (and very occasionally, "This is true"). She objected to Thurber's accounts of office politics and procedures, frequently noting that he could not know such things; after his disastrous stint as a Ross "jesus" in 1927, he hadn't spent much time in the office, though the book makes him sound like he'd been in every room. She even more strenuously objected to Thurber's portrait of Ross as an uncultured, naïve bumpkin. In the end, she annotated close to half of the pages in Thurber's book.

She also wrote to longtime colleagues, offering her opinion on Thurber's book as part of a private and communal shoring up of the magazine's legacy that everyone who'd known Ross engaged in over many rounds of letters. Rebecca West published a review in the London *Times* (laying into Thurber for portraying Ross as "a combination of Bottom the Weaver and a Siberian shaman, acting in a Western film written by Kafka"), which Katharine thought was the best critical opinion, and when she wrote to West to tell her so, West was enormously relieved. Thurber's book was a commercial success and had even been chosen as a Book-of-the-Month Club selection, which made West feel as if she'd gone mad, but Katharine's letter and others reassured her that the true history of the magazine was still there for the telling. But who would correct the record?

Katharine tried, but only halfheartedly, because she knew she could do nothing from within the magazine. A positive review of the book that appeared in *The Nation* seemed a decent pretext, so she dashed off a letter to the editor suggesting that, though a dead man can't be libeled, the magazine should not have amplified Thurber's "venomous attack" on Ross, with its "grossly untrue statements" about his integrity. She countered the view of Ross as an ignorant man by imagining how he would have edited the "dubious locutions" of the *Nation* review. But she sent the letter only to Shawn, telling him, "[It was] just to get it off my mind but of course it can't be sent. I enclose it for your amusement. Pl. throw it away." She and Andy tried to move past the unpleasantness, but Thurber made that difficult. He and Helen Thurber were, as Katharine reported to Shawn, writing to Andy nearly every day "with some sort of patronizing remark or mild dig (or worse than mild) at Andy," their misguided attempt to elicit a "loving answer" from Andy that testified to his esteem of Thurber's book, but also an expression of Thurber's perennial jealousy whenever Andy published a book, in this case *The Elements of Style*. Andy wearily joked that he was saving up material to write *My Years with My Years with Ross*. Neither Katharine nor Andy would publicly counter Thurber's portrait of Ross, but in the years to come, when not one but two biographers of Thurber came knocking at the North Brooklin farmhouse door, Katharine would not hold back. "Sooner or later Jim seemed, because of his deep antipathy to women, to attack his friends' wives when he was drinking," she would tell one biographer, Harrison Kinney, and she would give him what she considered the key to unlock Thurber's twisted relationship to writing: he "embroider[ed] and heighten[ed]" so well that he couldn't stop himself, and what worked for humorous effect in casuals like "My Life and Hard Times" was disastrous when it came to the actual history of the magazine. She made sure to save her annotated copy of *The Years with Ross* for posterity.

As she worked in the background, Katharine's letter of resignation—from the dreadful autumn of 1955 before Lobrano's death—was still metaphorically on Shawn's desk, and the two periodically revised the timing of her eventual retirement. Two days before the end of 1959, Katharine wrote to say: not yet. She had a very personal reason for wanting to stay on the payroll. That autumn, Elsie collapsed in her home in Piermont, New York, just precisely as she finished her biography of Robert Frost. Katharine rushed down on November 2 to be near her and ended up staying until Thanksgiving. Elsie suffered from heart trouble but her heart was too weak for the doctors to attempt surgery; she also had gallstones, anemia, and edema in the lungs. She resisted going to the hospital as long as she could, and when she finally was admitted, she stayed until almost Christmas. Even then Elsie couldn't return to her home, and so she checked into the Cosmopolitan Club in the city for a few weeks. Katharine paid the $10,000 hospital bill, and she told Shawn that she needed to work so she could afford to add a small wing to Elsie's rented house so her sister could live on one story, plus a full-time companion would have to be found. Katharine couldn't really know if these plans would come to fruition—"Elsie, when sick, is as stubborn as a mule, and she hates to take help or advice from her younger sister or even from her doctor"—but she postponed her retirement for a year on the strength of them.

In truth, there was another reason why Katharine wanted to remain at her post. She was then deep in the middle of editing the third collection of *New Yorker* short stories, and she was congenitally incapable of walking away until it was completed. As before, the collection was, as she called it, "a compromise selection, to suit the taste of five editors." As before, Katharine worked with the business office to determine the size and potential price of the book, and worked with the fiction department editors to collect and collate lists of stories. They agreed upon the writers who must be represented, and they brainstormed the stories that each could remember from the last decade with ease and pleasure. Then Katharine began tabulating. Simon & Schuster had given them a generous budget of 350,000 words, what would eventually number 778 pages of stories, and this allowed her to include six stories that were over 10,000 words long, including ones by McCarthy, Welty, Tucci, West, and Roth, and J. D. Salinger's "Raise High the Roof Beam, Carpenters" at 22,000 words. As before, the collection ran with only a short foreword signed by "The Editors," and as in the earlier collections they afforded themselves the privilege of defining the genre capaciously: "Narrative writers of the present generation have so often drawn upon the material of their own past that there is no longer a hard and fast line between fiction and autobiography, but we have included here autobiographical stories only where the facts are dealt with freely and imaginatively—in short, where the method used is the method of fiction, not of pure reminiscence." E. B. White was not included, but Roger Angell was, for the story that reworked his memory of the summer he and Nancy were stationed with a French family and their donkey while his parents went their separate ways. Katharine finished the book, *Stories from "The New*

Yorker" 1950–1960, in the spring, and it would be published that winter in time for the holiday.

This was turning into a year of books. Katharine flatly turned down two offers to edit books, even as she was putting the finishing touches on the story collection. The first was from Coward McCann, who wanted her and Andy to revise and reissue *A Subtreasury of American Humor* on the occasion of its twentieth anniversary, and the second was a proposal, out of the blue, from Looking Glass Library, a small publisher headed by Jason Epstein, Celia Carroll, and Edward Gorey, to edit a children's book of humor.

Katharine had far more ambitious plans for her next book. It would *not* be an edited collection of other people's writing. She envisioned a book authored under her own name, a book arising from her garden column, a book that would use those essays as source material for something much larger in scope and yet more personal. She outlined a book with thirteen chapters divided into four sections: 4 Hawthorn Street in Brookline, her childhood home; 82 Bridge Street in Northampton, home of her Sergeant relatives; places where she had picked wildflowers, including the Boston suburbs; and Woodstock, Connecticut, Aunt Poo's home before her move to Japan. The book would begin with a short introduction to establish the "modest background" of her Maine borders and beds in their telescoped growing season. "Place myself as an amateur with no special horticultural knowledge but with prejudices and preferences, and as a reader of catalogues." She listed other possible themes, such as "[her] imagined Florida garden." She edited this outline. Then she edited a third draft.

The idea coalesced in her mind as the year progressed, and by the autumn she started to mention it offhandedly in letters to Shawn and others. And then her fourth *New Yorker* column, "The Changing Rose, the Enduring Cabbage," attracted a letter that stood out from the pack. Alfred Knopf had begun sending her fan mail after her second essay. He was, in addition to being a colleague whom she knew professionally, an avid gardener at his house in Purchase, New York, and someone with an ear for well-turned and effective prose. Now he found her essay on flower fragrance to be "another fascinating article out of what would superficially appear to be most unpromising material." If Katharine should like to work them into a book, Knopf wrote, he would like to publish it.

Katharine and Knopf made a lunch date at the Four Seasons in the Seagram Building. Katharine didn't know at the time, but Knopf was then in the midst of an event of great professional and indeed industry-wide importance, the merger of Random House and Knopf. Nonetheless, he made time for this speculative volume of work, what Katharine called "this mythical, far-distant book." Her vision for the book was an uncategorizable blend of memoir, aesthetic theory, and commentary on contemporary garden trends. She had no title, no snappy, three-sentence description, just a strong narrative voice and enormous authority. Knopf was enthusiastic, and he continued writing to her with suggestions for nurseries and catalogs and invitations to discuss the book whenever she had the time.

How much was Katharine's conception of herself as an author influenced by Elsie's new book, *Robert Frost: The Trial by Existence*, just published in the summer of 1960? Probably not all that much—Katharine, after all, had other influences much closer to hand—but it was certainly a triumph for Elsie, who had begun the book in the 1940s, when Frost had granted his permission, and had worked full-time on it for over six years. A *New York Times* feature writer visited Elsie at her stone cottage in Piermont, "a cozy, fairy-tale retreat," and Elsie made a point to mention that she was no professional biographer and wrote about Frost as a friend and lover of poetry. She had included primary documents within the pages of the biography, such as Frost's letters, unpublished poems, reviews of his work, pages from his notebooks, even old Christmas cards, and that led several critics to dismiss the book as "little more than an affectionate scrapbook" or the work of someone with a "tendency to idolize her eminent friend." But just as many of them read it as "a warm, loving and sensitive biography of Robert Frost, written with authority from a long and rich personal acquaintance with the poet" and "a strikingly frank biography—one which, though devoted to its subject, creates no illusion of shielding it . . . Miss Sergeant's chronicle carries an authority no previous account has had."

Katharine's opinion of the book, naturally, went unrecorded, but she recognized it as an achievement deserving celebration, especially given Elsie's continual health battles—about that, Katharine could be endlessly sympathetic. The same month that Elsie's book was published, both sisters were honored by their alma mater. To celebrate its seventy-fifth year, Bryn Mawr drew up a list of seventy-five notable alumnae, to whom it would give Citations for Distinguished Service at a ceremony on June 4, 1960. (What Katharine didn't know at the time was that Elsie was actually the seventy-sixth alumna on the list; she hadn't originally been included, but her friend Hetty Goldman, an archaeologist and professor at Princeton's Institute for Advanced Study, had successfully campaigned to add Elsie to the roster.) The college was worried about some of its older and frailer alumnae, so they asked Katharine if she would travel from Maine down to New York to escort Elsie and Marianne Moore to West Philadelphia. Katharine agreed, though she found the idea of accepting an award quite tedious. She and Moore commiserated; Moore wrote that honors "are a problem—if not actually dastardly. They waste one's brain and vitality, extorting the utmost ingenuity, and a politeness absolutely alien under coercion." Ironically, it was the younger woman whose vitality was not up to the occasion; Katharine's recurring urological condition, complete with a fever of 104 degrees, meant that she needed to stay home. Nancy and her daughter Kitty traveled from nearby Easton to escort Elsie and Moore, and Nancy reported to her mother that the two writers were so energetic she could barely keep up with them.

Two awards arrived in the mail that month. The American Academy of Arts and Letters awarded Andy the Gold Medal for Essays and Criticism, given once every five years. He declined to attend the ceremony in New York, nor did he know quite what to do with the actual medal, which he said made him "uneasy." When Katharine's Bryn Mawr citation arrived in the mail, she too might have felt uneasy, or even angry, because the certificate omitted any mention of her writing for *The New Yorker* or her editing of *A Subtreasury of American Humor* and the three *New Yorker* short-story collections; it devoted one of its three paragraphs to an essay that E. B. White wrote about being married to a Bryn Mawr graduate. It was arguably a far greater honor to read the reviews, later that same year, of the third short-story collection when it was published in the early winter. She felt especially gratified by the review in the *New York Herald Tribune* because, in her words, "it so well demolished the old cliché about New Yorker short stories being all alike." The review goes out of its way to praise "the kind of editorial independence that is one with integrity," noting the mix of well-established and new names among its authors and the variety "in intention, mood and technique." It was as if the reviewer had seen right into her editorial soul.

By contrast, she wrote two furious letters to Shawn when she read the *New York Times* review, published on the front page of its Sunday book section. She called the assessment "pretty hard to take" and lashed the reviewer, Arthur Mizener, a professor of English at Cornell, for what she saw as cowardly criticism, "full of praise along with the scared retractions of this praise." The review maps out two distinct literary worlds, urban culture and the intellectual scene, and to Katharine, the reviewer was so beholden to "higher culture" that he was terrified he would lose credibility if he praised *The New Yorker*, which he relegated to the trash heap of "urban culture." She listed for Shawn's benefit all the stories in the collection that were not about "urban ways and mores," as well as the stories that were avant-garde, singling out Elizabeth Bishop's "In the Village" as an example of a piece that was both stylistically innovative and a realistic expression of its subject. "Ah, well," she concluded her letter. "One thing has come to me. After January 1st I'll be able to defend the New Yorker for the first time in 35½ years!" But Katharine's take on this review was a revealing misprision. Mizener sought not to place *The New Yorker* on one side of that culture divide but to praise the magazine for its ability to straddle it, to consistently attract stories of high quality precisely because of its criteria—he used the unfortunate word "limitation"—for stories that focused on urban, middle-class life told in "the tone of someone perfectly aware of the discouragement, the evils, the ironies of our world and ourselves, who is nevertheless prepared to deal with that world and to do so without shouting." Mizener directly criticized the knee-jerk rejection of *The New Yorker* by the too-defensive denizens of urban culture: "To get elbow room to be intellectuals, they have to fight free of that world" so vigorously that "almost by definition a good story is for them one that has been rejected by a big magazine and has then appeared in a little one." He argued that the third story collection demonstrated that *The New Yorker* was "the best literary magazine in the English-speaking world, big or little," surely words to gladden its editor, so why couldn't she hear them? Katharine's loyalty to the magazine was fierce and it made her overly defensive, and also, perhaps, ambivalent about freeing herself after so long within the magazine's ramparts.

The year was winding down and so was her career as magazine editor. Katharine spent the days before Christmas poring over her lists of writers and making detailed notes for the other editors about each contributor's productivity habits, recent hits and misses with submissions, amenability to editing, and need for follow-up. She mentioned personal issues that might prevent them from writing—Louise Bogan's daughter's husband had just died, Mary McCarthy had just divorced her third husband—and counseled the editors to remain steadfast in their encouragement. The notes are a glimpse into the dense networks that Katharine had woven over the years, as when she informed the *New Yorker* editors that the playwright George Kaufman was ill but had been sending "wistful messages" about publishing in *The New Yorker* through the woman who shampooed her hair and his. She didn't want any author to be left behind, for instance Philip Roth, for though she knew Shawn didn't care for his work, she herself thought he had a "potentially new background in that New Jersey suburban wealth[y] Jewish set of whom he sometimes writes." This was the heart of what she hoped to impart to the editorial team she was leaving behind: "I feel the newer editors give up too soon when a contributor has a period of writing badly. I can't help remembering the long years when Nancy Hale contributed such terrible stuff while she was in her period of breakdowns and when I kept in touch with her constantly encouraging and rejecting with gentleness. It pays off, and she has told me it did with her, in my case—sort of kept her going until Maxwell took over when she again began to be good." For Katharine's experience to mean anything, the other editors would need to pick up all the strands of this remarkable network and keep tugging on writers to elicit more stories, more essays, more reminiscences, more poems.

But now it was time for Katharine to retire, and she did with almost
no fanfare, embedded with her family in the old farmhouse in the middle of a Maine winter. Roger wrote a scant paragraph on the matter in
his letter to her that Christmas, merely gesturing toward the milestone:
"I guess I'm not quite the person to sum up all the reasons why this is
such a tremendously sad change for The New Yorker, but I can say what
I know to be true, which is that you will be terribly missed." He mentioned that Shawn had made no announcement of her retirement at the
magazine's offices and that he only knew it from her own letters. How
did Katharine take that news? "I must say she looks a little as though she
were entering Leavenworth," Andy wrote to a friend. But as Katharine
herself wrote to Louise Seaman Bechtel, the point of her retirement was
freedom, artistic and otherwise. She would "have more time for [her]
family and for [her] own writing—the New Yorker pieces and the book
[she] hope[d] to base on them."

Part VIII

Retirement
on *New Yorker*
Stationery

(1961–1977)

41.

Two days after the official end to her *New Yorker* life, Katharine was sitting at her desk on the third of January when dizziness suddenly struck her so forcefully she keeled over onto her papers. Her right arm went completely numb and she could not lift it for five minutes. If a novelist had given those particular afflictions to a fictional editor upon her retirement—her mind and her writing hand rendered useless—her real-life editor would have crossed it out as far too sodden with symbolism to be believed. But real life has a way of evading editors. The theme of these years might be best summed up by a phrase Katharine used a decade later when looking back at this time: "remarkable disasters," a series of unconnected health calamities dealt to her, one after another.

She and Andy thought she'd had a small stroke, but their local doctor ruled that out. He recommended that she travel down to New York for neurological tests, so at the beginning of February, in fear and suspense, Andy drove her to Harkness Pavilion. The provisional verdict was that her brain held a scar, embolism, or beginning tumor. She was prescribed Dilantin and phenobarbital and told to return in a few months. The Whites traveled on to Sarasota, Florida, without first returning to their farmhouse, while Katharine was in a daze from the medication. Her doctors sent them off with the hope that if it was a tumor, it was a slow-growing one that could perhaps be reabsorbed. So they waited.

And Katharine wrote. That was the other half of a note that sounded with unmistakable clarity in the beginning of January: she would be visited with extreme health troubles, but she would continue to work at the utmost limit of her energy. Her assistance with Andy's correspondence would have to be greatly curtailed, but she could still write to Shawn on her pet themes, and she followed up her Christmastime memo with another long one on "the seeking out of possible topnotch writers" by soliciting work and spending extra time to "save manuscripts" otherwise headed for rejection.

And she could still forge ahead with her next gardening essay. Even while her head and back pained her, even while she was packing for New York and Florida, she wrote. Even while she lay in her hospital in Harkness for a solid week after a lumbar puncture, head aching each time she lifted it, her sight gladdened by a bouquet that Elizabeth Lawrence had picked from her own garden in Charlotte, she managed to finish her sixth essay, which *The New Yorker* published that March.

"Green Thoughts in Green Shade" darkens the determined cheerfulness Katharine projects as a gardener in winter. She begins by conjuring up the water lilies of her childhood, the ones that she and her sisters picked from the canoe on Chocorua Lake, and then she imaginatively draws them forward into the future by speculating on the possibility of growing water lilies in the "lilyless" and "heart-shaped" pond in her Maine pasture, if she plants them in a sunken box in the very center, where the cows can't reach them. That image of the marooned lilies lingers in the mind as she pages through the catalog offerings for watery plants, until she punctuates the discussion: "From December to March, there are for many of us three gardens—the garden outdoors, the garden of pots and bowls in the house, and the garden of the mind's eye." This, of course, is what she had been writing about from the very beginning, the garden that existed when she thought it into being by browsing catalogs or reading antique garden manuals, and this year, it was helping her withstand the ordeal of hospitals and the anxiety of an imminent diagnosis. Despite her invalidism, she conveys enormous intellectual vigor. In a previous column, she had praised "broken" or striped tulips, but she subsequently discovered that their streaking was caused by a virus, and now in this column she writes about her "investigation and correspondence" with a government authority at the Department of Agriculture, a horticulturalist at Swarthmore, two Dutch growers, and finally a Dutch researcher, in order to give her readers accurate information about which bulbs to plant. She promises her readers that she will take up the subject of roses in her autumn column—but she would not be able to keep that promise.

Indeed, sitting at a desk in her Sarasota home was so difficult that she truly feared she'd never be able to write another word for *The New Yorker*. Alfred Knopf wrote to her after reading "Green Thoughts in a Green Shade" to say that he was glad her "book" was progressing, and Katharine felt compelled to tell him that the book on which she'd planned to spend the next decade was probably never going to be written.

One small bright spot that year came in May, when the Pulitzer Prizes were announced. Two of Katharine's authors were nominated for the poetry award, and though many thought that it should have gone to Ogden Nash, the prize went to Phyllis McGinley for her volume from Viking Press called *Times Three: Selected Verse from Three Decades*. The prize jury clearly wanted to recognize light verse, which came as something of a surprise to poets and readers, given that the previous year they'd awarded the prize to W. D. Snodgrass (also a *New Yorker* poet) for *Heart's Needle*, a volume that helped inaugurate confessional poetry, best practiced by Snodgrass's teacher, Robert Lowell. McGinley fully appreciated the exceptionality of her award and told Nash she believed that she'd won the Pulitzer on behalf of him, Dorothy Parker, Morris Bishop, and E. B. White—all *New Yorker* light verse masters.

In April, Katharine and Andy traveled by train back up to Harkness so she could spend another week there, undergoing more tests, and then they continued north to the farmhouse. Once again, the tests revealed nothing conclusive, though Katharine's condition worsened. Her time in New York, coming as it did after a particularly bad spell, prompted Nancy to take what she felt was an extraordinary step: she contacted Katharine's Manhattan physician, Dr. Dana Atchley, behind Katharine's back to ask him to meet with her and Roger. Nancy praised her mother's resilience, saying that she was impressed at how Katharine was squarely adjusting to a life that would never again be free of symptoms and medications. But she was worried that Andy would be wholly unable to care for her, and *that* would sink Katharine's spirits even more than her own illnesses. "She has times of considerable depression,"

Nancy wrote, "obviously intensified by Andy's reaction to her illness, in which he apparently mimics her symptoms, or is unable or unwilling to face the reality of the situation." She wanted to discuss with Dr. Atchley the possibility of making significant changes to the Whites' lifestyle.

Katharine spent most of the summer in bed with severe headaches, with no alterations to the farmhouse routine. Even her garden could provide no solace because for a short while she couldn't even bend down to pick flowers, much less wield a spade. She made plans to scale back her beds, and a very anxious and overworked Andy decided to sell the cattle ("There goes my source of manure," she wrote). As if that weren't enough, in July Katharine was rushed to the Blue Hill hospital for an emergency appendectomy and a fifteen-day hospital stay.

Finally, in September, when she returned to Harkness for a third time, she was given a test that she arguably should have received back in January, an angiogram, which revealed an occluded carotid artery, a potentially fatal condition but with a far better prognosis than a tumor. In October, she traveled to Rochester, New York, for a surgery with Dr. Charles Granville Rob, a pioneer of the technique to repair damaged blood vessels who had long treated Winston Churchill before being recruited to the United States. Nancy met Andy there to support him during the surgery. Katharine later said Dr. Rob "slit [her] throat" to remove the obstruction and she went into shock on the operating table and almost died, but the surgery was a complete success in the end.

While she was recuperating in the hospital, the Whites received news of James Thurber's death at the age of sixty-six. His last year had brutalized him. He suffered a series of small strokes but refused to see a neurologist, and his wife and friends were reduced to watching helplessly as he crashed into furniture and raged about in depression. He sent an unhinged five-page letter about Katharine to Roger when he heard of her illness, dredging up past conversations (including two occasions when—he said—Katharine burst into tears at him), analyzing a dream Katharine had recounted to him several years previously, blaming everything on the spring when she, Thurber, Andy, and Ernest were locked in romantic indecision, and bragging about his total recall and his mental telepathy, on the basis of which he was able firmly to diagnose Katharine's ailment as psychosomatic. Several months later, Thurber collapsed and was found in a pool of blood and rushed to the hospital, where surgeons successfully removed a hematoma from his brain. But he had lost much function and was confined to the hospital for what would be four mostly unresponsive weeks, until he lapsed into a deep coma and died on November 2, 1961. Because of Katharine's health, the Whites were not able to join the steady crowd of visitors to his bedside before his death. It was too late to repair the rupture that had riven their relationship.

Indeed, so bitter and distrustful was Thurber toward *The New Yorker* that a few months before his death he wrote to the magazine's lawyer to say that he feared what the magazine might publish for his obituary, and to request that the magazine simply reprint "The Secret Life of Walter Mitty" with a note saying this was the author's last request. Nobody took this seriously. William Shawn wrote an extravagant tribute to Thurber's influence on the magazine, holding nothing back, and then he turned the obituary over to Andy, who was no less fulsome in praise of his friend. "The whole world knows what a funny man he was, but you had to sit next to him day after day to understand the extravagance of his clowning, the wildness and subtlety of his thinking, and the intensity of his interest in others and his sympathy for their dilemmas." Andy noted that his favorite Thurber book—which worked as "his own best obituary notice"—was *The Last Flower*, for its expression of "his faith in the renewal of life, his feeling for the beauty and fragility of life on earth." *The New Yorker* did right by one of its own.

Katharine moved through her complicated grief and the long recovery from her surgery, and after another few months in Florida, she was again able to write an Onward and Upward with the Garden column. *The New Yorker* moved up her deadline by a month in order to make room for a new series of articles on pesticides by Rachel Carson—the first anyone would read of *Silent Spring*—which Katharine read in proof and excitedly discussed with gardening friends. Could some of her symptoms be explained not by her recovery from surgery but by DDT? Elizabeth Lawrence reported, only half in jest, that she had irritability, an aversion to work, a mental fog, and joint pains, and Katharine admitted to the same.

She wrote her new column not in joy and proficiency but in exhaustion. "It was a dreadful effort to get anything down on paper and I persisted, perhaps only to prove to myself that I could," she wrote to Lawrence. She got the jump on Carson by mourning the elms and bees and doves and robins who were dying "thanks to poison sprays." That would be the last column she would file for several years.

Katharine's birthday took place under the shadow of a new worry, one that sent her back into her own dark memories. That summer, Roger had announced his separation from Evelyn, a development that came just after a career breakthrough, the idea to write about baseball (it was a slow build from October 1961, when he first thought of starting a monthly sports column, to April 1962, when his first spring training essay was published). Katharine worried about all four of the Angells, but she deliberately offered no advice or pressure for a specific outcome, telling Roger only that he had seemed so much calmer upon the decision, as if he'd experienced "a great spiritual release."

But despite Katharine's best efforts to be steadfast for her son, over the next few months, the letters between her and Roger grew thick with negative emotions tangled around the nexus of anxiety, divorce, and money. Roger hated that his mother partially blamed herself for the end of his marriage. She simply couldn't help looking back to her own divorce and noting the parallels, as well as the discrepancies. The glaring difference to her was the relative ease with which she had established her own household as a working woman with a healthy paycheck, compared to Roger's struggle to afford alimony for Evelyn, who did not work. But could she please stop holding herself responsible by virtue of that long-ago decision to leave his father, Roger pleaded. "Neither you nor I believe in that kind of deterministic view (which utterly destroys my belief that I have been making my own life, good or bad, all this time)."

For her part, Katharine hated that she couldn't give him as much money as he needed, an issue inescapably bound up with her health. Nancy and Roger had each recently told her that they wished she could settle a substantial sum of money on them now, rather than leave it to them in her will. Katharine wrote at length about why she simply could not. She had been supporting elderly relatives with little income since the 1920s, she told Roger, and she didn't wish that on him. She was acutely aware that her health problems could lead to a stroke that would paralyze her, a fact she could face without self-pity. She'd paid for Elsie's recent hospitalization and might be called upon for more. Last year, a fourth of her income (an $11,000 pension, the last of some *New Yorker* back pay, and inheritances of $800 or $900 a year) had gone to relatives and a fourth had gone to doctors. And another thing she would voice to Roger, and Roger only: Andy's doctors told her that his mental health could become unstable enough to require hospitalization. She also revealed that she constantly toyed with the idea of selling the farmhouse, only to conclude, again and again, that it was cheaper than a New York apartment. If only they could access Andy's income from *Charlotte's Web*, still locked away from the IRS.

She did give Roger money for Callie and Alice's private school tuition, and she gave him $1,000 on his birthday to help with his new apartment and furnishings, along with another letter, separate from the dreary chronicle of financial details but included in the same envelope, telling him how proud she was of the way he'd handled his separation from Evelyn.

But Roger heard only her worry. He was desperate to reorient her attitude, not to mention his own relationship to her, so that he could tell the truth of his life without worrying that it would plunge her into depression or guilt. He needed her, and yet he was nervous to lean on her. Each one of his letters over the next year would sound the same theme: "I can't help wishing at times like that that you could force yourself or train yourself somehow to be a little more relaxed about the inevitable minor crises that life brings along." He knew very well, he told her, that it wasn't effective to tell someone just to not worry. But he couldn't help underscoring something that perhaps Katharine *could* reform: "this apparent pattern of exchanged anxiety and resultant sickness," that when Andy was low, she "sometimes appear[ed] to match or even to exceed his own worry or state of nerves, and that [might] compound the whole business."

What neither of them noticed was that Roger needed but was loath to depend on Katharine in the same way that she needed but was loath to depend on Andy. In fact, Roger might not have fully appreciated what lay behind the monologues he so dearly wished to silence. He would use the phrases "their exchanged symptoms," "joint hypochondria," and "their amazing sick-off" in an essay about Andy published in *The New Yorker* in 2006 and reprinted in *Let Me Finish*. But in September 1962, Katharine spelled it out for him: she talked endlessly about her health to Roger because she had no one else. She gave him an excruciating update on her all-too-real circulatory problems and then she explained *why* she was going into such detail. She said that she was scared for herself but could not confide in Andy in case his worry for her would tank his own mental health. She needed Andy to be strong, but she needed to reveal her own vulnerability. Roger was, to an extent he might not have realized, her safety valve and her backstop, even as his own life was coming apart for him to reassemble.

The following January in 1963, the Whites left for Sarasota as usual, but Katharine had trouble walking, and they feared she had a blocked femoral artery. Andy wrote to Roger that though she'd brought all her garden catalogs and books with her, she wasn't writing, and her spirit was "badly cracked" if not quite broken. "It is the saddest thing I have ever had to live with, to see her this way, after having done so much for so many, and now unable to do a small thing for herself. I sometimes think I would give everything I own for one garden piece, one book, and one restored lady." But he could hardly help, as he was going through a nervous breakdown of his own and had sworn off writing. The only thing that got them through was baseball, and Katharine was cheered by hobbling to her seat to watch games in the sun.

In fact, she did so much gentle walking in Florida that she restored some function to her leg and was able to avoid another surgery. The Whites returned to North Brooklin and on Independence Day, they received a phone call, which Katharine answered in the little telephone closet at the back of her office. It was Western Union with a telegram for Andy that she dutifully transcribed. But it was quite long, and after the first thirty or forty words, she interrupted the woman and demanded, "Is this a practical joke?" "The Western Union is not allowed to transmit practical jokes," the woman replied, and continued on with the long message from President Kennedy, congratulating Andy on being one of thirty-one people awarded the very first Presidential Medal of Freedom. Katharine took the message upstairs to the bathroom, where the newest recipient of the highest honor awarded to a civilian in peacetime was soaking in the tub.

That November, just as Andy was leaving for Blue Hill to mail his letter of regret to President Kennedy, he learned of his assassination. Katharine watched the news unfold on television and then had to take to her bed with a circulatory attack—wildly racing heart and massive headache—that she was certain would have been a stroke had she not had surgery. Exactly two weeks later, President Johnson awarded the medals at a White House ceremony. Andy did not attend and instead received the medal from Maine senator Edmund S. Muskie the following May, on President Kennedy's birthday, at a ceremony at Colby College. Katharine did not accompany him for this signal honor, presumably for health reasons.

Another signal event that Katharine missed that autumn: Roger's wedding to Carol Rogge, a secretary in the fiction department at *The New Yorker*. He and Evelyn had divorced that summer. He had been writing to Katharine about Carol since January, but even as late as September, he hadn't yet told Evelyn or his daughters about her—Callie was now sixteen, Alice twelve—so he hadn't been able to bring her to the farmhouse to meet the Whites (Elsie found out about her from Brendan Gill at MacDowell, and Katharine had to frantically scramble to contain her hurt at not hearing from Roger directly). Katharine's office grapevine sent back the overall impression that Carol was "warm and outgoing," and she told Roger, "Andy and I are going to love her." But there was no way she could travel down to the city for the ceremony. Roger and Carol were married on October 26, 1963, in the chapel of the Madison Avenue Presbyterian Church with just sixteen guests, all of whom traveled to Ernest and Betty Angell's Upper East Side town house for a champagne reception afterward. Katharine gave the bride and groom the money for their honeymoon, a two-week trip to Paris and London. And then in early December, the new couple made the pilgrimage up to Maine. Katharine gave them a party and everyone, friends and family alike, crowded into the farmhouse for the occasion. Katharine glowed to see her Maine circle accept Carol so easily, but then she paid a funny price for the successful event. She had so many return invitations to dinner in the wake of it that she exhausted herself with socializing before Christmas had even begun—and she smoked too much, because parties always had that effect on her.

And then like a thunderbolt Katharine was visited by the most remarkable disaster of them all, the one that would shape the rest of her life. Two days after Christmas, her skin exploded into a rash so severe that she was flown to Harkness Pavilion in New York, where she stayed for two weeks. She was given cortisone and eventually discharged, and she and Andy headed directly down to Sarasota. But within a month she was flown back to the hospital, and there she stayed for nine long weeks, what she described as "a very tortured time" when she had a high fever, nurses around the clock, and the mystery of her erupted skin, with painful pus-filled bubbles under the top layer. Finally, her doctors arrived at a diagnosis: subcorneal pustular dermatosis, an extremely rare condition whose only treatment was sulfa—to which Katharine was allergic. They gave her the drug anyway, which aggravated the very condition it was supposed to treat. Katharine's skin blistered all over her body and began to peel—she eventually shed an entire layer. Katharine found this experience painful, humiliating, and lonely. She couldn't bear to have anything touching her skin, so she lay in bed with sheets suspended over her, unable to have visitors other than doctors, nurses, and Andy.

The cortisone prescribed to contain the rash was her only option, but it made her skin swell. She lost her molars, and she lost hair by the handful. Over time, the cortisone would erode her health, specifically her bone strength, but she couldn't forgo it. When the Whites returned to Maine, Katharine tried for a while to subsist on a halved dose but eventually needed to return to the higher level. She was prescribed tranquilizers to counter the nervousness induced by the cortisone.

This remarkable disaster slashed into two of Katharine's deepest values: her work ethic and her dignity. Here was a woman who wore dresses and heels to pick flowers in her garden, and suddenly she could barely wear anything at all. She wrote to John Updike in the spring of 1964, "I slop about all ungirdled and wearing loose cotton but at least I have the pleasure of picking my daffodils and tulips and supervising the spring transplanting." She confided in Updike because he had just published *The Centaur*, featuring a character with a skin condition based on the author's own psoriasis ("For the innermost secret, the final turn of my shame was that the texture of my psoriasis—delicately raised islands making the surrounding smoothness silver, constellations of roughness whose uneven spacing on my body seemed living intervals of pause and motion—privately pleased me"). The two shared a few rueful words over their "mystical affliction" (she also wrote to thank him for dedicating *Telephone Poles and Other Poems*, published the same year, to her and Andy "in gratitude for good example and kind counsel"). But how remarkable that she wrote anything at all about her body and her clothes to the younger man, far away in Massachusetts. Wouldn't *that* seem to violate her sense of dignity? Sharing a glimpse of her ignominy was a bedrock principle of the reciprocity that she practiced as both an editor and a friend. To *not* mention her hardships would seem, to Katharine, almost snobbish but certainly pretentious, making her life seem easier or more rarefied than it actually felt to her.

While her body demanded her attention and prevented her work, Katharine dealt with the sudden and alarming decline of her sister Elsie. She had turned eighty in 1961, with a party at the Cosmopolitan Club hosted by her Bryn Mawr friend Pauline Goldmark. Katharine never ceased to worry about her, though Elsie lived comfortably in her stone house in Piermont and was surrounded by friends. Bessie Breuer obliquely referred to the trouble between the sisters as rooted in Elsie's "greed for life," her refusal to "rest in the dignity of her years, her charm and achievement." She counseled Katharine to set down the burden of worrying about Elsie, telling her, "You are truly brave, wanting so desperately to shelter others—and a great part of your strain has come from this anxiety for others. Elsie is acutely conscious of what a blessing you have been to her in all these years."

In August and September of 1964, Elsie was hospitalized at Harkness Pavilion. She was, in Katharine's words, "deranged" and plagued by hallucinations and paranoia about almost all her old friends. Mercifully,

Katharine was one of the few who escaped her suspicion, and she visited her sister nearly every day. Elsie was under the illusion that she was destitute, and she deputized people to sell her valuable old books and furniture to raise money for her care. One friend whom Elsie had known through Robert Frost, Dr. Jack Hagstrom, believed Elsie's story of penury and asked Katharine to meet him for lunch one afternoon. Katharine was distressed to hear how fully he enabled Elsie's delusions; in her mind, Hagstrom was himself unstable, and by butting into Elsie's financial and medical affairs, he prolonged Elsie's illness. Hagstrom had so alarmed her that she met with Elsie's lawyer and financial advisor, and learned to her relief that Elsie owned stocks, bonds, and savings worth nearly $100,000. In Katharine's narrative, once Hagstrom vanished from Elsie's bedside, she recovered. She moved to Sky View Rehabilitation in Croton-on-Hudson, surrounded by her remaining family furniture, and she became "almost her old self again," as Katharine described her to Nancy Hale, who knew Elsie from MacDowell. Katharine began the laborious process of cleaning out Elsie's house. "Elsie saved everything," she told Hale. "Cartons and cartons of family documents, old family letters, recent family letters, and a few unfinished projects and manuscripts."

The Whites visited Elsie in December on their way down to Florida. And then on January 27, 1965, they learned of her death. Elsie had been feeling well enough to visit New York, where she attended a meeting of the Analytical Psychology Club, had tea with a new friend, and stayed at the Cosmopolitan Club, but that night she collapsed in her room. Katharine had known that she might die at any moment; she had been so glad at Elsie's "comeback . . . a near miracle," as she wrote to a friend, but at least her death was "a glorious one—'triumphant' is a better word." She wrote to Roger, "I am thankful she died this way, instead of having a lingering half-life as might have been the case." Several of the obituaries described Elsie as "indomitable"—the same adjective Katharine used in a letter to Nancy Hale, as did May Swenson and Glenway Wescott.

Katharine's immediate reaction to Elsie's death was physical. The phone call, from Elsie's friend Anne Gugler, sent her heart racing and gave her a headache that meant she was nearly incoherent when she called Roger to tell him the news. She wrote to Agnes de Lima, Elsie's literary executor, "I miss her every day, especially on literary and family matters—books I would have wanted to send her or discuss with her, family news to report." In another letter to de Lima, she offered a precise kind of tribute: "She was a memoirist, an essayist, a critic, a portraitist, mostly of people she admired, and her marriage was to Literature with a capital L. She was a scholar too." Days later she collapsed at her desk from the strain of answering the dozens of letters. Over the next few days, Katharine's condition worsened, necessitating a higher dose of cortisone, and she asked Roger and Anne Gugler, the executor of Elsie's estate, to arrange Elsie's memorial service in her stead. Elsie had been very clear about her wishes—a small service *not* in a church, her remains cremated, music played by her friend Paul Nordoff, and speakers from both her literary and Jungian circles.

The small ceremony grew and grew as people learned of her death— Elsie had a real gift for friendship, Katharine observed. The Whites took the train to New York for the service that took place on Monday afternoon, April 12, 1965 at the Cosmopolitan Club, with Katharine standing by the door to welcome attendees. Bryn Mawr College president Katharine McBride introduced the speakers, including May Swenson, Glenway Wescott, and Robert Frost's daughter Leslie Frost Ballantine.

Katharine became the last survivor of her childhood family, the matriarch of the Sergeant-Shepley line. She felt the burden acutely, as she helped Anne Gugler and Agnes de Lima interpret Elsie's perplexing will and divide possessions among heirs and papers among libraries. Andy was touched to receive the books that Willa Cather had inscribed to Elsie. There were dressers and desks and an engraved silver porringer to sort out. And there was money, too. Katharine divided her own bequest among her three children, saving only enough to pay the gift tax.

Katharine found herself resenting in advance the time required to deal with the cartons of Elsie's papers that came to her, because she was eager to return to her gardening essays after such a long pause. But when she and Andy returned to North Brooklin after the service, she set herself to the task of sorting, notating, and disposing. "I would like my letters to her destroyed at once," she wrote to Agnes de Lima, saying that she didn't have the energy for "reading and destroying [her] own

nasty letters to her." But de Lima refused, sending Katharine all her own
letters, plus Elsie's letters to the family dating back to her very first trip
to Europe, as well as any other family-related letters, photographs, and
memorabilia that she could find. She sent Elsie's Frost and Cather manuscript materials to Bryn Mawr.

For Katharine, then, the summer of 1965 was spent stringently editing the family record in the name of preservation. She did destroy every
letter between the two sisters, and every mention of money, including
their father's will. She even ordered Harriet Walden at *The New Yorker* to
destroy the list of attendees at Elsie's memorial service, if only because
she couldn't imagine why anyone would want it. And then she wrote
notes on what remained and packed the cartons back up, sending them
to Yale University to create the Elizabeth Shepley Sergeant archive at
the Beinecke Library. It was the autumn of 1965 before Katharine could
finally return to what she considered her main job: writing.

42.

After a three-year hiatus, Katharine returned to the pages of *The New Yorker* in December of 1965 with "An Idea Which We Have Called Nature." She had been making notes for this essay, on and off, since the month after Elsie's death, writing through the grief and the logistics of saying goodbye to her sister. She turns her attention away from catalogs and toward garden books and the aesthetic philosophies that undergird them in "this age of modern architecture, crowded cities, and sprawling suburbs." She frowns at a modern garden planted outside a Brazilian hospital, and her opinion sounds distinctly editorial: "Too much fixed form in a garden, however abstract and imaginative, can be tedious." She mediates on the role a garden should play in the observer's mental health. "Wouldn't I prefer to look down, as I have during a long hospital stay, on a haphazard, unpatterned old-fashioned shrubbery and a few formal beds of roses or of spring bulbs, to be followed by summer annuals among which, one by one, the shrubs or flowers would come into blossom and offer me a new surprise for every week of a long convalescence?" For Katharine the gardener, overediting nature destroys the effect. Better to let imperfection and wildness remain, and to cultivate suspense.

Her column was becoming increasingly ambitious. She would produce seven essays for *The New Yorker* over the next five years—essays that stretched her as a writer by combining a gardener's appreciation of horticulture, a scholar's curiosity for how things have been done in other places and times, and, increasingly, a memoirist's nostalgia for the foundational experiences of her past. Her vision for a book began to accrete and deepen beyond simply a collection of her columns. In the meantime,

Simon & Schuster issued the three volumes of *New Yorker* stories as a boxed set, and Katharine wrote to Jean Stafford with pride: "That full page ad in the Sunday Times listing the table of contents is certainly varied. In a way it sums up my small career."

But soon *The New Yorker* was once again under attack. In 1965, Tom Wolfe published his instantly infamous two-part article in *New York*, the Sunday magazine supplement of the *Herald Tribune*, called "Tiny Mummies! The True Story of the Ruler of 43rd Street's Land of the Walking Dead." *The New Yorker* had run several satires of *New York* since its founding in late 1963 and Wolfe had taken offense. Now, on the occasion of *The New Yorker*'s fortieth anniversary, he published a faux profile of William Shawn in order to criticize *The New Yorker* as deathly boring and past its prime—not precisely a parody, since Wolfe worked hard to report his article, and not precisely a joke, since he had a ferocious agenda. He had been prevented at every turn from obtaining facts—Shawn had refused to be interviewed and staffers had followed his lead—but he nonetheless tried to play it both ways. Shawn was Ross's "hierophant" who used his quiet nature "like a maestro" to reign among "tiny giants" like E. B. White and James Thurber and all the others "pistling away their talents." It was a mocking portrayal of the magazine but with scrupulous details, such as the color-coded slips of paper used for routing articles—most of which were incorrect.

Katharine read the first article and furiously got out her pencil. The phrase "pure fiction" crops up repeatedly in her notes, and she spent half a page on "the big lie of the article—that Shawn is an embalmer out to preserve Ross's New Yorker in amber." She repeatedly calls Shawn an "innovator" and notes that he has published fiction that, in "its outspokenness, its experimentation," would never have gotten past Ross. She was outraged at Wolfe's highly inaccurate account of how *New Yorker* editors changed copy at their whim to produce a "mutation" of what their authors had submitted. She wrote to Jane Grant, "Never has a magazine spent so much time on getting contributors to make their own changes and never has any publication been so careful about requiring a signed and okayed author's proof before printing." She started to draft a letter to the editor but stopped after three righteous pages and instead wrote to Shawn to offer her support.

The *Herald Tribune* printed five letters of protest from *New Yorker* writers, including Andy, who labeled Wolfe's piece "sly, cruel, and to a large extent undocumented." In his view, the *Herald Tribune*'s "departure from the conventional weaponry of satire and criticism is unsettling; it shakes the whole structure of the free press, which depends ultimately on the good temper and good report of the people." Shawn and his lawyers decided against legal action. Two staff writers, Renata Adler and Gerald Jonas, fact-checked Wolfe's piece to within an inch of its life and published the results in the *Columbia Journalism Review*; Dwight Macdonald published a two-part essay in *The New York Review of Books* lambasting Wolfe's brand of journalism. But the clear winners of the fracas were Wolfe and *New York* magazine, whose ad revenue doubled over the next few months, so that when the *Herald Tribune* folded altogether in 1966, *New York* could carry on as an independent magazine. Five years later, *Ms.* magazine would begin as an insert in *New York*.

What no one mentioned at the time was the virulent misogyny of Wolfe's attack, his lengthy, sneering characterization of the magazine's casuals as "the wettest bathful of bourgeois sentimentality in the world," making *The New Yorker* "the perfect magazine fiction for suburban women." On and on he went: the women of "Larchmont, Dedham, Grosse Point, Bryn Mawr, Chevy Chase" thrill to *The New Yorker* for its predictable, safe stories of "Mother, large rural-suburban home with no mortgage, white linen valences, and Love that comes with Henry Fonda, alone, on a pure-white horse." Wolfe regarded Shawn, because he presided over the magazine in its heyday of mainstream popularity, as automatically effete and emasculated. Mass culture was gendered feminine—debased, easy to consume, culturally ineffectual or even placatory.

This was the moment the decades-old criticism of the *New Yorker* formula became almost irredeemably gendered. Readers had long worried about the gender politics of the magazine's fiction. Thurber told Katharine in 1938 the magazine was most characterized by "the pussy

cat quality of most of the males of most of the casuals," which con-
trasted so strongly with the times, otherwise dominated by Hemingway
and the hard-boiled detective novels of James Cain and Horace McCoy.
"We got to give 'em pokers to bend, women to lay, guys to smack in
the puss." He had acknowledged that he and Andy had led the trend
since the 1920s, when he'd been writing the Mr. Monroe stories about
a henpecked husband and Andy had published "Philip Wedge," about a
man whose neuroses lead him to withdraw from society. But complaints
like Thurber's dealt mostly with taste and market: was *The New Yorker*
publishing the best stories out there, and was it limiting its readership by
what it published? Now Wolfe stretched that criticism, claiming that, in
publishing such feminine fare, *The New Yorker* was emasculating readers,
threatening the potency of the American individual, and kneading rugged individuals into a soft and pliant mass. It was by now a familiar rhetorical turn—the gendering of the middlebrow critique—but the most
influential essay up to this point, Dwight Macdonald's two-part "Mass-
cult and Midcult" in *Partisan Review* in 1960, had spared *The New Yorker*
the force of the author's invective, largely because Macdonald had been a
staff writer for the magazine for eight years. Wolfe picked up what Macdonald dropped and made the attack more malicious and more personal.

This characterization of *The New Yorker*, far from being a flaw, was the
secret of its success since the height of the Jazz Age, a point proven three
times: by Katharine's 1940, 1949, and 1960 story collections. *The New
Yorker* reached—and kept—upper-middlebrow readers by appealing to
educated women, by publishing stories by women that engaged but often outstripped middlebrow literary conventions, and by disrupting empathy with its protagonists. The magazine achieved its widest circulation
to date in the postwar era when women readers began to outnumber
men. That was only a problem to those who considered women and their
interests to be unworthy of literature.

Wolfe ended his diatribe with a personal attack on Katharine, veiled
yet unmistakable. He accused her of building a dynasty by exerting dark
power over Ross and Shawn—her flunkies both—to hire E. B. White
and cultivate Roger Angell. He claimed, erroneously, that Shawn had
designated Roger as his successor. "It all *locks*, assured, into place, the

future, and pat pat pat pat pat pat pat pat patclap clap clap clap clap clap clap . . ." Of all the errors and insults and insinuations, Katharine was most offended by this casually snide undermining of Roger's two decades of editing experience.

The now-settled rhythm of the Whites' days proceeded along its bumpy track. They would spend the winter in Florida, and visit family and a friend or two on their road trips between Florida and Maine. Each morning, Katharine would settle at the desk in her office while her assistant perched at a tiny typewriter table set up in the living room behind her. Katharine would dictate letters—never into a machine, always to a secretary who would notate in shorthand—or would leave handwritten letters to be typed. She would read the final version of everything before it went out into the mailbag. Many of her letters offered visual proof of the split between the private and public Katharine Whites: the first few pages of a letter would be dictated and typewritten, and then before signing and mailing it, she would add handwritten lines that she didn't want her secretary to read, and that part would often fill several more pages. Her letters had a seasonality that arose from holidays and birthdays. There was always a gift to order, a letter to dictate.

Sometimes the Whites' day would start with an impossible injunction: "Andy isn't feeling well today. We must be quiet and not let the phone ring and bother him." The Whites' number was listed in the phone directory and anyone could call. Allene remembered that both of them hated the phone, but Andy could ignore it, while Katharine *had* to answer it. If it rang when she was in the living room, she'd pick up her walker, hold it over her head, and run to the dark little phone closet at the back of her office. "It might be from *The New Yorker!*" Allene pointed out. "Or from Roger!"

Katharine would also work on Andy's correspondence (she answered all his letters from children and signed his name), or she would make a meticulous list of spring bulbs to order, only to balk at the expense, start over again, and arrive at the same order. Since the United States' bombing campaigns in Vietnam, she'd been regularly sending letters of protest to the White House, only to get "stuffy, irrelevant" replies from the State Department. One time, a full eleven years before her death, Katharine asked her young secretary, Diane Allen Stewart, to type up the obituary she'd drafted, saying briskly, "You have to be prepared." A few minutes before lunch, Katharine would head out to the garden with her baskets and return with as many as seventy-five flowers, which she would arrange in five or six vases. Andy loved to watch her at this task because she was unsentimental and seemingly slapdash, "throw[ing] flowers at each other . . . as though she were playing darts in an English pub," but all the while following a firm internal vision.

The cook would put lunch on the table, which was the secretary's signal that her workday was over. Katharine would rest after lunch and perhaps write in the afternoon. Four o'clock was the martini hour, though Katharine's medications now prevented her from drinking, and then dinner, which the cook had left behind, and perhaps a television show upstairs in the TV room. Katharine liked *What's My Line?* because she knew Bennett Cerf and many of the contestants, and there she'd sit on the daybed with her hair down and one leg tucked up beneath her.

Some days, Katharine would ask her secretary or Henry to drive her into Ellsworth to get her long hair done, a wave and a rinse for the same thick bun she'd worn all her life, and perhaps she'd stop at the bank or the liquor store. Diane Allen Stewart recalled driving Katharine home from Ellsworth. Just when they'd get to the South Blue Hill turn on the way to Brooklin, Katharine would reach over, scoop out the cigarette butts she'd chain smoked, and toss them out the window, saying, "Oh, my, I must empty your ashtray," though Stewart preferred that she not litter. But most days Katharine worked, even when her skin condition flared up so that her chest and neck were red and she could barely tolerate her cotton clothes. She'd increase her cortisone, which would puff up her face and add weight to her body, and tell her secretary, "You know, I'm tense. Just don't pay any attention. I don't mean it against you."

Despite her intense physical discomfort, in 1966 she entered an unexpectedly fertile period of writing about gardens and flowers. That December she published a lengthy, detailed review of a glorious book, the start of the ten-volume *Wild Flowers of the United States* by the New York Botanical Garden. She also began writing and researching an essay about flower arranging—a seemingly modest subject, but not under

Katharine's pen, because its scope traveled "from before Christ to the present," as she told Nancy Hale. She planned to critique modern flower arranging as practiced in garden club shows around the country, though she knew it would render her name "mud in Sarasota *and* Maine."

The following year, she published three garden essays within five weeks of each other, the most productive moment of her entire writing career. The diatribe against garden clubs stretched across two essays. Her thesis: the American gardener is best at flower arranging when she (and to Katharine the gardener was always a woman) simply trusts her own instincts. The art had taken a wrong turn with club certification and judges who slavishly applied the arcane standards in the handbook of the National Council of State Garden Clubs. "Conformity stultifies art," she proclaimed, echoing all those critics of *The New Yorker*'s perceived formula for fiction. As predicted, her column produced several long and affronted letters—Katharine had touched a nerve. She wrote equally long letters to each of her critics, letters that she heavily revised and edited before sending. This was serious business to her. A few weeks later, she published her usual roundup of garden tomes, six of them in total, including a much-appreciated book on fragrance in the garden, though her own nose was "admittedly now unreliable because of years of smoking."

Now, though, the desire to shape the essays into a book, to supplement the garden columns with personal and family history, grew stronger and more urgent. Katharine wondered if she was running out of time. The amount of work daunted her—"correction, updating, amplification, and a couple of new chapters, etc." She assumed from Alfred Knopf's silence that he'd given up on her, but she mentioned the book constantly in letters to friends and testified to being under pressure to decide if the columns could be made into a book. She found herself living so much in the past, as she contemplated the book's shape, that the tiniest reference could release her into an expansive memory. She published two Department of Amplification columns, one about her father's whiskey lemonades and one about the Irish-moss blancmange of her childhood cook, and she told Shawn that these were mere trifles along the way to the "mythical book"—that phrase again. She wrote to May Sarton to discuss long-ago summers in New Hampshire as a potential backdrop to a chapter. She wrote to Roger to ask for family documents that might have come down to him, because she wanted to write about John Sergeant, the missionary in Stockbridge, as well as her family history in Northampton. Eventually, she produced a draft called "82 Bridge Street," about the Sergeant aunts who lived together in Northampton in a female-dominated society of tea parties, social calls, clubs, and committee meetings. Their world, "in possession of the Amazons," made such a distinct impression on the young Katharine that when her father gave her a copy of Elizabeth Gaskell's *Cranford* for her twelfth birthday, she mentally populated the novel with the scenes and characters of Massachusetts. The essay is suffused with affection, but it is short and unfinished—one way to discern its status is that it has almost no pencil edits, as if Katharine never had a chance to reread it. Too many things called her away from her book.

The remarkable thing about this couple with pressing work and every ailment in the alphabet from arthritis to ulcers was that they continually invited complexity into their lives. In the summer, even while feeling miserable, Katharine "gardened like fury" on every nice day, even if all she could do was water seedlings. July meant Andy's birthday and a family dinner. There were boat races to attend, and sometimes there were launches at Joel's boatyard. Each summer, Roger and Nancy and their families would come stay, and Katharine's life would revolve around them. Autumn proceeded from Katharine's and Roger's birthdays in mid-September through bulb-planting time. In October, Katharine would swath herself in tweeds and scarves and her overlong, threadbare raincoat and sit outside on a director's chair in the chilly wind for hours, consulting the intricate chart she'd labored over and pointing to where Henry should dig for the bulbs she'd ordered in the spring. Then Halloween, when the Whites would fill their kitchen table with candy and the neighborhood children could come in and choose what they'd like. But even before Halloween came the start of the Christmas season, the time of maximum complexity for Katharine and her beleaguered secretary. She gave gifts to absolutely everyone: her three children and eight grandchildren, of course, but also former *New Yorker* colleagues and contributors and secretaries, the household staff and some of their spouses and children, doctors and nurses, postal employees and butchers, and many others besides. She stored up mail-order catalogs and scrutinized ads in magazines for ideas, and she began placing orders in October, to publishers and New York department stores and specialty stores, and somehow she managed to keep track of everyone's clothing sizes and literary tastes, and each year, though Andy begged her to reduce the complexity and just give everyone checks, she carried on with selecting personalized gifts and dispatching them up and down the Eastern Seaboard. And then she and Andy wrote Christmas cards by the hundreds, often with a verse from Andy, always with a personalized line or two, and this project could not be trimmed without risking someone's hurt feelings; Katharine was aware of how much it meant to many people to get a card from the Whites.

In 1967, just before setting out for Florida, the Whites increased the chaos by acquiring not one but two puppies, and then they presided over the mayhem of a holiday with Joel, Allene, and their three children, who'd taken to spending Christmas in Florida each year, with a small pine tree and new-bought ornaments instead of the boxes of family ornaments at home in Maine. Andy was soon reduced to being a full-time kennel boy for Maggie, a little mongrel mutt, and Jones, a gloomy Norwich terrier imported from England. Jones charmed Katharine completely by curling up on her lap, while Maggie was a little too boisterous and would jump up and scratch Katharine's inflamed skin (she was soon given to Joel and Allene to raise). The day after Christmas, the project of sending thank-you notes began. The Whites' correspondence was monumental.

A central pillar of this correspondence was the letters between Katharine and Roger. They wrote to each other two or three times a month, long and newsy letters with criticisms of recent *New Yorker* pieces and gossip about mutual friends. Katharine consulted him frequently for help with birthday, graduation, and holiday gifts for his wife, Carol, and his children. And she worried. She followed with interest and anxiety the choices that Roger's daughters, Alice and Callie, made as they launched themselves through college and into young adulthood, and she devoted many pages to discussing their options. Could Roger get Callie a summer job at *The New Yorker*, as she and Andy had gotten him a job at *Country Life*? Would Roger allow her to pay for Callie's contact lenses?

What might they do to get Alice to study harder in high school? But she often caught herself in the midst of energetically brainstorming and stopped herself midstream, assuring Roger that she didn't mean to interfere or give advice. "I'm just ruminating," she wrote once, and another time: "I just felt I wanted to talk to you." She told Roger again and again that she admired him as a father, and she constantly sought to defuse what she saw as his anxiety about his children's response to his divorce.

But Katharine's worry made Roger worry for her. In a letter, he recalls a time she came to dinner at his house and he remarked that all children are hurt by divorce, and she "suddenly began to cry." His letter is desperate, almost impatient in its zeal to sweep away her pain. He states his position as baldly as he can: "I don't resent my past or blame you for anything to do with me. I don't believe I was particularly ill-treated or abused or overlooked as a child. I don't feel you shouldn't have divorced my father or lived your life differently than you did." He begs her to stop punishing herself on his account. Another day, she seemed so overwrought on the phone as they discussed Callie visiting her in Florida that he wrote to say he would not trouble her with news that would upset her, and that she must try to do something about her "deep ingrained habit of worry."

She replied with six closely written pages of meticulous prose, an extraordinary manifesto about the relationship between her heart and her mind, and perhaps unwittingly, a deeply affecting glimpse into the life of an elderly intellectual. She begins, as she does in every letter, with a statement of her health; she has recently been suffering neck soreness that makes it difficult to bend her head to write, but she refused her doctor's suggestion of painkillers, saying, "They make my brain fuzzy." Then on to the matter at hand: "You must allow me to feel concern about my granddaughters," she wrote. "Anxieties, if not self-centered, can even be useful, can be creative, can get things improved and changed." Anxiety, in her definition, is the proper expression of a thinking person's desire for a just and good future, for "the world and the planet and this country." Her biggest fear, even greater than death, was the thought of being mentally incapacitated, and what Roger had suggested, to keep from her news of his children's ups and downs, "indeed would be senility or death for [her]." She writes, "There's so much I want to accomplish before I die." Ambition expresses a thinking person's desire for the future, and she dearly wanted Roger to recognize it in her. "My children should understand me and take me as I am, faults and all, and above all not shield me but instead help me out on practical matters." And when she told Roger that she was merely ruminating, not giving him advice, she meant that she was not making a claim for his attention or expecting a certain response. The same could be said for all the itemized lists of medical woes that began every letter; she was not asking for pity or sympathy or even a response at all. She merely wanted to be heard.

That Roger was not persuaded by her disquisition on the merits of worrying can be seen in an essay he published in *The New Yorker* thirty years after Katharine's death on the topic of "her Olympic-scale worrying," her "bottomless worries and overthoughts." He affectionately imagines her at the head of the dinner table in Maine, Andy at the other end, his family in between, and he channels her inner monologue of fretting about family, the garden, the dessert, her authors, her ex-husband, *New Yorker* galleys, income tax, and it only ends when she puts down her fork and lights a cigarette.

Just in time for her seventy-fifth birthday in 1967, a new worry arrived on Katharine's desk. Two years after the Wolfe debacle, Corey Ford, one of the magazine's original satirists, published *The Time of Laughter*, his memoir of the twenties and thirties, with a chapter on *The New Yorker*. He made it clear in the book that he was writing against previous perceptions of Harold Ross as a "restless, exasperating innocent" (Thurber) or "virtually a maniac" (Gibbs). He made no mention of Tom Wolfe, but he implicitly countered him by crediting Ross's "balancing sense of humor about himself"; he was aware enough of his own faults to compensate for them with the people he hired. A secondary secret: "More than anyone else save Ross himself, Katharine S. and E. B. White were responsible for *The New Yorker*'s enormous impact on American letters. Their unerring taste guided it through the formative years." Katharine thanked Ford for his kind words about her and Andy, and even more for his "affirmative and enthusiastic" take on the magazine's history. "Of course I don't always agree with your opinions or even your facts," she went on. She winced over the now-fashionable sentiment that *The New Yorker* churned out "the self-analytic and pastel stories-without-plots" and pointed to the three *New Yorker* story collections as proof of its diverse offerings. And if they did publish "sensitive ladies," blame should be laid at Maxwell's feet; she herself published "the violent and sometimes difficult ones," like John O'Hara and Robert Coates. She did not agree that the magazine's long articles left no space for experimentation. Even now, she wrote, it "averages one or two unknown names to each issue." For instance, Roger had just that year published Donald Barthelme's "Snow White," a postmodern deconstruction of the fairy tale told by the seven dwarves (sample sentence: "Now she's written a great dirty poem four pages long, won't let us read it—refuses absolutely, she is adamant"), and Katharine, like many other readers, couldn't stop talking about its boundary pushing and experimentation. She loved it. Oh sure, she shuddered at the vulgarity of "Snow White's white arse," but she told Roger that she would have published it if it had passed across her desk.

Ford's memoir was followed by Jane Grant's, *Ross, "The New Yorker," and Me*, and though Grant consulted the Whites and they heavily corrected her page proofs, the manuscript went to press without their changes, prompting a horrified apology from Grant and the general feeling that the true book about Ross was still to be written. Many friends implored Katharine to do it. S. N. Behrman, Katharine's old friend and a playwright and *New Yorker* profile writer who'd been writing for the magazine since the late 1920s, offered to coauthor such a book with her. Ann Honeycutt, a *New Yorker* writer from the same era (and James Thurber's unrequited love), told Katharine, "You are the only one who could do that biography, the only woman he was ever in love with. You scared the bejesus out of him, of course, but you were the goddess." But Katharine was implacable in her refusal to consider such a project, even though, in the autumn of 1955 when she was frantically redesigning her job, she'd lobbied Shawn for the privilege of editing a book of Ross's letters chronicling the making of *The New Yorker*. This was not now the book she had in her mind's eye. Though there was little external sign of it, Katharine was wholly focused on her "mythical book." She wrote another column, published in December 1968, but it was a workaday review of ten gardening books, including a large illustrated volume about Winterthur in Delaware, as well as the reissue of her friend Elizabeth Lawrence's *A Southern Garden*. This was not an essay calculated to advance her literary project.

And then, yet another cascade of remarkable disasters befell her "freakish carcass," as she'd taken to describing herself. In Florida for the winter of 1969, Katharine fell, and because her bones had been weakened by years of cortisone at high doses, she fractured her spine. She hobbled around for a while in the hopes that the fracture would heal itself. But then she got shingles—for which the treatment was more cortisone—and then neuritis. Nancy offered to have Katharine and Andy move in with her and Louis, in what Roger privately called "a generous offer, if cuckoo."

Finally, Katharine's back pain was so bad that, once again, she abandoned Sarasota for her old haunt, the Harkness Pavilion, where she ended up staying for thirteen weeks. When she was finally released, an ambulance plane flew her home to Brooklin, where she slept in a hospital bed and moved around with a walker. She didn't know it yet, but she would never leave Brooklin again.

43.

The best thing is to just let the world come to you, as you do, and try to keep working and living.
　—Katharine to Frank Sullivan, 1974

The Whites had a "rather odd, uneasy" Christmas—Andy's words—during which Katharine was "as tense as an E-string" because of her high cortisone dose; she had also started taking digitalis for her heart. Nurses now cared for her almost around the clock. Both Katharine and Andy fretted over Joe, who was incommunicado while sailing a schooner across the South Atlantic and late for Christmas because of a blizzard in New York. Through it all, Katharine wrote another garden column, but she missed her December deadline because of "snow and gloom of night"—her words, which appear in the column's first sentence. But no matter, she asserted, because March was as good a time as December for the gardener to imagine their garden. She would keep working every day that she was physically able.

Her heart failed her the very week her essay was published. It was the day before Easter, and just after breakfast she found she couldn't breathe. Andy phoned the doctor, who rushed over and then called the volunteer ambulance corps. They arrived with an oxygen tank and drove Katharine to Blue Hill Hospital, where she was installed in an oxygen tent. Andy followed with all the things he'd gathered from the house that she might need, and he ruefully shook his head when she asked to bring with her into the oxygen tent the morning paper, the latest issue of *The New Yorker*, and her cigarettes. She managed to sleep all day and was noticeably better by Easter Sunday. She stayed in the hospital for a week so the doctors could enforce their prescription of bed rest, and soon enough, she was back to her regular routine of circumscribed but fervent activity.

The big event of the spring was the publication of *The Trumpet of the Swan*, which, against all odds and predictions, Andy had delivered to his editor, Ursula Nordstrom, the previous November. Katharine told William Maxwell that Andy had written it quickly and "without waiting the year he usually [did] for reconsideration," because her medical expenses were so great—and because he feared one or the other of them wouldn't be around to see it between covers if he waited too long. Katharine liked the book, especially Sam Beaver's diaries, which Andy had based on his own childhood journals, but Andy called it "his pot-boiler" and wished he'd never followed the one children's book that he truly loved with any other. Readers disagreed. John Updike gave the book a favorable review in *The New York Times*, calling it "a joy-ride through the gentle terrain of the highly unlikely," though he did concede that it lacked a little of the sprightliness and richness of E. B. White's prior two children's books. He marveled at the flimsiness of the tale's conceit—a honkless swan who must earn money to reimburse the store whose window his father broke when stealing a trumpet to compensate for Louis's silence. "If the author once winked during this accumulation of preposterous particulars, it would all turn flimsy and come tumbling down. But White never forgets that he is telling about serious matters." To Updike, *Trumpet* "glows with the primal ecstasies of space and flight, of night and day, of nurturing and maturing, of courtship and art." An erudite literary review of a simple children's book written by an old man—a book that fully resonated with the children for whom it was written. In 1971, *The Trumpet of the Swan* held the top slot on the *New York Times* bestseller list for children's books, and *Charlotte's Web* held the second slot.

Andy didn't much enjoy his success. Just after Updike's review appeared, he suffered a very near miss. He had appointments in Blue Hill, so he got ready for the eight-mile drive, a process that entailed taking his antihistamine for his July hay fever and also packing a thermos of coffee for when he inevitably felt drowsy from the medication. He had a strict protocol for such moments, even including a five-minute nap on the roadside if the coffee was ineffectual. But the cook was freezing a big batch of peas and he could not make his coffee. He hurried to his appointments, fell asleep at the wheel, and crashed into a telegraph pole on the right side of the road. A woman with her three children found him. How much worse it could have been; he sustained a broken nose, a black eye, and a broken rib. But a week later he was in the hospital for what Katharine called "a deep depression." He feared that he was losing control. He feared the most tangible symbol of that vulnerability—the revocation of his driver's license—but that didn't occur. He gained back some of the eleven pounds he lost after the accident.

The Whites stumbled through the year. One happiness was Roger and Carol's new baby boy, John Henry, whom they adopted at the age of six weeks, just in time for Roger's fiftieth birthday—though the Whites would not meet him until the following summer, when the Angells came to Maine and John Henry celebrated his first birthday. At the end of October, not long after a visit from Hannah Arendt, Mary McCarthy, and McCarthy's husband, Jim West, Andy took Katharine to Bangor to have a skin tumor removed from her right arm. Katharine prepared for the ordeal by placing all her Christmas orders.

Andy's outward success just kept rocketing up. In 1971, the National Book Committee selected him to receive its National Medal for Literature. Ursula Nordstrom wrote to him in jubilation: "It is always lovely when excellence is recognized. And also you are as pretty as Gloria Steinem on her best day." She told him that he'd beaten Vladimir Nabokov for the award, then she implored him to forget that she'd told him (Nabokov would win it two years later). Nordstrom made plans for him to receive the bronze medal and the check for $5,000 at Lincoln Center in front of a "small group of not more than 100." Harper would send a car to drive him and Katharine from North Brooklin down to New York. He needn't make a speech. He didn't make the trip at all; there was never a chance that he would. He deputized William Maxwell to accept the award on his behalf. Harper editor Cass Canfield spoke, and John Updike did too, praising his "unflickering tone of truth" and the steadiness of Andy's presence in his readerly life (he also spared a few sentences for Mrs. White, calling her "a warm fine mentor" and—yes, there it was—"a formidable woman"). Andy had earned literature's most prestigious honor, and yet he summarized the year thusly: "I'm glad it's over. I've never had such a bad time, never made more money, never done so few things that I wanted do to."

The world was passing the Whites by, occasional medals notwithstanding, as demonstrated by Shawn's rare rejection of an essay by Andy that September. Andy had written what he called a "parable" poking fun at the feminist campaign to cease the use of the pronoun "his" to mean "his or her." He meant only to be droll and he said he didn't much care that it was rejected. In that case, replied Roger, "discourage KSW from hitting Shawn with a thirty-page demurrer, no matter how right you think she is." Indeed, Katharine was outraged by the rejection, but she did not have the argumentative relationship with Shawn that she'd had with Ross, and it was now her policy not to interfere. Instead, her anger powered her through two long letters to Carol and Roger, the choicest parts reserved for the handwritten, private portions at the end of each. First, Shawn's rejection was abysmal editorial policy. He had told the Whites that he personally liked the piece and had had it set into proof, but had changed his mind when many women on the staff objected. Katharine was disgusted by his "pulse taking." She told Carol, "If an editor can't or doesn't dare publish what <u>he</u> likes, a magazine is doomed to failure." But then she learned that Roger was one of the staffers who lobbied against the piece, and she expounded to him at great and impassioned length on the second reason why he and Shawn were wrong to reject it: it was funny, and the feminist movement desperately needed humor in order to keep it from veering into eccentricity. The parable would have helped the movement; it was *pro*-feminist. She trotted out the old argument about the dream of equality under the sun of satire: "As Shawn put it, Women's Lib has become like the Negro race problem, you can't write humor on Negroes anymore. The subject is taboo for humor." Her word for Shawn's capitulation to the humorless women on his staff: "craven." "For Heaven's sake, Rog!" she burst out. "Satire and humor is <u>based</u> on writing about the small foibles or excesses of men and women." Roger argued right back: "That is nonsense." He agreed with her only that Shawn had mishandled Andy's expectations. Humor wasn't inherently disruptive or progressive: "Jokes about women's liberation perpetuate the old sexist ways—or most jokes about it do."

Katharine's voice, in these fiercely scrawled letters, is suffused with the fear of being misunderstood as outdated and conservative by her son, whom she so respected. She supports the goals of women's liberation, she tells him, especially equal pay for equal work. She believes that more women should enter politics and says, "[The] work of Women's Lib, as I see it, is to create in all the arts as well as men and to correct inequities of years of exploitation." But she also believes in (heteronormative) marriage and (women-raised) children, and she believes—since men and women are physically different—in the gendered differentiation of certain jobs, and that employers should be allowed to advertise jobs specifically for one or the other gender. "If an office needs to have a pretty receptionist so be it."

Her feminism had shifted slightly over time, or perhaps in response to her interlocutors. A few years previously, she had published a short essay in the alumni bulletin of the Winsor School (as it was now called) on the profession of writing, which ends by considering how to write alongside "the most important career of all—making a home and bearing and raising children." A few years later, she would say to a younger female writer, "I have been a liberated woman all my life and consider that I have had equal rights with men throughout my career"—but she always deplored the use of the title "Ms."

She repaired her small rift with Roger with a cheerful exchange of birthday letters. Katharine sent Roger a book on sailing, and he sent her *Maurice* by E. M. Forster. She couldn't resist getting in the last word—making a reference to a "convention led by 'chair persons'" and saying, "If that isn't ridiculous I don't know what is"—but she apologized for lecturing, allowed that Andy's piece probably hadn't been as well written as it could have been, and agreed to move on. "Anyway here endeth any more talk about this unhappy event."

It was around this time that Roger deliberately avoided another fraught conversation with his mother. He and Carol went to dinner one night at the Greenwich Village apartment of his old friend Peter Powys

Grey and a companion. As they sat around the table, Peter turned to his friend and said, "I'm going to tell him." "Are you sure you want to?" she asked. Peter faced Roger. "I'm your brother. We have the same father." Roger instantly reached over and hugged him. Carol said, "Roger, you said we weren't going to see anybody in your family for a change." Roger was stunned, but it all fell into place for him; he felt no inclination to repel this new information, because he could immediately see how it could have happened, knowing what he did about his father's infidelities. And after all, Peter looked like Ernest. In fact, the wife of Roger's best friend Walker Fields had noticed that when Roger and Peter played tennis together, they moved similarly and hit the ball in the same way. If Peter quite often won, it was because, as Roger now understood, "he had the advantage of knowing what it was all about, what we were really playing for." Roger told his father that Peter had revealed their kinship to him, and Ernest said that he was glad, that it was a relief. But Roger never once discussed Peter Grey with Katharine—he said he wouldn't dream of it—and he would never know what she knew or thought about any of this over the years.

Katharine could do nothing but let the world come to her. When her friends visited, they came away impressed with her steadfastness, even as they fully realized the obstacles she faced. Bessie Breuer, her writer friend since the 1930s, wrote, "I can conceive of your orderly mind and your noble soul arranging an ongoing productive life even as you are." Katharine likely felt as Breuer herself did, that as long as she could remain "vividly interested in what is happening in and to our country," if she could stay "moved by the incredible marvel of *life*," then she would be content. Nancy Hale visited for lunch, her first time seeing Katharine in Maine, and she wrote afterward, "My mind feels so easy and happy about you (in spite of all your troubles) because you look and seem and act as ever serene, beautiful and sort of regal."

Two projects consumed Katharine's working hours; her heart ailment had scared her into productivity. She urgently wished to finish the sorting and donating of her letters to Bryn Mawr; she told her attorney, "I expect to live to be ninety, but I might not," and she wanted to dispatch these letters and "go on to more interesting matters." But in true Katharine S. White fashion, this project swelled and amplified into something quite different from merely cleaning out her desk and filing cabinets. She thought hard about the meaning of the archive she was assembling. She was no literary celebrity; Katharine knew what a celebrity author looked like, and she often insisted to Scott Elledge, the professor of English at Cornell who had begun writing E. B. White's biography back in 1967, that she remain in the background of Andy's story as a helpmeet. Elledge offhandedly referred to his book "about the Whites." You'll write no such thing, Katharine replied. "The prospect of any book or piece 'about the Whites,' as if we were, say, the Lunts, dismays me for the Lunts are both creative artists where my role is not creative." She staunchly believed she did not warrant the spotlight. (But she also swiftly backed away from Elledge, telling him she didn't want to be a Jacqueline Kennedy and try to dictate his biography.)

She knew the history of *The New Yorker* like no one else—she was, after all, the only editor still alive who'd been with the magazine since the beginning—and she believed that *The New Yorker* would someday loom large in a literary history of the twentieth century. Given that, her perspective would be invaluable. She especially wanted to depict what she called the "editorial-personal letters" that formed the backbone of her editorial practice. She and William Maxwell argued gently about this as she enlisted his help with her archive. He told her that everything he knew about editing he'd learned from watching her write letters to Updike that were "so detailed and careful, and at the same time personal. He was getting ready to fly and [she was] encouraging him to do it." He did his best to emulate her concern for all dimensions of a writer. "I can't remember once shaving on a day I was going to the office and not feeling glad I was going there, in what is it? thirty eight years. To this many things contributed, of course, but the most important was the belief that the magazine was best served by what best served the writers I was working with. Which idea I got from watching you." He believed that only he continued in her tradition of the editorial-personal letter, with Roger and Bob Henderson conducting far more businesslike relationships with their authors. Katharine disagreed. She thought most of the magazine's editors had formed close friendships with their writers, that it was part of the magazine's culture. "As mother hen of the Fiction Dept. the personal-editorial letter was a habit I tried to instill in everyone," she wrote. "It's a New Yorker method I've always been proud of and it is rare among magazines." *This* was what she wanted preserved, the record of the relationships behind the casuals and poems and profiles and stories.

Once again, Katharine began to curate a collection. For someone so eager to box up her letters and get them out of her house, she did something extraordinary—she asked Harriet Walden and Ebba Johnson, the librarian at *The New Yorker*, to mail letters to her by the boxful. She wanted her personal archive at Bryn Mawr to show as robustly as possible how the magazine fostered its writers. She thought hard about which writers would be representative, and she decided to focus on John Updike, as a green and eager writer whose early career was entirely commensurate with the magazine itself. His file would serve as a transparent window onto the growth of an author. She thought to contrast him to Vladimir Nabokov, a writer highly accomplished in Russian and German who was just beginning to make a name for himself in English when she brought him over from *The Atlantic*. And she wanted her correspondence with Louise Bogan to demonstrate the workings of the magazine in the 1930s and 1940s. She felt a sense of urgency toward this project of gathering letters, too, because *The New Yorker* had done such a poor job of preserving its files and curating its own archive. The famous story, which Katharine related in many letters as she sought correspondence to round out her archive, is that during the war a well-meaning but clueless employee in the advertising department had responded to the wartime paper drive by donating almost all of the magazine's files from its early days. (When Ross heard about this, "there was a goddamming that could be heard as far as a Hundred and Tenth Street. He goddammed for three days without letup," according to Andy, and he would have "disemboweled [the employee] with a machete, except he didn't have a machete.") Now the files that survived lived downstairs in the furnace room of *The New Yorker*'s building at 25 West Forty-Third Street, where the carbon copies were slowly crumbling in the heat. It drove Katharine to distraction.

She did the work of a manuscript librarian: collecting letters, reading them, and writing short notes to indicate their importance and how they fit into the larger history. She had an absolute horror of seeming egotistical, and many of her notes defended against the imaginary accusation that she was burnishing her own legacy. She iterated in small and large ways her point that this donation was about *The New Yorker*'s history, not her own life. One exception was a cache of letters that she had written to her father when she was a college student. Might the Bryn Mawr library want them, though they were "of no value," but read simply as "period pieces" that might illuminate student life back in the 1910s? "I hasten to say that I did not have the vanity to preserve these letters myself," she assured the director of the library. "They turned up in a lot of boxes of material when my sister Elizabeth Sergeant died." Otherwise, she ruthlessly destroyed letters that she felt had no literary or historical significance. She enforced a tight definition of the archive: it would be solely about her work at *The New Yorker* and her and Andy's work on *A Subtreasury of American Humor*. Everything else was, to her, ephemeral.

This was her life's work: reading, rereading, adding and subtracting, growing and pruning in the same motion. She did it as easily as she breathed. She edited even while she wrote, and sometimes it drove her correspondents crazy. Frank Sullivan cried in despair, "Katharine, don't ever again write anything to me and then ink it out. You unsettled my reason for a full half hour by doing that in your note. I tried every way to decipher what you had inked out, held it against a strong light, used a magnifying glass, and if I had had some of those chemicals spies use to bring out secret messages I'd have used them too." He typed, "I must write you some time and then cross it out"—and he inked it over until it became almost but not quite illegible. Her editorial imagination did not stretch to include an understanding of what other people might find valuable about her life and work, how maddened and tantalized other people might be by what she omitted. She destroyed letters that she thought impugned someone's reputation. She was careful to note when she excised part of a letter. "3 pages more of this letter cut + destroyed by KSW Too personal about living members of my family KSW," she scrawled at the bottom of a letter she had written to Andy in 1945. She restricted the use of all the letters, requiring anyone who wished access to them to obtain permission from her or Andy, and from William Maxwell if the letter was from a *New Yorker* editor. She sealed several letters until the deaths of the authors discussed within them, and she expressed her overall condition that "living authors must be protected" and that "the feelings of editors, sometimes negative about its contributors must not be made public while a contributor is alive."

And even as she did so, she produced more letters to be restricted, as she reconceived old relationships and wrote honest assessments of her former authors now that they were no longer under her pencil. Nabokov, for one, had become "impossible" and "very swell-headed," and *Ada* was "well nigh unreadable" because he had started "parodying himself." She detested the sex scenes in John Updike's *Couples*. "I don't know what has come over Updike, my promising boy of so many years back," she lamented to Harriet Walden. "The new sexual explicitness seems to Andy and me to remove emotion and passion from novels on the same sort of sexual themes which will always continue in literature." She felt that both he and Cheever had become seduced by fame and caught up in the literary competition to be the greatest American writer. All three men seemed, to her, to conform to a pattern of fame and success that disappointed her, though she kept in loose touch with Updike and was friendly with Cheever and Nabokov as well.

Beyond her letters, Katharine also promised to Bryn Mawr all the first editions that authors had inscribed to her over the years, but she was not ready to part with them yet because she and Andy frequently consulted them when writing letters. Instead, she put little gummed stars inside the covers of all the books she intended for Bryn Mawr's bequest, and she began making a list of all her books. Then she began annotating the list with notes to explain the author's relationship to her, and then she added to the notes, and soon the notes were becoming pages and pages of stories and reminiscences, each author an entry whose name prompted a few polished anecdotes. She made and remade the lists as she found more books in every room and the attic, and she kept writing and amending her notes. "I could go on indefinitely writing little thumbnail sketches of some of these writers who were very dear to me," she mused. For instance, she said, "I had planned to write a piece on the four James Thurbers I have known." Her notes would eventually expand to six folders of lists with notes, supplemental lists, and indexes to the list.

Truly, *this* was Katharine White's autobiography. Her life story was best told through the detailed catalog of her relationships with writers. While she struggled with finding the right form to contain the family history that would give a bookish shape and heft to her garden columns, she had inadvertently discovered a way to release her memories onto the page, had discovered her genre—if only she'd realized it and had polished up this ad hoc memoir for readerly consumption.

She also decided to donate her world-class collection of garden books to Bryn Mawr, and to annotate that list, and it too stretched to seventy-five pages. It was a messy, disorganized process, conducted in fits and starts, and it made Katharine an enemy. The Whites had hired a young woman named Isabel Russell to act as secretary for Katharine, and occasionally for Andy, and she later wrote a memoir of her time with them. She was clearly besotted with Andy, but Katharine was a "pathetic, stout, quick-tempered, bemused invalid," a drama queen to Andy's dignified stoicism, someone who was "violently busy." Russell didn't use the word "formidable," but she makes palpable her resentment at being sent all over the house and up into the attic in search of books, and endlessly retyping lists, and suffering Katharine's "tiresome" digressions about her authors. Katharine, for her part, ended letters by dictating an apology for her "country secretaries," an apology that Russell then had to type neatly and mail.

In conditions far less than ideal, Katharine forged ahead, violently busy with her second project: E. B. White's collected book of letters. Harper had proposed the idea, and Andy had quailed before the task. He estimated he had written twenty-five thousand letters over his lifetime, but they wouldn't add up to a book. He didn't think his letters were amusing, plus he thought he might die any day. Katharine disagreed and knew they could excavate a book out of the larger morass. "I think he writes good letters," she wrote to Roger, "some funny and some very serious, and he has written them to every kind of person all over the land." The trick would be to find someone to edit the book—to do the exhausting logistics of tracking down letters with family and friends, the magazine, various universities, publishers, agents—and when the Whites got Harper to hire Dorothy Lobrano Guth, the daughter of Gus Lobrano, Andy felt marginally reassured. But he agreed to work with Dotty Guth on one condition: that if he died before she finished, the book was off. She almost immediately had a hard time performing her job, because she was beset with her own illnesses and family troubles. The work fell to Katharine. She soon reported that she was spending five to six hours a day working "for Andy."

The project instantly grew in scope. Harper conceived "a grandiose scheme for a uniform edition of Andy's selected works," in Katharine's words, "which [the Whites] probably [would] never live to complete." The collected letters would be second in the series, given its delays, followed by a volume of satire and casuals, and a volume of verse. The first book, which Katharine was now helping to assemble, was a collection of his essays, and both Whites worried that its contents would be all too familiar to Andy's readers. But they couldn't say no—they needed the money for Katharine's care. They sold a sliver of land to a neighbor.

Meanwhile, another member of their family was enjoying the triumph of a successful new book. In June of 1972, Roger published *The Summer Game*, a collection of his baseball essays, ten years after the first one appeared in *The New Yorker*. Roger's book unfurled every ounce of Katharine's motherly pride. She loved every word, loved his humor, his eye for detail, his affectionate and fair criticisms of players and teams and owners. And she also inhaled every review or bit of press, from an interview Roger did in Chicago to his appearance on the *Today* show, and his two reviews in the *New York Times*. She thought Christopher Lehmann-Haupt's review in the Sunday *Times* was fair, except for the last line: "Among baseball writers, Roger Angell is a sort of Al Kaline or Billy Goodman: no star of the brightest magnitude, he does it all well and makes it all look easy." Her response: "Let him name a brighter star! I can't think of *one*. I guess he just got mixed up in the wording of what he meant to say, which was that reading your pieces over the years he hadn't realized how great your writing was until it was put together in a book." Andy wrote to Roger to congratulate him, but he had to confess that he hadn't read it, because he hadn't managed "to pry the book out of the arms of the author's mother, where it is cradled day and night. She is a baseball nut and devoted parent." He added, "I have, of course, caught *glimpses* of the book," and he thought the book jacket was very nice indeed.

The Summer Game helped clinch Roger's reputation as a baseball writer. He had dedicated his book to his father, and toward the end of it, he offered a moving tribute to Ernest, in his eighties and still able to describe with sharpness and relish the gestures and quirks of the Cleveland Indian players he'd watched as a kid. Roger had grown up watching his father watch the game, and from Ernest's lifelong fascination he understood baseball as the most intensely *remembered* of all sports, an experience that lived on as "this inner game—baseball in the mind." The tribute to Ernest came just in time. A few months later, on January 11, 1973, Ernest Angell died in his town home on East Sixty-Sixth Street, where he had lived alone since his second wife's death in 1970. He had been suffering immobility and pain from arthritis, and he'd also had a heart condition. He was eighty-three.

Katharine was astonished to find that she had outlived her first husband; he was so healthy and vigorous and athletic. She wrote to Nancy and Roger on the day of his death to give them her condolences. She told Roger that what saddened her most of all was that "he hated [her] so and thought [her] a complete hypocrite." The tension between them lasted until the end of Ernest's life. Years before, when his wife Betty was drinking heavily, Ernest had left her in protest and come up to Maine to spend a week with Roger and Carol; the visit was very tense and fraught because of the sheer proximity of Katharine and Andy, one town over, though they didn't meet. They were never able to alter the pain of their connection. "You did try to be friends in later years," Roger wrote to her, "but of course it was impossible for him. If he had a blind spot, it was his pride, and in some blind, irrational way, he could never accept the end of your marriage and the beginning of your life with Andy." Roger called it "an obdurate and mountainous structure of harsh feelings," a structure that had no mirror in Katharine.

Several days after Ernest's death, Katharine turned to more practical matters. Roger and his half brother, Christopher, joint executors, would need to clean out two of Ernest's three houses, and Katharine offered her services as a family historian if they needed to sort furniture between the different sides of Ernest's families. The good Japanese prints that used to hang in their Ninety-Third Street house, she reminded Roger, were ones that Aunt Poo sent Ernest from Tokyo when he performed a legal task for her. (They went to Nancy.) Katharine also wrote to the grandchildren. She conceived her role as supplementing the dry obituaries, which lauded Ernest for his years chairing the American Civil Liberties Union and his several legal books. His grandchildren should also be proud of him for his counterespionage work, his establishment of the Willard Straight Post of the American Legion, and his happy and social second marriage to Betty. But there was one particular accomplishment missing from this list. When he'd been head of the ACLU, doing excellent work but making hardly any money, many people considered him a prime candidate to be a judge—but the fact that he'd fathered an illegitimate son would have sabotaged any such nomination. Roger called it "the tragedy of his life," because Ernest would have excelled at that career.

That winter, Ernest's children hosted a memorial service at the Century Association on Forty-Third Street, just down the street from the offices of *The New Yorker*. Roger spoke, making sure everyone at the well-attended gathering knew the less formal side of his father, "the civil libertarian at liberty, the great gent glimpsed in his sneakers," like the time just two winters previously when Ernest had jumped on a sled and raced down "bellywhoppers," trying to make it to the pond at the bottom of the hill. Katharine did not attend the service, nor did Peter Powys Grey.

That summer was a time of "haying, strangers, friends and neighbors dropping in etc. etc. No privacy." That year, she lay awake at night, stifling in the heat, unable to fall asleep until two o'clock in the morning because her brain was turning over the news of the day, restlessly composing letters she would never send about how to solve the Watergate affair. "My latest night plan," she wrote to Roger, "was to give immunity to everybody and ask them to come back and change their testimony and tell the truth so that it won't matter whether the President releases the tapes or not." That solved, she went on to worry about the youth; Andy's geese Liz and Apathy, who failed to hatch any goslings; fundraising for Blue Hill Hospital; and the change in *The New Yorker*'s dateline from Saturday to Monday. Everything about *The New Yorker* came under the purview of her worrying eye—the excessively long and somber articles that Shawn was publishing and that she felt were a mistake, whether or not he should retire, who could possibly replace him if he did. Her letters stretched on for pages—there was always so much to worry about.

44.

Everything is good here except that you are not here, and when you are not here the place has a hole right down through it from attic to cellar.
— Andy to Katharine

Nineteen seventy-five was the year of the fiftieth anniversary of *The New Yorker*, and though Katharine and Andy did not join the festivities, they may have caught NBC's coverage from the magazine's offices, which poetry editor Howard Moss gloomily thought looked "like the waiting room in a Morocco abortion clinic." Roger was far more ebullient in his report of the weekend. He took a group of editors to lunch in the Rose Room of the Algonquin, where a large cake waited for them with icing that spelled out "Happy Annivers-ery." "Being a born editor," Roger wrote, "I ate the typo." Then came the official party at the Plaza, which was only supposed to be for staff—no spouses, or even writers and artists—but plenty of people crashed and over three hundred people celebrated that evening. Even the extraordi-narily shy William Shawn attended, shook a few hands, and left, over-come with emotion. Then the Grolier Club hosted a cocktail reception and an exhibition of the magazine's works: drawings, covers, and books that had grown from *New Yorker* articles, including Andy's *The Second Tree from the Corner* and Roger's *The Summer Game*. Oddly, the anni-versary issue of *The New Yorker* contained a piece by Andy and a piece by John McPhee—two Maine articles in one issue, a rural *New Yorker* to commemorate fifty years at the center of Manhattan literary life. The anniversary was the mark of achievement and the end to an era. By the close of the year, a mandatory retirement policy forced the old guard, all of Katharine's hires and colleagues, to put down their pencils, including editors William Maxwell and Robert Henderson (though in typical *New Yorker* fashion they were all offered new offices "out of kindness and idiocy," as Roger put it).

To anyone checking the calendar, 1975 also meant it was high time for another history of the magazine and attendant controversy. Right on schedule, Brendan Gill published *Here at "The New Yorker"*—in fact, the timing of the book, the picture of Eustace Tilley on the cover, and the spot illustrations of Tilley at the head of each section made it seem as if the book were an authorized work for the anniversary, which it emphatically was not. This deception was only the first aspect of Gill's book that Katharine despised.

No one was ever as furious about a book as Katharine was about *Here at "The New Yorker."* It completely hijacked her thoughts. She shakily underlined it and penciled numbers along the margins that corresponded to pages and pages of notes. She told Harriet Walden that she was annotating it in case anyone wanted to sue Gill for libel (she believed she herself was libeled). She felt it urgent to provide corrections from someone who'd been at the magazine long before Gill.

Gill delivered the backhanded compliment of "formidable" and doubled down, calling Katharine "as stubborn—and, sometimes, as humorless— in pushing for the acceptance of her opinions as some weighty glacier working its way down a narrow Alpine pass." Katharine, according to Gill, intimidated Ross into agreeing with her, and if not, "held White as a sort of hostage" to get her way. As Nora Ephron wrote in her scathing *Esquire* review, Katharine wasn't the only one to be so disingenuously maligned: "The stories he tells, stories he seems to mean to be charming and affectionate, are condescending, snobbish and mean." Christopher Lehmann-Haupt noticed the same thing: friend or foe, everyone at *The New Yorker* "emerge[s] with teethmarks or tiny daggers in his or her flesh." Geoffrey Hellman gave a speech at the Grolier Club to refute Gill's portrait of Ross, and he sent Katharine a copy.

Katharine took comfort from these correctives, but the gossipy meanness continued outside the book covers. Roger read Gill's manuscript in galleys, and when he got to the passages about his mother, he pleaded with Gill to remove them, telling him that they'd kill her. So Gill had some inkling of how his stories would be received, but not only did he keep the offending passages in the book, he also seemed to believe they were true compliments. He invited the Whites to his book launch at publicist Benjamin Sonnenberg's Gramercy Park mansion ("Vulgarity Hall," said Roger, who arrived at the party in Woody Allen's stretch limousine). Though Katharine would have loved to see the inside of that storied house, she refused in horror.

Katharine was blindsided by this treatment. What had she ever done to earn Gill's enmity? She'd been the one to accept Gill's first casual back in 1936, and Gill had been so excited to receive Katharine's letter that he called her at home in the middle of the night. She had continued editing him for years; the note she'd written about him for the Bryn Mawr archive said he had "more bounce and more energy" than anyone else on the staff. Their friendship had even survived the hiccup of Gill's introduction of E. B. White's interview in *The Paris Review*, which he began with Andy's and Katharine's "imaginary" ill health: "It was always wonderful to behold the intuitive seesaw adjustments by which one of them got well in time for the other to get sick. What a mountain of good work they have accumulated in that fashion! Certainly they have been the strongest and most productive unhealthy couple that I have ever encountered, but I no longer dare to make fun of their ailments." Katharine and Andy let it slide at the time.

She was particularly incensed by Gill spreading the rumor that she had been "prepared to lead a palace revolution" against Ross. This was precisely backward, she fumed. "Everyone who knows me at all knows that my loyalty to Ross was almost fanatical. Instead of my going to Fleischmann to suggest ousting Ross, Fleischmann three times came to me." Gill's description of her as humorless and opinionated stung not only because it was personally insulting, but also because of how thoroughly he misrepresented the editorial culture of the magazine. She and Ross relished their arguments. But how could Gill have known that, given that he joined the magazine staff just when she left for Maine? It was another reminder that she was the only one left to testify about those early days.

Katharine mentioned the Gill book in every letter she wrote to family and friends for the next several months, warning them away from it, pleading with them not to take it seriously. She told Callie about the "ghastly picture of [her] old Grandmother," and launched into the story of Fleischmann's attempts to promote her: "I have always, because it sounds conceited, not told this; and I don't want to spread it around now. I don't even know whether your father knows it." George Core at *The Sewanee Review* approached her to review Gill's book, but Katharine turned him down. She had no interest in publishing her indictments, but she did want the story of Fleischmann's offers *known*, and so she told the story at length in her notes, repeating even in this secret spot that she didn't want the facts publicized. She was writing these stories for Shawn, and for posterity, and she kept promising to send them along to him as soon as she was finished.

She never finished. Several years after her death, Andy edited her notes, had them typed up, and sent them to Bryn Mawr with her annotated copy of Gill's book, adding his own note of agreement that the book was "offensive, gossipy, factually weak, and occasionally mean." Why did this book, with its spitefulness so transparent to most of its readers, upset Katharine so much? She became obsessive, and it took a clear toll on her mental health. "It has depressed me," she wrote to Evelyn McCutcheon, "and made my whole career seem not very worthwhile." She repeated this exact sentence in her notes to Shawn. Katharine's obsession with Gill's book was sad and regrettable, but in a way, she was right to be worried. Far more was at stake than her own reputation. Obscuring Katharine's contributions to *The New Yorker* was a blow to women's literary history, not to mention a larger story about women in the workforce between first- and second-wave feminism. Gill's book would indeed be influential in the telling of the magazine's history for the next few decades.

In November of 1976, Katharine underwent her most frightening health crisis yet. She was upstairs in her bedroom and called her nurse to help her plan the dinner party that she and Andy were giving that evening. Suddenly, Katharine turned to the nurse and said, "I can't breathe—please call Mr. White!" And then she collapsed into unconsciousness. That's all she remembered for the next two days. The fire department arrived within minutes and gave her oxygen, then the ambulance arrived and sped her to Blue Hill Hospital, where she was in the intensive care unit for thirty-six hours. The diagnosis: a buildup of fluid around her heart and lungs had caused congestive heart failure. She woke slowly through the haze of medication, and scared Andy with the strange things she said, at one point slapping her own head and crying, "Please, God; please, God; please, God." But her heart rhythm was strong, and she was sent home with a prescription for a daily diuretic. "The human body machine is pretty complex," she wrote in a joint letter to Roger, Nancy, and their spouses. "Mine is rusting."

Everyone, Katharine included, understood this to be a very near miss. Her rusting body was giving loud warning signs (weeks later, she had two teeth extracted, which crumbled under the dentist's fingers). Katharine, little given to sentimental or maudlin reflections, faced her mortality in a letter to her children: "At 83 I ought to be willing to go but I find I don't want to at all, and that I have far too much to accomplish for Andy on this book and on papers that I am sending to Bryn Mawr, and on family papers that have to be sent to Yale and Bowdoin College, to want to give up yet."

It was work that kept her here on earth. She insisted that Roger and his family still come to Maine for Thanksgiving. "Worst of all," she wrote to Evelyn McCutcheon, "I have not been able to order Christmas gifts in time to get here for my nurses and family and household help."

She was back at home in time for her and Andy's forty-sixth wedding anniversary, and if in 1954 his gift to her had been to tear down a building, now he promised her the construction of one, a greenhouse on their farm just south of her cutting garden with a stone foundation and a furnace. Though it wouldn't be built until the following year, by their forty-seventh anniversary she would be picking a bouquet of carnations from it. It was one of his most inspired presents and it gave her something to look forward to, another way to grow the garden of her mind, a way to live in the future. Friends and family augmented this gift the following year by sending delicate hothouse plants, such as orchids, and clay pots that could withstand the humidity.

As it happens, in 1976, just a few months after a third congestive heart episode and a week in the hospital, Katharine also gave what she called her "most successful gift of all time." She hadn't been able to play her Steinway baby grand piano for several years because of her eye trouble, and though she would miss Andy's occasional playing and their yearly Christmas carols, it was time to give the instrument to someone who could use it daily. Katharine gave it to Carol Angell, and the piano made the long journey from Andy's study to the Angells' fifth-floor apartment on the Upper East Side.

Incredibly, Katharine kept working, mostly on the nightmare that was Andy's book of letters. It had been a long slog, and though the book was in proofs, it was not close to completion, in part because it was far too long. Andy had never wanted to do the book in the first place (Katharine's word was that his publisher had "over-persuaded" him) and the three-year process only demoralized him further. Ursula Nordstrom at Harper & Row, the editor who had instigated it, had since retired, as had the publisher's assistant. The new assistant, Corona Machemer, stepped in, but Katharine found her to be too young and inexperienced, someone whose work needed supplementing, and Katharine helped Andy answer all her many, many queries on the proofs. Dotty Lobrano Guth had helped compile the letters, and her name would appear on the cover as editor, but the responsibility for the book's apparatus—the introductory essay, the shorter essays that headed each section, and the explanatory notes at the beginnings of letters that put them in context—fell heavily on Andy's shoulders. The process called out in him much that he disliked about writing, not least that he had to write about himself in the third person. And even as he tried to finish it, he chased the book's horizon, writing his usual letters to friends and family but asking them to save those letters in case he needed them for the book. Would it ever end? Andy and Katharine speculated on whether they could abandon the project and return the advance. Roger read the manuscript in proofs and liked it, and his opinion buoyed Andy at this dark hour. Still, it needed trimming, and an index. The publication date was moved back.

To readers, though, *Letters of E. B. White* showed no sign of the struggles to produce it when it was published in November 1976. Harper had only printed fifteen thousand copies at first, but by Christmas the book was a bestseller with fifty-five thousand copies in print. Wilfrid Sheed reviewed the book in *The New York Times* and praised it—but not without qualification. The letters revealed to Sheed the limitations of a writer who was "jumpy, edgy and nervous about just about everything," but he fully admired Andy's ability to create within such fetters. He connected this to the structures that gave shape to *The New Yorker*: "being inimitable within a formula is the very definition of White's genius."

Not incidentally, this book gave E. B. White's readers the most sustained portrait yet of Katharine S. White. She had, of course, appeared in his columns, where he referred to her as "my wife," and she was the inspiration for some of his fictional characters (she confessed to friends with mock embarrassment that she was Mrs. Mooney, an obsessive Giants fan, in his story "The Seven Steps to Heaven"). But Andy's mentions of Katharine obscured more than they revealed. As Roger would note in a 1997 foreword to *One Man's Meat*, "Because White is such a prime noticer it is a while before a reader becomes aware of how much he has chosen to leave out of the book. There is very little here about his wife, Katharine." Andy's brother Stanley once chastised him for the way he represented Katharine in his essays: "Of all the well-known contemporary characters, she has had by far the worst deal, being continually brought into the literary scene as nothing but a voice from the next room, a bodyless protest, or merely a diversion."

Now readers could catch more tantalizing glimpses of the way two careers had been intertwined within one long marriage. Andy's many letters to her—"Dear Kay"—showed how he relied on her, as when he asked about illustrators for *Stuart Little* or reported on his writing progress from New York or sent her drafts of the *Subtreasury of American Humor* apparatus for her to edit. His letters demonstrated his affection for her, even and perhaps especially the newsy letters of no emotional import that he wrote simply to make her laugh, such as his description of a peaceful day in the Maine country: "This is one of those mornings, the decibels working up to a crescendo, with many visiting boys all of them named Hawless. Dogs bark, sheep cry, domestics chatter, Howard and I stand three feet apart and yell directions at each other, the water pump and the coffee grinder run incessantly, and the young crows cry for the old life they once knew." It was easy to see the shared sense of humor that kept their marriage afloat through illness and disruption. It was less easy, from her husband's perspective, to see Katharine as a powerful member of New York's literary elite. The letters almost never referred to the circumstances of Katharine's career. Andy frequently used anecdotes about Katharine in his letters to others for comic effect, portraying his own bemusement and faint condescension at her foibles and weaknesses, as when he gave her a draft of a casual he'd written about their household staff, and by chance two of their servants were arguing on the floor below them. "Katharine finished reading the piece in tears, saying that she was no good as a housewife (she said she was no good as a mother either, just for heightened effect) and that she would have to give up her job and make a decent home for me. I told her to get the hell over to the office and win some more bread and stop her blubbering." Andy's letters book gives the cumulative impression that, just as he held himself to a standard of modesty and charming abasement, so did he have a policy of consistently downplaying his wife's role in his own professional life.

Katharine's eyesight was failing and she now read with a magnifying glass held in front of her reading glasses. For Christmas, Roger gave her the just-published second volume in the six-volume set of Virginia Woolf's letters, and though an ordinary person might have been fed up with letters—she was answering all the mail that flooded Andy upon the publication of his letters book, in addition to editing her own correspondence for university archives, and of course keeping up with her friends and family—she was well into the Woolf book when her eyesight worsened yet more, and she learned that she would soon be too blind to read or write. Roger wrote to her immediately. He knew he couldn't say anything to assuage her grief, but he focused on what would not be diminished—her "judgment and extraordinary intelligence"—and he drew a vivid picture of the life she could lead, with family members— "good readers and good talkers"—to surround her and secretaries to help keep up her correspondence. He argued his case: "I do firmly and earnestly believe that you can conquer this latest and worst piece of frightful luck—if you will let us all have a part in it." It was the last letter he ever wrote to her.

In the spring of 1977, she suffered another congestive heart failure. She recovered, just as she had the previous times, and came home to her tightly ordered routine. Her night nurse would wake her up each morning with her medication and help her to the bathroom. The nurse would leave at seven, and Andy would come into her bedroom at seven thirty with breakfast and the newspaper. The cook would come upstairs at eight forty-five to consult on the day's meals, and then the day nurse would arrive at nine to bathe her and apply her cortisone ointment. At ten thirty, Katharine would make her slow way downstairs on her canes, then switch to her walker for the trip to the living room. The north end of the living room sofa had been her seat of power for the past few years. Initially, she'd used a small round table to hold the morning mail and newspapers, and as she picked something up and finished it, she'd move it to the sofa on her left. The piles on the table and the sofa got higher and higher, a disorganized heap sliding to the floor, and still she'd implacably place a just-read letter on the top. Andy marveled at the order within the chaos: "Katharine sat quietly in the middle of the mess, dictating letters in a steady firm voice, never missing 'comma' and 'new paragraph.'" He tried to solve the problem by building Katharine a new coffee table, the length of the couch and painted the color of the living room. "Inside of a week, she had it groaning under the weight of seed catalogues, back issues of the New Yorker, carbons of letters to Senator Muskie, duplicates of orders to Hammacher Schlemmer, fly swatters, lengthy correspondence with department stores taking them to task for abandoning cotton and wool and substituting polyester, old copies of the Horn Book, a wooden glove box full of I don't know what, newspaper clippings of editorials she planned to take issue with, answered letters from grandchildren, and on and on."

She was looking forward to the summer, because Roger and Carol had finally purchased a cottage of their own in Brooklin, and she could enjoy having all three children at the farmhouse, and many of her nine grandchildren. And she did, for a short time that July.

On July 20, 1977, a day so hot that even healthy adults had a hard time catching their breath, Katharine woke up in distress. The night nurse brought Andy to her room, and indeed her pulse was extremely high. They called an ambulance and brought her to Blue Hill Hospital, and it soon became apparent that the medication was not going to help this time. Andy sat by her bedside, watching her heartbeat on the monitor, and he was there when she died that afternoon.

He drove himself home and told his family the news. The next day, he needed to return to the hospital to retrieve Katharine's belongings. Carol, knowing that it would be a difficult journey, offered to drive him, and she was touched to see that among Katharine's possessions was her bed pillow, which Andy had brought her the day before to make sure she was comfortable as she lay quietly dying in the ICU.

Three days after her death, the family held a small committal ceremony at the Brooklin Cemetery. It had been Katharine's wish to be cremated, and she didn't particularly care what happened to her ashes, but she thought the local cemetery would be the most appropriate place for them, as opposed to the Sergeant family plots in Northampton. Andy chose a spot in the far corner of the cemetery, away from all the other graves; some people would interpret this as snobbishness, but he told Roger that he intended not to intrude on the life of the townspeople—even after living in North Brooklin for more than four decades. Katharine wanted no church or home funeral, and so she had none, just a small gathering.

Andy did not attend his wife's service. He could not. But he did write a small piece for Roger to read. He paid tribute to what Katharine loved: the green earth; her friends and family; Brooklin, especially the Brooklin library, which was just down the road from her final resting place. He saluted her work ethic: "And until the very day of her death, last Wednesday, she was still loving and giving and writing and hoping. She never quit. Even in the most difficult circumstances—and they became, near the end, very difficult indeed—she continued to work for the things she believed in, and to keep in touch with the people she cared for." Then, as Katharine requested, he included a poem he had written for her forty years previously, "Lady Before Breakfast." Katharine had said, "It is a judgment about me—it's me as I was when I was vigorous and I like it."

> On the white page of this unwritten day
> Serena, waking, sees the imperfect script:
> The misspelled word of circumstance, the play
> Of error, and places where the pen slipped.
> And having thus turned loose her fears to follow
> The hapless scrawl of the long day along,
> Lets fall an early tear on the warm pillow,
> Weeping that no song is the perfect song.
>
> By eight o'clock she has rewritten noon
> For faults in style, in taste, in fact, in spelling;
> Suspicious of the sleazy phrase so soon,
> She's edited the tale before its telling.
> Luckily Life's her darling: she'll forgive it.
> See how she throws the covers off and starts to live it!

That summer, the stream of letters and cards of condolence to the North Brooklin farmhouse was "torrential," in Andy's words, and he could muster a reply to almost none of them. E. B. White may have been the decorated and nationally famous writer, but he marveled that Katharine's death prompted four or five hundred people to honor her by writing to him, everyone from college friends and *New Yorker* authors to her "strays," like a letter from a Finnish woman who used to clean for the Whites on Forty-Eighth Street decades earlier, who wrote to say how much it meant when Katharine gave her son a book. Andy couldn't keep up with the reminiscences.

But what he could do was order Katharine's gravestone, a plain slate with a round top, slim shoulders, and elegant Centaur type spelling out only her name and dates, and he could plant an oak tree, spindly and odd looking, in the empty corner of the cemetery where her monument lay. Eight years later, his own matching gravestone would stand next to hers, and both stones would weather poorly over time, and their grandchildren would replace them with dark gray stones, copies of the originals in shape and type, and decades later, the oak tree would rise seventy feet into the air with a lavish and symmetrical beauty, and more family members would be laid to rest around them, including Joel, their daughter-in-law Carol, their granddaughter Alice, and Roger.

But first, Andy would finish Katharine's work. Executing her estate meant finally packing up everything destined for the archives. Andy was consumed with inventories and appraisals. A Bryn Mawr librarian came and packed up five hundred fifty books from *New Yorker* writers, and by the fall the rest of Katharine's promised letters and family papers were finally donated.

And then there was the matter of Katharine's book. It took two years after her death, but Andy finally shepherded *Onward and Upward in the Garden* into publication with Farrar, Straus and Giroux: her fourteen garden columns, with an introduction by E. B. White, and a one-paragraph editor's note at the end to explain the "chapter missing from this book," Katharine's ardently dreamed of essay on the gardens of her childhood. Did Andy know that she'd once envisioned a much different book, the garden columns dug into and planted round with family history and reminiscence? He made no mention of this in the published version. He gave a loving portrait of the "turbulence" that ensued when an editor became a writer: "The editor in her fought the writer every inch of the way; the struggle was felt all through the house. She would write eight or ten words, then draw her gun and shoot them down. This made for slow and tortuous going. It was simple warfare—the editor ready to nip the writer before she committed all the sins and errors the editor clearly foresaw." The book's sales and reviews were strong enough that Andy felt he'd done his wife justice. Bryn Mawr mounted an exhibit of Katharine's papers in conjunction with the book, and Nancy Stableford spoke on behalf of the family (Andy fled to Florida). The book was well received and has stayed in print to this day, in a reissued volume from New York Review Books.

In the midst of it all, Andy was given a special citation from the Pulitzer Prize Board in 1978 "for his letters, essays and the full body of his work," and he wrote to an old *New Yorker* friend that it might have pleased Katharine, but he said, "Life without her is no bargain for me, awards or no awards. She was the one great award of my life and I am in awe of having received it." He felt adrift without her, because "she steadied [him] day and night." He said that after Katharine's death he had no desire to write anymore, and he also gave up hosting friends at the North Brooklin house. He broke his "no interview" rule once, but only to speak about Katharine, showing the reporter around the farmhouse and her cherished places, and even acting out her characteristic gestures, "his wife reaching for the phone with one hand and a cigaret [*sic*] with the other, rolling up her long hair 'around and around like this' and putting in many pins, cluttering up the sofa and coffee table with her papers."

Yet he still had his own work to do, collecting his writing if not producing new work. His ailments accumulated, and he worked steadily through them. He turned in a revised edition of *Elements of Style*, and the second volume in his uniform edition of works, *Essays of E. B. White*, was published the year of Katharine's death. The next volume, *Poems and Sketches of E. B. White*, took a few more years to collect, and for that he had enormous help from Corona Machemer, the Harper editor, who would become a dear friend and companion; it was published in 1981.

And Andy would have the signal experience of closely assisting his own biographer and living to read the book of himself. He had been hosting and corresponding with Scott Elledge for years, answering the most detailed questions about the furthest reaches of his past. His eyes began to fail him, but seventeen years after Elledge had first begun researching him, Andy read Elledge's biography in manuscript, prompting another flurry of quintessential E. B. White letters, elegant in their self-deprecation and their insistence on fact. "Congratulations on your manly attempt to make me into a literary character," he wrote. "It isn't going to work, but it makes great reading"—followed by dozens and dozens of corrections, tiny and large. He sat down with the published book and read it all over again, an experience that left him, as he wrote to Elledge, "exhausted but fulfilled," teary at the memories of Katharine, but also full of laughter at his own actions—and also at some of Elledge's interpretations. "Occasionally your explanation of what I was thinking about, or doing, gained by piecing together the wispy shreds of evidence, gave me a chuckle," he wrote—piercing right to a fear that lives in the heart of every biographer. "But that's inevitable in a book of this sort."

Just a few short months after the publication of his biography, E. B. White fell during a canoe trip on a nearby pond and then rapidly descended into senile dementia. He lived for another year, confined to the farmhouse under the care of nurses. Every day, his son, Joel, read to him, and the words that pleased him the most were his own, especially the book of letters that it had so bedeviled him to produce. He died on October 1, 1985, at his beloved farm. At the service later that month at the Blue Hill Congregational Church, the program carried another poem that Andy had written to Katharine—"Natural History," in which the speaker is a spider who, "In spider's web a truth discerning / Attach my silken strand to you / For my returning."

Epilogue

Katharine S. White Forgotten and Remembered

What an influence she was, what a builder! That Katharine, what a creation she was. Nobody stood more like a roof-tree for the magazine than she did. All she represented remains hers in memory and in value.
 —Janet Flanner to Roger Angell, 1977

What an achievement simply to have thought straight all her life.
 —Nadine Gordimer to Roger Angell, 1977

Katharine's obituaries also needed an editor. Her first name was spelled "Katherine" in *The Washington Post, The New York Times,* even *The Ellsworth* (Maine) *American,* whose editor, James Russell Wiggins, was a friend. She was described, yet again, as a Boston Brahmin. The truth stood revealed: Katharine Sergeant White didn't have a Katharine Sergeant White in her life, someone to worry for her and get things right—or to write a letter to the editor when things went wrong.

What if she'd had someone to facilitate her career, as she did for E. B. White? How much more could she have done—and, a more crucial question, would she have been happier if she could have done more? What might she have chosen to do? The contours of her life easily suggest unwritten books: the family reminiscence she never completed, the biography of Harold Ross, and the history of *The New Yorker*'s early years that she contemplated but discarded, all the edited collections that

publishers tried to solicit from her, but also books that she never imagined but might have, such as a collected book of her letters to authors
(an idea that Andy discussed with John Updike after her death but
indefinitely postponed). She once wondered to Jean Stafford, who was
teaching graduate students, if the best way to teach literature would be
to start with the draft of a story and then show its journey through the
editing process; such a craft book by a *New Yorker* bastion might have
sold millions. Or perhaps she would have put herself in the running for
the editor position after Ross's death, had her life circumstances been
different. There's no doubt she could have performed the role superbly.

One more counterfactual: what if Katharine had felt enough distance from her identity as a wife and mother actively to respond to the
new feminism? Early in *The Feminine Mystique*, Betty Friedan explains
how her own disillusionment with the postwar role assigned to American women came precisely from her work on mainstream magazines.
The many women who staffed the four major women's magazines—
Ladies' Home Journal, *Good Housekeeping*, *Woman's Home Companion*, and
McCall's—consciously sold their readers a hypocrisy: they were themselves career women (if often under male editors) who went to their
offices each day to publish articles that celebrated homemaking as wom-
en's highest calling. They effaced their own work and all the support
systems that made their careers possible. What if Katharine—who may
or may not have read *The Feminine Mystique* when it came out in 1963,
two years after her retirement—had decided to politicize the role of the
female editor, had felt energized to make visible her thirty-six-year career behind the scenes of a storied magazine? Who better to speak to the
history and future of women in the workforce than she, the only woman
on the masthead at *The New Yorker* at the end of her powerful career?

These are unanswerable speculations, and they sit alongside the near-
certain knowledge that Katharine died with enormous satisfaction in the
life she got to live. She likely felt that she'd had the substantial, worthwhile
life that she had anticipated when she graduated from Bryn Mawr in 1914,
and if she held any regrets, they likely focused on the ways that illness so
severely limited her. But she also died with some anxiety about how her
work would be remembered, an anxiety that would prove prescient.

When she began corresponding with librarians at Bryn Mawr about the donation of her papers, she stated the scope and contours of her legacy very clearly:

> What I am hoping to achieve is a sort of history and inside
> knowledge for future writers of the post World War I
> literary scene and especially of The New Yorker in its first
> two decades when it was responsible for developing and
> first publishing the writings of many of our best American
> writers and poets. The period is out of favor just now but it
> is sure to be studied and written about eventually. I am not
> interested in making these gifts a memorial to me.

She knew the story she envisioned was worth writing and she knew people would come looking for it. She preserved a history whose time had not yet come for the telling. She was only wrong about how eager those future readers would be for the story of *her* life. The historical is personal and there is no fulsome way to tell literary history without inquiring into the conditions and motivations for writing—and editing. Katharine's life offers so many windows into literary history, as the editor to important and forgotten writers, as the partner to a beloved writer and the mother to another one, as a late-blooming writer herself, as a curator of history.

Because of her self-effacement, part of her legacy must be inferred: her pride in her career, in her ability to craft a life that allowed her to work steadily through innumerable reasons not to. Though others—most notably her children—have ascribed guilt or regret to her, neither of those emotions can be found in the voluminous archive that she left behind. Perhaps she felt guilt and regret over her divorce, or over the amount of time *The New Yorker* took from homemaking and child rearing, and perhaps she edited those negative thoughts out of the official record. Or perhaps she never felt them, and they've been attributed to her by people who saw the toll that divorce and a supercharged career took on her and wondered if the cost was too high. Her marriage to E. B. White proves that she had no regrets after five years at *The New Yorker*, that she was willing to double down on her choices at a pivotal moment in her life. Their marriage assured that her career would be normalized and would function as part of the logic undergirding their family. She was proudly a working wife and mother, and though she would dash off a strident letter to me if she read this sentence, I consider her an artist for the way she wove together the parts of herself into a rich life of integrity.

It might surprise literary historians to read my claim that Katharine's career has largely been forgotten, because she is mentioned in every book and many of the articles about *The New Yorker* that cover the 1920s, '30s, '40s, and '50s. But most mentions are a kind of clerical due diligence, mere nods to the fact that she was in the room. These historians treat her as Harold Ross never did, as a token female, and few have bothered to ask what she brought to those editorial deliberations. In fact, the eclipse of Katharine White's career had so many causes as to be positively overdetermined.

American culture in the 1960s and '70s had reasons to erase her legacy and the legacies of those like her. White liberal feminists consciously looked back to suffragists for inspiration, but their "wave" metaphor, first used in a 1968 *New York Times Magazine* article, which periodized feminist activism, simultaneously obscured much of that history in order to portray so-called second-wave feminism as more radical and newly energized. They celebrated only the white women who focused single-mindedly on the vote, and they skipped entirely over the decades between the two "waves," from the Nineteenth Amendment in 1920 to Betty Friedan's *The Feminine Mystique*, almost exactly commensurate with Katharine's career. The clear losers in this rhetorical move were the socialist, anarchist, working-class, and queer feminists and feminists of color who organized for everything from labor rights to sexual freedom, not to mention the intersectional alliances dating all the way back to nineteenth-century coalitions of white suffragists and Black abolitionists. But second-wave feminists also needed to forget their immediate forebears; their narrative of twentieth-century discrimination against women could not admit the complexity of women who worked outside the home from the 1920s to the 1960s but who didn't call themselves feminists, politicize their own lives, or work for structural change. In-

deed, after a brief postwar drop, women's participation in the workforce
grew from 1947 onward, including married women with children at
home. The statistics tell a story of continuity, and this is arguably and
especially true of literary history, because publishing was one field where
women, long seen as arbiters of culture and the arts, were allowed to advance, in strong contrast to fields like business and law. The discontinuity,
over the course of Katharine's career, was in the attitudes toward women
in power and the tropes used to express those attitudes, a discourse in
which Katharine did not intervene.

Of course, Katharine was no Gloria Steinem, Diana Vreeland, or
Helen Gurley Brown—most definitely not a glamorous, single, or sex-
ually available woman in the public eye, nor was she an editor in chief.
She proudly deferred to Harold Ross, who exemplified the "charismatic
editor," one whose outsized personality guides the magazine and whose
social capital draws contributors to it. Katharine understood her brand
of editing to be most successful when least visible. She practiced many
kinds of subservience: to the institution of the magazine, to the demands
of the marketplace, and to the authors whom she wanted to keep submitting to her. Especially within a magazine that withheld author bylines and tables of contents, Katharine's career was never going to be
widely known or available for interpretation. Indeed, she might have said
that her legacy is precisely the absence of a discernible pattern among
the authors she curated—variety as her editorial signature, what style
was to E. B. White.

Other reasons for the opacity of Katharine's legacy stem from her own
choices, actions, and inactions. She might be more widely remembered
had she brought more women up behind her in the office hierarchy, but
though she hired many secretaries and manuscript readers, she hired only
one female editor, Rachel MacKenzie, whose own stellar career—she edited M.F.K. Fisher, Muriel Spark, Edna O'Brien, Isaac Bashevis Singer,
Saul Bellow, Philip Roth, Bernard Malamud, and Harold Brodkey—has
been more deeply buried than Katharine's. Even in her curation of so
many female writers whose main work was homemaking, Katharine up-
held gendered conventions for the division of labor, despite knowing all
too well the harm they caused women.

This concords with the fiction she edited. She placed herself on the leading edge of conventional, mostly realist fiction, rejecting the pat stories of her generation but also not overtly criticizing the white, upper-middle-class, liberal worldview into which she was born and educated. She was not a boundary pusher, not a patron of modernism or the avant-garde.

To anyone glancing at her only casually, she might have appeared a conservative matron presiding over her staff at the magazine and in her homes, a woman acting like a man by importing the norms of domestic management into the office. This picture of her, which surely fed into the portrait of her as "formidable," ignored what made her a magnificent editor. She sent her criticism along a network of fellow feeling, a through-line of trust built incrementally over the years. It was a substratum of emotion and reciprocity that was undetectable even to the people with whom she worked at the *New Yorker* offices, so that they could see her as formidable when her authors saw her as a generous magician. "Dear Katharine, I must sit down and write you *now* while the dream I woke from this clear autumn morning is still fresh," wrote the poet, novelist, and memoirist May Sarton in October 1960. "I dreamed that for some unknown reason you had given me a magic purse full of all sorts of sweet things in special pockets . . . I wish I could remember all the little things that were in this purse, all I do remember is that in the coin purse you had put something terribly wonderful *instead of* money, and I thought 'what a genius she is!'"

No, not a genius—something better. Katharine White's career irrefutably corrects the Romantic portrayal of literature as born from the innermost reaches of a genius creator. This myth swirled around Katharine even as she was in the process of demolishing it. In 1935, around the time that she designed *The New Yorker*'s first reading agreement, Thomas Wolfe published an essay in *The Saturday Review of Literature*, later issued as a book, that portrayed the writer as someone with "a huge black cloud" inside him, "loaded with electricity, pregnant," that finally "crested, with a kind of hurricane violence," onto the page (also "a great river thrusting for release inside [him]," also "burning lava from a volcano"). To that, he added a portrait of editorial genius, telling how he submitted his second novel, over a million and a half words, to his editor at Scribner, Maxwell

Perkins, who, with an effort every bit as monumental as Wolfe's own, like "a man who is trying to hang on to the fin of a plunging whale," sculpted it into its final, resplendent form. Katharine's legacy is to write a new story about literary creation and editorial revision. She defined herself not as a gatekeeper, a knife wielder, or a cocreator, but as a patron.

So much of the work that Katharine published was work that she called forth from her writers, not the product of primal or elemental forces that gushed from their bodies, but a response to the exterior world that solicited their perceptions and descriptions and storytelling and analysis and reporting and rhyming and parodying. So much of that work was written with other women in mind, and sometimes just one steadfast and receptive woman to stand in for them all. This writing, like Katharine's editing, was facilitated by an institution that gave structure, legitimacy, and value to their working lives. The institutional structure of art has not yet gotten its critical due, just as literature produced for the demands of a marketplace has often been denigrated by the assumption that capitalism compromises art. But magazines were crucial as an institution in the working lives of twentieth-century writers, especially beginning writers, especially women writers (and especially before the rise of MFA programs and the growth of teaching positions in the postwar era). Katharine relentlessly honed *The New Yorker*'s ability to meet her writers' needs because she peered directly into their lives, to the backstage of literary work, and she herself was the behind-the-scenes manager of her writer-husband's creative world. Far from working feverishly alone in a garret or off in Europe, as did Thomas Wolfe, these writers wrote amid constraints of family and health, as did Katharine. Their work was performed incrementally, in fits and starts, with sometimes grueling effort, but it often added up to something surprising, something with grace, something that showed no trace of strain or effort. As a patron, Katharine supported her writers by amplifying the sociality of their writing careers, not their solitude.

The cost of Katharine White's "personal-editorial" method of nurturing writers for *The New Yorker* was that she did not work with those whom she couldn't imagine lunching with at the Algonquin or hosting at her Turtle Bay home for cocktails. Her magnificent rapport and empathy mostly extended to those writers whom she perceived as likely to become friends, writers who shared her privilege as white, educated, and upper middle class, and so her legacy at *The New Yorker* needs to be outlined to make visible the close horizon of her intimacy. Highlighting this shortcoming is useful for the way it calls attention to what lies beyond her view, and so her rich and important career also serves as a tracking shot through the wider landscape of twentieth-century American letters, all those writers who tried and failed to publish in *The New Yorker* or who ignored it altogether. We can admire how this woman, born at a precise moment in history when opportunities for women were expanding, made full and abundant use of her freedom to work and raise a family, while also acknowledging how her curiosity stayed circumscribed within her privilege.

Katharine White's indisputable contribution to *The New Yorker* was to expand a regional humor magazine into a literary powerhouse, by campaigning for poetry, buying stories that were new and fresh and startling or more searching or dimensional, establishing elaborate back-office structures for finding, growing, and keeping new writers, defining the genre of casuals capaciously to include memoir, reminiscence, and fiction, and then keeping up alongside her writers as they played with this category to lasting effect. But she made the magazine more substantial while also keeping it buoyant, always insisting on humor, satire, parody, and light verse as necessary ingredients in the reader's diet, in part because they were such a necessary part of her own character and marriage.

She created an editorial ethos that outlived her, and nowhere is this better seen than in the long, distinguished, and satisfying career of her son. In one of the dozens of condolence letters that Roger Angell received from the broader *New Yorker* family as he sat in her office that summer in 1977, Frances Gray Patton remembered, "The first time I ever saw Katharine—way back in the winter of '48—she talked at length about her hopes for your future. What she wanted passionately was for you to become a really good and successful writer in your own right, and to be an editor of The New Yorker!" So many people marveled at how happy Roger seemed in the good life that echoed Katharine's own, as he too traveled between New York and Brooklin, as he balanced writing, editing, and parenting, and as he wrote the same brand of "personal-

editorial" letters to V. S. Pritchett, Ann Beattie, William Trevor, and
Donald Barthelme that William Maxwell, Rachel MacKenzie, and
others had adopted as their working method. The writer Alan Williams
called Katharine "the editor/encourager to the best of our time," but
mainly he was struck by how she was Roger's "own encourager, able as
so few brilliant parents are to inspire by whatever taut means a warm,
willing and surpassing emulation in the offspring."

Her influence was felt in the office long after her retirement, an influence so strong that even the young women who came after her wavered
when trying to describe her in modern terms. "I have always looked up
to her as the only woman ever to be really influential at the New Yorker,"
wrote one woman who never personally knew Katharine. "I don't know
how she felt about women's roles and feminism, but I hope she wouldn't
have been offended at being taken as a model. We all, of course, realized
that she was unique, but that didn't lessen her importance for us." Another woman who'd worked in the fiction department after Katharine's
time wrote, "All of us felt her presence and were proud to be there with
her." Rachel MacKenzie testified to Roger about both her relationship
to Katharine and her continuing influence: "Knowing your mother has
been one of the gifts of my life. The sense of her presence all these years
after she left the magazine is perhaps a measure of her stature. The taste
and intelligence, the humanity, the complexity have all left their mark
on those of us who knew and worked with her." No matter if Katharine
would have demurred about serving as a role model to so many ambitious literary women; they claimed her as the forebear they needed.

She spent nearly fifty years building a comfortable home life, editing out distractions, and smoothing obstacles so that E. B. White could
write, and the true story of that marriage and partnership will never be
told because so much of it was private between the two of them, as he
grappled with his anxieties and fears within the safety of her love and
understanding. How almost unimaginably different his life would have
been had Katharine not finally agreed to marry the man seven years her
junior. How much would he have been able to write?

I believe we can say with near certainty that he wouldn't have turned
his pen to children's stories had Katharine not made the field visible

for him with her thorough book reviews, and prodded him to write the stories in his head, and encouraged him to persist when the writing got tough, and put to good use her reputation among publishers to act as his literary agent and help convey his stories into the hands of readers (and then managed the daunting correspondence that poured back in from so many of those readers, young and old).

I am not the first to resuscitate Katharine's career. Just three months after Katharine's death in 1977, Andy White hosted a young woman named Linda Davis at his farmhouse. She arrived that autumn bearing a homemade apple pie and a list of questions that she wanted to ask him for her master's thesis on Katharine White's tenure at *The New Yorker*. She immediately got off on the wrong foot by knocking at the farmhouse's formal front door, which no one ever used. Andy came around the shrubbery, "looking displeased," as she later recalled in *The New Yorker*, and the first hour and a half of their visit was uncomfortable and stilted. But then Andy mixed a pre-lunch shaker of martinis and the cook brought in some crackers and cheese. Over lunch, he loosened up, launching into a tirade about Brendan Gill's book and confessing his own loneliness. When Davis drove away, she took with her a letter Andy had typed that afternoon, granting her permission to consult his papers at Cornell, and he would soon give her access to Katharine's papers at Bryn Mawr. Over the next six years, he and Davis would correspond often and she would visit about once a year. He would become a friend to Davis, congratulating her on her marriage and then the birth of her daughter, who happened to be born on Katharine White's birthday ("most adroit of you"). He stood by as Davis's thesis grew to a biography, and he died before it became a book, but he died knowing that Katharine's life was in magnificent hands. *Onward and Upward: A Biography of Katharine S. White* was published in 1987.

Surprisingly, both Andy's and Katharine's biographies would go out of print before the end of the twentieth century, and even more surprisingly, it would be Katharine who would receive this second biography. Or perhaps it's not so surprising, because E. B. White's work has remained in the public eye—read and reread around the world, all of it resplendently there for the finding—but Katharine's work has not. It is her career at *The New Yorker* that requires a double take and a reconsideration. Davis did not have the benefit of the *New Yorker* papers for her biography because they wouldn't be donated to the New York Public Library until 1991 and opened to scholars until 1994, so a full consideration of Katharine's work life and her influence was not yet possible. In 1985, William Leary was able to piece together the story of Katharine's decades-long relationship with Jean Stafford from other archives, which he published as an essay in *The Sewanee Review*. After the *New Yorker* papers became available, Nancy Franklin wrote a reassessment of Katharine's career, called "Lady with a Pencil," for *The New Yorker*, and Janet Carey Eldred devoted much of her book, *Literate Zeal: Gender and the Making of a "New Yorker" Ethos*, to a close reading of Katharine's editorial memos. These four works were the sources I devoured when I discovered Katharine, and they led me to glimpse the work that a full biography might perform, not just restoring Katharine's career to view but also changing the way we read the history of twentieth-century literature. It has been my good fortune to join this chain of supremely interesting people nervously knocking on descendants' doors, making their way to the North Brooklin farmhouse, and sitting in the sacred silence of the Manuscripts and Archives room at the New York Public Library, poring over a bottomless trove of letters.

It is amusing to speculate about how Katharine White might have wanted her story told—how she might have edited this very book. It would be shorter. It would have more one-liners. It might pay far less attention to matters of the heart, to the disappointments and betrayals that she worked so hard to surmount, given her own coping mechanism of purposefully forgetting pain and destroying letters referring to it. She might have wanted to focus only on the moments of connection, the successes.

But what she might consider overly sentimental or private, I consider political. Paying close attention to the patterns of her life has helped me see the patterns in what she published. As a pioneer of the work-from-home protocol, as someone who gave nearly her entire adult life to *The New Yorker*, who exemplified the magazine with unbreakable loyalty, her

home life was her work life—there was no separation. Her curation of
the magazine was an outgrowth of her own life and her position within
the culture. She was without doubt a literary feminist, and the twentieth-
century canon looks far richer when she is included in the frame, with
more emotional range, more women authors, and more attention to the
lived experiences of women. We benefit immensely from reading over
her shoulder.

Acknowledgments

I found Katharine Sergeant White when I went reading through twentieth-century literary history for a mentor; it turns out that writing a biography of an editor has been a splendid way to convene a community that approximates Katharine's support.

Two women were my first readers before I ever wrote a word: Leslie Daniels and Rachel Dickinson were crucial in helping me shape my thoughts into a proposal and my proposal into a book.

Katharine brought two new women into my life almost immediately. Geri Thoma at Writers House and Deanne Urmy at Mariner Books (formerly Houghton Mifflin Harcourt) are exactly the present-day mentors I craved, readers in the mold of Katharine herself and damn good at their jobs. All they lack is the perpetually burning cigarette. I'll always be grateful to Simon Lipskar, and I thank Susan Golomb for stepping in when Geri retired. How appropriate that an editor's biography should have two superb editors. Thank you, Jessica Vestuto, for bringing the book across the finish line with panache.

Without question, the biggest pleasure of writing this book was getting to know Roger Angell. He and his wife, Peggy Moorman, modeled generosity to me, and I loved every second of our conversations in New York and Maine and over the phone. This book would be so different without Roger's long memory, deep love and respect for his mother, and years as a *New Yorker* writer and editor. I miss him enormously. Peggy has stayed a dear friend and opinionated interlocutor on all things literary and artistic.

Thank you to Allene White and her daughter Martha for being such excellent keepers of the White legacy. I was so honored to meet Allene, hear her stories, flip through her photo album, and walk into her office to see Katharine's desk. Martha also showed me photos and old books and one gorgeous painting, and we spent quite a few long hours in beautiful Maine settings discussing her grandparents.

Jonathan Stableford and his wife, Cindy, hosted me in their mountaintop home in Vermont and told me much about the life of Nancy Stableford. Christopher Angell shared his memories of his father, Ernest Angell, and performed some truly impressive detective work on several old letters. Laura Engel stepped up with a big heart to take over her grandfather Roger's estate upon his death in 2022 and generously shared the letters and photographs that came her way.

I thank the current owners of the White farmhouse in North Brooklin, whose privacy I will protect but whose generosity in hosting my family and me one sylvan summer day must be acknowledged. Thank you for giving us a tour, along with the previous owners, and serving delicious food.

I am indebted to Eve Kahn and Julie Lasky for steering me to the Powys family. Thank you to Katey Grey for sharing memories of her childhood and her father, Peter Powys Grey. I'm also grateful to Kate Kavanagh, Chris Thomas, Charles Lock, and Alice Gerard for help with Snedens Landing and the Powys clan.

For helping to make my frequent travel to New York possible, I thank Railey Jane Savage. I thank my brother, Tim Reading, and my sister-in-law, Hallie MacDonald, plus Olympia and Wynn, for hosting me on research trips to Bryn Mawr. I thank Leslie Daniels and Andrew Knox for a special place in which to begin writing.

Every writer should have an excellent library and an excellent bookstore in their hometown. I have both: Tompkins County Public Library, where the librarians leap up and head to the hold shelf when they see me coming, and Buffalo Street Books, Ithaca's independent and community-owned bookstore. I have been privileged to serve on BSB's executive board for the duration of this project, which means I wrote a book about reading and writing while helping to shape the bookstore that would house it and put it in the hands of readers. Thank you to general manager Lisa Swayze, the bookstore staff, and fellow board members for all you do to foster book culture in Ithaca.

For enriching the reading and writing life, I am profoundly thankful for Jen Savran-Kelly, Jennifer G. Wilder, Angela and Ethan Macey-Cushman, Anisa Mendizabal, Karen Shepherd, Brian Arnold, Rebecca Peabody, Aisha Bastiaans, Emily Hopkins, Farr Carey, Bob Proehl, Heather Furnas, Sorayya Khan, Eleanor Henderson, Dina Bryan, Lizabeth Cain, and my sister, Stephanie Reading.

Thank you to Rob Vanderlan for reading early chapters, and an immense thank you to Aaron Sachs for reading the entire manuscript and giving this book the benefit of your intelligence.

Thank you, Sara Franklin, for reaching out to me as a fellow biographer of an editor and very quickly becoming so much more; and thank you for introducing me to Emily Van Duyne, for what turned into a substantial and sustaining three-way conversation. I'm grateful to Megan Marshall for early conversations about Katharine White and Elizabeth Bishop. David Michaelis is both a source on Katharine's life and an esteemed biographer himself; thank you for an energizing series of discussions and research leads.

I've benefited enormously from talking with three scholars who are working on Elizabeth Shepley Sergeant, and I thank Wendy Moffat, Patricia Loughlin, and Diane Prenatt for nerding out with me on all things Sergeant.

Anne Boyd Rioux became my accountability partner during the pandemic and a lovely long-distance friend. Anne also worked with Biographers International Organization to organize roundtables during the pandemic; my roundtable is still an enormous source of support, friendship, and inspiration, so I thank Carla Kaplan, Eve Kahn, Diane Prenatt, Christine Cipriani, Allison Gilbert, Sara Catterall, and Elizabeth Harris.

Another monthly support has been the Women Writing Women's Lives seminar from whose members I have learned so much. I was grateful to be able to present my work to this august group and thank Kate Calkin and Sydney Stern, as well as Sally Cook and Hilda Wright Rhodes for reaching out afterward with research leads.

I'm enormously beholden to Cara Dellatte and everyone at the Brooke Russell Astor Reading Room for Rare Books and Manuscripts at the New York Public Library, who retrieved endless boxes for me and made that beautiful room feel like an office away from home—and who generously provided scans to keep my writing going during the pandemic. Thank you to Eisha Neely and the staff at Cornell's Rare and Manuscript Collection for help with the E. B. White Papers. Marianne Hansen in Special Collections at Canaday Library was instrumental in helping me comb through Katharine White's archive, as well as research all three Sergeant women who attended Bryn Mawr.

Thank you to Evelyn Parker in Special Collections and Nanci Young in College Archives at Smith College; Margaret Warren, archivist at the Winsor School; Roberta Schwartz, archivist, and Sophie Mendoza, researcher, at Bowdoin College; Ginny Agnew for help in the Harry Ransom Center at the University of Texas at Austin; Sophia Duckworth Schachter at the Cosmopolitan Club in New York; Margaret Lacasse in Chicopee, Massachusetts, for generous and helpful legal research; Robin McElheny at Harvard University Archives for help with John Newberry; Marnie Goodbody at the Boston Public Library for devoting quite a bit of time to researching Charles Spencer Sergeant; Nora Ramsey at Syracuse University Libraries for help with Phyllis McGinley; Dean Rogers in the Special Collections at Vassar College for help with the Mary McCarthy and Elizabeth Bishop papers; David M. Hays, archivist at the Rare and Distinctive Collections, University of Colorado Boulder Libraries for help with the Jean Stafford papers; and Aaron M. Lisec for help with the Kay Boyle and Bessie Breuer papers at Southern Illinois University's Special Collections Research Center.

I am grateful to Stephanie Atwater, Nancy Randall, and Tracy Spencer at the Friend Memorial Public Library in Brooklin, Maine, for unearthing a box of interesting and useful documents on the library's history. Thank you to the staff of the Brooklin Keeping Society for hosting me one afternoon and showing me documents and artifacts, including Katharine's steamer trunk.

I was deeply honored to receive a National Endowment for the Humanities Fellowship in support of this book. Thank you to the Brush

Creek Foundation for the Arts, especially Sharon Hawkins and Lauren Creagan, for a productive month of writing in Wyoming. Thank you to the New York Public Library Short-Term Research Fellowship, especially Thomas Lannon, for funding to travel to the city. Thank you to the Robert B. Silvers Foundation for a grant to fund travel for research. Lesley Williamson and the Constance Saltonstall Foundation for the Arts provided crucial (and delicious) off-season support. A very big thank-you to Biographers International Organization and the Caros for a Robert and Ina Caro Research/Travel Fellowship, which funded a necessary and pleasurable trip to Maine.

Thank you to Frederick Courtright for detailed help with permissions.

I'm grateful to Erik Hoover for the book's title, which makes you two for two.

At Mariner Books, I am so lucky to have benefited from the expertise and eagle eyes of copyeditor Aja Pollock and senior production editor Evangelos Vasilakis. Thank you to Martin Wilson and Amelia Wood for getting the book out there in the world. Owen Corrigan and illustrator Eleanor Taylor made a striking cover which I love—and I bet Katharine would have too.

My daughter, Lucy Farmer, accompanied me on several New York trips, and was an able research assistant who discovered several of Katharine's pseudonymous works and unsigned children's book reviews. Lucy, you outperformed the digital search! Thank you to Shady, Lyra, Jay, Lucy, and Jasper for being my home.

Abbreviations

NAMES

BB	Bessie Breuer
CA	Callie Angell
CSS	Charles Spencer Sergeant
EA	Ernest Angell
EBW	E. B. White
EL	Elizabeth Lawrence
ESS	Elizabeth Shepley Sergeant
HR	Harold Ross
JT	James Thurber
KS	Katharine Sergeant
KSA	Katharine Sergeant Angell
KSW	Katharine Sergeant White
MMc	Mary McCarthy
RA	Roger Angell
SE	Scott Elledge
VN	Vladimir Nabokov
WS	William Shawn

BOOKS AND MANUSCRIPT COLLECTIONS

Access codes refer to box and folder numbers.

APM	*A Tribute to Our Common Past*, Annie Shepley Omori [colloquially known as "Aunt Poo's manuscript"], 1939, Shepley Family Papers, George J. Mitchell Department of Special Collections & Archives, Bowdoin College Library, Brunswick, Maine, 2.58
AT	*About Town: The "New Yorker" and the World It Made*, Ben Yagoda (Boston: Da Capo Press, 2000)
BM	Katharine Sergeant White Collection, Special Collections Department, Bryn Mawr College Library
BOW	Shepley Family Papers, George J. Mitchell Department of Special Collections & Archives, Bowdoin College Library, Brunswick, Maine
COLO	Jean Stafford papers, University of Colorado Boulder Libraries, Special Collections, Archives and Preservation Department

CU   E. B. White collection, #4619, Division of Rare and Manuscript Col-
                lections, Cornell University Library
CU-SE   Scott Elledge papers, #14/12/3592, Division of Rare and Manuscript
                Collections, Cornell University Library
EBNY   *Elizabeth Bishop and "The New Yorker": The Complete Correspondence*, ed.
                Joelle Biele (New York: Farrar, Straus and Giroux, 2011)
EBWB   *E. B. White: A Biography*, Scott Elledge (New York: W. W. Norton &
                Company, 1985)
GID   *Genius in Disguise: Harold Ross of "The New Yorker,"* Thomas Kunkel
                (New York: Random House, 1995)
LEBW   *Letters of E. B. White, Revised Edition*, ed. Dorothy Lobrano Guth, re-
                vised and updated by Martha White, foreword by John Updike (New
                York: HarperCollins Publishers, 2006)
LMF   *Let Me Finish*, Roger Angell (New York: Harcourt Inc., 2006)
LZ   *Literate Zeal: Gender and the Making of a "New Yorker Ethos,"* Janet
                Carey Eldred (Pittsburgh: University of Pittsburgh Press, 2012)
NYPL   New Yorker records, Manuscripts and Archives Division, New York
                Public Library
NYPL-HW   Harriet Walden New Yorker papers, Manuscripts and Archives Divi-
                sion, New York Public Library
NYPL-SNB   S. N. Behrman papers, Manuscripts and Archives Division, New York
                Public Library, Astor, Lenox and Tilden Foundations
NYPL-WS   William Shawn papers, Manuscripts and Archives Division, New York
                Public Library
OU   *Onward and Upward: A Biography of Katharine S. White*, Linda H. Da-
                vis (New York: Fromm International Publishing Company, 1989)
OUG   *Onward and Upward in the Garden*, Katharine S. White, edited and
                with an introduction by E. B. White (New York: New York Review
                Books, 1979)
SMITH   Nancy Hale papers, Sophia Smith Collection, Smith College, North-
                ampton, Massachusetts
SS   Elizabeth Shepley Sergeant, *Shadow-Shapes: A Wounded Journalist in
                WW I France* (Boston: Houghton Mifflin, 1920)
TG   *Two Gardeners: Katharine S. White and Elizabeth Lawrence—A Friend-
                ship in Letters*, ed. Emily Herring Wilson (Boston: Beacon Press, 2002)
TNY   *The New Yorker*, New York: F-R Publishing Company, 1925–
TOM   *This Old Man: All in Pieces*, Roger Angell (New York: Doubleday, 2015)
TYWR   *The Years with Ross*, James Thurber (New York: HarperCollins, 2001)
VASS   Louise Seaman Bechtel papers, Archives and Special Collections Li-
                brary, Vassar College Libraries
YALE   Sergeant family papers (MS 806), Manuscripts and Archives, Yale
                University Library
YALE-ESS   Elizabeth Shepley Sergeant papers, Yale Collection of American Liter-
                ature, Beinecke Rare Book and Manuscript Library

Notes

PROLOGUE: FEBRUARY 1953

ix   *"You know how"*: Frances Gray Patton to KSW, January 30, 1953, NYPL 722.24.

ix   *"All I can say"*: KSW to Frances Gray Patton, February 13, 1953, NYPL 722.24.

xi   *"a little family dinner"*: Frances Gray Patton to KSW, February 22, 1969, BM 9.12.

xii   *"It was almost as if"*: Frances Gray Patton to KSW, March 2, 1953, NYPL 722.24.

xii   *"you were safe"*: Frances Gray Patton, "The Game," TNY, May 9, 1953, 30.

xv   *"You've done a remarkably"*: Frances Gray Patton to KSW, September 15, 1957, NYPL 755.5.

xv   *"great sympathy"*: Frances Gray Patton to KSW, January 7, 1956, BM 9.12.

CHAPTER 1

3   *She was the only*: Births Registered in the Town of Brookline for the Year Eighteen Hundred and Ninety-Two, volume 422 (1892), 427, and *Index to Births in Massachusetts 1891–1895.*

5   *"had to carry a stepladder"*: OUG 105.

5   *"as good as live"*: OUG 165.

6   *"The stern paddle"*: OUG 129.

6   *"nuts, apples, peaches"*: OUG 299.

6   *"pallid lavender-white"*: OUG 310.

6   *"their heavenly fragrance"*: KSW to EL, March 17, 1960, TG 62.

7   *"Who will pick"*: OUG 260.

7   *Perhaps their similar*: "Katherine [sic] White, Ex-Fiction Editor of the *New Yorker,* Is Dead at 84," *New York Times*, July 27, 1977.

8   *"a lovely swamp"*: OUG 227.

CHAPTER 2

11   *"We read* Little Women*"*: APM, 85.

11   *"charmed circle"*: APM 91.

11   *"family glamour"*: APM 84.

12   *"a very superior set"*: APM 139.

13   *"quiet unassertive and saddish"*: ESS, "Autobiographical memoir (1st draft of 1st chapter)," undated [1964], BOW 2.35.

13   *"dominiser"*: ESS, "Another version . . . Garty," undated, YALE-ESS 18.394.

13   *"rousers of [her] inner"*: ESS, untitled manuscript, April 1, 1954, YALE-ESS 18.394.

14 *"You have great and unusual":* Bessie Sergeant to Anne Barrows, September 23 [n.d.], BOW 2.16.

14 *Charles paid $23,500:* Deed, Charles Spencer Sergeant (grantee), Brookline, MA, Norfolk County Registry of Deeds, June 15, 1898.

14 *"occupation or erection":* Quoted in "The Pill Hill Local Historic District: The Story of a Neighborhood" (Brookline, MA: Brookline Preservation Commission, 2009), 17.

15 *In Poo's mind:* APM 175.

16 *Elsie began her first:* Elizabeth Shepley Sergeant academic transcript, Bryn Mawr College, 1903.

16 *"So many things happened":* Unattributed [Katharine Sergeant], "The Teacup," undated manuscript, BM 30.13.

17 *Their father returned:* OUG 164.

17 *The Sergeants' cook:* Twelfth Census of the United States, June 2, 1900.

CHAPTER 3

18 *"My feeling for you":* Caroline Belle Sergeant to KSW, May 8, 1952, YALE 3.44.

18 *"really [her] mother":* KSW to EL, January 15, 1966, TG 155.

18 *"Aunt Crullie, I told":* Caroline Belle Sergeant to KSW, May 8, 1952, YALE 3.44.

19 *After graduating:* "Charles Spencer Sergeant," *Commercial and Financial New England Illustrated* (Boston: Boston Herald, 1906), 137. Other biographical details drawn from "Charles Spencer Sergeant," *Electric Railway Journal* 14 (October 1898): 615; Samuel Atkins Eliot, "Charles Spencer Sergeant," in *A History of Cambridge, Massachusetts, 1630–1913* (Cambridge, MA: Cambridge Tribune, 1913), 244; Albert Nelson Marquis, ed., "Charles Spencer Sergeant," *Who's Who in New England: A Biographical Dictionary of Leading Living Men and Women* (Chicago: A. N. Marquis and Company, 1915), 957.

20 *"thinking and reading":* APM 133.

20 *"the famous John":* KSW to Myra M. Sampson, February 2, 1968, BOW 2.13.

20 *John Sergeant graduated:* Reverend Samuel Hopkins, *Historical Memoirs Relating to the Housatonic Indians* (Boston: S. Kneeland, 1753, reprinted 1911), 13.

20 *"as fickle and irresolute":* John Sergeant quoted in Rachel Wheeler, *To Live upon Hope: Mohicans and Missionaries in the Eighteenth-Century Northeast* (Ithaca: Cornell University Press, 2008), 62.

20 *Stockbridge's most famous:* "Sergeant & Konkapot, 1972–1976," Norman Rockwell Museum, http://www.nrm.org/MT/text/Konkapot.html, retrieved 7/3/2018.

21 *He was a member: Official Bulletin of the National Society of the Sons of the American Revolution* 12 (June 1917): 45.

21 *"coming back without":* ESS, untitled and undated manuscript, YALE-ESS 18.395.

22 *"the family scapegrace":* KSW to S. N. Behrman, July 5, 1946, in *People in a Magazine: The Selected Letters of S. N. Behrman and His Editors at "The New Yorker,"* ed. Joseph Goodrich (Amherst: University of Massachusetts Press, 2018), 125.

22 *This Catharine:* "De Forest, Henry Alfred, A. B. 1832," *Biographical Memoranda Respecting All Who Ever Were Members of the Class of 1832* (New Haven, CT: Tuttle, Morehouse, and Taylor, 1880), 85.

22 *"Be sure to be so":* Quoted in Steven Mintz, *Huck's Raft: A History of American Childhood* (Cambridge, MA: The Belknap Press of Harvard University Press, 2004), 85.

22   *She moved to the South:* "Class of 1884: Sergeant, Caroline Belle, 1944," Classes
      of 1879–1890 records, Smith College Archives, CA-MS-01023, Smith College
      Special Collections, Northampton, Massachusetts, 1417.14.

22   *She taught at the Clarke:* KSW, "Caroline Sergeant, Daughter of Hamp, Dies at 93
      in Me.," *Daily Hampshire Gazette,* May 16, 1955.

23   *"a rare blessing":* Caroline Belle Sergeant to KSW, May 8, 1952, YALE 3.44.

CHAPTER 4

24   *"the romantic story":* KSW, "Books: How Dear to This Heart," TNY, December 11,
      1948, 123.

24   *"darksome forests":* KSW, "Books: Children's Books at Christmastime," TNY, De-
      cember 16, 1944, 78.

25   *"They are still":* KSW, "Children's Books: Between the Dark and the Daylight,"
      TNY, December 7, 1946, 128.

25   *Charles sent his:* KSW to Louise Seaman Bechtel, undated [1941], VASS 43.658.

25   *The city of Boston:* Leonard S. Marcus, *Minders of Make-Believe: Idealists, Entre-
      preneurs, and the Shaping of American Children's Literature* (Boston: Houghton
      Mifflin Company, 2008), 64, and "Mission & History," The Public Library of
      Brookline, https://www.brooklinelibrary.org/about/history/, retrieved August 3,
      2018.

25   *"Eliza Orne White":* KSW to Louise Seaman Bechtel, undated [1941], VASS 43.658.

25   *It was founded in 1873:* Marcus, *Minders of Make-Believe,* 67–68.

26   *William Falkner submitted:* Paul Rosta, "The Magazine That Taught Faulkner, Fitz-
      gerald, and Millay How to Write," *American Heritage* 37.1 (December 1985): 40.

26   *"for this was the best":* Quoted in *New Critical Approaches to the Short Stories of Ernest
      Hemingway,* ed. Jackson J. Benson (Durham, NC: Duke University Press, 1990), 88.

26   *"how many other":* "Notes and Comment," TNY, September 1, 1928, 9.

26   *"all soft and silky":* KS, "A Discovery (A True Story)," *St. Nicholas* 29 (August
      1902): 947–8, and KSW, "A Discovery (A True Story)," *Lion and the Unicorn* 19.2
      (1995): 232.

27   *"All the trees":* Elwyn B. White, "A Winter Walk," *St. Nicholas* 38 (June 1911): 757,
      and Melissa Sweet, *Some Writer!: The Story of E. B. White* (New York: HMH Books
      for Young Readers, 2016), 140.

27   *"a sinful hoax":* Rosamond Sergeant, *Wild Ducks, St. Nicholas* 30.2 (June 1903): 755,
      and KSW to S. N. Behrman, July 5, 1946, in Goodrich, ed., *People in a Magazine,* 125.

27   *"an amazing note":* EBW, "Onward and Upward with the Arts: The St. Nicholas
      League," TNY, December 8, 1934, 42.

27   *"often the ones":* KSW, "Children's Books: Between the Dark and the Daylight,"
      TNY, December 7, 1946, 127.

28   *"there was more to poetry":* KSW to RA, January 30, 1965, private collection.

28   *"Their comforts, their":* KSW to RA, March 6, 1967, private collection.

28   *"[Elsie] was a most important person":* KSW to RA, January 30, 1965, private collection.

29   *"preventative hot whiskey":* KSW, "Department of Amplification," TNY, June 18,
      1966, 112–14.

29   *When Charles celebrated:* "Used to Be a Bank Clerk: C. S. Sergeant's Word Now
      Law with Army of L Road Employees," *Boston Daily Globe,* June 12, 1901, and
      EBW to Linda H. Davis, October 22, 1981, BM 32.2.

29   *Ros was a tenth-grade:* KSW to EL, November 3, 1960, TG 81.
29   *How could Katharine:* Mary Pickard Winsor, "Miss Winsor's Speech," *Winsor Graduate Bulletin: Fiftieth Anniversary Issue* 3.2 (June 1936), YALE-ESS 15.351.
30   *She plunged right:* "Plan of Study," Miss Winsor's School for Girls, 1910–11.
30   *"liable at any time":* Winsor, "Miss Winsor's Speech," 5.
30   *The youngest Sergeant:* KSW, "A Few Jottings about Miss Winsor," undated, YALE-ESS 15.346.

CHAPTER 5

32   *She'd had a rocky:* Elizabeth Shepley Sergeant academic transcript, Bryn Mawr College, 1903.
32   *She graduated among:* KSA, "Elizabeth Shepley Sergeant," draft manuscript, undated [1920], Bryn Mawr Alumni Association folder.
32   *Elsie and Poo set sail:* APM 192–93.
32   *"Nervous strain":* Annie Shepley to CSS, March 12, 1904, YALE 4.32.
32   *"moral depression":* Unsigned, to CSS, June 8, 1904, YALE 4.31.
32   *Neurasthenia gave doctors:* Tom Lutz, *American Nervousness, 1903: An Anecdotal History* (Ithaca, NY: Cornell University Press, 1991), 3–7.
33   *"the mental activity":* George M. Beard, quoted in Lutz, *American Nervousness,* 4.
33   *"I have seen young girls":* Jane Addams, *Twenty Years at Hull House with Biographical Notes* (New York: The Macmillan Company, 1912), 118.
33   *"One of her troubles":* Annie Shepley to CSS, March 12, 1904, YALE 4.32.
33   *"brought back to E.":* Annie Shepley to CSS, March 9, 1904, YALE 4.32.
34   *"I must try to find":* Annie Shepley to CSS, April 13, 1904, YALE 4.32.
34   *Within an hour:* Annie Shepley to CSS, May 3, 1904, YALE 4.32.
34   *Had she been a man:* David G. Schuster, *Neurasthenic Nation: America's Search for Health, Happiness, and Comfort, 1860–1920* (New Brunswick, NJ: Rutgers University Press, 2011), 134–38.
34   *the "rest cure":* Ibid., 29–30.
35   *Sometime during this:* Marquis, ed., "Charles Spencer Sergeant," 957.
35   *He was offered:* KSW to CA, December 20, 1969, BM 29.1. But perhaps KSW was wrong and the two events were not related, because a contemporaneous letter suggests he declined the offer in late 1906, well after Elsie's return from Europe. See Speyer to CSS, January 2, 1907, YALE 4.27.
36   *Upon graduation:* "Sergeant, Rosamond," *The Graduate Club of Miss Winsor's School* (1910), 42.
37   *"raised his hand wearily":* KSW to EL, January 20, 1969, TG 187.
37   *Acceptance to Bryn Mawr:* Bryn Mawr Undergraduate College Catalogue and Calendar, 1910, 49–53.
37   *"a gentleman of ancient":* APM 198.
37   *Charles had similarly:* KSW to RA, April 22 and April 29, 1974, private collection.
37   *Yurin-en mainly served:* "Yurin-en: A Pioneer of Social Welfare Service in Japan," https://www.gllc.or.jp/en/history/index.html, retrieved October 15, 2019.
38   *"One of the strongest":* KSW, "A Few Jottings about Miss Winsor," 5.
38   *Katharine took an extra:* KSW to EL, January 4, 1966, TG 150.

CHAPTER 6

39   *Aunt Crullie took:* KSW to BB, September 10, 1973, BM 2.10.

39   *Family lore says:* LMF 32.

39   *Just before dawn:* "La Bourgogne Sinks at Sea," *New York Times,* July 7, 1898.

40   *"stretching as far":* EA, "Polly's Fourth (A True Story)," *St. Nicholas* 30.2 (August 1903): 855.

40   *"rewritten the worst":* LMF 51.

40   *"He was a very":* KSW to CA, January 20, 1973, BM 29.1.

40   *He tried out for both:* LMF 33.

41   *"mountain-climbing":* Stuart Chase to EBW, July 22, 1977, BM 29.9.

41   *"demurely love-lorn":* OUG 186–89.

41   *"a man-of-action":* "Our History: Over a Century of Giving," International Grenfell Association, http://www.grenfellassociation.org/who-we-are/history/, retrieved June 4, 2018.

41   *Ernest, toting a large:* LMF 35.

41   *At the end of that summer:* KSW to CA, January 20, 1973, BM 29.1.

41   *In their minds:* KSW to RA, September 20, 1976, private collection.

42   *He said yes:* "Engagements," *Boston Herald,* June 13, 1913.

42   *"like an Eskimo igloo":* KSW to CA, October 9, 1972, BM 29.1.

42   *That year, Ernest:* *The Harvard Graduates' Magazine* 19 (1910–11): 107, 116, 448, 468.

CHAPTER 7

45   *She quickly made:* "Mrs. Eleanor Washburn Emory," *Colorado Springs Gazette-Telegraph,* March 6, 1977.

46   *In Katharine's incoming:* *Bryn Mawr College Annual Report 1911–1912,* 23–26.

46   *Black applicants were:* To take an example relevant to Katharine: Jessie Redmon Fauset was poised to win the Bryn Mawr scholarship at the Philadelphia High School for Girls, but President Thomas secretly arranged to fund Fauset's tuition at Cornell, paying 10 percent herself and guaranteeing another 50 percent in subscriptions. Fauset flourished at Cornell (though she was not allowed to live in the dormitories and boarded with a professor) and graduated in 1905. She became the literary editor of the NAACP's magazine, *The Crisis,* where she helped cultivate the Harlem Renaissance and the careers of Zora Neale Hurston and Nella Larsen, among many others. There is no record indicating that she knew of President Thomas's machinations to keep from having to accept or reject Fauset. See Helen Lefkowitz Horowitz, *The Power and Passion of M. Carey Thomas* (New York: Knopf, 1994), 342–43.

46   *Mawrters' families:* Patricia A. Palmieri, "Here Was Fellowship: A Social Portrait of Academic Women at Wellesley College, 1895–1920," *History of Education Quarterly* 23.2 (Summer 1983), 195–214.

46   *Moreover, she was one:* *Bryn Mawr College Annual Report 1913–14,* 275.

46   *In early October:* Katharine Sergeant academic transcript, Bryn Mawr College, 1914.

46   *Katharine the freshman:* "Bryn Mawr College Yearbook. Class of 1914" (1914), *Bryn Mawr College Yearbook,* 45.

47   *"Can you not":* KS, "A Plea for the Satirical," *Tipyn o'Bob* 9.4 (March 1912): 13–14.

47   *Bryn Mawr made:* Barbara Miller Solomon, *In the Company of Educated Women: A History of Women and Higher Education in America* (New Haven: Yale University Press, 1985), 80.

47   *"but who cares":* KS to CSS, February 6, 1913, BM 29.11.

47   *"which, incidentally":* KS to CSS, February 16, 1913, BM 29.11.

48   *She joined:* "Collegiana: The Debating Society" and "The English Club," *Lantern 1913*, 96–97 and 100.

48   *"It is the most terrific":* KS to CSS, March 16, 1913, BM 29.11.

48   *"They say I play":* KS to CSS, April 6, 1913, BM 29.11.

48   *She was also the one:* "Editorials," *Tipyn o'Bob* 11.6 (January 15, 1913), 1.

49   *"I gulped and said":* Mrs. E. B. White, "1970 Bryn Mawr College Survey of the Alumnae and Alumni," Bryn Mawr Alumni Association Files.

49   *"We have all":* KS, untitled editorial, *Tipyn o'Bob* 10.3 (January 1913): 1–2.

50   *The miserable student:* Katharine Shippen, "Dodd's Doughty Debateers," *Bryn Mawr College Yearbook 1914*, 39–40.

50   *"shouted from the college":* KSW to Nancy Milford, December 5, 1973, BM 8.12.

51   *"bearing, carriage, address":* Charles Eliot, "President Eliot's Address of Welcome," *A Record of the exercises attending the inauguration of Caroline Hazard, LITT. D., as president of Wellesley College, III October MDCCCXCIX* (Cambridge, MA: Riverside Press, 1899), 14–17.

51   *"gentle breeding":* M. Carey Thomas, "The 'Bryn Mawr Woman,'" in *The Educated Woman in America: Selected Writings of Catharine Beecher, Margaret Fuller, and M. Carey Thomas*, ed. Barbara M. Cross (New York: Teachers College Press, 1965), 139–44.

51   *"some rather peculiar":* Eliot, "President Eliot's Address of Welcome," 15.

51   *"Adamless Eden":* Palmieri, "Here Was Fellowship," 214.

52   *"Our failures only":* Horowitz, *The Power and Passion of M. Carey Thomas*, 385.

52   *"Oh, Katharine, how":* OU 35.

52   *"Oh, you poor little":* Quoted in Horowitz, *The Power and the Passion*, 500 n43.

52   *Between 1889 and 1908:* Carroll Smith-Rosenberg, *Disorderly Conduct: Visions of Gender in Victorian America* (New York: Oxford University Press, 1985), 281.

52   *among the female:* "Table 143: Breadwinners Among Females," *Statistical Abstract of the United States* 33 (1910), 242.

53   *The first generation:* Solomon, *In the Company of Educated Women*, 95. See also Smith-Rosenberg, *Disorderly Conduct*, 177–78, and Lynn D. Gordon, *Gender and Higher Education in the Progressive Era* (New Haven: Yale University Press, 1990), 5.

53   *"She is a sweet":* Quoted in Bethany Hicok, *Degrees of Freedom: American Women Poets and the Women's College, 1905–1955* (Lewisburg: Bucknell University Press, 2008), 35.

53   *These smashes:* Horowitz, *The Power and the Passion*, 60–64.

54   *By the middle:* Smith-Rosenberg, *Disorderly Conduct*, 281.

54   *Among the classes:* "Table 22: Marital Status," in *A College in Dispersion: Women of Bryn Mawr 1896–1975*, ed. Ann Miller (Boulder: Westview Press, 1976), 105.

54   *Educated women:* Gordon, *Gender and Higher Education*, 196, and Hicok, *Degrees of Freedom*, 83.

54   *The easiest way:* Smith-Rosenberg, *Disorderly Conduct*, 281–84.

54   *"I guess there's no":* KS to CSS, February 16, 1913, BM 29.11.

54   *"oodles of girls":* KS to CSS, March 16, 1913, BM 29.11.

55   *"limp from the greatness":* KS to CSS, February 16, 1913, BM 29.11.

CHAPTER 8

56   *Looking back:* KSW to Janet Agnew, May 27, 1959, BM 30.1, and KSW to James Tanis, February 23, 1974, BM 31.1.

56   *"No Melville":* ESS, *Willa Cather: A Memoir* (Lincoln, NE: University of Nebraska Press, 1963), 10.

56   *It would arise:* D. G. Myers, *The Elephants Teach: Creative Writing Since 1880* (Chicago: University of Chicago Press, 2006), 104–121. See also Mark McGurl, *The Program Era: Postwar Fiction and the Rise of Creative Writing* (Cambridge, MA: Harvard University Press, 2009), 85–89.

57   *"aesthetic charm":* Quoted in Myers, *The Elephants Teach,* 26.

58   *"the style and methods":* Bryn Mawr College Calendar, 1913.

58   *"In looking over":* Martha Carey Thomas, "Chapel Talk," May 1, 1914.

58   *Moore had suffered:* Linda Leavell, *Holding On Upside Down: The Life and Work of Marianne Moore* (New York: Farrar, Straus and Giroux, 2013), 78.

59   *Elizabeth Bishop and:* Hicok, *Degrees of Freedom,* 107–9.

59   *"We editors have been":* Editorials, *Tipyn o'Bob* 11.1 (November 1, 1913): 1–2.

59   *Katharine and Winifred:* Virginia Wolf Briscoe, *Bryn Mawr College Traditions: Women's Rituals as Expressive Behavior,* diss. University of Pennsylvania, 1981, 550.

60   *"During vacations she must":* Editorials, *Tipyn o'Bob* 11.11 (April 1, 1914): 1–2.

60   *"The college papers":* Editorials, *Tipyn o'Bob* 11.14 (June 1, 1914): 2–3.

61   *"six shy, unassuming":* "In the Shrine and Out," *Bryn Mawr College Yearbook Class of 1914,* 93–95.

61   *For Katharine, no:* See Hicok, *Degrees of Freedom,* 41.

62   *The scale was immense:* See "May Day by the Scholars of Bryn Mawr, Saturday May the Ninth, 1914," *May Day Programs,* BM College Archives.

62   *There was a heavy:* "May Day at Bryn Mawr," *New Outlook,* May 23, 1914, 147.

62   *The Philadelphia Inquirer:* "Bryn Mawr in May Day Revel," *Philadelphia Inquirer,* May 10, 1914.

63   *"to [her] astonishment":* KS to CSS, May 25, 1914, BM 29.11.

CHAPTER 9

64   *"I am unmarried":* United States Passport Application, Form for Native Citizen, Issued, July 16, 1914.

65   *Beginning at the turn:* Smith-Rosenberg, *Disorderly Conduct,* 255.

65   *"Dust, Fumes, Monotony":* "Committee on Hygiene of Occupations," *Bulletin of the Women's Municipal League of Boston* 4.5 (April 1913), 17.

65   *"eczema on hands and arms":* KSW to CA, February 4, 1971, BM 29.1.

65   *Medicine suddenly seemed:* KSW to SE, September 10, 1970, CU 183.

66   *On May 22, 1915:* "Marriages Registered in the Town of Brookline for the Year Nineteen Hundred and Fifteen," 9.

66   *"two, possibly three":* KSW to CA, February 4, 1971, BM 29.1.

66   *"The first seven years":* KSW to CA, January 20, 1973, BM 29.1.

66   *Once back in Cleveland: Harvard College Class of 1911 Second Report* (Cambridge, MA: Crimson Printing Co., 1915), 57, and *The Cleveland Blue Book 1915,* 26.

66   *"I could only believe":* APB, "Department of Amplification," TNY, January 17, 1959, 80. That this was written by Katharine and about Ernest is proven by a contemporaneous letter in which Roger urges Katharine to write it, apparently after she

suggested he take on the topic of his father's self-talk. RA to KSW, December 26 [1958], private collection.

67 *The Angells began:* See Clare Virginia Eby, *Until Choice Do Us Part: Marriage Reform in the Progressive Era* (Chicago: University of Chicago Press, 2014), xviii and 37.

68 *Ros and John were married: Washington Post*, May 20, 1916.

68 *"a very pretty home wedding":* "Table Gossip," *Boston Daily Globe*, May 21, 1916.

68 *"Tris Speaker and I":* RA, "The Web of the Game," TNY, July 20, 1981, 105.

69 *The census had already:* Lucy Wright and Amy M. Hamburger, *Education and Oc-cupations of Cripples, Juvenile and Adult: A Survey of All the Cripples of Cleveland, Ohio, in 1916* (New York: The Red Cross Institute for Crippled and Disabled Men, 1918), 11.

69 *Though in later years:* Susan M. Schweik, *The Ugly Laws: Disability in Public* (New York: New York University Press, 2009), 234–40.

69 *"Men of Ohio!":* See photo, "Woman suffrage headquarters in Upper Euclid Avenue, Cleveland—A. (at extreme right) is Miss Belle Sherwin, President, Na-tional League of Women Voters; B. is Judge Florence E. Allen (holding the flag); C. is Mrs. Malcolm McBride," 1912, Library of Congress. https://www.loc.gov /pictures/item/97500065/.

69 *One important man:* "Thousand Men Wanted for Suffrage Parade," *Plain Dealer*, September 20, 1914; "Suffragists Plan Globe for Float," *Plain Dealer*, September 26, 1914; "Suffragists to Give Strong Jolt to Public Indifference in Parade of Ten Thou-sand," *Plain Dealer*, September 27, 1914, all clipped in *Woman Suffrage Party of Greater Cleveland: Scrapbooks; Newspaper Clippings* 4 (Campaign 1914): 8–9.

70 *"I think we should form":* June McCune Flory, *The Cleveland Play House: How It Began* (Cleveland: The Press of Case Western Reserve University, 1965), 5. See also Jeffrey Ullom, *America's First Regional Theatre: The Cleveland Play House and Its Search for a Home* (New York: Palgrave, 2014), 9–28.

70 *"businessmen and Bohemians":* Chloe Warner Oldenburg, *Leaps of Faith: History of the Cleveland Play House, 1915–1985* (Pepper Pike, OH: C. W. Oldenburg, 1985), 16.

70 *Katharine operated:* KSW to CA, February 4, 1971, BM 29.1.

71 *Sidney Howard was a close:* Arthur Gewirtz, *Sidney Howard and Clare Eames: Amer-ican Theater's Perfect Couple of the 1920s* (Jefferson, NC: McFarland & Company Inc., 2004), 12–13 and 82.

CHAPTER 10

72 *"My most vivid":* "Ernest Angell," *Harvard College Class of 1911 Decennial Report* (Boston: Four Seas Company, 1921), 10–11.

72 *He was recruited:* Paul H. Douglas, "War Risk Insurance Act," *Journal of Political Economy* 26.5 (May 1918): 461–83.

73 *"achieve[d] the effect":* KSA, "Doroshevitch," review of *The Way of the Cross* by V. Doroshevitch, *New Republic*, July 15, 1916, 286.

73 *She wrote an angry:* ESS, "Toilers of the Tenements: Where the Beautiful Things of the Great Shops Are Made," *McClure's Magazine* 35 (July 1910): 232.

73 *Elsie showed up:* ESS, *Willa Cather*, 31–43.

74 *Katharine would later:* KSW to CA, February 4, 1971, BM 29.1.

74   *Katharine assumed a leadership:* Virginia Clark Abbott, *The History of Woman Suffrage and the League of Women Voters in Cuyahoga County, 1911–1945* (Cleveland: np, 1949), 63.

74   *Katharine's job required:* KSW to CA, February 4, 1971, BM 29.1.

75   *Back in the summer: Fifty Years of Unified Transportation in Metropolitan Boston* (Boston: Boston Elevated Railway Company, 1938), 51, 74, and 84.

75   *In November of 1918:* Linda Davis, in *Onward and Upward* (48–49), states that Charles's salary was slashed from $20,000 to $6,000, and she suggests that Katharine would later portray his retirement more nobly than the "true events"—that he was partially responsible for the railway's financial mismanagement, that his retirement may have been forced, and that he retired in a cloud of shame. I could find nothing to support this. Charles was still making $20,000 a year in 1917 (even after the president's salary had been cut from $35,000 to $25,000); he remained second in command through several personnel changes; he was not mentioned in commission reports; and he retired at age sixty-six. See the Commonwealth of Massachusetts, *Proceedings of the Massachusetts Special Commission to Consider the Financial Condition of the Boston Elevated Railway Company,* March 1917, 170. Thank you to Marnie Goodbody, research librarian at the Boston Public Library, for help with this question.

75   *They were escorted:* "Mlle. de Vallette Killed by Grenade," *New York Times,* October 22, 1918, and "Miss Sergeant Injured," *New York Times,* October 25, 1918.

75   *"a stunning report":* SS 12.

75   *"for she made no sort":* Eunice Tietjens, *The World at My Shoulder* (New York: Macmillan, 1938), 162.

76   *"As so often":* SS 17.

76   *But when her injury:* Diane Prenatt, "Negotiating Authority: Elizabeth Shepley Sergeant's World War I Memoir," *Studies in the Humanities* 41.1–2 (March 2015): 69–99.

76   *"How bloodless and decent":* SS 117–18.

77   *"fine, frank, judicious":* SS 26 and 21.

77   *"the gallant comradeship":* SS 136.

77   *But Ernest stayed:* "Ernest Angell," *Harvard College Class of 1911 Decennial Report,* 10–11.

77   *She did not work for pay:* KSW to CA, February 4, 1971, BM 29.1.

78   *"propose to seek":* SS 110.

78   *On the advice:* KSW to HR, undated [1932], NYPL 170.7.

CHAPTER 11

79   *The Bryn Mawr Alumnae:* "Katharine Sergeant White," 1970 Bryn Mawr College Survey of the Alumni and Alumnae.

80   *On Sundays:* LMF 31–32.

81   *"I did remark":* John Cowper Powys to Marian Powys Grey, quoted in Jacqueline Peltier, "Emily Marian Powys: A Declaration of Independence," *Powys Journal* 17 (2007): 23.

81   *"so many close friends":* SS 125.

81   *That summer, he:* KSW to CA, Christmas 1976, BM 29.1.

81   *Ernest was the one:* Biographical facts of Marian Powys Grey come from Peltier, "Emily Marian Powys," 11–40.

82 *"adamant in her heroic"*: John Cowper Powys, *Petrushka and the Dancer: The Diaries of John Cowper Powys, 1929–1939*, ed. Morine Krissdóttir (New York: St. Martin's Press, 1999), 37.

82 *She may have deliberately*: See Morine Krissdóttir, *Descents of Memory: The Life of John Cowper Powys* (New York: Overlook Duckworth, 2007), 178, and Richard Perceval Graves, *The Brothers Powys* (New York: Scribner, 1983), 155.

82 *"neither absolutely black"*: John Cowper Powys quoted in Graves, *The Brothers Powys*, 155.

82 *That summer, Mrs. Ernest:* "Many Brooklinites Visit Quebec," *Standard Union*, August 22, 1922.

82 *"wishing that his"*: John Cowper Powys, August 7, 1938, in Krissdóttir, *Petrushka and the Dancer*, 279.

82 *Finally, as a Harvard:* Interview with Katey Grey, October 20, 2020.

83 *"making [her] sick"*: KSW to CA, Christmas 1976, BM 29.1.

83 *It's possible too:* Theodora Scutt, "Marian Powys Grey," *Powys Society Newsletter* 54 (April 2005): 36–37.

84 *Katharine's father, Charles:* Sergeant to Payson, Norfolk County Registry of Deeds, October 7, 1921, 531.

84 *"It became suddenly"*: Sidney Howard to ESS, September 10, 1921, quoted in Gewirtz, *Sidney Howard and Clare Eames*, 99.

84 *"complete hell"*: Sidney Howard to Jean McDuffie, April 12, 1922, quoted in Gewirtz, *Sidney Howard and Clare Eames*, 103.

85 *"bad mathematics"*: KSW to CA, February 4, 1971, BM 29.1.

85 *Ernest traveled first: Hearing Before a Select Committee on Haiti and Santo Domingo*, United States Senate, Seventy-Seventh Congress, First Session, August 5, 1921, 3.

86 *"insistence that the"*: KSA, "On Trial in Santo Domingo," *New Republic*, July 5, 1922, 157.

86 *Only* The Nation*:* Leon D. Pamphile, "The NAACP and the American Occupation of Haiti," *Phylon* 47.1 (1986): 91–100, and Tabe Ritsert Bergman, "Polite Conquest?: *The New York Times* and *The Nation* on the American Occupation of Haiti," *Journal of Haitian Studies* 17.2 (Fall 2001): 33–46.

86 *"brown and green"*: KSW to CA, February 4, 1971, BM 29.1.

86 *A poet friend:* KSW to William McGuire, June 4, 1976, SMITH 37.17.

86 *"very Germanic English"*: KSW to CA, February 4, 1971, BM 29.1.

86 *"more messed up"*: Ibid. See also Nancy Hale to KSW, August 4, 1976, and July 16, 1977, BM 5.6.

86 *Hinkle was a pioneer:* Jay Sherry, "Beatrice Hinkle and the Early History of Jungian Psychology in New York," *Behavioral Sciences* 3 (2013): 493, and Kate Wittenstein, "The Feminist Uses of Psychoanalysis: Beatrice M. Hinkle and the Foreshadowing of Modern Feminism in the United States," *Journal of Women's History* 10.2 (Summer 1998): 38–62. The manuscript that Katharine did not edit was Beatrice M. Hinkle, *The Re-Creation of the Individual: A Study of Psychological Types and Their Relation to Psychoanalysis* (New York: Harcourt Brace, 1923).

87 *"The picture which"*: KSA, "Being Respectable," *Nation* (July 18, 1923), 66. See also "Ervine's Impressions of His Elders," *Nation* (February 28, 1923), 248–49; "Balloons," *Nation*, April 4, 1923, 397; "The Soviet Leaders," *Nation*, May 9, 1923, 548; and "Miss Macauley in Lighter Vein," *Nation*, May 30, 1923, 634.

87   *She reviewed books:* KSA, "Told by an Idiot," *Atlantic Monthly*, June 1924, 14–16, and "Breezy Romance," *Saturday Review of Literature*, December 12, 1925, 403.

87   *She waxed rapturous:* KSA, "The Don Juan of the East," *Saturday Review of Literature*, September 5, 1925, 96.

CHAPTER 12

91   *Katharine walked into:* GID 119–20; Lois Long, "Tables for Two," TNY, February 19, 1927; Corey Ford, *The Time of Laughter* (Boston: Little, Brown & Co., 1967), 123.

92   *"I'd like to take off":* GID 79; TYWR 4; Simon Louvish, *Monkey Business: The Lives and Legends of the Marx Brothers* (London: Faber and Faber, 1999), 159; Frank Case, *Tales of a Wayward Inn* (New York: Garden City Pub. Co., 1940), 227; Margaret Case Harriman, *The Vicious Circle: The Story of the Algonquin Round Table* (New York: Rinehart, 1951), 51.

92   *"like a dishonest":* Louvish, *Monkey Business*, 159.

92   *Ross was given:* NYPL 123.5.

93   *"Somebody was using":* TYWR 19–20; GID 119; Corey Ford, *The Time of Laughter*, 117.

93   *"the outstanding flop":* TYWR 18.

93   *The artist Neysa McMein:* Janet Flanner, "Introduction: The Unique Ross," in Jane Grant, *Ross, "The New Yorker," and Me* (New York: Reynal and Company, 1968), 7–9.

94   *"always ornamented with":* Unsigned, "Paris Letter," TNY, September 12, 1925, 30. Judith Yaross Lee has corrected previous histories that say Flanner's first column appeared in the October 10 issue. See Lee, *Defining "New Yorker" Humor* (Jackson: University Press of Mississippi, 2000), 84.

94   *From the very first:* See Lindsay Starck, "Janet Flanner's 'High-Class Gossip' and American Nationalism Between the Wars," *Journal of Modern Periodical Studies* 7.1–2 (2016): 3, and Shari Benstock, *Women of the Left Bank: Paris, 1900–1940* (Austin: University of Texas Press, 1986), 101.

94   *Flanner never wrote:* Monica B. Pearl, "'What Strange Intimacy': Janet Flanner's Letters from Paris," *Journal of European Studies* 32.125–6 (2002): 315. The one time an editor slightly rewrote one of her letters and used the phrase "I think," Flanner wrote that it made her ill and was "utterly discouraging." Flanner, *Darlinghissima: Letters to a Friend*, ed. Natalia Danesi Murray (New York: Random House, 1985), 43.

94   *"Aw, why don't you":* Susan Henry, *Anonymous in Their Own Names: Doris E. Fleischman, Ruth Hale, and Jane Grant* (Nashville, TN: Vanderbilt University Press, 2012), 110.

94   *She'd lent her name:* Ibid., 168.

95   *As a member:* Thomas Vinciguerra, *Cast of Characters: Wolcott Gibbs, E. B. White, James Thurber, and the Golden Age of "The New Yorker"* (New York: W. W. Norton, 2016), 18–19, 23, 25–26.

95   *"Even if she has written":* Grant, *Ross, "The New Yorker," and Me*, 230.

95   *"Cabaret has its place":* Ellin Mackay, "Why We Go to Cabarets: A Post-Debutante Explains," TNY, November 28, 1925, 7–8.

96   *"one of the most":* Chandler Owen, "The Cabaret—A Useful Social Institution," *Messenger* 4 (August 1922): 461. See also Owen, "The Black and Tan Cabaret—

America's Most Democratic Institution," *Messenger* 12.2 (February 1925): 97–100.

96   *It sold out:* For accounts of the Mackay article that leave out Miller's and Grant's roles, see Ralph Ingersoll, *Point of Departure: An Adventure in Autobiography* (New York: Harcourt, Brace & World, 1961), 201–202; Vinciguerra, *Cast of Characters*, 26–27; and Ian Frazier, "The Cabaret Beat," TNY, February 23 and March 2, 2015, https://www.newyorker.com/magazine/2015/02/23/cabaret-beat, retrieved March 24, 2019.

97   *All three newspapers:* Grant, Ross, *"The New Yorker," and Me*, 230.

97   *"People simply have to":* Quoted in Erin Overbey, "Eighty-Five from the Archive: Ellin Mackay," https://www.newyorker.com/books/double-take/eighty-five-from-the-archive-ellin-mackay, retrieved March 24, 2019.

97   *A newspaperman named:* TYWR 27–28.

97   *"Modern girls are conscious":* Mackay, "The Declining Function: A Post-Debutante Rejoices," TNY, December 12, 1925, 15.

97   *"surrounded by women":* TYWR 5, and Ford, *The Time of Laughter*, 123.

97   *The New Yorker's pages:* AT 77–78.

98   *"I regret to say":* HR to Nannine Joseph, undated [1930], NYPL 5.6.

98   *"an infallible omniscience":* TYWR 7.

98   *Ross added Katharine's name:* NYPL 2.13.

98   *"Ross was furious":* KSW to SE, September 10, 1970, CU 180.

99   *Fully 20 percent:* LZ xiii.

99   *Women had been editors:* Patricia Okker, *Our Sister Editors: Sarah J. Hale and the Tradition of Nineteenth-Century American Women Editors* (Athens: University of Georgia Press, 1995). See her appendix for a list of white, Black, and Native women who edited magazines across the nation in the nineteenth century.

99   *In the 1920s:* Jayne Marek, *Women Editing Modernism: "Little" Magazines and Literary History* (Lexington: University Press of Kentucky, 1995), 12.

99   *Of utmost importance:* The most active female literary agents who submitted to *The New Yorker* in the 1920s and early 1930s were Ann Watkins, Lida McCord, Nannine Joseph, Elizabeth Nowell, Rowe Wright, Virginia Rice, Charlotte Barbour, Elsie McKeogh, Alma Levin at Brandt & Brandt, and Helen Everett at Curtis Brown.

CHAPTER 13

102   *If it was a Monday:* For the weekly schedule in 1927, see NYPL 3.5. The art meeting was later changed to Wednesday.

102   *"the more familiar":* KSA to HR, October 23, 1929, NYPL 148.13.

102   *She and Ernest ate:* KSA to Ralph Ingersoll, February 17, 1928, NYPL 139.17.

102   *He appeared in:* "Old Familiar Face," TNY, April 7, 1928, 17.

102   *"about the most significant":* KSA to Ralph Ingersoll, September 27, 1928, NYPL 139.16.

103   *Mrs. John D. Rockefeller Jr.:* KSA to HR, October 17, 1929, NYPL 148.13.

103   *A hot tip:* A. B. Bernd to KSA, September 26, 1929, and KSA to A. B. Bernd, October 2, 1929, Aaron Bernd papers, Stuart A. Rose Manuscript, Archives, and Rare Book Library, Emory University, 2.27. Thank you to Eleanor Henderson for the hot tip on Bernd.

103   *"This backwater hamlet"*: "Yo-Yo," TNY, November 9, 1929, 20–21.

103   *"manuscript, payments"*: KSW to Eugene Kincaid, February 10, 1967, NYPL-WS 16.7.

103   *"unsanitary and intolerable"*: KSA to Ralph Ingersoll, October 29, 1927, NYPL 139.17.

103   *"undergrments, 'functional'"*: KSW to Eugene Kincaid, February 10, 1967, NY-PL-WS 16.7.

103   *"honesty, decency, and believability"*: RF to KSW, January 6, 1961, BM 7.4.

104   *"Mr. Ross"*: KSA to HR, June 13, 1928, NYPL 139.16.

104   *"one of the best people"*: KSA to HR, June 14, 1928, NYPL 139.16.

104   *Her first* New Yorker *byline:* "The Men I Hate to Go Out With" and "The Men I Like to Go Out With," TNY, January 2, 1926, 33. Linda H. Davis was the one to identify Angelina as Katharine Sergeant Angell; see OU 72.

105   *"little lady"*: Angelina, "Poor Fish," TNY, June 26, 1926, 34–35.

105   *"March is the month"*: Unsigned, "Feminists' Confession," TNY, March 13, 1926, 45. See also "Thunder on the Left" and "Suburbanite's Spring," TNY, May 1, 1926, 40.

105   *"Your temper slightly"*: Angelina, "Sweetness and Light," TNY, March 13, 1926, 17.

106   *The magazine taught:* See Trysh Travis, "What We Talk About When We Talk About 'The New Yorker,'" *Book History* 3 (2000), 263, and Lee, *Defining "New Yorker" Humor*, 85–86.

106   *And the magazine:* Faye Hammill, "*The New Yorker*, the Middlebrow, and the Periodical Marketplace in 1925," in *Writing for "The New Yorker,"* ed. Fiona Green (Edinburgh: Edinburgh University Press, 2015), 17–19.

106   *Yet* The New Yorker *broke:* AT 46–52.

106   *"reviving the old feeling"*: Arthur Guiterman to HR, December 23, 1932, NYPL 169.6.

107   *Only in* The New Yorker: See Yeats, "Death," and Embry, "Bewitched Baby," in TNY, April 27, 1929, 21 and 28.

107   *Era-defining authors:* See Francis J. Bosha, "Hemingway and *The New Yorker*: The Harold Ross Files," *Hemingway Review* 21.1 (Fall 2001): 93–99, and Anne Margaret Daniel, "F. Scott Fitzgerald and the *New Yorker*, 1925–1941," *F. Scott Fitzgerald Review*, 11.1 (2013): 10–31.

107   *Edna St. Vincent Millay's agent:* KSW to Nancy Milford, October 5, 1973, BM 8.12.

108   *After she accepted:* KSW to Matthew Bruccoli, May 17, 1971, BM 2.14.

108   *"For one thing"*: KSA to Martha Banning Thomas, November 5, 1930, NYPL 152.18.

108   *"It will be what is"*: "The New Yorker Prospectus," NYPL 2.3.

109   *The magazine's readership:* On the peer culture of youth that structured the magazine, see Lee, *Defining "New Yorker" Humor*, 24–28.

109   The New Yorker *traded:* Jeffrey Gonzalez, "The Metropolitan as Master Subject: Janet Flanner's Paris Letters," *Mosaic* 43.1 (March 2010): 44–46.

110   *"Where is New York?"*: HR to James M. Cain, August 20, 1931, NYPL 14.15.

110   *"his demon checking department"*: KSW to Nancy Milford, October 5, 1973, BM 8.12. The Millay profile is Griffin Barry, "Vincent," TNY, February 12, 1927, 25.

110   *"a rather small, angry"*: KSW to Nancy Milford, December 5, 1973, BM 8.12.

110   *She listened to Mrs. Millay:* Cora Millay's original letter with Katharine's edits is in NYPL 1349.20, and the letter was published in TNY on April 23, 1927.

110   *"a prize hog"*: KSW to HR, undated [1933], NYPL 14.15.

111   *"The word toilet paper"*: HR to EBW, May 7, 1935, CU 85.

111   *"Oh dear, oh dear"*: KSW to Sally Benson, June 12, 1931, NYPL 154.9.

111   *"I have the reputation"*: KSW to Dorothy Parker, October 16, 1929, quoted in Lee, *Defining "New Yorker" Humor*, 63.

111   *"If anyone mentions"*: KSW to Will Cuppy, March 3, 1933, quoted in Vinciguerra, *Cast of Characters*, 62.

112   *"If honest, I must"*: KSA, "Home and Office," *Survey* 57 (December 1, 1926): 318–20.

CHAPTER 14

114   *"formidable"*: See for example John Updike, *Picked-Up Pieces* (New York: Knopf, 1975), 436; Harrison Kinney, *James Thurber: His Life and Times* (New York: H. Holt and Co., 1995), 359; Vinciguerra, *Cast of Characters*, 72; EBWB 110 and 150; and Katharine's son, Roger, in TOM 37. *New Yorker* writer E. J. Kahn Jr. called Katharine "a real *femme formidable*" in Michael Shnayerson's *Irwin Shaw: A Biography* (New York: Putnam, 1989), 236. For a discussion of the gendered use of this term to describe Katharine, see Nancy Franklin, "Lady with a Pencil," TNY, February 26 and March 4, 1996, 172–84, reprinted in *Life Stories: Profiles from "The New Yorker,"* ed. David Remnick (New York: Random House, 2007), 428–40.

114   *"intelligent, no-nonsense"*: GID 143.

114   *"a strong woman—too strong"*: Niccolò Tucci, quoted in OU 144.

114   *"a cold-blooded proposition"*: Danton Walker quoted in Vinciguerra, *Cast of Characters*, 72.

114   *"thrived on the role"*: Marion Meade, *Lonelyhearts: The Screwball World of Nathanael West and Eileen McKenney* (Boston: Houghton Mifflin Harcourt, 2010), 182–83.

115   *"Katharine was as"*: EBW to Ann Honeycutt, April 1, 1984, quoted in Kinney, *James Thurber*, 1050.

115   *"maternal"*: William Maxwell quoted in Franklin, "Lady with a Pencil," 184, and Jean Stafford quoted in Ann Hulbert, *The Interior Castle: The Art and Life of Jean Stafford* (New York: A. A. Knopf, 1992), 253. See also Dale Kramer, *Ross and "The New Yorker"* (New York: Doubleday & Company, 1951), 175.

115   *"complemented and admired"*: Edmund Wilson to JT, March 22, 1958, quoted in Kinney, *James Thurber*, 1044.

116   *"universal housemother"*: Hobart Weekes quoted in Kinney, *James Thurber*, 394.

116   *"Naturally, every time"*: KSW to HR, September 15 [1938–1940], NYPL 23.19.

117   *"She'd murder you"*: KSW, "Books to Go to Bryn Mawr College by Bequest," BM 34.2.

117   *Katharine's discovery of four:* Lee, *Defining "New Yorker" Humor*, 341.

117   *Long before E. B. White:* On the relationship between the female poets and the male authors of the Little Man archetype, see Lee, *Defining "New Yorker" Humor*, 349, and Catherine Keyser, *Playing Smart: "New Yorker" Women Writers and Modern Magazine Culture* (New Brunswick, NJ: Rutgers University Press, 2010), 71–72.

118   *Patience Eden was a single:* Biographical information on Martha Banning Thomas from Canadian Writing Research Collaboratory, https://cwrc.ca/islandora/object/ceww%3A17805916-ef0c-4203-ad70-677e27149eb7, retrieved May 14, 2020.

118   *"I have always had"*: KSA to Martha Banning Thomas, September 23, 1929, NYPL 148.11.

118   *"He wore a frock coat":* Elspeth, "Possibly," TNY, September 3, 1927, 22.

119   *"Do you like to know":* Elspeth MacDuffie to KSA, March 12, 1928, NYPL 141.2.

119   *"I'd rather be rejected":* Elspeth MacDuffie to KSA, undated [1929], NYPL 147.18.

119   *They used humor:* See Jessica Burstein, "A Few Words About Dubuque: Modernism, Sentimentalism, and the Blasé," *American Literary History* 14.2 (Summer 2002): 227–54, and Keyser, *Playing Smart,* 51–78.

119   *"The only thing I care":* Elspeth MacDuffie to KSA, undated [1928], NYPL 141.2.

119   *"Our list of prejudices":* The New Yorkers to Contributors, September 2, 1925, NYPL 2.8.

120   *"It seems to me":* Phyllis Crawford to KSA, March 28, 1928, NYPL 136.30.

120   *"In other words, this":* KSW to Baird Leonard, December 18, 1931, NYPL 159.5.

120   *"Ross would summon":* KSW, "Books to Go to Bryn Mawr College by Bequest," undated, BM 34.2.

120   *"should his wife have":* KSW to Sam Behrman, October 12, 1965, BM 1.12.

121   *"a time-consuming bother":* KSW, "Books to Go to Bryn Mawr College by Bequest," undated, BM 34.2.

121   *"Oh dear, Mr. S.S.":* KSW to Alexander Woollcott, July 23, 1930, NYPL 153.8.

121   *"went on talking":* Wolcott Gibbs quoted in Kinney, *James Thurber,* 398.

121   *"I always had a feeling":* Ibid., 570.

121   *"straight old-fashioned":* HR to KSW, undated [early 1940s], BM 10.11.

121   *"All right, all right":* KSW quoted in Jane Grant, *Ross, "The New Yorker," and Me,* 258.

121   *When Charles Lindbergh:* KSW to William Maxwell, undated [1962], BM 7.9.

CHAPTER 15

123   *"dead broke":* Anonymous [KSW], "Living on the Ragged Edge: Family Income vs. Family Expenses," *Harper's Monthly Magazine* 152 (December 1, 1925): 54–59.

124   *It galled Ernest:* RA, interview with author, March 6, 2019.

125   *In fact, not long:* Anne W. Armstrong, "Seven Deadly Sins of Woman in Business," *Harper's Magazine,* August 1926, 295–303, and John Macy, "Equality of Woman with Man: A Myth—a Challenge to Feminism," *Harper's,* November 1926, 705–13.

125   *Katharine was proud:* Rhoda E. McCulloch to KSA, February 24 and March 3, 1928, NYPL 141.7.

125   *What the essay:* KSW to CA, Christmas 1976, BM 29.1.

125   *One night, Ernest:* RA, interview with author, December 28, 2020.

125   *"that old romance":* James Thurber to EBW, July 1, 1953, reprinted in Harrison Kinney, ed., *The Thurber Letters: The Wit, Wisdom, and Surprising Life of James Thurber* (New York: Simon & Schuster, 2002), 596.

125   *Katharine perhaps knew:* Thank you to the Teads' grandson, David Michaelis, for this detail. Michaelis looked for traces of Katharine in his family's papers, to no avail, nor does she appear in Tead's professional papers at Cornell University. Michaelis was able to prove that Ernest Angell and Ordway Tead kept up a lifelong friendship, and that his mother, Diana, knew Ernest and his second wife, Betty. Ordway became the godfather to Ernest and Betty's son Christopher in 1944. In 1948, the Angells moved from East Ninety-Third Street to a farmhouse in Newtown, Connecticut, just a mile down the road from the Teads, and it may have been Ordway who influenced that location. In 1960, Ernest and Ordway published

articles in the same issue of *The Saturday Review of Literature*, and Ernest served
on the Briarcliffe College board of trustees after Clara's presidency and Ordway's
own tenure as chairman. Michaelis knew of no other affairs; the Teads had a happy
marriage until Ordway died in 1973 just months after Ernest's death.

125   *"I have always tended"*: KSW to Raymond Sokolov, April 16, 1976, BM 10.31.
126   *Katharine joined Elsie*: Sophia Duckworth Schachter to author, June 19, 2018.
127   *Family legend says*: LMF 101–102.
127   *"pretty sick about"*: KSW to Elsie McKeogh, December 30, 1932, NYPL 165.7.
128   *The sheer volume*: Vinciguerra, *Cast of Characters*, 44 and 75, and KSW to Harrison
      Kinney, March 23, 1973, BM 6.19.
128   *"But I shall never"*: John Mosher, "The Man with a Box," TNY, March 6, 1926, 18.
128   *"how few meanings"*: JCM, "The New German Picture," TNY, September 17, 1932,
      64. For the story of Katharine censuring Mosher about the review, see Vinciguerra,
      Cast of Characters, 45.
129   *Could Elspeth*: Elspeth MacDuffie to KSA, undated, and KSA to Elspeth Mac-
      Duffie, March 1, 1928, NYPL 141.2.

CHAPTER 16

130   *"In the name of John"*: EBW, "Child's Play," TNY, December 26, 1925, 17.
131   *"mak[e] for himself"*: EBW, "The Hotel of the Total Stranger," *The Second Tree from
      the Corner* (New York: Harper & Brothers, 1954), 214, quoted in EBWB 107.
131   *"Are you Elwyn"*: EBWB 109.
131   *"I sat there peacefully"*: Quoted in LEBW 70.
131   *"a small kingdom unto [them]selves"*: EBW, "The Art of the Essay, Number One,"
      Paris Review 48 (Fall 1969): 65–88.
131   *"Victorian mother"*: Lillian White Illian, quoted in EBWB 12.
131   *"never even knew"*: EBWB 12.
132   *"the golden time of year"*: LEBW 8.
133   *"a youth who persisted"*: John Hinterberger, "E. B.'s Baptism," *Seattle Times*, June 15,
      1983.
133   *"If the new 1925"*: EBW, "A Step Forward," TNY, April 19, 1925, 21.
133   *"burned with a low"*: Quoted in EBWB 100.
134   *"the tyranny of his modesty"*: Brendan Gill, "The Art of the Essay, Number One,"
      Paris Review 48 (Fall 1969): 65.
134   *"had a lot of back hair"*: EBWB 112.
134   *he left the country*: EBW to SE, August 8, 1969, CU 82.
135   *"She was then about sixteen"*: Untitled Newsbreak, TNY, July 19, 1930, 43. The
      quote comes from "A Millionaire's Girl," which was written by Zelda Fitzgerald
      and published under her husband's name just as she entered a hospital in Europe.
135   *"Prior to his return"*: This and subsequent newsbreaks from *Ho Hum: Newsbreaks
      from "The New Yorker,"* with a foreword by E. B. White (New York: Farrar & Rine-
      hart, Inc., 1931).
136   *"discarded sorrows"*: EBWB 133. See also Kinney, *James Thurber*, 316–17, 337–38.
136   *"And there comes an hour"*: EBW with manuscript edits by KSA, Comment, un-
      dated, NYPL 1349.31.
137   *No, probably not*: EBWB 147–48.

137   *"She's awfully sweet":* EBW, "Gramercy Park,"TNY, March 3, 1928, 27, and EBW, *The Lady Is Cold: Poems* (New York: Harper & Brothers, 1929), 16.

137   *No, that would be Rosanne:* EBWB 151–53.

137   *"Now grows my heart unruly":* Beppo [EBW], "Notes from a Desk Calendar,"TNY, January 14, 1928, 23, and White, *The Lady Is Cold*, 39–40, reprinted in EBWB 150.

138   *"You certainly stirred":* Elspeth MacDuffie to KSA, February 4, 1928, NYPL 141.2.

CHAPTER 17

139   *"This matter of fiction":* KSW to Morley Callaghan, December 19, 1928, quoted in Nadine Fladd, *Transnational Conversations: "The New Yorker" and Canadian Short Story Writers*, diss. University of Western Ontario, 2014, 78.

139   *Katharine thought:* AT 54.

140   *"Someone, I forget":* Sally Benson, "Apartment Hotel,"TNY, January 12, 1929, 16–17.

140   *"We are so glad":* KSA to Sally Benson, December 24, 1928, NYPL 135.15.

140   *Benson was an:* Maryellen V. Keefe, *Casual Affairs: The Life and Fiction of Sally Benson* (Albany: State University of New York Press, 2014), 95–116.

141   *"We feel that the effect":* KSA to Sally Benson, February 5, 1929, NYPL 145.5.

141   *"on the town":* Quoted in Keefe, *Casual Affairs*, 183.

141   *"Harold Ross vs. Sally Benson":* Wolcott Gibbs, "Theory and Practice of Editing New Yorker Articles," BM 4.14, quoted in GID 310 and 445.

142   *Like Benson and:* Richard Clarence Winegard, *Thyra Samter Winslow: A Critical Assessment*, diss. University of Arkansas, 1971, 1–37.

142   *"I am for neater":* Winslow, "Fewer and Neater Murders,"TNY, April 23, 1927, 31.

142   *"She took time":* Winslow, "But for the Grace of God,"TNY, October 13, 1928, 25.

142   *Winslow's voice was:* Judith Ruderman, *Passing Fancies in Jewish American Literature and Culture* (Bloomington: Indiana University Press, 2019), 69–84.

142   *In 1927, Katharine received:* Ken Cuthbertson, *Nobody Said Not to Go: The Life, Loves, and Adventures of Emily Hahn* (Boston: Faber and Faber, 1998), 68–70.

143   *"You're cattier than":* Quoted in Cuthbertson, *Nobody Said Not to Go*, 72.

143   *It wouldn't be until:* Emily Hahn to HR, July 23, 1929, NYPL 146.23, and Herbert Asbury to HR, undated, NYPL 149.7.

143   *Hahn's "Lovely Lady":* See Fitzgerald, "A Short Autobiography," TNY, May 25, 1929, 22–23, and HR to F. Scott Fitzgerald, April 26, 1929, NYPL 5.10.

143   *"All was quiet":* John C. Mosher, "That Sad Young Man,"TNY, April 9, 1926, 20–21.

143   *"As for Mrs. Angell":* F. Scott Fitzgerald quoted in Lee, *Defining "New Yorker" Humor*, 322.

143   *Fitzgerald would not maintain:* In late 1928, Ober asked Katharine, "Did you think of any suggestions for Scott Fitzgerald to do?" which prompted the idea of the Lardner profile. See Harold Ober to KSA, November 7, 1929, NYPL 147.17. Fitzgerald's story "Salesmanship in the Champs-Elysees" appeared in the February 15, 1930, issue of TNY. Zelda's story "The Continental Angle" appeared in the May 27, 1932, issue. Katharine rejected her next three stories and she does not appear to have submitted to TNY after that. See Wolcott Gibbs to Constance Smith, July 29, 1932, NYPL 172.11, and KSW to Constance Smith, February 22 and September 23, 1933, NYPL 187.11. In 1935, Katharine accepted Scott Fitzgerald's poem "Lamp in a Window" but rejected "For a Long Illness" as "a little too difficult to

understand." See NYPL 237.2. In 1936, she rejected the poem "Thousand and First Ship" for its "grave defects," including a "non-permissible rhyme in the fourth stanza." John Mosher rejected "Thank You for the Light" as "really too fantastic." See NYPL 260.4. Fitzgerald published two pieces in 1937, the poem "Obit on Parnassus" on June 5, 1947, and the casual "A Book of One's Own" on August 21, 1937.

144   *"We always have":* KSA to Rowe Wright, October 19, 1928, NYPL 136.33.

144   *"too much an inside":* KSW to Theodore Dreiser, November 11, 1929, NYPL 146.6.

144   *"just too obscure":* KSW to e. e. cummings, May 28, 1930, NYPL 149.29.

144   *"aroused [their] indignation":* KSW to Upton Sinclair, February 2, 1930, NYPL 152.14.

144   *Janet Flanner put:* Djuna Barnes, "Reproving Africa," TNY, May 5, 1928, 26–28.

144   *"as smart an idea":* Djuna Barnes to KSA, August 8, 1928, NYPL 135.10.

144   *"piece was pretty":* KSA to Djuna Barnes, November 1, 1928, NYPL 135.10.

144   *So triumphantly:* See 1931 and 1932 editorial correspondence in NYPL 163.6 and 174.9.

145   *Katharine not only turned:* See 1934 editorial correspondence in NYPL 196.5.

145   *Instead, Ross's de facto:* See Corey Ford's ten-part series that begins with "Blotters," TNY, May 9, 1925, 22, and James Thurber, "More Authors Cover the Snyder Trial," TNY, May 7, 1927, 69. Thurber included a parody within a review when he covered Eugene O'Neill's *Strange Interlude;* see James Thurber, "Cross-Country Gamut," TNY, February 11, 1928, 40.

145   *Taken together, these modes:* See Faye Hamill and Karen Leick, "Modernism and the Quality Magazines: *Vanity Fair* (1914–36); *American Mercury* (1924–81); *New Yorker* (1925–); *Esquire* (1933–)," in *The Oxford Critical and Cultural History of Modernist Magazines: Volume II: North America (1894–1960),* eds. Peter Brooker and Andrew Thacker (New York: Oxford University Press, 2012), 176–96; Daniel Tracy, "Investing in 'Modernism': Smart Magazines, Parody, and Middlebrow Professional Judgment," *Journal of Modern Periodical Studies* 1.1 (2010): 38–63; Hammill, "*The New Yorker,* the Middlebrow," 17–35.

145   *No writers of the Harlem:* Lee, *Defining "New Yorker" Humor,* 51, and AT 316.

145   *The magazine played into:* Lee, *Defining "New Yorker" Humor,* 51–54.

146   *For all the competing:* KSW to HR, September 16, 1930, and Daise Terry to Raymond Holden, November 13, 1930, both in NYPL 151.2.

146   *"It was a period":* Langston Hughes, quoted in Donald D. Dickinson, *A Bio-Bibliography of Langston Hughes, 1902–1967,* with a preface by Arna Bontemps (Hamden, CT: Archon Books, 1967), 34.

146   *Fauset edited* The Crisis: Carolyn Wedin Sylvander, *Jessie Redmon Fauset, Black American Writer* (Troy, NY: The Whitson Publishing Company, 1981), and Cheryl A. Wall, "Jessie Redmon Fauset: Traveling in Place," *Women of the Harlem Renaissance* (Bloomington: Indiana University Press, 1995), 33–84.

147   *"ambi-racially":* "Among the New Books," TNY, March 9, 1929, 86.

147   *One exception came:* KSA to HR, September 9, 1929, NYPL 148.13.

147   *White, as the acting:* Kenneth Robert Janken, *Walter White: Mr. NAACP* (Chapel Hill: University of North Carolina Press, 2006), 89–128.

147   *"come alive as":* KSW to Walter F. White, August 1, 1930, NYPL 153.5.

147   *A profile of James:* Robert Wohlforth, "Profiles: Dark Leader," TNY, September 30, 1933, 22.

148 *"would be not only"*: KSW quoted in Elizabeth Frank, *Louise Bogan: A Portrait* (New York: A. A. Knopf, 1984), 137.

148 *"rather long, rather"*: William Carlos Williams to KSW, October 12, 1930, NYPL 153.6, also quoted in AT 54.

148 *She had published:* Frank, *Louise Bogan*, 137.

149 *"I have written down"*: Louise Bogan quoted in Ruth Limmer, ed., *Journey Around My Room: The Autobiography of Louise Bogan* (New York: Penguin Books, 1980), xix.

149 *When the opportunity:* HR to Raoul Fleischmann, November 5, 1927, NYPL 3.3.

149 *Ernest's mother, Lily:* "Estates Appraised," *New York Times*, August 7, 1930.

149 *So highly regarded:* KSW to CA, March 10, 1975, BM 29.1.

CHAPTER 18

150 *"holy terror"*: KSW to CA, December 20 [1969?], BM 29.1.

150 *Ernest almost certainly:* Nancy remembered innocently asking her father why E. B. White was always at their house whenever Ernest left town. Roger began *Let Me Finish* with his remembrance of an automobile outing with his mother and Andy in 1928 when she stripped the gears of the family sedan on the Bronx River Parkway, but Katharine did not learn to drive until she went to Reno in 1929. See OU 80; LMF 5–6 and 18–19; and EBWB 171.

150 *Andy did not ask:* In fact, this was the only subject that would cause Andy to lean hard on his own biographer. He strongly urged Scott Elledge to omit two references to Ernest's infidelities, including a passage about giving up a longtime mistress in 1922. Andy was worried about how such mention would affect his own relationship with Nancy and Roger, and how it might expose Elledge to the umbrage of Ernest's heirs. Elledge complied. See EBW to SE, August 13, 1982, and April 25 [1983], CU 60.

150 *On June 15, 1928:* OU 78–79.

151 *"absolutely livid"*: Quoted in OU 78.

151 *Roger remembered being:* RA, interview with author, March 6, 2019.

151 *Katharine visited Janet:* KSA to Janet Flanner, August 15, 1928, NYPL 138.3, and Djuna Barnes to KSA, August 8, 1928, NYPL 135.10.

151 *"This is to introduce"*: KSW to SE, September 10, 1970, CU 183.

151 *"a last attempt to save"*: KSW to SE, August 9, 1970, CU 183.

151 *Katharine would later:* RA, interview with author, March 6, 2019.

152 *"Ernest wanted to be"*: EBW to SE, August 13, 1982, CU 82.

152 *"dead afternoon"*: EBW quoted in EBWB 156.

152 *Nancy, Roger, and their cousin:* RA, interview with author, March 6, 2019.

152 *"in such a whirl"*: RA, "Côte d'Azur," TNY, June 11, 1960, 36, and *Stories from "The New Yorker": 1950–1960* (London: Victor Gollancz, 1961), 454.

152 *"stand up party"*: EA to Sidney Howard, undated [1928], Sidney Coe Howard papers, BANC MSS 70/185 z, Bancroft Library, University of California, Berkeley, 2.24.

153 *"In the warm sun"*: EBW, *The Lady Is Cold*, 89; originally published in The Conning Tower, *World*, November 7, 1928.

153 *"Walking twice around"*: EBWB 159.

153   *"let a lot of cold"*: EBW to SE, February 17, 1970, CU 82.

153   *He was in love:* EBW to SE, February 1970, CU 82.

153   *"Then we got to"*: KSW to CA, Christmas 1976, BM 29.1.

154   *The Thurbers were having:* Kinney, *James Thurber*, 411–14.

154   *Just hours before:* Burton Bernstein, *Thurber: A Biography* (New York: Dodd, Mead, 1975), 177.

154   *Katharine couldn't muster:* KSW to SE, August 10, 1970, CU 183.

155   *Proof that marriage:* EBWB 160.

155   *Katharine had the bad:* Nelson Manfred Blake, *The Road to Reno: A History of Divorce in the United States* (New York: Macmillan, 1962), 64–65.

156   *Raymond Holden agreed:* Frank, *Louise Bogan*, 85.

156   *"I never had one"*: HR, quoted in Henry, *Anonymous in Their Own Names*, 173.

156   *So they learned:* Ibid., 187.

156   *When Katharine confided:* KSW to SE, August 9, 1970, CU 183.

157   *"a hard taskmaster"*: "KSW note on Daise Terry," undated, BM 12.8.

157   *Andy White then:* EBWB 161.

CHAPTER 19

158   *"in the most doubtful"*: KSW to Nancy Hale, January 8, 1935, NYPL 229.14.

159   *She heard that Ross:* GID 168–69.

159   *"I should like"*: KSA to EBW, July 17, 1929, CU 180.

160   *"suspended animation"*: KSA to EBW, May 31, 1929, CU 180.

160   *"critical judgment degenerates"*: KSW to EBW, July 28, 1929, CU 180.

160   *"A ranch wipes out"*: KSA to EBW, May 31, 1929, CU 180.

160   *"That I don't find"*: KSA to EBW, undated [1929], CU 180.

160   *"I wonder if I'll ever"*: KSA to EBW, June 18, 1929, CU 180.

160   *"Everyone you encounter"*: KSW to Nancy Hale, January 8, 1935, NYPL 226.14.

160   *"25, six feet"*: Agnes Boulton to Harold DePolo, May 31, 1929, quoted in William Davies King, *Another Part of a Long Story: Literary Traces of Eugene O'Neill and Agnes Boulton* (Ann Arbor: University of Michigan Press, 2013), 176.

160   *"a few beautiful ones"*: KSW to Nancy Hale, January 8, 1935, NYPL 226.14.

160   *"really just enjoying life"*: Agnes Boulton, "What Can I Give?," unpublished manuscript, quoted in King, *Another Part of a Long Story*, 196.

161   *"decided that this"*: KSW to Nancy Hale, January 8, 1935, NYPL 226.14.

161   *"You get away from"*: KSA to EBW, June 7, 1929, CU 180.

161   *"a distinction of which"*: KSA to EBW, undated [1929], CU 180.

161   *"I hope you are having"*: RA to KSA, May 18, 1929, private collection.

162   *"If only they'd leave"*: KSA to EBW, May 25, 1929, CU 180.

162   *"Andy, when you're around"*: KSA to EBW, June 22, 1929, CU 180.

162   *"[I] want you"*: KSA to EBW, May 31, 1929, CU 180.

162   *"outbursts of enthusiasm"*: KSA to EBW, June 18, 1929, CU 180.

162   *"Almost every woman"*: KSW to Nancy Hale, January 8, 1935, NYPL 226.14.

163   *"palpitating paragraphs"*: KSA to EBW, June 21, 1929, CU 180.

163   *"preeminently a writer"*: Ibid.

164   *"I thought I was"*: KSA to EBW, Monday evening [1929], CU 180.

164   *"Ontario is wonderful"*: EBW to KSA, August 1929, CU 60.

164   *"On account of the fact"*: EBW to HR, Friday [1929], NYPL 5.5.

164 *"fast awakening"*: Beatrice Hinkle, "The Chaos of Modern Marriage," *Harper's* 152 (December 1925): 6.

165 *"I hate to see"*: CSS quoted in OU 80.

165 *It was common*: George A. Bartlett, *Is Marriage Necessary: Memoirs of a Reno Judge* (New York: Penguin Books Inc., 1947), 13.

165 *"The purpose of all"*: Morris L. Ernst, *For Better or Worse: A New Approach to Marriage and Divorce* (New York: Harper, 1952), 157.

165 *Judges during this era*: Mary Ann Mason, *From Father's Property to Children's Rights: The History of Child Custody in the United States* (New York: Columbia University Press, 1994), 118–19.

166 *"civilized"*: KSW to CA, December 31, 1975, BM 29.1.

166 *"Their care, custody and"*: "Memorandum of Agreement," between EA and KSA, August 5, 1929.

166 *"never should have happened"*: RA, interview with author, March 6, 2019.

166 *"in essence renounced"*: SE, "Interview with Nancy and Louis Stableford," undated [1968], CU-SE 1.10.

167 *The idea of abandonment*: See for instance Scott Elledge's biography of E. B. White, where he describes Katharine as "a divorcée who had given custody of her children to their father" (EBWB 171).

167 *Her divorce would*: In "Lady with a Pencil," a 1996 *New Yorker* essay about Katharine, Nancy Franklin confesses that she was shocked by Katharine's divorce and elopement, saying, "But what shocks me more is how much my judgment of her as a mother affected my judgment of her as an editor, in a way that it never would have if she had been a man, and a father."

167 *"Defendant has treated plaintiff"*: Complaint, Katharine S. Angell, Plaintiff, vs. Ernest Angell, Defendant, Second Judicial District Court of the State of Nevada, County of Washoe, August 17, 1929.

168 *"deny each and every"*: Answer, Katharine S. Angell, Plaintiff, vs. Ernest Angell, Defendant, Second Judicial District Court of the State of Nevada, County of Washoe, August 17, 1929.

168 *"certain evidence"*: Findings of Fact, Conclusions of Law and Decree, Katharine S. Angell, Plaintiff, vs. Ernest Angell, Defendant, Second Judicial District Court of the State of Nevada, County of Washoe, August 19, 1929.

168 *None of them*: "Wife Sues Ernest Angell," *New York Times*, August 18, 1929; "Katherine Angell Files Divorce Suit," *Boston Daily Globe*, August 19, 1929; "Society Writer Files Reno Suit," *San Francisco Examiner*, August 18, 1929; and "Society Writer Sues Husband for Divorce," *Fort Worth Star-Telegram*, August 18, 1929.

CHAPTER 20

169 *"Travelling is more fun"*: Unsigned [KSA], Comment, TNY, September 7, 1929, 17.

169 *She found space*: Details on the furniture from the East Ninety-Third Street house come from KSW to RA, September 8, 1963, and January 25, 1972, private collection.

170 *She still used*: LMF 290.

170 *Katharine got a fast*: See exchange of letters between KSA and Janet Flanner in NYPL 146.14.

170 *"many a tedious"*: EBW to SE, February 17, 1970, CU 82.

170 *"like a floating"*: EBW to SE, August 9, 1970, CU 82.

171 *First they made:* Details of their wedding day come from ibid. and KSW to SE, August 10, 1970, CU 183.

171 *"By the way":* KSW to Gilbert Seldes, undated, NYPL 148.6.

171 *"I don't know whether":* Burke Boyce to KSW, May 7, 1930, NYPL 149.15.

172 *She was likely:* Roger told me he had no memory of the Walter Winchell incident, but in "Lady with a Pencil," her attempt to reevaluate Katharine's legacy, Nancy Franklin nonetheless wrote that this was how he learned of his mother's second marriage, and the story has subsequently been cited many times to demonstrate Katharine's tone-deaf parenting—including in Roger Angell's *New Yorker* obituary in 2022. See David Remnick, "Remembering Roger Angell, Hall of Famer," TNY, June 6, 2022. My conversation with Roger on this topic was on February 2, 2021. Winchell, "On Broadway," *New York Daily Mirror*, November 16, 1929. For the story of Hildegarde and Nancy, see OU 96.

172 *"Now, you have written":* White and Thurber, *Is Sex Necessary? Or, Why You Feel the Way You Do* (New York: Harper & Brothers, 1929), 65–67. For which chapters were written by White, see Bernstein, *Thurber*, 186.

CHAPTER 21

177 *"I've had moments":* EBW to KSW, undated [November 1929], CU 60 and LEBW 88.

177 *He did not find it as easy:* OU 97.

178 *"The spider, dropping down":* EBW, "Natural History," *Poems and Sketches of E.B. White* (New York: Harper & Row, 1967), 72.

178 *Naturally it was a:* Wolcott Gibbs to Herbert Asbury, March 18, 1930, NYPL 149.7.

179 *"White has been stewing":* EBW to KSW, undated [Spring 1930], CU 60 and LEBW 89.

179 *"Don't let Mr. White's":* EBW to KSW, October 31, 1930, CU-SE 1.36.

180 *One Saturday, the Gibbses:* "Woman Ends Life; Brooded over Play," *New York Times*, April 1, 1930.

180 *"Could you come":* KSW to Geoffrey Hellman, October 3, 1975, BM 5.16.

180 *He would move in:* Vinciguerra, *Cast of Characters*, 131–37.

181 *"[Katharine], Serena":* EBW to KSW, undated [postmarked July 5, 1930], CU 60.

181 *"I am standing on my ear":* KSW to BB, September 24, 1931, NYPL 155.2.

181 *"left 4 days a week":* EA to Hildegarde Angell, September 27, 1933, private collection.

182 *"Do you want":* EBWB 178.

182 *Ernest brought Roger:* EA to Hildegarde Angell, December 24 [1930], private collection.

182 *"White tells me":* EBW to Joe White, December 31, 1930, CU 60.

182 *"in complete charge":* EBW to Gus Lobrano, undated [early 1931], LEBW 100.

182 *He'd recently acquired:* E. B. White, "Home Movies," approximately minutes 3:40–7:20, private collection.

183 *She eased back:* See, for instance KSW to Janet Flanner, February 9, 1931, NYPL 157.6, and KSW to HR, February 10, 1931, NYPL 158.7.

183 *She took the three:* KSW to BB, April 16, 1931, NYPL 155.2.

183 *"I intend to have a talk":* EA to Hildegarde Angell, March 15 [1931], private collection.

184 *"You can't cooperate":* Ibid.

185 *"the whole New Yorker"*: Ibid.

185 *"He's been half sick"*: KSW to HR, June 23, 1931, NYPL 158.7.

185 *"Did we like Blue Hill?"*: KSW to Donald Moffat, October 2, 1931, NYPL 160.7.

186 *"He feeds crackers"*: EBW to KSW, October 6, 1931, LEBW 105.

186 *"Her life was full"*: EBW, "Obituary," TNY, March 12, 1932, 16.

186 *"the old fool"*: EBW to KSW, November 13, 1934, CU 60.

CHAPTER 22

187 *"the sort of person"*: Nancy Hale to Miss Carter [Linda H. Davis], December 18, 1977, BM 32.8.

187 *Hale and Katharine:* KSW, "Speech of Introduction for Nancy Hale, Cosmopolitan Club," January 1959, SMITH 18.10.

188 *"a bold adventuress"*: Nancy Hale, "Club Car," TNY, December 26, 1931.

188 *"In the United States"*: William Carlos Williams, "The Somnambulists," *transition* 18 (November 1929): 147, reprinted in *Critical Essays on Kay Boyle*, ed. Marilyn Elkins (New York: G. K. Hall & Co., 1997), 27.

188 *"Thoughts and menaces"*: Kay Boyle, "Kroy Wen," TNY, July 25, 1931, 13.

189 *Katharine began curating:* See AT 152–55 for a description of how *The New Yorker* sold "the more genteel strain of modernism."

189 *"Kroy Wen" was the first:* Joan Mellen, *Kay Boyle: Author of Herself* (New York: Farrar, Straus, & Giroux, 1994), 156.

189 *"the most persistent theme"*: KSW to Virginia Rice, June 12, 1931, NYPL 160.3.

189 *"rather not touch"*: Russell Lord to Virginia Rice, October 2, 1931, NYPL 160.3.

190 *"would be twenty"*: Kay Boyle, "White as Snow," TNY, August 5, 1933, 20.

190 *Katharine and Ross agreed:* KSW to Ann Watkins, April 26, 1933, NYPL 191.9, and Kay Boyle to Ann Watkins, May 17, 1933, NYPL 13.21.

191 *Even Vita Sackville-West:* See the Curtis Brown files for 1931 and 1932, NYPL 167.11.

191 *William Saroyan:* For Lowry, Saroyan, West, and Fante, see the Maxim Lieber files for 1933, NYPL 185.9.

191 *Lewis was a valued:* Alexander Woollcott, Shouts and Murmurs, TNY, July 19, 1930, 30.

191 *"When one lightly"*: Wyndham Lewis to Editors, August 2, 1930, NYPL 151.7.

192 *"that all [was] forgiven"*: Wyndham Lewis to KSW, October 16, 1930, NYPL 151.7.

192 *Circulation reached over:* AT 96–97.

193 *"do not hear"*: Conrad Aiken, "Prelude," TNY, February 6, 1932, 24.

193 *"put a mark down"*: Conrad Aiken, "Prelude," TNY, June 3, 1933, 16.

193 *"One can never"*: Conrad Aiken to KSW, October 26, 1932, NYPL 165.2.

193 *"was not attempting"*: Kay Boyle to KSW, April 18, 1932, NYPL 166.7.

193 *"I was extremely"*: Albert Einstein to Alva Johnston [translation in original folder], December 18, 1933, NYPL 182.12.

193 *"ought to serve"*: KSW to Conrad Aiken, November 26, 1932, NYPL 165.2.

193 *"It is a poem"*: KSW to William Rose Benét, April 16, 1932, NYPL 165.16.

194 *"red letter event"*: KSW to Clarence Day, February 16, 1933, NYPL 181.5.

194 *Day had published:* Clarence Day to KSW, July 10, 1933, NYPL 181.5.

194 *"Somehow your idea"*: Clarence Day to KSW, February 23, 1933, NYPL 181.5.

194 *"It does something"*: EBW, "Midwinter Madness," TNY, February 20, 1932, 42.

194 *There, amid many:* E. B. White, "Home Movies," approximately minutes 23:00–32:00, private collection.

195 *"anxiety plus energy":* RA, interview with author, December 4, 2019.

195 *In fact, 1932 was:* EBWB 181.

195 *As soon as Roger:* RA, interview with author, December 4, 2019.

196 *In February, the same:* "Prize for American Book Is Founded in France," *New York Herald Tribune*, February 19, 1932.

196 *"the most popular":* "Miss Cather Wins French Book Prize," *New York Times*, February 3, 1933.

196 *"one of our finest":* ESS, "The Prix Femina Americain," *Bookman*, March 1933, 76.

196 *"amuse or soothe":* Louise Bogan, "American Classic," TNY, August 8, 1931, 19.

197 *"a mother with children":* HR to Clifton Fadiman, October 5, 1936, NYPL 250.25.

197 *"Throw open the door":* EBW, "Children's Books," *Harper's*, January 1939; reprinted in *One Man's Meat* (Gardiner, ME: Tilbury House, 1997), 19.

197 *"With expensive paper":* KSW, "Books for Children," TNY, December 10, 1932, 92.

197 *"Tonstant Weader Fwowed up":* Dorothy Parker, "Far from Well," TNY, December 20, 1928, 98.

198 *"I don't know what":* KSW to BB, May 5, 1932, NYPL 166.11.

198 *"I imagine in your":* BB to KSW, undated [1932], NYPL 166.11.

198 *There is a home:* EBW, "Home Movies," approximately minute 42:30, private collection.

199 *"when we decided":* LEBW 99.

CHAPTER 23

200 *Before Katharine left:* KSW to Ralph Ingersoll, June 5, 1934, NYPL 206.4.

201 *Almost instantly the magazine's:* AT 98.

201 *"reflective pieces":* "Notice," The New Yorker Editors, October 17, 1934, NYPL 201.10.

201 *"to prove more":* KSW to Sherwood Anderson, November 5, 1936, NYPL 244.20.

201 *Though Bogan's husband:* Frank, *Louise Bogan*, 143. See also pages 211–19.

202 *"walking or reading":* Louise Bogan to KSW, undated [1934], NYPL 195.15.

202 *"they might give you":* Louise Bogan to Rolfe Humphries, July 2, 1935, in Ruth Limmer, ed., *What the Woman Lived: Selected Letters of Louise Bogan, 1920–1970* (New York: Harcourt Brace Jovanovich, 1973), 91.

202 *"I wish we could":* KSW to HR, April 28, 1934, NYPL 214.5.

202 *"looking as white":* KSW to HR, undated [1932], NYPL 170.7.

203 *"first to The New Yorker":* The New Yorker to Otto Soglow, November 16, 1932, NYPL 190.3.

203 *"I have been thinking":* KSW to HR and Raoul Fleischmann, December 8, 1935, NYPL 184.9.

204 *"his first loyalty":* KSW to HR, May 24, 1933, NYPL 187.5.

204 *Katharine bumped his:* KSW to Ogden Nash, May 30, 1933, NYPL 187.5.

204 *She reminded Everitt:* David Stuart, *The Life and Rhymes of Ogden Nash: A Biography* (n.p.: Taylor Trade Publishing, 2000), 33.

204 *They negotiated:* The New Yorker to Ogden Nash, December 1933, NYPL 187.5.

204 *"[their] leading artists ha[d]":* HR to James M. Cain, August 30, 1931, NYPL 164.9.

204 *"sound a warning":* HR to Eugene Spaulding, September 23, 1933, NYPL 180.12.

205 *"We have heard":* KSW to Maxim Lieber, November 27, 1936, NYPL 257.9.

205 *"This seems to":* KSW to Mr. Ross, Mr. Fleischmann, and Mr. Whedon, October 24, 1934, NYPL 199.5.

205 *What they were truly:* See Fiona Green, "Marianne Moore and the Hidden Persuaders," in Green, ed., *Writing for "The New Yorker,"* 171, and Travis, "What We Talk About When We Talk About 'The New Yorker,'" 269–71.

205 *For the third time: The New Yorker* to Ogden Nash, December 14, 1934, NYPL 225.14.

206 *This contract was called:* Ben Yagoda erroneously dates the innovation of the first reading agreement to 1938, and he improbably credits its invention to Gus Lobrano, a junior editor whom Katharine would hire that year. See AT 161.

206 *"I've never had such":* Ogden Nash quoted in Douglas M. Parker, *Ogden Nash: The Life and Work of America's Laureate of Light Verse* (Chicago: Ivan R. Dee, 2005), 43.

206 *"It's just another":* KSW to Elizabeth Nowell, February 10, 1936, NYPL 260.2.

206 *Sally Benson, still:* Wolcott Gibbs to KSW, undated [1934], and Wolcott Gibbs to Sally Benson, December 17, 1934, NYPL 195.8.

207 *Sure enough:* Sally Benson, "Wild Animals," TNY, July 20, 1935, 18–20.

207 *"for [their] reconsideration":* KSW to Arthur Kober, May 9, 1934, NYPL 207.6.

207 *Five months later:* Arthur Kober, "Rubia," TNY, November 17, 1934, 62.

207 *Day's nostalgic stories:* Yagoda attributes the inspiration for Thurber's series to Day's Father series in AT 104–5.

208 *"But I tell you":* Ralph McAllister Ingersoll to KSW, November 9, 1933, NYPL 184.8.

208 *"all are in the":* KSW to Ralph McAllister Ingersoll, November 19, 1933, NYPL 184.8.

208 *"appalled at the malice":* KSW to SE, September 10, 1970, CU 183.

209 *"face made of rubber":* "The New Yorker," *Fortune,* August 1934, 73–82+.

209 *Katharine had the:* The attribution of the parody idea to Katharine and subsequent details of the Ross-Luce battle come from Vinciguerra, *Cast of Characters,* 152–72.

209 *Editor St. Clair:* Katharine might have pointed out that Andy had already parodied *Time* in *The New Yorker.* See EBW, "Ballade of Meaty Inversions," TNY, March 11, 1933, 18.

210 *"Backward ran sentences":* Wolcott Gibbs, "Time . . . Fortune . . . Life . . . Luce," TNY, November 28, 1936, 20–25.

210 *"Time-Life was":* William Maxwell quoted in Vinciguerra, *Cast of Characters,* 162.

210 *"[It was] one of the best pieces":* HR quoted in Vinciguerra, *Cast of Characters,* 168.

211 *"the paucity of our literary":* Notes and Comment, TNY, November 25, 1933, 13.

CHAPTER 24

212 *"Everything is new":* LMF 54.

212 *"just the most terrible":* SE, "Interview with Nancy and Louise Stableford," undated [1968], CU-SE 1.32.

213 *"wrote hundreds of lines":* EBW to KSW, January 21, 1934, CU 60.

213 *"ten to twenty miles":* EBW to KSW, January 24, 1934, CU 60.

214 *"Each morning now":* KSW to EBW, January 25, 1934, CU 181.

214 *"it felt as soft":* EBW to KSW, March 28, 1934, CU 60 and EBWB 186.

214 *"I'm glad you":* KSW to EBW, undated [1934], CU 180.

214 *"and that's what caused"*: Robert Coates to KSW, June 2, 1934, NYPL 198.2.

215 *"These last few weeks"*: KSW to Robert Coates, June 27, 1934, NYPL 198.2.

215 *"a cat, a puppy, Nancy"*: Ibid.

215 *"Oh no, Nancy"*: SE, "Interview with Nancy and Louis Stableford" [1968], CU-SE 1.32.

216 *Entering from the front:* This description of the White house comes from photographs in a family album taken just after Andy's death in 1985. With great thanks to Allene White for showing me the photos—and Katharine's desk, now her own.

216 *"I never heard of"*: KSW quoted in Nancy Stableford, "Bryn Mawr–April 4, 1979," CU 16.1.

216 *"She is taking a pre-medical"*: KSW to Jean Batchelor, October 12, 1934, NYPL 194.14.

217 *"I am awfully tired"*: KSW to BB, January 17, 1935, NYPL 223.4.

217 *"going around like"*: Blake Bailey, *Cheever: A Life* (New York: Knopf, 2009), 81.

217 *"make a living out"*: Ibid., 81–82.

217 *"I wish he'd try"*: KSW to Maxim Lieber, June 18, 1935, NYPL 233.4.

218 *"Dress or not"*: *The New Yorker* invitation, undated [March 1935], NYPL 236.5.

218 *"It is going to be hardest"*: KSW to Robert Coates, March 22, 1935, NYPL 224.15.

218 *"You deserve much"*: Janet Flanner to KSW, undated [March 1935], NYPL 227.21.

218 *"she would never suggest"*: Anonymous, "Interview: Roger Angell discusses Katharine S. White," December 6, 1978, private collection.

219 *"I have seen so"*: KSW to Phyllis McGinley, March 10, 1934, NYPL 209.12.

219 *"We encountered a writer"*: Notes and Comment, TNY, March 3, 1934, 13.

219 *"That's the penalty"*: Phyllis McGinley to KSW, March 21, 1934, NYPL 209.12.

220 *"the prettiest lady"*: Phyllis McGinley to KSW, April 2, 1935, NYPL 234.19.

220 *"There's not only"*: Louise Bogan to KSW, February 4, 1935, NYPL 222.19.

220 *One writer bemoaned:* Phyllis McGinley to KSW, October 23, 1935, NYPL 234.19. McGinley's first marriage and divorce have not been independently confirmed. She remained in the Catholic Church, wrote frequently about her faith in poems and essays, and was chosen on the basis of her faith to serve on a New York State bipartisan committee on abortion.

220 *Hale had placed:* KSW to HR, October 5, 1933, NYPL 184.9.

220 *"one of the great"*: KSW, "Speech of Introduction for Nancy Hale, Cosmopolitan Club," January 1959, SMITH 18.10.

221 *"It is so nice to think"*: Nancy Hale to KSW, undated [1935], NYPL 229.14.

221 *"Ever since being"*: KSW to Nancy Hale, January 8, 1935, NYPL 226.14.

221 *What would you:* KSW to Nancy Hale, October 22, 1936, NYPL 253.16.

222 *Joel, who was only:* Joel White quoted in Bill Mayher, *Joel White: Boatbuilder, Designer, Sailor* (Brooklin, ME: Noah Publications, 2002), 17.

222 *"a constant delight"*: EBW to KSW, June 9, 1935, LEBW 116.

222 *"light, well-rounded"*: KSW to EBW, undated [July 11, 1935], CU 181.

223 *"a good old-fashioned"*: KSW to EBW, September 20, 1935, CU 181.

224 *"I think of you"*: KSW to EBW, September 19, 1935, CU 181.

224 *"the future and more babies"*: KSW to EBW, September 21, 1935, CU 181.

224 *"to start fresh"*: KSW to EBW, September 27, 1935, CU 181.

224 *"Just packed specialty"*: EBW to KSW, September 1, 1935, CU 60.

225 *"wearing [his] finest"*: EBW to KSW, September 19, 1935, CU 60, LEBW 121.

225   *"Got your note":* EBW to KSW, September 20, 1935, CU 60, LEBW 122.

225   *"I wrote ten thousand":* A. Scott Berg, *Max Perkins: Editor of Genius* (New York: New American Library, 2016), 295.

225   *"Do walk down":* KSW to Nancy Hale, November 15, 1935, NYPL 229.14.

225   *"a small but distinguished":* EBW quoted in Pamela Hanson, *Manhattan's Turtle Bay* (Mount Pleasant, SC: Arcadia Publishing, 2008), 25.

CHAPTER 25

226   *"met there many":* Franklin P. Adams, The Conning Tower, *New York Herald Tribune*, December 21, 1935.

226   *Ross held court:* Kinney, *James Thurber*, 610.

226   *"beaker or two":* Franklin P. Adams, The Conning Tower, *New York Herald Tribune*, October 26, 1935.

227   *"a wallet and a gold watch":* Langston Hughes, "Why, You Reckon," TNY, March 17, 1934, 22.

227   *"Since I must":* Langston Hughes quoted in Arnold Rampersad, *The Life of Langston Hughes, Volume I: 1902–1941* (New York: Oxford University Press, 2002), 299.

227   *"I laughed myself":* Maxim Lieber quoted in Faith Berry, *Langston Hughes: Before and Beyond Harlem* (Westport, CT: L. Hill, 1983), 221.

228   *"convinced that this":* Wolcott Gibbs to Maxim Lieber, January 28, 1935, NYPL 233.5.

228   *"as colorful a story":* KSW to Maxim Lieber, March 1, 1935, NYPL 233.5.

228   *"The remoteness of the setting":* KSW to Maxim Lieber, March 9, 1935, NYPL 233.5.

228   *"Can't you persuade":* William Maxwell to Geraldine Mavor, December 8, 1938, NYPL 299.18.

228   *"Those are O. Henry":* Wolcott Gibbs to Sally Benson, September 7, 1934, NYPL 195.8.

228   *O. Henry was, of course:* Paul March-Russell, *The Short Story: An Introduction* (Edinburgh: Edinburgh University Press, 2009), 39.

229   *"I wish they were":* Sally Benson to Wolcott Gibbs, September 12, 1934, NYPL 195.8.

229   *Benson did, in fact:* Keefe, *Casual Affairs*, 167.

229   *"more literary and artificial":* KSW to Maxim Lieber, February 21, 1936, NYPL 257.9.

229   *The story was seen:* Andrew Levy, *The Culture and Commerce of the American Short Story* (New York: Cambridge University Press, 1993), 86–87.

230   *"unity of effect":* Edgar Allan Poe, "Review of *Twice Told Tales*," in *The New Short Story Theories*, ed. Charles May (Athens: Ohio University Press, 1994), 60.

230   *"The editor's function":* Edward J. O'Brien, *The Dance of the Machines: The American Short Story and the Industrial Age* (New York: The Macauley Company, 1929), 149.

230   *"least common denominator":* Edward O'Brien, *The Advance of the American Short Story* (New York: Dodd, Mead and Co., 1931), 6.

230   *"a thin trickle in a deep":* Edward O'Brien quoted in Levy, *The Culture and Commerce of the American Short Story*, 50.

231   *Soon, New Yorker authors:* "Index of Best American Short Stories, 1915–1999," *The Best American Short Stories of the Century*, eds. John Updike and Katrina Kenison (Boston: Houghton Mifflin, 1999), 797–835.

231 *"somehow selling [his]"*: Morley Callaghan, quoted in Fladd, *Transnational Conversations*, 67.

231 *"new sort of material"*: KSW to Morley Callaghan, November 7, 1928, quoted in Fladd, *Transnational Conversations*, 68–69.

232 *"too many coincidences"*: KSW to Morley Callaghan, February 26, 1937, quoted in Fladd, *Transnational Conversations*, 90.

232 *"I'm just all in"*: KSW to Janet Flanner, February 25, 1936, NYPL 251.16.

233 *"I think . . . your page"*: HR quoted in AT 43.

233 *"personal 'Judge'"*: KSW to HR, August 10, 1937, NYPL 21.5.

233 *"In a moment of low"*: KSW to Clifton Fadiman, April 24, 1936, NYPL 250.25.

233 *"Please check my"*: EBW to Christopher Morley, April 27, 1936, LEBW 125.

233 *Yet another jesus:* GID 259–60.

234 *"Nation contributor, English Instructor"*: Clifton Fadiman to KSW, May 10, 1936, NYPL 250.25.

234 *"We none of us"*: KSW to Clifton Fadiman, May 27, 1936, NYPL 250.25.

234 *"except most dilettantishly"*: HR to KSW, undated [1936], NYPL 250.25.

234 *"might at least"*: KSW to Raoul Fleischmann, May 29, 1936, NYPL 251.18.

235 *Trilling kept trying:* See correspondence in NYPL 286.19.

235 *"probably be hell"*: Janet Flanner to KSW, May 9, 1935, NYPL 227.21.

235 *"Just too fascinating"*: KSW to Janet Flanner, April 26, 1935, NYPL 227.21.

235 *The resulting profile:* Janet Flanner, "Führer—I," TNY, February 29, 1936, 20; "Führer—II," TNY, March 7, 1936, 27; and "Führer—III," TNY, March 14, 1936, 22.

235 *"We never go in"*: HR quoted in Annalisa Zox-Weaver, "At Home with Hitler: Janet Flanner's Führer Profiles for the *New Yorker*," *New German Critique* 102, no. 34.3 (Fall 2007): 107.

236 *"the only job that I"*: Janet Flanner to KSW, October 19 [1938], BM 4.6.

236 *"Mrs. White smiled"*: William Maxwell quoted in Barbara Burkhardt, *William Maxwell: A Literary Life* (Urbana: University of Illinois Press, 2005), 63.

236 *And when Ross:* AT 171–72, OU 119–22, and KSW to HR, September 8, 1937, BM 10.11.

237 *Katharine had already:* Louise Bogan to WS, December 9, 1941; Limmer, ed., *What the Woman Lived*, 225.

CHAPTER 26

238 *"I have the greatest"*: EBW to Gus Lobrano, July 15, 1935, LEBW 118.

238 *"All that can be done"*: EBW to KSW, May 1, 1936, LEBW 126–27.

239 *"Things haven't changed"*: EBW to Stanley Hart White, undated [1936], LEBW 129–30.

239 *"I will be walking"*: EBW, "My Physical Handicap, Ha Ha," TNY, June 12, 1937, 20.

239 *"The ear must be"*: Notes and Comment, TNY, April 24, 1937, 13.

240 *"Everyone is old"*: KSW to EBW, September 7, 1936, CU 181.

240 *"amazingly well outwardly"*: KSW to EBW, March 28, 1937, CU 181.

240 *"She's a funny gal"*: KSW to EBW, April 2, 1937, CU 181.

241 *"I want to see what"*: EBW to Stanley Hart White, March 13, 1937, LEBW 144.

241 *And perhaps Andy:* See Kinney, *James Thurber*, 614–15 and 620.

242 *"delicate spiritual tremor"*: EBW to KSW, May 31, 1937, LEBW 145–48.
243 *"year of grace"*: Ibid., 145.
243 *"one of the most sensible"*: EBW quoted in EBWB 211.
243 *"It scared me to death"*: KSW to Carol Angell, March 30, 1973, private collection.
243 *"The dizziness had nearly"*: KSW to HR, August 10, 1937, NYPL 21.5.
244 *"had definitely decided"*: KSW to Rosemary Carr Benét, September 22, 1937, NYPL 268.6.
244 *She also took on:* "Prize of $5,000 Is Projected to Reward Poets," *New York Herald Tribune*, June 28, 1937.
244 *"I can't see any"*: KSW to Norman de Rocheville, November 20, 1936, BM 3.19.
244 *"Is Aunt Elsie my aunt"*: KSW to EBW, September 1937, CU 181.
245 *"Was glad to get"*: EBW to KSW, early September 1937, LEBW 152.
245 *"[Stay] if you are doing"*: KSW to EBW, early October 1937, CU 181.
245 *"I wouldn't know"*: EBW to KSW, early September 1937, LEBW 151.
245 *"Greatly to my surprise"*: KSW to EBW, September 1937, CU 181.
246 *"three or four new men"*: KSW to Janet Flanner, January 20, 1938, NYPL 295.4.
246 *"how to edit copy"*: KSW, handwritten note on Gibbs's "Theory and Practice of Editing New Yorker Articles," November 22, 1969, BM 4.14.
246 *"Editing on manuscript"*: Wolcott Gibbs, "Theory and Practice of Editing New Yorker Articles," c. 1937, BM 4.14, reprinted in GID 442–46.
246 *"in a limp beaten"*: EBW to James Thurber, January 8, 1938, LEBW 159.
247 *"I wondered again why"*: EBW to KSW, December 30, 1937, CU-SE 1.36.
247 *"I have been struggling"*: KSW to JT, January 13, 1938, NYPL 306.16.
247 *Charles Spencer Sergeant died:* "Charles Sergeant Dead in Florida," *Boston Daily Globe*, February 27, 1938.
247 *"homely and sweet"*: Caroline Belle Sergeant to KSW, March 8, 1938, YALE 3.45.

CHAPTER 27

249 *"an unholy mess"*: EBW to JT, January 8, 1938, LEBW 158–59.
249 *"ready and eager"*: EBW to KSW, December 31, 1937, LEBW 157.
249 *"Don't despair of not"*: KSW to EBW, December 30, 1937, CU 181.
249 *"I haven't produced"*: EBW to JT, January 8, 1938, LEBW 158–59.
249 *"I was not reluctant"*: KSW, handwritten notes on Brendan Gill's *Here at "The New Yorker"*, undated [1975], BM 30.15.
249 *"I felt I had"*: Nan Robertson, "Life Without Katharine: E. B. White and His Sense of Loss," *New York Times*, April 8, 1980.
250 *"This is not a time"*: JT to EBW, undated [October 6, 1937], reprinted in Kinney, ed., *The Thurber Letters*, 251.
250 *"a stubborn inhabitant"*: EBW, "You Can't Resettle Me: A Defense of New York City by a Stubborn Inhabitant," *Saturday Evening Post*, October 10, 1936, 8.
250 *"The health argument"*: JT to KSW, February 23, 1938, reprinted in Kinney, ed., *The Thurber Letters*, 278.
251 *"They have said"*: KSW to Janet Flanner, February 17, 1938, NYPL 295.4.
251 *"After 'thinking it over'"*: Raoul Fleischmann quoted in Kinney, *James Thurber*, 653–54.
252 *"On a day like this"*: EBW to KSW, undated [May 3, 1938], BM 29.4.
252 *"Any money at all"*: EBW to Ik Shuman, summer 1938, LEBW 167.

253 *"nicely dressed, courageous"*: EBWB 253.

253 *"Don't let Andy neglect"*: Day quoted in EBWB 254.

253 *"I've been thinking"*: KSW to EBW, December 30, 1937, CU 181.

254 *A few years previously*: Raoul Fleischmann to KSW, January 12, 1937, and May 2, 1928, BM 4.7.

254 *"premier cliché artist"*: KSW to Gus Lobrano, undated [1938?], BM 7.2.

CHAPTER 28

257 *"a form of rebellion"*: RA quoted in Joe Bonomo, *No Place I Would Rather Be: Roger Angell and a Life in Baseball Writing* (Lincoln: University of Nebraska Press, 2019), 9.

258 *"Great bandleaders"*: Willing Davidson, "Baseball, Fiction, and Life: Roger Angell's Era Spanning Career at *The New Yorker*," February 16, 2020, https://www.newyorker.com/culture/the-new-yorker-interview/baseball-fiction-and-life-roger-angells-era-spanning-career-at-the-new-yorker, retrieved August 3, 2023.

259 *"considering how little"*: KSW to EA, May 15, 1938, private collection.

259 *"My life here"*: KSW to Ruth McKenney, August 29, 1938, NYPL 301.10.

260 *North Brooklin, Maine, had*: See Brooklin Keeping Society, *Images of America: Brooklin*, 2003.

260 *Luckily the Whites*: See KSW to RA, June 7, 1972, and April 8, 1976, private collection.

261 *Katharine would receive*: KSW to CA, January 2, 1976, BM 29.1.

261 *"I don't think he'll learn"*: KSW to HR, September 15 [1938], NYPL 23.19.

261 *"I thought his first"*: KSW to HR, September 15 [1938], NYPL 23.19.

262 *"just a doctorer"*: KSW to Ik Shuman, August 9, 1938, NYPL 23.17.

262 *"But the best thing"*: KSW to HR, September 15 [1938], NYPL 23.19.

262 New Yorker *staffers met*: Ik Shuman to HR, April 27, 1939 [incorrect date, likely 1938], NYPL 23.17.

263 *"faults, repetitions, typos"*: KSW's 1972 note appended to HR to KSW, undated [1938], BM 10.11.

263 *"never read a more"*: KSW to HR, "Report on Issue of Feb 22, 1941," undated, NYPL 964.20.

263 *"so slight and delicate"*: KSW to HR, "Report on Jan 1, 1941 Issue," undated, NYPL 964.20.

263 *"an obviously minor effort"*: KSW to HR, "Report on Issue of Feb 22, 1941," undated, NYPL 964.20.

263 *"We're turning into"*: KSW to HR, September 15 [1938], NYPL 23.19.

263 *"the great Christmas present"*: KSW to HR, "Report on December 10, 1938 Issue," undated, NYPL 964.20.

264 *"Just tell the boys"*: KSW to HR, September 15 [1938], NYPL 23.19.

264 *"destructive post-mortems"*: KSW to HR, "Report on December 31, 1938 Issue," undated, NYPL 964.20.

265 *"The age of specialization"*: Unsigned [KSW], "Children's Books," TNY, December 8, 1938, 87.

265 *"every day of the year"*: KSW to HR and WS, June 3, 1940, NYPL 23.19.

265 *"too-definitive, too strenuous"*: HR to KSW, June 7, 1940, NYPL 23.19.

265 *"How can one choose"*: KSW to HR, undated [summer 1940], NYPL 23.19.

266 *"the exciting thing"*: KSW to Eugene Saxton, June 23, 1940, CU 181.

266 *"the finest in children's"*: Quoted in "Friend Memorial Public Library: The First Hundred Years," https://friendml.org/library-history/, retrieved August 3, 2023.

266 *"batting away"*: KSW to HR, January 10, 1939, NYPL 23.19.

266 *"Close physical contact"*: EBW, *One Man's Meat*, 20.

267 *"the Grand Panjandrum"*: KSW, undated typed note in Louise Bechtel folder, BM 1.10.

267 *"If a story was imaginative"*: Frances Clarke Sayers, *Anne Carroll Moore: A Biography* (New York: Atheneum, 1972), 127.

267 *"Not recommended for purchase"*: Lepore, *The Mansion of Happiness: A History of Life and Death* (New York: Random House, 2013), 42.

267 *"You will be shocked"*: EBW to Eugene Saxton, March 1, 1939, LEBW 182.

267 *"I think Ernest"*: KSW to EBW, March 1939, CU 181.

268 *"My wife is nagging"*: EBW to Eugene Saxton, April 11, 1939, LEBW 184.

268 *"I am afraid"*: EBW to Anne Carroll Moore, April 25, 1939, LEBW 185.

268 *"I've decided that"*: KSW to Anne Carroll Moore, quoted in Lepore, *The Mansion of Happiness*, 50.

CHAPTER 29

269 *But just under half:* Of the 101 women who published short stories in *The New Yorker* from the summer of 1938 through the end of 1943, 42 had been previously published in the magazine and 1 (Katherine Mansfield) was published posthumously. Of the 58 new authors, 40 published three or fewer stories, leaving 18 who might be termed Lobrano and Maxwell's discoveries. This group notably includes Shirley Jackson, who will be discussed later. It includes Ida Treat, Katharine's friend from Cleveland, and Rebecca West, whom Ross edited. It also includes Carson McCullers and Marjorie Kinnan Rawlings, who each published a small handful of stories before dropping out of the magazine. These statistics were compiled using the *New Yorker* Fiction Index at newyorkerfiction.com.

270 *"Paris became German"*: Unsigned, Notes and Comment, TNY, June 22, 1940, 11.

271 *"lost jewels which lie"*: EBW to Frank Sullivan, May 26, 1939, LEBW 186.

271 *"a subtreasury designed"*: EBW and KSW, eds., *A Subtreasury of American Humor* (New York: Coward-McCann, 1941), xi.

271 *"If it is good"*: KSW to Jerome Weidman, September 7, 1940, NYPL 346.13.

271 *"This would be a book"*: KSW to HR and Ik Shuman, November 7, 1939, NYPL 23.17.

272 *"a distinguished collection"*: Ibid.

272 *"the world's living authority"*: KSW to HR and Ik Shuman, undated [1939], NYPL 346.13; TOM 53; LEBW 234.

272 *He'd spent one summer:* LEBW 234.

273 *"At the time the magazine"*: Unsigned draft of foreword, undated, NYPL 346.13.

274 *"The odds are"*: "Display Ad 38," *New York Herald Tribune*, December 5, 1940.

274 *"The New Yorker has"*: "Miss Cather's New Novel and Other Recent Fiction," *New York Times*, December 8, 1940.

274 *"form a profound"*: Rose Feld, review of *Short Stories from "The New Yorker,"* *New York Herald Tribune*, December 8, 1940.

CHAPTER 30

275 *The original Brooklin Library:* "Centennial Celebration, Brooklin, Maine," July
1949, Brooklin Keeping Society. Other details of the Whites' history with the library come from "Friend Memorial Public Library."

276 *"the functional regulation":* *The Collecting Net* 14.122 (August 5, 1939): 112.

276 *"seem[ed] to have safety":* KSW to Eugene Saxton, July 1, 1940, CU 181.

276 *Nancy finished her:* George W. Pierson, *A Yale Book of Numbers: Historical Statistics
of the College and University, 1701–1976* (New Haven: Yale University, 1983), 160
and 171.

276 *"cornered":* KSW to EBW, July 1941, CU 181.

276 *She had some advice:* SE, "Interview with Nancy and Louis Stableford," 1968,
CU-SE 1.32 and OU 130.

277 *"My great hope":* KSW to EA, May 8, 1941, private collection.

277 *"Aren't the facts":* KSW to EA, May 21 [1941], private collection.

277 *Nancy and Louis were married:* "Nancy Angell Married," *New York Times*, September 9, 1941.

277 *Katharine responded:* SE, "Interview with Nancy and Louis Stableford," 1968,
CU-SE 1.32.

278 *Too frequently:* RA to KSW, January 16, 1939, private collection.

278 *"a darling":* KSW to Eugene Saxton, July 1, 1940, CU 181.

278 *It was a monumental:* RA, interview with author, January 12, 2021.

279 *"two silences":* RA, interview with author, March 6, 2021.

279 *"It is rich":* Stanley Walker, "Anthology of Laughter," *New York Herald Tribune*, November 16, 1941.

279 *"serious and inspired":* Ole H. Lexau, "Millions of Chuckles," *Atlanta Constitution*,
May 24, 1942.

279 *The book soon began:* "Best Sellers for the Week," *New York Times*, March 16, 1942,
and Fanny Butcher, "Books: 43 Books Top 100,000 Mark in 1942 Sales," *Chicago
Daily Tribune*, December 30, 1942. On the book's selection as a BOMC dividend,
see KSW to Eugene Saxton, March 22, 1942, in CU 181.

280 *"a parlor strategist":* KSW to EBW, February 4, 1942, CU 181.

280 *"a little too remote":* KSW to Eugene Saxton, January 14, 1942, CU 181.

280 *"by a committee":* Ralph Ingersoll to KSW, April 30, 1942, BM 6.9.

280 *When the Japanese:* Bonomo, *No Place I Would Rather Be*, 11, and LMF 184.

281 *"the very patriotism":* EBW, *One Man's Meat*, 221.

281 *"100 pounds of wool":* EBW, *One Man's Meat*, 265.

281 *"suit the President":* EBW quoted in EBWB 233.

282 *"these baboons":* KSW to EBW, February 17, 1942, CU 181.

282 *"One reason I don't":* KSW to Eugene Saxton, February 19, 1942, CU 181.

283 *"The first personal singular":* See for instance Irwin Edman, "Earthy, Humorous, Ac-
cessible: E. B White Creates a Wise Personal Art of Discourse," *New York Times*,
June 14, 1942, and MAS, "One Way of Life," *Hartford Courant*, July 5, 1942.

283 *"one of the most useful":* Clifton Fadiman, "In Praise of E. B. White, Realist: The
Light-Fingered Humorist Is Also a Light-Giving and Original Thinker," *New
York Times*, June 10, 1945.

283 *"political implications":* EBW to Stanley Hart White, June [1944], LEBW 243.
Sales figures are from EBWB 229.

284 *Nancy and Louis moved:* *The Collecting Net* 18.153 (November 1943): 6.
284 *"It is all breathtaking":* KSW to EBW, October 3, 1942, CU 181.
285 *"This operation is going":* KSW to EBW, March 10, 1943, CU 181. See also letters from KSW to EBW on February 26, 27, and 18, 1943.
286 *Andy wrote to his editor:* EBWB 237.
286 *And he handily:* KSW to HR, undated [September 1943], NYPL 958.7.
286 *"My admiration for your":* HR to EBW, May 7 [1943], in Thomas Kunkel, ed., *Letters from the Editor: "The New Yorker"'s Harold Ross* (New York: Modern Library, 2000), 211.
286 *"McKelway, Cooke":* HR to EBW, undated [June 1942], in Kunkel, *Letters from the Editor*, 184.
286 *"Damned if I know":* HR to KSW, September 14 [1942], in Kunkel, *Letters from the Editor*, 186.
286 *"Whatever White wants":* HR to KSW, Sunday [summer 1943], BM 10.11.
287 *"Our system for":* HR to KSW, October 19, 1942, in Kunkel, *Letters from the Editor*, 191.
287 *It took time to iron:* On EBW's arrangement, see EBWB 239. On KSW's arrangement, see KSW to HR, April 25, 1944, and T. M. Brassel to HR, January 14, 1944, NYPL 958.7.
287 *"nervous crack-up":* EBW to Harry Lyford, October 28, 1943, LEBW 236.
287 *As a nerve:* EBWB 237.
288 *"There seems to be a kite":* EBW to Stanley Hart White, March 2, 1944, LEBW 239.
288 *"take frequent shower":* EBW to Harry Lyford, October 28, 1943, LEBW 236.
288 *"Joe looked so sweet":* KSW to EBW, early July 1943, CU 181.
289 *"fully awake, instead":* EBW, *One Man's Meat*, xii–xiii.

CHAPTER 31

293 *"all the little 4f's":* Unsigned, *The Conflict* 2 (January 18, 1943): 1, NYPL 389.6.
293 *From 1941 to 1945:* For the increase in subscriptions, see AT 211. For Grant's pony edition, see AT 181 and GID 366. For Ross's desperation for submissions, see Kunkel, *Letters from the Editor*, 209.
294 *"meandering thru the halls":* Daise Terry to KSW, Sunday [undated], BM 12.8.
294 *"Gosh, Mr. Fleischmann":* Daise Terry to KSW, Friday [undated], BM 12.8.
294 *"The New Yorker is":* EBW to Stanley Hart White, March 2, 1944, LEBW 239.
295 *"I wouldn't do that":* KSW to Cornelia Otis Skinner, April 28, 1944, NYPL 410.21.
295 *"Half a lifetime":* EBW, "A Weekend with the Angels," TNY, January 22, 1944, 18, and EBW, *Second Tree from the Corner*, 3.
295 *"a clear-cut victory":* EBW to Stanley Hart White, undated [mid-January 1944], LEBW 237.
295 *"lack an enemy":* EBW, *The Wild Flag: Editorials from "The New Yorker" on Federal World Government and Other Matters* (Boston: Houghton Mifflin Company, 1946), xii.
296 *"Carson McCullers":* BB to William Maxwell, undated [1942], NYPL 388.6.
296 *"fiction that is art":* KSW to BB, May 19, 1944, NYPL 402.22.
297 *Katharine noted, for instance:* William Maxwell to Bernice Baumgarten, January 21, 1943, NYPL 388.5.
297 *"I don't expect you":* Ann Watkins to Gus Lobrano, December 1, 1943, NYPL 400.7.

297 *"There's something unpleasant"*: William Carlos Williams to Charles Pearce, April 16, 1943, NYPL 400.19.

298 *"[fought] like a tiger"*: HR to KSW, 1943, quoted in AT 216.

298 *Jackson's best-known work*: On "The Lottery," see Ruth Franklin, *Shirley Jackson: A Rather Haunted Life* (New York: Liveright Publishing Corporation, 2016), 221–37.

298 *That first year*: See the Leland Hayward files in NYPL 392.8, 406.12, 420.3, and 434.2.

299 *"Is her stuff flatly"*: Stanley Edgar Hyman to Gus Lobrano, October 2, 1946, NYPL 448.23.

299 *Editor Robert Henderson*: Robert Henderson to Ann Mason, October 2, 1947, NYPL 450.11, and Gus Lobrano to Eleanor Kennedy, August 11, 1948, NYPL 465.5.

300 *But he dropped*: See NYPL 341.15, 379.13, and 395.18.

301 *"she had written"*: Frances Kiernan, *Seeing Mary Plain: A Life of Mary McCarthy* (New York: W. W. Norton & Co., 2000), 209, and "Mary McCarthy, Edmund Wilson, and the Short Story That Ended a Marriage," https://www.newyorker .com/books/page-turner/mary-mccarthy-edmund-wilson-and-the-short-story -that-ruined-a-marriage, retrieved August 7, 2023.

301 *"extraordinarily brilliant"*: KSW to MMc, May 8, 1945, NYPL 416.14.

301 *"highly irregular"*: Harold Ross to KSW, May 14, 1945, NYPL 416.14.

302 *"almost unvarying ritual"*: MMc to Linda Davis, September 29, 1978, BM 32.10.

304 *"I can't begin to tell"*: KSW to MMc, May 23, 1957, NYPL 754.2.

304 *"like the one [she]"*: Edmund Wilson to KSW, May 13, 1944, NYPL 414.11.

304 *"I'm sorry the sum"*: KSW to Edmund Wilson, June 2, 1944, NYPL 414.16.

CHAPTER 32

306 *"to [her] mind and without"*: KSW to HR and Gus Lobrano, June 18, 1945, NYPL 427.21.

306 *Katharine fervently wanted*: For Pearce and KSW's early correspondence with Bishop, see EBNY 3–13.

307 *"so extravagantly emotional"*: KSW to Henry Volkening, March 31, 1944, NYPL 412.4. See also Hyman's effort on Ellison's behalf in NYPL 418.12. "In a Strange Country" was published in *Tomorrow* in 1944 and later collected in *Flying Home and Other Stories*.

307 *"rather too melodramatic"*: William Maxwell to Henry Volkening, November 8, 1946, NYPL 439.10.

307 *Richard Wright, W.E.B. Du Bois*: For Wright, see NYPL 400.26; for Du Bois, see 418.8.

307 *"Of course, I know"*: Alex Haley to Gentlemen, November 27, 1945, NYPL 419.27.

308 *"I suspect those ears"*: KSW to Christine Weston, June 8, 1944, NYPL 414.7.

309 *"mice in the subconscious"*: EBW to Stanley Hart White, undated [January 1945], LEBW 249.

309 *"With death at hand"*: EBW, "The Librarian Said It Was Bad for Children," *New York Times*, March 6, 1966, quoted in EBWB 254.

309 *"a nightmare"*: EBW to Morris Bishop, undated [1949], LEBW 287; see also EBW to Dorothy W. Sanborn, April 18, 1961, LEBW 436.

310   *"Only another children's"*: Ursula Nordstrom, "Stuart, Wilbur, Charlotte: A Tale of Tales," *New York Times*, May 12, 1974.

310   *She sent a contract*: Ursula Nordstrom to KSW, March 30, 1945, in Leonard S. Marcus, ed., *Dear Genius: The Letters of Ursula Nordstrom* (New York: HarperCollins, 1998), 8.

310   *"If ever there was"*: E. B. White, "A Reporter at Large: The Eve of St. Francis," TNY, May 5, 1945, 44.

310   *"It seemed more"*: E. B. White, "A Reporter at Large: Beautiful Upon a Hill," TNY, May 12, 1945, 45.

311   *"Looks as if"*: KSW to EBW, undated [May 7, 1945], CU 181.

311   *"The first season"*: KSW, "Children's Books: Fairy Tales and the Postwar World," TNY, December 9, 1945, 120.

312   *"not much bigger"*: EBW, *Stuart Little* (New York: Harper & Row, 1945), 1.

312   *"non-affirmative, inconclusive"*: EBW, "The Librarian Said It Was Bad for Children," *New York Times*, March 6, 1966.

312   *"Well, what's the matter"*: KSW quoted in Lepore, *The Mansion of Happiness*, 218n58.

313   *"But I can't help"*: KSW quoted in LEBW 252.

313   *"shook up"*: EBW, "The Librarian Said It Was Bad for Children."

314   *"Children can sail"*: Ibid.

314   *"Let us not overstimulate"*: KSW, "Children's Books: Between the Dark and the Daylight," TNY, December 7, 1946, 127.

CHAPTER 33

315   *"a dream-duplex"*: Louise Bogan to Morton D. Zabel, January 4, 1948, in Limmer, ed., *What the Woman Lived*, 258.

316   *"I'm disgusted that"*: KSW to BB, April 9, 1946, NYPL 430.21.

316   *"excessively happy"*: Joel White quoted in Mayher, *Joel White: Boatbuilder, Designer, Sailor*, 16.

316   *"just about forever"*: RA, "Brooklin Memories," 2021, https://www.youtube.com/watch?v=U18abLFhfbc, retrieved February 15, 2024.

317   *"I really enjoyed"*: RA to KSW, September 7, 1946, private collection.

317   *What Andy intended*: Samuel Zipp, "Raising *The Wild Flag*: E. B. White, World Government, and Local Cosmopolitanism in the Postwar Moment," *Journal of Transnational American Studies* 4.1 (2012).

318   *"It is for one"*: Marianne Moore to KSW, March 24, 1946, NYPL 437.10.

318   *She and a few other*: See Louise Bogan to Allan Tate, January 16, 1945, in Limmer, ed., *What the Woman Lived*, 245, and Leavell, *Holding On Upside Down*, 326–27.

320   *Katharine told Weston's*: KSW to Henry Volkening, September 23, 1946, NYPL 439.10.

320   *"That really gripes me"*: Christine Weston to KSW, July 18, 1946, BM 15.6.

321   *"I really feel"*: KSW to William Maxwell, July 4, 1947, BM 7.19.

322   *"You probably won't"*: KSW to Peter Powys Grey, July 16, 1947, NYPL 959.4.

322   *Senator Greenleaf sits*: Peter Powys Grey, "Shadows of the Evening," *Story* 32.129 (Summer 1948), 34–40.

323   *Roger sternly lectured*: RA to KSW, July 5, 1957, private collection.

323   *"It's been nightmarish"*: KSW to Christine Weston, May 16, 1947, NYPL 456.19.

CHAPTER 34

324 *His editing was:* Charles Pearce to VN, undated [1943], NYPL 396.18, and VN, "On Discovering a Butterfly," TNY, May 15, 1943, 26.

324 *"electric":* KSW to Véra Nabokov, July 11, 1977, BM 8.22. On KSW's initial cultivation of VN, see KSW to HR, January 7, 1944; KSW to Louis Forster, April 11, 1944; KSW to VN, June 2, 1944, NYPL 410.11; and Brian Boyd, *Vladimir Nabokov: The American Years* (Princeton: Princeton University Press, 1991), 73.

324 *"laggards in a cross":* VN to KSW, March 21, 1945, NYPL 423.13.

325 *"the pattern showing":* VN to KSW, January 1, 1946, NYPL 437.19.

325 *"full of exciting":* KSW to VN, June 9, 1947, NYPL 452.2.

325 *"To my intense delight":* KSW to VN, August 2, 1947, NYPL 452.2.

325 *"almost decided to stop":* VN to Edmund Wilson, August 29, 1947, in *Dear Bunny, Dear Volodya: The Nabokov-Wilson Letters, 1940–1971,* ed. Simon Karlinsky (Berkeley: University of California Press, 1979), 219.

326 *"I think you have":* VN to KSW, August 8, 1947, NYPL 452.2.

326 *Around this time:* Edmund Wilson to VN, April 7, 1948, in Karlinsky, *Dear Bunny, Dear Volodya,* 225.

326 *"I feel almost":* KSW to VN, February 15, 1951, NYPL 511.11.

326 *"Great sympathy":* VN, "Appendix," *Speak, Memory: An Autobiography Revisited* (New York: Everyman's Library, Alfred A. Knopf, 1999), 259.

326 *"Commas in The New Yorker":* EBW, "The Art of the Essay No. 1," 65.

326 *"incurably deranged":* VN, "Symbols and Signs," TNY, May 15, 1948, 31.

327 *"I've decided to ask":* KSW to VN, July 10, 1947, NYPL 452.2.

327 *"a good sample":* VN to KSW, July 15, 1947, NYPL 452.2.

327 *"so carefully mutilated":* VN to KSW, March 13, 1948, NYPL 466.16.

327 *"dummy wordings":* KSW to VN, March 22, 1948, NYPL 466.16.

327 *You have already:* VN to KSW, March 17, 1951, NYPL 511.11.

328 *Critics have found:* Much has been written about the KSW-VN correspondence regarding this story, including several essays in Yuri Leving, ed., *Anatomy of a Short Story: Nabokov's Puzzles, Codes, "Signs and Symbols"* (New York: Continuum International Publishing Group, 2012), but this volume is riddled with errors, such as the claim that KSW left her career at *The New Yorker* in 1949.

329 *"she had closed":* Jean Stafford, "Children Are Bored on Sunday," TNY, February 21, 1948, 23.

330 *"I find myself":* KSW to Jean Stafford, August 29, 1948, COLO 27.9.

331 *"Patient Disappeared After":* Frank Sullivan to KSW, April 25, 1948, BM 12.3.

331 *A fellow patient:* LMF 64–65.

332 *"I always think":* KSW to Jean Stafford, April 30, 1948, COLO 27.9.

332 *"[We] are earnestly waiting":* KSW to Henry Volkening, December 17, 1948, NYPL 468.17.

332 *"positively heavy":* KSW to Edmund Wilson, November 3, 1948, NYPL 470.32.

333 *"the constant cooperation":* KSW, "Books: How Dear to This Heart," TNY, December 11, 1948, 122.

333 *"a few friends":* KSW to Jean Stafford, December 20, 1948, COLO 27.9.

CHAPTER 35

334 *"derogatory and insulting":* Madison S. Jones Jr. to *The New Yorker* Editors, September 14, 1948, COLO 24.21.

334 *"any other phraseology":* *The New Yorker* to Madison S. Jones Jr., September 16, 1948, COLO 24.21.

335 *"Don't let it get":* KSW to Jean Stafford, September 29, 1948, NYPL 469.12.

336 *"Nothing—nothing":* Honor Canou to Editor of *The New Yorker*, July 1949, COLO 24.21.

336 *"We consider it":* *The New Yorker* to Lucinda Bukeley, August 11, 1949, COLO 24.21.

336 *"anti-racial prejudice":* KSW to HR, undated [1946], NYPL 959.4.

336 *"She was an old-fashioned":* Frances Gray Patton, "The Falling Leaves," TNY, November 22, 1947, 37.

337 *"at least all of the following":* F-R Publishing Corporation, "*The New Yorker*: Editorial Policy and Purpose" (New York, 1946), 3, quoted in Mary Corey, *The World Through a Monocle: "The New Yorker" at Midcentury* (Cambridge, MA: Harvard University Press, 1999), 10.

337 *"never been able":* KSW to HR, September 15 [1938], NYPL 23.19.

337 *"Negroes enjoy a certain":* EBW to Mr. and Mrs. Z——, January 9, 1951, LEBW 301–302.

338 *"representative":* "Foreword," *55 Short Stories from "The New Yorker"* (New York: Simon & Schuster, 1949), ix.

338 *She explained to Simon & Schuster:* KSW to Jack Goodman, April 14, 1949, NYPL 483.11.

339 *"The land where":* KSW to EBW, undated [May 1949], CU 181.

339 *The very instant:* Katherine Gauss Jackson to KSW, September 22, 1949, BM 6.11.

339 *"the summer of the grandchildren":* EBW to Stanley Hart White, July 15, 1949, LEBW 283.

340 *"a disappointment":* KSW to Jean Stafford, July 26, 1949, COLO 27.9.

340 *"some form of memoir":* Delmore Schwartz, "Smile and Grin, Relax and Collapse," *Partisan Review* 17.3 (1950): 293.

341 *It sought to use:* This definition comes from Joan Shelley Rubin's influential book *The Making of Middlebrow Culture* (Chapel Hill: University of North Carolina Press, 1992).

342 *"are edited (or edit)":* Stephen Spender, "The Situation of the American Writer," *Horizon* 19.111 (March 1949): 173.

342 *"takes his culture":* Russell Lynes, "Highbrow, Lowbrow, Middlebrow," reprinted in *The Wilson Quarterly* 1.1 (Autumn 1976): 153. Subsequent scholars of American twentieth-century middlebrow culture have largely agreed with Lynes. Trysh Travis uses the term. George H. Douglas, Catherine Keyser, Faye Hammill, and Karen Leick characterize the magazine as "smart," though Hammill elsewhere names it "a distinctly middlebrow institution," as do Daniel Tracy and Tom Perrin. Travis, "What We Talk About," 254; Douglas, *The Smart Magazines: 50 Years of Literary Revelry and High Jinks at "Vanity Fair," "The New Yorker," "Life," "Esquire," and "The Smart Set"* (New York: Archon Books, 1991), 1–3; Keyser, *Playing Smart: New York Women Writers and Modern Magazine Culture* (New Brunswick, NJ: Rutgers

University Press, 2010), 5–11; Hammill and Leick, "Modernism and the Quality Magazines," 185–90; Hammill, "*The New Yorker*, the Middlebrow," 30–31; Tracy, "Investing in 'Modernism,'" 40–41; Perrin, and "On Blustering: Dwight Macdonald, Modernism, and *The New Yorker*," 228–29, all in Green, *Writing for "The New Yorker."*

342   *The magazine's circulation grew:* AT 211.

343   *"I can't find any other":* KSW to Isabel Bolton, August 5, 1947, LZ 92.

343   *"the pretentious":* KSW, "Wolfe Call: Letter to the Editor," *New York Times*, February 5, 1961.

343   *Where middlebrow literature:* See Beth Driscoll, "The Middlebrow Family Resemblance: Features of the Historical and Contemporary Middlebrow," *Post45*, July 1, 2016.

344   *"middlebrow personalism":* Janice Radway, *A Feeling for Books: The Book-of-the-Month Club, Literary Taste, and Middle-Class Desire* (Chapel Hill: The University of North Carolina Press, 1997), 283.

344   *"I do not think":* VN to KSW, November 10, 1947, NYPL 452.2.

345   *"pointless and inane":* Edmund Wilson to KSW, November 12, 1947, BM 15.12.

345   *"the vast number":* HR to KSW, November 4, 1947, BM 10.11.

345   *"It's entirely your":* KSW to Christine Weston, January 9, 1948, NYPL 468.18.

346   *"What bothers us":* KSW to Isabel Bolton, undated [August 1947], BM 2.6. For an excellent discussion of this exchange between KSW and Bolton, see LZ 83–97.

346   *In 1951,* The New Yorker: EBW to Larry Eisenberg, February 25, 1952, LEBW 322.

347   *"She's the kind":* KSW to Bernice Baumgarten, October 18, 1948, NYPL 459.11.

347   *"like knocking [her] shins":* Elizabeth Taylor to KSW, March 16, 1949, NYPL 36.1.

347   *"I agree with":* Rumer Godden to KSW, January 31, 1949, NYPL 476.9.

347   *"wondering if there":* Rumer Godden to KSW, April 7, 1949, NYPL 476.9.

347   *"grave risk":* KSW to Rumer Godden, April 20, 1949, NYPL 476.9.

348   *"a howling fury":* Roald Dahl to Howard Moss, April 14, 1949, NYPL 36.1.

348   *"All morning, people":* EBW, "H. W. Ross," TNY, December 15, 1951, 23.

348   *"Andy! An-dy!":* GID 432.

349   *"darling Kay, Oh yes":* Janet Flanner to KSW, December 13, 1951, BM 4.6.

349   *"such a bunch":* EBW to Elmer Davis, December 16, 1951, as well as EBW to Frank Sullivan, [December 17?, 1951], LEBW 318–19.

350   *"William Shawn has accepted":* Raoul Fleischmann quoted in AT 256.

350   *"never forgave Shawn":* EBW to SE, August 25, 1982, CU 82.

350   *The editorial staff:* KSW to Nadine Gordimer, October 17, 1952, NYPL 712.14.

CHAPTER 36

351   *"the door would presently":* EBW to JT, April 6, 1952, LEBW 326.

352   *"thinking that she might":* KSW to Louise Bogan, April 7, 1952, NYPL 710.22.

352   *"I feel rather":* KSW to Adrienne Rich, June 1, 1953, NYPL 723.8.

353   *Rich took her advice:* See Adrienne Rich to KSW, October 10, 1954; KSW to Rich, October 11, 1954; and Rich to KSW, December 18, 1954, NYPL 731.4, and Hilary Holladay, *The Power of Adrienne Rich: A Biography* (New York: Doubleday, 2020), 114.

353   *"extremely neat, pointed":* KSW to Bernice Baumgarten, May 7, 1952, NYPL 710.26.

354 *She wrote to Maxwell:* For details of her illness, see KSW to Gus Lobrano, July 21 and 31, 1952, NYPL 717.8, and KSW to William Maxwell, August 1, 1952, NYPL 522.13.

354 *"ten sheep, eighteen":* EBW to the Pupils of 5-B, December 26, 1952, LEBW 335.

355 *Katharine would ask:* Jonathan Stableford, interview with author, July 16, 2019.

355 *"to relax a trifle":* RA to KSW, September 15 [1950s], private collection.

355 *"anti-snobs":* Jonathan Stableford, interview with author, July 16, 2019.

356 *"continual never-ending":* KSW to EA, August 31 [1952], private collection.

357 *"something of a hoax":* KSW to WS, September 8 [1952], NYPL-WS 17.3.

358 *What so many people:* My thoughts here have been heavily influenced by Janet Carey Eldred's sympathetic and feminist analysis of the ways Katharine's body has been discussed over the years and her willingness to see this issue through Katharine's own needs and desires. Both of us, reading the same letters, have been struck by what previous writers have not seen: how *hard* Katharine worked through debilitating illnesses. See LZ 145–60.

358 *"warm browns and grays":* KSW to Jean Stafford, November 1, 1952, COLO 27.4.

359 *"are not words":* KSW to Mrs. George F. Murray, April 27, 1949, quoted in OU 140, but it is Michael Sims who identified it as the source for Andy's final line. See *The Story of "Charlotte's Web": E. B. White's Eccentric Life in Nature and the Birth of an American Classic* (New York: Bloomsbury Publishing, 2012), 206–7 and 157–207. For Margaret F. Murray's letter, see "Life in America," *New York Times*, March 20, 1949, and for Andy's rebuttal, see "'Typical' Brooklin," *New York Times*, April 17, 1949.

359 *"Any Harper book":* Ursula Nordstrom to EBW, March 19, 1951, in Marcus, *Dear Genius*, 36.

360 *"I step into real":* Anne Carroll Moore, "The Three Owls' Notebook," *Horn Book*, December 19, 1952, https://www.hbook.com/story/three-owls-notebook, retrieved February 18, 2022.

360 *"reservations about Stuart Little":* Ursula Nordstrom to EBW, October 23, 1952, in Marcus, *Dear Genius*, 55.

360 *To this day:* Melissa Block, "Charlotte A. Cavatica: Bloodthirsty, Wise, and True," *All Things Considered*, National Public Radio, August 4, 2008.

361 *"Geography must be":* Elizabeth Bishop to KSW, October 10, 1952, EBNY 85.

361 *"Try it for something":* Elizabeth Bishop to KSW, September 12, 1952, EBNY 84.

361 *"I hope you won't":* Elizabeth Bishop to KSW, October 25, 1952, EBNY 89.

361 *"A scream, the echo":* Elizabeth Bishop, "In the Village," TNY, December 19, 1953, 26.

362 *"lovely prose poem":* KSW to Elizabeth Bishop, November 12, 1952, EBNY 96.

362 *"I wanted to give":* Elizabeth Bishop to KSW, November 23, 1952, EBNY 98.

362 *"I am really":* KSW to Elizabeth Bishop, January 20, 1953, EBNY 101.

363 *"emotional family crises":* KSW to Elizabeth Taylor, March 25, 1953, BM 12.5.

363 *Joe had met Allene:* Martha White, email to author, March 16, 2022.

363 *"a wise arrangement":* KSW to CA, undated [Christmas 1976], BM 29.1.

363 *"Clean":* Allene White, interview with author, August 13, 2019.

364 *"This purchase of this":* KSW to Elizabeth Bishop, July 29, 1953, EBNY 114.

364 *"He is not a very":* VN to KSW, July 26, 1953, NYPL 722.14.

364 *"acute distress":* VN to KSW, March 10, 1952, NYPL 714.18.

365 *"What to do? It is a cata-stroph!":* VN, "Pnin," TNY, November 28, 1953, 45.

365 *"It is not the enormous":* VN to KSW, September 29, 1953, NYPL 722.14.

365 *"We all of us like":* KSW to WS, September 8, 1953, NYPL-WS 17.5.

366 *"Your annoyance with"*: KSW to Elizabeth Bishop, September 24, 1953, EBNY 116.
366 *"millions of conventional"*: KSW to Elizabeth Bishop, November 20, 1953, EBNY 120.
366 *"to help get that"*: KSW to Elizabeth Bishop, January 7, 1954, EBNY 126.

CHAPTER 37

367 The New Yorker *had:* Corey, *The World Through a Monocle*, 40–57.
369 Boyle herself had: Charles Trueheart, "Documents Show FBI Kept Files on Leading U.S. Writers," *Washington Post*, September 30, 1987.
369 *Over the next few:* See Boyle to WS, March 21, 1953, in *Kay Boyle: A Twentieth-Century Life in Letters*, ed. Sandra Spanier (Urbana, IL: University of Illinois Press, 2015), 501–7, and Brenda Wineapple, *Genêt: A Biography of Janet Flanner* (New York: Ticknor & Fields, 1989), 224–32. Interestingly, no correspondence between KSW and Kay Boyle in the 1950s has been preserved in either the Bryn Mawr or *New Yorker* archives.
369 *"political naivete"*: Gus Lobrano to Whom It May Concern, October 3, 1952, NYPL 718.20. The description of WS's letter is found in Kay Boyle to Ann Watkins, September 26, 1952, in Spanier, *Kay Boyle*, 491–93.
369 *"syphilitic fascism"*: Janet Flanner to KSW, undated [1953], BM 4.6.
369 *"[her] oldest friend"*: Ibid.
369 *"read and edited"*: KSW to Janet Flanner, October 18, 1953, in Rai Peterson, "A Question of Loyalty: 'The New Yorker' and Kay Boyle," *Journal of the Midwest Modern Language Association* 40.1 (2007): 64–74.
370 *"It made me happy"*: ESS, *Willa Cather*, 40.
370 *"But she was"*: Ibid., 2.
370 *"marred for [Katharine]"*: KSW to Nancy Hale, July 6, 1976, BM 5.6.
370 *"Edmund Wilson said"*: KSW to William McGuire, May 17, 1976, SMITH 198.10. For a near-identical sentiment, see "KSW handwritten note on Nancy Hale," undated, BM 5.6.
370 *Might she profile:* See the letters to and from Harold Ober Associates in NYPL 526.10 and 722.17.
371 *"a long-drawn-out"*: EBW to Stanley Hart White, March 11, 1954, LEBW, 356.
371 *"about the most confused"*: KSW to Christine Weston, May 11, 1954, NYPL 732.29.
372 *"Most New Yorker work"*: KSW to May Sarton, February 25, 1954, NYPL 731.14.
372 *When Andy wrote:* EBW to Stanley Hart White, March 11, 1954, LEBW 355–56. On the publication of *The Second Tree from the Corner*, see LEBW, 352–54, and EBWB 309.
372 *"very special reasons"*: Véra Nabokov to KSW, December 9, 1953, NYPL 722.14.
373 *"My advice would be"*: KSW to Véra Nabokov, February 1, 1954, BM 8.22.
373 *"I am afraid the book"*: VN to KSW, February 3, 1954, NYPL 730.6.
373 *"more unpleasant than amusing"*: KSW to VN, February 15, 1954, NYPL 730.6.
374 *"Too bad he was"*: "K. S. White's Note on Vladimir Nabokov," 1977, BM 8.23.
374 *"She tips the scales"*: EBW to Bristow Adams, March 29, 1954, LEBW 357.
374 *"[her] favorite of all people"*: KSW to Louise Seaman Bechtel, April 14, 1954, VASS 43.659.
374 *"more dead than alive"*: KSW to Jean Stafford, July 14 [1954], COLO 27.4.
375 *"You are my precious stone"*: EBW to KSW, July 18, 1954, LEBW 364.
375 *"feeding on anti-histamines"*: KSW to WS, August 1, 1954, NYPL-WS 17.1.

376 *"a set-up for suicide":* Ibid.
376 *She'd read a story:* For both Hardwick and Lessing, see "Writers: Removed from Potential List," NYPL 134.8.
377 *"mild promise":* KSW to Gus Lobrano, undated [summer 1954], NYPL 134.8.
377 *"I loved that magazine":* Updike, *Picked-Up Pieces*, 35. Updike's biographer, Adam Begley, writes that Updike's critics thought of him as such a typical *New Yorker* writer, it was "as though he had been concocted in-house, the product of a singularly fruitful editorial meeting." I prefer the metaphor of the school because it provides an intersection of Updike's careful study of the magazine and Katharine's patient labor to grow promising writers into reliable contributors. Adam Begley, *Updike* (New York: Harper Perennial, 2015), 120.
378 *Updike, she observed:* KSW to BB, March 2, 1972, BM 2.11.
378 *In total that year:* Begley, *Updike*, 80.
378 *"The patient and abundant":* John Updike to KSW, September 2, 1954, NYPL 732.20.
378 *"Your letter of September 2nd":* KSW to John Updike, September 15, 1954, NYPL 732.20.
378 *Andy made light:* EBW, "Our Windswept Correspondents: The Eye of Edna," TNY, September 25, 1954, 39.
379 *Katharine, on the other:* KSW to Jean Stafford, undated [September 1954], NYPL 732.11.
379 *"hospitalitis—the food":* KSW to Jean Stafford, October 29, 1954, NYPL 732.11.
379 *"a nervous hurry":* John Updike to KSW, November 26, 1954, NYPL 732.20.
379 *"treatise on punctuation":* KSW to John Updike, December 1, 1954, NYPL 732.20.
380 *All this for a ten-line:* John Updike, "The Clan," TNY, December 18, 1954, 119.
380 *"like a mother retriever":* John Updike to KSW, September 16, 1970, BM 14.1.
380 *"It was all quite":* KSW to Ida Treat Bergeret, January 6, 1955, NYPL 734.11.
380 *"being a grandmother":* KSW to Frances Gray Patton, December 30, 1954, NYPL 730.18.
380 *"Dear John Updike":* KSW to John Updike, March 21, 1955, NYPL 740.6.

CHAPTER 38

383 *"a repair job":* KSW to Ida Treat Bergeret, February 16, 1955, NYPL 734.11.
383 *"I do, except—":* KSW to Frances Gray Patton, April 15, 1955, NYPL 738.20.
383 *"followed a familiar pattern":* KSW, "Caroline Sergeant, Daughter of Hamp, Dies at 93 in Me.," *Daily Hampshire Gazette*, May 16, 1955.
384 *"much too swish":* KSW to Jean Stafford, August 31 [1956 or 1957], COLO 27.9.
384 *"Never has so much":* EBW to Allene White, July 7, 1955, LEBW 375.
384 *When* Punch *invited Andy:* OU 170.
385 *"A shot of Mrs. White":* JT quoted in Kinney, *James Thurber*, 982.
385 *Despite this, they met:* Ibid., 1050.
385 *Their vacation immeasurably:* KSW to Jean Stafford, August 31 [1956 or 1957], COLO 27.9.
386 *They visited the Updikes:* Begley, *Updike*, 117.
387 *"I am at the end":* KSW to WS, August 13, 1955, NYPL-WS 17.1.
387 *"so many queer things":* KSW to WS, October 4, 1955, NYPL-WS 17.1.

388   *And so Katharine gave:* See KSW's note to her letter to Jean Stafford, December 22, 1955, COLO 27.9, and OU 6–7.

388   *"a passion of self-loathing":* Jean Stafford, "The Mountain Day," TNY, August 18, 1956, 32.

389   *"No matter what":* Elizabeth Hardwick to KSW, May 20, 1955, NYPL 736.13.

389   *"This I would love":* KSW to WS, undated [1955], NYPL-WS 17.1.

390   *"anywhere at all":* KSW to WS, October 11, 1955, NYPL-WS 17.1.

390   *"at times extremely":* Gus Lobrano to KSW, undated [1955], NYPL-WS 17.1.

390   *"I have done":* KSW to WS, October 25, 1955, NYPL-WS 17.1.

391   *"After January first":* KSW to Elizabeth Bishop, December 7, 1955, EBNY 162–63.

392   *"a shiver of desolation":* May Sarton to KSW, December 3, 1955, BM 10.17.

392   *"I don't think I can":* Frank Sullivan to KSW, February 13, 1956, BM 12.3.

392   *"No editor I've worked":* Bernice Baumgarten to KSW, December 2, 1955, BM 1.9.

392   *"Please do not jump":* KSW to WS, undated [1955], NYPL-WS 17.1.

393   *"supremely good as a critic":* May Sarton to KSW, December 3, 1955, BM 10.17.

393   *There, Roger replicated:* RA, interview with author, December 28, 2020.

394   *"stinky old couch":* Katey Gray, interview with author, October 22, 2020.

394   *"food and drink":* EBW to Stanley Hart White, January 21, 1956, LEBW 380.

CHAPTER 39

395   *"heavenly":* KSW to Jean Stafford, March 13, 1956, COLO 27.4.

395   *"frightfully difficult":* KSW to WS, March 3, 1956, NYPL-WS 17.1.

395   *"for it is love":* Unsigned [E. B. White], "G. S. Lobrano," TNY, March 10, 1956, 155.

396   *"Every time there's":* Janet Flanner to KSW, undated [1936?], BM 4.6.

396   *She agreed to head:* KSW to William Maxwell, March 11, 1956, BM 7.19.

396   *"If you had retired":* Mollie Panter-Downes to KSW, April 15, 1956, BM 9.10.

396   *"If you know of":* KSW to Frances Gray Patton, June 30, 1956, NYPL 746.5.

397   *"I suppose he has":* KSW to Diarmuid Russell, May 28, 1956, NYPL 746.20.

397   *"No chance":* KSW, handwritten note on Christine Weston to KSW, undated [May 1957], BM 15.6.

397   *"enormous":* KSW to Harriet Walden, September 28, 1956, NYPL-HW 5.5.

397   *"The experienced men":* KSW to Jean Stafford, June 29, 1956, COLO 27.4.

398   *"the amateurishness":* RA to KSW, September 14 [1955], private collection.

398   *"that [their] being there":* KSW to WS, March 10, 1956, NYPL-WS 17.1.

398   *"Sell your stock!":* RA to KSW, undated [summer 1956], private collection.

399   *"Thanks for holding":* RA to KSW, March 2, 1976, private collection.

399   *"There seems to be":* RA to EBW, August 29, 1957, NYPL 757.16.

399   *"I realize that his death":* KSW to V. S. Pritchett, May 21, 1956, NYPL 746.11.

400   *"All over the world":* KSW to Elizabeth Hardwick, June 27, 1956, NYPL 743.25.

400   *"He is a strange man":* KSW to Jean Stafford, June 29 [1956], COLO 27.4.

400   *"I was so impressed":* Jean Stafford quoted in Raymond Sokolov, *Wayward Reporter: The Life of A. J. Liebling* (New York: Harper & Row, 1980), 275.

400   *In July, a happy:* EBW to Frank Sullivan, July 20 [1956], LEBW 386–87.

401   *They wanted to settle:* Allene White, interview with the author, August 13, 2019.

401   *Joe bought a boat:* Mayher, *Joel White*, 21–22.

401   *After years as:* Jonathan Stableford, interview with the author, July 16, 2019.

401 *That summer Katharine:* Last Will and Testament of Caroline B. Sergeant, March 26, 1954, NYPL 134.2.

402 *"a most personal":* KSW to ESS, June 17 [1956], private collection.

403 *"states of mind":* KSW to Jean Stafford, March 18, 1955, COLO 27.9.

403 *"the nick of time":* KSW to WS, March 15, 1957, NYPL-WS 17.5.

403 *"scandalously lazy month":* KSW to Elizabeth Hardwick, April 2, 1957, NYPL-WS 17.5.

403 *Roger could not:* Tom Gorman to KSW, March 8, 1957, BM 5.1.

403 *"Which is a real tribute":* KSW to VN, March 25, 1957, BM 8.24.

403 *"[her] jauntiest granddaughter":* KSW to VN, September 25, 1958, BM 8.24.

404 *A college friend sent:* EBW to H. A. Stevenson, April 1, 1957, LEBW 400 and EBWB 325–32.

404 *"She is a truly gifted":* EBW to Edward W. Weimar, November 11, 1957, LEBW 409.

404 *"the inestimable advantage":* EBW to J. G. Case, November 3, 1958, LEBW 415.

405 *"husbands and wives":* JT to KSW, May 3, 1957, reprinted in Kinney, ed., *The Thurber Letters*, 671-675.

405 *"I can't remember":* KSW to JT, May 13, 1957, BM 12.9.

406 *"some short stories":* KSW to Shirley Jackson, January 24, 1957, NYPL 752.19.

406 *"I think of you":* KSW to Phyllis McGinley, May 13, 1957, NYPL 754.4.

407 *"I ended up a complete":* KSW, "Books to Go to Bryn Mawr College by Bequest," undated, BM 34.2.

407 *Clearly the baton:* Ann Petry, "Has Anybody Seen Miss Dora Dean?" TNY, October 25, 1958, 41.

407 *"In this one month":* KSW to Frances Gray Patton, August 30, 1957, BM 9.12.

409 *"impersonal":* Adrienne Rich to Howard Moss, March 3, 1958, NYPL 763.11.

409 *"I am disturbed":* KSW to WS, January 31, 1958, NYPL-WS 17.5.

409 *"I have written Roger":* KSW to WS, October 18, 1957, NYPL-WS 17.5.

409 *"iconoclastic suggestion":* KSW to WS, December 20, 1958, NYPL-WS 17.2.

410 *"remarkably prosperous":* P. B. Bart and J. H. Rutledge, "Urbanity, Inc.: How the *New Yorker* Wins Business Despite Air of Disdain," *Wall Street Journal*, June 30, 1958, quoted in AT 309.

CHAPTER 40

412 *"The two interests":* OUG 83.

412 *"clean-cut, of interesting":* OUG 3.

413 *"Don't blush":* William Harris to KSW, May 17, 1965, BM 5.11. See also Jane Grant to KSW, May 18, 1965, BM 5.2.

413 *"I hate to sound":* KSW to Louise Seaman Bechtel, March 20, 1960, VASS 43.659.

414 *"with love":* EL to KSW, undated [January 1959], TG 14. See also pages 18 and 27 for expressions of antisentimentalism.

414 *"had never thought":* EBW, "Introduction," OUG viii.

415 *"suddenly at a very high":* RA, interview with author, November 4, 2019.

415 *"degenerated awfully":* KSW to WS, November 9, 1960, NYPL-WS 17.2.

415 *"had dreams of glory":* KSW to EL, July 2, 1958, TG 8.

416 *"As I write":* OUG 21.

416 *"the penalty one pays":* OUG 45.

416 *"The tests proved":* KSW to Louise Seaman Bechtel, March 20, 1960, VASS 43.659.

417 *"the phrase that pops":* EBW, "Khrushchev and I," TNY, September 26, 1959, 39.

417   *"a name to conjure with"*: OUG 65.

417   *"in fairly constant touch"*: KSW to WS, March 16, 1959, NYPL-WS 17.2.

418   *"a combination of Bottom"*: Rebecca West, "Ross Misprized," review of *The Years with Ross* by James Thurber, *Sunday Times*, July 19, 1959. See letters between KSW and West in BM 15.5.

418   *"venomous attack"*: KSW to The Editors of The Nation [unsent], undated [summer 1959], NYPL-WS 17.4.

418   *"[It was] just to get it off"*: KSW to WS, June 19, 1959, NYPL-WS 17.4.

419   *"with some sort of"*: KSW to WS, undated [summer 1959], NYPL-WS 17.4.

419   *"Sooner or later Jim"*: KSW to Harrison Kinney, March 23, 1973, BM 6.19.

419   *Two days before:* KSW to WS, December 29, 1959, NYPL-WS 17.4.

420   *"Elsie, when sick"*: KSW to EL, December 28, 1959, TG 53.

420   *"a compromise selection"*: KSW to EL, March 17 [1960], TG 61.

420   *"Narrative writers"*: The Editors, "Foreword," *Stories from "The New Yorker" 1950–1960* (New York: Simon & Schuster, 1960), unpaginated.

421   *Katharine flatly turned:* See Robert Mabry to KSW, May 17, 1960, BM 7.9, and Clelia Carroll to KSW, June 16, 1960, BM 2.17.

421   *"modest background"*: KSW, "Possible themes of chapters in my book—Probably not in this order," undated, BM 25.11.

421   *"another fascinating article"*: Alfred A. Knopf to KSW, March 14, 1960, BM 20.14.

422   *"this mythical, far-distant"*: KSW to Alfred A. Knopf, April 15, 1960, BM 20.14.

422   *"a cozy, fairy-tale"*: Nona Balakian, "The Author at Home," *New York Times*, June 16, 1960.

422   *"little more than"*: Unsigned, "Books: Late Frost: Witty, Wise, and Young," *Time*, July 4, 1960, and Glauco Cambon, "Revolution and Tradition," *Poetry* (April 1962), 53.

422   *"a warm, loving and sensitive"*: Unsigned, "Robert Frost: Trial by Existence," *Kirkus Reviews*, June 1, 1960, and James M. Cox, "Robert Frost Alone Is Space," *Virginia Quarterly Review* 36.3 (Summer 1960), 470.

423   *"are a problem"*: Marianne Moore to KSW, January 11, 1960, BM 8.15.

423   *"uneasy"*: EBW to Dorothy Lobrano, June 14 [1960], LEBW 428.

424   *"it so well demolished"*: KSW, handwritten note, 1972, BM 16.2.

424   *"the kind of editorial"*: John K. Hutchens, "Stories from *The New Yorker*," *New York Herald Tribune*, November 10, 1960.

424   *"pretty hard to take"*: KSW to WS, undated [December 23, 1960], and December 24, 1960, NYPL-WS 17.1.

424   *"the tone of someone"*: Arthur Mizener, "The Voice Is Quiet, the Eye Is Sharp: With Its Stories *The New Yorker* Offers Notes and Comment on Our Urban Culture," *New York Times*, December 18, 1960.

425   *"wistful messages"*: KSW to WS, December 20, 1960, NYPL-WS 17.2.

426   *"I guess I'm not"*: RA to KSW, December 30, 1960, private collection.

426   *"I must say she looks"*: EBW to Morris Bishop, undated [January 2, 1961], LEBW 432.

426   *"have more time"*: KSW to Louise Seaman Bechtel, September 12, 1961, BM 1.11.

CHAPTER 41

429   *Two days after:* Details of her health troubles for the year 1961 come from KSW to Louise Seaman Bechtel, September 12, 1961, BM 1.11, KSW note, undated [1972], BM 16.1, and LEBW 432–34.

430 *"the seeking out"*: KSW to WS, January 10, 1961, NYPL-WS 17.1.

430 *"lilyless"*: OUG 130.

431 *Alfred Knopf wrote:* TG 100.

431 *"She has times"*: Nancy Stableford to Dana Atchley, April 15, 1961, private collection.

432 *"There goes my source"*: KSW to EL, August 3, 1961, TG 109.

432 *"slit [her] throat"*: KSW to Véra Nabokov, October 16, 1961, BM 8.22.

432 *His last year:* Details of Thurber's final illness and death come from Bernstein, *Thurber*, 479–505, and Harrison, *James Thurber*, 1071–77.

433 *Indeed, so bitter:* Bernstein, *Thurber*, 485–86.

433 *"The whole world"*: Unsigned [E. B. White], "James Thurber," TNY, November 11, 1961, 247.

434 *"It was a dreadful"*: KSW to EL, June 5, 1962, TG 122.

434 *"thanks to poison sprays"*: OUG 160.

434 *"a great spiritual release"*: KSW to RA, August 19, 1962, private collection.

434 *"Neither you nor I"*: RA to KSW, September 5 [1962], private collection.

435 *She was acutely:* KSW to RA, September 15 [1962], private collection.

435 *She did give:* KSW to RA, September 16, 1962, private collection.

435 *"I can't help wishing"*: RA to KSW, January 18 [1963], private collection.

435 *"this apparent pattern"*: RA to KSW, January 18 [1963] and February 1 [1963], private collection.

436 *"their exchanged symptoms"*: RA, "Andy," TNY, February 14, 2005, 140, and LMF 125–26.

436 *She gave him:* KSW to RA, September 15 [1962], private collection.

436 *"badly cracked"*: EBW to RA, April 5, 1963, LEBW 452.

436 *"Is this a practical joke?"*: EBW to Howard Cushman, July 9, 1963, LEBW 456.

437 *"warm and outgoing"*: KSW to RA, September 8 [1963], private collection.

438 *"a very tortured time"*: KSW to EL, November 18, 1964, TG 144.

438 *"I slop about all"*: KSW to John Updike, May 13, 1964, BM 14.2.

439 *"For the innermost secret"*: John Updike, *The Centaur* (New York: Alfred A. Knopf, 1979), 54.

439 *"mystical affliction"*: John Updike to KSW, September 10, 1963, BM 14.1.

439 *"greed for life"*: BB to KSW, September 30, 1961, BM 2.11.

439 *In August and September:* Details of ESS's last few months come from KSW's letters to Nancy Hale, March 31, 1965; May 28, 1965; and July 14, 1965, SMITH 18.10.

440 *"almost her old self again"*: KSW to Nancy Hale, July 14, 1965, SMITH 18.10.

440 *"Elsie saved everything"*: KSW to Nancy Hale, July 26, 1965, BM 5.6.

440 *"comeback . . . a near miracle"*: KSW to Agnes de Lima, February 12, 1965, private collection.

440 *"I am thankful"*: KSW to RA, January 30, 1965, private collection.

440 *"indomitable"*: See Helen Mitchell, "Elizabeth Shepley Sergeant," *New Magazine of Rockland County*, April 1964, 15; KSW to Nancy Hale, March 31, 1965, SMITH 18.10; May Swenson to KSW, March 10, 1965, YALE-ESS 19.409; and Thornton Wilder, untitled draft of memorial speech, YALE-ESS 19.409.

441 *"I miss her"*: KSW to Agnes de Lima, February 12, 1965, private collection.

441 *"She was a memoirist"*: KSW to Agnes de Lima, May 30, 1966, private collection.

441 *"I would like my letters"*: KSW to Agnes de Lima, June 26, 1965, private collection.

CHAPTER 42

443 *"this age of modern"*: OUG 193.

444 *"That full page ad"*: KSW to Jean Stafford, November 9, 1965, COLO 27.9.

444 The New Yorker *had run*: J. Q. Purcell, "Jimmy Bennett Doesn't Work Here Anymore," TNY, March 14, 1964, and unsigned [Lillian Ross], "Red Mittens!" TNY, March 6, 1965. For Wolfe's account of the origins of the *New York* articles, see "Foreword: Murderous Gutter Journalism," in Wolfe, *Hooking Up* (New York: Farrar, Straus and Giroux, 2000), 249–54.

444 *Ross's "hierophant"*: Tom Wolfe, "Tiny Mummies! The True Story of the Ruler of 43rd Street's Land of the Walking Dead," *New York*, April 11, 1965, and Wolfe, *Hooking Up*, 255–67.

444 *"the big lie of the article"*: KSW, undated notes, BM 16.1.

444 *"Never has a magazine"*: KSW to Jane Grant, May 27, 1965, BM 5.2.

445 *"sly, cruel, and to a large"*: EBW to John Hay Whitney, April 12, 1965, LEBW 482, and "Aftermath: Tom Wolfe on *The New Yorker*," *New York Herald Tribune*, April 25, 1965.

445 *Two staff writers*: Renata Adler, *Gone: The Last Days of "The New Yorker"* (New York: Simon & Schuster, 1999), 84–90; Renata Adler and Gerald Jonas, "The Letter," *Columbia Journalism Review*, Winter 1966, 29–34; Dwight Macdonald, "Parajournalism, or Tom Wolfe & His Magic Writing Machine," *New York Review of Books*, August 26, 1965, 3–5; and Dwight Macdonald, "Parajournalism II: Wolfe and *The New Yorker*," *New York Review of Books*, February 3, 1966, 18–24.

445 *"the wettest bathful"*: Tom Wolfe, "Lost in the Whichy Thickets: *The New Yorker*," *New York*, April 18, 1965, reprinted in Wolfe, *Hooking Up*, 280.

445 *"the pussy cat quality"*: JT to KSW, February 23, 1938, reprinted in Kinney, ed., *The Thurber Letters*, 278.

446 *It was by now*: On Macdonald's curious stance toward *The New Yorker*, see Tom Perrin, "On Blustering: Dwight Macdonald, Modernism and *The New Yorker*," in Green, *Writing for "The New Yorker*," 228–48.

446 *That was only a problem*: See LZ 80–83 and 129–38; Corey, *The World Through a Monocle*, 151; and Travis, "What We Talk About When We Talk About *The New Yorker*," 259.

447 *"Andy isn't feeling well"*: Sanford Phippen and Farnham Blair, "Onward and Upward in Brooklin, Maine: Interview with Diane Allen Stewart," *Puckerbrush Review* 9.1 (Winter 1989): 40–51.

447 *"It might be from"*: Allene White, interview with the author, August 13, 2019.

447 *"stuffy, irrelevant"*: KSW to S. N. Behrman, July 25, 1968, NYPL-SNB 27.2.

448 *"throw[ing] flowers at each"*: EBW, "Introduction," OUG xvi.

448 *"Oh, my, I must"*: KSW quoted in Phippen and Blaire, "Onward and Upward in Brooklin, Maine," 50.

449 *"from before Christ"*: KSW to Nancy Hale, July 24, 1967, BM 5.6.

449 *"Conformity stultifies art"*: OUG 273.

449 *"correction, updating, amplification"*: KSW to Evelyn McCutcheon, November 18, 1967, private collection.

449 *She published two*: KSW, Department of Amplification, TNY, July 10, 1965, 70–71, and June 18, 1966, 112–14. See also KSW to WS, June 10, 1966, NYPL-WS 16.7.

450 *Eventually, she produced*: KSW, "82 Bridge Street," undated, BM 22.3.

451 *Andy was soon reduced:* EBW to Carol and RA, January 9, 1967, in Martha White, ed., *E. B. White on Dogs* (Thomaston, ME: Tilbury House, 2013), 158–62.

452 *"I'm just ruminating":* KSW to RA, March 3, 1966, and March 6, 1967, private collection.

452 *"suddenly began":* RA to KSW, September 16 [ca. 1966], private collection.

452 *"deep ingrained habit":* RA quoted in KSW to RA, January 30, 1968, private collection.

452 *"They make my brain":* KSW to RA, January 30 [1968], private collection.

453 *"her Olympic-scale worrying":* LMF 268.

453 *"restless, exasperating innocent":* Ford, *The Time of Laughter*, 130.

453 *"affirmative and enthusiastic":* KSW to Corey Ford, September 23, 1967, BM 4.9.

454 *"Now she's written":* Donald Barthelme, "Snow White," TNY, February 18, 1967, 38.

454 *"Snow White's white arse":* KSW to RA, undated [February 1967], private collection.

454 *Ford's memoir was:* Jane Grant to KSW, March 17, 1968, BM 5.2, and EBW to Edward Weeks, March 12, 1968, LEBW 508.

454 *S. N. Behrman, Katharine's:* S. N. Behrman to KSW, October 17, 1965, BM 1.12.

454 *"You are the only one":* Ann Honeycutt to KSW, undated [summer 1967], BM 6.3.

454 *"mythical book":* KSW to EL, October 17, 1969, TG 195.

455 *"freakish carcass":* KSW to RA, September 15, 1969, private collection.

455 *In Florida for the winter:* Details of Katharine's health crises in the winter and spring of 1969 come from LEBW 525–28, TG 194–95, and KSW to Eleanor Mc-Cutcheon, March 17, 1969, and May 2, 1972, private collection.

455 *"a generous offer, if cuckoo":* RA to KSW, January 15 [1969], private collection.

CHAPTER 43

456 *"rather odd, uneasy":* EBW to Helen Thurber, January 9, 1970, LEBW 542.

456 *"snow and gloom":* OUG 333.

456 *Her heart failed her:* EBW to Greta Lee Banzhaf, April 1, 1970, LEBW 547–48.

457 *"without waiting the year":* KSW to William Maxwell, July 6, 1970, BM 7.19.

457 *"a joy-ride through":* John Updike, review of *The Trumpet of the Swan*, New York Times, June 28, 1970.

457 *Andy didn't much enjoy:* Details of Andy's accident come from KSW to William Maxwell, July 27, 1970, BM 7.19, and KSW to SE, July 24, 1970, CU 183.

458 *At the end of October:* EBW to RA, October 24, 1970, LEBW 556.

458 *"It is always lovely":* Ursula Nordstrom to EBW, November 12, 1971, in Marcus, *Dear Genius*, 320–21.

458 *"unflickering tone of truth":* Updike, *Picked-Up Pieces*, 435.

459 *"I'm glad it's over":* EBW quoted in EBWB 349.

459 *"discourage KSW from":* RA quoted in EBWB 349.

459 *"pulse taking":* KSW to Carol Angell, September 15, 1971, private collection.

459 *"For Heaven's sake":* KSW to RA, September 22, 1971, private collection.

459 *"That is nonsense":* RA to KSW, September 20 [1971], private collection.

460 *"the most important career":* KSW, "The Young Writer," *Winsor School Alumnal Bulletin*, Spring 1964, 4.

460 *"I have been a liberated":* KSW to Nancy Milford, December 5, 1973, BM 8.12.

460 *"convention led by":* KSW to RA, October 1, 1971, private collection.

461 *"I'm going to tell him":* RA, interview with author, December 28, 2020.

461   "*I can conceive*": BB to KSW, undated [1970], BM 2.10.

461   "*My mind feels so easy*": Nancy Hale to KSW, September 11, 1971, BM 5.6.

462   "*The prospect of any book*": KSW to SE, September 9, 1967, CU 183.

462   "*so detailed and careful*": William Maxwell to KSW, undated [July 1970], BM 7.16–18.

462   "*I can't remember once*": William Maxwell to KSW, undated [August 6, 1974], BM 7.16–18.

463   "*As mother hen*": KSW to William Maxwell, July 27, 1970, BM 7.19.

463   *She wanted her personal:* See KSW to William Maxwell, January 22, 1971, and April 24, 1972, BM 7.19.

463   "*there was a goddamming*": EBW to Frank Sullivan, May 14, 1964, LEBW 472–73.

464   "*of no value*": KSW to James Tanis, April 2, 1971, BM 31.1.

464   "*Katharine, don't ever again*": Frank Sullivan to KSW, undated, BM 12.3.

464   "*3 pages more*": KSW handwritten note on KSW to EBW, April 28, 1945, CU 181.

465   "*living authors must*": KSW quoted in Leo M. Dolenski to EBW, September 26, 1977, BM 30.4.

465   "*impossible*": KSW note, undated, on Edmund Wilson to KSW, December 27, 1971, BM 15.12. See also KSW, note, October 22, 1969, on William Maxwell to KSW, October 20, 1969, BM 7.16.

465   "*I don't know what*": KSW to Harriet Walden, undated [June 1968], NYPL-HW 5.6.

465   "*I could go on*": KSW to James Tanis, April 2, 1971, BM 31.1.

466   "*pathetic, stout*": Isabel Russell, *Katharine and E. B. White: An Affectionate Memoir* (New York: W. W. Norton & Co., 1988), 21.

466   "*country secretaries*": KSW to James Tanis, April 2, 1971, BM 31.1.

466   "*I think he writes*": KSW to RA, June 7, 1972, private collection.

467   "*a grandiose scheme*": KSW to BB, September 10, 1973, BM 2.11.

467   "*Among baseball writers*": Christopher Lehmann-Haupt, "Angell Wings over Baseball," *New York Times*, June 6, 1972.

467   "*Let him name*": KSW to RA, June 7, 1972, private collection.

468   "*to pry the book out*": EBW to RA, May 15, 1972, LEBW 587.

468   "*this inner game*": RA, *The Summer Game* (New York: Viking Press, 1972), 292.

468   *A few months later:* "Ernest Angell, Lawyer, Dead; Former Chairman of ACLU," *New York Times*, January 12, 1973.

468   "*he hated [her] so*": KSW to RA, January 11, 1973, private collection.

468   *Years before:* RA, interview with author, April 23, 2021.

468   "*You did try*": RA to KSW, January 17, 1973, private collection.

469   *His grandchildren should:* KSW to CA, January 20, 1973, BM 29.1.

469   "*the tragedy of his life*": RA, interview with the author, December 28, 2020.

469   "*the civil libertarian*": RA, *Ernest Angell Memorial Booklet*, private collection.

469   "*haying, strangers*": KSW to RA, July 12, 1973, private collection.

469   "*My latest night plan*": KSW to RA, July 23, 1973, private collection.

CHAPTER 44

471   "*like the waiting*": Quoted in RA to KSW and EBW, February 24, 1975, private collection.

471   "*Being a born editor*": RA to KSW, February 24, 1975, private collection.

472   "*out of kindness and idiocy*": RA to KSW, December 19, 1975, private collection.

472 *She told Harriet:* KSW to Harriet Walden, May 20, 1975, NYPL-HW 6.1.

472 *She felt it urgent:* KSW to WS, April 2, 1975, NYPL-WS 16.8.

472 *"as stubborn—and, sometimes":* Gill, *Here at "The New Yorker,"* 289–90.

472 *"The stories he tells":* Nora Ephron, "Somewhere at *The New Yorker*," *Esquire*, June 1975, 30.

472 *"emerge[s] with teethmarks":* Christopher Lehmann-Haupt, "A Swarm of Affectionate Bees," *New York Times*, February 10, 1975.

473 *"more bounce and more":* KSW, "Note on Brendan Gill," undated, BM 4.15.

473 *"It was always":* Gill, "E. B. White: The Art of the Essay No. 1," 65.

473 *"Everyone who knows me":* KSW, untitled and undated notes, BM 30.15.

474 *"ghastly picture":* KSW to CA, March 10, 1975, BM 29.1.

474 *She was writing: Here at "The New Yorker"* had a long afterlife. When it was reissued in paperback ten years after Katharine's death, Gill included a new introduction in which he addressed Mrs. White's indignation; his essay was also published in *The New York Times.* He said he had "lavish[ed] much praise" upon her, but that the "old warrior" was not satisfied with what he wrote, and "subsequently mounted a strenuous campaign of falsehoods" against him. "How much remains to be said about Mrs. White!" he wrote, and then concluded with a story of her "indomitable competitiveness," when Bryn Mawr, on the occasion of its seventy-fifth anniversary, drew up a list of seventy-five alumni to honor, including Elsie Shepley Sergeant but not Katharine, who then raised hell to get on the list, which was then extended to seventy-six honorees.

   Gill got this story wrong, as Leo Dolenski, a librarian at Bryn Mawr, explained in a letter to the *Times.* Katharine was on the original list, and Elsie's friend Hetty Goldmark successfully petitioned the college president to include Elsie. Gill was forced to issue a correction, his first in fifty-three years of journalism, but he continued to insist that he simply made a mistake and was not mean-spirited or unjust to Katharine. See Gill, "Still Here at *The New Yorker*," *New York Times*, October 4, 1987; "White at *The New Yorker*," *New York Times*, November 1, 1987; and Michael Bamberger, "Gill vs. White: Smear at *The New Yorker*?," *Washington Post*, October 31, 1987.

474 *"offensive, gossipy":* EBW, "A Note by EBW," September 1981, BM 30.15.

474 *"It has depressed me":* KSW to Evelyn McCutcheon, April 11, 1975, private collection.

475 *"I can't breathe":* KSW to Roger and Carol Angell and Nancy and Louis Stableford, November 10, 1975, private collection.

475 *"Worst of all":* KSW to Evelyn McCutcheon, December 18, 1975, private collection.

476 *"most successful gift":* KSW to RA, July 2, 1976, private collection.

476 *"over-persuaded":* KSW to Evelyn McCutcheon, October 14, 1976, private collection.

477 *"jumpy, edgy and nervous":* Wilfrid Sheed, review of *Letters of E. B. White, New York Times*, November 21, 1976.

477 *"Because White is such":* RA, "Foreword," *One Man's Meat*, ix.

477 *"Of all the well-known":* Stanley Hart White to EBW, January 20, 1947, CU 185.

477 *"This is one":* EBW to KSW, undated [spring 1941], LEBW 200–201.

478 *"Katharine finished reading":* EBW to Joseph Bryan III, November 30, 1937, LEBW 156.

478 *"judgment and extraordinary":* RA to KSW, May 5, 1977, private collection.

479 *"Katharine sat quietly":* EBW to WS, August 12, 1977, private collection.

480 *Carol, knowing that:* RA, interview with the author, May 7, 2021.

480 *Andy chose a spot:* Ibid. See also LMF 268.

480 *"And until the very day":* EBW, "Precis on KSW," undated [July 1977], BM 31.1.

481 *"On the white page":* EBW, "Lady Before Breakfast," *The Fox of Peapack,* reprinted in *Poems and Sketches of E. B. White,* 70.

482 *"The editor in her fought":* E. B. White, "Introduction," OUG viii–ix.

483 *"Life without her is no":* EBW to Gluyas Williams, May 8, 1978, LEBW 620.

483 *"his wife reaching":* Nan Robertson, "E. B. White's Loss Wrenches a Love Letter from His Soul," *Chicago Tribune,* April 28, 1980.

483 *"Congratulations on your":* EBW to SE, May 25, 1982, LEBW 648.

483 *"exhausted but fulfilled":* EBW to SE, February 10, 1984, LEBW 676.

EPILOGUE: KATHARINE S. WHITE
FORGOTTEN AND REMEMBERED

487 *"What I am hoping":* KSW to Mrs. Spitzer, November 31, 1969, BM 30.7.

488 *These historians treat:* An example is Thomas Vinciguerra's *Cast of Characters: Wolcott Gibbs, E. B. White, James Thurber, and the Golden Age of "The New Yorker."* Vinciguerra mentions Katharine White frequently and her portrait even appears on the cover, but she is not included in his "cast of characters," which he defines as the three men upon whom Ross most relied.

488 *White liberal feminists:* There are many critiques of the "wave" metaphor. See, for instance, Nancy A. Hewitt, "Feminist Frequencies: Regenerating the Wave Metaphor," *Feminist Studies* 3.3 (Fall 2012): 658–80, and Katherine M. Marino and Susan Ware, "Rethinking 'First Wave' Feminisms: An Introduction," *Signs* 47.4 (Summer 2022): 811–16.

489 *The statistics tell:* For a broad overview of women in the workforce between the two "waves," see Stephanie Coontz, *The Way We Never Were: American Families and the Nostalgia Trap* (New York: Basic Books, 1992), esp. chapter 7; Coontz, *A Strange Stirring: "The Feminine Mystique" and American Women at the Dawn of the 1960s* (New York: Basic Books, 2011), esp. chapter 4; and Joanne Meyerowitz, ed., *Not June Cleaver: Women and Gender in Postwar America* (Philadelphia: Temple University Press, 1994). One example of the publishing industry's amnesia can be seen in the 2018 obituary for literary agent Elaine Markson, which erroneously claimed she was "among the first women to own a literary agency"; see Sam Roberts, "Elaine Markson, Literary Agent for Feminist Authors, Dies at 87," *New York Times,* June 1, 2018.

489 *"charismatic editor":* Matthew Philpotts, "The Role of the Periodical Editor: Literary Journals and Editorial Habitus," *Modern Language Review* 7.1 (2012): 39–64.

490 *"Dear Katharine, I must":* May Sarton to KSW, October 6, 1960, BM 10.17.

490 *"a huge black cloud":* Thomas Wolfe, *The Story of a Novel* (New York: Charles Scribner's Sons, 1936), 37, 52, and 57.

492 *"The first time":* Frances Gray Patton to RA, September 2, 1977, private collection.

493 *"the editor/encourager":* Alan Williams to RA, July 27 [1977], private collection.

493 *"I have always looked":* Kathy [Barth?] to RA, August 18 [1977], private collection.

493 *"All of us felt":* Nancy Gerstein Novogrod to RA, undated [1977], private collection.

493 *"Knowing your mother":* Rachel MacKenzie to RA, July 25, 1977, private collection.

494 *"looking displeased":* Linda H. Davis, "The Man on the Swing," TNY, December 27, 1993, 91.

495 *In 1985, William Leary:* William Leary, "Jean Stafford, Katharine White, and the 'New Yorker,'" *Sewanee Review* 93.4 (Fall 1985): 584–96.

Photo Credits

Index

ABOUT
MARINER BOOKS

MARINER BOOKS traces its beginnings to 1832, when William Ticknor cofounded the Old Corner Bookstore in Boston, from which he would run the legendary firm Ticknor and Fields, publisher of Ralph Waldo Emerson, Harriet Beecher Stowe, Nathaniel Hawthorne, and Henry David Thoreau. Following Ticknor's death, Henry Oscar Houghton acquired Ticknor and Fields and, in 1880, formed Houghton Mifflin, which later merged with venerable Harcourt Publishing to form Houghton Mifflin Harcourt. HarperCollins purchased HMH's trade publishing business in 2021 and reestablished their storied lists and editorial team under the name Mariner Books.

Uniting the legacies of Houghton Mifflin, Harcourt Brace, and Ticknor and Fields, Mariner Books continues one of the great traditions in American bookselling. Our imprints have introduced an incomparable roster of enduring classics, including Hawthorne's *The Scarlet Letter*, Thoreau's *Walden*, Willa Cather's *O Pioneers!*, Virginia Woolf's *To the Lighthouse*, W.E.B. Du Bois's *Black Reconstruction*, J.R.R. Tolkien's *The Lord of the Rings*, Carson McCullers's *The Heart Is a Lonely Hunter*, Ann Petry's *The Narrows*, George Orwell's *Animal Farm* and *Nineteen Eighty-Four*, Rachel Carson's *Silent Spring*, Margaret Walker's *Jubilee*, Italo Calvino's *Invisible Cities*, Alice Walker's *The Color Purple*, Margaret Atwood's *The Handmaid's Tale*, Tim O'Brien's *The Things They Carried*, Philip Roth's *The Plot Against America*, Jhumpa Lahiri's *Interpreter of Maladies*, and many others. Today Mariner Books remains proudly committed to the craft of fine publishing established nearly two centuries ago at the Old Corner Bookstore.